Managing in Times of Disorder

Organization Science

Series Editor: Arie Y. Lewin

Books from Sage Publications,
Organization Science, and the
Institute for Operations Research and the Management Sciences

The Sage Publications **Organization Science** book series reprints expanded Special Issues of *Organization Science*. Each individual volume is based on the original Special Issue that appeared in *Organization Science*. It includes all-new introductions by the editors as well as several chapters that did not appear in the original Special Issue. These new chapters may include reprints of papers that appeared in other issues of *Organization Science*, relevant papers that appeared in other journals, and also new original articles.

The book series is published by Sage Publications in partnership with INFORMS (the Institute for Operations Research and Management Sciences) the publisher of *Organization Science*. The Series Editor is Arie Y. Lewin, the Editor in Chief of *Organization Science*.

Organization Science was founded in 1989 as an international journal with the aim of advancing the field of organization studies by attracting, then publishing innovative research from across the social sciences. The term "Science" in the journal's title is interpreted in the broadest possible sense to include diverse methods and theoretical approaches. The editors of *Organization Science* believe that creative insight often occurs outside traditional approaches and topic areas, and that the role of *Organization Science* is to be broadly inclusive of the field by helping to integrate the diverse stands of organizational research. Authors are expected to describe theoretical concepts that give meaning to data, and to show how these concepts are relevant to organizations. Manuscripts that speculate beyond current thinking are more desirable than papers that use tried and true methods to study routine problems.

Initial books in this series:

Longitudinal Field Research Methods: Studying Processes of Organizational Change
   Edited by George P. Huber and Andrew H. Van de Ven

Organizational Learning
   Edited by Michael D. Cohen and Lee S. Sproull

Cognition Within and Between Organizations
   Edited by James R. Meindl, Charles Stubbart, and Joseph F. Porac

Managing in Times of Disorder: Hypercompetitive Organizational Responses
   Edited by Anne Y. Ilinitch, Arie Y. Lewin, and Richard D'Aveni

For information on subscriptions to *Organization Science*, please contact INFORMS at 940-A Elkridge Landing Road, Linthicum, MD 21090-2909, 800-446-3676. For submission guidelines, contact INFORMS at 290 Westminster Street, Providence, RI 02903, 800-343-0062.

Managing in Times of Disorder

Hypercompetitive Organizational Responses

Anne Y. Ilinitch
Arie Y. Lewin
Richard D'Aveni
Editors

Organization Science

SAGE Publications
International Educational and Professional Publisher
Thousand Oaks   London   New Delhi

For information:

SAGE Publications, Inc.
2455 Teller Road
Thousand Oaks, California 91320
E-mail: order@sagepub.com

SAGE Publications Ltd.
6 Bonhill Street
London EC2A 4PU
United Kingdom

SAGE Publications India Pvt. Ltd.
M-32 Market
Greater Kailash I
New Delhi 110 048 India

Printed in the United States of America

Library of Congress Cataloging-in-Publication Data

Managing in times of disorder: Hypercompetitive organizational responses / edited by Anne Y. Ilinitch, Arie Y. Lewin, and Richard D'Aveni.
p. cm. -- (Organization science)
Includes bibliographical references and index. ISBN 0-7619-1018-2 (acid-free paper). -- ISBN 0-7619-1019-0 (pbk.
acid-free paper)
1. Competition. 2. Organizational effectiveness. I. Ilinitch, Anne Y. II. Lewin, Arie Y., 1935- . III. D'Aveni, Richard A. IV. Series: Organization science (Thousand Oaks, Calif.)
HD41.M334 1998
658--dc21   97-45402

This book is printed on acid-free paper.
98 99 00 01 02 03 04 10 9 8 7 6 5 4 3 2 1

Acquiring Editor: Harry Briggs
Editorial Assistant: Anna Howland
Production Editor: Sanford Robinson
Production Assistant: Denise Santoyo
Designer/Typesetter: Rose Tylak
Cover designer: Candice Harman
Indexer: Jean Casalegno

Contents

Part II: HYPERCOMPETITIVE RESPONSES: NEW ORGANIZATIONAL FORMS AND STRATEGIES

Part III: OTHER PERSPECTIVES

Preface

The ideas in this book are the culmination of more than three years' collaborative work by several hundred organizational scholars, practicing managers, and consultants to the largest corporations in the world. The idea began with a call for papers for a special issue of *Organization Science,* which followed up on and broadened the scope of a 1993 Academy of Management showcase symposium on vertical integration and outsourcing. In the views of symposiums panelists Anne Y. Ilinitch, Richard D'Aveni, and Brian Quinn, business environments were changing dramatically and thus merited revolutionary organizational forms and strategies. We also realized, however, that some of the most relevant and creative new work on organizational forms and strategies was in an embryonic stage, and thus identifying such papers and developing them through the review process would involve nontraditional and much more intensive approaches than most reviewers had experienced. We were fortunate to create a group of more than 150 reviewers representing roughly 75 colleges and universities worldwide who were willing to rise to this challenge and were able to look first for the "jewel" in the papers rather than for reasons to reject them. We allowed authors almost a year to respond to the call, as well as actively seeking out relevant working papers in a variety of disciplines. Our goal was to stimulate as well as discover fresh, boundary-spanning research (Meyer, Goes, and Brooks 1995). Ultimately, the call for papers generated more than 100 submissions from authors representing 11 countries (France, United States, Canada, The Netherlands, Sweden, Norway, Japan, Korea, Singapore, Greece, and the United Kingdom).

Perhaps the single most important event in assuring that the research being undertaken was relevant as well as rigorous was the creation of the

Whittemore Conference on Hypercompetition, co-sponsored by the Amos Tuck School at Dartmouth College and *Organization Science*. The conference brought together academics, senior executives, and consultants to discuss together the issues facing firms operating in increasingly chaotic environments. Time and energy spent reviewing, critiquing, and building on each other's work, both at the conference and in the subsequent revision cycles, enabled authors to develop stronger, more robust, and more elaborated theoretical and methodological themes. The process challenged authors to cycle between inductive and deductive approaches, theory and practice, to arrive at a final product that was enriched by multiple perspectives. Many authors were asked to undertake the unusual step of incorporating ideas from other papers into their own empirical studies and theoretical work.

A final challenge was to overcome the inherent riskiness in asking researchers to work on a new, unproven theme with no assurance that a broader intellectual market would emerge for their scholarship. It is increasingly apparent, however, that organization and strategy scholars are beginning to engage the themes presented in this volume, not because of the volume per se, but simply because researchers are interested in addressing issues that "matter."

The final culmination of these activities are two volumes of a special issue of *Organization Science* addressing "New Organizational Forms and Strategies for Managing in Hypercompetitive Environments" (May-June, 1996 and July-August, 1996) and this book, which both illuminates and extends the concepts presented in the special issue. The process of identifying, developing, organizing, and publishing this research has spanned nearly four years and required multiple virtual and actual editorial consultations in locations throughout the world (including Atlanta, Dallas, Vancouver, Mexico City, Hanover, Seattle, the Research Triangle area of North Carolina, and Tokyo).

We greatly appreciate the leadership of *Organization Science* and Sage Publications for their patience with and moral and financial support of this endeavor; the Amos Tuck School of Dartmouth College, the University of Washington Seattle's School of Business Administration, the University of Washington Bothell's Management Program, and the Fuqua School of Duke University for their financial and administrative support; and the Whittemore family for their generosity in funding the conference on Hypercompetition. Our deepest thanks, however, are reserved for the conference participants, authors, reviewers, and colleagues listed in the following pages, whose ideas and perspectives have brought this project to life and have created a body of work that can potentially lead both managers and academics in new directions.

REFERENCE

Meyer, A. D., J. B. Goes, and G. R. Brooks (1995), "Organizations Reacting to Hyperturbulence,"
    in G. P. Huber and A. H. Van de Ven (Eds.), *Longitudinal Field Research Methods:
    Studying Processes of Organizational Change,* Thousand Oaks, CA: Sage.

Acknowledgments

1994 Academy of Management
Vertical Integration Symposium Panelists, Atlanta

Rich Bettis, Kenan-Flagler Business School, University of North Carolina
Alfred Chandler, Harvard University
Rich D'Aveni, Amos Tuck School, Dartmouth College
Kathy Harrigan, Columbia University
Charles Hill, University of Washington
Anne Y. Ilinitch, Kenan-Flagler Business School, University of North Carolina
Brian Quinn, Amos Tuck School, Dartmouth College
David Ravenscraft, Kenan-Flagler Business School, University of North Carolina

Fall, 1995 Whittemore Conference Participants,
Amos Tuck School, Dartmouth College

Organization Science Workshop

Dong Jae Kim, Yonsei University, Korea
Bruce Kogut, Wharton School, University of Pennsylvania
Tim Craig, University of Victoria
Anne Smith, Florida Atlantic University
Ken Smith, University of Maryland
Greg Young, North Carolina State University
Ming Jer Chen, Wharton School, University of Pennsylvania
Julia Liebeskind, University of Southern Carolina
Rob Grant, Georgetown University
Henk Volberda, Erasmus University
Lacy Glenn Thomas, Emory University
Avie Figenbaum, Technion

Javier Gimeno, Texas A&M University
Kathy Eisenhardt, Stanford University
Charles Galunic, INSEAD
Paul Hirsch, Northwestern University
James Richardson, University of Hawaii
Arjen Van Witteloostulin, University of Limburgh
Paul Schoemaker, University of California at Irvine
Session Chairs
Claudia Bird Schoonhoven, Amos Tuck School, Dartmouth College
Fred Webster, Amos Tuck School, Dartmouth College
Brian Quinn, Amos Tuck School, Dartmouth College
Syd Finkelstein, Amos Tuck School, Darmouth College
Phil Anderson, Amos Tuck School, Dartmouth College
Ian McMllan, Wharton School, University of Pennsylvania
Bill Joyce, Amos Tuck School, Dartmouth College
Kathy Harrigan, Columbia University
Vijay Govindarajan, Amos Tuck School, Dartmouth College
Conference Speakers
Jim Abeglan, Gemini Consulting
Paul Walsh, Pillsbury
Arie Y. Lewin, Fuqua School, Duke University
Stephan Haeckel, IBM
Richard D'Aveni, Amos Tuck School, Dartmouth College
George Cattermole, DuPont
Hiroyuki Itami, Hitotsubashi University
Peter Neupert, Microsoft
David Martin, Texas Instruments
James Bailey, Citibank
David Ulrich, University of Michigan
Andrew Sigler, Champion International
Tom Peters, Tom Peters Group
Terry Neill, Andersen Consulting
Rita McGrath, Columbia University
Chris Argyris, Harvard University
Rosabeth Moss Kantor, Harvard University
George Day, Wharton School, University of Pennsylvania
Jay Galbraith, University of Southern California

Corporate Participants

Bobby V. Abraham	Chairman and Chief Executive Officer	Paragon Trade Brands
Carl J. Brentley	President	CPS Distributors, Inc.
Robert Bradford	Principal	Parthenon Group
Yale M. Brandt	Vice Chairman	Reynolds Metals Co.
Mel G. Brekhus	Vice President	Texas Industries
James B. Bruhn	Vice President–Commercial Products	Weirton Steel
William J. Cadogan	Chairman, President and Chief Executive Officer	ADC Telecommunications, Inc.
C. Lloyd Carpenter	Vice President, Business Operations	Westinghouse Electric Electronics Systems Group

Geoffrey A. de Rohan	Vice President, Health Care Business Development	Wheaton, Inc.
James F. Dicke, II	President	Crown Equipment Corporation
Frank Doczi	President and Chief Executive Officer	Home Quarters Warehare
Gerald L. Elson	Vice President and General Manager	General Motors Inland Fisher Guide Division
William S. Epstein	Deputy President and Chief Operation Officer	First New Hampshire Bank
Lucille N. Evans	Senior Vice President—Finance and Administration	Swift Textiles, Inc.
Peter C. Forster	President and Chief Executive Officer	George Hyman Construction Co.
Gerald G. Garbacz	Chairman and Chief Executive Officer	Baker and Taylor
Ekkehard Grampp	President	Rohm Tech., Inc.
Rita Grisham	President	T&N Industries
Alan L. Hainey	Executive Vice President and General Manager	General Electric Capital Mortgage Services, Inc.
Robert J. Hauser, Jr.	President and Chief Operations Officer	Commonwealth Land Title Insurance Company
David J. Hirt	Chief Executive Officer and President	Batesville Casket Company
David R. Holmes	Chairman, President and Chief Executive Officer	Reynolds and Reynolds Co.
Michael S. Hunt	Vice President, Pharmaceutical Strategy Planning	Eli Lilly
Guy R. Jillings	Head of Strategic Planning, Royal Dutch/Shell Group Company	Shell International Petroleum
Richard G. Klein	General Manager	John Deere Harvester Works
Thomas A. Krake	Chief Financial Officer	Eli Lilly, Canada
Charles R. Kreter	General Manager and Chief Financial Officer	Ellicott Machine Corporation
Robert A. Lauer	Managing Partner for Change Management, the Americas	Andersen Consulting
T. Scott Leisher	Group Vice President	CCC Information Services
Fred L. Marion	Vice President, Business Development and Advanced Systems, Electronics, and Missiles Group	Martin Marietta Technologies, Inc.
Erik Matson	Managing Partner	PHH Fantus Consulting
Charles H. McGill	Vice President, Acquisitions	Dun & Bradstreet Corporation
H. H. Meijer	Member of the Executive Board	Royal Nedlloyd Group, N.V.
John A. Miller	Network Systems Strategy Officer	AT&T
W. S. Montgomery, Jr.	President, Chief Executive Officer and Treasurer	Spartan Mills
Richard H. Morehead	Vice President, Corporate Planning/ Development	Abbott Laboratories
Michael C. Murr	President, Progressive Partners and Chief Investment Officer	Progressive Corporation
Pamela M. Neuhaus	Vice President, Strategic Business Development and Planning	GTE Information Services, Inc.
Charles Perrottet	Vice President and Director of Corporate Consulting	The Futures Group
Robert C. Purcell, Jr.	Executive in Charge of Corporate Strategy Development	General Motors Corp.

Joyce M. Roche	Vice President, Global Marketing	Avon Products
Anthony T. G. Rodgers	Executive Director	Zenecca Group PLC, UK
James N. Rosse	President and Chief Executive Officer	Freedom Communications, Inc.
Steven B. Rossi	Executive Vice President and General Manager	Knight-Riddle, Inc. *The Philadelphia Inquirer* and *Philadelphia Daily News*
Walter B. Schaffir	President	Growth Dynamics, Inc.
Peter E. Schwab	President and Chief Executive Officer	Foothill Capital Corp.
Claibourne D. Smith	Vice President, Technology and Professional Development	E.I. Du Pont de Nemour & Company
John M. Stropki	Senior Vice President—Sales	Lincoln Electric Company
Lawrence B. Swerling	Director of Strategic Planning	Rohm & Haas
Charles E. Tingley	President and Chief Executive Officer	Transamerica Leasing, Inc.
William A. Wallace	Vice President	CH2M Hill, Inc.
James D. Walsh	Director of Market Analysis and Business Planning	Electronics Data Systems, Inc.
Ken L. Watman	President	Kao Corporation of America
Richard B. Wilkins	President	RFS Business Forms
Daniel P. Wilson	President	Interlake Corporation, Interlake Material Handling Division

Adminsitrative Support

Dwayne Helleloid, University of Washington
John Down, University of Washington
Gloria Finkelstein, Amos Tuck School, Dartmouth College

Organization Science Special Issue on Hypercompetition

Reviewers

ADLER, PAUL, University of Southern California
AMBURGEY, TERRY, University of Kentucky
ANDERSON, CARL, University of North Carolina
ANDERSON, PHILLIP, Dartmouth College
ARGOTE, LINDA, Carnegie Mellon University
BALAKRISHNAN, SUNDAR, University of Washington-Bothell
BARKER, VINCE, University of Wisconsin
BARR, PAM, Emory University
BARTUNEK, JEAN, Boston College
BASS, BERNARD, Binghamton School of Management
BATEMAN, THOMAS, University of North Carolina
BAUGHN, CHRIS, Wayne State University
BOEKER, WARREN, London Business School
BOLTON, MITCHELE, San Jose State University
BOULDING, WILLIAM, Duke University
BOURGEOIS, JAY, University of Virginia
BOYNTON, ANDREW, University of North Carolina
BRITTAIN, JACK, University of Texas at Dallas
BROMILEY, PHILLIP, University of Minnesota
BURTON, RICHARD, Duke University
CHAKRAVARTHY, BALA, University of Minnesota
CHEN, MING JER, University of Pennsylvania
CHENG, JOSEPH, Ohio State University
COLLINS, PAUL, University of Washington
COLLIS, DAVID, Harvard University
COOPER, RANDY, University of Houston
CRAIG, TIM, University of Victoria
DACIN, TINA, Texas A&M University
DAVIS-BLAKE, ALISON, University of Texas

DAY, DIANA, Rutgers University

DAY, GEORGE, University of Pennsylvania

DEEDS, DAVID, Temple University

DELBECO, ANDRE, Santa Clara University

DESS, GREGORY, University of Texas
at Arlington

DOUGHERTY, DEBORAH, McGill University

DOZ, YVES, INSEAD

DRAZIN, ROBERT, Emory University

DUTTON, JANE, University of Michigan

EISENBEIS, ROBERT, University of North
Carolina

EISENHARDT, KATHLEEN,
Stanford University

FALKENBERG, JOYCE, Norwegian School
of Economics

FIEGENBAUM, AVI, Technion

FINKELSTEIN, SYDNEY, Dartmouth
College

GARUD, RAGHU, New York University

GELETKANYCZ, MARTA, Penn State
University

GERSICK, CONNIE, University of California
at Los Angeles

GIMENO, JAVIER, Texas A&M University

GOES, JAMES, University of Alaska

GOLDEN, BRIAN, University of
Western Ontario

GOMES-CASSERES, BENJAMIN, Harvard
University

GRANT, JOHN, University of Pittsburgh

GRANT, ROBERT, Georgetown University

GRAY, BARBARA, Pennsylvania State
University

GUTH, WILLIAM, New York University

HABIB, MOHAMMED, Temple University

HAGUE, GERALD, University of Maryland

HARRIGAN, KATHRYN, Columbia University

HART, STUART, University of North Carolina

HATFIELD, DONALD, Virginia Polytechnic

HAVEMAN, HEATHER, Cornell University

HEDLAND, GUNNAR

HEELEY, MICHAEL, University of Washington

HELFAT, CONSTANCE, University of
Pennsylvania

HELLELOID, DUANE, University of
Washington

HENDERSON, REBECCA, MIT

HENNART, JEAN-FRANCOIS, University of
Illinois

HILL, CHARLES, University of Washington

HIRSCH, PAUL, Northwestern University

HITT, MICHAEL, Texas A&M University

HOUGHTON, SUSAN, Georgia State
University

HREBINIAK, LAWRENCE, University
of Pennsylvania

HUBER, GEORGE, University of Texas

HURRY, DILEEP, Southern Methodist
University

IRELAND, DUANE, Baylor University

JAIN, VINOD, Texas Christian University

JELINEK, MARIANN, College of William
& Mary

JEMISON, DAVID, University of Texas

JONES, CANDACE, Boston College

JOYCE, WILLIAM, Dartmouth College

JUDGE, WILLIAM, University of
Tennessee

KAZANIJIAN, ROBERT, Emory University

KING, WILLIAM, University of Pittsburgh

KOGUT, BRUCE, University of Pennsylvania

KOTHA, SURESH, University of Washington

LAVERTY, KEVIN, University of Washington-
Bothell

LAWLESS, MICHAEL, Duke University

LEI, DAVID, Southern Methodist University

LEVINTHAL, DANIEL, Univeristy of
Pennsylvania

LIEBERMAN, MARVIN, University of
California at Los Angeles

LIEBESKIND, JULIA, University of
Southern California

LUMPKIN, THOMAS, University of Texas at
Arlington

MAHONEY, JOSEPH, University of Illinois

MARCUS, ALFRED, University of Minnesota

MEYER, DALE, University of Colorado

MEZIAS, STEPHEN, New York University

MILES, RAYMOND, University of California
at Berkeley

MILLER, KENT, Purdue University

MITCHELL, WILLIAM, University of
Michigan

MOLDOVEANU, MICHAEL, Harvard
University

NANDA, ASHISH, Harvard University

NARAPAREDDY, VI, University of Denver

NONAKA, IKUJIRO, Hitotsubashi University

OLIVA, TERRENCE, Temple University

OLIVER, CHRISTINE, York University

OLK, PAUL, University of California at Irvine

PARAYRE, ROCH, Southern Methodist University
PARKHE, ARVIND, Indiana University
PAUN, DOROTHY, University of Washington
PENG, MIKE, University of Hawaii
PETERAF, MARGIE, University of Minnesota
PETERSON, RICHARD, University of Washington
PHAN, PHILLIP, York University
POPPO, LAURA, Washington University
RAJAGOPALAN, MANDINI, University of Southern California
RAPP, WILLIAM, University of Victoria
RAVENSCRAFT, DAVID, University of North Carolina
REED, RICHARD, Washington State University
REGER, RHONDA, University of Maryland
RICHARDSON, JAMES, University of Hawaii
ROMANELLI, ELAINE, Georgetown University
ROSE, ELIZABETH, University of Southern California
RUEFLI, TIMOTHY, University of Texas
SAKSON, JANE, University of Washington
SCHOEMAKER, PAUL, University of California at Irvine
SHARMA, ANURAG, University of Massachusetts
SINGH, JITENDRA, University of Pennsylvania
SLATER, STANLEY, University of Washington–Seattle
SMITH, ANNE, Florida Atlantic University

SMITH, KENNETH G., University of Maryland
SNOW, CHARLES, Pennsylvania State University
SPENDER, J.-C., New York Institute of Technology
STEPHENS, CARROLL, Virginia Polytechnic
STEWART, ALICE, Ohio State University
STOPFORD, JOHN, London Business School
STOUT, SUZANNE, University of Texas at Dallas
SULLIVAN, JEREMIAH, University of Washington
TAYLOR, SUSAN, University of Maryland
THOMAS, L. G., Emory University
THOMAS, TOM, University of Washington
TUSHMAN, MICHAEL, Columbia University
UNGSON, GERARDO, University of Oregon
UZZI, BRIAN, Northwestern University
VAN WITTELOOSTUIJN, ARJEN, University of Limburgh
VICTOR, BART, IMD, Switzerland
VOLBERDA, HENK, Erasmus University
WALKER, GORDON, Southern Methodist University
WALSH, JAMES P., University of Michigan
WILLIAMS, JEFFREY, Carnegie Mellon University
WOO, CAROLYN, Purdue University
YOUNG, GREGORY, North Carolina State University
ZAHEER, AKBAR, University of Minnesota
ZEITHAML, CARL, University of Virginia
ZHARA, SHAKER, Georgia State University

Administrative Support

Tracy Flynn Scott, Amos Tuck School, Dartmouth College
Mike Peng, University of Hawaii
Jon Down, University of Washington
Pam Roberson, former Managing Editor, *Organization Science*
Sue Yager, former Managing Editor, *Organization Science*
Candita Gerzsevitz, Technical Editor, INFORMS

Managing in Times of Disorder

Administrative Support

Harry Briggs, Editor, Sage Publications
Sue Yager, former Managing Editor, *Organization Science*
Tracy Flynn Scott, Amos Tuck School, Dartmouth College

Introduction

ANNE Y. ILINITCH
ARIE Y. LEWIN
RICHARD D'AVENI

The language and metaphors of today's managers make one point abundantly clear: They are experiencing the strongest and most disruptive competitive forces of their careers. Rather than a game, business has become war. Rather than an honorable fight with the best firm winning, the goal has become extermination of the enemy. CEOs from industries ranging from telecommunications to auto parts describe the competition they face as "brutal," "intense," "bitter," and "savage" (D'Aveni, 1995). In the words of Andrew Grove, the CEO of Intel, "only the paranoid survive" (Grove 1996) in a world of hypercompetition (also Neupert, Chapter 5, this volume). Increasingly, managers are turning to academics and consultants to understand why the nature of competition is changing and for insights about how to compete in chaotic and disorderly times.

This book is an exploration and interpretation of the profound changes that are affecting the character of competition today. From our own research and from the research showcased in this collection, we feel that we have gained several important insights into the phenomenon called "hypercompetition" (D'Aveni 1994). First, hypercompetition is not the force driving environmental change; rather, it is an expected response in times of increasing disorder—albeit a response that accelerates managerial perceptions of disorder, stress, and unpredictability. Second, although hypercompetition is an expected response to increasing environmental disorder in which some firms are becoming creators of change, organizations are experimenting with a range of new organizational forms and strategies to adapt to or manage those changes. Third, the form of response most likely to be chosen, as well as the success of that response, depends at least in part on a firm's competitive position at the time of the change, its historical capabilities, and its preferred adaptive style. Finally, we believe that the natural forces shaping the environment are not linear; rather, they unfold over very long periods of time. When viewed from the inflection point where one cycle ends and the next begins, extreme disorder should be expected. Viewed from the broader perspective of decades and centuries, however, this inflection point is part of a cycle in which new order emerges, although it may resemble what has gone on before or what has been predicted ("Electronic Commerce Survey" 1997). The following sections elaborate on these insights, using research in this volume to enrich and illuminate the discussion.

THE NATURE OF HYPERCOMPETITION

Scholars differ with respect to the nature and extent of the disorder perceived by managers today. Porter (1996), for example, suggests that extreme environmental changes and the resulting hypercompetitive responses are limited to a special subset of firms, typically those operating in high-tech environments. Others may be exaggerating the potential impact of hypercompetition, suggesting that "corporate anarchy" is the ultimate end result (Canger 1995; Zohar and Morgan, Chapter 20, this volume). Despite these relatively extreme positions, conventional wisdom suggests that changes in the nature of competition, like changes in the economy and society, tend to occur in cycles or waves (Ross 1989), which build, crest, and retreat with some degree of regularity over a period of decades. The inflection points associated with the end of one cycle and the beginning of another historically have been associated with cataclysmic shifts, which provide significant economic opportunities but which also may have serious social consequences (Schumpeter 1934; Weber 1910). History would predict higher levels of disorder at inflection points such as the one joining the end of the post-World War boom cycle and the beginning of the information technology cycle than at other points along these "long waves."

Although some historians argue that the inflection point of the 1990s varies little from others, such as the beginning of the industrial revolution (Maney 1997), several characteristics of this point may be unique relative to those seen in the past. For example, recent dislocations have led to the emergence of a temporary and contingent workforce, which has heightened income disparities rather than created shared economic benefits (Victor and Stephens, Chapter 19, this volume). Also, the rate and scope of information technology diffusion, along with its rapidly decreasing cost, have allowed emerging nations and small firms to enter markets with greater speed, more knowledge, and less financial capital than ever before ("Electronic Commerce Survey" 1997; "The Hitchhiker's Guide to Cybernomics" 1996). Because of relatively open markets, U.S. firms are for the first time facing global rivals and the need to establish and manage truly global operations.

Interestingly, the disorder and stress of hypercompetition may be felt earlier and far more keenly in the United States than in most other countries, because the U.S. business system (that is, the culture, institutional structure and management systems) is more vulnerable to and has been more profoundly affected by these changes. Itami (Chapter 3, this volume) suggests that the United States has not benefited from workforce and demand stability, forces that have tempered the effects of "excessive" competition in Japan. In addition, information technology has diffused much more broadly and rapidly in the United States than in other countries, such as Japan, Britain, or Germany ("Electronic Commerce Survey" 1997), presenting firms with the capability to obtain and share information and process that information much more swiftly than many of their global counterparts. Whereas U.S. firms may be on the leading edge of trends that will eventually become universal and thus may be farther down the learning curve, they are also having to invent new forms and strategies for harnassing and coordinating these powerful forces in constructive ways. The high levels of anxiety, uncertainty, and dislocation experienced by U.S. managers and workers today may be the transition cost of gaining long-term global competitive advantage.

This book leads off with a chapter that documents the hypercompetitive shift that has taken place in the U.S. economy over the past three decades. In a study of 200 manufacturing industries over the 1958-1991 time frame, Thomas (Chapter 1, this volume) finds that dynamic resourcefulness (that is, the ability to create new strategic assets) varies greatly across industries, due to differences in supply and demand characteristics, knowledge base, and entry conditions. Consistent with traditional economic theory, in relatively static industry environments, high levels of rivalry are associated with poor market performance. In industries with high dynamic resourcefulness, however, escalations in rivalry actually improve market performance, up to a point. In addition, dynamically resourceful industries experience more hypercompetitive firm behavior as well as wider variances in individual firm performance. Like Thomas's research, Young, Smith and Grimm's study

(Chapter 2, this volume) of rivalry in the hypercompetitive software industry during the 1980s also challenges key assumptions of industrial organization economics. Contrary to theory, their results suggest that industry-level cooperation does not reduce firms' competitive behavior or positively impact their performance. Rather, individual firms that cooperated were able to increase both their competitive activity and their performance. Itami's discussion of competition in Japan (Chapter 3, this volume) further substantiates Thomas's findings, illustrating how moderate levels of domestic rivalry can increase both firm and industry learning and thus enhance national competitive advantage in global markets. Taken together, these three chapters begin to document the emergence and nature of hypercompetition, challenge basic assumptions of the traditional structure-conduct-performance models, and raise issues that future empirical studies of hypercompetitive industries can address.

ORGANIZATIONAL RESPONSES
TO ENVIRONMENTAL SHIFTS

As the increasing variance in firm performance within industries suggests, firms are responding to shifts in their environments with a broad array of new strategies and organizational forms. The research in this book suggests that organizational responses fall on a continuum (hypocompetitive to hypercompetitive) ranging from denial to aggressively breaking the rules (see Figure I.1). We will first discuss these two extreme responses on the continuum and then examine adaptive and management responses falling in the middle of this range.

DENIAL

James Bailey, Executive Vice President of Citibank, addresses the questions of how a dominant player in the industry could have missed the signs of radically changing industry rules and how difficult it is to regain lost market share. In a candid discussion of Citibank Bankcard's painful reorientation, he suggests that the firm's historical success blinded management to the hypercompetitive moves introduced by new entrants. As a new entrant itself into the bankcard industry in the late 1970s, Citibank's "deep pockets" enabled it to change the rules of the credit card industry invented by American Express and established a beach head from which to expand future interstate lending operations. What Citibank did not understand was that having unleashed hypercompetition in an industry, the leader cannot stand still. Their seemingly unassailable position was eroded by new competitors, including Discover, AT&T, and GM using "irrational," "bound to fail" rule-breaking strategies. It took the loss of nearly a quarter of their market share and hundreds of millions of dollars to bring the perceived value of their product into line with their competitors' and to recapture the momentum that they had lost. Bailey offers early warning signs and techniques to prevent other firms from falling prey to similar "blind spots."

ACCELERATION

As the Citibank case illustrates, some firms already have transformed their strategies to become hypercompetitive. Consequently, they become accelerators of hypercompetition within their industries. Andrew Grove, CEO of Intel, acts on the belief that in hypercompetitive environments, firms succeed by gaining continuous temporary advantages (Grove 1996). In practice, this means that Intel has next-generation products ready for rollout as soon as a new generation of products is introduced. Similarly, Peter Neupert (Chapter 5, this volume), Senior Director of Strategic Relationships for Microsoft, describes Microsoft's strategy as "the willingness to take a long-term approach, but always taking the short-term tactical action to win in the next few months . . . we never get beat on pricing even though we're the market leader." The chapters by Kim and Kogut and Nault and Vandenbosch (Chapter 6 and Chapter 8, respectively, this volume) provide empirical and theoretical support for these sorts of behaviors. Using a sample of semiconductor firms, Kim and Kogut show how firms that develop proprietary know-how in the form of technological platforms can quickly develop a range of related products to take advantage of emerging markets. The tacit knowledge amassed by Microsoft in both operating system software and applications software platforms illustrates this point. Technical platforms, however, also provide firms with the capability to quickly develop and introduce new generations of technologies that then allow them to dramatically drop prices on existing product lines. This strategy, used brilliantly by Intel, causes problems for competitors in two ways: First, they are forced to catch up on the technology side and second, they have less money with which to do it, given the need to respond with price cuts of their own. Nault and Vandenbosch's model (Chapter 8, this volume) of the product cannibalization decision also supports Intel's strategy that firms in intensely competitive industries gain competitive advantage by launching pre-emptive strikes, even if they lose money at the margin.

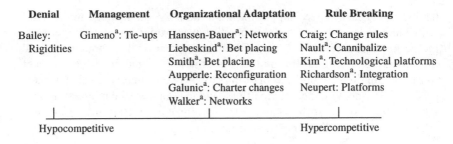

Denial	Management	Organizational Adaptation	Rule Breaking
Bailey: Rigidities	Gimeno[a]: Tie-ups	Hanssen-Bauer[a]: Networks Liebeskind[a]: Bet placing Smith[a]: Bet placing Aupperle: Reconfiguration Galunic[a]: Charter changes Walker[a]: Networks	Craig: Change rules Nault[a]: Cannibalize Kim[a]: Technological platforms Richardson[a]: Integration Neupert: Platforms

Hypocompetitive   Hypercompetitive

Figure I.1. Organizational Responses to Hypercompetition
a. These works have multiple authors.

Some firms adopt a hypercompetitive stance out of necessity. The case study by Craig (Chapter 7, this volume) suggests how the desperate condition of the Asahi Brewing Company caused it to break the rules that characterized competition in the brewing industry in Japan. By launching Super Dry, Asahi changed the rules to competing on the basis of new product introduction. Market leader Kirin's reluctance to cannibalize existing sales not only allowed Asahi to quickly become the market leader, but the development of similar capabilities involved two painful years for Kirin (and other competitors). Richardson (Chapter 9, this volume) tells a similar story about the fashion apparel industry, where firm success or failure depends on the ability to respond quickly to supply and demand imbalances and rapidly changing market preferences. In this industry, where value chain activities are increasingly dispersed throughout the world, information technology (IT) provides vertically integrated firms with the flexibility and control to quickly link and manage the value chain, and The Limited was among the first to develop and exploit such capabilities successfully. Unlike the two-year advantage that new product introduction capabilities gave Asahi, however, IT advantages are likely to be much more transient because of their ease of imitation and followers' ability to adopt IT products off the shelf so quickly (Hunter, DeSanctis, Lewin, Sakano, and Carroll 1997).

MANAGEMENT

One response to extreme hypercompetitive behavior is to try to reduce or manage it. Porter (1980, 1985, 1996) has long argued that classic industrial economic solutions such as increasing barriers to entry and gaining market power over rivals, suppliers, and buyers will reduce rivalry within an industry. Gimeno and Woo (Chapter 10, this volume) provide insights into two forces that affect the intensity of hypercompetitive rivalry. Their study of the airline industry demonstrates that although similar strategies may increase competitive intensity, multimarket tie-ups tend to reduce it. Their findings not only provide insights into existing empirical conflicts regarding the relationship between strategic similarity and rivalry, they also provide guidance to managers regarding short-term strategies for avoiding costly price wars. The widespread and long-term viability of tie-up strategies may be limited, however, at least in part because they assume a relatively equal distribution of financial and physical resources and constraints across competitors. Competitors such as Southwest have managed to defeat this strategy by choosing much cheaper alternative locations that allow travelers to trade small inconveniences for dramatic savings.

ORGANIZATIONAL ADAPTATION

Perhaps the most difficult response to changing environmental conditions and the hypercompetitive reactions of competitors is organizational adaptation. "Adaptor" firms are aware of the changes affecting their environment and face the challenge of responding to the hypercompetitive conditions created by "accelerators." Grant and Volberda (Chapter 12 and Chapter 11, respectively, this volume) develop organizing frameworks that synthesize several theoretical approaches for a more thorough understanding of the organization capabilities of flexibility, adaptivity, and knowledge creation.

Specifically, Volberda explores the "paradox" of flexibility that causes "friction between change and preservations," developing in the process a dynamic logic for the discovery of new forms. He conceptualizes flexibility as both a managerial and an organizational design task: The managerial task is to provide dynamic capabilities for organization flexibility and change, whereas the design task is to configure technology, structure, and culture for preservation and control. The "metaflexibility" of a firm combines three types of flexibility: operational (reactive), structural (adaptive), and strategic (radical). The four resulting organizational forms (rigid, planned, flexible, and chaotic) represent a continuum of points along the opposite trajectories of routinization (control) and revitalization (flexibility). Those flexibilities and forms provide a dynamic approach to restructuring in response to cycles of competition.

Grant focuses on how organizations develop the capabilities necessary for revitalization and how they integrate specific capabilities to achieve routinization. Beginning with the assumption that firm resources are the primary source of competitive advantage and that knowledge creation is the firm's most important resource, he suggests that the Volberda flexibility paradox may be resolved by acquiring specific knowledge efficiently and by applying many areas of specialized knowledge integratively. Competitive advantage depends on more than integration efficiency, however; it also requires breadth and flexibility, which Grant argues may be best supplied by network forms. Whereas the Grant and Volberda chapters begin to outline the domain for creating dynamic capabilities, other chapters in this volume illustrate at least four ways that firms develop flexibility within current boundaries and structural constraints: network forms, bet placing, charter changes, and spontaneous reconfiguration.

Networks probably represent the latest management "fad" for responding to uncertain and dynamic environments. Quinn (1994), Miles and Snow (1994), and others have suggested a variety of flexible network forms that are assumed to enable firms to better cope with the increasingly complex and rapidly changing conditions both created and reinforced by globalization and the widespread diffusion of information technology. Walker, Kogut, and Shan; Liebeskind, Oliver, Zucker, and Brewer; and Hanssen-Bauer and Snow (Chapters 13, 15, and 14, respectively, this volume) examine various aspects of both the benefits and limitations of network forms.

Walker et al. explore two sides of networks: the institutional or social capital side, which revolves around interorganizational social structures, and the structural hole side, which explores potential entrepreneurial linkages between (rather than within) relationships. Networks that rely on social capital tend to be stable and closed, promoting efficient cooperative linkages, speed, and the ability to protect proprietary information (Walker et al., Chapter 13, and Liebeskind et al., Chapter 15, this volume). In contrast, networks that exploit structural holes may offer greater economic payoffs because firms in such networks have greater latitude in their cooperative strategies. Firms that form relationships in open networks could be viewed as hypercompetitive accelerators, initially free-riding on the social capital of their existing relationships to launch new ones, although they could, over time, lose this social capital due to their violation of network norms and commitments (Walker et al., this volume). Such open network relationships in the software industry may be responsible for higher firm-level performance (Young et al., Chapter 2, this volume). Interestingly, Walker et al.'s results suggest that in the biotech industry, network formation is better explained by social capital than structural hole theory, perhaps because of the importance of long-term relationships in the industry and the relative imbalance in partner sizes.

The social networks described by Hanssen-Bauer and Snow (Chapter 14, this volume) and Liebeskind et al. (Chapter 15, this volume) illustrate further benefits and constraints of the organizational form. Certainly, the regional learning network formed by Norwegian firms promoted knowledge creation and sharing among firms with different sizes and resource availability, establishing relationships that particularly benefited small firms and firms with lower levels of organizational slack. The stability of such networks, however, depends on strong institutional norms, which, in the case of Scandinavian firms, are deeply embedded in the national culture and history. In more individualistic cultures, such as that of the United States, not only are the institutional norms to support such a network weaker, but also the drive to exploit structural holes through forming open networks may be stronger. Thus, in the United States, these factors may serve as limiting conditions on network forms.

Liebeskind et al. (Chapter 15, this volume) offer an interesting explanation of the persistence of social networks in the biotechnology industry. In addition to providing strong norms for protecting proprietary investment over long time periods, such networks offer member firms efficient ways of locating, evaluating, and placing bets on a much wider variety of technical knowledge than could be accomplished either within the boundaries of a single firm or through independent market transactions. Describing bet-placing behavior of a totally different and seemingly random nature, Smith and Zeithaml (Chapter 16, this volume) describe how two "Baby Bells," also facing a turbulent and opportunity-rich environment, engaged in bet-placing in numerous international markets to gain the skills and perspective needed to compete in a deregulated domestic telecommunications environment. Unlike firms in the biotech industry, which had shallow pockets and a need to tap into expertise throughout the world, however, the Baby Bells tended to exploit structural holes through the establishment of open network relationships. Not only did open networks offer the Baby Bells greater opportunity for gaining and transferring knowledge to their central cores, but they also presented less downside risk, due to the relatively sparse population of telecommunication regions and the new Bell companies' relatively low accumulation of social capital.

Two final examples of adaptation illustrate the feasibility and viability of internal structural flexibility. Galunic and Eisenhardt's (Chapter 17, this volume) analysis shows how large, diversified firms change divisional charters rather than organizational structure to adapt and respond to risky start-ups, rapid growth, and mature industry conditions. Although this type of flexibility can enable firms to respond with speed to changing conditions, stabilize divisional profits, maintain their geographic presence, and promote commitment to the organization, it also can exact high political and psychological costs. Thus, the role of leaders in the process of charter changes is critical to its success, not only because of their "matchmaking" function, but perhaps more important, for creating and maintaining an organizational culture in which knowledge can be retained and recombined.

Aupperle (Chapter 18, this volume) views the spontaneous reconfiguration of the Spartan mercenaries in Xenophon's Anabasis as perhaps the ultimate example of embedded routines of adaptation. Using the Greek supraculture as a metaphor, he describes how, when faced with a sudden and complete loss of the army's command structure, the Spartans were able to call up routines that were deeply embedded in their military "playbook," reconfigure them, and self-organize a successful retreat. Grant (Chapter 12, this volume) argues that such organizationally embedded routines offer significant advantages over both explicit directions and standard operating procedures because they increase both the speed of organizational response and the ability of organizational units to self-adapt to a broad range of circumstances. Because these routines are embedded in the collective memory of organizations and cannot be well-articulated by individual members (Cohen and Bacdayan 1994), however, tapping into the flexibility that such routines provide may involve maintaining a high degree of cultural and workforce stability (see Itami, Chapter 3, this volume, for a discussion of this "paradox"). Both Aupperle's and Itami's work suggests that a collectivist culture can be important for learning and activation of adaptive routines.

HYPERCOMPETITION AND EQUIFINALITY

Despite the similar environmental changes and hypercompetitive shifts that most industries are facing, chapters in this volume as well as in the business press suggest that firms are responding and adapting in radically different ways. Post-positivists might argue that order-destroying conditions give rise to idiosyncratic responses that are not amenable to being studied as normal science (McKelvey 1997). Yet, as McKelvey points out, positivism (or realism) is the only scientific approach that protects organization science from false theories. The concept of equifinality may provide direction not only for integrating these two seemingly contradictory positions into a single, "quasi-natural" view of organization science, but also for combining a seemingly random group of idiosyncratic organizational responses into a more focused and predictable set (McKelvey 1997). In organization science, equifinality has come to mean that final organizational states or performance levels can be reached from different initial conditions and by a variety of different paths (Gresov and Drazin 1997). Thus, in the context of this book, equifinality suggests that a firm's response to environmental disorder might take very different forms, depending on the degree of hypercompetitive acceleration in the firm's environment, its competitive position at the time it recognizes the need to respond, and its historical capabilities and preferred adaptive style.

The concept of equifinality contrasts sharply with contingency theory, which has long been an underlying assumption of the strategy and organization theory fields and that emphasizes the importance of creating a fit between the firm's environment, strategy, and structure. Gresov and Drazin (1997) suggest that in organizations with relatively simple functions and a narrow range of structural options, contingency theory may still hold. That is, "ideal profiles" may exist, which result in optimal strategy-environment fit and thus high performance. The regional learning networks in Norway described by Hanssen-Bauer and Snow may suggest such a form, given the relatively straightforward network goal and the narrow and culturally perfected structure for achieving it (Hanssen-Bauer and Snow, Chapter 14, this volume).

Given the increase in complex organizations and structural options open to firms, however, Gresov and Drazin (1997) argue that some form of equifinality rather than contingency will more likely prevail, resulting in a range of adaptive organizational forms and responses. For example, the divisional charter changes described by Galunic and Eisenhardt (Chapter 17, this volume) are an alternative to structural change for organizations with complex functions and a relatively wide latitude of structural options, a type of equifinality that Gresov and Drazin term "configurational." In this case, multiple ideal patterns can be expected; choosing among them involves trading off structures and functions. Similarly, biotech firms' use of social networks as a means of "bet placing" (Liebeskind et al., Chapter 15, this volume) may illustrate "suboptimal" equifinality; however, given the resource constraints of the firms and the social constraints of the networks, such closed networks may offer the most efficient method of protecting investments and prospecting for new technologies. Finally, the bet-placing behavior of the Baby Bells seeking new knowledge and ways of competing in deregulated environments suggests "trade-off" equifinality, in which the international divisions were created to pursue focused opportunities free of the structural constraints imposed by the focal organization conditioned to operating under regulatory regimes.

Hypercompetitive acceleration and denial responses also suggest the importance that competitive position, degree of disorder, and adaptive preference may play in strategic choice. For example, Asahi was in a desperate competitive position; happened to have developed, in house, a series of new products; and had selected a new CEO who was willing to break the rules by introducing new product-based competition to the Japanese beer industry. Conversely, Citibank's inability to process competitors' rule-breaking strategies can be explained by its inward focus due to its past competitive successes, its seeming immunity to environmental change, and its history of excellence and market leadership. Finally, Microsoft's initial denial and then abrupt turnaround of its Internet strategy reflects its historic capability of "embracing, extending, and exterminating" rivals (Gold and Ilinitch 1997; Neupert, Chapter 5, this volume).

At a time of increasing disorder, it is not wise to speculate on whether an optimal form or structure exists that will ensure success in environments characterized by hypercompetitive responses. The generic strategies of cost, differentiation, and focus are unlikely to provide sustainable competitive advantage, because in hypercompetition, advantages are temporary. Rather than embracing contingency theory and "fit" as a model, the cases and analysis contained in this book as well as the examples from practicing consultants and managers suggest that the concept of equifinality better explains the anticipated emergence of new organizational forms. In hypercompetitive environments, competitive advantage will increasingly derive from a firm's ability to develop new capabilities to meet rapidly changing market conditions. Interestingly, as firms increasingly compete and differentiate on the basis of knowledge and flexibility, the boundaries between form and strategy will become increasingly blurred, as will the boundaries of firms, further negating the value of traditional tools such as industry analysis. If knowledge integration is the goal or strategy of firms competing in dynamic environments, as Grant (Chapter 12, this volume) suggests, then organizational form is central to creating and exploiting knowledge and translating it into capabilities.

FUTURE DIRECTIONS

In our view, the period of disorder and chaos in organizational environments is set to take off, and, as yet, we know very little about creating organizations and strategies which institutionalize capacities for change. The dominant paradigms in organization theory are based on stability seeking and uncertainty avoidance through organization structure and processes, whereas the dominant paradigms in strategic management are based on rivalry reduction through competitive actions that restrict entry and signal oligopolistic bargains. We as academics are just beginning to ask the important questions that must be answered to enable organizations to successfully transition to these new times. For example, from an organizational forms perspective, how can organizations develop and manage their actions to exploit flexibility in knowledge creation? How can firms reinvent themselves as they move along the flexibility trajectory? And, more generally, what do "disposable organizations" (March, 1995) that routinize change look like? From a strategic management perspective, what are the necessary and sufficient conditions for hypercompetition and how does it differ from current constructs? What factors drive the cycles of competitive escalation and de-escalation? Does de-escalation raise profits in the short run, only to weaken firms in the long run? How do government policies, national heritage, history, and culture inhibit or enhance the abilities of firms to compete in chaotic environments? How can small or weak organizations win against much larger or stronger competitors? How do some firms succeed in rewriting industry rules? Which models of strategy will become obsolete in hypercompetitive environments?

Finally, from an ethical or moral perspective, how do organizations balance the need for a fierce will to prevail against loyalty to group or organizational norms? How does society balance the potential benefits of aggressive organizational forms and cultures against their dark side, that is, their human costs and their propensity to overreact and undertake extreme actions? Is hypercompetition a metaphor "gone wild," as Zohar and Morgan (Chapter 20) suggest in this volume? Or does their reaction to a world based on creative destruction and market disruption represent an unfounded fear of the future?

The challenges to both academic researchers and practicing managers attempting to make sense of such disorderly and chaotic environments are substantial. From an academic standpoint, new theoretical frameworks are needed to organize and understand the variation, experimentation, transience, adaptation, and flexibility that increasingly characterize the organizational designs, strategies, and management practices being invented by managers. In addition, we should continue modeling strategic organizational responses to increasingly chaotic environments with the goal of providing better categorizations, typologies, and generalizable theories about the conditions in which new organization forms and strategies can succeed. New methods and metrics will have to be developed and adapted to test these theories (such as complexity theory and rate analysis proposed by McKelvey 1997). From a managerial perspective, the task at hand is to intensify exploration, experimenting and innovating with new organizational forms. Our experience with this project suggests that it is the iterative nature of the process, the information sharing across disciplines, and the integration of theory building, theory testing, and observation of actual practice that will strengthen both the rigor of our research into these important new phenomena and the relevance of our research to managerial practice. The chapters in this volume not only demonstrate that such work is possible, but they also provide fresh insights into how it can be done.

REFERENCES

Canger, J. (1995), "Executive Commentary," *Academy of Management Executive, 9, 3, 57-59.*

Cohen, M. D. and R. Bacdayan (1994), "Organizational Routines are Stored as Procedural Memory: Evidence from a Laboratory Study," *Organization Science, 5, 4, 554-568.*

D'Aveni, R. (1994), *Hypercompetition: Managing the Dynamics of Strategic Maneuvering,* New York: Free Press.

_____ (1995), "Coping with Hypercompetition: Utilizing the New 7S Framework," *Academy of Management Executive, 9, 3, 45-60.*

"Electronic Commerce Survey Report" [Special Section]. (1997), *The Economist,* May 10, 56-74.

Gold, A. and A. Ilinitch (1997, October), *Viewing Dynamic Industries Through Multiple Conceptual Lenses: The Case of Microsoft and Netscape,* paper accepted for presentation at the Strategic Management Society Annual Meeting, Barcelona.

Grove, A. (1996), *Only the paranoid survive,* New York: Doubleday.

Gresov, C. and R. Drazin (1997), "Equifinality: Functional equivalence in organization design," *Academy of Management Review, 22, 2, 403-428.*

Hunter, S., G. DeSanctis, A. Y. Lewin, T. Sakano, and T. Carroll (1997), "Information Technology and New Organizational Forms: A Cross-Cultural Analysis Working Paper," Durham, NC: Duke University, Center for Research on New Organization Forms, Fuqua School of Business.

Maney, K. (1997), "Technology Moving Too Fast? Be Glad It's Not the 1840s," *USA Today,* January 30, 28.

March, J. G. (1995), "The Future, Disposable Organizations, and the Rigidities of Imagination," *Organization Science, 2, (3/4), 427-440.*

McKelvey, B. (1997), "Quasi-natural Organization Science," *Organization Science, 8, 4, 352-380.*

Miles, R. and C. Snow (1994), *Fit, Failure, and the Hall of Fame: How Companies Succeed or Fail,* New York: Free Press.

Porter, M. E. (1980), *Competitive Strategy,* New York: Free Press.

_____ (1985), *Competitive Advantage,* New York: Free Press.

_____ (1996), "What Is Strategy?" *Harvard Business Review, 74, 6, 61-78.*

Quinn, B. (1994), *The Intelligent Enterprises,* New York: Free Press.

Ross, M. (1989), "Economic Long Waves in Retrospect," in *A Gale of Creative Destruction: The Coming Economic Boom 1992-2020,* New York: Praeger, 33-57.

Schumpeter, J. (1934), *The Theory of Economic Development,* Cambridge, MA: Harvard University Press.

"The Hitchhiker's Guide to Cybernomics." (1996), *The Economist,* September 28, 3-46.

Weber, M. (1978, orig. 1910), *Economy and Society* (G. Roth and C. Wittich, Trs.), Berkeley: University of California Press.

Part I

FORCES DRIVING
HYPERCOMPETITION

1

The Two Faces of Competition

Dynamic Resourcefulness and the Hypercompetitive Shift

L. G. THOMAS, III

Competition in the American economy has fundamentally changed over the last few decades, from static to dynamic. This study labels this important change the *hypercompetitive shift,* and documents it across 200 industries of the U.S. manufacturing sector during 1958 to 1991. For industries that undergo a hypercompetitive shift, there is an increase in the cross-firm variance in performance and a rotation in the value-rivalry relationship from a negative association to an inverted-U. As a consequence of these competitive changes, the strategic focus of firms shifts from careful exploitation of given, highly durable strategic assets to the steady creation of many new, rapidly depreciable ones.

The key driver of hypercompetitive shift is the *dynamic resourcefulness* of an industry, or the ease with which new strategic assets can be created. Determinants of dynamic resourcefulness include the dynamism of related transactors (notably consumers and suppliers), the knowledge base of the industry, and structural conditions that promote easy entry.

(HYPERCOMPETITIVE SHIFT;
DYNAMIC COMPETITION;
SCHUMPETERIAN COMPETITION;
DYNAMIC RESOURCEFULNESS)

AUTHOR'S NOTE: This chapter is adapted from L. G. Thomas, III's presentation at the Whittemore Conference on Hypercompetition, September 1994.

INTRODUCTION

Competition has two faces, or two distinct impacts on firms. On one side, *static competition* takes technology as given, thereby forcing firms to compete on price and costs. Static competition reduces the value of the firm by denying it cashflows. Greater competition lowers prices and/or raises costs of providing services, thus reducing profits and depreciating strategic assets. On the other side, *dynamic (or Schumpeterian) competition* changes technology at various points of the value chain, challenging firms to compete in completely new ways. As firms in an industry transform their technologies, they create different strategic assets that bring them new streams of cashflows. Thus competition can be a benefit or a detriment to a firm depending on whether it is primarily static or dynamic.

Which face does competition really show? This study examines this question for industries of the U.S. manufacturing sector during 1958 to 1991. The principal finding is that the overall nature of competition in the U.S. economy has dramatically changed during these three and one-half decades. In the early years of the study, static competition dominated. But by the final, most recent years, dynamic competition clearly dominates. This change from static to dynamic competition, a trend ignored by most strategy models, is called the *hypercompetitive shift*, a term adapted from D'Aveni (1994). In addition to this trend over time, the study finds that whether competition is static or dynamic varies with the instruments of rivalry among firms and with the structural propensity of an industry to produce new strategic assets. The latter propensity is described as the *dynamic resourcefulness* of an industry.

The plan of this chapter is as follows. The next two sections provide theoretical context. The distinction between static and dynamic competition is examined in more detail, and the concept of dynamic resourcefulness of an industry is defined and explored. Three conditions are identified under which competition in an industry is likely to be dynamic: (1) hypercompetitive industries, having structural features that promote dynamic competition, (2) the hypercompetitive shift, as competition becomes more dynamic with a secular trend on average across all industries, and (3) hypercompetitive behaviors, instruments of rivalry that are likely to trigger dynamic competition. Then the methodology of the study is outlined in terms of measurement, data sources, and estimation issues. After the empirical findings are reported, the conclusion summarizes the findings on the hypercompetitive shift and notes their strategic implications. Appendix A presents in detail the estimation technique (maximum pseudo-likelihood) and Appendix B examines various limitations and extensions of the empirical findings.

THEORY: THE TWO
FACES OF COMPETITION

What makes a firm successful relative to others in an economy? Few issues are more hotly debated in strategic management and industrial economics (for reviews of this debate, see Grant 1991a, Winter 1995, and Porter 1991). To place this in the context of that debate, two well-known models of corporate success are contrasted, though of course other versions of these models and even other models could be comparably used.[1]

On the left in Figure 1.1 is the Five Forces restatement of the Structure-Conduct-Performance model by Porter (1979a, 1980), and on the right is the Diamond model by the same author (1990a, 1990b). At first glance, they are the same "model," in that both are nothing more than an iteration of participants in an industry, with a few quirks. Consumers of a firm's products and services are listed twice in each model, as "substitutes" and "buyer power" in the Five Forces model and as "demand conditions" and "related industries" in the Diamond model. (This last point is also made by Grant 1991b.) Further, these models offer very Anglo-Saxon iterations in which government, capital markets, and the institutions of science are excluded and invisible. A more comprehensive listing of industry participants is given in Figure 1.2.

Clearly, the important differences between the Five Forces and Diamond models cannot lie in the particularities of how the more comprehensive iteration of industry participants in Figure 1.2 is reduced to specific listings in Figure 1.1. Rather, the difference between the two models is in the assumed underlying nature of competition itself. In the Five Forces model, we are in a world of static or non-Schumpeterian competition, with given strategic assets. The focus is on cashflows from higher prices and restrained costs, achieved by low rivalry among a given and clearly identifiable set of competitors. Competition is damaging to success in the world represented by this model. Such turbulence reduces the ability of firms to tacitly collude for higher prices and restrained costs, and it interferes with the ability of current competitors to successfully exclude new entrants despite the high profits of existing firms. In this world of static technology, rivalry unambiguously reduces the value of the firm to its owners. Additionally, strong buyers, strong suppliers, activist government, and strong labor organizations undermine success for firms by reducing their ability to collude/exclude and by creating countervailing bilateral monopolies.

Porter's own words leave no doubt as to the static nature of competition in the Five-Forces model. "Competition in an industry continually works to drive down the rate of return on invested capital toward the competitive floor

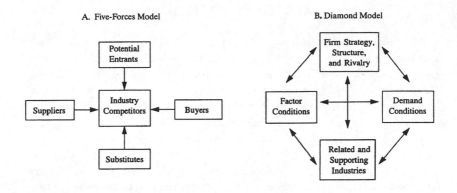

Figure 1.1. Two Models of the Determinants of Corporate Success

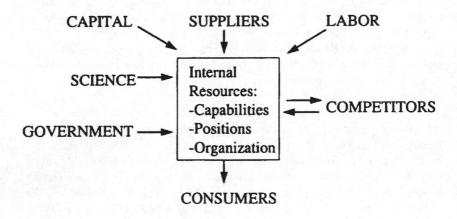

Figure 1.2. The Network Model: The Firm as Resources in a Network of Relationships

rate of return" (1980, p. 5; also 1979a, p. 137). It is not just direct rivalry that threatens profits in this world of static technology. "Suppliers can exert bargaining power on participants in an industry by raising prices or reducing quality. Powerful suppliers can thereby squeeze profitability out of an industry." And "customers likewise can force down prices, demand higher quality or more service, and play competitors off against each other—all at the expense of industry profits" (both Porter 1979a, p. 140; also 1980, pp. 24,

27). The bottom line under such circumstances is that "the corporate strate-gist's goal is to find a position in the industry where his or her company can best defend itself against these forces" (Porter 1979a, pp. 137, 145; also 1980, pp. 4, 29). The completely static nature of the underlying technology in this world is transparent. Especially note Porter's summary injunction to find *a position* (clearly static) on which to found corporate strategy.

The non-Schumpeterian nature of the Five Forces model is sometimes obscured by confusion over use of the term "dynamic." The actual mechanics of competition in the Five Forces model, of course, occur over time. Collu-sion, exclusion, and bargaining with powerful related transactors such as key suppliers thus acquire "dynamic" aspects such as reputation, signaling, promises/threats, and so on. Nonetheless, for rivalry, entry, and related transactors to unambiguously damage the value of the firm requires a world of static technology and non-Schumpeterian competition. Note the semantic ambiguity of the term "dynamic competition" as meaning either competition over time or competition through innovation, with only the latter constituting dynamic competition in the sense of Schumpeter (1934).[2]

In the Diamond model, however, we are in a world of truly dynamic, Schumpeterian competition. The focus of the model is on the creation of new strategic assets at various points of the value chain, driven by rivalry among a shifting set of powerful firms. Rivalry is essential to corporate success in this brave new world. Competitive challenge is what compels firms to break down old ways of business and what enables them to create new ways of doing business. Further, powerful related transactors such as strong buyers, strong suppliers, activist government, and strong labor organizations are critical to success in dynamic competition. Their strength and dynamism add to the challenge facing firms, and these strong external transactors offer their own new technologies and new approaches.

Again, Porter's own words leave no doubt as to the dynamic or Schum-peterian nature of competition in the Diamond model. "Companies achieve competitive advantage through acts of innovation" (1990b, p. 74). "Innova-tion and change are inextricably tied together. But change is an unnatural act, particularly in successful companies; powerful forces are at work to avoid and defeat it" (1990b, p. 75). Innovation is seen as powered by intense rivalry and by strong related transactors. "Rivalry creates pressure on companies to innovate and improve. Local rivals push each other to lower costs, improve quality and service, and create new products and processes" (1990b, p. 82; also 1990a, p. 118). And "demanding buyers provide a window into advanced customer needs; they pressure companies to meet high standards; they prod them to improve, to innovate, and to upgrade into more advanced segments" (1990b, p. 79; also 1990a, p. 89). By 1990, Porter's ultimate strategic commandment of 1979/1980, that firms should find "a position" to shield themselves from competitive forces is now seen as one of the "all-too-easy escape routes that appear to offer a path to competitive advantage, but are actually short-cuts to failure" (1990b, p. 89). Instead, the new strategic injunction is for managers to provide "leadership that harnesses and amplifiers competitive forces to promote innovation and upgrading" (1990b, p. 89).

How do we reconcile these two very different views of competition? Let us begin with the pronounced irony that Schumpeter (1942) himself argued that innovation is best advanced by reduced rivalry, contrary to the Diamond model. Indeed, for decades of empirical research in industrial economics, the "Schumpeterian hypotheses" meant precisely the argument that large firms in highly concentrated industries are more innovative than other firms. Schumpeter posed his hypotheses out of concern about the very basic question of how firms raise the necessary cashflows to fund creation of new strategic assets. His concerns appear to be a mix of the cashflow issues of the Five Forces model and the challenge issues of the Diamond model. And indeed, Schumpeter's concerns would seem to have significant validity. For example, Chrysler's development of minivans and purchase of the Jeep division of American Motors saved and transformed the firm. The near bankruptcy of Chrysler in 1979 certainly challenged the firm to develop these new competitive niches, but a U.S. government bailout was a necessary antecedent (Reich 1985). Similarly, Airbus has developed significant capabilities and market positions in the commercial aviation market. The price for development of those resources was some $20 billion in loans from various European governments (Tyson 1992). As a third example, low domestic prices for ethical drugs set through government regulations have certainly challenged French pharmaceutical firms—right into competitive oblivion—by denying them adequate resources to perform R & D for major innovations (Thomas, 1994). Clearly, the cashflow issues that are the focus of static competition do not suddenly evaporate simply because dynamic competition occurs.

Thus we see that Schumpeterian rivalry really shows both faces of competition. Dynamic effects from rivalry challenge firms to develop new strategic assets generating future cashflows, but static effects remain, reducing current cashflows. An important reconciliation of those two effects of rivalry was provided by Scherer (1967b, 1980), whose argument is adapted in Figure 1.3.[3] At low levels of rivalry, the dynamic effects of rivalry dominate (see the top panel of Figure 1.3). Increases in rivalry from zero would do little to change the cashflows from present strategic assets (minimal static effects), but would importantly spur firms to create new strategic assets that would generate future cashflows (large dynamic effects). Thus at low levels of rivalry, rivalry and innovative effort (hence the value of the

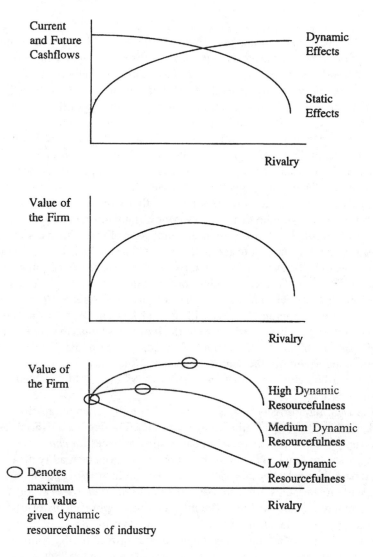

Figure 1.3. Rivalry, Cashflows, and Value

firm) would be positively correlated. At very high levels of rivalry, however, static effects dominate. The dynamic benefits from greater rivalry plateau, while the static costs mount. Thus at high levels of rivalry, rivalry and innovative effort (hence firm value) are negatively associated. Overall, the rivalry-innovation relationship would be "inverted-U," with some optimal level of rivalry (see the middle panel of Figure 1.3).[4] Thus both faces of competition are incorporated in the model. Scherer (1967a) provided empirical support for his inverted-U hypothesis, subsequent theory development was offered by Kamien and Schwartz (1976), and further empirical confirmation was provided by several researchers, including Scott (1984) and Levin, Cohen, and Mowery (1985). For excellent surveys of these issues, see Cohen and Levin (1989) and Cohen (1995).

The first postulated main effect of the theory is the inverted-U relationship. The second postulated main effect arises from recognition of the high variance in performance across firms in dynamic competition, so that not all firms benefit. Dynamic competition involves the introduction of new products, new processes, and new organizations that will become new strategic assets for the firm—if the firm is lucky. Many, if not most, of such innovative efforts by firms in fact fail. As a consequence, some firms gain in competitive position and their immediate competitors lose. The analysis to this point has considered only the average impact of rivalry. Here we see that though rivalry may well increase the average value for firms in an industry (the left arm of the inverted-U), it will increase the variance as well. As the experiences of firms diverge, corporate success will depend less and less on the "shared assets" (to use Porter's 1979b term) of the industry such as the general price level and the intensity of demand. Instead, as an industry undergoes a hypercompetitive shift, the source of corporate success moves internal to the firm, toward its ability to create new strategic assets as old ones depreciate ever more rapidly.

The two main effects in this study thus concern changes in firm stock market values due to escalating industry rivalry. The dependent variables for analysis are industry means and intra-industry variances for *changes in stock market value* of firms in the industry. Those values can be readily measured, and indeed several alternate measures are examined in Appendix B. The independent variables for analysis are *escalations in rivalry,* for which measurement is more difficult. The most common approach historically has been to proxy the level of rivalry at a given point of time, not changes in rivalry over time. That traditional approach has proved highly controversial and ultimately unimpressive. The early investigations of the "Schumpeterian hypotheses" in industrial economics, for example, used concentration as a crude inverse proxy for rivalry. A series of studies have cast severe doubt on the validity of that proxy, including those by Demsetz (1973) documenting the diversity of returns among firms in concentrated industries, by Peltzman (1977) and Salinger (1990) documenting that increased concentration reduces industry prices, and by Porter (1979b), Ravenschraft (1983), and

Schmalensee (1985) documenting that concentration reduces industry profitability. These newer studies all challenge the traditional interpretation that concentration is associated negatively with rivalry, and strongly suggest that concentration is instead a result of efficiency differences across firms.

Fortunately, for this study we are not directly interested in measuring rivalry per se. Instead we are concerned with measuring the challenge that rivalry exerts for firms in an industry. The static effects of challenge are reduced current cashflows and the dynamic effects are the future benefits of innovations. For both static and dynamic effects, then, we do not measure rivalry directly, but rather measure the impact of rivalry on cashflows. For example, the most obvious measure of challenge arises when prices fall while industry output and unit costs are constant (in formal terms, prices fall *ceteris paribus*). By far the most likely cause of declining prices *ceteris paribus* is indeed increased rivalry among firms in the industry. As a consequence, the core independent variables of this study are changes in unit sales, prices, and costs—all of which drive industry cashflows.[5] A reduction of industry prices *ceteris paribus* implies escalating industry challenge and signals greater competition, as do increases of unit costs *ceteris paribus*.

The two core empirical issues examined in this study are the mean value-rivalry relationship for firms in an industry and the within-industry variance around that mean. If competition is primarily static, escalating rivalry (reduced cashflows) will lower the average value of firms in an industry and the intra-industry variance in performance will be small. Essentially, current cash-flow effects shared by all firms in the industry will dominate any effects of changes in technology that are heterogeneous across firms. Conversely, if competition is primarily dynamic, the value-rivalry relationship will be an inverted-U, so that rivalry will increase average firm value at least initially, and the intra-industry variance in performance will become larger. Firms will be forced by escalating rivalry to innovate and to create new strategic assets, and those dynamic effects will augment value for firms on average, though with higher variance.

Figure 1.4 summarizes the two main effects that are the core expectations of the study. Under static competition, increased rivalry will monotonically decrease the stock market value of firms on average, and the realized effects on individual firms will not deviate much from the industry average effect. The mean effect on firms in the industry is denoted by the heavy declining line; one standard deviation around the mean effect is denoted by the shaded area around the line. Under dynamic competition, increased rivalry will have a nonlinear impact on the average stock market value for firms, but with much greater variance in impact.

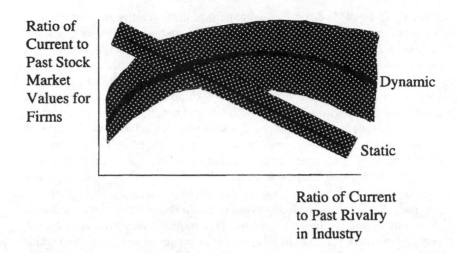

Figure 1.4. Two Main Effects
NOTE: Mean performance denoted by heavy line. Range of one standard deviation denoted by shaded area.

THEORY: DYNAMIC RESOURCEFULNESS
AND HYPERCOMPETITION

The argument thus far is that under static competition, expected firm value monotonically declines with rivalry and has little variance, whereas under dynamic competition, expected changes in firm value are related to escalating rivalry with an inverted-U shape and the interfirm variance is high. These two discrete models can be linked by positing a contingency factor: the innate propensity of an industry to create new strategic assets, here called the *dynamic resourcefulness* of the industry. Dynamic resourcefulness varies widely across industries. In an industry where it is low, the creation of new strategic assets is very difficult. For such industries, competition is essentially static as there are few or no dynamic benefits from rivalry. Rivalry and firm value are then unambiguously negatively related (see the bottom panel of Figure 1.3). In industries of medium dynamic resourcefulness, rivalry will generate some dynamic effects, though the value-rivalry curve will be rather flat. In industries of high dynamic resourcefulness, here called *hypercompetitive industries,* we observe the true inverted-U (again, see the bottom panel of Figure 1.3).

It is useful to contrast the concept of dynamic resourcefulness with two other concepts in strategic management. First, the *resource-based view of the firm* presents corporate success as derived from firm-specific efficiency rents as opposed to industry-wide monopoly rents. The latter (monopoly) approach is of course the basis of the Five Forces model. In contrast, hypercompetition is driven by the rapid creation of new firm-specific resources, and thus represents a dynamic application of the resource-based view of the firm—hence the term "dynamic resourcefulness." But note that hypercompetitive industries also involve the rapid depreciation of strategic assets, be they based in efficiency or in monopoly. Hence, though hypercompetition is consistent with the resource-based view of the firm, the reverse need not be true—a completely static industry with no monopoly but stable, large efficiency rents would not in fact be hypercompetitive. Such an industry (one of static efficiency) seems to be the type described by Demsetz (1973). Note then that this study cannot be construed as providing evidence for the historical validity of the Five Forces model, but merely evidence that whatever validity it may once have had has depreciated with time. The study findings indicate a shift away from static competition, be it monopoly based or efficiency based.

The second related concept in strategic management is *resource munificence.* An industry is munificent in resources if firms have large cashflows from either efficiency or monopoly sources. Essentially, resource munificence is *static resourcefulness,* or the static equivalent of dynamic resourcefulness. Resource munificence refers to the presence of strategic assets. Dynamic resourcefulness refers to the ability to generate new strategic assets that will generate future cashflows. A dynamically resourceful industry has a balance between resource munificence (static resourcefulness) and challenge, as discussed previously.

Hypercompetitive Industries

What attributes of an industry are likely to make it more dynamically resourceful than most other industries, and thus more likely to be hypercompetitive? Several recent studies can be adapted to answer this question. In the strategic management literature, D'Aveni (1994) identified four industry factors as drivers of hypercompetition: (1) consumer demand, (2) the knowledge base of firms and associated workers, (3) the declining height of entry barriers, and (4) the increasing frequency of alliances among firms—one driver for each of his "arenas." In the industrial economics literature, numerous "post-Schumpeterian" studies (for surveys, see Cohen and Levin 1989 and Cohen 1995) have identified three sets of industry factors associated with high levels of innovative activity: appropriability conditions, consumer demand, and technological opportunity. Those three factors are in addition to firm size and industry concentration that were the focus of "traditional Schumpeterian" industrial economics.

The intersection of these sets of studies suggests three industry factors that make some industries more dynamically resourceful than others.

1. *Transactor dynamism,* or features of demand and supply that both push and nurture innovation in an industry. An example of how related transactors forced innovation is provided by how the dynamism of demand forced a hypercompetitive shift in the U.S. petroleum industry in the 1930s (Comanor and Scherer 1995).[6] Among the many factors used in the neo-Schumpeterian literature as empirical proxies for the dynamism of related transactors are (1) the growth rate of demand, which facilitates new technologies and firms and rewards innovation, (2) the inelasticity of demand, which makes possible higher prices and greater rewards for innovation, and is proxied by the percentage of final demand due to consumers (versus industry and government), and (3) the technical sophistication of suppliers, which both challenges and aids firms in the industry to innovate, and which is inversely proxied by the percentage of supply due to raw materials.

2. *Knowledge base,* or the dynamism and depth of the knowledge base of an industry. Proxies for this driver of hypercompetition include (1) the percentage of the workforce that is professional, indicating the capacity of workers in the industry to innovate, and (2) the productivity growth rate for the industry, a rather direct measure of innovative activity.

3. *Entry conditions,* or the dynamism of market structure. An important example of how entry triggers industry innovation and competitive renewal is provided by the wave of imports and minimills that beset the American steel industry in the 1970s (Comanor and Scherer 1995). Proxies for this driver of hypercompetition include (1) growth in the industry concentration ratio, an inverse proxy for ease of entry, and (2) growth in industry imports, a direct proxy for ease of entry.

These variables are expected to be reasonable measures of dynamic resourcefulness with the exception of imports for which minimal effect is expected. Imports reduce cashflows and challenge firms (static effects) without readily enabling innovative response (dynamic effects). Imports are discussed further below in the subsection on hypercompetitive behaviors. Formal hypotheses, one for each main effect, follow.

H1. *More dynamically resourceful industries have a more pronounced inverted-U in the relationship between mean growth in stock market value and escalating rivalry; less dynamically resourceful industries have a traditional monotonically declining performance-rivalry relationship. Dynamic resourcefulness is associated with seven variables that encourage innova-*

tiveness: three for transactor dynamism, two for knowledge base, and two for entry conditions.

H2. *More dynamically resourceful industries have higher intra-industry variance across firms in the growth of firm stock market values.*

The two hypotheses are summarized in Table 1.1.

Hypercompetitive Shift

From the preceding arguments, dynamic resourcefulness is expected to increase generically over time. The study sample covers the years 1958 to 1991. At the beginning of the sample, technology evolved rather slowly and creating new strategic assets was difficult (D'Aveni 1994). Transportation costs were high, and the U.S. economy was essentially closed to foreign competition. Communication and data processing costs were high, and information moved slowly. Under those circumstances, strategic assets were very durable. Consider some examples. In the soft drink industry, the five major firms each purveyed only one brand, which had been introduced decades earlier. In the telecommunications industry, AT&T maintained a vertical and horizontal monopoly, established by 1909, for much of the United States. In the automobile industry, General Motors dominated the American market with the twin strategies of vertical differentiation (from Chevrolet up to Cadillac) and vertical integration of production. Both GM strategies were established in the 1920s. The internal organization of such firms as Coca-Cola, AT&T, and General Motors was rigidly focused on intensive exploitation of their historic strategic assets.

By 1991, that calm and stable economic environment had quite disappeared for most American firms (D'Aveni 1994). Falling transportation, telecommunication, and data processing costs had globalized many markets. The top panel of Figure 1.5 demonstrates the steady rise over time of trade as a share of GDP for the United States. This globalization simultaneously depreciated historic, national strategic assets and fostered the creation of new, global strategic assets. The rapid change of technology facilitated the proliferation of new products and new competitors, again depreciating old strategic assets. The bottom panel of Figure 1.5 traces the steady, slow deterioration of competitive position for firms in the U.S. manufacturing sector after 1950. From a postwar high of 40 percent, ROA (return on total capital) slowly declined until the 1980s where it plateaued. A recent paper (Thomas and Waring 1995) documents that the stabilization and turnaround of ROA for U.S. manufacturing firms was due to the rise of firm-specific innovations that mark dynamic competition. The steady trend in increasing

TABLE 1.1 Hypotheses, Method of Testing, and Findings

Number	Hypothesis	Method	Finding
Hypercompetitive industries			
H1	More resourceful industries have an inverted-U for the value-rivalry relationship; less resourceful industries have a monotonically negative relationship.	Six industry factors have appropriate signs in Table 1.7: sales growth (+), consume (+), raw materials (-), professional (+), productivity (-), concentration (-).	Correct sign, significant in 4 of 6 cases.
H2	More dynamically resourceful industries have higher intra-industry variance in firm performance.	Five industry factors have appropriate signs in Table 1.6: consume (+), raw materials (-), professional (+), productivity (+), concentration (-).	Correct sign, significant in 5 of 10 cases.
Hypercompetitive shift			
H3	The value-rivalry relationship moves from monotonically negative in early years to an inverted-U relationship in more recent years.	Estimated minimum of value-SGA relationship $(-\alpha_3/\gamma_3)$ falls above most observations in early years; estimated maximum $\{-[\alpha_3 + \beta_3{}^*(t-68)] / \gamma_3 + \delta_3{}^*(t-68)]\}$ lies near median of observations in later years.	Confirmed; see Figure 1.8.
H4	The intra-industry variance of firm performance increases over time.	Coefficient on year term is positive in Table 1.6.	Positive and significant.
Hypercompetitive behaviors			
H5	Growth in industry shipments and industry prices has smaller impacts on firm values over time.	Coefficients on time-interaction terms for growth in shipments and prices are negative in Tables 1.4 and 1.5.	Negative and significant.
H6	Rivalry in unit-SGA costs is more likely to have an inverted-U relationship with firm values in recent years than are other forms of rivalry in the same time period.	Estimated maximum $\{-[\alpha_3 + \beta_3{}^*(t-68)] / [\gamma_3 + \delta_3{}^*(t-68)]\}$ for SGA-growth lies near median of observations in later years; comparable estimated minimum or maximum lies outside range of most observations for CGS and prices.	Confirmed; compare Figures 1.7, 1.8, and 1.9.
H7	Growth in industry shipments and prices reduces the intra-industry variance in firm performance.	Coefficients on terms for growth in shipments and prices are negative in Table 1.6.	Negative and significant in 3 of 4 cases.
H8	Growth in unit-CGS and unit-SGA increases the intra-industry variance in performance.	Coefficients on terms for growth in unit-CGS and unit-SGA are positive in Table 1.6.	Positive and significant in 3 of 4 cases.

A. U.S. Merchandise Trade as Share of GNP

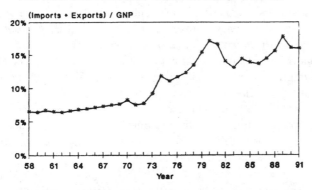

Source: U.S. Statistical Abstract (1994)

B. Returns and Costs of Capital, U.S. Manufacturing Sector

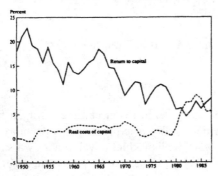

Source: Blair and Litan (1990)

Figure 1.5. Examples of Underlying Secular Trend Generating a Hypercompetitive Shift

competitive intensity for American manufacturers was driven by underlying changes in technology that precipitated entry by new competitors and new modes of competition among current competitors-that is, an increase in the general dynamic resourcefulness of U.S. manufacturing industries.

The preceding argument suggests a steady, almost linear increase in the dynamic resourcefulness of many U.S. industries during the 1958 to 1991 span of the study, a linear trend that was itself driven by the effectively linear increase in the underlying determinants of dynamic resourcefulness: trans-actor dynamism, knowledge base, and entry conditions. The exogenously generated increase in dynamic resourcefulness caused a hypercompetitive shift from static to dynamic competition over the time period. Hence, a simple linear time trend interacted with key variables is used as a proxy for the general intertemporal increase. Over the time period of the study, shared factors for all firms in the industry (such as prices) would have steadily smaller impact on firm performance. At the same time, the rivalry-value relationship would flatten and in the extreme become an inverted-U. Finally, the intra-industry variance for performance would increase over time. For-mal hypotheses for each main effect follow.

H3. *The relationship between the average growth in firm stock market value and escalating rivalry is monotonically negative for the early years of the sam-ple, but over time shifts to an inverted-U in later time periods.*

H4. *The intra-industry variance of stock market growth for firms in an industry increases over time.*

These hypotheses are summarized in Table 1.1.

Hypercompetitive Behaviors

A final determinant of dynamic resourcefulness for an industry is the instruments through which rivalry is expressed. Rivalry may occur through price wars, marketing wars, new product development wars, and so on. All of those instruments of rivalry produce static effects on cashflows, and thus challenge the firm. The real issue, however, is how readily each of the quite different instruments (or arenas) of rivalry produces dynamic effects through creation of new strategic assets.[7] Contrast, for example, the consequences of an industry war in new product development with the consequences of a sharp increase in the price of a key raw material. Both developments reduce short-term cashflows (static effects) and challenge firms. Yet new product development by its very nature is much more likely to generate new strategic assets that will help firms cope with the challenge over the long term. Similarly, contrast the consequences of a competitive invasion by foreign firms through imports and an invasion by the same firms through local transplants established by direct investment. Again, both developments challenge established local firms and produce negative static effects for them. Yet studies by Porter (1990a) for a variety of industries and Thomas (1994) for the global pharmaceutical industry demonstrate that firms learn far more rapidly from localized rivalry. Nearby rivals, competing under the same general conditions, learn readily from each other. Imports come from rivals obscured by geography, culture, language, and other profound differences of the competitive environment that impede learning and other dynamic responses.

Both the intertemporal and cross-sectional effects discussed previously vary by the instrument of rivalry. Some instruments are a common experience of all firms in the industry (such as price levels). Those shared instruments will have a steadily smaller effect on firm values over time because of the hypercompetitive shift, will be unlikely to have an inverted-U relationship with value, and will be associated with lower intra-industry variance in firm stock market performance. Other instruments are by their nature much more firm specific (such as new product launches) and will have opposite effects. The most important instruments are the marketing and R & D expenses that are aggregated in SGA (selling, general, and administrative expenses). Hence:

H5. *The impact of changes in industry shipments and industry prices on changes in average firm stock market values declines over time.*

H6. *Increased rivalry in unit-SGA expenses is likely to have an inverted-U relationship with average increases in firm stock market performance, whereas increased rivalry in prices or in unit-CGS (cost of goods sold) is more likely to retain a monotonically negative relationship.*

H7. *The impact of growth in industry shipments and industry prices on the intra-industry variance in stock market performance across firms is negative.*

H8. *The impact of growth in unit-CGS and unit-SGA on the intra-industry variance in stock market performance across firms is positive.*

Again, these hypotheses are summarized in Table 1.1.

Summary

The theory for this study is restated and extended in Figure 1.6. An industry undergoes a hypercompetitive shift when exogenous changes in technology make the industry more dynamically resourceful, by making the creation of new strategic assets easier. The more rapid creation of new strategic assets is accompanied by the more rapid depreciation of older ones. These exogenous changes in technology are expected to have three impacts, as indicated in Figure 1.6. Only the last two are examined formally in this study (denoted by double arrows). First, there will be an increase in rivalry—through emergence of new competitors, the development and deployment of new instruments (or arenas) of rivalry, and increased use of old instruments.

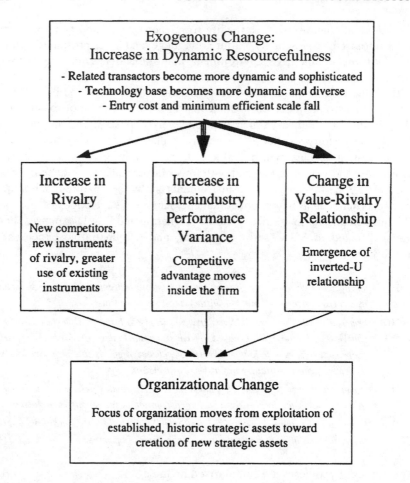

Figure 1.6. Summary of Theory

Second, there will be an increase in the variance of performance across firms in an industry. Third, the effect of rivalry on the expected value of firms will change from an unambiguous negative association to an inverted-U. As a final effect, these changes in the industry will force changes inside the firm itself, as it reorganizes to adapt to its new competitive environment. Reorganization refocuses the firm from intense exploitation of old, given strategic assets toward a new goal of ever more rapid creation of new strategic assets. Internal reorganization is perhaps the most critical step in the realization of dynamic benefits from rivalry.

METHOD

Sample and Data Sources

Data for this study are pooled cross-section time-series. Individual observations are single 4-digit SIC manufacturing industries in single years during 1958 to 1991. Table 1.2 provides an overview of the data with descriptive statistics and variable correlations. Variable definitions and sources are summarized in Table 1.3. Data were drawn from four sources. First, industry changes in sales, prices (wholesale price indices), and sales per worker (productivity) were taken from the excellent NBER (National Bureau of Economic Research, Cambridge, MA) dataset maintained by Wayne Gray, of NBER and Clark University. The importance of the NBER data is that they are consistent over the various changes in SIC definitions during the three decades. The NBER dataset spans the years 1958 to 1991 and thus provided the time limits for the study. Second, average industry changes in stock market values, in unit cost of goods sold (CGS), and in unit selling, general, and administrative expenses (SGA) were drawn from two versions of Standard & Poor's Compustat. Firms are linked across the two Compustat datasets by cusip-code (a six-digit numerical identifier). Third, changes in concentration ratios and import/sales ratios were taken from Salinger (1990). Finally, unlike all other data which vary by both industry and year, data for industry features used as proxies for industry dynamic resourcefulness were taken for a single year, 1987. From the Annual Input-Output Tables for the United States, for each 4-digit SIC, data were taken for the proportion of final demand due to consumers (as opposed to business or government demand) and for the proportion of inputs that are raw materials (from agriculture and mining). From the Current Population Survey, data for each 3-digit SIC were taken for the proportion of workers in an industry that are professional. The variable glossary in Table 1.3 gives further details of variable definition.

Operationalization

Most variables are of the form of one-year and ten-year growth rates: $\ln(X_t / X_{t-1})$ for one-year growth and $\ln(X_t / X_{t-10})$ for 10-year growth. For the one-year changes data run from 1959 to 1991, as the first year of data is lost in computing the growth ratios. For the 10-year changes data run from 1968 to 1991, as the first ten years of data are lost. For the one-year changes, static competition is expected to prevail; too little time elapses in a single year to allow the benefits of challenge and of technical evolution that would offset

TABLE 1.2 Data Overview: Sample Attributes, Descriptive Statistics, and Variable Correlations

Sample attributes	1-Year Growth Rates	10-Year Growth Rates
Number of raw data points (firm/year)	60,960	26,386
Number of observations (industry/year)	6,682	4,648
Total number of years	33	24
Average number of firms per industry	9.1	5.7
Average number of industries per year	202	194

Descriptive statistics (Mean at left, standard deviation at right)	1-Year		10-Year	
1. ln(grow(stock market value))	.124	.370	.986	.902
2. ln(grow(industry shipments))	.026	.103	.253	.369
3. ln(grow(unit cost of goods sold))	.003	.043	.010	.114
4. ln(grow(unit selling and administrative costs))	.020	.095	.116	.245
5. ln(grow(wholesale price index))	.040	.054	.472	.281
6. ln(grow(shipments per worker))	.023	.065	.227	.217
7. ln(grow(4-firm concentration))	.011	.032	-.040	.505
8. Percentage final demand to consumers	.141		.204	
9. Percentage inputs from raw materials	.030		.107	
10. Percentage workforce professional	.076		.056	

22

Variable Correlations

(Variable numbers immediately above; one-year correlations at bottom left of matrix;
10-year correlations at top right of matrix)

	1.	2.	3.	4.	5.	6.	7.	8.	9.	10.
1.		.04**	-.23**	.05**	.02	.09**	.00	.07**	.06**	.07**
2.	-.02		-.00	-.12**	-.38**	.39**	.08**	-.02	-.07**	.18**
3.	-.15**	-.02		-.25**	-.00	.02	.02	-.01	-.02	.04**
4.	-.04*	-.12**	.00		.02	-.07**	-.12**	-.02	.01	.00
5.	.02	-.25**	.00	.03*		-.55**	.03*	-.10**	-.01	-.05**
6.	.04**	.62**	-.06**	-.09**	-.32**		.05*	.19**	.07*	.18**
7.	.01	.01	-.01	.00	.01	.01		-.04*	-.03	-.04**
8.	.01	-.01	-.01	-.00	-.03*	.05**	.02		.08**	-.32**
9.	-.00	-.02	-.00	.02	-.02	.02	.05	.08**		-.20**
10.	.03*	.06**	-.00	-.00	-.02	.06**	.03*	-.23*	-.20**	

TABLE 1.3 Variable Glossary

Functional forms

grow(X_t) Ratio of variable X in year t to either X in year $(t-1)$ for one-year changes, or to X in year $(t-10)$ for 10-year changes.

ln(grow(X_t)) Natural logarithm of grow(X_t).

Computation and sources

Stock market value	For each firm, stock market value of common equity is computed as shares of common equity outstanding times calendar year-end closing price. Data for this variable are derived from Compustat. Values for 1974-1991 are taken from Compustat PC Plus, including research (defunct) firms. Values for 1958-1975 are taken from the Black Compustat tapes, including the full coverage, PST, and research files. Firms are matched across the two files by the 6-digit cusip code. One-year and 10-year growth ratios are computed for each firm, and the average is taken over all firms in the 4-digit SIC industry.
Shipments	Value of shipments in an industry, deflated by the industry-specific wholesale price index; taken from the NBER database based on original census data.
Prices (PPI)	Industry producer price deflator (PPI), from the NBER database based on census data.
Unit-CGS	Unit cost of goods sold is the ratio of cost of goods sold to sales for each firm. This variable has the same computation method and source as stock market value.
Unit-SGA	Unit selling, general, and administration expense is the ratio of SGA expense to sales for each firm. This variable has the same computation and source as unit-CGS.
Productivity	Constant dollar shipments divided by number of workers in the industry, from the NBER database based on census data.
Concentration	Four-firm concentration ratio, taken from Salinger (1990).
Imports	Ratio of imports to industry shipments, taken from Salinger (1990).
Consumer	Ratio of consumer demand to total demand, taken from the Annual Input-Output Tables of the United States for 1987 only.
Raw material	Ratio of inputs from agriculture and mining to total inputs, taken from the Annual Input-Output Table of the United States for 1987 only.
Professional	Percentage of workers in an industry that are professional, taken from the *Current Population Survey* for 1989 only.

---

the current cashflow impacts of greater competition. For the 10-year changes, whether static or dynamic competition prevails is an empirical equation.

To allow for the hypothesized secular trend, key variables are interacted with (year-59) for the one-year changes and (year-68) for the 10-year changes. All estimation includes fixed effects for years (binary variables included for each year). The coefficients for the year binary variables are not of interest and are not reported.

To allow for nonlinearity that creates an inverted-U, the regressions are specified in the following form:

$$\ln(Y) = \alpha + \beta^* \ln(X) - \gamma^* X.$$

That functional form implies that as X increases, Y initially increases and reaches a maximum when $X = (-\beta/\gamma)$. If the signs for β and γ are reversed, then Y is a minimum at $X = (-\beta/\gamma)$.

Estimation

The two key regression specifications follow.

$\ln(\text{SMV}_t/\text{SMV}_{t-1})$
$= \alpha_0 + \alpha_1 \ln(\text{Ship}_t/\text{Ship}_{t-1})$
$+ \alpha_2 \ln(\text{Unit\_CGS}_t/\text{Unit\_CGS}_{t-1})$
$+ \alpha_3 \ln(\text{Unit\_SGA}_t/\text{Unit\_SGA}_{t-1})$
$+ \alpha_4 \ln(\text{PPI}_t/\text{PPI}_{t-1})$
$+ \beta_1 \ln(\text{Ship}_t/\text{Ship}_{t-1})^*(t-59)$
$+ \beta_2 \ln(\text{Unit\_CGS}_t/\text{Unit\_CGS}_{t-1})^*(t-59)$
$+ \beta_3 \ln(\text{Unit\_SGA}_t/\text{Unit\_SGA}_{t-1})^*(t-59)$
$+ \beta_4 \ln(\text{PPI}_t/\text{PPI}_{t-1})^*(t-59)$
$+ \gamma_1(\text{Ship}_t/\text{Ship}_{t-1})$
$+ \gamma_2(\text{Unit\_CGS}_t/\text{Unit\_CGS}_{t-1})$
$+ \gamma_3(\text{Unit\_SGA}_t/\text{Unit\_SGA}_{t-1})$
$+ \gamma_4(\text{PPI}_t/\text{PPI}_{t-1})$
$+ \delta_1(\text{Ship}_t/\text{Ship}_{t-1})^*(t-59)$
$+ \delta_2(\text{Unit\_CGS}_t/\text{Unit\_CGS}_{t-1})^*(t-59)$
$+ \delta3(\text{Unit\_SGA}_t/\text{Unit\_SGA}_{t-1})^*(t-59)$
$+ \delta_4(\text{PPI}_t/\text{PPI}_{t-1})^*(t-59).$ (1)

$\ln(\text{SMV}_t/\text{SMV}_{t-10})$
$= \alpha_0 + \alpha_1 \ln(\text{Ship}_t/\text{Ship}_{t-10})$
$+ \alpha_2 \ln(\text{Unit\_CGS}_t/\text{Unit\_CGS}_{t-10})$
$+ \alpha_3 \ln(\text{Unit\_SGA}_t/\text{Unit\_SGA}_{t-10})$

$+\ \alpha_4\ \ln(PPI_t/PPI_{t-10})$

$+\ \beta_1\ \ln(Ship_t/Ship_{t-10})*(t-68)$

$+\ \beta_2\ \ln(Unit\_CGS_t/Unit\_CGS_{t-10})*(t-68)$

$+\ \beta_3\ \ln(Unit\_SGA_t/Unit\_SGA_{t-10})*(t-68)$

$+\ \beta_4\ \ln(PPI_t/PPI_{t-10})*(t-68)$

$+\ \gamma_1(Ship_t/Ship_{t-10})$

$+\ \gamma_2(Unit\_CGS_t/Unit\_CGS_{t-10})$

$+\ \gamma_3(Unit\_SGA_t/Unit\_SGA_{t-10})$

$+\ \gamma_4(PPI_t/PPI_{t-10})$

$+\ \delta_1(Ship_t/Ship_{t-10})*(t-68)$

$+\ \delta_2(Unit\_CGS_t/Unit\_CGS_{t-10})*(t-68)$

$+\ \delta_3(Unit\_SGA_t/Unit\_SGA_{t-10})*(t-68)$

$+\ \delta_4(PPI_t/PPI_{t-10})*(t-68).$ (2)

Estimates for Eqs. 1 and 2 are reported in Tables 1.4 and 1.5, respectively. If there is no inverted-U (H1, H3, and H6), then the γ and δ sets of coefficients will all be zero. If there is no time trend (H5), then the β and δ sets of coefficients will all be zero. Note how the relationships between value and the four instruments of rivalry vary over time. For example, from regression Eq. 2, in 1968 at the start of the sample, the relationship between stock market value (SMV) and rivalry in unit SGA (selling, general, and administrative costs) is:

$\ln(SMV_t/SMV_{t-10})$

$=\ \alpha_3\ \ln(Unit\_SGA_t/Unit\_SGA_{t-10})$

$+\ \gamma_3(Unit\_SGA_t/Unit\_SGA_{t-10}).$ (3)

By the end of the sample period in 1991, the relationship is:

$\ln(SMV_t/SMV_{t-10})$

$=\ (\alpha_3+\beta_3*23)\ln(Unit\_SGA_t/Unit\_SGA_{t-10})$

$+\ (\gamma_3+\delta_4*23)(Unit\_SGA_t/Unit\_SGA_{t-10}),$ (4)

as 23 years have elapsed since 1968. Because of the proliferation of coefficients in the specification, we interpret the appropriate relationships by plotting them at the start (1968) and end (1991) of the sample. In other words, we plot the curves given by Eqs. 3 and 4.

The estimation for the study is complicated by the hypothesized changes in variances (H2, H4, H6, and H8). Ordinary least squares analysis assumes that variances across observations are uniform. Yet four of the hypotheses are precisely that variances differ over time (an increasing secular trend), across industries (being higher in more resourceful industries), and across instruments of rivalry (being lower for shared instruments such as prices and higher for heterogenous instruments such as SGA expense). At the minimum we have a rich heteroscedasticity problem. Even more fundamentally, however, we expect the mean and variance of performance across industries to be positively correlated, as both increase with a hypercompetitive shift. Thus the dependent variables cannot be normally distributed, as variances do not depend on the mean for normally distributed variables.

Appendix A gives the estimation procedure in full detail. It is sufficient here to say that the mean and the variance regressions are estimated together, so that the estimated variances can be used to correct for the nonuniform and nonnormal nature of the dependent variable. The estimated variance regressions are reported in Table 1.6.

A final estimation issue is how to allow industry dynamic resourcefulness variables to alter the functional shape of the value-rivalry relationship. By this point, with time trends, nonlinearity, and nonnormal errors, the estimation verges on being overly complex. Rather than proliferate additional coefficients for industry variables, we can apply the following more straightforward procedure. Because greater dynamic competition and industry dynamic resourcefulness are expected to be present mostly in recent years, we will examine only the 10-year growth rates for the last one-half of the sample, growth rates ending in 1980 to 1991. The expected most likely source of nonlinearity is the value-SGA rivalry relationship. We therefore estimate the following regression equation for the mean 10-year growth rates during those last 11 years.

$$
\begin{aligned}
\ln(SMV_t/SMV_{t-10}) \\
&= \alpha_0 * SHIFT + \alpha_1 \ln(Ship_t/Ship_{t-10}) \\
&+ \alpha_2 \ln(Unit\_CGS_t/Unit\_CGS_{t-10}) \\
&+ \alpha_3 \ln(Unit\_SGA_t/Unit\_SGA_{t-10}) * SHIFT \\
&+ \alpha_4 \ln(PPI_t/PPI_{t-10}) \\
&+ \gamma_2(Unit\_CGS_t/Unit\_CGS_{t-10}) \\
&+ \gamma_3(Unit\_SGA_t/Unit\_SGA_{t-10}) * SHIFT \\
&+ \gamma_4(PPI_t/PPI_{t-10}) \quad\quad\quad\quad\quad\quad\quad\quad\quad (5)
\end{aligned}
$$

$$
\begin{aligned}
SHIFT \\
&= \theta_1 * \ln(grow(Shipment)) + \theta_2 * Consume \\
&+ \theta_3 * Raw\_Material + \theta_4 * Professional
\end{aligned}
$$

$+ \theta_5 * \ln(\text{grow}(\text{Shipment per Worker}))$

$+ \theta_6 * \ln(\text{grow}(\text{4-Firm Concentration})).$

That specification allows for greater or less estimated nonlinearity in the impact of SGA rivalry on value, per Figure 1.3. The results are reported in Table 1.7. The shift term estimation included a variable for growth of the import-sales ratio for the industry. Unfortunately, because of the limitations of U.S. government data collection, import values are missing for some 30 percent of sample observations. The import variable proved insignificant in every specification tried, and was therefore ultimately excluded from estimation. Because we do not expect any effect of imports (as discussed in the preceding subsection on hypercompetitive behaviors), and because so many observations lack import data, the results with the import variable are not reported.

The estimation approaches used to test each of the eight hypotheses are summarized in Table 1.1. Estimation results are reported in the next section.

FINDINGS

The empirical findings are summarized in Table 1.1 and reported for the one-year growth rates in Tables 1.4 and 1.6 and for the 10-year growth rates in Tables 1.5 and 1.6. Recall that regressions for the mean and variance of growth in stock market value for firms in an industry are estimated together. The dependent variable is $\ln(\text{grow}(\text{SMV}))$ in regressions for Tables 1.4 and 1.5, where SMV stands for stock market value and $\ln(\text{grow}(\text{Shipment}))$ gives the natural logarithm of the one-year or 10-year growth rate. The dependent variable for Table 1.6 is the natural logarithm of the squared residuals from the associated mean regression of Table 1.4 or 1.5. Again, for details of the statistical procedure, see Appendix A.

Hypercompetitive Industries

The cross-sectional differences across industries in the nature of competition are largely as expected. Under H1, seven industry factors were examined for their impact on the value-SGA rivalry relationship, the relationship most expected to trigger hypercompetition. Results are reported in Table 1.7. One of those factors, imports, was not expected to affect the relationship, and in fact did not. Results with the import variable are not reported. Of the six remaining factors, four performed well: the percentage of final demand from consumers (a proxy for the inelasticity of demand), the percentage of

TABLE 1.4 Mean Regressions, Basic Variables, One-Year Growth Rates, 1959-1991

| | Without Nonlinearity | | With Nonlinearity | |
	Basic Variable	Basic Variable Interacted with Time	Basic Variable	Basic Variable Interacted with Time
Intercept	.18**		−.06	
	(4.50)		(−.07)	
ln(grow(shipments))	.66**	−.014**	.81**	−.021
	(7.02)	(−4.23)	(3.56)	(−1.71)
grow(shipments)			−.23	.002
			(−.91)	(.45)
ln(grow(unit-CGS))	−1.37**	.001	−2.51	−0.51
	(−9.49)	(.51)	(−.91)	(−1.11)
grow(unit-CGS)			.94	.014
			(.47)	(1.03)
ln(grow(unit-SGA))	−.55**	−.002	−1.33**	.004
	(−5.66)	(−.52)	(−2.80)	(.67)
grow(unit-SGA)			.55	−.004
			(.92)	(−.75)
ln(grow(price))	.93**	−.021**	1.03**	−.033
	(5.56)	(−3.77)	(9.48)	(−1.73)
grow(price)			−.07	−.04
			(−.44)	(−.76)
F-tests	9.20**: null hypothesis: coefficients for 4 time interaction terms = 0.		1.57: null hypothesis: coefficients for 8 nonlinear terms = 0.	
Pseudo-R^2	.56		.56	
Observations	5,364		5,364	

NOTES: Dependent variable is ln(grow(SMV)); SMV denotes stock market value. T-statistics are given parenthetically. Regressions include a full set of binary variables for years, though these binary coefficients are not reported. Estimation technique is pseudo-maximum likelihood; estimates of the variance relation are in Table 1.6. Significance levels: ** at 1 percent, * at 5 percent.

the workforce that is professional, the 10-year productivity growth (both proxies for the technological base), and the 10-year growth in concentration (an inverse proxy for ease of entry). A fifth variable, 10-year growth in industry shipments (a proxy for dynamism of demand) was correctly signed but insignificant. That outcome may be due to the fact that ln(grow(Shipment)) already appears in the basic relationship, as well as in the shift term; further, the 10-year growth in shipments and 10-year growth in productivity are correlated at the .50 level—not highly, but perhaps enough to mask the true effect of growth in sales. The raw materials variable (an inverse proxy for sophistication of supply) did not perform well.

TABLE 1.5 Mean Regressions, Basic Variables, Ten-Year Growth Rates, 1968-1991

	Without Nonlinearity		With Nonlinearity	
	Basic Variable	Basic Variable Interacted with Time	Basic Variable	Basic Variable Interacted with Time
Intercept	.86** (17.46)		-4.06** (-5.98)	
$\ln(grow(shipments))$	.72** (12.55)	-.011** (-5.38)	.57** (7.60)	-.012 (-1.17)
$grow(shipments)$			.02 (.66)	-.002 (.91)
$\ln(grow(unit\text{-}CGS))$	-1.22** (-8.49)	-.027** (-3.51)	-10.51** (-6.91)	.217** (4.17)
$grow(unit\text{-}CGS)$			6.94** (4.96)	-.151** (-7.94)
$\ln(grow(unit\text{-}SGA))$	-.35** (-3.66)	-.012 (-.52)	-2.11** (-9.19)	.239** (8.12)
$grow(unit\text{-}SGA)$			1.35** (5.00)	-.186** (-9.58)
$\ln(grow(price))$	.93** (6.84)	-.059** (-5.06)	.64* (2.06)	-.105** (-5.63)
$grow(price)$			.63** (4.15)	-.014 (-.97)
F-tests	7.65**: null hypothesis: coefficients for 4 time interaction terms = 0.		17.61**: null hypothesis: coefficients for 8 nonlinear terms = 0.	
$Pseudo\text{-}R^2$	35		.41	
Observations	3,520		3,520	

NOTES: Dependent variable is $\ln(grow(SMV))$; SMV denotes stock market value. T-statistics are given parenthetically. Regressions include a full set of binary variables for years, though these binary coefficients are not reported. Estimation technique is pseudo-maximum likelihood; estimates of the variance relation are in Table 1.6. Significance levels: ** at 1 percent, * at 5 percent.

Under H2, six industry factors were examined for their impact on the intra-industry variance of stock market growth. Results are reported in Table 1.6. By far the best-performing measures are those for the knowledge base of the industry: percentage of the workforce that is professional and the growth rate of labor productivity. The market structure variables are mixed. Increases in concentration are associated with decreased variance, as expected. As import data were missing for almost 30 percent of the sample and the import variable was not statistically significant when used, the specifications including imports are not reported. The demand/supply vari-

TABLE 1.6 Variance Regressions

	One-Year Growth Rates 1959-1991		Ten-Year Growth Rates 1968-1991	
	Without Nonlinearity	With Nonlinearity	Without Nonlinearity	With Nonlinearity
Intercept	−5.31	−5.33	−2.30	−2.44
	(−23.60)	(−23.51)	(−4.24)	(−5.45)
Predicted value of industry mean	1.50	1.33	.25	.27
	(5.23)	(4.79)	(2.77)	(2.47)
Number of firms in industry	−.05	−.05	−.04	−.04
	(−9.10)	(−9.77)	(−8.03)	(−7.28)
Year	.014	.014	.021	.023
	(4.22)	(4.09)	(3.62)	(3.93)
ln(grow(shipments))	−.84	−.95	.12	.13
	(−2.63)	(−2.97)	(.95)	(1.07)
ln(grow(unit-CGS))	5.07	5.56	3.20	2.17
	(3.55)	(4.56)	(7.60)	(3.29)
ln(grow(unit-SGA))	.60	.43	.56	.79
	(.99)	(.73)	(3.11)	(4.44)
ln(grow(price))	−2.19	−1.78	−.91	−.86
	(−3.80)	(−3.31)	(−6.27)	(−5.51)
Percentage final demand consumer	.03	.03	.09	.05
	(.45)	(.61)	(1.08)	(.76)
Percentage supply raw materials	−.20	−.13	.12	.31
	(−1.99)	(−1.26)	(1.13)	(2.14)
Percentage workforce professional	.82	.81	.67	.67
	(3.67)	(3.72)	(2.91)	(2.78)
ln(Grow(shipments per worker))	.25	.17	.76	.68
	(.92)	(.59)	(5.45)	(5.75)
ln(Grow(4-firm concentration))	−.01	−.03	−.12	−.14
	(−.47)	(−.67)	(−2.81)	(−1.98)
Observations	5,344		3,506	
Source of coefficients Used for estimation	Table 1.4		Table 1.5	

NOTES: For estimation procedure, see statistical appendix. *T*-statistics in parentheses. Dependent variable is ln(residual**2); residuals taken from the indicated table.

TABLE 1.7 Regression Results, Industry Factors Shift Value-Rivalry Relationship

Ten-Year Growth Ratios, 1980-1991			
Basic Relationship		Shift Parameters	
ln(grow(shipment))	.51**	ln(grow(shipment))	.53
	(8.22)		(1.36)
ln(grow(unit-CGS))	−1.38**	Percentage final demand consumer	.45**
	(−6.11)		(2.77)
grow(unit-CGS)	.78**	Percentage supply raw materials	−.13
	(2.84)		(−.64)
ln(grow(unit-SGA))	.55**	Percentage workforce professional	1.25**
	(3.75)		(3.37)
grow(unit-SGA)	−.77**	ln(grow(shipments per worker))	.34**
	(−5.50)		(4.02)
ln(grow(price))	−1.05**	ln(grow(4-firm concentration ratio))	−.13*
	(−3.51)		(−2.04)
grow(price)	.71**		
	(5.45)		
Pseudo-R^2		.44	
Observations		1,560	

NOTES: The dependent variable is ln(grow(SMV)), where SMV indicates stock market value; regressions include a full set of binary variables for years; coefficients for these binaries are not reported. Estimation technique is pseudo-maximum likelihood; estimates of the variance regression are not reported. Significance levels: ** at 1 percent, * at 5 percent.

ables contribute little to explanation of differences across industries in internal variance of performance.

Hypercompetitive Shift

The intertemporal shifts between 1958 and 1991 in the nature of competition are largely as expected. Under H3, the value/SGA-rivalry relationship was expected to be monotonically negative for the one-year growth rates and to shift from monotonically negative to an inverted-U for the 10-year growth rates. Results are reported in Table 1.4 for the one-year growth rates and Table 1.5 for the 10-year growth rates. The findings in Table 1.5 are plotted in Figure 1.7. First, there is no relevant nonlinearity in the findings in Table 1.4 for the one-year growth rates. Specifically, if we formally test the null hypothesis that all eight nonlinear coefficients (the γ and δ sets of coefficients in Eq. 1) are all equal to zero, we can not reject this hypothesis at the 5 percent level. That result is expected, as a single year is arguably too short a period for the dynamic effects that cause nonlinearity to be realized.

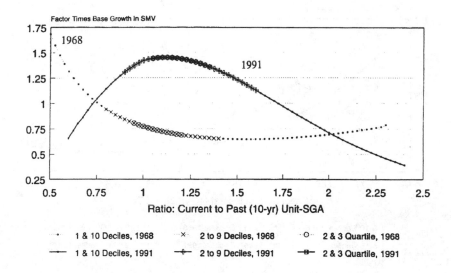

Figure 1.7. Effect of Rivalry in Unit-SGA on Mean Growth in Firm Value (SMV)

Turning to the 10-year growth rates and the nonlinear relationship reported on the right of Table 1.5, we find that most of the coefficients allowing
for nonlinearity are highly significant. Interpretation of the nonlinear findings is difficult by simply looking at Table 1.5. Finding an inverted-U
relationship requires not only an appropriate pairing of coefficient signs, but
also an appropriate distribution of the independent variable around the
maximum. For example, if all observations are on the left of the estimated
inverted-U maximum, we have merely found a concave, positively sloped
relationship. To assist in interpretation of the findings, the estimated value-
rivalry relationships for unit-SGA costs are plotted in Figure 1.7, which gives
the estimated relationship in 1968 and the subsequent relationship in 1991.
In 1968, the value-SGA-rivalry relationship is monotonically negative for
more than 95 percent of the sample, consistent with static competition. In
1991, however, we have a true inverted-U as expected for dynamic competition. Note that industries with no change in unit-SGA have a value of 1.0 for
the 10-year growth rate in unit-SGA. As shown in Figure 1.7, those median
industries perform significantly better than ones with much lower or much
higher SGA growth.

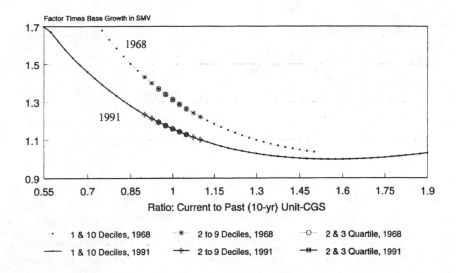

Figure 1.8. Effect of Rivalry in Unit-CGS on Mean Growth in Firm Value (SMV)

For H4, the hypothesized positive secular trend for intraindustry variance in performance is strongly documented in Table 1.6. As reported, the coefficient on the linear-time variable has a positive significant estimate.

Hypercompetitive Behaviors

As hypothesized, different competitive behaviors differ sharply in impact. Under H5, the impact of escalations in shipments and in prices becomes steadily lower over the sample period. In Table 1.4 for the one-year growth rates, the time-trend coefficients (the βs of Eq. 1) are highly significant and negative for shipments and output prices. By 1991, the effect of those two variables on the mean industry valuation growth, though still positive, is markedly lower. Clearly, the "shared assets" of industry sales and industry price have much less impact today than in the 1950s, even on a one-year growth basis. Note that there is no significant change over time in the impact of unit cost of goods sold (CGS) or unit selling, general, and administrative costs (SGA). The comparable coefficients for the 10-year growth rates are reported in Table 1.5 and show similar results, with one important difference. This difference arises from the estimated value-price rivalry relationship in 1991, at the end of the sample period. In Table 1.4, the estimated effect of

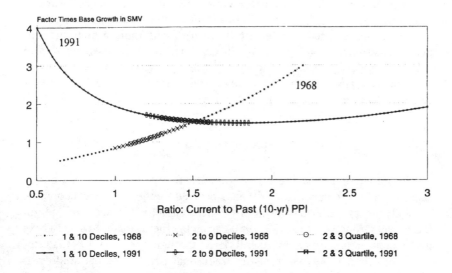

Figure 1.9. Effect of Rivalry in Price on Mean Growth in Firm Value (SMV)

price changes is positive and significant in 1991; in Table 1.5, the estimated effect of price changes becomes negative after 1983, and is negative and significant by 1991.[8] Given that a positive value-price rivalry relationship is at the core of the Five Forces model, which is one of the most prominent in strategic management, this result is unexpected and perhaps even startling.

Under H6, escalations in SGA expense are much more likely to trigger dynamic competition than other competitive behaviors. To assist in interpretation of the findings, the estimated value-rivalry relationships for unit-SGA, unit-CGS, and the producer price index are plotted in Figures 1.7, 1.8, and 1.9 respectively. Each figure shows the estimated relationship in 1968 and the subsequent relationship in 1991. For rivalry in unit-CGS as plotted in Figure 1.8, the estimated relationship is monotonically declining for virtually all sample observations, both in 1968 and in 1991. However, for rivalry in unit-SGA, the findings are quite different. By 1991, we have a true inverted-U as expected for dynamic competition. Finally, the value-price rivalry relationship is plotted in Figure 1.9. Here we see a shift from a monotonically increasing relationship in 1968 to one that is monotonically declining in 1991 for more than 95 percent of sample observations. The "nonlinear" results for prices on the right of Table 1.5 are thus really not so different from the "linear" results on the left.

Under H7 and H8, we expect asymmetries in the impacts of various instruments of rivalry on the intraindustry variance in stock market growth. The results are reported in Table 1.6. Industries with rapid growth in firm-specific instruments such as rivalry in CGS and SGA are associated with higher intraindustry variance. Industries with rapid growth in shared instruments such as prices and shipments have lower variances (though shipments have no effect for the 10-year growth rates).

CONCLUSION

This study has pulled together arguments from a variety of sources to assert that a hypercompetitive shift has occurred for the American economy. The study theory is drawn from the structure-conduct-performance paradigm (Bain 1959 through Porter 1979, 1980), from the literature on firm networks and dynamic competition (Marshall 1920 through Freeman 1993, Porter 1990, and Thomas 1994), from the traditional Schumpeterian studies of industrial economics (notably Scherer 1967), from the recent steam of neo-Schumpeterian research (including Levin, Cohen, and Mowery 1985, and Levin et al. 1987), and from D'Aveni's (1994) important monograph on hypercompetition. While D'Aveni initially identified the hypercompetitive shift, the present study spells out theoretically what the shift entails, ties the theory to underlying literatures, and empirically verifies that the shift is generally present among some 200 industries of the U.S. manufacturing sector.

The study theory is summarized in Figure 1.6. The dynamic resourcefulness of the average industry in the U.S. manufacturing sector has steadily increased. Fundamental exogenous changes in the underlying technologies for commerce have made the creation of new strategic assets significantly easier. The inescapable flip-side of more rapid creation of new strategic assets is the more rapid depreciation of older, established strategic assets. Thus, the increase in dynamic resourcefulness triggers a hypercompetitive shift, from static to dynamic competition. That shift entails greater competitive rivalry (not examined here), greater variance in competitive outcomes, and the rise of an inverted-U for the value-rivalry relationship.

The empirical findings document the existence of the hypercompetitive shift in multiple and consistent ways.

- Shared aspects of competition in an industry, such as industry prices and industry demand growth, are shown to be much less important for firm performance today than in the 1960s, only 30 years ago. Despite the academic prominence accorded by certain models to the role of high prices as a source of corporate success, by 1991 industry prices had an estimated minimal, and in some cases, even negative, relationship to long-term firm performance.

- For rivalry in SGA-costs, the value rivalry relationship is shown to have shifted from a monotonic decline expected under static competition to an inverted-U expected under dynamic competition. SGA expense, encompassing marketing and research activities, is the instrument of rivalry most likely to be associated with the creation of new strategic assets.

- Industries with a stronger knowledge base, more dynamic related transactors, and easier conditions of entry are more associated with hypercompetitive shift. The strongest evidence is for the technology base of an industry.

- The within-industry variance of firm performance is increased by dynamic competition: over time, across rivalry instruments, and across the industry factors.

The second and third sets of findings suggest the particular importance of knowledge base in triggering the hypercompetitive shift. They suggest that of D'Aveni's four arenas of competition, his knowledge arena is by far most likely to be associated with dynamic competition. Again, comparison of Figures 1.7, 1.8, and 1.9 shows the unique importance of the knowledge arena.

The strategic implications of the findings are that the basis of competitive advantage for contemporary firms has moved steadily away from the "shared assets" of common features in an industry toward unique firm- specific aspects of innovation. Correspondingly, the focus of internal organization for firms has shifted from thorough exploitation of given strategic assets toward new organizational forms that facilitate the creation of new strategic assets. With the rise of the resource-based view of the firm, the strategic management profession seems to have intuitively sensed and anticipated that fundamental shift, though it has not yet fully recognized the implications of constant resource competition, erosion, and recreation.

The study is only a small start toward the necessary empirical studies of hypercompetition. In a period when American firms have radically altered their strategies and organizations to shift from static to dynamic competition, much of American academe remains mired in models that are valid only under static competition. It is time for researchers who study strategic management to join American firms with our own hypercompetitive shift.

Appendix A: Statistical Method

The growth rate of stock market value for firms in an industry (denoted Grow(SMV)) is a random variable with a highly nonnormal distribution. First, the growth rates are skewed, with most firms achieving moderate growth and a small number of firms achieving truly enormous growth. Second, the variance of the random variable is heteroscedastic. And third, the means and variances of realizations are positively related. An industry in which firms undergo moderate growth will have low variance in Grow(SMV), whereas industries in which firms undergo spectacular growth will have great volatility. Therefore, the relationship between Grow(SMV) and rivalry cannot be estimated by ordinary least square techniques, as OLS presumes a uniform normal distribution. Further, were the relationship to be investigated by maximum likelihood techniques, a potentially complex density function would be specified.

Not only are maximum likelihood techniques cumbersome, but the need to choose an explicit density function poses risks of misspecification. For example, Grow(SMV) might initially be regarded as distributed by gamma, where variance is proportionally related to the square of the mean. Yet the gamma density function cannot be expressed in closed form, and thus maximum likelihood estimation would require cumbersome numerical integration. Further, the gamma distribution requires that the variance of Grow(SMV) be exactly proportional to the square of the mean of Grow(SMV), a strong assumption. The variance of Grow(SMV) might instead be regarded as proportional only to the mean, rather than its square. Yet the classified distribution reflecting such linear proportionality is the Poisson, whose density is for discrete distributions, not continuous random variables such as Grow(SMV). Hence, there is a trade-off. On the one hand we might specify simpler densities (such as the unmodified exponential, a closed-form member of the gamma family) with associated likelihood functions, but simpler density functions pose risks of misspecification, and the resulting maximum likelihood estimates will be inconsistent. On the other hand, we might specify modified classical densities for Grow(SMV) with associated likelihood functions that are extremely complex and cumbersome to estimate.

The use of quasi-likelihood and pseudo-likelihood techniques vastly reduces the force of this tradeoff. With those methods, we do not specify the density function for Grow(SMV), but only the relationship between the means and variances of the dependent variable. If that specification is valid, the resulting estimates are consistent and asymptotically normal (Carrol and Rupert 1988). The estimates are conveniently obtained through iteratively weighted nonlinear least squares, using standard routines. When the exact relationship between the mean and variance of the dependent variable is known and weighted least squares are iterated to convergence, the resulting estimates are called maximum quasi-likelihood estimates (McCullagh and Nelder 1986, Carroll and Rupert 1988). When the exact mean-variance relationship is unknown, with parameters of some functional mean-variance relationship to be estimated, the fully iterated weighted least squares estimates are called maximum pseudo-likelihood estimates (Carroll and Rupert 1988). Thus, surprisingly enough, these techniques are at once less restrictive and less prone to misspecification and at the same time significantly easier to implement than maximum likelihood estimation.

Because the exact mean-variance relationship is not known, and indeed is a focus of study, we must use pseudo-likelihood techniques. The mechanics of the pseudo-likelihood method are as follows. For a given number k of independently distributed random variables Y with a vector of realizations $\mathbf{y}$ (and components y), we specify given scalar functions M and V such that the expected value and variance of each y is:

$$EV(y) = M(\mathbf{b}) \tag{A1}$$

$$\mathrm{Var}(y) = \sigma^2 V(M(\mathbf{b}), \mathbf{a}) \tag{A2}$$

where σ^2 is an unknown scalar dispersion parameter, where $\mathbf{b}$ is a vector of p unknown parameters to be estimated, and $\mathbf{a}$ is a vector of q unknown parameters. If we knew the parameter vector $\mathbf{a}$ exactly, we could directly use quasi-likelihood estimation. Here we must not only estimate the parameter vector $\mathbf{b}$ for the mean relationship in A1 but also the parameter vector $\mathbf{a}$ for the variance relationship in A2. For purposes of this study, we further specify M and V such that:

$$\ln(EV(y)) = \ln(M(\mathbf{b})) = \mathbf{bx} \tag{A3}$$

$$\ln(\mathrm{Var}(y)) = a_0 + a_1 * \ln(M(\mathbf{b})) + a_2 * N_{\mathrm{firm}} + a_3 * \mathrm{Year} + \mathbf{cz} \tag{A4}$$

where $\mathbf{x}$ is a vector of p known independent covariates (including instruments of rivalry), $\mathbf{z}$ is a vector of $r < 0$ q known independent covariates (including instruments of rivalry and industry resourcefulness proxies), and $\mathbf{c}$ is a subvector of $\mathbf{a}$ with r parameters to be estimated. When $a_0 = 0$, then $a_1 = 0$ is consistent with a unit normal distribution for y, $a_1 = 1$ is consistent with the Poisson distribution, and $a_2 = 2$ is consistent with the exponential distribution (again, a closed-form member of the gamma family).

To estimate the parameters $\mathbf{b}$ and $\mathbf{a}$ we must first obtain start-values. OLS regression of equation 1 in the text produces initial star values for the $\mathbf{b}$ vector. Saving the residuals from this OLS regression, squaring them, and using them as the dependent variables in OLS estimation of Eq. 2 in the text produces initial start-values for the **a** vector. Second, using those start-values, we form the variance function as in A3 and perform iteratively weighted nonlinear least squares as follows.

dependent variable: y

regression function: $M(\mathbf{b})$

weights: $1/V(M(\mathbf{b}), \mathbf{a}^*)$.   (A5)

Third, saving parameter estimates $\mathbf{b}^*$, or equivalently saving the results and predicted values $M(\mathbf{b}^*)$, pseudo-likelihood estimation executes a second round of iteratively weighted least squares to obtain new estimates of the variance function parameter vector $\mathbf{a}^*$ as follows.

dependent variable: $\ln[(y - M(\mathbf{b}^*))^2]$

regression function: $\alpha_0 + \alpha_1 * \ln(M(\mathbf{b}^*)) + \alpha_2 * \text{Nfirm} + \alpha_3 * \text{Year} + \mathbf{cz}$

weights: 1.0.   (A6)

Because of the specification of the variance function, ordinary (unweighted, linear) least squares can be used here. The sole problem with that approach arises from extremely good fits, whereby the "dependent variable" in A6 becomes the logarithm of nearly zero. Such so-called "inliers" are clearly visible on a diagnostic plot of a logarithm of the squared residuals against a logarithm of the predicted means. In the study, roughly 15 (of more than 5000) observations were clear inliers, with the logarithm of squared residuals having value less than -15. Those few observations have been deleted in variance function estimations (only) reported in Table 1.6. Finally, the last two steps are repeated in their entirety, with updated estimates of **b** and **a,** until convergence is achieved. Inference about the parameter vector **b** can be based on the asymptotic coefficient standard errors and asymptotic **t**-statistics reported in weighted least squares outputs of statistical packages. Carroll and Ruppert (1988) label that tactic "Wald inference." Inference about the parameter vector **a** is usually more complicated, because of the dependence of the distribution of **a** on estimates of **b.** In the case where the intercept variance term a_0 is small, as it is here, the complications are eased and the asymptotic t-statistics reported from the OLS regressions employed in A6 may be used for approximate Wald inference. Inference in the variance regression, however, is not well established.

Appendix B: Limitations and
Extensions of Empirical Findings

Several additional analyses were executed to test the limitations of the study. The full results of the analyses are not reported, but the approach and findings are described here.

DIVERSIFICATION. To examine the impact of rivalry on individual firms, and hence stock market values, we must match firms to industries. For an undiversified firm, the matching is straightforward. A diversified firm, however, operates in multiple industries, and matching its performance with industry characteristics becomes problematic. As the degree of diversification for American firms steadily and markedly increased over the study period, some of the study findings may be due less to a hypercompetitive shift than to a downward secular trend in data quality.

To discern the extent of the problem posed by diversification, data from the Compustat *Industrial Segment File* were examined for 1989. Of the more than 6000 firms listed there, almost 75 percent operated in only a single 4-digit SIC. For only 2 percent of those firms (roughly 300) did the largest 4-digit business segment (SBU) account for less than 50 percent of total corporate sales; for only 80 firms (1.3 percent) did the largest SBU account for less than 40 percent; and for only 15 firms did the largest SBU account for less than 30 percent. Those very highly diversified firms are of course among the very largest in the U.S. economy, so their economic impact is much greater than that indicated by this simple "headcount." Nonetheless, the study employed unweighted averages of firms in an industry, which precisely reflect the headcount. Hence, diversification, which on a corporate-sales-weighted basis has a large impact on the U.S. economy, had a small impact on the study.

As a check on the reported empirical findings, the Compustat data (covering the variables stock market value, unit-CGS, and unit-SGA) were recomputed after deletion of any firm that in 1989 had more than 20 percent of corporate sales outside its largest SBU. From the preceding discussion, it is no surprise that the empirical findings are virtually unchanged when even moderately diversified firms are excluded from the analysis. This approach is hardly definitive, as the roster of firms in 1989 is not a complete roster of all firms in the 1958 to 1991 period. Further, the diversification level for many firms changed over time. Unfortunately, a complete SBU breakout for all firms over the 33 years of the study is not available.

VALUE RATIOS VERSUS VALUE LEVELS. The study examined the growth in the levels of stock market values. This approach was taken because dynamic competition may well involve a tradeoff of lower margins for higher growth that increases firm value. Nonetheless, it is useful to check whether the findings are still valid when different formulations of the dependent variable are used. Two new variables were computed for each firm: SMV/S or the ratio of stock market value to sales and SMV/B or the ratio of stock market value to book value of common equity. Industry means and variances for these two new variables were computed and the reported analyses were replicated. The reported findings were not materially changed.

FIRM VERSUS INDUSTRY UNIT OF ANALYSIS. The study used industry averages as dependent variables, because the rivalry phenomenon of interest occurs at an industry level. The analysis was replicated with individual firms as observations. The results differed marginally, and in expected ways. The pseudo-R^2 statistic was much lower (.15 versus .40), but because there were 10 times as many observations with individual firms, the t-statistics were higher. In the variance regressions, the effect of number of firms in the industry was lower and the effect of the mean on the variance was higher (indicating greater nonnormality). Key findings were unchanged.

CORPORATE LEVERAGE. The debt-equity ratio for nonfinancial U.S. firms measured in book value terms rose slowly from 50 percent in 1960 to 65 percent in 1974. It then fell sharply back to 50 percent where it remained until 1984. After 1984, corporate America aggressively retired equity and issued new debt so that the debt-equity ratio rose to 75 percent by 1989 (for these data, see Blair and Litan 1990). That is hardly a smooth secular trend, but it is an upward trend that may account for some of the reported findings. As a check on the empirical work of the study, a new variable In(grow(Debt)) was computed, where Debt refers to the book value of outstanding long-term debt for firms in an industry. The new independent variable was linearly added to the analysis. The estimated coefficient for the debt variable was insignificant. Perhaps the aggregate financial restructurings, like diversification, were heavily skewed to a few large firms. The size-weighted impact on the economy is large, but the unweighted average effect on most firms is much smaller.

ACKNOWLEDGMENTS

The author is indebted to Huggy Rao, Geoffrey Waring, and the editors and referees of this special issue for patient comments on an early draft of the article. Conversations with Richard D'Aveni on theory and Richard Colombo on statistical method were extremely helpful. The views and errors of the article are those of the author alone.

NOTES

1. The Five Forces model is a restatement of the Structure-Conduct-Performance model that dates at least back to Bain (1959), though Scherer (1980) cites Mason (1939) as the fountainhead for this enormous stream of research. The Diamond model restates an old argument that firms locally cluster together and thus share performance attributes. That argument dates back to

Marshall (1920, Chapter X, Section 3), who cited three rules governing the process: "good choice of workers" (factor supply), "subsidiary trades" (related industries), and shared "mysteries of the trade" (technology base). Had Marshall been more of a popularizer, he would perhaps have called his model the "Marshallian triangle."

2. A third meaning of the phase "dynamic competition" is provided by D'Aveni (1994). In his discussion of four different arenas (or instruments) of rivalry, he characterizes a slow pace of competition as static and a more rapid pace as dynamic. Some of his arenas/instruments are non-Schumpeterian and others are clearly Schumpeterian. There is little point in trying here to reconcile the three different meanings of "dynamic competition," as each is sensible in its own realm. In this article, the term "dynamic" refers exclusively to the Schumpeterian sense of competition.

3. Scherer's 1967 paper examines the relationship between market structure and the average research intensity of firms in an industry, a key concern of the traditional industrial economics studies of the "Schumpeterian hypotheses." The reasoning of Scherer's important work is adapted and applied to the broader issues raised here.

4. There is no expectation whatsoever that firms in industry will somehow attain this optimal level of rivalry. The careful collusion among firms that would be necessary to adjust industry rivalry toward the optimum is highly unlikely, particularly given the uncertainty and hetero-geneity that inherently characterize innovation. The actual determinants of any given level of industry rivalry are an issue well beyond the scope of this article.

5. The actual levels of profitability would be very poor proxies for rivalry and challenge. First, profitability is arguably a much closer proxy to the dependent variable, stock market value, than to the independent variable, rivalry. Second, some of the core hypotheses are that the value-rivalry relationship is an inverted-U under dynamic competition, and that the nature of competition shifts from static to dynamic across industries and across time. Hence, it would be nearly impossible to map a given level of profits to a given level of rivalry in advance, prior to the empirical analysis, so that the mapping could be used as an independent variable. Instead, cashflows were disaggregated into their key components: revenues (prices and inflation-adjusted sales) and costs (for manufacturing and for selling/innovation). Once we execute this disaggre-gation, we are forced to use change measures, as it is difficult to tell in advance whether a given price level is "high" or "low" or whether a given level of SGA expense indicates mild or intense rivalry. The empirical analysis relates changes in rivalry to changes in stock market value.

6. Comanor and Scherer (1995) contrast the evolution since 1911 of U.S. Steel, which survived an antitrust challenge intact, and the trust-busted fragments of Standard Oil Company. From a Five Forces perspective, the petroleum industry in the U.S. "lost" the antitrust case and suffered greater rivalry. Yet Comanor and Scherer demonstrate that in the long-run, Standard Oil "won" its antitrust battle. In the 1930s, driven by an exogenous shift in demand from kerosene to gasoline, smaller firms grew and competition sharply intensified, forcing the Standard Oil spinoffs to adapt. With their innovations of manufacturing technology and organization, the spinoffs stopped the aggregate loss of market share that had set in for Standard Oil even before the divestiture order, drove many smaller and weaker firms from the industry, and attained a level of competitive excellence that remains preeminent in the world today. In contrast, the dominant U.S. Steel maintained a price umbrella over its competitors, encouraging minimal competition, and suffered continuous loss of market share until the 1990s. By the 1970s, the U.S. Steel industry had lost its leadership position to the Japanese. Ultimately, hammered by imports and by new minimills using recycled steel, the large and established U.S. steel firms were forced to become more adaptive and competitive. This example suggests that a hypercompetitive shift comes eventually to all industries, but arrives sooner in some industries than in others. Indeed, in the U.S. petroleum industry, the hypercompetitive shift appears to have occurred in the 1930s.

7. The dynamic resourcefulness of an industry is thus a product of the year in history, industry factors, and the instruments of rivalry. All three factors matter in combination. For example, Porter (1990) argued that the challenge provided by high wages in Germany has added value and success for German firms. This may well be true. But the domestic institutions of German labor markets are quite distinct from those of the United States (Freeman 1993). Because of extensive worker training programs (including government technical schools and corporate apprenticeship programs), strong worker organizations (including pervasive work councils and, in larger firms, union codetermination), and stringent regulation of layoffs and separations, it is plausible that higher German wages may indeed lead to new strategic assets based on high productivity uses of labor. Wright (1987) argued that such upgrading occurred in the American South with the advent of the 1930s New Deal labor regulations. In contrast, the United States in the 1990s maintains minimal worker training, extremely high job mobility across firms, decimated unions, and (in states such as Georgia) laws that still allow workers to be fired without cause (Freeman 1993). It is implausible under these circumstances that higher U.S. wages will accomplish much beyond reduction of corporate wealth. Thus, even in the same year and with the same instrument of rivalry, the degree of dynamic resourcefulness of an industry may vary dramatically.

8. Note for the one-year growth rates that $.93 - 32 * .021 = .26$, as there are 32 years separating 1959 and 1991, and a test for the null hypothesis that $\alpha_4 + 32 * \beta_4 = 0$ can not be rejected at the 5 percent level. Note for the 10-year growth rates that $.93 - 23 * .059 = -.43$, as there are 23 years separating 1968 and 1991, and a test for the comparable null hypothesis of zero is rejected at the 1 percent level.

REFERENCES

Bain, J. S. (1959), *Industrial Organization,* New York: John Wiley.

Blair, M. M. and R. E. Litan (1990), "Corporate Leverage and Leveraged Buyouts in the Eighties," in J. B. Shoven and J. Waldfogel (Eds.), *Debt, Taxes, and Corporate Restructuring,* Washington, DC: Brookings.

Carroll, R. J. and D. Ruppert (1988), *Transformation and Weighting in Regression,* New York: Chapman and Hall.

Cohen, W. M. (1995), "Empirical Studies of Innovative Activity," in P. Stoneman (Ed.), *The Handbook of Economics of Technical Change,* London: Basil Blackwell.

——— and R. C. Levin (1989), "Empirical Studies of Innovation and Market Structure," in R. Schmalensee and R. Willig (Eds.), *Handbook of Industrial Organization,* Amsterdam: North Holland.

Comanor, W. S. and F. M. Scherer (1995), "Rewriting History: The Early Sherman Act Monopolization Cases," *International Journal of Economics and Business,* 2, 2.

D'Aveni, R. A. (1994), *Hypercompetition: Managing the Dynamics of Strategic Maneuvering,* New York: Free Press.

Demsetz, H. (1973), "Industry Structure, Market Rivalry, and Public Policy," *Journal of Law and Economics,* 16, April, 1-10.

Freeman, R. B., Ed. (1993), *Working Under Different Rules,* New York: Russell Sage.

Grant, R. M. (1991a), "The Resource-Based Theory of Competitive Advantage: Implications for Strategy Formulation," *California Management Review,* 33, Spring, 114-135.

——— (1991b), "Porter's 'Competitive Advantage of Nations': An Assessment," *Strategic Management Journal,* 12, 535-548.

Kamien, M. I. and N. L. Schwartz (1976), "On the Degree of Rivalry for Maximum Innovative Activity," *Quarterly Journal of Economics,* 90, 245-260.

Levin, R. C., W. M. Cohen, and D. C. Mowery (1985), "R & D Appropriability, Opportunity, and Market Structure: New Evidence on some Schumpeterian Hypotheses," *American Economic Review,* 75, May, 20-24.

—— A. K. Klevorick, R. R. Nelson, and S. G. Winter (1987), "Appropriating Returns from Industrial R & D," *Brookings Papers on Economic Activity,* Microeconomics, 783-820.

Marshall, A. (1920), *Principles of Economics,* 8th ed., London: Macmillan.

Mason, E. S. (1939), "Price and Production Policies of Large-Scale Enterprise," *American Economic Review,* 29, March, 62-74.

McCullagh, P. and J. A. Nelder (1986), *Generalized Linear Models,* New York: Chapman and Hall.

Peltzman, S. (1977), "The Gains and Losses from Industrial Concentration," *Journal of Law and Economics,* 20, October, 229-263.

Porter, M. A. (1979a), "How Competitive Forces Shape Strategy," *Harvard Business Review,* March-April, 137-145.

—— (1979b), "The Structure Within Industries and Companies Performance," *Review of Economics and Statistics,* 61, May, 214-227.

—— (1980), *Competitive Strategy,* New York: Free Press.

—— (1990a), *The Competitive Advantage of Nations,* New York: Free Press.

—— (1990b), "The Competitive Advantage of Nations," *Harvard Business Review,* March-April, 73-93.

—— (1991), "Towards a Dynamic Theory of Strategy," *Strategic Management Journal,* 12, Winter, 95-118.

Ravenscraft, D. J. (1983), "Structure-Profit Relationships at the Line of Business and Industry Level," *Review of Economics and Statistics,* 65, February, 22-31.

Reich, R. B. (1985), "Bailout," *Yale Journal of Regulation,* 2, 2, 163-224.

Salinger, M. A. (1990), "The Concentration-Margins Relationship Reconsidered," *Brookings Papers on Economic Activity,* Microeconomics, 287-335.

Scherer, F. M. (1967a), "Market Structure and the Employment of Scientists and Engineers," *American Economic Review,* 57, 574-631.

—— (1967b), "Research and Development Resource Allocation under Rivalry," *Quarterly Journal of Economics,* 81, 359-394.

—— (1980), *Industrial Market Structure and Economic Performance,* 2nd ed., Chicago: Rand McNally.

Schmalensee, R. (1985), "Do Markets Differ Much?" *American Economic Review,* 75, June, 341-351.

Schumpeter, J. A. (1942), *Capitalism, Socialism, and Democracy,* New York: Harper.

—— (1934), *The Theory of Economic Development,* Cambridge, MA: Harvard University Press.

Scott, J. T. (1984), "Firm versus Industry Variability in R & D Intensity," in Z. Griliches (Ed.), *R & D, Patents, and Productivity,* Chicago: University of Chicago Press.

Thomas, L. G. (1994), "Implicit Industrial Policy: The Triumph of Britain and the Failure of France in Global Pharmaceuticals," *Industrial and Corporate Change,* 3, 2, 451-489.

—— and G. Waring (1995), "The Depreciation of Competitive Advantage for U.S. Manufacturing Firms, 1950-1993," working paper, Emory University. Copy available from author.

Tyson, L. D. A. (1992), *Who's Bashing Whom? Trade Conflict in High Technology Industries,* Washington, DC: Institute for International Economics.

Winter, S. G. (1995), "Four R's of Profitability: Rents, Resources, Routines, and Replication,"
    in C. Knudsen and C. Montgomery (Eds.), *Evolutionary and Resource-Based Approaches
    to Strategy: Towards a Synthesis,* Kluwer.
Wright, G. (1987), "The Economic Revolution in the American South," *Economic Perspectives,*
    1, Summer, 161-178.

2

"Austrian" and Industrial Organization Perspectives on Firm-Level Competitive Activity and Performance

GREG YOUNG
KEN G. SMITH
CURTIS M. GRIMM

Drawing on the Austrian school of economics and the structure-conduct-performance (s-c-p) paradigm of industrial organization, the authors present and test a dynamic model of competitive activity and performance. They examine the model in two stages. First, they explore the influence of industry-level and firm-level cooperative mechanisms on firm-level competitive activity. Second, they examine the effect of firm- and industry-level competitive activity on firm performance.

The authors use the dynamic model of competitive activity to examine the complex linkages between the firm's environment, its actions, and its performance outcomes. They report a longitudinal analysis of a sample of 1,903 competitive moves undertaken in the software industry. Hypothesis testing supports the relationships in the model argued from the Austrian perspective, but provides only partial support for those derived from the s-c-p paradigm. Firm-level cooperative mechanisms are found to increase the firm's competitive activity, and firm-level competitive activity is related positively to the firm's return on assets and return on sales. Contrary to expectation based on the s-c-p paradigm, industry-level cooperative mechanisms are not related to the firm's competitive activity or to its performance. Consistent with the IO paradigm, however, a measure of industry rivalry that directly captures industry-level competitive activity is related negatively to firm-level performance.

(AUSTRIAN ECONOMICS;
DYNAMIC STRATEGY; HYPERCOMPETITION;
INDUSTRIAL ORGANIZATION ECONOMICS;
INTERFIRM COOPERATION; PERFORMANCE)

That firm-level competitive action is at the core of business strategy and competitive positioning is well accepted (Chen et al. 1992, Mintzberg 1978, Porter 1980: ch. 5, Thompson and Strickland 1993, p. 77). Indeed, the dynamic strategy research stream focuses on the relationship between competitive action and competitive advantage (e.g., Bettis and Weeks 1987, Chen et al. 1992, MacMillan et al. 1985, Smith et al. 1992). The more recent hypercompetition concept builds on that dynamic view of strategy to address market environments characterized by extremely vigorous competitive action, in which sustainability of competitive advantage depends on the speed of action and the extent of competitive rivalry (D'Aveni 1994, p. 217).

Dynamic firm-level competitive action in hypercompetitive environments has three important characteristics. First, competitive advantage is short lived because frequent aggressive firm-level action disrupts causal linkages between competitive conduct and performance outcomes established in the market status quo. Second, firms must undertake series of actions to continuously recreate competitive advantage. Finally, in a hypercompetitive marketplace, firms with more competitive activity theoretically will have superior performance over time in relation to rivals with less activity (D'Aveni 1994, pp. 12, 258, 364).

The key role of firm-level action in the hypercompetitive market is consistent with the emphasis on market processes described by the Austrian school of economics (see, e.g., Jacobson 1992; Kirzner 1976, 1979, 1992; Schumpeter 1934). According to Austrian economics, organizational action (1) constitutes the *critical* market process, (2) can disrupt linkages between competitive conduct and performance found in the status quo of the marketplace, and (3) can convert otherwise neglected opportunity to the advantage of the acting organization, and by diffusion to the larger marketplace.

The focus on organizational action and its role in market processes is a major contribution of the Austrian school that has informed the dynamic strategy research stream (Smith et al. 1992, p. 4) as well as the hypercompetition concept (D'Aveni 1994, p. 365). The strategy literature, however, has largely failed to subject the Austrian approach to critical empirical examination (Jacobson 1992, p. 784). Moreover, theoretical tension between the Austrian school and the structure-conduct-performance (s-c-p) paradigm of industrial organization (Bain 1951), a well-researched root discipline of the strategy field, lends urgency to the task of testing the propositions of the Austrian school.

The tension between the s-c-p paradigm and the Austrian school arises from the common focus of the two perspectives, namely the linkages between the market environment, competitive conduct, and performance outcomes. The perspectives diverge in several respects, but two important differences paramount to our present research concern (1) competitive conduct outcomes arising from cooperative mechanism between rivals, and (2) performance outcomes expected from competitive conduct.

Drawing from the Austrian school, D'Aveni (1994, pp. 333-341) argues that in hypercompetition firms use horizontal cooperative mechanisms, or relationships with rivals for mutual benefit (e.g., joint product development, joint distribution, product licensing), as a means to *escalate* their individual competitive activity. Conversely, according to the s-c-p tradition, horizontal cooperative mechanisms create interfirm linkages that allow *reduction* of rivalrous behavior (Stigler 1964).

According to D'Aveni (1994), firms in a hypercompetitive environment must undertake frequent competitive activity over time to create and recreate competitive advantage. A well-established stream of IO literature (see Scherer and Ross 1990), argued from the industry level of analysis, supports the opposite view that high levels of competitive conduct lead to lower performance of firms within an industry.

The theoretical tension between the Austrian school and the traditional industrial organization paradigm warrants efforts toward resolution. We examine the influence of horizontal cooperative mechanisms on firm-level competitive activity, and the relationship between firm-level competitive activity and performance outcomes. More specifically, we propose a dynamic model of competitive activity that relates cooperative mechanisms and competitive action at both the firm and industry levels of analysis and describes firm-level performance as a function of those multilevel dimensions.

A sample of 1,903 competitive moves undertaken over a nine-year period in the U.S. software industry was used to test our model. As suggested by D'Aveni (1994, p. 2), competitive conduct in the U.S. software industry provides a uniquely comprehensive view of the way competitors act to build their own advantage.

A DYNAMIC MODEL
OF COMPETITIVE ACTIVITY

We introduce a dynamic model of competitive activity that explicitly treats firm-level competitive action as a consequence of firm participation in cooperative mechanisms and as an antecedent of firm performance, within the larger context of industry cooperation and rivalry. The model, depicted in Figure 2.1, thus incorporates cooperative and competitive aspects of firm-level action with comparable concepts of cooperation and competition at the industry level. In Figure 2.1 we intentionally omit relationships between firm- and industry-level cooperation and between firm- and industry-

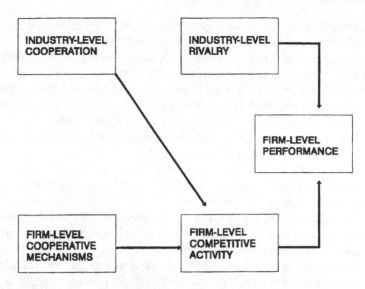

Figure 2.1. Dynamic Model of Competitive Activity

level cooperation and industry-level rivalry and firm-level performance. We control for those relationships in hypothesis testing.

Our research segments conduct into two components, the cooperative and competitive activity of the individual firm and the cooperative and competitive activity of that firm's rivals (referred to as industry cooperation and competitor rivalry). Our focus, as represented by the arrows in Figure 2.1, is on the influence of firm- and industry-level cooperation on firm-level competitive activity and the influence of firm- and industry-level competitive activity on firm-level performance.

The multilevel framework allows integration of the Austrian school with the structure-conduct-performance paradigm from IO economics. Importantly, the s-c-p paradigm treats the industry as the primary unit of analysis, whereas in our present model primary attention is on the individual firm. The change of focus from industry conduct to individual-firm activity is consistent with recent development in IO theory. For example, game-theoretic techniques that model rivalry have applied industry-level theory to the examination of competitive conduct at the firm level (Fraas and Greer 1977, Saloner 1991), providing additional support for the disaggregate perspective. Porter (1981) noted the shift in the unit of analysis in industrial organization research to include both the firm and the industry. That development should not be theoretically surprising, as the importance of market structure is that it induces firm-level conduct (Caves 1972).

Firm-level competitive activity is defined here as the total number of competitive actions a firm takes in a given year. That approach is consistent with D'Aveni's (1994), as well as with IO literature suggesting that competitive actions among industry incumbents are the fundamental core of competitive conduct (Caves 1984, Porter 1980). Drawing on literature concerning competitive moves and advantage (Caves 1984, D'Aveni 1994, Khandwalla 1981, Pennings 1981, Porter 1980, Salop and Scheffman 1983, Schmalensee 1978), we consider competitive activity to include product introductions and announcements, as well as marketing and promotion campaigns (including price cuts).

We define the level of competitive activity in the industry (industry-level rivalry) as the aggregation of firm-level competitive activity minus the competitive activity of the focal firm. When the number of competitive actions between all firms in the industry is high, rivalry will be intense. Our definition is consistent with the IO literature suggesting that rivalry be framed as a sequence of competitive moves among industry incumbents (Caves 1984, Porter 1980). Rivalry has been similarly defined in several recent studies (Schomburg et al. 1994, Smith et al. 1992).

We define firm-level cooperative mechanisms to be formal interfirm agreements including equity purchases, mergers, technology licenses, and participation in trade associations and technology consortia (Bresser 1988, Dollinger 1990, Harrigan 1985, Koh and Venkatraman 1991). That definition focuses on the linkages between organizations over which flow communication and resources. We recognize that some types of cooperative mechanisms may be difficult to distinguish from competitive action. For example, a cooperative mechanism may position a focal firm in some hybrid organization to compete in a broader scope of product-markets. The purpose of our article, however, is to examine the contrasting arguments about the relationship between horizontal interfirm linkages and competitive activity. Hence, it is important to focus on the theoretical distinction between the two constructs.

In the IO tradition, according to the s-c-p paradigm, the proliferation of cooperative mechanisms between all firms in an industry is an important dimension of industry structure (Bain 1951, Stigler 1964). We define the level of cooperative mechanisms in the industry (industry-level cooperation) as simply the aggregation of firm-level cooperative mechanisms minus those of the focal firm. That is, when the number of cooperative mechanisms involving firms in an industry is high, the level of industry cooperation will tend to be high.

The model depicted in Figure 2.1 thus reflects both the firm-level emphasis of the Austrian school and the industry-level focus of the industrial organization perspective. In the next section we develop hypotheses describing the relationships portrayed in Figure 2.1 in more detail. The hypotheses specify how, within the context of industry cooperation and competitor rivalry, the cooperative activity of the firm will influence its competitive activity, and how the firm's competitive activity will in turn influence its performance.

HYPOTHESES

The Influence of Industry- and Firm-Level
Cooperative Mechanisms on Firm-Level Competitive Activity

Cooperative mechanisms are actions of one firm that form connections or coalitions with other firms in the industry (Porter 1980, p. 88; 1985, p. 57). The consequences of cooperation differ with the level of analysis (industry vs. firm).

As is consistent with the s-c-p paradigm of the IO tradition and the industry level of analysis, we expect cooperative mechanisms to provide opportunities for industry participants to communicate and to learn about each other's goals and incentives (Stigler 1964). Scherer and Ross (1990) argued that firms can move their industry in the direction of greater overall industry cooperation by increasing the level of industry communication. One mechanism for achieving such communication is cooperative agreements between firms. Hence, as the number of cooperative agreements between firms in the industry increases, the ease of communication between firms would increase and the resultant social structure of the industry would become more cooperative.

The proliferation of cooperative mechanisms at the industry level increases opportunities for informal collusion or tacit cooperation between firms (Bresser 1988, Oster 1990, Stigler 1964) and decreases the vulnerability of firms to threats from competitor rivalry. As a result, firms can establish higher prices and achieve higher performance from any given portfolio of competitive activity than would otherwise be possible (Koh and Venkatraman 1991; Nielsen 1988; Scherer and Ross 1990, pp. 213, 226). Further, formal cooperative agreements in an industry serve as rules for behavior that make competitiveness more predictable (Gottfredson and White 1981), thereby reducing the firm's risk associated with expected returns from competitive activity. Thus, in a cooperative industry context, firms can achieve performance objectives with fewer competitive actions than would be necessary in a less cooperative environment.

H1. *As the number of industry-level horizontal cooperative mechanisms increases, firm-level competitive activity decreases.*

Our expectation in H1 is that the industrywide proliferation of cooperative mechanisms will constrain or have a negative influence on each firm's competitive activity. In contrast, consistent with the Austrian perspective, we expect firm-level cooperative mechanisms to have a positive impact on each participant's tendency to undertake competitive activity (D'Aveni 1994; Kirzner 1976, p. 85; Rizzo 1982, pp. 58-59). Horizontal cooperative mechanisms give participants access to both tangible and intangible complementary resources, including knowledge, technology, and/or physical assets (Koh and Venkatraman 1991, Mariti and Smiley 1983, Nielsen 1988). For example, a firm with strong product development skills but relative weakness in marketing may license its innovative products to a competitor with distribution strengths.

As Lenz (1980, p. 228) has argued, firm-level competitive activity is a function not only of the resources a firm directly owns, but also of resources it can access from relationships and interactions with other organizations in its environment. Cooperative mechanisms provide means whereby participating firms can compete for position more economically than firms that must acquire resources unilaterally. Thus, cooperative mechanisms enable each participant to undertake more competitive activity than is possible with the resources accessible to any participant alone (D'Aveni 1994, p. 338; Koh and Venkatraman 1991; Lenz 1980, p. 228; Mariti and Smiley 1983; Nielsen 1988).

H2. *As the number of horizontal cooperative mechanisms in which a firm participates increases, competitive firm activity increases.*

Following the dynamic model in Figure 2.1, we next develop hypotheses addressing the influence of industry- and firm-level competitive activity on firm performance.

The Influence of Industry Rivalry and Firm-Level Competitive Activity on Firm-Level Performance

Framing firm performance as a consequence of firm action is consistent with IO literature suggesting that rivalry be framed as a sequence of competitive actions among industry incumbents (Caves 1984, Porter 1980). Importantly, the s-c-p paradigm of IO posits that the conduct of firms in an industry will in turn affect performance. Researchers in that tradition, however, usually infer rather than directly measure rivalry (Porter 1981).

According to the s-c-p paradigm of IO economics, an industry characterized by high levels of rivalrous competitive conduct has negative consequences for firm performance. Intense rivalrous competition in an industry can drive up the acquisition costs of scarce resources or spur suppliers to extend distribution to rivals (Barney 1991, Mahoney and Pandian 1992, Peteraf 1993). In addition to competition for resources, there may be competition for product/market positioning as rivals attempt to respond to or deter competitive action.

The IO perspective is that firm-level activity may provoke industry rivalry that dissipates potential performance outcomes in a competitive battle. Strategy scholars also have used game theoretic formulations of the prisoner's dilemma model to demonstrate that high levels of rivalry lead to low profits for competitors (Bettis and Weeks 1987, Porter 1980, Schomburg et al. 1994, Smith et al. 1992). Too much activity, in the aggregate, hurts firm-level performance.

In short, the level of industry rivalry affects profitability prior to strategy implementation (ex ante) by increasing the costs of resource acquisition and affects it after implementation (ex post) by increasing the cost of defending against product/market rivals. Thus, the threat of competitive retaliation reduces the expected benefit associated with competitive action, thereby reducing the profit incentive to undertake competitive activity (Astley and Fombrun 1983, Khandwalla 1981, Scherer and Ross 1990, Stigler 1964).

A rich array of IO empirical studies have found inferential support for that notion by showing a positive linkage between industry concentration and industry profitability (Scherer and Ross 1990, pp. 422-423). Although the degree of rivalry was not measured directly in those studies, the s-c-p paradigm implies that high concentration produces lower levels of rivalry and thereby higher profits.

A more recent line of strategy research has operationalized the conduct construct, affording a direct test of the relationship between rivalry and performance. Schomburg et al. (1994) found a negative relationship between rivalry, defined as the frequency of new product introductions by industry participants, and profitability in the beer, telecommunications, and personal computer industries. Similarly, Smith et al. (1992) demonstrated that competitor rivalry, defined in terms of the frequency of competitive action, was related negatively to industry profitability in the airline industry.

H3. *The greater the level of industry-level competitive activity, the lower the firm-level performance.*

D'Aveni (1994, pp. 10-12) argues that, in a hypercompetitive environment, firm performance is an outcome of a series of competitive actions. That conceptualization is consistent with the Austrian school, which emphasizes that opportunity for profit is the most important incentive for a firm to undertake competitive action (Kirzner 1976, 1979, 1992; Schumpeter 1934). The Austrian school's emphasis on aligning the firm's action with opportunity is well accepted in the strategy field (e.g., SWOT analysis). "Austrian" roots also are evident in the hypercompetition perspective of a firm's performance as an outcome of a series of competitive actions (D'Aveni 1994, pp. 10-12). For example, product introductions and marketing moves are typical strategic thrusts that companies use to seize the initiative in their markets (see Porter 1980, pp. 159; Schomburg et al. 1994), whereas product announcements can create market disruption by unsettling opponents (D'Aveni 1994, p. 279).

Competitive activity of the firm creates internal organizational assets in the form of skills, routines, and knowledge as well as assets that cross the organizational boundary such as contracts, relationships, brand images, and networks (Nelson and Winter 1982, p. 99; Porter 1991, p. 102). Maintaining or enhancing the productive asset base of the firm requires undertaking activities (Porter 1991, p. 103). In building on asset strengths, the cost of taking action is lower for the firm that has efficiencies derived from a rich history of prior activity. Importantly, the firm with a rich history of activity-derived learning not only has lower costs of supporting superior performance, but also is capable of undertaking more activities in a given time period.

To illustrate the beneficial effect of undertaking more action in a given period of time, Figure 2.2, adapted from D'Aveni (1994, p. 12), portrays a series of firm-level actions and their associated cumulative profitability over time. Reflecting the arguments of the Austrian school, each trapezoid in Figure 2.2 represents a firm's action to exploit a specific opportunity, and its volume represents profits earned by the firm for having acted to seize that opportunity.

The greater the number of trapezoids (actions) and the larger their volume (profits), the greater the firm's performance over time. In a hypercompetitive environment, the erosion of profit for each action (the declining right leg of each trapezoid) comes very soon in time. Thus, in a hypercompetitive industry, the firm that undertakes more actions generates a higher level of performance. We summarize the preceding discussion in the form of a testable hypothesis.

H4. *As competitive firm activity increases, firm performance increases.*

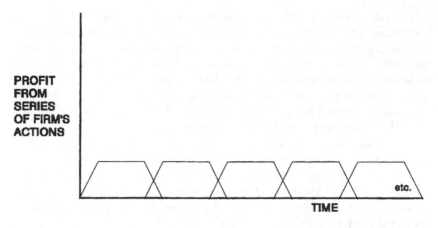

Figure 2.2. A Series of Competitive Actions Adds to a Firm's Total Performance Outcome
SOURCE: Adapted from D'Aveni 1994: 12

METHODS

To test the hypothesized relationships, we constructed a dataset for publicly owned firms in the computer software industry (SIC 7371, 7372, 7373) from two sources. In building the sample, we used information on individual firms, industry structure affecting all firms, and longitudinal dynamics of competition.

Sample

The sample consisted of publicly owned single-business firms in the U.S. computer software industry during the period from 1983 to 1991. Those years were formative ones, for the software industry emerged from the computer hardware industry as a distinct market around 1980 (Standard and Poor's Industry Surveys 1977, 1980, 1984). As *Fortune* noted, "until the Eighties, the computer software business was dominated by vertically integrated companies . . . that made every element of their products, from silicon to software" (Sherman 1993). Moreover, computer software is a singularly important domestic U.S. industry, one that sets the direction for the global computer industry (Manasian 1993). An example of the dominance of the U.S. industry is evident in Europe: Of the top ten independent software vendors operating there, seven are U.S. firms (McCormick and Greenbaum 1992).

Limiting the sample to firms primarily in a single industry ensures that all firms are exposed to the same environment, an important consideration in any strategy research. Unique industry characteristics may be critical in explaining the relationship among important variables (Hansen and Hill 1991), and the components of competitive advantage in one industry may not be appropriate in other industries characterized by different environments. For research on hypercompetition, it is extremely important not to sample unintentionally from more passive industry environments.

For continuity over the period 1983 to 1991, we considered firms to be in the computer software industry if their primary SIC assignment was any of the computer software codes (7371, 7372, or 7373).[1] Such an approach is consistent with the assumption in the literature that organizations in a four-digit standard industry category are horizontally interdependent and share one market (Kim et al. 1989; Palepu 1985; Pennings 1981, p. 434).

We took a conservative approach to defining software firms and accepted only those identified by both the Standard and Poor's Corporate Directory and the Disclosure database of SEC filings. Firms for which the primary SIC assignments were in agreement in the two sources were accepted as a consensus list of firms in the computer software industry. That approach resulted in 365 firm-year observations for the period from 1983 to 1991.

One firm was dropped from the sample because it appeared in only one year and reported accounting losses equal to more than six times sales. After we dropped 19 other firms because of missing data, the final sample consisted of 345 firm-year observations with 1,903 actions over the period 1983 to 1991.

Notably, the final sample encompassed more than 63% of all industry sales for the 1983-1991 period (based on all 10-K and annual reports classified with the software SIC codes by Disclosure); hence, most of the industry economic activity was captured in the sample. In addition, annual firm profitability, quick ratio test of liquidity, and year-to-year industry growth did not differ significantly between the research sample and the industry norms published by Dun and Bradstreet, as indicated by pairwise t-tests. We therefore concluded that the research sample was representative of the industry.

Firm- and Industry-Level Competitive Activity

The focus of our study was on competitive firm activity. Our measure of firm activity followed the recent stream of strategy research on dynamic competition (Bettis and Weeks 1987, Smith et al. 1992), which has introduced a direct measure of competitive actions undertaken by the firm.

Competitive actions were identified by a structured content analysis of published articles (Jauch et al. 1980), a technique used in other studies of dynamic strategy (e.g., Chen et al. 1992; Smith et al. 1991, 1992). We applied a comprehensive, multiple source method and examined citations of the sample firms appearing in the Predicasts F & S Index for the 1983-1991 period. We coded all cited moves of product introductions, product announcements, and marketing/promotion campaigns, typical strategic thrusts that companies use to seize the initiative in their markets (e.g., see D'Aveni 1994, p. 279; Porter 1980, pp. 17, 76; Schomburg, Grimm, and Smith 1994).

Our method identified *a total of 1,903 rivalrous actions* in the computer software industry for the 1983-1991 period. We selected a random subsample of 2 percent of the 1,903 competitive moves to assess the validity of the published citations observed for the sample. Fifty-eight percent of the subsample had multiple sources. In each and every case in the subsample, agreement between multiple sources was 100%.

The measure of firm-level competitive activity was expressed quantitatively as the annual sum of each firm's moves, an approach that captures the series of competitive activities typically found in a hypercompetitive environment (see Figure 2.2). The industry-level measure of competitor activity (industry-rivalry) was expressed as the aggregation of firm moves to the industry level minus the focal firm's own competitive activity. Our approach was consistent with that of Kwoka (1979), who aggregated sample market share data to construct industry concentration values.

Firm- and Industry-Level Horizontal Cooperative Mechanisms

Horizontal cooperative mechanisms are business moves undertaken jointly by competitors. We included only cooperative moves that create mechanisms for interfirm communication but are not directly tied to a competitive activity. Building on previous work, we defined horizontal cooperative mechanisms to be equity arrangements, mergers, technology licenses, and participation in trade associations and technology consortia (Bresser 1988, Dollinger 1990, Harrigan 1985, Koh and Venkatraman 1991). Each Predicasts F & S Index citation of such a move in the software industry was counted as one cooperative mechanism for each of the participating firms in the sample. Thus, the measure captured the influence of cooperation for each participating firm without any definitional overlap with competitive activity. The industry-level measure of cooperative mechanisms was expressed as the aggregation of firm-level cooperative mechanisms to the industry level minus the focal firm's own cooperative activity.

Firm Performance

We used two commonly accepted financial measures of firm performance, return on sales and return on assets. The data were collected from annual SEC filings as reported by the Disclosure database. Because the legal requirements associated with SEC filings mandate accurate reporting that fairly reflects business conditions, that data source is highly reliable.

Control Variables

Following prior research, we controlled for the size and age of the firm, which may influence the firm's flexibility of action (Aldrich and Auster 1986; Baker and Cullen 1993; Buzzell, Gale, and Sultan 1975; Buzzell and Wiersema 1981; Cool et al. 1989; Fombrun and Ginzberg 1990; Nelson and Winter 1982, p. 310; Smith et al. 1989). The size of the firm was measured by the dollar sales of the firm, as reported in the Disclosure database of SEC filings. That measure is transformed with a log function. The age of the firm was measured in years since original corporate founding, as reported in Standard Corporate Descriptions (S & P 1992) and the Corporate Technology Directory (Corptech 1991).

In addition, we controlled for industry rivalry when examining the influence of industry cooperative mechanisms on firm-level competitive activity. When examining the influence of industry rivalry and firm-level competitive activity on performance, we controlled for industry- and firm-level cooperative mechanisms.

Correlated error terms are common in studies with longitudinal data (Kennedy 1985, Smith et al. 1991). Following Fombrun and Ginzberg (1990), we corrected serial correlation by including as a separate independent variable the dependent variable lagged one period. Table 2.1 displays correlations for all major variables.

Tests and Data Analysis

We tested hypotheses by applying multiple regression analysis, a typical approach to estimating economic models of firm conduct (Scherer and Ross 1990, p. 413). Independent measures were lagged one time period behind dependent measures to account for causal relationships implied by the hypotheses.

The dependent variable for H1 and H2 was the number of competitive actions of the focal firm in a year of observation, a continuous measure of firm competitive activity. The entire model was lagged one year to examine directly the causal linkage hypothesized between firm activity and perfor-

TABLE 2.1 Pearson Correlation Coefficients of Major Variables[a]

Variables	Mean	S.D.	1	2	3	4	5	6	7
Firm level									
1. Competitive activity	5.35	12.19							
2. Cooperative mechanisms	.42	.78	.46***						
3. Return on assets	.06	.32	.22***	.17**					
4. Return on sales	.06	.24	.24***	.20***	.77***				
Industry level									
5. Competitor rivalry	264.55	99.69	−.02	−.03	−.05	−.04			
6. Cooperative mechanisms	20.64	5.63	.02	−.09	−.00	−.03	.86***		
Controls									
7. Firm size (*natural log*)	11.01	1.53	.43***	.35***	.33***	.35***	.12*	.10	
8. Firm age	12.83	7.48	−.13*	−.06	−.01	−.01	.12*	.10	.23***

a. Two-tailed test of significance. $N = 345$.
*$p < .05$; **$p < .01$; ***$p < .001$.

mance. The following hypothesized research model for H1 and H2 was specified for regression analysis.

Firm-level Competitive Activity$_{t-1}$

$$= b_0 + b_1 \text{ firm-level cooperative mechanisms}_{t-2}$$
$$+ b_2 \text{ industry-level cooperation}_{t-2}$$
$$+ b_n \text{ control variables}_{t-2}$$
$$+ e \tag{1}$$

where b_1 = parameter to be estimated, $t-n$ = years lagged, and e = error term.

H3 addresses the influence of competitor rivalry on firm performance, and H4 examines the influence of the firm's competitive activity on its performance. We tested those hypotheses with a second model similar to that specified in Equation 1. Both competitive firm actions and competitor rivalry were specified as the independent variables of interest, and firm performance (measured by return on assets and return and sales) was the dependent variable of interest. Firm- and industry-level cooperative mechanisms were included as controls.

Firm-level Performance$_t$

$$= b_0 + b_1 \text{ firm competitive activity}_{t-1}$$
$$+ b_2 \text{ industry rivalry}_{t-1}$$
$$+ b_3 \text{ firm cooperative mechanisms}_{t-1}$$
$$+ b_4 \text{ industry cooperative mechanisms}_{t-1}$$
$$+ b_n \text{ control variables}_{t-1}$$
$$+ e \tag{2}$$

RESULTS

H1 and H2

Table 2.2 reports the statistical results for H1 and H2, in which industry- and firm-level cooperative mechanisms at time $t-2$, respectively, are independent variables of interest and competitive activity at time $t-1$ is the dependent variable. H1 is not supported. That is, cooperative mechanisms at the industry level are unrelated to a firm's competitive activity. In contrast, H2 is supported. As the cooperative mechanisms in which the firm participates increase, competitive firm activity increases (beta = .08, $p < .05$).

H3 and H4

Table 2.2 also reports the regression results for the models that examine the influence of competitor rivalry (H3) and competitive activity (H4) on firm performance. In those models, firm competitive activity and industry competitor rivalry were entered as the principal independent variables of interest. Return on assets was the dependent measure of firm performance in the first model and return on sales was used in the second.

As argued in H3 the competitor rivalry measure is significant and negative (beta = $-.22$, $p < .05$ for ROA, beta = $-.21$, $p < .05$ for ROS). H4 also is supported, as the influence of firm competitive activity on relative firm performance is positive and significant (beta = .22, $p < .01$ for ROA; beta = .22, $p < .01$ for ROS).

Note that the results are stable despite the collinearity between firm-level horizontal cooperative mechanisms and competitive activity observed in our sample ($r = .46$, $p < .001$, Table 2.1). The relationships between industry-level competitive activity and firm performance (H3) and between firm-level competitive activity and firm performance (H4) reported in Table 2.1 are the same when firm-level horizontal cooperative mechanisms are not included

TABLE 2.2 Results of Regression Analysis[a]

Variables	Competitive Activity[b]	Performance[c]	
		ROA	ROS
Firm level			
Competitive activity		.222**	.222**
		(.001)	(.001)
Cooperative mechanisms	.075*	−.001	.027
	(.526)	(.018)	(.016)
Industry level			
Competitor rivalry	−.115	−.221*	−.209*
	(.012)	(.000)	(.000)
Cooperative mechanisms in the industry	.055	.122	.146
	(.161)	(.004)	(.004)
Firm-level controls			
Size (*natural log*)	.030	−.091	−.074
	(.375)	(.011)	(.011)
Firm age	−.059*	−.008	−.084
	(.067)	(.002)	(.002)
Competitive activity (*lagged*)	.877***		
	(.041)		
Performance (*lagged*)	.452***	.376***	
	(.051)	(.054)	
Adjusted R^2	.89	.29	.22
F	196.88***	14.04***	10.23***

a. Standardized regression coefficients reported; one-tailed test of significance. Standard errors in parentheses.
b. Dependent variable is the firm's competitive moves (product introductions plus marketing and promotion moves) for year t–1. Independent variables are for year t–2. $N = 148$.
c. Dependent variable is the firm's performance (either return on assets or return on sales) for year$_t$. Independent variables are for year t–1. $N = 229$.
*$p < .05$; **$p < .01$; ***$p < .001$.

in the regression model. Further, firm-level horizontal cooperative mechanisms do not become significant when firm-level competitive activity is removed from the model.

DISCUSSION

The purpose of our study was to test hypotheses about competitive firm activity that were derived from the Austrian school of economics and industrial organization economics. We developed a model of competitive activity to examine the influence of industry- and firm-level cooperative mechanisms on firm-level competitive activity, and the link between industry- and firm-level competitive activity and firm performance. Importantly, we found evidence that engaging in firm-level cooperative mechanisms has a positive effect on the firm's competitive activity and that competitive firm activity is related positively to firm performance. Three of our four hypotheses are supported.

Our results show that firm performance increases as competitive firm activity increases, but declines as the intensity of competitor rivalry in the industry increases (see Table 2.2). An examination of the coefficients, however, shows that unless competitor rivalry provoked by a move is extreme, the positive effects of the competitive move will outweigh the possible negative consequence of competitor rivalry.[2] The relative importance of the competitive activity coefficient versus the competitor rivalry coefficient (an industry measure adjusted for the focal firm) highlights the significance of firm action for performance. In particular, it suggests that firm action, for which managers have significant control, can be vital to achieving superior performance even in the face of competitive rivalry.

Recent strategy literature (e.g., D'Aveni 1994, Schomburg et al. 1994, Smith et al. 1992) has encouraged managers and scholars to consider competitor rivalry in terms of the intensity of competitive action and counteraction. Consistent with IO literature, our study empirically demonstrates the negative relationship between industry rivalry and firm performance. Thus, the dynamic action model provides an approach for examining the sources of firm performance in the presence of competitor rivalry.

The model could be extended to examine more comprehensively the determinants of firm competitive activity and industry-level rivalry, as well as to include a link between the amount of firm activity and the level of competitor rivalry. More specifically, firms are not independent in the marketplace; they are affected by each other's actions and are prone to react (Porter 1980, Smith et al. 1992). In addition to the positive effect of competitive activity (observed in the test of H4), there could be a negative aspect if competitive activity leads to increased competitor rivalry.

We are encouraged by the results of our study, but recognize the resource-based argument that sustainable superior performance is associated with moves dominated by the use of imperfectly mobile resources (Barney 1991, Peteraf 1993). Also, the Austrian school has argued that the rate of firm activity depends on variations across firms in luck and the distribution of skills (Kirzner 1979, pp. 135, 154). For example, the ability to anticipate and exploit profit opportunities, a core concept of the Austrian school, is a valuable resource that may be relatively immobile. Researchers could usefully draw on Hall's (1993) framework of linkages between intangible resources and sustainable competitive advantage to examine imperfectly mobile resources as they relate to competitive activity. The amount of explained variance in our study suggest that unspecified, perhaps intangible, variables influence firm activity.

We examined the dynamic model of competitive activity within the context of the software industry. Future research should explore the generalizability of the model to other environmental contexts. For example, the role of cooperative mechanisms in fast-paced and complex high-tech industries may be different from that in more stable and simpler low-tech industries. Further, Smith and Grimm (1987) found a significant relationship between types of strategy and performance outcomes after, but not before, deregulation in the railroad industry, suggesting that firm action influences performance more when regulatory constraints are removed.

The relationship between firm activity and performance outcomes may also be linked to the number of markets in which firms face each other in competition. For example, software firms may compete in more than one market as the software industry becomes more segmented by customer group and computer platform. Multimarket competition makes the cooperative and competitive interconnections between firms more complex, and competitive activity may be less attractive if rivals have multiple loci for retaliation (Gimeno and Woo 1996). The dynamic model of competitive activity proposed here could be extended to consider the effects of multimarket competition.

Future research also could usefully consider the association between industry structure, firm resources, and firm performance in the context of the individual firm's portfolio of competitive move types and sequencing. For example, some set or sequence of competitive activity may yield more performance benefits or evoke more rivalrous countermoves.

CONCLUSION

We draw on the Austrian school of economics and the structure-conduct-performance paradigm of industrial organization to add insight to our understanding of the actecedents and consequences of firm-level competitive activity. Our study results indicate the competitively active firm is likely to participate in cooperative activities. Importantly, we find that competitively active firms outperform less active firms. We submit that the dynamic model of competitive activity provides a framework that is grounded in theory, empirically supported, and particularly suited to the examination of how competitors act in the marketplace to build their own advantage.

NOTES

1. Prior to 1987, such firms were identified by a single four-digit SIC segment, computer programming (7372). After 1987, the computer programming industry was divided into three SIC codes: computer programming services (SIC 7371), prepackaged software (SIC 7372), and computer integrated system design (SIC 7373). Firms in the original (pre-1987) SIC 7372 later appeared in any of the three new classifications.

2. For example, the coefficients when firm performance is measured by return on sales indicate that a unit change in the competitive activity variable has a .222 effect on the dependent variable, whereas a unit change in the competitor rivalry variable has a −.209 effect on the dependent variable. However, in interpreting the relative magnitude of the coefficients, it is important to recall that standardized betas are reported. The standard deviation of the firm activity variable is 12.19, whereas the standard deviation of the competitor rivalry variable is 99.69. Thus, the positive effect of an individual move is more than eight times the negative effect of a theoretical single rival competitive move, which might be in response to the firm's move.

REFERENCES

Aldrich, H. and E. R. Auster (1986), "Even Dwarfs Started Small: Liabilities of Age and Size and Their Strategic Implications," *Research in Organizational Behavior,* 8, 165-198.

Astley, W. G. and C. J. Fombrun (1983), "Collective Strategy: Social Ecology of Organizational Environments," *Academy of Management Review,* 8, 576-587.

Bain, J. S. (1951), "Relation of Profit Rate to Industry Concentration: American Manufacturing, 1936-1940," *Quarterly Journal of Economics,* 65, 293-324.

Baker, D. D. and J. B. Cullen (1983), "Administrative Reorganization and Configurational Context: The Contingent Effects of Age, Size, and Change in Size," *Academy of Management Review,* 36, 6, 1251-1277.

Barney, J. B. (1991), "Firm Resources and Sustained Competitive Advantage," *Journal of Management,* 17, 99-120.

Bettis, R. A. and D. Weeks (1987), "Financial Returns and Strategic Interaction: The Case of Instant Photography," *Strategic Management Journal,* 8, 549-563.

Bresser, R. K. F. (1988), "Matching Collective and Competitive Strategies," *Strategic Management Journal,* 9, 375-385.

Buzzell, R. D., B. T. Gale, and R. G. Sultan (1975), "Market Share —A Key to Profitability," *Harvard Business Review,* 53, January-February, 97-106.

———— and F. D. Wiersema (1981), "Modelling Changes in Market Share: A Cross-sectional Analysis," *Strategic Management Journal,* 2, 27-42.

Caves, R. E. (1972), *American Industry: Structure, Conduct, Performance.* (3rd ed.), Englewood Cliffs, NJ: Prentice Hall.

———— (1984), "Economic Analysis and the Quest for Competitive Advantage," *Paper and Proceedings of the 96th Annual Meeting of the American Economic Association,* 127-132.

Chen, M. J., K. D. Smith, and C. M. Grimm (1992), "Action Characteristics as Predictors of Competitive Responses," *Management Science,* 38, 439-455.

Cool, K., I. Dierickx, and D. Jemison (1989), "Business Strategy, Market Structure and Risk-return Relationships: A Structural Approach," *Strategic Management Journal,* 10, 507-522.

Corptech (1991), *Corptech Directory of Technology Companies,* Woburn, MA: Corporate Technology Information Services.

D'Aveni, R. A. (1994), *Hypercompetition: Managing the Dynamics of Strategic Maneuvering,* New York, Free Press.

Dollinger, M. J. (1990), "The Evolution of Collective Strategies in Fragmented Industries," *Academy of Management Review,* 15, 266-285.

Fombrun, C. J. and A. Ginsberg (1990), "Shifting Gears: Enabling Change in Corporate Aggressiveness," *Strategic Management Journal,* 11, 297-308.

Fraas, A. G. and D. F. Greer (1977), "Market Structure and Price Collusion: An Empirical Analysis," *Journal of Industrial Economics,* 26, 1, 21-44.

Gimeno, J. and C. Y. Woo (1996), "Do Similar Firms Really Compete Less? Strategic Distance and Multimarket Contact as Predictors of Rivalry Among Heterogeneous Firms," *Organization Science,* 7, 2, 323-341.

Gottfredson, L. S. and P. E. White (1981), *Interorgainzational Agreements,* New York: Oxford University Press.

Hall, R. (1993), "A Framework Linking Intangible Resources and Capabilities to Sustainable Competitive Advantage," *Strategic Management Journal,* 14, 8, 607-618.

Hansen, G. S. and C. W. L. Hill (1991), "Are Institutional Investors Myopic? A Time-Series Study of Four Technology-driven Industries," *Strategic Management Journal,* 12, 1-16.

Harrigan, K. R. (1985), "An Application of Clustering for Strategic Group Analysis," *Strategic Management Journal,* 6, 55-73.

Jacobson, R. (1992), "The 'Austrian' School of Strategy," *Academy of Management Review,* 17, 782-807.

Jauch, L. R., R. N. Osborn, and T. N. Martin (1980), "Structured Content Analysis of Cases: A Complementary Method for Organizational Research," *Academy of Management Review,* 5, 517-526.

Kennedy, P. (1985), *A Guide to Econometrics,* Cambridge: MIT Press.

Khandwalla, P. N. (1981), *Properties of Competing Organizations,* New York: Oxford University Press.

Kim, W. C., P. Hwang, and W. P. Burgers (1989), "Global Diversification Strategy and Corporate Profit Performance," *Strategic Management Journal,* 10, 45-58.

Kirzner, I. M. (1976), "Philosophical and Ethical Implications of Austrian Economics," in E. G. Dolan (Ed.), *The Foundations of Modern Austrian Economics,* Kansas City, MO: Sheed & Ward.

────── (1979), *Perception, Opportunity, and Profit: Studies in the Theory of Entrepreneurship,* Chicago: University of Chicago Press.

────── (1992), *The Meaning of Market Process: Essays in the Development of Modern Austrian Economics,* New York: Routledge, Chapman and Hall.

Koh, J. and N. Venkatraman (1991), "Joint Venture Formations and Stock Market Reactions: An Assessment in the Information Technology Sector," *Academy of Management Journal,* 34, 869-892.

Kwoka, J. E. (1979), "The Effect of Market Share Distribution on Industry Performance," *Review of Economics and Statistics,* 61, 101-109.

Lenz, R. T. (1980), "Strategic Capability: A Concept and Framework for Analysis," *Academy of Management Review,* 5, 2, 225-234.

MacMillan, I., M. L. McCaffrey, and G. Van Wijk (1985), "Competitor's Responses to Easily Imitated New Products: Exploring Commercial Banking Product Introductions," *Strategic Management Journal,* 6, 75-86.

Mahoney, J. T. and J. R. Pandian (1992), "The Resource-Based View Within the Conversation of Strategic Management," *Strategic Management Journal,* 13, 363-380.

Manasian, D. (1993), "A Survey of the Computer Industry," *The Economist,* February 27-March 5, S1-S18.

Mariti, P. and R. H. Smiley (1983), "Co-operative Agreements and the Organization of Industry," *Journal of Industrial Economics,* 31, 437-451.

McCormick, J. J. and Greenbaum, J. (1992), "Microsoft Gets a European Accent," *Information Week,* June 1, 38.

Mintzberg, H. (1978), "Patterns in Strategy Formation," *Management Science,* 24, 934-948.

Nelson, R. R. and S. G. Winter (1982), *An Evolutionary Theory of Economic Change,* Cambridge, MA: Belknap Press.

Nielsen, R. P. (1988), "Cooperative Strategy," *Strategic Management Journal,* 9, 475-492.

Oster, S. M. (1990), *Modern Competitive Analysis,* New York: Oxford University Press.

Palepu, K. (1985), "Diversification Strategy, Profit Performance, and the Entropy Measures," *Strategic Management Journal,* 6, 239-255.

Pennings, J. M. (1981), *Strategically Interdependent Organizations.* New York: Oxford University Press.

Peteraf, M. A. (1993), "The Cornerstones of Competitive Advantage: A Resource-Based View," *Strategic Management Journal,* 14, 3, 179-191.

Porter, M. E. (1980), *Competitive Strategy,* New York: Free Press.

———— (1981), "The Contributions of Industrial Organization to Strategic Management," *Academy of Management Review,* 6, 609-620.

———— (1985), *Competitive Advantage: Creating and Sustaining Superior Performance,* New York: Free Press.

Rizzo, M. J. (1982), "Mises and Lakatos: A Reformulation of Austrian Methodology," in I. M. Kirzner (Ed.), *Method, Process, and Austrian Economics,* Lexington, MA: Lexington Books.

Saloner, G. (1991), "Modeling, Game Theory, and Strategic Management," *Strategic Management Journal,* 12, 119-136.

Salop, S. C. and D. T. Scheffman (1983), "Recent Advances in the Theory of Industrial Structure," *American Economic Review,* 73, 2, 267-271.

Scherer, F. M. and D. Ross (1990), *Industrial Market Structure and Economic Performance,* Boston: Houghton-Mifflin.

Schmalensee, R. (1978), "Entry Deterrence in the Ready-to-Eat Breakfast Cereal Industry," *Bell Journal of Economics,* 9, 305-327.

Schomburg, A. J., C. M. Grimm, and K. G. Smith (1994), "Avoiding New Product Warfare: The Role of Industry Structure," in *Advances in Strategic Management, Vol. X, Part B,* Greenwich, CT: JAI.

Schumpeter, J. A. (1934), *The Theory of Economic Development,* Cambridge, MA: Harvard University Press.

Sherman, S. (1993), "The New Computer Revolution," *Fortune,* June 14, 56-80.

Smith, K. G. and C. M. Grimm (1987), "Environmental Variation, Strategic Change and Firm Performance: A Study of Railroad Deregulation," *Strategic Management Journal,* 8, 363-376.

————, ————, and M. J. Gannon (1992), *Dynamics of Competitive Strategy,* London: Sage.

————, ————, ————, and M. J. Chen (1991), "Organizational Information Processing, Competitive Responses, and Performance in the U.S. Domestic Airline Industry," *Academy of Management Journal,* 34, 60-85.

————, J. P. Guthrie, and M. Chen (1989), "Strategy, Size and Performance," *Organizational Studies,* 10, 63-81.

S & P (1992), *Standard Corporate Descriptions,* New York: Standard & Poor's.

Stigler, G. (1964), "A Theory of Oligopoly," *Journal of Political Economy,* 72, 44-61.

Thompson, A. A. and A. J. Strickland III (1993), *Strategic Management,* Boston: Richard D. Irwin.

3

Hypercompetitive Strategies, Japanese Style

HIROYUKI ITAMI

I was asked to talk about the hypercompetitive strategies of Japanese firms, and I will divide this into three parts. In the first part, I'll be explaining what Japanese firms do. Of course, I will be talking about Japanese firms in general; therefore, there will be many exceptions. Still, I will be telling about what at least a majority of Japanese firms may have been doing during the past 30 years or so. I have been doing research on the development of Japanese industries during the past 40 to 50 years after the war. This year I'll be writing about the automobile industry; several years ago I wrote a book on the chemical industry in Japan. The chemical industry and the automobile industry are very, very different industries. In the chemical industry, Japan is not doing very well. In the automobile industry, Japan is doing very well. One of the questions that I was asking in my book was about the chemical industry. Why was it not doing well? Here is an answer. The chemical industry actually is an industry in which capability building is very difficult. It takes such a long, long time; much longer than the automobile industry. Perhaps that's one of the reasons why European firms are still very good at chemicals: They started a long, long time ago.

I will talk about what Japanese firms do first, and then I'll talk about how Japanese firms can sustain their very hypercompetitive activities. When I was asked to talk about hypercompetition, I didn't know the term. As I began to understand what the term means, it was very familiar to me. That is the way Japanese firms behave. So, I think I am in a position to talk about the hypercompetitive strategies of Japanese firms in some detail.

AUTHOR'S NOTE: This chapter is adapted from Hiroyuki Itami's presentation at the Whittemore Conference on Hypercompetition, September 1994.

The third thing I will address is the question of how these hypercompetitive activities emerged in Japan, and why Japan has been that way for such a long time, without killing anybody in the process. That's going to be an interesting question to ponder to determine who might gain the global hypercompetitive edge.

Hypercompetition as a term was new to me, but as a content or a reality, it is very familiar to me. For example, the number of firms in Japan in any particular industry seems very large compared with the number of firms competing in the same industry in the United States. Take the automobile industry: The United States has three firms making passenger cars. Japan has nine firms producing passenger cars. But depending on the way you count, the nine may become seven or six. This is the way hypercompetitive firms have been exporting to the rest of the world during the past 30 years.

An amazing number of firms have been exporting an amazing number of cars throughout the past 35 years or so. First, of course, there was Toyota, then Nissan. Honda and Mazda followed. Then came Mitsubishi. Then came Subaru. Then came Suzuki. It's almost an endless number of firms. This is not only true of the automobile industry. In the semiconductor industry, for example, there are about three or four major firms in the United States producing and selling semiconductor chips. We have about 9 or 10 firms doing the same thing in Japan. The chemical industry is a bit extreme. We have about 16 firms producing ethylene or cracking ethylene and producing all kinds of polyolefin-type products. I don't know the equivalent number of firms in the United States, but in Japan, it's just too many. I have a potential theory that a country the size of Japan may want to have about six or seven firms competing in a particular industry. The magic number seems to be somewhere between five and seven. With that kind of number, it seems to me, the competition becomes very healthy, but at the same time not too destructive.

Another feature of Japanese competitive behavior is to produce or put out many variations of a particular product. If we compare passenger car model variations in Japan, the United States, and Germany using 1985 data sources, the United States has had about 300 passenger car model variations throughout the past 20 to 30 years. Germany started small, perhaps 100 variations, and has now come up to 400. Japan started around 1965 with a very small number, about 40. Now they are producing around 1,000 variations. You can see how much variety Japanese firms have in this category of industry. This variety is true not only for consumer goods such as automobiles. In the petrochemical industry, for example, in many kinds of plastics, Japanese firms tend to produce five to six times more varieties and grades in their technology than their U.S. counterparts. It's almost ridiculous, and it is certainly costly to do so—and the cost has to be borne by someone.

Because of the large number of firms producing such a variety of a particular type of product, we tend to use the term "excessive competition" in Japan, rather than "hypercompetition." Now, in excessive competition, firms tend to use the three weapons that they can use: price, product, service. They try not to compete on prices. The firms may be producing low-end products, but for a particular product, unless they are trying to enter a particular market, they try not to use price as their major weapon, because they know that once you start price wars, everyone will be killed. The firms try to compete on product, by putting out many varieties, satisfying small niches by producing all kinds of products. Third, they compete on service. Fiercely. This is perhaps the greatest competitive weapon that the Japanese tend to have—service for cars, service for repairs—all kinds of things. This is also one of the reasons why in the chemical industry, Japanese firms have not been able to do very well overseas. The type of service competition in Japan seems to be quite different from service competition overseas.

Turning to strategies, it is amazing that many Japanese firms in the same industries tend to follow the same strategies. There is not much strategy differentiation. Therefore, firms look very homogeneous from the outside. With this kind of very homogeneous strategy and emphasis on the same three kinds of weapons, it may be a bit surprising to see very little exit from a particular industry, even if some firms may not be making a lot of money. For example, in the chemical industry where there are 16 firms producing ethlyene, about 12 of them have not been making any profit for the past three years. Still, somehow they survive.

This description may give you the idea that Japanese firms may be progressing a little slower than you might think, but that's not the case. If you look at the Japanese automobile industry's productivity and improvement from 1972 to 1989 compared to the United States and Germany using the same scale, the points will be much more concentrated. I don't know if I would call the improvement dynamic or crazy, but Japan improved labor productivity, and they improved value in a given time period. I want to point out the very rapid-fire movement of Japanese industry in a particular time frame. They move fast. How they can do this is the question, and in answering it, let me point out one thing. Very often they can go too far, and they did in the 1980s. One of the reasons why this Japanese industry is in trouble right now in the 1990s is the excess that they experienced in the 1980s. They increased the value added per Japanese car—which means they raised the price. The way they raised the prices was not by just announcing the higher prices; they decided to develop slightly different cars. A little attachment here, a little attachment there, and they raised the price. That's the trick they did, and now they're a victim of this trick.

Certainly this type of excessive nonprice competition and too many variations of products have many types of costs: costs to produce, costs to develop. Interestingly enough, because Japanese firms can put out many variations of products for a particular segment of the market, consumers in Japan seem to be in an ironic situation where they have abundant opportunities to make small choices. Choices are packed into a small range; they don't have much opportunity to have a wide selection over a wide range. This may be better than having no choice at all, but the way Japanese firms tend to differentiate their products seems to be too narrowly segmented.

Japanese firms have been using this kind of strategy for the past 20 or 30 years. How could they do it is the next question that I want to address, and the basic answer is that they did it by capability building within the firm. No fancy marketing gimmicks. No fancy strategy. Just very basic capability building. Toyota is a good example. At Toyota, labor productivity is king. They really care about flexible and efficient production systems, and their thinking seems to be shared by many Japanese firms in the following sense: Once you have very efficient and flexible production systems and product develop systems in place, whatever happens in the market, you can follow. You can experiment even in the marketplace. You put out a product, and if it is not very successful, you just pull it and replace it with something new. If you can do that kind of thing quickly and perhaps inexpensively, you are not going to have to worry about how to forecast the market five years from now. You just go to the market and experiment.

This may sound a bit crazy, but there's what I call the paradox of hypercompetition in the sense that firms need stability in their system to be fiercely competitive and to have a rapid-fire movement in their behaviors. As I have stated, Japanese firms have been moving very quickly for productivity improvement, for product development, but they have been, in a sense, protected by stability of two kinds. One is the stability of human networks provided by highly stable employment patterns. If we compare employment stability in the automobile industry in three countries, employment in the United States fluctuates much more than in either Germany or Japan. Japan's very stable employment pattern, of course, helps the accumulation and repayment of the know-how and experience of people. This is true not only in the automobile industry, but in many other industries as well. The same pattern holds for the steel industry. Employment fluctuates much more in the United States. Many people might say that is because of exports, that Japan has exported to absorb the shocks in domestic demand. That is not the case.

The annual domestic demand for each of the three countries is also very different. Domestic demand fluctuates much more in the United States than in Japan. If firms become hypercompetitive in a U.S. kind of environment, many people will "die." In a downturn, not too many firms can survive. In Japan, however, demand is very stable; the market is very stable. Downturns are certainly downturns, but they are small, and therefore people can survive. That seems to be a paradox of hypercompetition. If you want to have hypercompetition, you need stability in employment and demand. This is counterintuitive.

I stated there are two kinds of stability that we need. I explained about human networks and about the reason why the Japanese firms can have stability in their human networks both within the firm and with their suppliers. The demand is very, very stable. Now, this very stable demand will provide a basis for capability building in many ways. The stable demand provides very smooth flow of cash and allows very stable relationships with suppliers. It also allows very stable learning by doing. Obviously, you can use the market to offset instability by acquiring another firm or acquiring a skill accumulated by someone else by paying the price. Certainly markets can use existing capabilities that exist elsewhere. But, it's only organizations of human beings who accumulate capabilities, and this nurturing of this accumulation process seems to be very important if you want to have hypercompetitive firms.

The third part of my story is about why this type of competition emerged in Japan, perhaps naturally. There seem to be two concepts of competition. One is a concept of competition commonly explained in economics textbooks, the other one is not. An example is the competition to gain admission to MBA programs. Students will be competing against each other for admission to the Tuck School if both of them apply only to the Tuck School. But, if one is applying to Harvard and the other one is applying to Tuck, still they may compare their notes and test scores and feel like they're competing with each other. The first concept of competition is competition as taking something from others. If you get something, the other will not. It's a zero sum game. You won't cooperate because if you take something from someone else, then someone else may take something from you, too. So you try to create niches and try to reduce the degree of competition. Now, Japanese firms share another concept of competition on top of the first concept. This type of competitive sort of interaction leads to dialogue among competitors, unspoken dialogue, actually, it's not a cartel. You put up some kind of a product. A competitor will reply, and in the process, each of you will learn about the path of future product development. This type of competition perhaps was necessary for Japan as a small nation with a large population and limited mobility. If you begin to play a zero sum game in that kind of environment, you end up killing each other. Planet Earth may be getting smaller and more crowded. That may be one of the basic reasons why we will have to talk about the concept of hypercompetition in the coming decades.

Part II

HYPERCOMPETITIVE RESPONSES:
NEW ORGANIZATIONAL
FORMS AND STRATEGIES

4

The Paralysis of Deep Pockets

JAMES L. BAILEY

It's always a pleasure to talk about the business I grew up in, the credit card business. Whereas many presentations are about how-tos and success stories about creating competitive advantage, I thought it would be interesting to tell the dark side of the story, the story of how the same deep pockets that built your business can blind you to threats and paralyze you into inaction. This paralysis is life threatening. It threatens your business; it threatens your career. If you let it go too far, it will be fatal. I've been there, and I can tell you it's a place you never want to be. Fortunately, in many cases it can be prevented, and it can be cured. This talk is about what those threats are . . . and the cures.

THE EARLY OPPORTUNITY

To understand how we got ourselves into a corner despite our success, it helps to understand how we came to be successful in the first place. Fifteen years ago in the late 1970s, Americans paid for purchases a lot of different ways. They paid cash; they wrote checks; they used a store charge. And, although it pains me to say it, they even used their American Express cards. The one thing they didn't do much was used a bankcard.

Where others might have seen an unbeatable opponent in Amex, we saw a terrific opportunity. From the customer's point-of-view, bankcards were cheaper, more flexible, and more convenient than the alternatives. From Citibank's perspective, bankcards looked like an ideal way to get beyond the physical limitations of the branch banking business and the interstate bank-

---

AUTHOR'S NOTE: This chapter is adapted from James L. Bailey's presentation at the Whittemore Conference on Hypercompetition, September 1994.

ing laws. It was a nationwide business in an envelope, and we were one of the first banks to see the opportunity and put resources into developing it.

We laid out a vision to have 20 million accounts and the number one share position in the industry. And by 1981, we were so successful that we had signed up 5 million accounts and lost more than $175 million in just three years. There are lots of explanations for those losses. The country was in a recession. Our cost of funds was higher than the rates we could charge. Mass market mailings and new operations centers do not come cheap, and we experienced some growing and learning pains on the credit side. But whatever the explanation, the losses were still losses. We can all look at the bankcards industry today and know that $175 million was money well spent. But at the time it was not such a sure thing. It's testimony to the company's commitment to our vision—and the deep pockets to sustain those losses—that we kept on going.

Over the next few years, we worked hard to build the business. We pioneered a number of techniques in direct response advertising. We got a lot better at credit granting, particularly so we could say the magic words, "You have already been approved." We built three state-of-the-art operations centers from the ground up, centers that today take more than half a million calls a day. We also built the industry's first co-branded reward program in partnership with American Airlines. The business grew and prospered. By 1990, we had signed up more than 20 million accounts, which spent more than 40 billion dollars, generated more than three and a half billion dollars in revenues, and earned more than half a billion dollars in profits a year, up from nothing at the beginning of the decade.

Whereas the advances in credit and marketing were critical, for our purposes it's worth taking a look at the operating leverage that scale allows. Over the course of the decade, we reduced our operating expenses from nearly one and half times revenues to just over 25%. To this day, there are customer service advances, such as the PhotoCard, which are difficult for competitors to copy, not so much because the technology is proprietary, but because very few companies have the scale to use them cost-effectively.

To close out this section, Citibank Bankcards parlayed the commitment and the capital of the corporation into an industry leadership position. We finished the '80s with the number one position in share and profitability, fueled by advances in credit scoring, mass marketing, customer service, and operations. We had also begun using our profits and many of the same techniques to take on many of Citibank's consumer markets abroad. By 1990, we had nearly 5 million accounts overseas generating $500 million in revenues in their own right. But I'm not here just to talk about our success, I'm here to talk about the problems it caused.

CLOUDS ON THE HORIZON

Everyone who has a mailbox or a TV knows that the credit card category has changed dramatically over the past five years. Let me take a minute to trace that history.

The first cloud on the horizon was the launch of the Discover card in 1986. Discover was one of the first mass market no-fee cards, and the only one with a cash rebate. We thought Discover wasn't much of a threat. We thought it was a bad deal for consumers (which it is) and that it would be too expensive to create a merchant network from scratch. We never imagined that they would spend a billion dollars building the network and hundreds of millions more on marketing. But they did, and soon they had more cards in circulation than anyone. The good news was that when we looked for the impact on our portfolio, we looked in vain. We couldn't trace any loss of customers, revenues, or profitability to Discover. And everyone knew you couldn't make money on no-fee customers.

AT&T came next. Whereas Discover was initially targeted as a companion to the Sears card, AT&T was a full frontal assault on banks like us. They offered a no-fee card and the AT&T heritage for service quality. We were good and mad, but we still didn't see the threat. We weren't interested in no-fee customers, and we thought our products and customer service were sufficiently superior to justify the fee.

AT&T really opened the floodgates. GM followed shortly thereafter, with a breakthrough idea and the biggest promotional launch budget in the history of financial services. GE followed, and then a raft of focused price competitors who targeted Citibank by picking out our best customers and mailing them better deals.

Over the next three years, we lost about a million cardmembers and something like two share points. Our revenues flattened, we stopped making progress on costs, and, owing in large part to the significant recession, we saw credit losses soar. Although the business was still very profitable by most standards, absolute profits dropped more than $100 million from 1990 to 1991. Profits recovered the following year, but core business momentum— account growth—was gone.

Part of what happened was simply that it's hard to be number one. Everyone needs an enemy, a target to go after. In the 70s and early 80s Amex was everyone's enemy. By the late '80s it was us. But part of what happened we did to ourselves. Day to day, we didn't think these guys were much of a threat. What we didn't see was that they took our strategy for changing the category—a better customer offer and big marketing dollars—and used it against us.

At this point you're probably asking yourself, didn't they notice what was happening? Why didn't they do something? What were they thinking? I'll tell you what we were thinking. Here's what we said:

> It's the recession. When the economy picks up, account growth will resume and people will start paying their bills again. We'll be back on track.

> We cut back on new account acquisitions on purpose.

> No-fee cardmembers are low revenue and high risk. We're glad they've gone somewhere else.

> None of those other guys are making any money. They'll have to add fees to stay in business.

> We have better, differentiated products. Consumers will pay a premium to carry our cards. The price pressure doesn't apply to us.

> We can't afford a $200 million hit.

This is the paralysis of deep pockets. The inability of highly successful companies to see threats clearly, particularly changes in the competitive frame. The more successful you are, the harder it is to anticipate that someone else will do you one better. For years, everyone said the United States couldn't support a fourth broadcast television network, and that teens and twenty-somethings were too tough an audience. But Fox Broadcasting did it. The tendency is to push the old tools harder, even if they don't seem to work any more. Worse yet, there is the urge to retreat altogether. I think the auto companies are trying to learn this. The difficulty of trying something different, even when the threat has you by the throat. IBM was on the public critical list for at least five years. It even had some sense of what it needed to do. But they couldn't push forward. Sometimes an upstart is just an upstart. But sometimes your business is on the line. How can you tell? And what do you do?

DIAGNOSIS

The first thing you have to do is pay attention. Listen to yourself. What stories do your people tell about what's happening? Watch the fundamental signals your business is giving. Pay attention to your customers. Listen hard. Pay attention to the marketplace, especially to competitors who are growing very rapidly. Everywhere you look, see and hear what's really there, not what you want to see. The absolute worst thing you can do is keep telling yourself stories about how there isn't really a problem. Second, no matter how painful it seems, you have to take action. Things don't get better with time they get worse. So, pay attention. Take action. It sounds easy. I assure you these will be the hardest decisions you ever make. I'm going to give you examples from my business and others of how smart, reasonable people looked the data in the eye and saw blue instead of green and tell you how we ultimately broke the cycle.

The first place to look is the stories you tell. Do any of these sound familiar? Is all the bad news really good news in disguise? My favorite is, "We didn't want those customers anyway." Look where that got some of the automotive companies. Do people say, "It's not our fault?" Do you think your competitors don't know what they're doing? I can assure that your competitors think you're the one that's out to lunch. And they'll hang in there a lot longer than you think to prove it. The major airlines have been waiting for the price cutters to go out of business for years. This takes me to my favorite, that your products are superior and immune from price competition. We said this a lot. It's true, category leaders do sometimes sustain brand premiums. But overall price levels are set by the market, not by you. Get too far out of line, and your customers will resent you, they'll leave in droves, and they're hell to win back. AT&T has this problem in spades in their long distance business. Does any of this sound familiar?

After sizing up the conventional wisdom, you have to get to the root cause of the problem so you can figure out what to do. The best technique I know for doing this is benchmarking. Benchmarking, along with quality management, is becoming a widely misunderstood business fad. To a lot of people, benchmarking means you measure some costs and calculate some financial ratios. That's not how I see it. First, costs are just part of the picture. A lot of companies have cut pretty deeply over the past few years and their unit costs look pretty good. But their revenue productivity stinks. Second, the numbers are not an end in and of themselves, they just give you clues as to where to look. Real benchmarking is about the process and strategy which creates good numbers, not about the numbers. Benchmarking is not something you do once, and you have to benchmark *pre*scriptively, not just *de*scriptively. Good benchmarking can help you cure paralysis or even keep it from setting in in the first place. Bad benchmarking just gives you more ways to explain bad news away.

Now for some examples of good and bad benchmarking in different areas of the business. I'll tell you in advance that in almost every case, the difference wasn't the data we looked at, but what we saw there. My first example is how traditional cost comparisons can lead one astray. When we compared our costs for a range of operations functions versus an average for other large bankcard issuers, we were below industry average, sometimes by as much as 60%. This was good news.

Then we looked at some upstarts. We had a better ratio of costs to revenues, but in absolute terms, the upstarts had lower unit costs than we did. This was not good news. This is also happening in the airline industry, where the majors have been comparing costs per seat-mile to each other, while Southwest has established a new level. Even more disturbing than the cost position itself was what we found when we tried to understand why we were high. There were someplaces where our competitors had better practices than we did, and we do have a broader and more complex product line than they do. But the fundamental explanation for the difference turned out to be that they were stretching their costs over a rapidly growing account base while our business was shrinking, driving our unit costs up.

How were we going to restart growth? By taking a good, hard look at our products and price points, not by cutting our costs. Apple Computer, prior to last fall's across-the-board price cuts, was in a similar position. Volume was down, their cost position was rising, and they were accumulating a lot of unsold inventory. It's true that they had to do some serious price cutting to support lower price points. But their growth was stalled because they had a flawed idea about what price premium their products could command, not because their cost position was out of line.

Another thing that we looked at was our credit losses, which you may be surprised to learn are a larger item in our P&L than expenses. Historically, we knew we went deeper into the market than other issuers, and it followed that we would have higher credit losses. But we had good profitability on those incremental customers, and so as long as losses came in about where we had predicted, we were satisfied. But in 1992-1993, we took a closer look at how we were doing versus our competitors. In early 1992, our loss rates were about 30% higher than the industry average, and we thought we wanted to be at about 20% higher. As if that wasn't bad enough, many of the upstarts we were so concerned about were achieving loss rates below industry levels.

First, we wanted to understand whether these guys had discovered some new magic in credit granting that we'd missed. When we looked, we did find some differences—they did have some new techniques. This was a blow, because we had always thought of ourselves as the pioneers. But here again, the biggest factor explaining the difference in performance wasn't a new approach to the discipline. What was happening was that competitors were growing, and we were shrinking. And they were growing by singling out our best customers and giving them a better deal. So, not only were we behind because we were spreading our loss dollars over a shrinking portfolio, but the average quality of the portfolio itself was deteriorating.

Although this may sound like a problem unique to a lending business, I assure you it is not. Any time you have relatively low marginal costs, even if the absolute number of dollars required for start up is high, the industry leader is vulnerable to losing its best customers to a determined entrant at a new price point. And often, the thing you notice first is the bump in unit costs. But if you let yourself funnel all your energies into a cost-cutting exercise, you run the risk of entering a vicious circle where you go through round after round of cost cuts but can never quite catch up with the shrinking customer base. Before you know it, 15%-25% of your customers will be gone, or even more.

I'm not saying that you don't need to pay attention to costs, you do. And sometimes you have to cut costs deeply just to survive. But you can't cost cut your way to prosperity. You have to have a customer strategy which enables you to grow. Compare and contrast the fortunes of two of America's auto manufacturers. Both had a terrible cost problem, and both of them went through wave after wave of massive cost cuts. But even while it went through the pain of layoffs and the embarrassment of a government bailout, one really went to work on its product line. And so they have seen the better turnaround in share and results.

Monday afternoon quarterbacking is easy. But as it turns out, we had direct evidence we were ignoring. By way of background, remember that we maintained a steady price structure through out the 1980s: a $20 fee, a 19.8% interest rate. We adopted a lower, variable rate structure in 1992, which brought us down to 15.4%, but by mid-1993, most of the offers in the mail were for no-fee cards, and every eligible mailbox in America had a low-rate offer of 11.9% or better in it. Until then we said the things I mentioned earlier. You have to charge a fee to get a good customer. You can't make money at those prices. Our customers will stay for our products. After all, only 5% of customers that left said they liked our competitors' products better.

Then we looked at the data again. Several things really got our attention. First, if you include the customer accounts we closed for credit reasons, customers were disappearing at a 15% annual rate. At that rate, our entire marketing budget went toward replacing the customers who left; we didn't have a penny left over to sign up new accounts. Second, although departing customers had always complained about price, when the noise level got to 70% it was too loud to ignore.

We took another look at our annual customer satisfaction survey. Customers ranked our products as being pretty close to competitors' on some key factors, like timely and accurate statements and timely approval of purchases. But we had large gaps in important factors like customer service and credit line and a yawning gulf in our pricing structure. We finally woke up to the fact that our account base was shrinking, while the category was growing at growing at double-digit rates. As Pepsi realized when they looked beyond sodas to see the explosive growth in what they call alternative beverages, there was a boom going on out there and it was leaving us behind. We knew something had to give.

This is what I mean by prescriptive benchmarking. Look at everything; not just costs but revenues, processes, customers. Pick the right competitors and comparisons. And, above all, see what's really there, no matter how painful or embarrassing it is. One of the things I fault us for most was ignoring the evidence we had. As early as 1988, customers were telling us that they preferred our competitors' no-fee offers to our offers with fees. I wonder sometimes what would have happened if we had led on fee elimination, not followed.

RESPONSE

Once you know what to do, you have to act. We knew we had to cut price and deliver greater value to customers. But as you know, taking action can be a lot harder than figuring out what to do. For us, it was excruciating. We stalled. We said again that no-fee customers carried too much credit risk. We said we couldn't take the hit, which, given Citicorp's public commitment to build its capital base, was true. The one thing we didn't say, although some do, was that we'd settle for a smaller business to maintain our returns. Let me tell you, the share loss doesn't stop. Not every customer leaves the first time a better offer comes along. Some truly believe your products are better. But they know you're charging them more, and I doubt they like it. In time they'll go too. IBM, Xerox, and more other companies than I could name have all learned this the hard way.

You have to take the hit. It seems expensive now, but it's cheaper and easier than rebuilding your share and your reputation later. We're right in the middle of it; we're signing up customers for $50 or $100 apiece that we paid $30 for the first time. Our high-price image lingers, and some customers will never come back. And it's not just us. I got an offer in the mail at home the other day from AT&T offering to pay me $50 to change my long distance service back to them. So, starting in early 1993, we did it. We eliminated the fee on most of our basic products that still had fees. That cost about $150 million. But we saved some money consolidating collection centers. We adopted a lower-cost funding strategy. Last but not least, now that we had a better story to tell, we stepped up spending on new customer acquisitions. We put a record number of new offers in the mail with the new no-fee price. Like Compaq does after every round of price cutting, we came out swinging.

I don't mind telling you that the fee decision was the hardest decision I've ever made. The corporation that had funded us in the early '80s had spent 1991-1992 in intensive care. As we say around the place, by mid-1993, the patient was just beginning to sit up and take solid food. But it wasn't a sure thing that we had the financial strength or the credibility to sustain the move. We had to make the capital ratios we'd sworn we would make. We were afraid the analysts wouldn't understand and would take a couple of points off the stock. Right up to the end, I worried we weren't going to do it . . . and I stayed up nights worrying that we would.

Nine months later, as far as we can tell, we're headed in the right direction. Customer satisfaction surveys show we're doing better. Not best by a long shot, but better. Voluntary attrition has dropped in half. We're on track to add about one and half million accounts this year, a rate we've not seen in five years. We're holding our own on share and we're on our way to a record year financially, even though revenues are more than $100 million behind where we had wanted to be.

LESSONS

That's our story of deep pockets, good and bad. In the late 1970s through the mid-1980s, we used deep pockets and a single-minded focus on our vision to define the bankcards industry. But when others came along, with more money to spend and a new way to play, we were slow to react. We didn't take them seriously at first, and once we did we were afraid of the consequences. We maintained our course for at least three years when we had clear evidence that we had lost our competitive edge. We had what I call a financial success but a customer failure. It took a significant share loss—more than 10% of our position—to get our attention. But by mid-1993, we knew our future was slipping away despite our terrific financials. In late 1993, we used this position of relative strength to act, restructuring our customer offer so we could begin growing again.

We've been talking about the paralysis of deep pockets, the tendency for successful companies to be slow to recognize threats and to postpone taking action even when the threat clearly challenges their future. This is a natural tendency. Successful companies aren't successful by accident. They have built their position by driving single-mindedly toward their vision. An effective challenge often requires a change in the competitive frame. The same ability to shut out the doubters, the very beliefs that made the company strong, make them see changes to the competitive frame as just so much noise.

What can you do to prevent this paralysis, or to cure it once it sets in? You have to set aside your most dearly held beliefs and get a good, clear, hard grip on the facts. What do your customers really think? How do your products and the processes you use to deliver them stack up against them? What are your financials really saying? You have to benchmark. And you have to benchmark proactively, with the intent of doing something with what you learn. And then you have to act. The threat isn't going away. You react or you die.

There are two last points I would like to make. One is that you can't live from crisis to crisis. Managing in a crisis tends to get our adrenaline going, but it's much easier to deal with something before it gets to be a crisis. You have to be vigilant. You have to look for trouble when there doesn't seem to be a cloud in the sky. You have to benchmark proactively as an integral part of how you do business.

The second point is that you have to keep straight what are the ends and what are the means. Benchmarking is just a tool for getting to the bottom of your issues. Deep pockets just help you carry out your vision. No amount of benchmarking or deep pockets can compensate for a bad customer strategy. At Citibank, we did a lot of benchmarking and our resources certainly made a difference at a difficult time. But we didn't turn things around until we got our customer strategy back on the right track.

5

Building a Leadership Position
in a Hypercompetitive Technology Market

PETER NEUPERT

I would like to talk about how Microsoft has built its leadership position. When I thought long and hard about this chapter, I first wanted to learn what "hypercompetition" was. So, I started reading Rich D'Aveni's book. Then it occurred to me: This all sounds very familiar. This has been the environment that we have been living in since I started with the company in 1986, and certainly Microsoft has been in this environment even before that time. So I affirm that everything that I read about technology markets, or at least the things that I have direct personal experience in, suggests that they are very hypercompetitive. Technology markets are very much global. We worry about winning in every marketplace around the world. Intense global competition has certainly been the way we have been living.

I do not think there is a simple answer to how you build or maintain a leadership position in these sorts of markets. I will use some of Bill Gates's and Steve Ballmer's words, rather than my words, to give sort of the insider view of what is important, or what the critical success factors are, in our business. I only add one thing, and that is smart leadership, because Bill and Steve do not take credit for it.

The key thing is a set of attributes, two or three of which I will address. One of the most important from my point of view, and I use the extreme example: We are paranoid; we are competitive, and we are paranoid. There is no lead that is not surmountable. We have never been financially oriented. We have always focused on financial or market share as a measure of our

AUTHOR'S NOTE: This chapter is adapted from Peter Neupert's presentation at the Whittemore Conference on Hypercompetition, September 1994.

success, but we have never looked at a very concrete analysis of what return are we going to get. That has not been the focus. The focus has been on the technology—the category—how do we win in the category; is this going to be an important emerging trend; do we have to be there; if we are not there, what's going to happen to us. And we are always looking over our shoulder. I think this attribute really starts at the top, and so I will start with leadership.

LEADERSHIP

There has been a lot written about Bill Gates. Some of it is true, some of it is not true. He makes an amazing difference in our company, and it is hard to overestimate that. He is very hands-on; he has the right set of values; he focuses on what we call "vision." We had a vision from the very beginning: a computer on every desk and in every home. That drove us a long way in the later 1980s. That was very much graphical user interface. Now in the later 1990s, we have a different vision, but we have always had something keeping us focused on the next platform change; how can we use that to our advantage; what are the core competencies that we have to have. It has been very focused from the technology point of view. Bill does a great job using his position to stay very outwardly focused. He talks at conferences; he talks to customers. Up until 1992, he went to every subsidiary in the world every year, and we have 25 of them. He reviewed their operations; he was very much in touch, and, he is very good at synthesizing information. That's Bill's role.

Steve Ballmer's contribution is the bias to act. Steve is a marketing guy, a sales guy. When I first started in 1986, he was doing Windows® for $100.00, it was just like a used car salesman act, it was just incredibly funny. But he is the one who really developed the "Do-it-try-it-fix-it." If we don't do something, we won't know, so let's do it. That has made an important difference in our getting in the marketplace—keep on trying, keep on trying to make it work. It is a willingness to change strategy if we are not being successful. The long-term approach has given us time to make those things happen. It doesn't all work if results don't matter. So results really matter. But it matters how you measure them, and this is always against the competition. We are very focused on how we are doing against our competition and against our potential competition. How we view our competition has changed dramatically in the past two or three years, and that's an important thing to continue to evolve.

This is the message that Bill and Steve and Mike Maples were giving to our employees. We had a record year; we exceeded our analysts' expectations again. But, what they focused on was on the competition. How are we doing against the competition? Now on one hand, we look at it and say, "Gee, what do we have to do?" We have been telling the analysts we are going to grow more slowly every year, and we generally do because of the law of large numbers. But for us to grow at 20%, we have to grow another Lotus every year. That's a big challenge. Our applications revenue, just in the past two years, is what really has made us the dominant player. We are really focused on competition with Lotus Notes®. We are way behind; we have been behind for a couple of different reasons, but we think we have a strategy that will help change the rules and get to the next level when we introduce our new set of products. We hope to be able to take our position on the desktop and leverage it into the network, and we think that will be good both for us and for customers.

We have been focused on benchmarking measures of how well we are using our resources. We have gone through a growth phase and a restructuring phase and so forth. We have done both, and you have to do them at the same time. One of the key people who helped our financials was Jon Shirley, who was the president of the company for a few years. We reduced our cost-to-goods-sold each year for four years, as we were growing the company at 40% a year. And that was really, really important. Not very many people cared about it, it wasn't a technology thing, but it got the company moving in a direction that has paid a huge benefit in the past few years. I think you can do both, it doesn't have to be one, doesn't have to be growth, it doesn't have to be restructuring or cost containment, you have to do them both at the same time.

INDIVIDUAL EXCELLENCE

That was the leadership piece. A second key tenet of our company is individual excellence. That comes through in lots of different ways. The good news, and perhaps we have an unnatural advantage here, is that in the software business, it is reasonably easy to let individual excellence show through. A good example is David Weiss. This was back in 1988—I was managing a joint development with IBM. We were doing OS/2; we had just released Windows Version 2.2. We were way late on OS/2; we weren't being able to meet the expectations; the development was taking longer. We still believed; we were firmly committed to OS/2; we had more developers on OS/2, more money, more marketing on OS/2 than anybody else. We wanted OS/2 to succeed. Bill and Steve wanted OS/2 to succeed. But we had this nagging problem that it wasn't meeting the customer requirement. It wasn't meeting the reality of the machines. And this guy, David Weiss, just kept working on Windows. The team was down to less then 10 people on Windows now; we had everybody else on OS/2. He figured out how to break the 640K memory barrier in Windows, and created Windows 3.0. One guy. I had four architects on my team who said it never could be done; he figured out how to do it. And with that, we had the opportunity to take Windows and continue on to meet customer requirements and move forward, and he changed our whole strategy over the next three and one half years. But my point is, one person—individual excellence—can make a difference. People know that story in our company, and they know we expect individuals to make a difference. In the software business, perhaps like other knowledge businesses, one really great person is worth 200 not so great people. So, we have had a recruiting and people management activity purposely focused to make sure we got the best people.

Brian Quinn, in one of his books, *The Intelligent Enterprise* (1994), I think really captured the essence of how important this is to the long-term health of a business. Learning is exponential, the best people like to work on the hardest problems, good people like to work around the best people, and it's a self-fulfilling cycle. You bring everybody up, and once you are ahead, you are always ahead, until you screw up and miss the platform change. That has been our approach when we want to get into a business or a technology area. We go out and get the best people to start a core group and then build around them and take the time. We won't go buy existing technology very often, because that doesn't really help, unless it is the only way we can get the best people.

Passion for technologies is another important commitment. We always paid less than others and gave stock, so monetary awards typically do not happen. What David is, fundamentally, is like a Fellow in other organizations. He has continued to work on the successive versions of Windows and is the chief architect. He does not have a title; he does not report to a vice president, but he works on what he wants to work on and makes a difference. An individual contributor does not manage a group. We have never made the best technical guys managers, or we kept their scope of management relatively small when they needed it. The best example of this is Dave Cutler. When we needed to go build Windows NT, Dave Cutler became available. Fifteen other people from Digital Equipment in the western region all came; he had a whole team. They managed that team and built the foundation for Windows NT, which was a multiscaleable, multiprocessor-based architecture. It is his fourth implementation; there are now 300 people around him, but he manages a small team. He just manages the core.

The way we reward individuals is that we make them share in the success of the company. We do not have very sophisticated management bonus systems. The current compensation has not been a significant piece of it. We have always heard the story that the stock cannot continue to go on; it's making less of impact. People don't value it. We have got to increase blah-blah-blah. . . . We haven't changed. And I think we're going to continue on this track. Bill's solution has been 17% in vested and unvested options. He has been willing to accept that level of dilution to support this compensation technique. I forget how much money that was last year, but I think it's on the order of 750 million dollars of option grants that went out to employees. Gotta keep it working.

Another thing that lets individual excellence matter or make a difference is an incredibly flat organization. We are a very flat organization even though we have 15,000 people now. It's fairly straight forward: We use e-mail. We live and die by it. That is the way we communicate. That's the way Bill communicates. Any employee can communicate with Bill. We use it reasonably effectively as a mechanism to keep the organization flat, to keep in touch with what our customers are saying, to keep in touch with how the engineers feel, to understand how to make quick strategy decisions, and to make sure that the small team of four or five people all understand what's going on.

LONG-TERM APPROACH, BUT SHORT-TERM TACTICAL ACTION

Perhaps as the result of the controlled ownership, perhaps as the result of a passion for products and technology, we've taken a long-term approach to investments and certain decisions. We have the courage of our convictions. People look today at Windows as a success, but in 1985 when they initiated Windows 1.0, it was a joke. Windows 2.0 in 1987 was bigger joke. Customers didn't like it. It didn't fit the requirements. Bill never lost sight that graphical user interface was a better solution that the character interface and that somehow we were going to get it to work on the IBM PC platform. And that would be important. We focused all of our resources in making that a reality. We did the same thing in CD-ROM; it's now changed, it's now called the multimedia. But back in 1986-1987, we said that was going to be important, and we just kept plugging along. One of the things we did smart in this CD-ROM stuff was that we kept costs low. We just sort of had an effort: limp along, limp along, limp along. But in 1993 when it started to take off, we were there. We had a tool, we had branding strategy, we had some properties under development, and in the next 12 months we'll produce a hundred titles in the consumer division for CD-ROM. That patience, and a little bit of market timing, is what really made it for us. It is not as if we have dominated the software business over the history of the software business. We were behind in the DOS applications. We were behind in many respects in networking and continue to be behind. We were behind in lots of communications areas. We have come from behind frequently to a leadership position, not always being the first mover in that piece, and it has paid off.

We're using that approach to a future investment in the information highway. We see this other huge evolutionary change coming. I'm in the advanced technology group working for Nathan Myhrvold. We are trying to build all the systems infrastructure and applications infrastructure, if you will, for the information highway. That's what we see as the next major evolution that is going to impact all of our businesses. I don't care what business you are in, the convergence of communications and computing is going to impact your core competencies, how you do business, how you interact with customers; it's going to be an important event in the next 10 years. When it's going to happen, we don't know. Our focus is on the core skills we need to have to be a winner from a technology point of view. We have efforts going on to either acquire technology or acquire core expertise, or build on the foundation that we have in each of these areas. There has been a lot in the press about the convergence of media and the convergence of networking, so I don't want to spend a lot of time, but that's the foundation. We see it coming, we've started an advance technology group, we've built some research around it, and we are now starting to build some products and some alliances to make sure that we're there when the timing's right, and to try to derive how some of the people define what's accomplishable.

One of the interesting things is that we always address things from a software point of view. Depending on which vendor you talk to, they have the solution to the information highway. Oracle thinks it's a database problem; AT&T thinks of it as a hardware problem. We think of the Internet as a software problem. We want to take the personal computer industry, microprocessors, standard components, low-cost manufacturing, and 500 different printers, as the right model for the information highway. So, we're going to take an approach that makes it a distributed computing network as opposed to just a video distribution system or a video-on-demand distribution system. The endgame may be five years from now, but the game may be won two or three years from now.

One of the things that I think has made Microsoft unique is that we are willing to take a long-term approach, but we always take the short-term tactical action to win in the next few months. We do not want to lose any beachheads. We do not get beaten on pricing, even though we're the market leader. We do not like to lose. That balance between taking the hill and maybe taking some setbacks by taking the hill, and staying focused on continuing to do that has helped us establish where we are, both in the operating systems business and in the applications business. I think it's just the way we operate. We hope it will make us successful in the information highway business. We are working with customers. We are investing hundreds of millions of dollars a year to make this as real as we can this year. But, if it doesn't happen until the year 2000, we'll be O.K., and in the meantime, we will have learned, and we will have created those relationships with customers, and we will have had user interfaces and applications and some activities in place to know how to tweak it the next time. A lot of users joke, never buy the first version of a Microsoft product, they only get it right on the third time. There is some merit to that, but we don't know a better way. We don't know a better way to get the third time right, and we've done lots of usability tests, and lots of analysis to make sure that we can do the first version better, but it takes that sort of evolution, at least in our business, to make the real results happen.

We do not feel like we have a divine right to win the information highway. We're worried to death about it. It keeps Bill up at night. As I said, we're paranoid. We're worried about every risk you can imagine—we don't get our products done, we miss the opportunity, or we wanted to charge too much for a particular sale that would have cemented a relationship. We worry about legislation coming down that makes it impossible for us, or anyone, to make any money on the systems software infrastructure, which is a 100 million dollar-a-year investment. Somebody's got to be able to make money out of it. Where I think that we have an advantage is that we're bold enough, or audacious enough, to think through the soup-to-nuts of how to do it. We're not going to be in the network engineering business; we're not going to lay any cable. We don't want to own any pipes, so we're not going to compete with AT&T or MCI. But the question then is, how do you take all the infrastructure that they have, and the resources that they have, and make them as valuable as you can, when there are 40 million personal computers connected up? The big risk is that we'll be late, we'll have made a mistake, or somehow that in a monopoly play by an access cable company in a monopoly-driven environment right now, the best technology may not be what matters. That's one thing that keeps us up at night.

SUMMARY

To sum up, the information highway is a long-term play, and we recognize that one thing that we are doing differently now is that we are spending a lot early, because we think that time-to-market will be very important. It always is in the system infrastructure business. There are a lot of pieces that have to come together from a technological point of view: graphics, communications, the ATM technology. Our approach in the system software business is always to focus on how can we establish standards to build the market. One of the key things is, will there be one or many highway platforms that applications providers will have to choose among? And, how will that slow the market? An example that I always use is that if you look at the Japanese personal computer market, there were five different DOS platforms up until last year, and as a result, application providers always spent their time porting from one platform to the other and not investing because they could not make a return. If we make that same mistake in the information highway because that is the way evolution happens, I think it will retard the growth of it. We are focused on how can we establish standards and at the same time make a return, but recognize that we have got to make the majority of our money on the application services side of the business. What we get from being in the systems software side is the courage of our convictions that we know what to invest in, what can be done, in the application side.

We have been able to create a position of leadership through vision, some technology, and, most important, one of the things that I think is a real customer asset: execution now. We are very reliable. We may not be the first one, we may not be the innovators, but we know where to invest our money, we deliver quality products, and I think that's made a big difference to a lot of corporations in our business markets. That is something that has evolved by knowing about individual excellence, knowing about passion for products, and knowing how to build an organization that knows how to build software. We have turned those core competencies into a low-risk choice for the customer. Hey, you can't go wrong buying a Microsoft software product.

I think that Bill and Steve in the leadership make a big difference in getting the best people and keeping us focused on being global in fighting this, and that you have to be relentless. If you don't win the first time, you've got to keep trying, and you've always got to be paranoid. And, you've got to worry about the guy who's coming up behind your back—who will change the rules of the game on you.

REFERENCE

Quinn, B. (1994), *The Intelligent Enterprises,* New York: Free Press.

6

Technological Platforms
and Diversification

DONG-JAE KIM
BRUCE KOGUT

As the invention of fundamental new sciences spawns subsequent research, discovery, and commercialization, core technologies branch into new applications and markets. Some of them evolve over time into many derived technologies, whereas others are essentially "dead ends." The pattern of evolution and branching is called a "technological trajectory." An intriguing question is whether some firms can ride the trajectory by developing proprietary experience in a "platform technology." Because the knowledge is proprietary, firms that originate in industrial fields based on a platform technology acquire the technological skills to diversify and to mimic the branching of the underlying technological trajectory.

The ability to compete in hypercompetitive markets depends on the acquisition of know-how that is applicable to a wide set of market opportunities. Such capabilities serve as platforms into quickly evolving markets. To respond rapidly to market changes, a firm must have already acquired fundamental competitive knowledge. In a high-technology industry, such knowledge invariably is derived from experience with the underlying science and related technological fields.

The authors examine capabilities as platforms by analyzing the temporal sequence of diversification as contingent on market opportunities and previous experience. The pattern of diversification of firms reflects the evolutionary branching of underlying technologies. In that sense, the aggregate decisions of firms are driven by the technological trajectories common across an industrial sector. Certain technologies have wider technological and market opportunities, and consequently experience in those technologies serves as a platform for expansion. The authors propose that a firm's experience in platform technologies increases the likelihood of diversification when environmental opportunities are favorable.

The proposition is tested with the sample of 176 semiconductor startup companies founded between 1977 and 1989. Evidence from multidimensional scaling of expert opinion and from an analysis of patent records was gathered to identity relatedness among subfields and the evolutionary direction of the technologies. A discrete hazard model is specified to estimate the effect of technological histories on subsequent diversification. The results confirm the relationship between relatedness and directionality of technologies and the industrial path of diversification. The finding that diversification depends on technological experience and market opportunity has important implications for firms' entry decisions. The authors discuss those implications by describing experience as generating options on future opportunities and distinguishing between the historical path by which the stock of knowledge is accumulated and the path by which new knowledge is generated and commercialized.

(PLATFORM TECHNOLOGY; DIVERSIFICATION;
TECHNOLOGICAL TRAJECTORY;
KNOWLEDGE ACCUMULATION; OPTION)

Competing in rapidly evolving industries poses the complex problem of choosing what capabilities should be developed for highly uncertain and volatile markets. Freeman (1987) has observed that forecasting the class of future technologies has proven to be easier than identifying future markets and products. The implication of that seemingly innocuous observation is rather radical. Developing competence in new but broad-based technological skills is an investment in a platform to participate, by a process of expansion and diversification, in the evolution of future opportunities. In contrast, forecasting demand for specific products may lead to the development of capabilities poorly suited for the markets that eventually prove to be economically interesting.

Industries in which competitive advantages of innovations quickly erode are commonly called "Schumpeterian" or "hypercompetitive." In such an environment, the capability to upgrade products and diversify into related segments is often built on the accumulation of experiential know-how that allows for expansion during windows of opportunity.[1] The initial experiences of firms provide platforms, or options for diversifying into new markets when the timing is right.

We explain the pattern of diversification of startup firms in rapidly growing industries as linked to the evolutionary branching of technologies and market opportunities. A central idea in research on the evolution of firm capabilities is that the local search process builds on previous knowledge that can be transferred to new fields. Our conceptual contribution is to link the path of a firm's diversification to the development of the underlying technological trajectory. The notion of a trajectory implies that technologies differ in their potential to generate new paths of development and to serve as platforms into new markets. Some technologies provide a starting point or platform for the exploration and development of new resources and have a high potential to spawn new markets. Other technologies are specific to certain applications and represent essentially dead ends for further major development.

We predict that firms with experience in platform technologies have a significantly greater opportunity and tendency to diversify into related sub-fields than firms with products narrowly dedicated to a market. Experience with a platform technology generates the organizational capability to compete in related fields, but it does not guarantee that a firm will, in fact, diversify or succeed. That process is not uniquely driven by technology, but by firms' efforts to grow in the presence of competition and the expansion of new market opportunities. In that sense, the accumulation of experience provides platforms to enter future but uncertain markets whereas the *timing of diversification* should depend on the growth of the related subfields.

We develop and test the proposition that the pattern of diversification reflects the branching of the underlying technologies contingent on market opportunity. An overview of the literature on technological evolution establishes two points: that a trajectory is the cumulative knowledge resulting from local search, and that the knowledge may be specific and proprietary to firms because of experimental learning or system effects. It is only when the knowledge from the search is proprietary and firm-specific that technological branching and diversification should be related. After a brief review of the history of technological branching in the semiconductor industry, we analyze the subfields to determine their "relatedness" and "directionality." An application of multidimensional scaling to questionnaire data shows that experts differentiate subfields of semiconductors into distinguishable clusters. We then analyze the subfield distribution of patent histories of 53 startup firms. The analysis shows clear directional differences in the frequency, speed, and subfield diversity of patent activity according to the technological origins of the startup firm.

Longitudinal regression tests were applied to a sample consisting of the diversification and survival histories of 176 startup semiconductor firms founded between 1977 and 1989. We find strong support for the idea that particular subfields, as suggested by the technical literature and by the MDS and patent results, serve as platforms into other markets. Our discussion broadens the investigation by considering whether firms make entry decisions myopically or with foresight.

OVERVIEW

The argument we present consists of three parts:[2]

1. Technologies follow an observable trajectory. Some technologies are more likely to serve as platforms into new markets than others. The trajectory and the platform can be identified empirically.

2. Organizations differ in their points of origin and in their accumulation of know-how with different technologies. Those that gain experience in platform technologies will be more likely to diversify into new markets than those with experience in nonplatform technologies.

3. Organizations tend to diversify into new markets when the markets are growing.

A common approach in studies of diversification is to relate a firm's portfolio of businesses to a measure of relatedness, or to relate a firm's diversification decision to such a measure. We have two wider objectives. The first is to explain dynamically the path of a firm's diversification history in terms of its acquisition of related knowledge in a particular industry or subfield. The second is to show that the pattern of diversification at the firm level corresponds to a broader technological trajectory in which particular technologies act as platforms into more specialized applications. A key element in that explanation is the relationship between firm-level diversification into distinct markets and macro technological trajectories. To make that connection, we develop three points: that trajectories are defined by both technological and market opportunities, that knowledge accumulates in response to a firm's experience in solving particular problems, and that a firm's diversification history is linked to the trajectory because knowledge is proprietary.

Technological Trajectories

Potential technological developments can be seen as a transition matrix in which current technologies evolve into new ones. The matrix can be considered the potential technological space. If there were no logic to technological development, the transition would be essentially random. The notion of a trajectory suggests the contrary: that technological evolution is influenced by the past. The term "technological opportunity" captures the idea that not all transitions are equally likely and that some are favored by the inherent richness, or evolvability, of a technology.

Nelson and Winter (1982, pp. 255-256) make a similar observation:

> In many technological histories the new is not just better than the old; in some sense the new evolves out of the old. One explanation for this is that the output of today's searches is not merely a new technology, but also enhances knowledge and forms the basis of new building blocks to be used tomorrow.

The choice of a technology is determined not only by current capabilities and technological bottlenecks to be solved. Technologies must also be accepted for use. The selection process may be determined abstractly by a market, but market forces are outcomes of the institutional environment, including government policies (which were influential in the early history of semiconductors). The historical record supports the importance of the coincidental effects of current technical capabilities and socioeconomic conditions on opportunities for future expansion (Mowery and Rosenberg 1981, Bijker and Pinch 1987).

The union of organizational factors that create a "technological push" and environmental conditions that create a "market pull" underlies the notion of what Nelson and Winter (1977, 1982) and Dosi (1982) have called "technological trajectories." Such trajectories represent the expansion of a core set of solutions (e.g., mechanization of production) that are favored by the institutional forces that condition their selection and survival. The revealed trajectory is the conjunction of both technological and market factors, and is determined by neither individually.

A trajectory implies that early investments in a technology reap increasing returns. One expansion of that dynamic is the tendency toward increasing specialization, or divergence. Occasionally, specialized technologies converge in new combinations, which then follow a pattern of specialization. The repeated application of a particular set of technologies or organizing principles eventually exhausts the set of potential combinations and market opportunities. Because opportunities are limited, the expansion of a trajectory is both constrained and finite.

Local Adaptation and Diversification

A trajectory is tied to the local search efforts of firms. There is an interesting analogy between the trajectory in technologies and the observed pattern in diversification. Diversification is the outcome of temporally ordered decisions to adapt or acquire knowledge for exploitation in new markets. The fact that diversification from a given industry is not randomly distributed over all other industries suggests that industry experience guides the evolution of technological and product market choices of individual firms (Teece et al. 1994).

The dependence of the capability to expand by diversification on the history of industry experience of firms supports a view of evolution by adaptive search. Firms are not strictly inert, but diversify and adapt by learning within the developmental constraints of their current capabilities. An organization is developmentally constrained in its acquisition of both new information and new ways of doing things. Consider, for example, the research on the acquisition of knowledge by technology transfer and innovation. A common observation in studies on technology transfer has been the importance of prior experience in determining the adopter's capabilities to absorb the technology (Teece 1976, Contractor 1981, Pavitt 1987). Similar conclusions have been reached about the process by which knowledge is accumulated and learned (Cohen and Levinthal 1990, Henderson and Clark 1990, Helfat 1994).

History in a particular industry appears to govern the opportunities for diversification for individual firms. In industries where technological capability is an important determinant of competitive advantage and market success, the diversification pattern of a firm is coupled to its ability to tap into the technological trajectory of its industry. In that case, the analogy between diversification and technological evolution is not metaphorical, but reflects a link between the diversification path of the firm and a technology's trajectory.

Because search is local, it is not surprising that innovations are often recombinations of existing ideas and practices (Kogut and Zander 1992). Schumpeter (1968, pp. 65-66) argued that, in general, innovations are new combinations of existing "materials and forces." Usher (1971, p. 50) called the process of invention a "cumulative synthesis of many items which were originally independent."[3] The explanation of why innovations tend to be recombinations lies partly in the domain of what individuals can know and partly in the fact that what organizations know and learn is delimited by their rigidity in changing their information and structuring of roles.

Platform Technologies and Diversification

A trajectory suggests direction in technological development. It is a simple step to proceed from the notion of a trajectory branching into new applications and markets to an explanation for the diversification path of firms. However, one point in the logic must be clarified: Why and when should an individual firm replicate the branching of a trajectory through its own diversification pattern?

The notion of an adaptive search is part of the basis for understanding the bridge between trajectories and diversification paths of firms. In general, the diversification literature, following Penrose (1959), has stressed the importance of related diversification to performance. In the tradition of the seminal study by Rumelt (1974), that literature has focused primarily on the cross-sectional relationship between relatedness and performance. The evidence tends to show that firms enter industries related to their current lines of business (Montgomery and Hariharan 1991).

The findings on relatedness are consistent with a process by which a firm's diversification path is coupled to a technological trajectory.[4] However, there is a difference. A trajectory implies that diversification should follow a broad *direction*. Relatedness at a point of time is only a cross-section of the dynamic relatedness across time. The points of divergence and convergence in a trajectory represent opportunities for established firms to diversify into new subfields. The creation of those critical junctures often depends on the efforts of new firms, but the subsequent development of the resultant subfields tends to show a clear mixture of entry by both entrepreneurial and established firms (Tushman and Anderson 1986). Relatedness does not establish that a given firm needs to span different markets.

However, both relatedness and direction are necessary to isolate a trajectory. Any temporal series of changes in technology or diversification will suggest a path. For a sufficient number of observed changes, a conservative approach is to test whether the series follows a random path. Such tests often plagued by low power is a statistical sense. An alternative method is to identify relatedness of a technology at Time 1 to that at Time 2 by looking at measures of their relatedness. (That approach is equivalent to saying there is systematic serial correlation in diversification over time.) It is the combination of direction with a determination of relatedness that defines a trajectory empirically.

One way to think about those issues is to distinguish between technologies that are specialized to particular subfields and those that can serve as platforms into new markets and applications. A platform technology represents the development of a capability that maps onto a wide variety of market opportunities, a capability that is consequently characterized by a high degree of intertemporal relatedness to a wide expanse of new markets. We call such dynamic relatedness the *"directionality"* of a technology.

What makes a technology a platform is its formative influence on a newly evolving trajectory that is characterized by increasing returns to investment in further exploration. The increasing returns are achieved either through network externalities of components in a wider technological system (e.g., the rotary converter in electrical grids) or through the accumulation of learning by doing that is useful for the generation of new products. Those two dynamic factors of network evolution and learning, separately and jointly, lead to self-organizing and irreversible historical patterns (Arthur 1985, David 1975, Silverberg et al. 1988). When they are proprietary, they tie the expanding trajectory to the diversification paths of firms.

Proprietary learning in design and production is the basis for viewing some semiconductors as "technology drivers." As Howell and his coauthors (1988, p. 28) explain:[5]

> The significance of learning economies has imparted a tremendous strategic importance to certain types of semiconductors for which significant unit demand exists— and which can thus be produced in high volumes—but which are also highly complex. The mass production of such extremely complex devices generates "learning" about complex production processes which can be applied to a much wider range of other device types which are produced by a company in lower volume. Such high complexity, high volume "technology drivers" are widely viewed as a prerequisite to remaining competitive in semiconductors over the long run. Consequently, these product areas have been the principal areas of international competition in microelectronics since the early 1970s.

Udayagiri (1993) has shown that learning economies in one generation of semiconductors lowers the costs of subsequent generations. When those learning economies are also useful for application to other markets, we should expect the branching of a platform technology into new and related subfields.

System dependence and proprietary learning, independently or jointly, tie the opportunity of a firm to the overall success of its trajectory. Only if the platform is proprietary will technological relatedness be reflected systematically in the diversification pattern of the firm. If the benefit of the externality of learning is entirely public, trajectories will still occur, but there would be no advantage for firms experienced in the technology to be the engine of growth through diversification. For that reason, proprietary learning in the absence of network externalities commonly serves as a platform into new markets. In the absence of a learning advantage, network externalities can serve as an entry into other markets for a firm in an environment where patent or regulatory protection is provided. The microprocessor used in personal computers is a classic example of a network externality that expanded over time with the proliferation of computers and is proprietary because of patent protection and the installed base.

We can summarize our discussion in two propositions. Technologies develop on the basis of current capabilities and the influence of market opportunities. Those two forces—the push of current capabilities and the pull of environmental signals—shape the direction of search. By the argument of firm adaptability, we would expect the variances in problem-solving experiences to lead to differential diversification capabilities conditional on environmental opportunities. We therefore suggest the following propositions.

P1. *Technological Platform: A firm with experience in a platform technology is more likely to diversify into the exploration and generation of new markets than a firm that has developed narrowly based skills.*

P2. *Market Timing: The pattern and timing of entry into a subfield are related positively to the growth of the market.*

The propositions correspond closely to notions of hyper- and Schumpeterian competition. In rapidly evolving industries, competitive capabilities are transitory and opportunities are quickly closed by competitors. An implication of a trajectory is that the ability to compete on timing is contingent on the acquisition of the relevant know-how. In environments where future opportunities are uncertain, there is value in owning proprietary know-how that acts as a platform for rapid expansion.

DATA AND METHODS

To test the claims, we first establish the trajectory of technology in a given industry, semiconductors, and identity the technologies that can be characterized as platforms. We then construct event history records of startup companies in the semiconductor industry to record their initial subfield entry and their subsequent timing of diversification. The event of diversification is the dependent variable to be related to a firm's technological experience.

Sample and Data

The main source of our data is Dataquest, a market research firm based in San Jose, California. Primary data and technical details about semiconductors were collected through field research. One author visited three semiconductor plants; the other conducted 50 hours of telephone interviews and served as teaching assistant for a course on circuitry taught in the department of electrical engineering. Presentations of the research were made to a meeting of industry analysts and to the planning staff of a large electronics firm.

The initial list of 180 startup firms founded between 1977 and 1989 was acquired from Dataquest publications (1988, 1990). Because startup firms enter with a restricted product range, the research design has the obvious advantage of tracking the effect of a firm's initial experience on its subsequent path of diversification. The design also has the advantage of concentrating on a sample of firms where technology is likely to be one of the most important considerations; in a wider sample of incumbents, other capabilities such as marketing skills would certainly require further analysis. Using the Dataquest list, we contacted the startup firms and collected complete histories of entry at the subfield level (i.e., product diversification records). We could not collect complete data for four of the firms, which were dropped from the sample. Therefore, 176 startups firms form the sample for our study.

Table 6.1 provides a list and description of the primary subfields of semiconductor devices. The shipment data for the subfields were retrieved from unpublished or proprietary records. Digital signal processors (DSP) did not have shipment data. Gallium arsenide devices (GaAs) had shipment data only for 1984 through 1988. Both of those subfields were dropped in the final regression analysis.

In Table 6.2, the raw ratios of initial and subsequent entry to total entries for the sample firms are given. Substantial variation is evident, with memory and gallium arsenide devices showing the highest proportion of initial entrants. Because subsequent entries occur in significant proportions only for application-specific integrated circuits (ASICs), microcomponents, optoelectronics, and telecommunication, the regression analysis applies to those subfields.

TRAJECTORIES IN SEMICONDUCTORS

Before reporting the regressions, we describe the historical trajectory in semiconductors, and then determine the pattern of relatedness and evolutionary direction among the subfields. That is, even if currently there are two

TABLE 6.1 Technological Subfields—Primary Product Segments

Subfield	Product Segments
Analog	Operational amplifiers, comparators, data conversion products, interface products, voltage regulators, and sensors
ASICs	Gate arrays, cell libraries, and progammable logic devices (PLDs)
DSP	Single-chip DSP microprocessors, microprogrammable devices, special function circuits, and ASIC DSP products
Discrete	Diodes, transistors, power field-effect transistors (FETs), and thyristors
GaAs	Discretes (small-signal transistors and power FETs), optoelectronics (light-emitting devices, detectors, and integrated opto devices), and other applications (analog and digital)
Memory	Dynamic random access memory (DRAM), static random access memory (SRAM), read only memory (ROM), erasable programmable read only memory (EPROM), and ferro-electric memory
Micro	Microprocessors, mass storage, system support, and key/display chip sets
Opto	Light emitting devices (LEDs), light sensing devices, optocouplers, and photodiodes
Telecom	Dialers, modem, line interfaces, codec/filter, and switch arrays

SOURCE: Dataquest (1988, 1990).

TABLE 6.2 Ratio of Initial and Subsequent Entry

	Analog	ASIC	DSP	Discr	GaAs	Memory	Micro	Opto	Tele
Initial entry	.65	.46	.43	.75	.95	.83	.43	.36	.21
Subsequent entry	.35	.54	.57	.25	.05	.17	.57	.64	.79

subfields, we need to provide evidence of an asymmetry: experience in one subfield serves as a platform for expansion into the other, but not vice versa. Simple relatedness is not sufficient for understanding the evolutionary pattern of diversification.

Descriptive Overview

The notion of a trajectory can be illustrated by analyzing the recent history of technological development in the semiconductor industry. The industry grew out of the laboratories of AT&T, but the early demand for the devices was driven by the growing appetite for military applications (Nelson 1962, Brittain and Freeman 1980). In the United States, the increasing importance of computers gradually shifted supply to the production of digital devices, especially memory; in Japan, the growth of consumer electronics pulled the local industry toward specialization in analog semiconductors (Malerba 1985). The reorientation of Japanese producers to digital production occurred only in the mid-1970s. That example of a successful transition in specialization from analog to digital devices also illustrates the importance of the selection environment. The MITI policy of favoring Japanese computer makers effectively pulled production toward the development of digital capabilities (Anchordoguy 1989). Another important difference was the role played by startup companies in the United States and by established firms in Japan.

The history of technological branching of the industry can be represented by a dendrogram, as shown in Figure 6.1. A dendrogram is a model (in contrast to a theory) that "is a more or less accurate representation of the path of evolution" (McKelvey 1982, p. 296).[6] Our classification traces the divergence of the basic technology by market segmentation, as opposed to being a strict classification by technical trait. It thus resembles Hannan and Freeman's (1987) pragmatic approach of identifying classes of organization by niches. (Subsequently, we validate the classification by statistical procedures.) There are obviously other ways to construct the tree, such as by the electrochemical properties (e.g., MOS) or by manufacturing sophistication (as used by Schoonhoven et al. 1990).

The trunk of the tree is the basic discovery of the discrete transistor (and related discrete components) and integrated circuit. Integrated circuits developed entry along two lines associated with analog and digital encoding. Another way to distinguish the evolutionary branching is by use of material or, more generally, by tracing the evolution of materials as "co-evolving" with the applications. Early use of germanium gradually was dropped in favor of silicon. An alternative material, gallium arsenide, was introduced with slow acceptance. By the early 1970s, the industry began to divide into new subfields, first memory and then microprocessors. The divergence of semiconductor technologies evolved into the newer subfields of digital signal processors (DSPs, used to replace some analog devices in consumer electronics) and ASICs (used for customized functions).

An especially interesting subfield is telecommunications, for which a semiconductor device is a hybrid of digital and analog technologies. Similarly, the properties of gallium arsenide have proven to be useful for optoelectronics. Those subfields are outcomes of "convergent" technologies.[7] In evolutionary biology, a dendrogram (or "cladist" taxonomy) is a strictly hierarchical tree whose branches always diverge and never converge again (Dawkins 1986, pp. 258-259). Innovation, in contrast, as the outcome of recombining elements, produces both divergent and convergent technological trajectories.

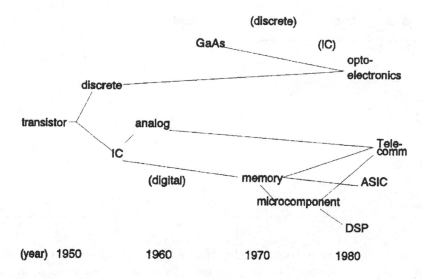

Figure 6.1. Evolution of Semiconductors

Technological Relatedness and Directionality

Before testing the propositions, we validated the relationships posited in Figure 6.1. History provides a kind of demonstration proof by showing that a particular evolution is feasible. We are interested in a stronger statement, namely, that the historical patterns represent a tendency toward increasing specialization stemming from technologies that embody the greatest opportunities. Some technologies have proven to be less fecund; others have failed entirely. In essence, we want to show that the historical evolution represents a *directional tendency* that should be mapped onto the diversification paths of firms.

We first drew on our interviews and technical literature to assemble a set of priors on the relatedness among the subfields and branches, and then turned to more formal methods to validate those impressions. To establish a stronger claim to directionality, we also reviewed the patent histories of startup firms that reported patents to analyze the evolutionary pattern of technological diversification in the patent record. The details of that analysis are given in Appendix 1.

Summary of Findings on Relatedness and Directionality

Our analysis of the technical literature, expert opinions, and patent histories serves as a method of triangulation to establish patterns of relatedness

TABLE 6.3 Matrix of Entry Sequence (predicted)

From \ To	ASICs	Micro	Opto	Teecom
Analog				(+)
ASICs				
DSP		(+)		
Discrete			(+)	
GaAs			(+)	
Memory	(+)	(+)		(+)
Micro				
Opto				
Telecom				

at a point of time and directionality over time. Table 6.3 summarizes the overall results. As noted in the discussion of the sample, we are analyzing the effects of previous technological experience on subsequent entries. Our hypotheses are applied to entry into ASICs, microcomponents, optoelectronics, and telecom ICs, where subsequent entries occurred in significant numbers. The principal finding is that memory is related to several other subfields, both cross-sectionally and dynamically. Analog experience is expected to be significant in entering telecom ICs. Following the strong suggestion of the technical literature and expert opinions, we hypothesize that experience in discrete and GaAs devices should help firms enter optoelectronics. Patent analysis does not clearly capture those relationships, however. All three analyses suggest strong relatedness between DSP and microcomponents, but the issue is directionality. Patent analysis reveals strong directionality from DSP to microcomponents but not vice versa; hence we hypothesize that relationship.

The method of triangulation is important because each technique analyzes different data, yet reveals similar patterns. The technical literature provides a straightforward look at the technological evolution of semiconductors. The multidimensional scaling relies on the opinions of experts about both technological and market relatedness. (See Appendix 2 for questionnaire.) Finally, the analysis of patents provides insight into directionality, as well as technological opportunity. Table 6.3 is a distillation of the findings of the three approaches.

We next test whether the pattern of technological relatedness and directionality is replicated in the diversification histories of individual firms. Even though the innovation of memory semiconductors preceded ASICs chronologically, the analysis looks at firms that have entered at a time when those subfields were conterminous. It is not surprising that subsequent fields should be shown to be related to historically precedent industries, but the historical ordering is hardly accidental. There is no historical necessity for startup firms in our sample to replicate history, other than the fact that there is an experiential relationship between the capabilities gained in the platform technologies and the other subfields. Nevertheless, as reported subsequently, advancing the historical clock (that is, beginning the observations at a later date so that all subfields begin in the same calendar year) does not influence the results.

REGRESSION ANALYSIS

The regression analysis of the link between the diversification path and the direction of the underlying trajectory is longitudinal and at the firm level, with all variables time-varying. The dependent variable is entry into a subfield at a given time and is set to one if the firm entered and zero otherwise. The experiential acquisition of the firm's technological capability is captured by dummy variables for each subfield, equal to one if the firm was currently active in the area. In addition, as larger firms might have greater resources than smaller ones, we collected data on the size of the startup firms, linearly interpolating the estimates for years for which we lacked data. **SIZE** is measured by the number of employees.

The munificence of the selection environment is indexed by two variables, density and growth of shipments. The variable growth of a subfield (**SHIP-MENT GROWTH**) is measured by the yearly rate of changes in shipment volumes. **DENSITY,** as a measure of competitive effects, is a count of the number of all firms listed as making sales in a subfield. As many studies have found that entry and density have a quadratic relationship, we also included the square of density.[8]

Method of Analysis

One of our central claims is that a firm accumulates experience by operating in one subfield that may serve as a platform in other subfields. Because we do not have direct observations on the stock of experience, we use a method that proxies it in two ways. First, we record by a dummy variable whether a firm is active in a particular subfield. Second, we analyze the conditional waiting time, or hazard, from the time a firm is first recorded as existing to the time of its entry into another field. We expect firms that are active in an industry based on a platform technology to diversify more rapidly into related fields. Accordingly, we specify the regression as estimating the hazard, or conditional waiting time, to diversification.

A discrete time hazard model was used to calculate the hazard rate of diversifying among the startup firms (Allison 1984). That method defines the set of startup firms at risk for each annual cross-section or time spell, that is, those firms that had not previously entered a subfield. Because the period of observation lasted from 1977 through 1989 and we treated each year as a spell, there were 13 discrete time spells. The 13 cross-sections were then stacked. That discrete method is similar to continuous-time estimation by partial likelihood, though the two models do not exactly converge to the same specification (Cox and Oakes 1984, Allison 1984).

To test the effects of explanatory variables on the hazard rate, we used a logit specification. For each subfield, a binomial model was used to estimate the effects of the covariates.[9] If T is an integer-valued random variable showing the waiting time from the inception of a startup firm to the diversification event, the hazard rate is defined as the probability of an event at time t given no previous diversification in the subfield:

$$P_t = Pr(T = t \backslash T \geq t).$$

The logit model for estimating the effects of the covariations on the discrete hazard is specified by:

$$\log\left[\frac{P_{it}}{1 - P_{it}}\right] = \alpha + \beta X_{it}$$

where P_t is the probability of the firm diversifying into subfield i at time t, α is a constant, β is a vector of coefficients, and X is a vector of time-varying covariates. The changes in the hazard rate are restricted in this model to arise from changes in the time-varying covariates; the intercept α is assumed fixed. That restriction can be relaxed, but the inclusion of year dummies shows that the results are not very sensitive to such a specification.

The appeal of a hazard specification is that it captures the effects of both the technological push and the environmental pull. Experience in certain subfields can be expected to accumulate faster and to be more closely related than that in other areas, and hence should lead to a more rapid rate of diversification. Further, we would expect the timing of diversification to depend on the favorability of market conditions. We capture both effects by

TABLE 6.4 Discrete Time Logit Regression Estimates[a]

	ASIC	Micro	Opto	Telecom
Constant	−5.20	−9.90	75.8	−93.13**
	(−.65)	(−.57)	(.61)	(−2.32)
Analog	.190	1.36	−15.3	2.77***
	(.26)	(1.47)	(−.009)	(3.82)
ASIC		.801	−476	.735
		(1.16)	(−.40)	(1.13)
DSP	−16.9	−.371	−14.7	1.01
	(−.005)	(−.28)	(−.006)	(.96)
Discrete	−16.6	.095	1.05	.396
	(−.005)	(.06)	(.76)	(.39)
GaAs	.094	.301	2.38**	−14.8
	(.10)	(.26)	(2.44)	(−.007)
Memory	1.43***	3.73***	−.107	1.29*
	(2.18)	(4.56)	(−.09)	(1.77)
Micro	−.997		.652	2.40***
	(−1.17)		(.51)	(3.26)
Opto	−16.4	−13.2		−15.0
	(−.005)	(−.006)		(−.005)
Telecom	−15.8	−12.4	−14.3	
	(−.003)	(−.004)		
Shipment growth	.026**	.033**	−.065	.102**
	(2.05)	(2.45)	(−1.25)	(2.41)
Density	.137	.323	−5.34	4.92**
	(.48)	(.38)	(−.57)	(2.12)
Density	−.001	−.006	.089	−.070**
	(−.77)	(−.62)	(.51)	(−2.06)
Firm size	.007	.003***	−.008	−.006
	(.52)	(3.70)	(−1.02)	(−.58)
Log-likelihood	−67.547	−58.395	−35.062	−46.254

a. t-statistics in parentheses; two-tailed test.
*prob. < .10; **prob. < .05; ***prob. < .01.

use of a hazard model with time-varying covariates that pick up the differences in experience accumulation and market opportunities across subfields.

Regression Results

Table 6.4 reports the discrete time logit regression estimates. Shipment growth significantly increases the likelihood of entry into ASICs, microcomponents, and telecommunication ICs, but is not significant in optoelectronics. Density measures are significant only in the telecommunication subfield.

TABLE 6.5 Matrix of Entry Sequence (actual)[a]

From \ TO	ASICs	Micro	Opto	Telecom
Analog				(+)***
ASICs				
DSP		(+)		
Discrete			(+)	
GaAs			(+)**	
Memory	(+)**	(+)***		(+)*
Micro				[+]***
Opto				
Telecom				

a.(): hypothesized; []: not hypothesized.
*prob. < .10; **prob. < .05; ***prob. < .01.

Firm size is significant only in microcomponents. The primary factor explaining the *timing of diversification* is the growth of the market.

Table 6.5 is a more concise summary of the effects of competing in one subfield on subsequently diversification. Memory emerges clearly as a technological platform. The effect of experience in memory subfields is shown to be significant and positive in increasing the hazard of entry into the ASICs, microcomponents, and telecommunication IC subfields. Experience with discrete semiconductors, however, does not seem to be a significant factor in explaining entry into optoelectronics, whereas gallium arsenide experience proves to be significant in entry into that subfield. DSP experience is not significant in entry into microcomponents. Analog experience is a significant platform for entering the telecommunication IC market.

The relationships between the prior and subsequent entry are consistent with the broad distinction between analog and digital technologies. There are no crossovers in those two clusters of technologies. It is especially interesting that entries in the subfield of telecommunication devices—which embody both digital and analog technologies—are significantly related to prior entry in microcomponents and memory (i.e., digital technologies) as well as in analog circuits. As expected, the superior optical property of gallium arsenide in comparison with silicon serves as a platform into the optoelectronics subfield.

Although all of the subfields existed at the beginning of our period of observation, certain products, especially memory devices, originated much earlier. Some industries only had new firm entries until a few years after the beginning our analysis period. To validate the results, we ran the regressions starting at a later date, 1983. The results summarized in Table 6.4 were replicated.[10]

DISCUSSION

Specific Observations

Initial entry into the memory subfield serves as a particularly broad platform by which to enter other subfields. Yet, no subfield serves as a significant entry point into memory. In contrast, experience in ASIC production appears to be a sink, with no indication that it can be used as a way to gain entry into other subfields. Industry growth has a significant effect on attracting entry of startup companies that began in other markets. Thus, although the costs of entry into ASICs appear low, the competitive pressures on startups are substantial.

That inference is supported in Table 6.6, where the exit ratio for the total entrants (i.e., 180 startups) into each subfield is calculated. ASIC firms have two times the exit rate of firms making gallium arsenide devices, which have the next highest rate. ASIC startups face a difficult task of developing competitive capabilities in their own markets against the head start of entering companies from other subfields.

To test the significance of that claim, we ran a partial likelihood analysis on the exit (hazard) rates of startup firms that began in the four subfields of memory, microcomponents, telecommunications, and ASICs; the covariates were the same as before, but market growth represented the growth of the initial subfield. (The results are available on request.) Given the low number of exits, the results are poor. However, the result of interest is that the effect of being begun in the ASIC industry significantly raises the hazard of exiting; beginning in the other subfields has no significant effects.

Successful ASIC firms are in a quandary. Their success in their initial market cannot be applied easily for entry into other subfields, and yet entry into their market is easy for other firms. They illustrate the classic dilemma of a competency trap. Not surprisingly, as indicated in Table 6.6, acquisition rates of ASIC startup firms are considerable. Such firms have nowhere to go, and the acquisition of their subfield experience is valuable for firms diversifying into the industry.

TABLE 6.6 Exit Ratio by Subfield[a]

	Analog	ASIC	DSP	Discr	GaAs	Memory	Micro	Opto	Tele
Dissolution	.031	.200	.000	.143	.182	.050	.000	.111	.000
Merger and acquisition	.063	.133	.063	.000	.000	.100	.091	.000	.000
Total	.094	.333	.063	.143	.182	.150	.091	.111	.000

a. Total number of exit/total number of entry (for 180 startup firms founded between 1977 and 1989).

General Observations: Myopia Versus Foresight

The results support the explanation of firm diversification as the evolution of a stock of experiential knowledge that provides a platform by which to enter related fields. The relatedness among technologies and markets appears to map onto the path of diversification of firms. That path is not entirely foreseeable, for it depends on both the uncertain attractiveness of future markets and the success of the firm in its current activities.

The concept of technological platforms has significant consequences for understanding that what a firm does lays the foundation for what it can be. In his analysis of the historical development of nineteenth century American industries, David (1975, p. 4) similarly proposes that "choices of technique become the link through which prevailing economic conditions may influence the future dimensions of technological knowledge."

The "link" raises two fundamental issues about the nature of uncertainty and foresight of organizations. Rumelt (1984) notes that even in a stringent model whereby success is determined initially by some random draw, startup firms over time differentiate themselves. He writes (p. 565):

> Which activities should the entrepreneur combine? The general answer is, *those that will exhibit strongly dependent postentry efficiencies.*

Dependent post-entry efficiency, which is synonymous with path dependence, is the cornerstone of the concept of a trajectory and has a subtle implication. Given that the investment and entry an organization makes today form its subsequent capabilities, current decisions have what can be called an "option" quality. Entering the memory market provides a wider set of options to enter other subfields than entry into ASICs (see Appendix 3).

The option consideration runs counter to the mainstream treatment of risk explored in the tradition of Cyert and March (1963), in which organizations are described as creating buffers against uncertainty. It is consistent with the distinction between exploitation and exploration made by March (1991) and Hedlund and Rolander (1990). An established firm has the choice to exploit its resources in its current activities or to explore new markets. Because of heterogeneity in their accumulated experiences or in slack resources, firms may differ in the extent to which they divert resources from current activities to the accumulation and recombination of experience.

An important issue raised by the argument and results of our study, therefore, is whether organizations follow myopic and forward-looking policies, both in the initial choice of entry and in the subsequent path of development. The large number of entrants into the ASIC market suggests that impediments to entry are low, but the high rate of exit and low rate of diversification suggest that such easy entry is coupled with high risk to survival. Profitability may be higher in that industry than in others, but survival rates are less favorable.

High entry and exit rates conform with a Lippman and Rumelt (1982) model in which post-entry dependence—that is, the option value for subsequent diversification—is low. In that model, a firm pays an entry fee to see whether it is (randomly) assigned a profitable technology. Because ASIC production can be contracted out so that the capital investment is only in design, entry and exit costs are not high. If diversification options generated from the initial technology are low, a high exit rate should be expected. (See Klepper and Graddy 1990 for a formal treatment.)

The relationship between current profitability and diversification options corresponds closely to D'Aveni's (1994) notion of a hypercompetitive environment in which know-how and timing are important. In such an environment, the profitability of a given product quickly evaporates, forcing competitors to be constantly developing and exercising options for product improvements or diversification into fields related to the current experiential stock or know-how. In the absence of options, hypercompetition results in high exit rates, as in the ASIC subfield.

An option approach is a handy way to analyze the case of hypercompetition when timing and know-how advantages matter. D'Aveni (1994, p. 22) notes that "one way to escape [the] cycle of competition on price and quality is to enter a new market or launch a new product. Timing of market entry and the know-how that allows entry form the second arena for competitive interaction."

In our study, the know-how is the learning by doing that is accumulated in the source industry. We can think of the value of remaining in that industry as $V(s)$, where s is the cash flows from current and future production. The value of cash flows from diversifying into a new target industry, or introducing new product or service changes, is $V(d)$. Normally, we treat value of the firm as $V = V(s) + V(d)$. However, because experience in producing S is useful for producing the target industry product, additivity is no longer obeyed; there are interactions among the projects, such that $V = V(s) + V(d\backslash s)$. The second term captures what Myers (1977) called a "growth option." To incorporate the timing dimension, we would need to add time subscripts.[11]

Several subtle issues must be refined, especially in relation to the selection environment and experimentation. For example, a forward-looking strategy would suggest that by diverting resources to experimentation, an organization gains incremental experience that provides a platform to launch into new industries. However, although such expansion may enhance a firm's long-range opportunities, it also diverts resources and thus may increase the hazard of failure in the short-run.

A critical contextual variable, then, is the stringency of competition, which may limit a firm's ability to divert resources to the accumulation of new learning. To the extent that risk-taking and exploratory search require slack resources, organizations that have entered competitive environments are handicapped in their abilities to develop the requisite flexibility and diversity of resources.[12] The findings of Carroll and Hannan (1989) on the negative effects of competitive environments on survival during a firm's early years are consistent with that view. It is not surprising that incumbent semiconductor firms have won share in ASICs. Regressions not reported here show no effect of the number of competitors or industry growth on exit rates of startup firms. That finding is not surprising, for the ASIC subfield, in which so many exits have occurred, is still growing rapidly. Given the rather high exit rates, the findings suggest that unobserved organizational capabilities play an important role in the evolution of new subfields.

The radicalness of a technology is specific to firms' organizational capabilities to explore new fields given their accumulated knowledge and incentive structure. New technological opportunities often represent "organizational discontinuities" to some firms; to others, they represent an opportunity for diversification and growth. Understanding the relationship between technological opportunity and organization capability is one of the more intriguing challenges raised by the differential failure and success of startup companies in diversifying and growing.

CONCLUSIONS

A subtle implication of our study is the arbitrariness of the exact path of technological trajectories. Platform technologies represent the coincidence of market and technological opportunities. They are likely to be more formative in their influence during the early history of an industry, when markets are yet not well defined. In growing new markets populated by firms with uncertain but differentiated capabilities, a rule that promotes searching in the environs of current practice is likely to lead to diversification for firms whose technologies impinge on a wide set of market opportunities.[13] For firms whose research experience is unrelated to other markets, that rule is self-limiting over time.

As market opportunities are filled, the platform value of a technology diminishes. Because market opportunities change over time, the inherent opportunities in a technology are historically conditioned. What has been a platform in the past may not be one in the future. The fact that history conditions opportunities is a fundamental limitation on projecting the past into the future.

The finding that experience in memory production has been historically useful for diversification is no guarantee that it will be in the future. The volume of microprocessor production has greatly increased over the past decade. The relatedness among new flows of technological progress is no longer the same as the relatedness that drove the accumulation of the stock of technological knowledge. In principle, a firm can repeat the exact historical path of technological learning by focusing on memory production and then branching into other (but no longer new) markets. Whether future market opportunities and the current set of evolving technologies would be suited to the replication of historical lessons is unlikely. The observation is an old one: one can enter the river once, but never the same river twice.

ACKNOWLEDGMENTS

Paul Almeida's research assistance and participation made an important contribution to the article, for which the authors thank him. They also acknowledge the comments of the anonymous referees, and Erin Anderson, Bill Barnett, Jacques Delacroix, Richard D'Aveni, Drew Harris, Rebecca Henderson, Dan Levinthal, Marvin Lieberman, Bill McKelvey, Marshall Meyer, Ron Sanchez, and Gordon Walker on previous drafts and of Sid Winter on the various mutations. Carolyn Doles and Dataquest are gratefully acknowledged for their cooperation. Financial support for the project was provided by a grant from AT&T under the auspices of the Reginald H. Jones Center at the Wharton School. The authors thank the Amos Tuck School of Dartmouth College for awarding the Whittemore Prize to this article.

Appendix 1: Triangulation:
Relatedness and Directionality

RELATEDNESS: LITERATURE ANALYSIS

The initial review of the literature provides some simple expectations about relatedness in the industry. We find a very obvious distinction between discrete and integrated circuits and, within integrated circuits, between devices that rely on digital or analog signals.

There are a few straightforward implications for the subfields. Optoelectronics originated through the combination of optics and electronics technologies. Technically, optoelectronic devices are a special application of discrete semiconductor technology. Yet, optoelectronics is a distinct subfield because it provides a significantly different technological solution—by combining optics and electronics—to meet new (i.e., light-related) problems in the semiconductor industry. Similarly, GaAs is considered a distinct subfield given the potential of the field and the unique demands that the use of the compound places on design and wafer fabrication. Though GaAs chips are faster, use less power, and have greater radiation hardness than silicon, the material is brittle and has low heat capacity. Those properties make the compound difficult to handle and result in low yields. The primary uses are in defense, aerospace, and telecommunications. Gallium arsenide, because its optical property is superior to that of silicon, has been used heavily in optoelectronic devices.

Within the category of integrated circuits, analog and digital signaling are the two primary branches of the technology. Digital technology can be further divided into memory, microcomponent, and application-specific integrated circuits (ASICs). The three subfields share a common characteristic in terms of their principal end market, computers.

There is fairly wide consensus that memory has acted as a platform. The preceding quotation on technology drivers ends with the conclusion that "at present, the most common 'technology drivers' are advanced computer memory devices for which high volume demand exists—dynamic and static random access memories (DRAMs and SRAMs) and erasable programmable read only memories (EPROMs)" (Howell et al. 1988, p. 28). Similarly, Borrus et al. (1983, p. 214) write that "MOS (metal oxide silicon) memory ICs are complex circuits that require technically sophisticated design and production capabilities. Technical sophistication here is transferable to the design and production of other complex products."

Memory, like all of our subfield classifications, is an aggregation of many products. Particular products may be more important drivers than others. Moreover, the function may change over time. In his study on Intel, Burgelman (1993) noted that Intel dropped DRAM production when SRAM was discovered to serve as a substitute for driving the learning in design and testing for both memory and microprocessor devices. The switch from DRAM to SRAM does not change our memory category as a critical platform for gaining experience relevant to other subfields.

The importance of memory devices to the microcomponents subfield, especially microprocessors, is evident in its origins. (Other areas of microcomponents such as mass storage and graphic chip set are basically extensions of memory technologies.) The microprocessor was created when a Japanese company wanted to develop a semiconductor to provide certain logical functions to support a new range of calculators. It turned to a newly founded company, Intel, that had "expertise in the design and manufacture of memory chips." (Braun and MacDonald 1982, p. 108). Since then, the current investment required to produce DRAM has moved beyond the resources of new firms, but SRAM have grown in importance and have become a high volume product serving as a driver for many firms (Wolf 1986, p. 619).

A similar relationship is evident between memory and ASICs subfields. For example, standard cells, often called "cell libraries," the most recent product segment of ASICs, are customer-specified combinations of a number of functional cells, from logic gates to memories and even complete processing units. Memories are almost always included as part of the device.

Digital signal processing (DSP) is another subfield in which digital technologies are applied. The fundamental technological problem of the DSP subfield has been real-time implementation of digital technologies in miniature (Mitra and Mondal 1987). Technological advances in integrated circuits around memory and microprocessors have been a major driver of that new application area (Oppenheim 1975).

Finally, telecommunication integrated circuits were originally a segment of analog integrated circuits, as the data to be processed in telecommunications have been mostly analog (i.e., continuous signal). Recent applications of telecommunication ICs to office automation through networking personal computers, however, seem to be pushing the technological boundary of the subfield toward digital areas.

MULTIDIMENSIONAL SCALING OF EXPERT OPINIONS: RELATEDNESS

There is danger of being too glib about the messy issue of the subfield classification that we adopted from industry convention. Because the claim of shared learning implies a potential symmetry among subfields, it suggests the possibility that a platform switch such as that from DRAM to SRAM within memory could occur across subfields. Recall that the revealed technological branching represents the conjunction of technological accumulation and market opportunity. It is not surprising, therefore, that once technological learning has accumulated, changes in market opportunity (e.g., a large demand for microprocessors that generates sufficient experience effects independent of memories) can shift the revealed relatedness in diversification.

Such potential switching among subfields implies that the classifications should be built up from a multidimensional scaling of product characteristics. We take a middle ground by maintaining the historical classifications, but validating a structure of relatedness among them by a statistical analysis of a distance metric across several dimensions. The distances were derived by sampling expert opinions. A questionnaire was sent to a small number of selected industry experts. Six institutions were chosen on the basis of their reputation and ease of access: two marketing research firms (Dataquest and Integrated Circuits Engineering), two industry associations (Electronics Industry Association and Semiconductor Industry Association), a manufacturing company (AT&T), and an academic institution (School of Engineering at the University of Pennsylvania). The questionnaire was sent to a person identified through personal telephone calls. Of the six, five responded (the expert from the Semiconductor Industry Association did not respond).

We asked the experts to rate technological relatedness between subfields on a scale of 1 (not related) to 5 (highly related). A total of 36 combinations of pairs (i.e., $_9C_2 = 36$) were used to estimate technological "distance" between any two subfields. The data were then analyzed by multidimensional scaling techniques (MDS), a method commonly used to map perceptual (or psychological) distance among a number of objects (Green and Tull 1978: chapter 14, Kruskal and Wish 1978, Davies and Coxon 1983).

We ran the MRSCAL (metric scaling) program of the MDS(X) package with the data on technological relatedness. MRSCAL is a metric distance scaling program that positions a set of stimulus objects as points in a spatial map. The input data for MRSCAL are the lower triangle, without diagonal, of a square symmetric data matric—average (dis)similarity scores of the respondents.

The results of the scaling can be represented spatially to show the hidden structure. The spatial representation consists of a geometric configuration of points, which correspond to the objects analyzed. The larger the dissimilarity between two objects, the farther apart they are in a spatial map.

Figure 6.2 is the spatial representation of the nine semiconductor subfields—the two-dimensional map of technological relatedness. (See Kim 1992 for an analysis of the dimensionality and stress and a Shepard diagram of fit.) The inference from the literature is clearly confirmed in the scaling derived from the expert opinions. There is a distinct but overlapping division between the digital and analog clusters. Memory, ASICs, microcomponents, and DSP form a cluster of digital technologies. Telecommunication integrated circuits are between the digital and analog clusters. Discrete semiconductors are separated from integrated circuits (digital and analog) clusters. Optoelectronics and gallium arsenide, as expected, form another cluster.

PATENT EVIDENCE: DIRECTIONALITY[14]

The preceding section examines the relatedness between technological subfields based on the history of subfield evolution. Through the use of patent data, we can

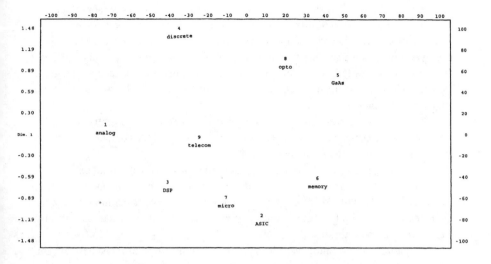

Figure 6.2. Multidimensional Scaling Analysis: Metric Scaling

analyze not only the relatedness but also the "directionality" of subfields. That analysis provides further support for our propositions: (1) subfields in the semiconductor industry differ in the extent to which they facilitate technological diversification and (2) some subfields (namely, memory devices) serve as technological platforms for entry into other subfields whereas others (such as ASICs) are less likely to facilitate diversification.

The population considered was the 180 startup firms in the semiconductor industry established between 1977 and 1989. We examined the patenting histories of those by using the computerized patent database available of LEXUS, which contains complete details (other than technical drawings) of all U.S. patents granted from 1974 to date. For the purpose of the analysis, only firms that had been granted three or more patents by May 1993 were selected. A total of 53 firms fit into that category.

For each of the 53 firms, we developed a patent profile showing the distribution of the patents across time and across technologies (the nine technological subfields in the semiconductor industry). The year of patent application (commonly accepted as the year of innovation in patent analysis) was available directly from the front page of the patent, but classification along technological subfields was challenging. The patent classification system is based on technology and contains about 400 primary classes and up to a 100,000 subclasses. Such classification of the patents did not facilitate categorization along the technological subfields we were considering.

For the purpose of the study, therefore, we examined individually more than 750 patents belonging to the 53 firms. Two electrical engineers read the detailed patent documents and, according to their primary field of application, classified each patent along one of the nine semiconductor subfields. The more general patents and ones that did not fit nearly into any of the subfields were placed in a special category, "other." Thus, we obtained the complete patent history of the 53 firms across time and across technology.

The 53 firms were assigned to their subfield of initial market entry. For each category the percentage of total patents in each subfield and the percentage of firms patenting in each subfield were calculated.

Table 6.7 is a comparison of patenting activities of firms with initial experience in different technologies. The firms belonged primarily to the memory, ASICs, analog, and GaAs subfields. Discrete, telecom ICs, DSP, and microcomponents were represented by only a few firms (four or fewer) and no firm in the sample initially belonged to optoelectronics.

The pattern of patenting activities shows that memory devices best fit the description of a platform technology. The patents of memory firms on average are diversified across the highest number of fields (as indicated by technological diversification) and those firms are also the fastest to patent in a field outside their own subfield. The time to diversification is 2.3 years for memory, the least among all subfields. The patenting activity also suggests memory firms are likely to diversify into ASICs and to a lesser extent into analog, DSP, and telecommunications.

ASIC firms have less diversified patenting records than memory firms and are slower to patent outside their own field. The only likely field of diversification (for ASIC firms) as indicated from patent data is DSP, GaAs experience can aid entry into analog and DSP is related to microcomponents (primarily microprocessors). Patent diversification of firms with original experience in the discrete and microcomponent subfields is narrow.

Similar to memory firms, analog companies have a diverse patent history, with patent activity especially high in telecommunications and DSP fields. However, the patent diversification is less notable than that for memory firms.

We checked also whether patents preceded or followed market diversification. In 35 cases, startup firms field patents in areas other than the original subfield in which they were founded. In 29 of the 35 cases, patents were granted prior to entry into that market (i.e., technology came first). In only three cases was the patent obtained after market entry (i.e., market came first), and the remaining three patents were granted in the same year as market entry. Those trends indicate that technological knowledge is acquired prior to market diversification.

Overall, the findings support the expectation that experience in memory increases opportunities for technological diversification over a wide range of fields. Experi-

TABLE 6.7 Platform Technologies—Evidence from Patents

Subfield of Granted Patent[a]		Subfield of Initial Entry							
		Memory (15 firms) %	ASICs (9 firms) %	Analog (11 firms) %	GaAs (9 firms) %	DSP (4 firms) %	Telecom (2 firms) %	Discrete (2 firms) %	Micro (1 firm) %
Memory	A	**24**	**5**		**2**	**11**			
	B	73	22		11	25			
ASICs	A	**18**	**63**	**1**	**4**	**6**			
	B	40	78	9	11	25			
Analog	A	**17**	**1**	**49**	**24**				
	B	27	11	82	44				
GaAs	A				**36**				
	B				67				
DSP	A	**7**	**12**	**18**	**10**	**37**			
	B	27	56	36	22	75			
Telecom	A	**5**	**5**	**15**	**3**		**100**		
	B	27	22	27	33		100		
Discrete	A			**1**				**67**	
	B				18			100	
Micro	A	**3**	**1**			**26**			**100**
	B	13	11			50			100
Other	A	**26**	**12**	**16**	**22**	**20**		**33**	
	B	73	56		64	78	50	100	
Patents per firm		16.7	16.1	16.8	12.2	8.8	13	9	3
Technological diversification*		2.1	1.8	1.5	2	1.8	0	1	0
Time to diversification**		2.3	3.7	4.9	2.6	4.3		4	

a. A and B indicate percentages along columns, that is, along subfields of initial entry. A = % of patents granted belonging to a particular technological subfield (columns should sum to 100). B = % of firms with patents granted within a particular subfield.
*Mean number of subfields in which patents were granted for a typical firm (excluding own subfield).
**Mean number of years before first successful patent application in a new subfield.

ence in other fields, such as ASICs, did not lead to a broad or rapid pattern of patenting. Whereas memory firms may easily gain technological expertise in ASICs, the converse is not true. Such asymmetry supports the claim of directionality in the development of a trajectory.

Appendix 2:
Expert Opinion Questionnaire

According to the Dataquest, there are nine product subfields in the semiconductor industry. (Please see Table 6.1 for the list of product segments.)

How much are the following subfields technologically related to each other?

	Not Related				Strongly Related
1. analog - ASIC	1	2	3	4	5
2. analog - DSP	1	2	3	4	5
3. analog - discrete	1	2	3	4	5
4. analog - GaAs	1	2	3	4	5
5. analog - memory	1	2	3	4	5
6. analog - micro	1	2	3	4	5
7. analog - opto	1	2	3	4	5
8. analog - telecom	1	2	3	4	5
9. ASIC - DSP	1	2	3	4	5
10. ASIC - discrete	1	2	3	4	5
11. ASIC - GaAs	1	2	3	4	5
12. ASIC - memory	1	2	3	4	5
13. ASIC - micro	1	2	3	4	5
14. ASIC - opto	1	2	3	4	5
15. ASIC - telecom	1	2	3	4	5
16. DSP - discrete	1	2	3	4	5
17. DSP - GaAs	1	2	3	4	5
18. DSP - memory	1	2	3	4	5
19. DSP - micro	1	2	3	4	5
20. DSP - opto	1	2	3	4	5
21. DSP - telecom	1	2	3	4	5
22. discrete - GaAs	1	2	3	4	5
23. discrete - memory	1	2	3	4	5
24. discrete - micro	1	2	3	4	5
25. discrete - opto	1	2	3	4	5
26. discrete - telecom	1	2	3	4	5
27. GaAs - memory	1	2	3	4	5
28. GaAs - micro	1	2	3	4	5
29. GaAs - opto	1	2	3	4	5
30. GaAs - telecom	1	2	3	4	5
31. memory - micro	1	2	3	4	5
32. memory - opto	1	2	3	4	5
33. memory - telecom	1	2	3	4	5
34. micro - opto	1	2	3	4	5
35. micro - telecom	1	2	3	4	5
36. opto - telecom	1	2	3	4	5

Appendix 3: Hypercompetition
and Growth Options

As noted in the text, the attribution of technological accumulation implies that a firm acquires an option to diversify into related fields. That option has two features. One is a modified experience effect, whereby the accumulated experience in one field (i) such as memory lowers the production costs of another field (j), say ASICs. More formally, we can write

$$C(Q_{j,t}) = ce^{-\sigma \sum_0^t Q_{i,t}}.$$

The second feature is the growth of the target industry (e.g., ASICs). We can think of growth as proxying a stochastic process that governs the price of ASICs. One representation is simply geometric Brownian motion, whereby

$$\frac{dP}{p} = p\, dt + \sigma\, dz.$$

If the price of ASICs crosses a particular threshold (P^*), entry is worthwhile.

The problem is similar to the analysis of learning curves by Majd and Pindyck (1989). To fit the model, production of memory devices must depend on a known and certain price. Experience effects would then be deterministic. Analytical solutions are possible for that case.

A more complicated characterization is to let the price of the currently produced product (memories) and that of the target industry (ASICs) be governed by two distinct stochastic processes. (In reality, they would probably share a common disturbance term.) Solving for two stochastic processes is numerically tractable, but more complicated than solving for the single process of Majd and Pindyck. A simplifying solution is to view the firm as resource constrained and consequently faced with the choice between producing in the source industry or diversifying. In that case, using a single process to describe the ratio of the prices of the two industries can suffice.

In our empirical study, we do not analyze the value of the option but rather the hitting time distribution, or hazard rate. Leaving aside industry and other effects, the hazard model corresponding to a Wiener process is the inverse Gaussian. To include time-varying covariate effects, we would set either the mean or variance or both to be a function of the covariates. We avoid the difficult specification issues associated with that parametric approach by working with the semiparametric discrete hazard model. Thus, the underlying option model is not transparent, because we work with the hitting time distribution and we do not specify that distribution parametrically.

To return to the Majd and Pindyck model, we implicitly follow the case of a single stochastic process for the price of the target industry, which we proxied by shipment growth. We assumed that experience accumulates in some way from the time of entry in the source industry. The experience effect is captured by time-varying dummy variables that serve as the state variables. The other principal state variable is price. When price, proxied by the growth rate (with other covariates held constant), crosses some threshold, the firm enters the target industry. The other covariate effects (i.e., density) are added to the reduced-form equation, but are derived (ad hoc) from a structural model in which price is partly endogenous to market structure.

An important issue, given that characterization, is when the firm should diversify. That question is the same as asking whether the hitting time is when the option is exercised. A formal way to understand hypercompetition in terms of timing and know-how is in a dynamic context where difficult-to-imitate assets are accumulated by experience, and entry is the hitting time when market growth, or price, hits a critical threshold.

To add more strategic content to the formulation, we would consider competitive interactions, as highlighted by D'Aveni, and the choice to allocate resources to learning. Competitive interactions in an option context are especially complex, because price becomes endogenous. Kulatilaka and Perotti (1994) provide an analysis of the related question of whether to maintain the wait option or early exercise of entry. Learning is analyzed in Kogut and Kulatilaka (1994; paper available from the authors upon request).

NOTES

1. See D'Aveni (1994) on hypercompetition and chapters 2 and 4 for a discussion of the conversion of know-how to stronghold advantages. See also Eisenhart (1990) on high-velocity environments.

2. We thank an anonymous reviewer for consolidating this argument.

3. See the operationalization of new knowledge in Schoonhoven et al. (1990).

4. Not only technology, but also the applicability of other capabilities such as marketing and distribution, may drive diversification to the new industry.

5. We thank Naren Udayagiri for bringing this quote to our attention.

6. See Dawkins (1986, p. 258ff.) for a discussion and Barley (1990) for another use of a dendrogram.

7. David and Bunn (1990) call the innovations that bridge technological branches "gateway technologies"; Sahal (1981) has called such convergence "creative symbiosis."

8. See, for example, Hannan and Freeman (1987) and Carroll and Hannan (1989). Theoretical issues are associated with the use of the density squared measure (Klepper and Graddy 1990), primarily concerning misspecification due to omission of demand effects. We include demand effects in our model. Also, density squared is highly correlated with concentration,

which is an alternative though still problematic measure. The density squared measures does not affect any other estimates and it is included for control and to enhance comparability with other studies.

9. A multinomial model cannot be implemented because it would entail using a subfield as both a dependent and an explanatory variable.

10. The only change was a significant relationship between analog and microprocessors. Both of those subfields predate the start of the longer period (used for Table 6.4) and were not of concern in investigating the 1983 truncated sample.

11. That characterization also suggests a way to define hypercompetition. Let us define a hypercompetition index as $I_{HP} = V(s,d)/V(s)$. A hypercompetitive environment is one in which the index tends toward a high value over time, that is, when current competition has eroded profits but the accumulated and proprietary learning is valuable to entry into new growth markets. There are degenerative cases when both current operations and future opportunities are equally poor because of competition; then it would be more reasonable to define the numerator as the "representative industry" or to redefine the index as Tobin's Q.

12. See Singh (1986) for one study showing a positive relationship between risk-taking and slack resources.

13. See Kauffman's (1993, pp. 76-95) discussion on rugged landscapes with "generatively entrenched" genes.

14. This section is based on research by Paul Almeida. See Almeida (1992) for details. (Paper available from the authors upon request.)

REFERENCES

Allison, P. D. (1984), *Event History Analysis: Regression for Longitudinal Data*, Beverly Hills, CA: Sage.

Almeida, P. (1992), "Note on Directionality in the Patent Histories of Semiconductor Start-ups," mimeo, Wharton School.

Anchordoguy, M. (1989), *Computers Inc.: Japan's Challenge to IBM*, Cambridge, MA: Harvard University Press.

Arthur, W. B. (1985), "Competing Technologies and Lock-in by Historical Events: The Dynamics of Allocation under Increasing Returns," Center for Economic Policy Research, Paper 43, Stanford University.

Barley, S. R. (1990), "The Alignment of Technology and Structure through Roles and Networks," *Administrative Science Quarterly*, 35, 61-103.

Bijker, W. E. and T. Pinch (1987), "How the Sociology of Science and Sociology of Technology Benefit Each Other," in W. E. Bijker, T. P. Hughes, and T. Pinch (Eds.), *The Social Construction of Technological Systems*, Cambridge: MIT Press.

Borrus, M., J. E. Millstein, and J. Zysman (1983), "Trade and Development in the Semiconductor Industry: Japanese Challenge and American Response," in J. Zysman and L. Tyson (Eds.), *American Industry in International Competition*, Ithaca, NY: Cornell University Press.

Braun, E. and S. MacDonald (1982), *Revolution in Miniature*, 2nd ed., New York: Cambridge University Press.

Brittain, J. W. and J. H. Freeman (1980), "Organizational Proliferation and Density Dependence Selection," in *The Organizational Life Cycle*, J. R. Kimberly, R. H. Miles et al. (Eds.), San Francisco: Jossey-Bass.

Burgelman, R. (1993), "A Process Model of Internal Corporate Venturing in the Diversified Major Firm," *Administrative Science Quarterly,* 28, 223-244.

Carroll, G. R. and M. T. Hannan (1989), "Density Dependence in the Evolution of Populations of Newspaper Organizations." *American Sociological Review,* 54, 524-541.

Cohen, W. and D. Levinthal (1990), "Absorptive Capacity: A New Perspective on Learning and Innovation," *Administrative Science Quarterly,* 35, 128-152.

Contractor, F. J. (1981), *International Technology Licensing,* Lexington, MA: Lexington Books.

Cox, D. R. and D. Oakes (1984), *Analysis of Survival Data,* London: Chapman and Hall.

Cyert, R. M. and J. G. March (1963), *A Behavioral Theory of the Firm,* Englewood Cliffs, NJ: Prentice Hall.

Dataquest (1988), *A Decade of Semiconductor Companies,* San Jose, CA.

———— (1990), *A Decade of Semiconductor Start-ups,* San Jose, CA. D'Aveni, R. (1994), *Hypercompetitive: Managing the Dynamics of Strategic Maneuvering,* New York: Free Press.

David, P. A. (1975), *Technical Choice, Innovation, and Economic Growth,* Cambridge, UK: Cambridge University Press.

———— and J. A. Bunn (1990), "Gateway Technologies and the Evolutionary Dynamics of Network Industries: Lessons from Electricity Supply History," *Evolving Technology and Market Structure,* A Heertje and M. Perlman (Eds.), Ann Arbor: University of Michigan Press.

Davies, P. M. and A. P. M. Coxon (1983), *MDS(X) User Manual: The MDS(X) Series of Multidimensional Scaling Programs,* University of Edinburgh.

Dawkins, R. (1986), *The Blind Watchmaker,* New York: W. W. Norton.

Dosi, G. (1982), "Technological Paradigms and Technological Trajectories," *Research Policy,* 11, 147-162.

Eisenhardt, K. (1990), "Speed and Strategic Choice: How Managers Accelerate Decision Making," *California Management Review,* 32, 3, 39-54.

Farrel, J. and G. Saloner (1985), "Standardization, Compatibility, and Innovation," *Rand Journal of Economics,* 16, 70-83.

Freeman, C. (1987), *Technology Policy and Economic Performance: Lessons from Japan,* London: Pinter.

Green, P. E. and D. S. Tull (1978), *Research for Marketing Decisions,* 4th ed., Englewood Cliffs, NJ: Prentice Hall.

Hannan, M. T. and J. Freeman (1987), "The Ecology of Organizational Founding: American Labor Unions, 1836-1985," *American Journal of Sociology,* 94, 910-943.

Hedlund, G. and D. Rolander (1990), "Action in Heterachies: New Approaches to Managing the MNC," in *Managing the Global Firm,* C. A. Bartlett, Y. Doz, and G. Hedlund (Eds.), London: Routledge.

Helfat, C. (1994), "Evolutionary Trajectories in Petroleum Firm R & D," *Management Science,* 40, 1720-1747.

Henderson, R. M. and K. B. Clark (1990), "Architectural Innovation: The Reconfiguration of Existing Product Technologies and the Failure of Established Firms," *Administrative Science Quarterly,* 35, 9-30.

Howell, T. R., W. A. Noeliert, J. H. MacLaughlin, and W. A. Wolff (1988), *The Microelectronics Race: The Impact of Government Policy on International Competition,* Boulder, CO: Westview.

Kauffman, S. A. (1993), *The Origins of Order: Self-organization and Selection in Evolution,* New York: Oxford University Press.

Kim, D.-J. (1992), "Technological Accumulation, Sequential Entry, and Exit of Start-up Companies in the Global Semiconductor Industry," unpublished Ph.D. dissertation, Wharton School, University of Pennsylvania.

Klepper, S. and E. Graddy (1990), "The Evolution of New Industries and the Determinants of Market Structure," *Rand Journal of Economics,* 21, 27-44.

Kogut, B. and N. Kulatilaka (1994), "What is a Capability? History, Complementarities, and Organizational Discontinuity," mimeo.

———— and U. Zander (1992), "Knowledge of the Firm, Combinative Capabilities, and the Replication of Technology," *Organization Science,* 3, 3, 383-397.

Kulatilaka, N. and E. Perotti (1994), "Strategic Investment Timing Under Uncertainty," discussion paper no. 145, London School of Economics.

Kruskal, J. B. and M. Wish (1978), *Multidimensional Scaling, Quantitative Applications in the Social Sciences,* 07-011, Newbury Park, CA: Sage.

Lippman, S. and R. Rumelt (1982), "Uncertain Imitability: An Analysis of Interfirm Differences in Efficiency under Competition," *Bell Journal of Economics,* 13, 418-453.

Majd, S. and R. S. Pindyck (1989), "The Learning Curve and Optimal Production under Uncertainty," *Rand Journal of Economics,* 20, 331-343.

Malerba, F. (1985), *The Semiconductor Business The Economics of Rapid Growth and Decline,* Madison: University of Wisconsin Press.

March, J. G. (1991), "Exploration and Exploitation in Organizational Learning," *Organization Science,* 2, 71-87.

McKelvey, B. (1982), *Organizational Systematics,* Berkeley: University of California Press.

Mitra, S. K. and K. Mondal (1987), "Scanning the Issue," *Proceedings of the IEEE,* 75, 9, 1139-1140.

Montgomery, C. and S. Hariharan (1991), "Diversified Expansion by Large Established Firms," *Journal of Economic Behavior and Organization,* 15, 71-89.

Mowery, D. C. and N. Rosenberg (1981), "Technical Change in the Commercial Aircraft Industry, 1925-1975," *Technology Forecasting and Social Change,* 20, 347-358.

Myers, S. (1977), "Determinants of Corporate Borrowing," *Journal of Financial Economics,* 5, 147-175.

Nelson, R. R. (1962), "The Link between Science and Innovation: The Case of the Transistor," National Bureau of Economic Research.

———— and S. G. Winter (1977), "In Search of Useful Theory of Innovation," *Research Policy,* 6, 36-76.

———— and ———— (1982), *An Evolutionary Theory of Economic Change,* Cambridge, MA: Harvard University Press.

Oppenheim, A. V. (1975), "Scanning the Issue," *Proceedings of the IEEE,* 63, 4, 548-549.

Pavitt, K. (1987), "International Patterns of Technological Accumulation," in *Strategies in Global Competition,* N. Hood and J. E. Vahlne (Eds.), London: Croom Helm.

Penrose, E. (1959), *The Theory of the Growth of the Firm,* New York: John Wiley.

Rumelt, R. (1974), *Strategy, Structure, and Economic Performance,* Boston, MA: Harvard Business School.

———— (1984), "Toward a Strategic Theory of the Firm," in *Competitive Strategic Management,* R. B. Lamb (Ed.), Englewood Cliffs, NJ: Prentice Hall.

Sahal, D. (1981), *Patterns of Technological Innovation,* Reading, MA: Addison-Wesley.

Schoonhoven, C. B., K. Eisenhardt, and K. Lyman (1990), "Speeding Products to Market: Waiting Time to First Product Introduction in New Firms," *Administrative Science Quarterly,* 35, 177-207.

Schumpeter, J. (1968), *The Theory of Economic Development,* Cambridge, MA: Harvard University Press (first published in 1911).

Silverberg, G., G. Dosi, and L. Orsenigo (1988), "Innovation, Diversity and Diffusion: A Self-Organisation Model," *Economic Journal,* 98, 1032-1054.

Singh, J. V. (1986), "Performance, Slack, and Risk Taking in Organizational Decision Making," *Academy of Management Journal,* 29, 3, 562-585.

Teece, D. J. (1976), *"The Multinational Corporation and the Resource Cost of International Technology Transfer,* Cambridge, MA: Ballinger.

———— , R. Rumelt, G. Dosi, and S. Winter (1994), "Understanding Corporate Coherence: Theory and Evidence," *Journal of Economic Behavior and Organization,* 23, 1, 1-30.

Tushman, M. L. and P. Anderson (1986), "Technological Discontinuities and Organizational Environments," *Administrative Science Quarterly,* 31, 439-465.

Udayagiri, N. (1993), "Learning Curves: Cross Product Spillovers and Firm Differences," unpublished Ph.D. dissertation, Carlson School of Management, University of Minnesota.

User, A. T. (1971), "Technological Change and Capital Formation," in *Economics of Technological Change,* N. Rosenberg (Ed.), Harmondsworth: Penguin.

Wolf, S. (1986), *Silicon Processing for the VLSI Era, Vol 2: Process Integration,* Sunset Beach: CA: Lattice.

7

The Japanese Beer Wars

Initiating and Responding to
Hypercompetition in New Product Development

TIM CRAIG

In the mid-1980s, the Japanese beer industry, a stable oligopoly in which competition had traditionally been limited to well understood nonprice dimensions, experienced an outbreak of new product "hypercompetition" which saw a ten-fold increase in the industry's new product introduction rate, produced a major shake-up in firms' competitive positions, and forced firms to transform themselves in fundamental ways in order to compete effectively. Surprisingly, this hypercompetition occurred despite heavy government regulation of the industry. Driving it were a variety of demographic, dietary, social, economic, and distribution trends which affected demand for beer, plus the existence of a major player, Asahi, on the edge of bankruptcy and therefore sufficiently desperate to risk a frontal attack on the industry leader, Kirin.

At the firm level, substantial internal change and the building of new organizational capabilities were required both to initiate and respond to hypercompetition. Examining in detail the process and difficulty of overcoming inertia and effecting change within the Asahi and Kirin organizations, two distinct types of hypercompetition-appropriate capabilities are identified. One is *specialized* capabilities, which allow a firm to compete effectively on the competitive dimension that a particular *round* of hypercompetition is based on (such as new product development). The other is *general* capabilities which allow a firm to efficiently carry out the continual recombination and reemployment of resources which a hypercompetitive *state,* in which shifts in the nature of competition are frequent and continuous, requires. Both types of capabilities are shown to be difficult to build and imitate, and for this reason to be potential sources of sustainable advantage.

The chapter identifies three broadly defining characteristics of hypercompetition: (1) continuing, nonmarginal change in the nature of competition, (2) required nontrivial organizational change, and (3) significant effects on firm performance and competitive position. Conceptually, it is argued that hypercompetition is Schumpeterian in nature, featuring recurring and fundamental competitive change, but that hypercompetition is most accurately seen as a particular combination of Schumpeterian, Industrial Organization, and Chamberlinian competition, with Schumpeterian instability weakening, but not replacing, the more stable aspects of Industrial Organization and Chamberlinian competition.

(HYPERCOMPETITION;

JAPANESE BEER, NEW PRODUCT DEVELOPMENT;

ORGANIZATIONAL CAPABILITIES)

INTRODUCTION

Capitalism . . . is by nature a form or method of economic change and not only never is but never can be stationary. (Schumpeter 1950, p. 82)

The fundamental impulse which sets and keeps the capitalist engine in motion comes from the new consumers' goods, the new methods of production or transportation, the new markets, the new forms of industrial organization that capitalist enterprise creates. (p. 83)

It is not [price competition within a static set of production methods and organizational forms] which counts but the competition from the new commodity, the new technology, the new source of supply, the new type of organization—competition which commands a decisive cost or quality advantage and which strikes not at the margin of the profits and the outputs of the existing firms but at their foundations and their very lives. This kind of competition is as much more effective than the other as a bombardment is in comparison with forcing a door. (p. 84)

Schumpeter, writing in 1950 of the "perennial gale of creative destruction" that drives capitalism, offers three key insights. The first is that capitalism is a continually changing process. The second is that the economic structure is changed not from outside but *from within,* by capitalist enterprises themselves. The third is that competition comes in many forms, and that certain kinds are far more powerful than others.

These ideas have profound implications for industries and for firms. At the industry level, they warn of the potential breakdown of what appear to be stable, oligopolistic arrangements which confine industry competition to within well-understood boundaries. When one firm, either industry member or outsider, mounts an attack based on a type of competition not "ordinarily" used in the industry, a fundamental change in the nature of industry competition can result. For individual firms, what is required to initiate or respond to such an attack, and to compete successfully in an environment marked by continuing attacks and shifts in competitive modes, differs greatly from what is needed for success in more stable and predictable environments. Particularly critical in such situations is the ability of firms to transform themselves. Firms must not only develop the particular skills, resources, and capabilities that a new mode of competition requires; they must also become more efficient at making and responding to subsequent strategic moves, in order to keep pace with an intensely competitive and fast-paced environment. This is because today's "new" mode of competition may be supplanted tomorrow by a "newer" mode, which will require still different skills, resources, and capabilities.

While these ideas accurately describe the continuously shifting nature of competition in many industries today, they are in sharp contrast with much of the thinking and research that has traditionally dominated the field of strategic management. Strategy theorists have tended to view the competitive environment as relatively static, or as evolving in systematic and predictable fashion, with, in turn, predictable implications for firms' strategic and organizational choices. The purpose of SWOT analysis, for example (e.g., Andrews 1971), is to devise strategies which achieve a good "fit" with an external environment and internal resources and capabilities which are, for the most part, given. Porter (1980) views the competitive environment as evolving, but in a way that can be predicted through the use of analytical techniques such as the "five forces" model or the industry life cycle.

The competitive environment described by Schumpeter, however, is neither static nor predictable. It more closely resembles what is today known as hypercompetition, which D'Aveni (1994) describes as a condition of "rapidly escalating competition . . . (in which) the frequency, boldness, and aggressiveness of dynamic movement by the players accelerates to create a condition of constant disequilibrium and change." In hypercompetitive situations, the potential to succeed through superior environment analysis and strategy formulation by management, as traditional approaches emphasize, is restricted, as the environment and the ways firms compete change at a fast rate and in unpredictable ways. Instead, firm efficiency at adjusting internal

skills, resources, and capabilities to allow implementation of strategic requirements dictated by the shifting nature of competition becomes a key
competitive requirement.

One industry which has experienced hypercompetition during the past
decade is the Japanese beer industry. From the end of the second World War
through the 1970s, Japan's beer industry was a typical oligopoly, consisting
of a small and stable number of firms, protected by high entry barriers, and
governed by well-understood rules designed to avoid "excessive competition." During the 1980s, however, the established pattern of competition
broke down when one firm, against a background of environmental change
which had increased latent demand for new products, introduced a new beer
which fundamentally altered the competitive landscape. Asahi's *Super Dry,*
the world's first "dry" beer, touched off a period of hypercompetition in new
product development that produced a tenfold increase in the rate of new
product introduction and resulted in a major realignment of competitive
position. This chapter describes the results of an investigation of this industry
and its four major firms during this period. Presented first is an industry-level
analysis which examines the causes, course, and effect on firm position and
performance of the period of new product hypercompetition. The next two
sections focus on organizational change and capability building inside two
individual brewers: Asahi, the primary initiator of the new product boom and
its major beneficiary, and Kirin, the company hurt most by Asahi *Super Dry*
and the one which required the greatest internal adjustment in order to
respond successfully to the emergence of hypercompetition. The final section of the chapter relates the case findings to existing theory and addresses
broader questions concerning the nature and causes of hypercompetition and
the organizational characteristics it requires of firms. (Appendix 1 describes
the research methodology employed in this study.)

JAPAN'S BEER INDUSTRY
AND THE "NEW PRODUCT WAR"

Industry Competition Prior to the New Product War

Japan's four major brewers, Kirin, Asahi, Sapporo, and Suntory, make up
a stable oligopoly protected by high entry barriers in distribution, advertising
costs, and government regulation. Since the 1949 break-up of Dai Nippon
Beer into today's Asahi and Sapporo, carried out under Japan's anti-monopoly
law which was imposed after the war by the United States for the purpose of
dissolving Japan's financial cliques or *zaibatsu,* only two firms have at-

tempted entry. One was Takara, a distillery, which entered the beer market in 1957 and withdrew eleven years later after failing to achieve a viable position. The other was whiskey maker Suntory, which entered in 1963 and has survived, despite rarely showing a profit in the beer business.

Nonprice competition is the industry rule, an arrangement that has been supported by the Japanese government, which puts high priority on a stable business environment and reliable, low-cost taxation of alcoholic beverages. (In 1989, beer taxes provided 2.5% of total Japanese government revenues.) Though "free pricing" exists in principle, in practice the four producers strictly maintain a standard retail price for beer, with Kirin, which holds a dominant market share, acting as price leader.

In the absence of price competition, Japan's brewers, through the early 1980s, competed with each other by means of advertising, quality (i.e., keeping fresh, not old, beer on retail shelves), and development and control of distribution channels (Ogihara 1979). These means of competition favored the strong; Kirin's dominant share, built up over three decades, gave it a cost advantage due to scale effects in production, advertising, distribution, and bottle recycling, and the strong reputation of the Kirin brand, once established, caused many drinkers to equate Kirin with beer and order Kirin automatically.

Prior to the 1980s, product development in the industry was confined to marginal, unpublicized adjustments in the taste of existing brands, and packaging-based product differentiation. In the latter category fall what were known as the "draft wars" and the "container wars." Until 1964, all canned and bottled beer produced in Japan was heat pasteurized, or what is known in Japan as "lager."[1] As alternative nonheat technology was developed to remove yeast and microorganisms and thus make the canning and bottling of "draft" beer possible, companies sought to gain market share by introducing canned and bottled draft. Suntory marketed the first pure draft beer in 1967, using a microfilter developed by NASA. Asahi introduced its draft in 1968, followed by Sapporo in 1977, and, finally, Kirin, which had resisted introducing draft for fear of cannibalizing its top-selling *Lager,* in 1981. Although draft's share of the market grew steadily during this period, reaching 41% by 1985, no company was able to significantly increase its market share by introducing draft.

The "container war," which began in the late 70s, was a period of attempted product differentiation through packaging innovation. Begun by Asahi and Suntory, then soon joined by Sapporo and Kirin, this round of competition featured the marketing of beer in cans and bottles of various sizes, shapes, and designs; there were take-home mini-barrels for parties, rocket-shaped containers called space shuttles, and cans and beer ads featuring cartoon penguins and raccoons. As was the case with the "draft war," however, this packaging-based product differentiation strategy had little effect on market share. In the early 1980s it was, for the most part, abandoned.

The draft and container wars illustrate a pattern that, after a number of repetitions, had come to be well understood in the industry. When Asahi, Sapporo, or Suntory introduced a product innovation, it would be quickly imitated. If the innovation threatened Kirin's market share, the industry leader would come out with a similar product and use its advantage in reputation, distribution, and financial resources to overwhelm the originator. Thus, a certain balance was maintained; the three smaller brewers avoided directly attacking Kirin for fear of retaliation, while Kirin, for its part fearful that further share gains would draw the attention of Japan's anti-monopoly authorities, restrained itself from doing anything to further weaken its rivals.[2]

Initiating Hypercompetition: Environmental Trends Plus Competitive Attack

The new product hypercompetition that rocked Japan's beer industry in the 1980s resulted from a combination of external environmental change and a competitive attack, which took advantage of that change, by a single brewer. By the early 1980s, a variety of demographic, dietary, social, economic, distribution, and competitive trends had occurred or were underway (see Table 7.1) which held, for this industry, implications of two kinds. First, these trends were producing in Japan powerful but latent demand for new types of beer; this underlay the hypercompetition in new product development which would soon emerge. In addition, several of these trends would affect the industry in a broader way. The market entry of foreign beers, the increase in consumer choice and power, and rationalization of the distribution sector not only helped increase demand for new products, but also intensified firm rivalry and opened up new potential modes of competition. This meant that hypercompetition in the Japanese beer industry would not necessarily end when the new product war died down. Rather, it was increasingly likely that this particular "round" of competition would be followed not by a new equilibrium and period of stability, as in the past, but by a subsequent hypercompetitive "round," equally intense but based on different competitive dimensions. This is indeed what happened, as we shall see below.

The response of Japan's brewers to these environmental trends produced the "new product war," a period of intense competition in new product development which began around 1985 and saw a dramatic jump in the rate of product introduction. Between 1964 and 1984, an industry average of 0.76

TABLE 7.1 Changes in the External Environment Underlying the New Product War

---

Demographic trends. The generation consuming the most beer in Japan was no longer the generation born before the war, who had grown up drinking strong, bitter tasting Kirin *Lager,* the industry's dominant brand, but a new post-war generation with their own "modern" tastes and eager to distinguish themselves from their old-fashioned elders.

Dietary changes. The Japanese diet had grown richer (the amount of oil and fats purchased per household doubled between 1965 and 1985), resulting in a trend toward lighter-tasting drinks and side dishes (the amount of sugar and salt used by Japanese dropped by 50% over the same period).

Social change. More women were drinking beer, particularly young working women who played a major role as trend setters. Women's tastes in beer were believed to differ somewhat from men's.

Economic change. Economic prosperity and rising incomes had brought in an era of consumer choice, in which "keeping up with the Suzukis" was being replaced by self-expression, and many products, including beer, were seen less as commodities and more as ways to express and satisfy individual tastes.

Changes in distribution. With more singles and young couples living in urban apartments with limited storage space, fewer people were having liquor shops deliver cases of beer and more were buying a few cans at a time from convenience stores, supermarkets, and vending machines. This led to increased experimentation with different brands on the part of the buyer who, standing in front of a vending machine or reach-in display case in a store, was faced with an array of labels to choose from.

Changes in competition. By the mid-80s, foreign brands such as Budweiser and Heineken had worked their way into Japanese stores and vending machines and were being widely advertised. The *chu-hai* boom of 1985—a *chu-hai* is a light cocktail made from *shochu* (a potato-based wine similar to vodka), soda, and fruit flavoring—cut into beer sales and drove home the point that demand existed for greater novelty and variety in alcoholic beverages.

---

new beers were put on the market per year; from 1985 to 1993, the new product introduction rate averaged 7.56 per year (see Figure 7.1).[3]

The first, pre-*Super Dry,* phase of the new product war took place in 1985-1986 as the Japanese brewers recognized and responded to external trends indicative of increasing consumer demand for variety. Because no single new product had ever dramatically affected market share in this industry, the aim of most product development during this period was to create and fill new niches. "Many varieties, small volume" summed up the product strategy, and the accepted industry definition of a "hit" new product was one that sold one million cases in a year. Kirin, Sapporo, and Suntory all developed and marketed "light" and all-malt beers during this period. The most successful new product of this phase was Suntory's *Malts,* an all-malt introduced in 1986 which sold two million cases its first year on the market.

The only brewer to buck the "niche" trend during this period was Asahi. By industry standards, Asahi had historically been active in product innova-

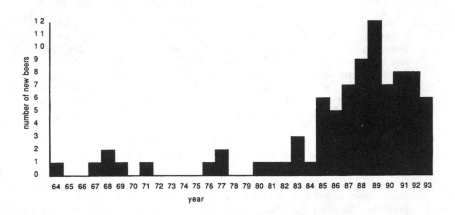

Figure 7.1. Number of New Product Introductions in the Japan Beer Industry by Year, 1964-1993

tion, introducing Japan's first canned beer in 1958, the industry's first bottled draft in 1968, and the mini-barrel that touched off the "container war" in 1977. Yet none of these innovations boosted market share; thanks to strong brand loyalties and rapid imitation by rivals, the innovations cannibalized Asahi's own products rather than taking sales away from the other brewers (Kagono and Yoshihara 1983). Echoing the words of Schumpeter concerning competition that strikes at the margin versus that which strikes at the foundation, Asahi product development manager Makoto Sugiura characterized such product innovation as "niche marketing, competing around the edges, not a frontal attack at the center of beer taste range" (Sugiura interview).

By the early 1980s, Asahi fortunes had fallen to an all-time low. In 1981, poor profitability forced the company to implement an early retirement program for 550 employees, and a stock repurchase rescue by Sumitomo Bank and a friendly chemical company were needed to save Asahi from a "greenmail" attempt. Market share, continuing a long downward trend, fell below 10%, considered the break-even point in the industry. Because of its precarious position, Asahi dared, or was forced out of desperation, to risk a product strategy of competing not around the edges, but at "the dead center of the consumer taste range." This meant making a major change in the taste of the company's main product, Asahi *Draft*. Sugiura explains:

In 1984-1985, when we were considering giving up competing at the edge and going instead for the dead center of the taste range, this was a big risk. The case of Coca Cola changing the taste of Coke shows what can happen when a food or beverage maker changes the taste of its main product. Since this would be a major frontal attack, if we failed it would be all over for Asahi. But our market share had dropped to under 10%, so if we did nothing there would be a good chance of Asahi disappearing from the market anyway. For this very reason, we were able to carry out the bold marketing we did, changing the taste of our beer and shooting for what we hypothesized was a new taste center. (Sugiura interview)

Asahi product planners hypothesized that the center of the taste preference range had shifted away from where it was generally said to be, that is away from the bitter, strong flavor that characterized the industry's top seller, Kirin *Lager.* This hypothesis was based on the idea that beer taste preferences are related to dietary makeup, and that as the Japanese diet had become richer (see Table 7.1), consumer craving for strong, rich flavor in beer had weakened, since strong, rich-tasting food is better complemented by lighter-tasting drinks (Suguira interview, Usuba 1989). (A similar trend was seen in other taste products: milder cigarettes and less sweet cakes and desserts had gained popularity over the previous two decades.)

To test this hypothesis, Asahi in 1984 conducted a 5,000 person taste preference survey, by far the largest in industry history. Beer drinkers were asked what makes a beer delicious, and Asahi found that their answers fell mainly into two categories. One was *koku,* which means rich taste, and the other was *kire,* which means refreshing, sharp, stimulating to the throat when swallowed. Challenging conventional wisdom which held *koku* and *kire* to be incompatible—a beer could have a rich taste or a sharp, refreshing taste, but not both—Asahi's marketing side product developers asked their R & D counterparts to create a beer that was a little more *koku* than the most *koku* beer on the market, Kirin *Lager,* and at the same time a little more *kire* than the most *kire* beer on the market, Sapporo *Black Label* draft. Such a beer, they reasoned, would be close to the center of the modern Japanese beer drinker's taste range (Sugiura interview). After repeated experimentation and test brewing, a beer that matched this taste concept was created. The new beer, known as *koku-kire* and promoted with the slogan "rich in taste, yet also sharp and refreshing" (*koku ga aru no ni kire ga aru*), was put on the market in place of Asahi's existing draft in February 1986, and helped produce a 12% increase in sales for that year.

Encouraged by the success of the new Asahi draft and feeling they were moving in the right direction taste-wise, Asahi's product planners next hypothesized, again based on taste preference surveys, that consumer tastes in beer were moving further away from *koku* and toward *kire*. Accordingly, the taste concept for the beer that would be *Super Dry* was created: similar to the new draft but with an even sharper, clearer, more refined taste.

When *Super Dry* was put on the market in March 1987, it quickly became Asahi's top seller. Production could not keep pace with demand, and at one point Asahi prohibited its employees from buying *Super Dry* in order to save it for customers. Kirin, Sapporo, and Suntory, hoping that "dry" beer was a fad which would fade when winter came, were slow to respond with their own versions of dry. *Super Dry's* popularity continued to grow, however, prompting the other brewers to prepare dry brands for launching in early 1988. Learning that the rival drys had names and labels similar to those of *Super Dry,* Asahi blocked their market entry, forcing them to make last-minute labeling and advertising changes by threatening to take legal action for copyright infringement. By the time Asahi's competitors got their dry brands in stores, *Super Dry* had become synonymous with dry beer in the minds of consumers, and it continued to far outsell its imitators.

13.5 million cases of *Super Dry* sold in 1987, rewriting the industry definition of a hit new product. Asahi's sales for 1987 jumped 33%, and by 1989, thanks almost entirely to *Super Dry,* Asahi's market share had risen to 24.8% from just 10.3% three years earlier. *Super Dry* allowed and sales outlets, and for the first time in 28 years, Asahi passed Sapporo to reach second place in market share. In 1989, *Super Dry* accounted for more than 20% of all beer consumed in Japan.

The scale of *Super Dry's* success revolutionized thinking in the industry. Not only did it confirm that Japanese drinkers were open to new and "modern" beers with fresh images and tastes that matched the times; equally important, *Super Dry* demonstrated that what was at stake was not just the loyalty of any particular niche, such as the fashion-conscious young, but a mass market, including Japan's "main users." *Super Dry* succeeded primarily at the expense of the industry's dominant brand, Kirin *Lager*; during the 1986-1989 period when Asahi's market share rose 14.5 points, Kirin's fell 11.2 points. (Sapporo's share fell 2.4 points, and Suntory's 0.9 points.) Further, *Super Dry* boosted the level of new product competition through its effect on consumer expectations; the *Super Dry* story was widely told in the media, generating high public interest in the "beer wars" and further increasing consumer eagerness to try new beers. *Super Dry* was called a "home run," and the brewers responded by redoubling their product development efforts, each seeking to be the next to hit a home run. As a result, new product introduction frequency increased; product strategy changed from "many varieties, small volume" to "many varieties, medium/large volume;" and sales targets rose, as the accepted definition of a hit product jumped from one million to 10 million cases.

Responding to Hypercompetition:
Catch-Up, Wind-Down, and Next Attack

The years following the appearance of *Super Dry* saw a sustained high rate of new product development and introduction, as it was considered impossible for a brewer to compete in the industry without participating aggressively in the new product race. Twenty-one new beers were marketed in 1988-1989, with Kirin and Sapporo launching eight each. For Kirin, the move to what it called a "full line" strategy represented a sharp shift in direction from its historically conservative approach to new products, designed to avoid cannibalizing *Lager.* Industry-wide sales of 1988-1989's new beers were disappointing, however, the only notable hit being Sapporo's seasonal *Fuyu Monogatari* ("Winter Tale"), a 5.5% alcohol brew created especially for drinking in winter and sold only from October to February.

Especially striking was the failure of the copycat dry beers; none sold well, and by 1993 all had been discontinued, conceding the dry segment entirely to still-strong *Super Dry.* *Super Dry*'s success, it turned out, was due to more than good marketing and a skillfully nurtured first-mover advantage in name recognition; equally important was *Super Dry*'s superior taste, and causal ambiguity surrounding that taste. When *Super Dry* appeared, "dry" beer was defined as beer that is fermented to a higher degree than ordinary beer, giving it a higher alcohol content (*Super Dry* was 5% compared to the usual 4.5%), less sugar, and a smooth but sharp taste. This is how rival drys were brewed, both in Japan and abroad. This was a very incomplete understanding of the brewing process for *Super Dry,* however, as Makoto Sugiura, who was involved in the beer's development, explained in 1991:

> For the first one or two years after *Super Dry* came out, we kept a lot of secrets about how we developed and brewed it; for example how to make the wort, whether we used hulled or unhulled malt, and so on. Now, the other brewers are moving in the same direction as us tastewise, so naturally they're doing the same sort of things we did to get that taste. But when *Super Dry* came out, "dry" was taken to mean only degree of fermentation. This, of course, is one way to get a *kire*-type taste, and it's part of how *Super Dry*'s taste is produced. But we weren't worried about the other brewers' dry-type beers, as they were all called, because there's a lot more to it than that. In order to produce a deep, really good [*oku-bukai*] taste, you have to do a lot more than just upping the degree of fermentation. (Sugiura interview)

A key advantage that Asahi held over its competitors in the early years of the new product war lay in its capability to develop a beer that was not only attractive imagewise, but whose taste was sufficiently good and well-matched to consumer palates that sales continued to grow even after the newness had worn off. By contrast, the new beers rushed onto the market by Kirin, Sapporo, and Suntory in 1988-1989 in a strictly strategic response to *Super Dry*'s popularity were not backed up by a strong organizational capability to create and market new beers that consumers would truly welcome. Asahi was the first brewer to build such a capability—this is described in detail below—and for the period of time it took Asahi's rivals to strengthen their own product development, *Super Dry* remained unrivaled by other new products and continued to provide Asahi with gains in market share.

By around 1990, Kirin, Sapporo, and Suntory had developed new product capabilities to rival Asahi's and as a result, new beers in or near *Super Dry*'s class began to appear. The biggest success was Kirin's *Ichiban Shibori* (literally "first extract"; the beer is sold abroad as *Ichiban,* or "Number One"). Launched in 1990 with a first-year sales target of 10 million cases, *Ichiban Shibori* sold 35 million cases its first year on the market, breaking *Super Dry*'s new product record. Combined with still-strong *Lager, Ichiban Shibori* gave Kirin two solid "pillars" around which to anchor its broad lineup, and helped the company gain market share for the first time in six years. 1991 saw three more new beers with strong first-year sales: Asahi's "Z" (19 million cases), Sapporo's *Ginjikomi* (18 million cases), and Suntory's *Beer Ginjo* (10 million cases).

By 1993, however, the new product war was beginning to show signs of winding down, or at least of shifting in nature. Domestic demand for beer, which had grown at an average annual rate of 7.15% from 1987 through 1990, leveled off in the early 90s, and declined by 1.8% in 1993, the first drop since 1984. Japan's continuing recession was partly to blame, and brewers were reevaluating the wisdom of continuing to introduce new products, believing that "in times of recession, consumer tastes return to the basics" (*Yomiuri Shimbun,* January 28, 1994). Consumer interest in new beers also appeared to be fading, with customers tiring of the constant parade of new brands showing up in stores and on TV. These trends were read as signaling that the potential for another hit along the dimensions of *Super Dry* or *Ichiban Shibori* had diminished significantly. New product introduction and consumer response in 1991-1993 added weight to this view. In 1992, established brands *Ichiban Shibori, Super Dry, Black Label,* and *Malt's* showed healthy sales increases while sales of 1991's new beers fell by roughly half in 1992, their second year on the market. Of the 14 new beers marketed in 1992-1993, none were major hits, and in 1993 the only company to see a growth in sales was Sapporo, the sole brewer *not* to introduce any new products.

Among the brewer managers were many who welcomed the prospect of an end to the new product hypercompetition, which was costly even when big hits were forthcoming, and unjustifiably so when they were not. The head of R & D in Sapporo's production division expressed the following concern about the continuing new product race and the competitive dynamics it created:

> The current level of new product development is quite expensive. It takes a lot of money to develop an original new beer, and on top of that many of the recent new brands require materials or production methods that are more costly than those used to brew the old standards. Plus, to give a new product a chance to become a hit, you need to advertise it heavily, and that costs money.[4] We seem to be caught in this cycle where if one company tries to differentiate itself by bringing out a new beer or packaging innovation, then the three others also have to do it. The originator gets a temporary advantage, but it's copied quickly, and the industry as a whole ends up hurting itself by having to do all these extra things that cost more but give no advantage over the competition. The result is that consumers end up drinking expensive beer. (Murakami interview)

Hypercompetition has proved difficult to call off, however, as environment trends, both existing and new, continue to provide opportunities for, and require, firms to find and employ new modes of competing. In the area of new product development, a shift back toward niche beers has become evident, with a number of low-calorie, seasonal, and regional beers among the 1992-1994 new entries. In 1994, Asahi in particular was enjoying success in marketing regionally restricted brews such as *Hakata Kuradashi,* which had cut Kirin's market share in the Kyushu region (previously 70%) by almost ten percentage points.

Perhaps more significant is the influence on competitive conditions of continued rationalization of the distribution sector, increased entry by foreign brands, yen appreciation, and deregulation, which together have set the stage for a new round of hypercompetition based on cost competitiveness. Beginning in 1994, sales of imported beer priced 20%-40% below domestic brands expanded sharply, thanks to appreciation of the yen. A relaxation of licensing requirements was making it easier for large liquor discounters, big supermarkets, and convenience store chains to obtain retail liquor licenses, adding fuel to a shift in distribution away from traditional small-scale general liquor stores, which traded service for a fixed price structure, to large-scale outlets with discount pricing strategies and the bargaining power to support them.[5] These trends increased pressure on the beer companies to lower costs, and in March of 1994, Kirin launched a new competitive "attack," announcing that it had entered a full-scale alliance with Anheuser-Busch which would enable Kirin to significantly reduce procurement costs for imported beer and cans. Rather than brew its own "ice" beer, which would require substantial investment in facilities for freezing the beer during the production process to remove impurities, Kirin was planning to import ice beer from Busch's Los Angeles plant and market it in Japan under the Kirin label. Kirin also planned to import US-made beer cans from an Anheuser-Busch affiliate at half the unit cost of Japanese cans (Ishizawa 1994). The winding down of the new product war thus did not mean that *Super Dry,* and the company that brewed it, would now be competing in a stable, nonhypercompetitive environment. Rather, the nature of competition was changing again. Just as Asahi had redefined the terms of competition by initiating the new product war, Kirin was now doing the same thing by shifting competition to cost reduction, with factors such as firm ability to establish and manage beneficial relationships with foreign brewers emerging as key new competitive weapons.

Outcomes: The Effect of Hypercompetition on Performance and Competitive Position

In addition to profitability, market share is widely used by Japanese corporations as a key measure of competitive position and strength (Abegglen and Stalk 1985). Market share is particularly important in the brewing industry because of the cost advantage that volume provides due to scale effects in production, advertising, distribution, and bottle recycling. A share of 10% is considered to be the break-even mark in the industry.

As Figure 7.2 and Table 7.2 show, new product hypercompetition had a pronounced effect on profitability and market share; the years 1987-1989 saw Asahi's market share and profitability soar, while those of its rivals fell. While there had been clear trends in share movement over the post-war period, with Kirin's share climbing while those of Asahi and Sapporo declined, these took the form of gradual change. In sharp contrast, the performance effect that the new product boom produced was sudden and very large, with Asahi's market share jumping from 10.3% in 1986 to 20.7% in 1988 and 24.8% in 1989, and operating profits rising to three times their pre-new product boom levels. After a two-year disruption, however, market shares stabilized again at new levels; the profitability of Asahi's competitors recovered, while Asahi's profits remained far above pre-*Super Dry* levels.

This suggests a pattern that may be generally true of periods of hypercompetition: first, a major shake-up and substantial gain by the initiating firm, which has successfully attacked using a new competitive weapon (in this

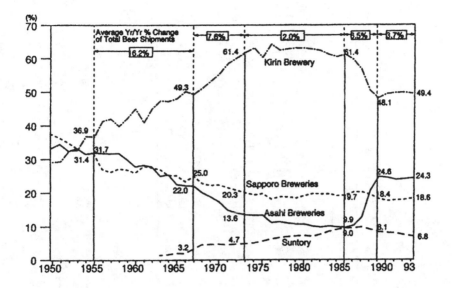

Figure 7.2. Historical Market Shares of Japanese Beer Companies

case, new product competition); next, a continuing but diminishing gain by the initiator as the potential performance benefits of the initial advantage are used up; and finally, a new equilibrium as other companies respond with strategies and newly developed capabilities that allow them to compete successfully in whatever competitive mode it was that the initiator introduced to set off the "war." Underlying this pattern is a significant first-mover advantage, born of a strategy and, more importantly, a capability to implement that strategy, that the initiating firm possesses and which other firms, at the beginning, do not. This first-mover advantage lasts as long as it takes responding firms to develop similar capabilities, or to launch new attacks based on different, but effective, strategies and capabilities. The reaching of a new equilibrium in competitive position marks the end of the first-mover advantage and may also signal an impending wind-down to the particular round of hypercompetition, as the potential for major gains vis-à-vis rivals is diminished. In hypercompetitive environments, however, the new equilibrium is likely to be a temporary one, lasting only until a new round is initiated by a new attack or counterattack along a different competitive dimension.

In order for a capability to provide the initiator of hypercompetition with sustained advantage, it must be valuable in exploiting opportunities, rare, imperfectly imitable, and without strategically equivalent substitutes

TABLE 7.2 Comparative Performance of Japanese Beer Procedures, 1979-1992 (unit: billion yen)

	1979	1980	1981	1982	1983	1984	1985	1986	1987	1988	1989	1990	1991	1992
ASAHI														
Sales	181.0	185.2	198.4	201.8	214.8	224.4	236.4	259.4	345.1	544.9	655.1	730.8	739.1	770.6
Operating profit	4.1	3.9	4.6	3.0	4.2	4.3	4.4	2.6	3.5	14.5	11.1	15.1	18.8	35.9
Current Profit	2.8	3.2	3.4	2.1	2.4	2.8	3.3	5.3	9.4	15.0	18.7	17.2	17.4	14.0
KIRIN														
Sales	830.5	955.9	984.8	1041.7	1069.8	1151.8	1210.9	1221.8	1266.3	1178.8	1199.8	1355.8	1315.7	1366.1
Operating profit	31.6	40.4	42.4	50.0	47.0	60.7	65.5	72.1	69.6	41.1	39.3	63.1	64.7	69.9
Current profit	31.6	42.3	45.0	45.2	49.8	66.6	73.3	79.3	80.8	64.7	64.6	84.9	86.4	82.7
SAPPORO														
Sales	251.2	276.5	330.4	347.8	362.2	379.9	402.6	436.0	467.0	489.7	463.6	492.6	533.3	551.7
Operating profit	5.4	8.7	11.9	11.4	9.8	12.2	12.2	15.1	14.5	5.0	(3.7)	5.4	6.4	12.7
Current profit	4.4	6.6	9.0	9.2	8.5	9.8	10.7	12.4	13.1	13.5	7.5	8.4	9.1	10.7

SOURCE: Kaisha Shikiho (Japan Company Handbook).
NOTE: Performance data for Suntory's beer operations not available.

(Barney 1991). The new product development capability that Asahi created fulfilled these requirements: It was valuable in exploiting the opportunity that increasing demand for new beers presented; it was rare—for a period of two years or so, Asahi alone had such a capability; although ultimately imitable, imitation was difficult and took time, for reasons explained below; and there were no substitutes for excellent product development if a company sought to participate successfully in the new product race.

Concerning the relationship between capabilities, advantage, and performance, a comparison between the new product hypercompetition and the earlier draft and container wars is instructive. Because the draft and container wars centered on packaging differentiation, with the beer itself remaining largely untouched, they did not strike at the "foundations" of firm performance, as Schumpeter might say. The appeal of packaging innovation was limited and imitation was easy, requiring not the building of complex new capabilities but simply new packaging ideas plus the solution, within the production function, of any technical problems presented by their implementation. For this reason, imitation was swift, significant first-mover advantages were absent, and effect on relative performance was virtually nil. In contrast, the product concepts that drove the new product war were not marginal, but represented entirely new beers, different physically, in taste, and in image from existing products. *Super Dry* and other successful new brands such as *Malt's, Fuyu Monogatari,* and *Ichiban Shibori* gave consumers a stronger reason to switch than the attraction of drinking old beer in new bottles. Further, a product such as *Super Dry* could not be quickly created or copied. The other brewers tried, but creating *Super Dry* was a complex and time-consuming task, which required a product development capability that itself was complex and time-consuming to create. By being the first to build this capability, Asahi gained a critical advantage: a two-year lead in product development capability which allowed Asahi to dominate the dry sector. Because the copycat dry beers did not come out of well-developed new product capabilities, they could not compete with *Super Dry,* and they therefore failed to survive.

Thus far, we have examined the actions of Japan's brewers from the outside. To limit the analysis to this level, however, would be to miss a central part of the story, since, as Schumpeter argues, the forces that change industries and the nature of competition are not only external, but come as well *from within* capitalist enterprises. Of particular interest are the nature and dynamics of the capability-based advantage held by the initiator of hypercompetition, an advantage that rivals must match if they are to compete successfully under hypercompetitive conditions. The following two sections illuminate this issue by looking more closely at capability creation inside Asahi and Kirin, focusing on internal challenges faced and internal changes made which allowed Asahi to initiate and gain from the period of new product hypercompetition, and Kirin, after a time, to respond successfully. These case studies show why effective new product capability took so much time to create. They also suggest that two distinct types of organizational capabilities are of value in hypercompetitive conditions: *specialized* capabilities which allow a firm to compete effectively on a particular competitive dimension, such as new product development; and more *general* hypercompetition- appropriate capabilities which help a firm continuously respond to and influence the frequent changes in industry and competitive conditions that characterize hypercompetition.

INSIDE ASAHI: BUILDING NEW PRODUCT DEVELOPMENT CAPABILITY

Pre-Hypercompetition Conditions at Asahi

While demographics, taste preferences, and retailing methods were undergoing shifts in the 1970s and early 80s that were increasing latent demand for new beers in Japan, none of Japan's four brewers was prepared to carry out the level and type of new product development that new conditions called for. Product development was in the hands of brewmasters who were out of touch with customer needs; information gathering systems were underdeveloped; and existing employee attitudes selected against newness and blocked needed cross-functional cooperation.

Conditions at Asahi were particularly ill-suited for effective, consumer-oriented new product development. One critical problem was that the taste of Asahi beer was the exclusive domain of what is called the "production side," that is the brewmasters in charge of R & D and brewing at the beer plants. This was territory that was off limits to marketing, as "marketing side" product developer Makoto Sugiura explains:

> When it came to the matter of our beer's taste, production was in charge and we marketing people couldn't say anything. The production people were the specialists, the pros, and they used a lot of technical terms for analyzing beer that we didn't know. When we asked them something concerning taste, they would pull the wool over our eyes, speaking in a technical language that we couldn't understand. They had a monopoly on the matter of what good taste was; they'd say 'this is good taste, this is Asahi beer.' The system was they'd make it and we'd try our hardest to sell it. The criterion for how Asahi beer should taste was the personal preference of a

certain high level manager on the production side. Everyone adjusted to him; if he said a certain kind of beer was delicious, then that became, for Asahi, what delicious beer was. (Sugiura interview)

A related weakness was that market data on consumer tastes and behavior played virtually no role in product development. The only taste surveys carried out at Asahi were questionnaires given to visitors touring Asahi brewing plants, and these were analyzed by the production side and used not to develop new beers but to make minor taste adjustments in existing ones (Usuba interview).

Such a product development system, if it can be called that, may have been adequate for the "niche marketing" of the packaging-based draft and container wars, which required little more than the solution of technical problems such as how to can or bottle "draft" beer and how to package existing beers in new containers of various shape and size. But it was ill-suited for the kind of consumer needs-driven product development that Asahi marketers, sensitive to changing consumer tastes and behavior, felt was needed in the marketplace of the 1980s.

The production-marketing rivalry over control of product development was exacerbrated by a high degree of "sectionalism" and mistrust among the different functional areas at Asahi (Ishiyama 1987). Relations were especially bad between the production and marketing divisions, with each blaming the other for the company's poor performance. Production people felt: "No matter how good the beer we make is, it doesn't sell because the sales force does such a poor job that it sits in the distribution channels and the taste deteriorates." Sales people felt: "If the production people were less egocentric and more in touch with consumer tastes, our beer would taste and sell better" (Kokuryo 1989).

Solving these problems required two levels of change within Asahi. One falls under the category of organizational design: "on paper" changes in the boundaries and responsibilities of organizational units and the setting up of new procedures and systems for gathering and using consumer information and guiding the product development process through its various necessary steps. The second type of change, more difficult to make but vital for successful implementation of an aggressive new product strategy, involved changes in thinking and behavior: improving cross-functional relationships, changing employee attitudes, and, for key participants in the product development process, developing new kinds of communication skills and knowledge.

Securing a Role for Marketing and Designing
a Product Development Organization

The first imperative was to end production's strangle-hold on product development and secure for marketing a central role in the product development process. The door to marketing's participation in new product development was opened by Asahi president Tsutomu Murai, who, when he took over in 1982, set out to revitalize the company by initiating a corporate identity (CI) campaign centered around a new corporate philosophy. One of two explicit statements that formed the basis of the new philosophy was: "Considering the wants and needs of our customers" (Usuba 1989). Marketing-side product developer Sugiura explains what this did for marketing's participation in product development:

> The CI concept itself was to give the consumer what he wants most, so from this point on making delicious beer was something both the production and marketing sides were deeply involved in. For the first time, marketing had a voice; we were the consumer. (Sugiura interview)

In order to implement marketing's involvement in developing new beers, a new organization for product development was created. Two sections in charge of product development were set up, one organizationally a part of the larger production division, the other a part of the larger marketing division. New product development is carried out jointly by these sections, through a process described as "playing catch with each other." This arrangement was adopted to give product developers a needed degree of independence and authority and at the same time achieve integration with the broader production and marketing functions whose cooperation was essential in getting newly developed beers brewed, packaged, promoted, and put on retail shelves. One of the biggest changes that the new arrangement brought about was that consumer surveys were now conducted and interpreted not just by brewmasters, but by production and marketing people in concert. Managing Director Hisashi Usuba, one of the designers of the new setup, explained why this is important:

> When you conduct a taste survey, the data are not always clear, not easy to interpret, so different people read it quite differently. If, as before, production does the surveying, they read the results in a way that is convenient for them, that matches their beliefs and thinking. The organizational change was made to prevent this; having marketing and production carry out surveys together resulted in a change from a "what suits production" to a "what do consumers want" approach to new product development. (Usuba interview)

The marketing-side section played the leading role in creating new product concepts and coordinating the overall process. Also, much of the hierarchy that once stood between the people developing new products and top management was removed. Sugiura explains:

> Now, we dozen or so people in the production- and marketing-side product development sections can go almost directly to the top with our ideas. Before, we needed a lot of *hanko* (seals, the equivalent of a superior's signature of approval) before our ideas got a hearing at the top. This is a big change from before, and very important, as speed and timing are critical in introducing new beers. When I talk with managers in jobs similar to mine at other, nonbeer, companies, I find they are surprised by how quickly we can go from proposal to action. (Sugiura interview)

The new system was also consumer data-intensive. A variety of information-gathering and market-contact routines were developed, such as the annual 5,000-person taste survey and systematic after-hours scouting of drinking establishments and customers by product developers. In total, these features served to provide visibility, specialization, authority, information access, fresh ideas, and speed to the product development process, characteristics which were notable by their absence in product development at any Japanese brewer prior to the new product boom.

Changing Behavior and Thinking

Redrawing organizational boundaries and reporting relationships and establishing new information-gathering routines were important first steps toward creating a better product development system, but these alone did not ensure that product development would function smoothly and effectively. A more difficult challenge was to build positive attitudes and relationships among functional areas that needed to cooperate in developing, producing, and marketing the new products. Such changes in attitude and thinking were required at two levels: that of the new product development units, and that of the broader organization.

1. *Building Effective Communication Among Product Developers.* Hisashi Usuba talked about the importance of good communication between the marketing and production personnel who now found themselves working together to develop new beers, and some of the barriers that had to be overcome to achieve it.

> Marketing people generally have a broad view of the world and are tuned in to consumers, to opinions out in the street Production people, by contrast, spend more

time shut up inside the plant or the lab, and are more conservative. They're often called "technology crazy," meaning they're locked up in their own universe and don't know what's going on in the real world. The two groups even drink differently after work; technical people stick to one or two bars they know while marketing people drink around, try a lot of new places, and are therefore quick to pick up trends and information.

Successful new product development depends very much on effective communication between these two groups. The characteristics of a beer are hard to measure and state clearly, unlike, for example, the specs of an automobile. To create a "product plan" for a new beer, words are needed which capture and convey accurately the product concept. Marketing people are not especially good at this; production people, on the other hand, have the technical vocabulary to express a beer's characteristics much more precisely.

To overcome these gaps in knowledge and vocabulary, our production- and marketing-side product developers have spent a lot of time and effort building a common vocabulary for describing and creating beers, and educating each other, the production people teaching the marketing people about technical aspects of beer brewing, and the marketing people making the production people more aware of trends in the marketplace. One thing we do a lot of to achieve this is "*nomi*-nication" ("drinking communication," *nomi* is the Japanese word for drinking). People from the two product development sections get together in the same room to drink beer and analyze data. In Japanese companies, there's a wall between marketing and production, but with this organizational set-up and our efforts to build communication and understanding, we've been very successful in tearing down this wall. (Usuba interview)

Each Monday evening, around 30 marketing- and production-side personnel involved in product development meet together to taste and talk about beer. One purpose is to build a common vocabulary concerning taste that both marketing and production specialists can understand. The difficulty of this was attested to by a product planner who stated: "We've been having these Monday meetings for four or five years now, and only recently have we come to be able to communicate effectively" (Tokumaru 1990, p. 92). During the development of Asahi's new draft in 1984-1985, it was through these meetings that the two sides reached a common understanding of what *koku* and *kire* meant. Repeatedly; the production side would produce a beer and the two groups would sample it together, asking "is this more *koku* than Kirin, is it more *kire* than *Black Label*?" (Sugiura interview).

Twice-monthly "*nomi-nication*" meetings between marketing and technical product developers are also held at Asahi's Central Research Laboratory for what Sugiura calls technological seed development: "I have the R & D side working on a few brewing method variations, or 'seeds'; because there's always a chance we'll use such seeds in our pursuit of a certain taste. We marketing side people are pure amateurs technically, and these meetings are a learning opportunity for us, a chance to be educated by the R & D people about technical aspects of brewing" (Sugiura interview).

2. *Creating Company-Wide Attitudes to Support Product Development.* While development of good-tasting new beers by the core product development units is essential, this alone does not ensure market success. Launching of a new brand has to be OK'd by top management, and positive cooperation and support must be forthcoming from the various other people and sections that play a role in getting a new beer brewed, packaged, distributed, promoted, and sold. Two types of inertia blocked this type of support at Asahi.

One was general resistance to change. For many people and sections, the increased number of new products as well as some of their specific brewing, packaging, and promotional features meant that unwelcome changes would have to be made in work routines. Usuba explains:

> Our production and sales people, like people everywhere, basically like to do things the same way they did them yesterday, that's easiest. They are conservative, and strongly resist change. For this reason, new products were not welcomed; they were likely to be troublesome, so new product development was neglected. (Usuba interview)

The other source of inertia centered around certain unhealthy aspects of Asahi's organizational heritage: the hostile cross-functional (particularly marketing-production) relations that have been described above, and what Hirotaro Higuchi, who succeeded Murai as president in 1986, calls the company's "order of merit"—the fact that the opinions of a highly-ranked person carry much greater weight than the opinions of a lower-ranked person. According to Higuchi, this was the biggest barrier to successful new product development in the "old" Asahi, making it impossible to change the taste of Asahi beer from below. When a new beer was developed it had to go up through the ranks for approval, and sooner or later it would run into a vice-president or director who, given a choice between Asahi's original beer and the new one, would pick the old because that was what he had come to love in his years at Asahi (Hayakawa 1989).

In order to create needed company-wide cooperation and support for new product development, new attitudes and behavior had to be developed: openness to innovation and change, belief that change was needed, and a corporate culture marked by positive cross-functional cooperation. Two forces helped foster these attitudes at Asahi. One was *external* pressure; the role that deteriorating performance, being "at the edge," played in facilitating change at Asahi has been described above. The other was *internal* pressure, in the form of Asahi's corporate identity campaign and the leadership of top management.

The corporate identity campaign that Murai carried out to revitalize Asahi included a number of activities designed to "heal" an organization marked by riskaverse attitudes and poor cross-functional relations. Task forces composed of managers from all functional areas were put in charge of designing and carrying out CI activities and given responsibility for dealing with issues such as data use, employee suggestions, and customer complaints (Kokuryo 1989). Company retreats were also used to break down functional walls. Six hundred Asahi managers were split into cross-functional groups and sent on four-day outings of business (discussion about Asahi and what was needed to revive company fortunes) mixed with pleasure (eating, drinking, hot-spring soaking). Participants reported that production and sales people, thrown together, were at odds the first day or two, but by the end had come to understand each other better and to feel closer, more like fellow Asahi employees and less like mistrustful adversaries (Ishiyama 1987).

The CI campaign is also credited with creating an atmosphere in which change was viewed with less alarm than before, and in which managers accepted facts objectively rather than resisting or filtering out negative or inconvenient reality (Hayashi 1989). This had a direct and beneficial effect on product development; concerning the controversial idea of changing the taste of Asahi's main product to better match the perceived, but unproven, shift in consumer taste preferences, Marketing Division General Manager Yasuo Matsui states: "We were very fortunate that CI activities were under way. People were willing to question taboos" (Kokuryo 1989, p. 11).

Top management support for innovation and the ideas of younger employees also played an important role in turning around Asahi's culture. A personnel manager says:

The biggest thing in my opinion was the leadership of top management. They emphasized quality and originality and demanded these of workers. For the product developers, a tremendous motivator was top management's willingness to use the fruits of their labor, to market the products they created. Under the old system, the young people developing new products were stymied; their proposals had to be evaluated and decided on by a series of upper managers, who made judgments based on their own established values. The new things that younger people tried were rejected, as they rose toward the top, in favor of the old and traditional. What Higuchi did when he came in was to start actively and directly using ideas and proposals from near the level of the organization at which they originated. The distance between the people actually doing new product development and top management became much shorter. (Ninomiya interview)

It was Higuchi who made the decision to launch *Super Dry,* over his own concern that marketing another new brand so soon after the new Asahi draft would only cannibalize the draft. The product development team pushed hard, however, and after drinking the new beer and finding it tasted good, Higuchi gave *Super Dry* the go-ahead. Higuchi also increased R & D spending and strongly supported Asahi's new products with enlarged budgets for advertising and promotion.

The efforts at Asahi to improve cross-functional relations and create a stronger customer orientation paid off at a critical point in the development of Asahi's new draft beer, as marketing head Matsui explains:

> At the time that we on the marketing side created the product concept for *koku-kire* and asked the brewmasters to create a beer of this type, a top production-side manager said to me: "In order to brew the kind of beer you are asking us to make, it will be necessary not just to change ingredients, but to re-do the entire production process from start to finish. We'll even have to develop a new yeast. That will be very tough." At that point I thought there was no way he would agree to what we were proposing. But to my surprise he continued: "But, let's give it a try." At this moment I strongly felt the effect of our CI campaign, a main theme of which was to throw out certain old ways and values and to respond to consumers by making products that meet their needs. (Matsui 1990)

This account of internal change at Asahi is not just the story of a successful company turnaround; it also highlights the importance of organizational capability and change as both a defining feature of hypercompetition and a source of first-mover advantage for the initiator of a hypercompetitive round. Prior to the new product boom, Asahi's organizational capability to conduct consumer-driven new product development was poor, but not uniquely so; no Japanese brewer possessed the organization, systems, and attitudes that were needed to create and bring to market the new beers that would drive the new product boom. By being the first to create such a capability, however, Asahi was, for a time, unique; and in this uniqueness, which took the form of a capability gap between Asahi and its rivals, lay the source of Asahi's performance gains. What it took to reduce that gap was the development of similarly effective new product development capabilities on the part of other brewers. To examine this process, we next look briefly at product development-related change and capability-building in Asahi's largest rival, Kirin.

INSIDE KIRIN: RESPONDING
TO HYPERCOMPETITION

Pre-Hypercompetition Conditions at Kirin

In order to respond to Asahi's *Super Dry* attack and the changed nature of industry competition, Kirin, like Asahi before it, had to overcome inertia and carry out change that would strengthen its capability to create and market new beers that consumers would welcome. Ironically, if resistance to change at Asahi was exacerbated by a *poor* performance record, Kirin faced inertia for the opposite reason: because its performance had been extremely *good.* Like many dominant companies in oligopolistic industries, Kirin was, by the early 1980s, a bureaucratic organization characterized by a strong seniority system and risk-averse thinking and behavior by employees. Existing ways were believed to be best, as these had carried the company to industry dominance. The corporate culture was intolerant of failure, and penalized the trying of new things. Management was "allergic" to negative information. Diversity and creativity had been bred out of the work force, selected against in recruiting and discouraged through acculturation and training, with the result that Kirin employees were known as *kintaro-ame,* after a candy stick that has the same pattern inside no matter where you slice it (Esaka 1988a).

An industry analyst writes: "Kirin's middle management in the 1980s were the people who had been on the front line during Kirin's 'golden age,' and they learned too many things too well from Kirin's success. For Kirin to regain its competitive strength, it was necessary for its management class to go through the difficult process of 'unlearning' many of the lessons of the company's past success" (Esaka 1988a, pp. 231-232). Kirin product development leader Yoshiaki Takano concurred in 1990: "There has been an emphasis in the company on 'unlearning' some of the values and ways of thinking that characterized Kirin in the past. Before, for example, failure was not allowed; the attitude was this is Kirin, failure doesn't happen here" (Takano interview).

Advocates of aggressive product development were blocked by strong strategic inertia in the fear of cannibalizing Kirin *Lager,* the industry's best selling brand. Protect-*Lager* thinking had stifled creativity, and Kirin rarely introduced a product innovation ahead of its rivals. Company president Hideyo Motoyama said in 1988: "It's true that we responded slowly to the trends toward canned and draft beer. But you must remember that Kirin's red label bottled *Lager* accounted for over half the beer drunk in Japan. Our number one priority was to avoid hurting sales of our main, dominant product" (Esaka 1988a, p. 238). In 1966, then-president Masuo Tokikuni had gone even further, stating: "There are no new products in beer. You can change the size or shape of the bottle, but what's inside does not change" (Kagono and Yoshihara 1983, p. 9).

Changing Thinking at Kirin

In the more stable, predictable, and reliability-rewarding competitive environment of past years, Kirin's corporate culture had been an asset. But in the faster-placed, hypercompetitive environment of the 1980s, certain aspects of this culture were dysfunctional. To change this was a difficult process, requiring a long, sustained, and multifaceted effort.

When Hideyo Motoyama became president in 1984, he is reported to have believed that Kirin's conservative and bureaucratic culture had become a liability, and that there was a need for a new kind of thinking, a greater willingness among Kirin employees to take risks and try new things. He thus began a series of activities and measures aimed at "internal revitalization." As at Asahi, this revitalization included both formal organizational change and measures aimed at bringing about a change in employee thinking and orientation.

Formal change included a switch from a functional to a product division structure; "rationalization" of administrative staff; the organizational separation of new product development from sales, where the protect-*Lager* mentality reigned; and the creation of cross-functional new product teams to carry out and coordinate the development of individual new beers. These organizational changes were made not only for their intrinsic value as more effective work arrangements, but also for their stimulative effect on Kirin employees. Yoshiaki Takano states: "Rules and organization are made to be changed. This is one way to shake up and stimulate people and the company" (Takano interview).

Changing employee thinking and orientation was an especially thorny challenge at Kirin. Initial measures taken in 1984—the setting up of a special section to direct revitalization efforts and a CI campaign aimed at rousing employees from complacency—failed: The patient, steeped in traditional Kirin ways, could not cure himself (Kubo 1991, Esaka 1988a).

In 1985, outside consultants were brought in to assess the state of Kirin's organization. Conducting over 1,100 interviews inside the company, the consultants found that employees did not feel Kirin faced a crisis, nor did they believe Kirin's stable prosperity would be threatened in the next ten years. The large scale of the interviewing, though, provided impetus to revitalization efforts by starting talk within the company that "management is up to something big" (Kubo 1991).

Over the latter half of the 1980s, what might be called a "preaching" campaign was employed by management to try to influence employee thinking and behavior. Employees repeatedly heard, from management and the company union, the message that the world had changed and that for Kirin to continue to prosper, new ways of thinking and working were required. The following quotation from a pamphlet distributed to all Kirin employees in 1990, was typical:

> Over the past few years Kirin has faced, it is no exaggeration to say, the most difficult circumstances in company history. It can be said that one of the main reasons for these circumstances lay in our inability to respond sensitively to drastic changes in the social and competitive environment. To put it another way, the thinking and behavior and values that we Kirin employees have possessed up to now no longer fit or are accepted by today's society.
>
> The world changes quickly. The age when ten years was a long time has passed. Today, three years is a long time. Things change a lot in three years. That's how fast-paced change is now. What would happen, in such an age, if we kept doing the same things in the same way that we did last year? We would undoubtedly become known as a company that is behind the times. (Kirin Breweries and Kirin Labor Union, *Shin Jiritsu Sengen*)

Views critical of Kirin management, once forbidden, were published in the company newsletter *Kirin*. Employee transfers and promotions were also used to stimulate change. For the first time, union members and younger workers were promoted to section chief rank, and managers from nonbeer operations such as the soft drink division and subsidiary Kirin-Seagram, which had never enjoyed the luxury of holding a dominant market position, were transferred to the beer division to inject new ideas and attitudes (Nagaoka et al. 1989).

In 1990, efforts to reinforce and further push internal change were being centered around a new personnel system, whose centerpiece was a new evaluation and reward system which provided greater incentives for taking risks and trying new things and lesser rewards for preservation of the status quo. Personnel Department Head and Managing Director Kazunori Nakano explained: "You can tell people to be responsive to change, but if the evaluation and reward system is one that penalizes employees for failure, no one is going to take the risk of trying new things" (Kubo 1991, p. 258).

Despite the magnitude and variety of these internal measures, there is general agreement that internal efforts alone were insufficient to bring about real change at Kirin, and that, as at Asahi, external pressure in the form of deteriorating performance also played a critical role. Yoshiaki Takano states: "The organizational and management changes that were made could not have happened had it not been for *Super Dry* shock" (Takano interview). Asahi's Sugiura agrees: "Starting last year (1990) Kirin really changed from being a conservative defender to being an attacker. It took a 10% drop in share to enable them to do this" (Sugiura interview).

By the early 1990s, while few would argue that Kirin had achieved a complete transformation from bureaucratic dinosaur to responsive innovator, it was clear that the company's efforts at revitalization had born fruit—in organization, culture, employee behavior, and performance of Kirin products in the marketplace. Yoshiaki Takano spoke about these results in 1990:

> Young people's ideas are seen as more important than they once were. In the past, younger workers and older workers, higher ranking employees and lower ranking employees, did not discuss things on the same level. The voices of the older and higher ranked people carried far more weight. Now, the two groups communicate with each other on much nearer the same level. Another big change is that failure is viewed differently than it once was; it is OK if we learn from it. This change was necessary to get people to be original and try new things, and it has been a big back-up for our new product development. (Takano interview)

The openness to new ideas and the empowerment of younger employees, who staff the new product development teams, paid off in the development of *Ichiban Shibori*. *Ichiban Shibori* is brewed using only the first extract of malt and not the second, which produces tannin and adds a bitter taste. (Other beers use both the first and second extracts.) For this reason, it is costlier to produce; if two extracts produce 100 units, one provides only 90. According to Kirin managers, had the campaign to change thinking at Kirin not been made, traditionally strong cost considerations would have prevailed, blocking *Ichiban Shibori;* there would not have been young product developers boldly pushing a new beer that was more expensive to produce, and there would not have been upper management ears open to what those younger voices were saying (Sakurai interview, Kubo 1991).

By around 1989, the new product development capability gap between Asahi and Kirin had been eliminated. Kirin's new product system was not an exact replica of Asahi's, but in terms of ability to create and market new beers that matched consumer needs, the two were similar. As was the case with Asahi, it took Kirin considerable time and effort to overcome inertial forces that blocked the development of an effective new product development capability, but the task was doable. Once done, not just at Kirin but also at Sapporo and Suntory, where similar product development capabilities were created, Asahi's capability-based advantage was neutralized, and a new equilibrium was reached, one reflected in a restabilization, for the time being, of competitive position.

Organizational capabilities have been defined as a company's skills at combining and coordinating individual resources for a particular productive use (Hill and Jones 1994), and as the integration of specialist knowledge to perform a discrete productive task (Grant 1996). Capabilities provide an important source of competitive advantage because they are intangible and difficult to imitate (Lippman and Rumelt 1982, Nelson and Winter 1982, Barney 1986a). The Asahi and Kirin cases illustrate two levels of capabilities which are important in providing competitive advantage in hypercompetitive environments. One is *specialized* capabilities, required to effectively perform a particular task, such as new product development. As the above accounts have shown, the effective integration and application to the task of new product development of individual resources— information, ideas, financial resources, the specialist skills of technical and marketing side product developers, and support from other departments and top management—required fundamental change in corporate culture and values, the unlearning of hidden routines and attitudes, changes in formal organization and procedures, and the acquisition of new knowledge, under-standing, and communication tools. Achieving these is not easy, making the creation of an effective specialized capability in new product development a formidable and time-consuming challenge. Specialized capabilities are important in hypercompetition because they enable a firm to initiate and compete successfully in a round of hypercompetition based on a particular competitive dimension.

A second level of capability evident in the Asahi and Kirin stories is a more *general* capability to efficiently combine and activate resources to allow effective competition on new dimensions, not just once but continu-ally. This kind of capability enables a firm to respond swiftly and proactively to the rapid-paced changes, opportunities, and threats that characterize hypercompetitive environments. A capability of this nature, also, is not easy to build. The themes of inertia and resistance to change emerge very strongly from the accounts of Asahi's and Kirin's efforts at transformation. In order to enhance their ability not only to compete in new product development but to initiate and respond to subsequent hypercompetitive rounds against a background of continuing environmental change, these firms needed in their organizations several fairly rare and difficult-to-develop traits: vision and the ability to spread that vision throughout the company; sensitivity and openness to environmental change and its effect on current strategies and resources; positive attitudes toward change in company strategies, poli-cies, and territorial charters; broadly cooperative cross-functional relations; top management mastery of methods and tools for effecting internal change; and forward-looking, attack-minded thinking oriented as strongly toward creating new advantages as defending old ones. These traits constitute a complex capability that is difficult not only to create, but also to maintain, and Kirin demonstrate, while failure and difficulty provoke change, success heightens complacency (Hedberg 1981).

Such a capability is both rare—because it is difficult to create and maintain—and valuable in giving a firm an edge in the ability to continually generate new advantages. D'Aveni (1994) argues that such an ability is the only sustainable advantage in hypercompetitive environments, where continuous change reduces the sustainability of any particular specialized capability-based advantage. Kirin's first-in-industry response to downward price pressures via its alliance with a foreign brewer is evidence that this company has come a long way toward developing such a general capability. It seems unlikely that the old Kirin, complacent, riskaverse, and fearful of straying from proven ways, would have acted so aggressively, playing not the defender but the attacker and proactive shaper of the nature of industry competition.

DISCUSSION

While the emphasis in this chapter has been on Schumpeterian aspects of the Japanese beer industry's new product war, hypercompetition in this (and other) industries can perhaps most accurately be seen as a particular combination of Schumpeterian, industrial organization (IO), and Chamberlinian competition. (See Barney 1986b for an exposition of these three views of competition.) Prior to the new product war, the Japanese beer industry was characterized by a combination of IO and Chamberlinian competition. Structural features emphasized by IO theory—high entry barriers, the small number of firms, a regulatory environment supportive of the status quo, and the existence of a dominant firm with power over weaker rivals as well as an incentive to keep them in business—resulted in competition being centered on nonprice dimensions which worked to the leader's advantage while keeping collective industry rents high. Consistent with a Chamberlinian view, firms possessed unique but overlapping resources, which had produced an equilibrium in competitive means and the distribution of economic returns; Kirin's scale and reputation advantages underlay strategies which produced for that company a sustained period of superior performance. Schumpeterian competition was absent.

When Schumpeterian competition emerged in the 1980s in the form of the new product war, it did not *replace* IO and Chamberlinian competition so much as add to these a new type of competition which significantly reduced the effectiveness of strategies and resources created in and for an IO/Chamberlinian competitive setting. The industry's oligopolistic structure did not change, firm resource uniqueness did not disappear, and product differentiation remained a source of economic rents. What changed was the effectiveness of particular kinds of product differentiation, with the reputation attributes of established brands like Kirin *Lager* becoming less meaningful and the taste, image, and newness attributes of new brands increasing in importance. Accompanying this was a corresponding change in the value of certain unique resources and capabilities, with those supportive of effective new product development increasing in value and those hindering it becoming a liability. Moreover, the shift in competitive dimensions employed by firms did not end with the new product war, but has continued. The recent emergence of cost-based competition can be seen as another Schumpeterian shock, which again changes the value of established strategies, resources, and capabilities.

Concerning the causes of hypercompetition, a useful distinction may be made between the factors which produce a "round" of hypercompetition, based on a particular competitive dimension, and those which underlie a broader hypercompetitive "state," in which competitive change is continual and multiple rounds succeed one another with little respite in between. The round of new product hypercompetition in the industry studied was caused by a combination of environmental trends which increased demand for new kinds of beer, plus a competitive attack by an industry player which took advantage of those trends and that change in demand. More generally, it can be said that a round results when (1) environmental change of some sort makes possible or more attractive a mode of competition that had been previously dormant, and (2) a competitor "attacks" by employing that competitive mode effectively.

The causes underlying a state of hypercompetition are broader trends which work to increase the intensity of competition, the pace of change, and the variety of competitive dimensions on which firms can, or must, compete. These decrease the likelihood that an industry, once a round ends, will settle back into stability and equilibrium. In the case of Japan's beer industry, these trends include forces described by Porter (1980), such as greater bargaining power by buyers (larger distributors, pickier consumers with more choices) and an increase in substitutes (the *chu-hai,* more foreign beers), plus deregulation. These form the broader, dynamic background against which competition continues to evolve in new directions even as the new product war winds down.

The role of government regulation deserves comment as, although recent deregulation is influencing ongoing competitive change, hypercompetition first broke out in this industry within and despite a highly regulated environment. Because of the importance of beer taxes as a source of government revenue, the industry has been strictly regulated through licensing requirements aimed at securing the advantages of low-cost and reliable tax collection from a few large, healthy brewers rather than from numerous smaller, weaker ones. For decades, this regulatory environment supported a stable oligopoly led by a dominant firm able to orchestrate competition in a way that worked to its advantage while providing a piece of the pie for everyone. Cooperative firm behavior designed to preserve collective health was practiced; for example, Asahi allowed Suntory to share its distribution system when the latter entered the industry in the 1960s, and Kirin discontinued all advertising for four years during the 1970s when its market share rose to unprecedented levels. This competitive arrangement worked only as long as each member was viable, however. Suntory's perennial weak performance— its beer operations have shown a profit only once, in 1984—was mitigated by the fact that beer accounts for only a quarter of total company sales. But when Asahi, a firm dependent on beer for around 80% of sales, fell to a state where its continued existence was in doubt, the result was an unstable situation featuring a desperate firm with nothing to lose. This desperation helped trigger new product hypercompetition by pushing Asahi to carry out a "frontal" attack which a more secure firm might not have risked.

One might argue that Kirin could have prevented Asahi from launching the new product war by propping Asahi up before it became so desperate. However, while this might have postponed hypercompetition, it seems doubtful that the industry leader could have prevented hypercompetition from happening altogether, for the environmental trends that underlay it were and are strong, creating opportunities for effective competition on new dimensions that rivals were bound to take advantage of at some point. Even Asahi, while benefitting greatly from the new product war, was incapable of controlling what it had set in motion. It was not Asahi's intention when it introduced *Super Dry* to initiate hypercompetition; the company would no doubt have preferred to enjoy the enhanced performance and strengthened position that *Super Dry* brought it in a less intense competitive environment than that which exists today.

The question of why hypercompetition broke out when it did, in 1985 rather than, say, 1965 or 1995, has important normative implications for other industries. The answer would seem to lie in external change; it was during the 1980s that the various environmental trends described in this paper converged to produce both the round of new product hypercompetition and the continuing hypercompetitive state with its shifting array of emerging opportunities and threats for firms. When Kirin's president stated in 1966 that "there are no new products in beer," he was probably right; *at that time* there were not, because demand for them was weak. Twenty years later, however, the environment had changed, demand had shifted, and the situation was ripe for a competitor to respond by launching a new beer that would transform the rules of competition and the value of firm resources and capabilities.

The study I have described was of hypercompetition in an oligopolistic, highly regulated, and relatively low-tech industry. To what extent the findings can be generalized to industries with different structural features and technology levels is a question that can best be answered by continued research on a broader range of hypercompetitive industries. The primary goal of this paper has been to contribute to a better understanding of the nature of hypercompetition, its causes, and its organizational and performance implications for firms. In summarizing the findings of the study, three characteristics emerge which I argue to be defining features of hypercompetition. First, hypercompetition involves nonmarginal change in the dimensions along which firms compete. This change is continual and results from a combination of environmental trends and competitive attacks by firms. Second, hypercompetition requires firms to transform themselves in nontrivial ways, and in particular to create new and complex organizational capabilities. Third, hypercompetition has significant performance effects, which derive from difficult-to-imitate specialized capabilities at the round level, and more general but rare capabilities at the state level. While the speed of change in hypercompetitive environments weakens (but does not eliminate) the sustainability of specialized capability-based advantage, it increases the importance of the advantage provided by general hypercompetition-appropriate capabilities, which remain valuable as long as broader hypercompetitive conditions persist in an industry.

ACKNOWLEDGMENTS

The author would like to gratefully acknowledge the financial support received for this research project from the Fulbright Program of the Japan-United States Educational Commission. Special also thanks go to the people of Asahi Breweries, Ltd., Kirin Breweries, Ltd., Sapporo Breweries, Ltd., and Suntory, Ltd., who generously provided their time, insights, and cooperation in this research; to Tom Roehl of University of Illinois, Charles Hill of University of Washington, and Hideki Yoshihara and the members of his seminar at Kobe University for their guidance and support; and to Ali Dastmalchian, Tom Lawrence, and Will McNally of University of Victoria and four anonymous reviewers for their thoughtful comments and criticisms concerning this manuscript.

Appendix 1:
Research Methodology

Design:

Qualitative multiple case study, following procedures outlined by Glaser and Strauss (1967), Mintzberg (1979), Jick (1979), Eisenhardt (1989), and Yin (1989).

Firms investigated:

Asahi Breweries, Ltd.; Kirin Breweries, Ltd.; Sapporo Breweries, Ltd.; Suntory, Ltd.

Data sources:

(1) Documentary evidence: books; articles from newspapers, magazines, and academic journals; materials published by the Brewers Association of Japan; internal documents provided by the brewers. (2) Semistructured interviews with firm managers. (3) A questionnaire survey conducted at each firm.

(Appendix 2 lists interviewees and questionnaires returned for each firm.)

Data Gathering and Analysis Sequence

1. A set of research questions concerning both the new product hypercompetition (the forces underlying it, its dynamics, its outcome) and the actions of individual firms (strategic moves, organizational changes, resistance to change) was written to anchor the data gathering. These questions were used along with extant literature on innovation and inertia to create an initial list of variables to be investigated. This list was used in extracting and recording information from documentary evidence, and as a basis for developing interview questions and questionnaire items.

2. Documentary evidence was gathered and analyzed to establish as much industry and firm knowledge as possible to internal data collection.

3. Semistructured interviews were designed and conducted at each firm with managers from selected functions. A total of 18 interviews was conducted. The managers interviewed were of section chief, department head, or higher rank, and all had worked in the functional areas of interest during the period 1982-1990, that is from just prior to the outbreak of new product hypercompetition through its height. Interview questions were developed for each functional area and sent to all interviewees prior to interviewing. The questions were written by the researcher in Japanese, then checked by 12 employees of a major Japanese corporation and, where necessary, revised to ensure accuracy and clarity. The interviews were conducted in Japanese, and lasted from 30 minutes to two hours each. In addition to covering the prepared questions, the interviews were used to clarify firm-specific issues which had surfaced during the prior investigation of documentary evidence. All interviews

were recorded on tape. Rough written notes were also taken during the interviews, and the "24-hour rule" (Bougeois and Eisenhardt 1988) was followed; impressions and as much detail as could be recalled were recorded within one day of the interview. The interview tapes were later transcribed, and used extensively in writing up the research results.

4. The questionnaire was designed to supplement the interviewing by sampling the views of a larger number of persons than it was possible to interview. (Sampling problems ruled out a questionnaire-based statistical comparison among firms.) Questionnaire items were similar to the interview questions, with several allowing for open-ended answers. An initial draft of the questionnaire was revised following the interviewing to include additional items whose relevance the interviews had revealed. After checking for clarity and accuracy (by the same native Japanese speakers who had checked the interview questions), questionnaires were distributed at each firm to employees in new product development, R & D, production, advertising, and sales. Questionnaire responses were coded, recorded by item for each firm, and incorporated into the research results.

5. The first step of the data analysis was to combine data from the secondary materials, interviews, and questionnaire to write detailed accounts of the findings for each firm. These accounts followed a common format and were purely descriptive; in fact, analysis was consciously avoided in order to record as objectively and neutrally as possible what occurred at each firm and for what reasons. These descriptions served to give the researcher and other readers an in-depth familiarity with the particulars of each case, as well as to provide an easily accessed data bank to use in cross-case and industry analysis. Once the descriptive account was completed for an individual company, a within-case analysis was written, discussing the case findings in terms of the research questions, and making note of significant results or insights provided by the particular case. The final steps involved cross-case comparison, and theory development along the lines described by Eisenhardt (1989, p. 541): "From the within-site analysis plus various cross-site tactics and overall impressions, tentative themes, concepts, and possibly even relationships between variables begin to emerge."

Flexibility and Reliability. In contrast to laboratory experiments or surveys, the data collection procedures in case study research are not completely routinized, as continuous interaction between theoretical issues and data being collected requires adaptiveness and flexibility of the researcher and the data collection design. Accordingly, the initial data collection plan was modified as the investigation proceeded to include additional variables and respond to particular information access issues that arose. Reliability in data collection and analysis was promoted using tactics recommended by Yin (1989): (a) using case study protocol, (b) developing a case study database, and (c) having key informants review the draft case study report to check and corroborate essential facts.

Appendix 2: Interviewees and
Questionnaire Respondents, by Firm

Asahi

Interviewees
Makoto Sugiura—marketing, new product development Ninomiya—personnel
Hikojiro Suzuki—personnel
Hisashi Usuba—production, R & D
Masato Nakagawa—production, R & D
Number of questionnaire respondents: 24

Kirin

Interviewees
Toshihiro Kanazawa—secretary to president Shigeo Sakurai—planning and
control department
Yoshiaki Takano—R & D, new product development
Masaki Harada—personnel
Number of questionnaire respondents: 8

Sapporo

Interviewees
Izumi Kitaoka—publicity department
Tadao Murakami—production, R & D
Masumi Nozaki—personnel
Toshiaki Oka—new product development
Number of questionnaire respondents: 16

Suntory

Interviewees
Makoto Inoue—manager, office of the president
Shun-ichi Naito—personnel
Akihisa Hirabayashi—marketing, new product development
Kazuo Nakatani—R & D
Hiroaki Ono—marketing, office of the president
Number of questionnaire respondents: 10

NOTES

1. In Japan, beer that is heat pasteurized is called "lager," while beer that isn't is called "draft." Heat pasteurization is done to destroy microorganisms that shorten shelf life; this makes bottling and home consumption possible. In the case of canned or bottled "draft," this is achieved by brewing in sterile conditions and maintaining refrigeration, or by processes such as ceramic filtration.

2. Kirin's market share first exceeded 60% in 1972, prompting speculation in 1973 that the company might be declared a monopoly and broken up. Kirin responded by suspending all advertising from 1974 to 1978, for fear of the consequences of further industry domination (Nagaoka et al. 1989).

3. A "new product" is defined here as one in which the beer is physically different—in ingredients and/or brewing method—from products previously offered by the producer. The beer must also be advertised as a new beer. The following are not counted as new products: unpublicized adjustments in the taste of existing beers; a previously marketed beer offered in a new type or size of container; new foreign brands produced under license by Japanese brewers in Japan.

4. Industrywide, marketing expenses as a percent of beer sales (weighted average of four brewers) rose from 3.86% in 1983 (pre-new product boom) to 5.67% in 1987 (mid-new product boom).

5. The combined share of the liquor retail business controlled by convenience stores, chains, retailers, discounters, and other new entrants climbed from 5.8% in 1983 to 28.2% in 1993, while the share of traditional general liquor stores fell from 76.2% to 55% (Morgan Stanley 1994).

REFERENCES

Abegglen, J. C. and G. Stalk, Jr. (1985), *Kaisha: The Japanese Corporation,* Tokyo: Charles E. Tuttle.

Andrews, K. R. (1971), *The Concept of Corporate Strategy,* Homewood, IL: Irwin.

Barney, J. B. (1986a), "Organizational Culture: Can It Be a Source of Competitive Advantage?" *Academy of Management Review,* 11, 3, 656-665.

———— (1986b), "Types of Competition and the Theory of Strategy: Toward an Integrative Framework," *Academy of Management Review,* 11, 4, 791-800.

———— (1991), "Firm Resources and Sustained Competitive Advantage," *Journal of Management,* 17, 1, 99-120.

Beer Shuzo Kumiai (1989), *Beer Hyakka* (Beer Encyclopedia), Tokyo: Beer Shuzo Kumiai.

Bourgeois, L. J. and K. M. Eisenhardt (1988), "Strategic Decision Processes in High Velocity Environments: Four Cases in the Microcomputer Industry," *Management Science,* 34, 7, 816-835.

D'Aveni, R. A. (1994), *Hypercompetition: Managing the Dynamics of Strategic Maneuvering,* New York: Macmillan.

Eisenhardt, K. M. (1989), "Building Theories from Case Study Research," *Academy of Management Review,* 14, 4, 532-560.

Esaka, A. (1988a), "Kirin Beer: Eiko no 'shinwa' wo torimodosu joken" (Kirin Beer: Conditions for Reviving a Success Story), *President,* April 1988, 226-247.

———— (1988b), "Beer Senso (I)" (The Beer War, I), *President,* December, 276-296.

———— (1989), "Beer Senso (II)" (The Beer War, II), *President,* January, 316-323.

Glaser, B. G. and A. L. Strauss (1967), *The Discovery of Grounded Theory: Strategies for Qualitative Research,* London: Weidenfeld and Nicholson.

Grant, R. M. (1996), "Prospering in Dynamically-Competitive Environments: Organizational Capability as Knowledge Integration," *Organization Science,* 7, 4, 375-387.

Hayakawa, K. (1989), *Asahi Beer Higuchi Kotaro no Super Keieijutsu* (The "Super" Management of Asahi Beer's Higuchi Kotaro), Tokyo: Seikai Bunka Sha.

Hayashi, H. (1989), "Shinshohin kaihastsu no soshiki to taisei" (The Organization and System of New Product Development), *JPI Journal,* 27, 10, 9-13.

Hedberg, B. L. T. (1981), "How Organizations Learn and Unlearn," in Paul C. Nystrom and William H. Starbuck (Eds.), *Handbook of Organizational Design,* Vol. 1, New York: Oxford University Press.

Hill, C. W. L. and G. R. Jones (1994), *Strategic Management,* Boston: Houghton Mifflin.

Ishiyama, J. (1987), *Asahi Beer no Chosen* (The Challenge of Asahi Beer), Tokyo: Nihon Noritsu Kyokai.

Ishizawa, M. (1994), "Kirin, Busch Go for Another Round," *The Nikkei Weekly,* March 14, 9.

Jick, T. D. (1979), "Mixing Qualitative and Quantitative Methods: Triangulation in Action," *Administrative Science Quarterly,* 24, 602-611.

Kagano, T. and H. Yoshihara (1983), *Ashai Beer,* Nomura Management School, Japan.

Kirin Brewery and Kirin Labor Union (1990), "Jiritsu sengen" (Independence Declaration), Company pamphlet.

Kokuryo, J. (1989), *Asahi Breweries, Ltd.,* Boston: Harvard Business School.

Kubo, H. (1991), "Kirin wo yomigaeraseta 'Tokkoyaku' " (The Medicine that Revived Kirin), *Zaikai Tenbo,* August, 254-259.

Lippman, S. A. and R. P. Rumelt (1982), "Uncertain Imitability: An Analysis of Interfirm Differences in Efficiency under Competition," *Bell Journal of Economics,* 23, 418-438.

Matsui, Y. (1990), Speech given at Matsushita Electric Industrial Co., Ltd., Osaka, Japan.

Mintzberg, H. (1979), "An Emerging Strategy of 'Direct' Research," *Administrative Science Quarterly,* 24, 582-589.

Morgan, Stanley (1994), "Beer," *Investment Research Japan & Asia/Pacific,* October 5, 1994.

Nagaoka, F., T. Nakagawa, K. Sakai, and Y. Honma (1989), "Kirin Beer: 'Seiko no fukushi' ni nayamu Gulliver" (Kirin Beer: The Price of Past Success for Gulliver), *Nikkei Business,* June 19, 6-21.

Nelson, R. R. and S. G. Winter (1982), *An Evolutionary Theory of Economic Change,* Cambridge, MA: Belknap Press of Harvard University Press.

Ogihara, K. (1979), *Beer, Seishu, Whiskey Gyokai* (The Beer, Sake, and Whiskey Industries), Tokyo: Kyoikusha Shuppan Service.

Porter, M. (1980), *Competitive Strategy,* New York: Free Press.

Schumpeter, J. A. (1950), *Capitalism, Socialism, and Democracy,* 3rd ed., New York: Harper & Row.

Tokumaru, S. (1990), "Aji, message, shokubunka: dore go kakete mo ikinokorenai" (Taste, Message, and Food Culture: Survival Requires All Three), *Dime,* April 5, 89-95.

Usuba, H. (1989), "Asahi Super Dry Beer—Its Identity and History," *MBAA Technical Quarterly,* 26, 85-88.

Yin, R. K. (1989), *Case Study Research: Design and Methods,* London: Sage.

Yomiuri Shimbun (January 28, 1994), "Beer Brand Kesho-naoshi" (Beer Brand Facelifts).

8

Eating Your Own Lunch

Protection Through Preemption

BARRIE R. NAULT
MARK B. VANDENBOSCH

Recent discussions of management practices among successful high-technology companies suggest that one key strategy for success is to "eat your own lunch before someone else does." The implication is that in intensely competitive, or hypercompetitive markets, firms with a leading position should aggressively cannibalize their own current advantages with next-generation advantages before competitors step in to steal the market. Given the pace of technological and other types of change, such strategy often requires creating next-generation advantages while the current advantages are still profitable—that is, trading current profits for future market leadership.

We capture the tradeoff between a market leader's willingness to reap profits with its current set of advantages and its desire to maintain market leadership by investing in the next generation. Using a competitive model that determines the equilibrium launch time of a next generation advantage, we find that, in absence of lower launch costs for an entrant, the incumbent will be first to launch to maintain its market leadership. That is, regardless of the severity of penalties for being a follower in the next generation, it is optimal for the incumbent to preempt the entrant by launching early—even if the incumbent consequently loses money at the margin. We derive a straightforward condition to determine when an incumbent will make negative incremental profits from its investment in the next-generation advantage. The fact that the condition does not depend on the size of the incumbent's investment costs indicates that the severity of competition, rather than the costs of developing and introducing a next-generation advantage, is what forces firms to cannibalize at a loss.

Finally, we find that a preemptive launch can result in an earlier launch of the next generation than is socially optimal, and provide a sufficient condition for that to occur. Although customers are better off as a result of an earlier launch, their gain may be outweighed by the additional costs firms incur from launching prematurely.

(FIRST-MOVER; HYPERCOMPETITION;

MANAGEMENT PRACTICES;

COMPETITIVE STRATEGY)

INTRODUCTION

We address the question of whether it is better to sustain a current advantage or preempt it with a next-generation advantage. A recent *Fortune* article discussing the management practices of successful high-technology companies such as Intel, Hewlett Packard, and Microsoft gave one of the key strategies for success as "eat your own lunch before someone else does" (Deutschman 1994). This strategy suggests that in intensely competitive, or hypercompetitive, markets, firms with leading or dominant market positions should cannibalize their own current advantages—advantages in product, process, knowledge, and so on—with next-generation advantages before competitors step in to steal the market. Given the pace of technological and other types of change, such strategy often requires investing in and launching next generation advantages while current advantages are still profitable—that is, trading current profits for future market leadership. It has been employed successfully by Hewlett Packard to dominate both the laser and inkjet printer markets, and by Intel in its microprocessor business. In contrast, Seagate Technology, which did not cannibalize its favorable position in 5.25 inch disk drives with the emerging 3.5 inch format, and National Semiconductor, which delayed the upgrade to its market-dominating ethernet chipset, lost millions of dollars and market position by *not* "eating their own lunches."

The actions of several leading firms support an "eat your own lunch" strategy. Motorola began using "self-obsoleting tactics" when its frequency modulation (FM) development cannibalized its AM car radio business in the 1940s (Slutsker 1994), and continues to do so today in its paging and cellular phone businesses. Bell Northern Research, the research arm of Northern Telecom, uses an approach it calls "backcasting," working backward from the required market launch to track the progress of next-generation development projects (*Telesis* 1993). Many firms, such as Hewlett Packard, are investing in processes that reduce their product development times (House and Price 1991), whereas other firms, such as Intel, maintain their product development readiness by simultaneously working on several successive product generations (*Business Week* 1995a).

The preceding examples illustrate the appeal of a strategy we call "protection through preemption." We believe such a strategy is necessary to maintain market dominance. That is, a competitive advantage in an intensely competitive market can be sustained only by a series of preemptive moves designed to stay ahead of competitors. Each of those moves has the potential to cannibalize current strengths. D'Aveni (1994) supports that notion by suggesting that a protection-through-preemption strategy is appropriate in hypercompetitive markets. He argues that because no barriers are sustainable, to be successful, a firm must organize to create a series of temporary advantages, with self-cannibalization being one approach to building such an advantage.

Though many of our examples are of technology-intensive industries that have frequent introductions of next-generation products, our model results apply to any multigenerational setting where next-generation advantages of any kind can supersede current advantages. Examples of our protection-through-preemption strategy in nontechnology-intensive product markets include Sealed Air Corporation's launch of "uncoated" bubble wrap to thwart potential competitors (Dolan 1982) and Hanes Corporations introduction of L'Eggs panty hose. Advantages outside product markets include information systems (e.g., American Airlines' SABRE reservation system and Wal-Mart's inventory management system), supply chain management (e.g., Compaq), scale of R & D investment (e.g., Samsung in the DRAM market), manufacturing and management processes (e.g., Boeing Corporation), and service delivery (e.g., Walt Disney).

Despite being successful in practice, a protection-through-preemption strategy runs counter to many of the findings in the economics and marketing literature suggesting that incumbents should delay their launch of the next generation (e.g., Ghemawat 1991; Kamien and Schwartz 1982; and Reinganum 1983, 1985). The rationale for those results, which pertain almost exclusively to product markets, is that the incumbent will damage its current rent stream by launching the next generation. Because the entrant has less to lose by launching the next generation than the incumbent, the entrant will be compelled to launch first.

Ghemawat's (1991) model is typical of models supporting a delayed launch strategy by the incumbent. He develops a modified patent race model that allows for overlapping generations and imitation of the next generation by followers. The key result is that the incumbent (i.e., AT&T in the voice-only PBX business) is unwilling to innovate and launch the next generations (voice and data PBX technologies). As the entrant has little to lose by innovating and entering the next generation, doing so is in its best interest. Hence, the incumbent may be better off by not competing with the entrant in the next generation, thus limiting self-cannibalization. Such strategy is argued to be optimal in hotly contested markets—markets similar to those in which self-cannibalization strategies are now being practiced.

The limited empirical research on protection-through-preemption strategy provides mixed findings. While some empirical research has been done on first-mover advantage (Kerin et al. 1992), pioneering (Golder and Tellis 1993) and timing of entry (Lilien and Yoon 1990), most of the work has examined the performance of firms entering markets in a particular order rather than the entrant-incumbent interaction we study. Nonetheless, some of the findings are relevant. Analyzing 112 products from 52 French firms, Lilien and Yoon (1990) found that firms are more successful when they enter a market in the introduction phase of the product life cycle, but first entrants are not as successful as followers. Like other research on pioneering and timing of entry, the study concerned only the firm's entry into the market. Lilien and Yoon do not analyze the influence of changes and modifications in the firm's offerings *after* market entry. Therefore, it is difficult to determine whether self-cannibalization by incumbent firms has an effect on performance. In a study of the American diagnostic imaging industry, Mitchell (1991) found that incumbents in a segment have better performance than true entrants when a new segment is opened. For example, market leaders in computer tomography (CT) scanners are also leaders in magnetic resonance imaging (MRI) scanners even though they were not the first to enter the MRI market. To the degree than MRI scanners are the next-generation technology, Mitchell's findings run counter to our protection-through-preemption strategy—even if incumbents are late, assets they are able to transport from the current generation such as brand name, distribution, and experience allow them to succeed in the next-generation market. However, Mitchell found that when only incumbents are considered, there is a first-mover advantage. That result is consistent with our suggested strategy.

The objectives of our chapter are to determine conditions under which an incumbent will use a protection-through-preemption strategy and to refine those conditions to show when an incumbent will preemptively launch a next-generation advantage at a loss to preserve its market leadership. To achieve our objectives, we build a model in which competition between an incumbent (the recognized leader in the deployment of the current generation advantage) and an entrant (a challenger in the next generation) determines the equilibrium launch time of a next-generation advantage. In doing so, we capture the tradeoff between the market leader's willingness to reap profits on the current generation and its desire to maintain market leadership by launching the next generation. We assume that the launch of the next-generation advantage incurs a one-time fixed cost for R & D and other costs necessary to bring the advantage to market, which we model as declining in real terms over time. In addition, firms' launch costs and profit flows are common knowledge. We employ the modeling approach and solution concept from games of timing by Fudenberg and Tirole (1985, 1986). That approach is general enough to accommodate differences in the diffusion processes between generations.

The results of our model indicate that regardless of the severity of penalties for being a follower in the next generation, it is optimal for the incumbent to preempt the entrant by launching early—even if the incumbent consequently makes lower overall profits after the next generation launch. We also provide a straightforward condition to determine when the incumbent's preemptive launch of the next generation makes negative profits at the margin. The condition does not depend on launch costs, but rather on the severity of competition, which therefore determines when firms will cannibalize at a loss. We also show that competition can result in a preemptive launch that is earlier than would be socially optimal, and derive a sufficient condition for that to occur. The results have significant implications for practicing managers and policymakers. For managers, our results imply that firms in intensely competitive industries should be willing to launch next-generation advantages preemptively to maintain market leadership, even if they lose money at the margin. For policymakers, our results imply that leaving next generation launch timing to the market may not be socially opitimal.

The remainder of the chapter is organized as follows. In the next section we discuss our model formulation and prior research. We then outline our notation and assumptions. In the subsequent section we provide the details of our model and report our main results, followed by an analysis of the welfare implications and limitations of our model. In the final section we discuss managerial implications, how our model could be validated, and directions for future research.

MODEL FORMULATION
AND PRIOR RESEARCH

Our model formulation incorporates standard assumptions and results from the marketing literature. Studying multigeneration product diffusion,

Norton and Bass (1987) found that sales of each generation followed a single peaked distribution over time. Subsequently, Wilson and Norton (1989) found that the optimal time to launch a product line extension is either early in the original product's life cycle or not at all. Their results depend on the relationship between the sales of the two products, their relative margins, and the length of the firm's planning horizon relative to the original product's diffusion time. Purohit (1994) found that if the firm can decide the extent of innovation then a product replacement strategy (discontinuing the current product) is more profitable than a line extension. Our model's assumptions and results are consistent with those findings. Other research has examined the diffusion process as a function of such variables as price, quality, and promotion expenditures that are under the control of the firm (Kalish and Lilien 1986). Our model is formulated in terms of profit flows rather than unit sales, prices, and costs, and accounts for diffusion effects in the relationships among the profit flows over time and across generations. Although not explicitly part of our formulation, an equilibrium setting of marketing mix variables is reflected in our profit flows.

Although the problem we model is similar to the one modeled by Ghemawat (1991), discussed previously, our results are opposite to his because we model the problem differently. In our formulation the launch of next-generation advantages is a timing decision rather than a binary launch/no launch decision, so preemption is admitted as a strategy. In addition, the rivalry component in our model is less severe as we allow differentiated competition between the two generations, and declining launch costs play a role in our analysis.

Our approach is rooted in research in which irreversible capital commitments are viewed as a way to deter entry. That stream began with a static model showing that excess capacity could deter a new entrant by giving an incumbent a credible threat to expand output and reduce marginal cost, thereby lowering price (Spence 1977). Then Spence (1979) found that from a static view of a dynamic solution to entry deterrence through investment, firms overinvested, illustrating that entry-deterring investment that was not rational in a static setting could be rational in the larger dynamic context. Eaton and Lipsey (1980) extended the finding by showing that if capital is not durable, then an incumbent monopolist protecting its position may need to replace capital (e.g., plant) before the capital is economically obsolete. Thus, the protection of its incumbency under the threat of a new entrant forces the monopolist to invest earlier than it would otherwise choose to do. Dixit (1979, 1980) modeled excess capacity as deterrence where full use of the capacity is not precommitted and found that a new entrant could be deterred if the incumbent set output just over a threshold level. Fudenberg and Tirole (1983) developed a model based on Spence's (1979) and established the existence of a set of perfect equilibria. Being unable to refine the set, they developed the solution concept we use here as a response. In our model the combination of timing dynamics and the threat from the entrant forces the incumbent to launch earlier than it would prefer to do, and Fudenberg and Tirole's equilibrium concept is necessary to resolve that combination of effects.

Although we characterize our model differently it also follows in the spirit of "an endless race" described by Aoki (1991). His results suggest that if returns on investment in technology are deterministic, then a firm may cease to compete even if it is only one generation behind. It returns are stochastic, however, then a firm may invest in technology even if it is more than one generation behind because a future launch by a competitor may fail. Aoki's formulation fixes launch costs over time, makes technology proprietary, and most important, restricts positive profits to a single generation. In our model next-generation advantages have deterministic payoffs, launch costs decline in real terms over time, the entrant can launch the next generation without having launched the current generation, and both generations can generate positive profits simultaneously.

Our model is also related to work on first-mover advantage. Kerin et al. (1992) point out that the presence and magnitude of first-mover advantages are contingent on a number of economic and behavioral factors. We assume that there are positive first-mover advantages, which may be the result of technological leadership, preemption of scarce resources, and the introduction of buyer switching sots (Lieberman and Montgomery 1988). The magnitude of those advantages is reflected in the firms' profit flows resulting from the launch of the next generation.

Although we do not study probabilistic payoffs to next-generation advantages, another important stream of research addresses uncertainty as the key issue in managing new generations. For example, several articles have examined how much costly information firms should gather prior to launch when the profitability of an innovation is unknown (Mamer and McCardle 1987; McCardle 1985). Timing is not a factor because there are no first-mover advantages, but firms gather information to lessen the chance of launching an unprofitable innovation and may modify their decisions because of potential competition. Our case is precisely the opposite—profitability resulting from next-generation launches is known and, because there may be first-mover advantages, timing is critical.

TABLE 8.1 Profit Flows

Time	Incumbent	Entrant
$0 \leq t \leq \min \{T^I, T^E\}$	$\pi_0^I(t)$	$\pi_0^E(t)$
$T^I \leq t \leq T^E$	$\pi_1^I(t)$	$\pi_2^E(t)$
$T^E \leq t \leq T^I$	$\pi_2^I(t)$	$\pi_1^E(t)$
$t \geq \max \{T^I, T^E\}$	$\pi_3^I(t)$	$\pi_3^E(t)$

NOTATION AND ASSUMPTIONS

For ease of communication, we describe the setting as a duopoly consisting of an incumbent that markets a product or service based on the current-generation advantage and an entrant that may also have a current-generation advantage. The firms compete to launch the next-generation advantage. Our modeling of the setting, however, is less restrictive as we allow many firms to compete to launch the next generation. Our concentration on one incumbent and one entrant, as we define them, entails no loss of generality in our analysis, as the equations that determine our results involve only those two firms. Omitting additional firms has no effect. The assumptions we require for our results follow.

We represent the incumbent by superscript I and the entrant by superscript E. Let T^i be the launch time of firm $i \in \{I, E\}$. The notation in Table 8.1 gives the profit flows at a given time t for each firm, exclusive of the launch cost. $\pi_0^i(t)$ is the pre-launch profit flow, $\pi_1^i(t)$ is the profit flow to firm i when only that firm has launched, $\pi_2^i(t)$ is the profit flow to firm i when only the other firm has launched, and $\pi_3^i(t)$ is the profit flow when both firms have launched.

Our first assumption is partly definitional and partly a restriction on firms' relative profits. Assumption 1 defines the incumbent as the firm with the largest differences in the present value of profit flows between having launched the next-generation advantage and having had a competitor preempt that launch—the firm with the most to lose if it does not preempt. If there are more than two firms, then the entrant is the firm with the next largest difference. Assumption 1 requires that we rank the firms by the magnitude of the difference,

$$\int_T^\infty \left[\pi_1^i(t) - \pi_2^i(t) \right] e^{-rt} dt$$

ASSUMPTION 1.

$$\int_{T}^{\infty}\left[\pi_1^I(t) - \pi_2^I(t)\right] e^{-rt}dt$$

$$> \int_{T}^{\infty}\left[\pi_1^E(t) - \pi_2^E(t)\right] e^{-rt}dt > 0.$$

The assumption orders firms by what Katz and Shapiro (1987) call the incentive to preempt: which firm benefits the most from being the first mover. The restriction embedded in the assumption is that firms can be ordered in a way that does not depend on the time T when the ordering is computed. Thus, in absence of an exogenous event that affects only a proper subset of firms, we believe the order of the difference in profit flow between being first and being preempted should be a function of relative firm characteristics rather than the time of launch. For example, Intel, the market leader with an 80 percent share of the PC microprocessor business, would be classified as the incumbent because it has the most to lose from being preempted by the launched of a superior PC-based processor.

Assumption 1 follows directly when the incumbent is the only firm with a current-generation advantage. In this case, prior to the entrant's launch, profit flows for the entrant are zero $\pi_0^E(t) = \pi_2^E(t) = 0$. We can then rearrange Assumption 1 into

$$\int_{T}^{\infty}\pi_1^I(t)\, e^{-rt}dt > \int_{T}^{\infty}\left[\pi_2^I(t) + \pi_1^E(t)\right] e^{-rt}dt.$$

That inequality is true because, for a product-market example, a two-product monopoly has profits greater than the joint profits from two differentiated products offered by competing firms. Because the next generation supersedes the current generation, the resulting vertically differentiated competition lowers the profitability of current generations. Although not necessary for our analysis, it is plausible that the leader with the current generation advantage is the incumbent in our model. However, our analysis extends to situations in which the firm with the most to gain from being the first mover is not the market leader in the current-generation. For example, on the basis of its strong brand and inkjet printing capabilities, Hewlett Packard went from nowhere to being one of the leading firms in the plain paper fax market.

Kim and Kogut (1996) show that some technologies offer a better starting point, or platform, than others for the exploration and development of new advantages in different markets. The incumbent defined by Assumption 1 could be the leading firm in a second market where it has experience with a promising technology platform, a platform from which it could become the leader in the first market. As such, that firm has the most to lose by not being first to enter the new market.

Let r be the discount rate. Assumption 2 makes the discount rate strictly positive.

ASSUMPTION 2.

$$r > 0.$$

Let $K(t)$ be the present value of the cost of launching the next generation at time t. There is no superscript on launch costs because we give neither firm a launch cost advantage. Assumption 3 specifies that the nominal cost of launching the next generation falls over time at a decreasing rate. The launch costs reflect the improvement in technology—product or process—from basic research, which reduces current costs of development and launch. That feature is included to model the reality that, over time, the skills necessary to successfully complete R & D on a specific technology improve and become more widely available. Moreover, related technologies become further developed with time.

ASSUMPTION 3.

$$\frac{d[K(t)e^{rt}]}{dt} < 0 \quad \text{and} \quad \frac{d^2[K(t)e^{rt}]}{dt^2} > 0,$$

$$\forall t < \infty; \; \liminf_{t \to \infty} K(t) = 0.$$

From Assumption 3 the present value of launch costs, which we use subsequently, falls over time:

$$\frac{d[K(t)e^{rt}]}{dt} = \frac{dK(t)}{dt}e^{rt} + K(t)re^{rt} > 0$$

(1)

$$\Rightarrow \frac{dK(t)}{dt} < -K(t)r < 0.$$

Using (1), we can show that their present value falls at a decreasing rate:

$$\frac{d^2[K(t)e^{rt}]}{dt^2} = \frac{d^2K(t)}{dt^2}e^{rt} + 2\frac{dK(t)}{dt}re^{rt} + K(t)r^2e^{rt} > 0$$

(2)

$$\Rightarrow \frac{d^2K(t)}{dt^2} > -r\frac{dK(t)}{dt} > 0.$$

The assumption is satisfied, for example, by exponential costs of the form $K(t) = e^{-(r+\beta)t}$, where β is the rate of current cost decay (Fudenberg and Tirole 1985).

The conditions in our next assumption in essence preclude a second launch of the next-generation advantage. We argue that there are several forms of competition in which we expect those conditions to hold.

ASSUMPTION 4. *When firm i is second to launch the next generation,*

$$(a) \left[\pi_2^i(T^i) - \pi_3^i(T^i) \right] e^{-rT^i} - \frac{dK(T^i)}{dT^i} > 0,$$

$$(b) \int_T^\infty \left[\pi_2^i(t) - \pi_3^i(t) \right] e^{-rt} dt + K(T) > 0.$$

Assumption 4(a) is stated in terms of the time of the second next-generation launch, T^i. It implies that when the cost of launch is factored in for the follower, differentiated competition is more profitable than direct competition between the follower's and the leader's next generations. Because the last terms in Assumption 4(a) and (b) are positive, the profit flows from entering the next-generation market for the follower can be greater than those from not entering at all, but not enough greater to alter the launch decision.

This condition is weaker (i.e., less restrictive) than the scenario of direct and unencumbered Bertrand competition in the next-generation market, which would imply that profits from the next generation are zero, $\pi_3^i(t) = 0$. If the entrant and incumbent are able to differentiate their next-generation advantages, Assumption 4 implies that they are not sufficiently differentiated to cover launch costs. Bertrand competition can support profits between two undifferentiated goods if there are decreasing returns to scale from production, for example capacity constraints (Tirole 1988). In that case, Assumption 4 implies that those profits do not exceed the costs of launch. Traditional Cournot analysis is really a choice of capacity with subsequent price competition, and Assumption 4 could again imply that the profits do not cover launch costs. (Tirole argues that the assumption of Bertrand competition is more appropriate for fairly flat marginal cost production and Cournot competition is more appropriate with sharply rising marginal cost. We believe that high-technology firms, for example, are likely to have high fixed and low marginal costs of production.)

This condition is also weaker than the result from Judd (1985), employed by Ghemawat (1991) to set $\pi_3^i(t) = 0$, where, in a product-market scenario, an incumbent would rather not compete directly with an entrant that markets a differentiated product because the direct competition in the differentiated product cannibalizes profits from the current product. That result is one in which profits can increase due to abandonment of a product, in our case the incumbent not launching the next-generation product. It is also supported by Purohit (1994), who found that a product-replacement strategy—discontinuing sales of the current generation in favor of the next generation—was more profitable than a line extension where both generations are sold.

Finally, after the first mover launches its next-generation advantage, the first mover's goal will be to drive down the potential profits of any new entrant in the next generation quickly, providing a credible threat to prevent entry. In the particular case of the entrant that does not have a current-generation advantage, if the entrant is second with the next generation, then it may not be able to set the price of its offering higher than marginal cost.

Consistent with our Assumption 4, in his study of the Japanese beer industry, Craig (1996) found firms that launched copycat dry beers—second introductions of the next generation—all discontinued their dry beer brands within a few years because they did not sell well. Without Assumption 4, our model would yield very different results, a point we reexamine subsequently.

Assumptions 5 and 6 are used to ensure that the next generation is launched in the interior of the solution space. Assumption 5 ensures that no firm launches the next generation at time zero. The profit flows for the incumbent are used in Assumption 5.

ASSUMPTION 5.

$$\int_t^\infty \left[\pi_1^I(t) - \pi_2^I(t) \right] e^{-rt} \, dt < K(0).$$

Assumption 6 ensures that the next generation is launched in finite time. The profit flows for the entrant are used in Assumption 6.

ASSUMPTION 6.

$$\inf_t \left\{ K(t) e^{rt} \right\} < \int_t^\infty \left[\pi_1^E(t) - \pi_2^E(t) \right] e^{-rt} \, dt.$$

In the fully general case, payoffs to firm i are

$$g_1^i(T^i, T^j) = \int_0^{T^i} \pi_0^i(t) \, e^{-rt} \, dt + \int_{T_i}^{T^j} \pi_1^i(t) \, e^{-rt} \, dt$$

$$+ \int_{T^j}^\infty \pi_3^i(t) \, e^{-rt} \, dt - K(T^i)$$

when firm i launches first and

$$g_2^i(T^i, T^j) = \int_0^{T^j} \pi_0^i(t) \, e^{-rt} \, dt + \int_{T^j}^{T^i} \pi_2^i(t) \, e^{-rt} \, dt$$

$$+ \int_{T^i}^\infty \pi_3^i(t) \, e^{-rt} \, dt - K(T^i)$$

when firm i launches second, where the superscript j means "not i."

MODEL

Equilibrium Launch Times

We begin by establishing the time of the second next-generation launch. That time is the solution to maximizing the payoffs to launching second by choosing when to launch, $\max_{T^i} g_2^i(T^i, T^j)$. Using Assumption 4(a), we know that the first derivative, marginal revenue less marginal cost, is positive for both the incumbent and the entrant,

$$\frac{\partial g_2^i(T^i, T^j)}{\partial T^i} = \left[\pi_2^i(T^i) - \pi_3^i(T^i) \right] e^{-rT^i} - \frac{dK(T^i)}{dT^i} > 0,$$

recognizing that in this case $\pi_3^i(t)$ applies to firm i being the second mover with the next generation. Therefore, because the payoffs are increasing as firm i waits longer, there is never a second time when the next generation is launched. That is, either only one firm launches the next generation or the next generation is launched simultaneously by both firms.

Solving for the optimal launch time assuming the other firm has not yet launched is equivalent to maximizing the payoffs from being first to launch by choosing when to launch, $\max_{T^i} g_1(T^i, T^j)$. For each firm, the necessary first-order condition equating marginal revenue and marginal cost is

$$\left[\pi_0^i(T^i) - \pi_1^i(T^i) \right] e^{-rT^i} - \frac{dK(T^i)}{dT^i} = 0. \tag{3}$$

The second-order condition sufficient for (1) to define a maximum is

$$\left[\frac{d\pi_0^i(T^i)}{dT^i} - \frac{d\pi_1^i(T^i)}{dT^i} \right] e^{-rT^i} - r\left[\pi_0^i(T^i) - \pi_1^i(T^i) \right] e^{-rT^i} - \frac{d^2K(T^i)}{[dT^i]^2} < 0. \tag{4}$$

Using (2) and (3), we know that the last two terms in (4) together are negative. Because profit flows are sure to increase at the time of the next-generation launch, $(d\pi_1^i(T^i)/dT^i) - (d\pi_0^i(T^i)/dT^i)$ is positive. Thus, (4) is satisfied.

Using T to represent the time of the next-generation launch, we can define payoff functions for the first firm to launch the next generation as L (leader), for the second firm to launch the next generation as F (follower), and for simultaneous launch of the next generation by both firms as M. Those payoff functions are

$$L^i(T) = \int_0^T \pi_0^i(t)e^{-rt}\,dt + \int_T^\infty \pi_1^i(t)\,e^{-rt}\,dt - K(T),$$

$$F^i(T) = \int_0^T \pi_0^i(t)e^{-rt}\,dt + \int_T^\infty \pi_2^i(t)\,e^{-rt}\,dt, \text{ and}$$

$$M^i(T) = \int_0^T \pi_0^i(t)e^{-rt}\,dt + \int_T^\infty \pi_3^i(t)\,e^{-rt}\,dt - K(T).$$

For both firms, leading with the next generation yields higher profits than simultaneous launch of the next generation, $L^i(T) > M^i(T)$. Using Assumption 4(b), we know that following is also more profitable than simultaneous launch, $F^i(T) > M^i(T)$. Therefore, we can safely stop further analysis of simultaneous launch as neither firm would choose it in equilibrium. We note that, in general, a simultaneous launch is not an equilibrium in models of this type (Fudenberg and Tirole 1985, Reinganum 1981).

For there to be a single time when each firm is indifferent between launching and not launching—that is, for the leader and follower functions to intersect only once—we require that four conditions be satisfied. We can describe them intuitively as follows. At time zero, payoffs to leading must be less than those to following (i.e., waiting). Later, there must be a time when leading is more profitable than following. Because of the nature of decay in launch costs and because of discounting of profit flows, for next-generation launch times far into the future the payoffs to leading must converge with those of following. Finally, once a time is reached when payoffs to leading are greater than those to following, payoffs to leading at any subsequent time are greater than payoffs to following. We can express Conditions 1 through 4 mathematically as follows.

Condition 1: $L^i(0) - F^i(0) < 0$.

Condition 2: $\exists T$ such that $L^i(T) - F^i(T) > 0$.

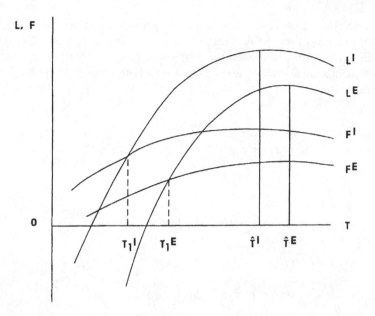

Figure 8.1. Leader and Follower: Functions for the Incumbent and the Entrant

Condition 3: $\lim \inf_{T \to \infty} L^i(T) = 0$.
Condition 4: $L^i(T) - F^i(T)$ is strictly quasi-concave.

In our model, Condition 1 is

$$\int_T^\infty \left[\pi_1^i(t) - \pi_2^i(t) \right] e^{-rt} \, dt - K(0) < 0.$$

Condition 1 for the incumbent is directly satisfied by Assumption 5. Use of Assumptions 1 and 5 shows that Condition 1 is also satisfied for the entrant. Condition 2 for the two firms is

$$\int_T^\infty \left[\pi_1^i(t) - \pi_2^i(t) \right] e^{-rt} \, dt - K(T) > 0.$$

Condition 2 for the entrant is directly satisfied by Assumption 6. Assumptions 1 and 6 are sufficient for Condition 2 to be satisfied for the incumbent.

Condition 3 is satisfied for both firms because the limits of integration over profit flows converge and the next-generation launch costs approach zero from Assumption 3.

Taking first and second derivatives of the function $L^i(T) - F^i(T)$, we can determine that Condition 4 is satisfied. Setting the first derivative to zero, we get

$$-\left[\pi_1^i(T) - \pi_2^i(T)\right] e^{-rT} - \frac{dK(T)}{dT} = 0 \tag{5}$$

and

$$-\left[\frac{d\pi_1^i(T)}{dT} - \frac{d\pi_2^i(T)}{dT}\right] + r\left[\pi_1^i(T) - \pi_2^i(T)\right] e^{-rT} - \frac{dK^2(T)}{[dT]^2} < 0. \tag{6}$$

Using (2) and (5), we know that the last two terms together in (6) are negative. From our discussion of (4), profit flows increase at the time of the next-generation launch so $d\pi_1^i(T)/dT$ is positive. $d\pi_2^i(T)/dT$ is nonpositive because a firm's current generation cannot be more profitable when the other firm launches the next generation.

We use T_I^i to denote the unique time when each firm's leader and follower functions intersect, that is, when the payoffs to leading are equal to those from following. The following lemma determines the ordering of T_1^I and T_1^E.

LEMMA 1 T_1^I occurs prior to T_1^E.

PROOF. T_1^i is defined by $L^i(T_1^i) = F^i(T_1^i)$. Using Assumption 1, we know that at the same T, $L^I(T) - F^I(T) > L^E(T) - F^E(T)$. Therefore, at T_1^E, $L^I(T_1^E) - F^I(T_1^E) > 0$. As a result, $T_1^I < T_1^E$.

The intuition is captured directly by Figure 8.1. Because the incumbent has a larger gain from launching the next generation versus being preempted than does the entrant (Assumption 1), the incumbent can launch (i.e., lead) with positive profits earlier than the entrant. Consider the case in which the entrant does not have a current-generation advantage. In a product market, for example, if the incumbent leads with the next-generation product, then it has a two-product monopoly. In contrast, if the entrant leads with the next generation, then it faces differentiated competition from the incumbent's current-generation product. Hence, the incumbent's leader function is suffi-ciently above the entrant's leader function that the time when payoffs to leading are equal to those from following is earlier for the incumbent. Using Lemma 1, we determine the equilibrium launch time of the next generation.

> THEOREM 1. *The unique perfect preemption equilibrium is when the incumbent launches the next generation at T_1^E and the entrant never launches.*
>
> PROOF. See Appendix.

Theorem 1 applies if $T_1^E \leq \hat{T}^I$, where $\hat{T}^I$ solves the first-order Condition (3) that represents the optimal time for the incumbent to launch in absence of competition. Otherwise, the incumbent launches at the same time as it would if the entrant were not present, T^I, the entrant never launches, and the equilibrium is not preemptive. We do not pursue the latter case because competition from the entrant plays no role in the incumbent's decision of when to launch.

Figure 8.1 also provides the intuition for Theorem 1. At any time beyond T_1^E, if the next-generation advantage has yet to be launched, then the entrant should immediately launch the next generation because leading is more profitable than following and a launch by the incumbent is imminent. At T_1^E, the entrant is indifferent between launching and not launching. However, at T_1^E the incumbent is better off leading than following, and can determine that the entrant's launch is imminent. Therefore, the incumbent launches the next generation precisely the instant before the entrant would unambiguously prefer to lead rather than follow. That result itself is not surprising because it is driven by our Assumptions 1 and 4, which give the incumbent the advantage and preclude a second launch of the next generation. What is surprising is the number of different models of competition, from various forms of Bertrand to Cournot that we discussed previously, under which those two assumptions hold. Moreover, we do not require additional assump-tions about the diffusion process within or between generations. Theorem 1 holds regardless of the rate of migration of customers to the offering that incorporates the next-generation advantage.

The result holds as long as launch costs do not favor the entrant suffi-ciently to reverse the ordering of times when each firm's payoffs to leading are equal to those from following. We state that point as a necessary condition in a corollary.

> COROLLARY 1. *A necessary condition for the entrant to launch the next genera-tion is that the entrant has lower launch costs than the incumbent.*

PROOF. For the entrant to launch first requires that at some T, $L^E(T) - F^E(T) > L^I(T) - F^I(T)$. From Assumption 1, that is possible only if $K^E(T) < K^I(T)$.

Cannibalizing at a Loss

Although the incumbent is the first and only firm to launch the next generation, it does not necessarily follow that the incumbent makes positive incremental profits with the next generation. Consider a calculation of the post-launch profit flows for the incumbent that isolates the marginal profit flow obtained from launching the next generation. Taking the incumbent's profit flow after launch less the pre-launch profit flow that would have occurred if the launch had not taken place, $\pi_{new}(t)$, we have

$$\pi_{new}(t) = \pi_1^I(t) - \pi_0^I(t). \tag{7}$$

At the equilibrium launch time for the next generation, T_1^E, the incumbent prefers to lead rather than follow, which means that

$$\int_{T_1^E}^{\infty} \left[\pi_{new}(t) + \pi_0^I(t) \right] e^{-rt} dt - K(T_1^E) > \int_{T_1^E}^{\infty} \pi_2^I(t) e^{-rt} dt > 0,$$

after substitution for $\pi_1^I(t)$ from (7). Reorganizing, we obtain the following inequalities:

$$\int_{T_1^E}^{\infty} \pi_0^I(t) e^{-rt} dt + \int_{T_1^E}^{\infty} \pi_{new}(t) e^{-rt} dt - K(T_1^E) > \int_{T_1^E}^{\infty} \pi_2^I(t) e^{-rt} dt > 0.$$

If the present value of profits from the current generation for the incumbent should there be no launch of the next generation is larger than the present value of profits from the current generation for the incumbent should the entrant have launched the next generation,

$$\int_{T_1^E}^{\infty} \pi_0^I(t) e^{-rt} dt > \int_{T_1^E}^{\infty} \pi_2^I(t) e^{-rt} dt,$$

then it is possible that

$$\int_{T_1^E}^{\infty} \pi_{new}(t) \, e^{-rt} \, dt - K(T_1^E) < 0.$$

(8)

In other words, the net present value of the marginal profits obtained by launching the next generation is negative. Assumption 1 is sufficient, but certainly not necessary over all t, for the condition prior to (8) to occur. We can prove a surprising theorem about when an incumbent will launch the next generation losing money at the margin.

THEOREM 2. *A necessary and sufficient condition for the incumbent to make negative profits at the margin from the next generation is that, at the time of launch, the present value of additional profit flows from the next generation for the incumbent is less than the present value of the difference in profit flows between leading and following with the next generation for the entrant.*

PROOF. Using the definition of the marginal profit flow from the next generation provided in (7) and substituting into (8) gives

$$\int_{T_1^E}^{\infty} \left[\pi_1^I(t) - \pi_0^I(t) \right] e^{-rt} \, dt - K(T_1^E) < 0.$$

But we know T_1^E is defined as the time when the payoffs to leading are equal to those of following for the entrant, $L^E(T_1^E) = F^E(T_1^E)$, which is

$$\int_{T_1^E}^{\infty} \left[\pi_1^E(t) - \pi_2^E(t) \right] e^{-rt} \, dt - K(T_1^E) = 0.$$

Combining and rearranging the preceding equations gives

$$\int_{T_1^E}^{\infty} \left[\pi_1^I(t) - \pi_0^I(t) - \pi_1^E(t) + \pi_2^E(t) \right] e^{-rt} \, dt < 0.$$

Therefore, we have the following relation between profits flows:

$$\pi_1^I(t) - \pi_0^I(t) < \pi_1^E(t) - \pi_2^E(t).$$

Theorem 2 is important because it does not depend on launch costs. Thus, it shows that the incumbent cannibalizing its current-generation advantage at a loss with the next generation, or *eating its own lunch,* depends on the nature of competition.

When the entrant does not have a current-generation advantage, the necessary and sufficient condition in the theorem is that, at the time of launch, the present value of profit flows for the incumbent from the current generation advantage (status quo) is greater than the present value of the difference between profit flows for the incumbent from leading with the next generation and profit flows for the entrant from leading with the next generation. In that case, cannibalization at a loss depends on the returns to an incumbent that has acquired both the current- and next-generation advantages versus the intensity of competition should the entrant be first to launch the next-generation advantage.

WELFARE AND LIMITATIONS

Welfare Results

General results from prior research in several disciplines suggest that if prices and diffusion patterns do not change, then customers are better off when they receive the benefits of the next-generation advantage earlier (Balcer and Lippman 1984, Gaimon 1989). If having a common provider across generations also increases customer welfare because of continuity in style, design, operation, and service, then the incumbent would carry an additional advantage across generations. Whether customers are actually better off depends on the extent to which the incumbent can derive economic rents from providing such continuity. Those economic rents are captured in the profit flows.

The social welfare equation is made up of a producer component as well as a customer component. On the producer side, launching early—the preemption result—dissipates profits simply as a result of higher launch costs because real launch costs fall over time. The costs of early launch are higher because related technology and expertise may not be sufficiently developed, and some basic research relating to the advantage may be incomplete. On the customer side, if we assume prices and diffusion patters are not altered, then customers are better off with an earlier launch unless the early launch causes some type of product failure that would not occur if the next generation were launched later.

Writing social welfare as a function of the launch time T, we have

$$W(T) = CS^i(T) + L^i(T),$$

where the present value of social welfare, $W(T)$, is the sum of the present value of customer surplus, $CS^i(T)$, and the leader's profits, $L^i(T)$. Customer surplus is decreasing with a later launch time, or larger T, and is used instead of consumer surplus as the beneficiaries of the next-generation advantage may be in an industrial rather than a retail market. Both of the latter terms have the superscript i because they depend on which firm launches the next-generation advantage. The socially optimal time for the next generation to be launched solves the first-order condition equating marginal social benefit with marginal cost,

$$\frac{dW(T^*)}{dT^*} = \frac{dCS^i(T^*)}{dT^*} + \left[\pi_0^i(T^*) - \pi_1^i(T^*)\right]e^{-rT^*} - \frac{dK(T^*)}{dT^*} = 0,$$

$$\tag{9}$$

where the firm that launches is the one that yields the greatest welfare at its optimal launch time. Thus, the social optimum specifies which firm launches and the time of that launch. Using (4), we know that the condition $d^2CS^i(T^*)/[dT^*]^2 < 0$ is sufficient for concavity. The last two terms in (9) are identical to those in the first-order condition for the firm's optimal launch time, (3). Because customer surplus is decreasing in T, the socially optimal launch time is earlier than the optimal launch time of either firm. That is, for the firm that launches in the social optimum, the socially optimal launch time is earlier than the time it would otherwise choose.

Reinganum (1989) suggests that because each firm ignores the effect of its actions on others, the industry is less profitable, as above, and that the social good may be reduced. Hence, an important question is whether the next generation is launched earlier than is socially optimal because of preemption in response to the intensity of competition. The following theorem provides a sufficient condition for the preemptive launch to occur earlier than is socially optimal. It requires that we account for the possibility that in some cases launch by the entrant is socially optimal and in other cases launch by the incumbent is socially optimal.

> THEOREM 3. *Case (i): If launch by the entrant is socially optimal, then a sufficient condition for the preemptive launch to occur earlier than is socially optimal is that, at the time of the preemptive launch, the difference in the present value of the entrant's profit flow between the status quo and being the follower with the next generation is greater than the marginal loss in customer surplus.*
>
> *Case (ii): If launch by the incumbent is socially optimal, then a sufficient condition for the preemptive launch to occur earlier than is socially optimal is that, at the time of the preemptive launch, the difference in the present value of the incumbent's profit flow between the status quo and being the follower with the next generation is greater than the marginal loss in customer surplus AND that the difference in the present value of the incumbent's profit flow between leading and following with the next generation is smaller than the marginal decline in launch costs.*

PROOF. The condition in case (i) is identical to the first condition in case (ii). That condition is

$$\left[\pi_0^i(T_1^E) - \pi_2^I(T_1^E)\right] e^{-rT_1^E} > -\frac{dCS^i(T_1^E)}{dT_1^E}.$$

Adding $[\pi_1^i(T_1^E) - \pi_0^i(T_1^E)]\, e^{-rT_1^E}$ to both sides gives

$$\left[\pi_1^i(T_1^E) - \pi_2^i(T_1^E)\right] e^{-rT_1^E} > -\frac{dCS^i(T_1^E)}{dT_1^E} + \left[\pi_1^i(T_1^E) - \pi_0^i(T_1^E)\right] e^{-rT_1^E}.$$

Multiplying by -1 and rearranging the last term on the right hand side yields

$$-\left[\pi_1^i(T_1^E) - \pi_2^i(T_1^E)\right] e^{-rT_1^E} > \frac{dCS^i(T_1^E)}{dT_1^E} + \left[\pi_0^i(T_1) - \pi_1^i(T_1^E)\right] e^{-rT_1^E}. \tag{10}$$

Now consider case (i). Let T^{LF} be the T defined by (5) for the entrant. Using the definition of T_1^E, together with the strict quasi-concavity of $L^E(T) - F^E(T)$, we know that $T_1^E < T^{LF}$. Again using the strict quasi-concavity of $L^E(T) - F^E(T)$

and the fact that (5) defines the extrema of $L^E(T) - F^E(T)$, we know that the following inequality must hold.

$$-\left[\pi_1^E(T_1^E) - \pi_2^E(T_1^E)\right]e^{-rT_1^E} > \frac{dK(T_1^E)}{dT_1^E}.$$

For case (ii) the second condition directly assumes that inequality for the incumbent. Combining it with (10), we get

$$\frac{dCS^i(T_1^E)}{dT_1^E} + \left[\pi_0^i(T_1^E) - \pi_1^i(T_1^E)\right]e^{-rT_1^E} - \frac{dK(T_1^E)}{dT_1^E} > 0.$$

From (9) and the concavity of the social welfare function, $T_1^E < T^*$.

Theorem 3 is important because it signifies a lose-lose outcome as a result of hypercompetition that results in a preemptive launch. That is, producers' profits are dissipated from competition to such an extent that the losses are larger than the gains customers receive from an earlier launch of the next-generation advantage. Consequently, society loses as well.

Thus, we find that customers are always better off with an earlier launch, meaning that the earlier launch is a wealth transfer from firms to customers. If the customers' gain is greater than the firms' loss from launching prematurely, then society is better off. At some point, however, the customers' gain is less than the firms' loss, and at that point society begins to lose. Although strictly outside our model, should we choose to define society as a country, then society could be better off even when customers' gain is less than firms' loss if the premature launch preempts a foreign entrant from launching the next-generation advantage, possibly preventing a loss of jobs and technological know-how.

Limitations

Aside from conditions that ensure an interior solution to the launch-timing game—neither firm launches immediately and a launch is made eventually—our results rely on two key assumptions, Assumptions 1 and 4. We believe those assumptions are representative of a large number of cases. Assumption 1 embodies the presence of a strong first-mover advantage with the next generation by strictly ordering the gains to preemption versus the losses from being preempted. It allows us to determine unambiguously which firm launches the next generation first. Assumption 4 captures the futility of following. It ensures that after the first launch of the next generation there will not be a following launch of the same generation, and helps us restrict the range of our analysis. Relaxing Assumption 4 is the focus of our future efforts.

As we discuss through the main steps of the analysis, Assumptions 1 and 4 are even less severe when the entrant does not have a current-generation advantage. In that case, Assumption 1 should be automatic: In a product-market scenario, the profit flow from a two-product monopoly is larger than the combined profit flows of two firms competing with differentiated products. Assumption 4 is also supported in that case. First, Assumption 4(a) directly relies on differences in profit flows at the time of the second next-generation launch. Second, in the absence of positive externalities, differentiation, or decreasing returns to scale, the result of Bertrant competition would preclude positive profits from the next generation. If the entrant were the follower, then at the time of the second next generation launch the entrant would have no externalities with which to work, and it would be in the incumbent's interest to see that none are gained by being willing to undercut the entrant temporarily until the entrant is forced to exit. If the incumbent were the follower, then the differentiated competition result from Judd (1985) would apply: Being second with the next generation would intensify competition for its current generation, so the incumbent may be better off not following with the next generation.

The profit flows, and our assumptions about relationships between them, are flexible enough to incorporate the effects of a diffusion process on market demand. Moreover, we made no assumptions about launch cost asymmetries between firms—neither firm has a launch cost advantage. We address that point in the corollary to Theorem 1: It is not possible for the entrant to launch the next generation first without a launch cost asymmetry in its favor.

DISCUSSION

The results of our model have clear implications for firms competing in intensely competitive markets. Individual advantages are not sustainable and market leadership may require the development of a series of temporary advantages. In product markets, for example, older products are continually being replaced by next-generation products that typically provide superior functionality. Although gaining a competitive advantage in a particular generation may be very profitable, continued investment must be made in the development and launch of future generations to protect the original advantage. Without subsequent launches of more advanced generations, a firm can expect to be leapfrogged by a competitor. Our results validate the "eat your own lunch before someone else does" strategy outlined by

Deutschman (1994). However, our results go further by implying that to protect the gains created by a competitive advantage, it may be necessary for the next generations to loose money at the margin. That is, a firm may incur incremental losses from the launch of the next-generation advantage to maintain its leading position in the market. In addition, our welfare results imply that preemption can cause a next-generation advantage to be launched earlier than is socially optimal. In other words, because society bears the cost of a premature introduction, social welfare may be reduced by hypercompetitive forces that lead to an early launch of the next-generation advantage. Therefore, not only can firms be forced to eat their own lunches, they can be forced to eat society's lunch as well.

The conditions under which our series of results is obtained are reasonably intuitive. For a given firm to employ a protection-through-preemption strategy requires that the firms be the one with the most to lose if it does not preempt, that the time value of money be accounted for, that launch costs fall at a decreasing rate over time, and that following by another firm is futile. In addition, for the incumbent to cannibalize at a loss requires that the present value of the incumbent's additional profit flows from the next-generation advantage be less than the difference in profit flows between leading and following for the entrant—essentially the incumbent is forced to launch to maintain its current leadership.

Thus, our results suggest that firms in hypercompetitive markets cannot afford the luxury of extending the life of a current advantage. The market dynamics are such that firms must become accustomed to repeatedly leap-frogging their own current advantages with next generations to maintain market dominance. Those dynamics serve to shift the distribution of profits within the life cycle toward the early stages, as in the case of personal computers where most of the profits from a given generation are made within months, and some times weeks, of launch (*Business Week* 1995b). Similarly, firms competing on their expertise in supply chain management find that the process of improvement can never stop as early advantages are competed away by rivals that employ similar or more advanced strategies (Henkoff 1994).

The managerial prescription implied by our model is straightforward: When there is competition to be first in a market, incumbents should strive to maintain leadership in the next generation even if they must cannibalize their current (market-leading) advantages. That prescription is consistent with Craig's (1996) observation that hypercompetition can play out in a series of hypercompetitive "rounds"—periods of intense competition on a particular dimension—similar to the setting we model. In the Japanese beer industry, Craig found that following an initial market share loss as a result of a competitor's preemptive strike, the Kirin brewery retained its market leading status by instituting a series of self-cannibalizing moves—moves that maintained rather than increased market share and profitability. Those findings, obtained from a detailed case study—a vastly different methodology than the one we employ—are consisted with our results in Theorems 1 and 2. Together, those theorems indicate that a preemptive launch of a next-generation advantage can be optimal, not necessarily resulting in increased performance, but rather protecting the firm's market position.

Despite the clarity of the prescription, several practical difficulties make implementation of a protection-through-preemption strategy difficult. One difficulty is the fact that the competition to be first to market leads to a premature market entry. That is, rather than waiting for the optimal launch time (when profits related to the current-generation advantage decline and launch costs fall), a firm is forced to launch early because of competition. The implications is that firms in rapidly evolving markets must be well organized to execute a preemptive strategy effectively. As noted in the Introduction, several leading companies appear to be instituting policies that enable them to carry out such a strategy.

A second impediment that firms face in implementing a strategy of protection-through-preemption is that the returns to the next generation may be significantly less than the return to the current generation. In fact, as outlined in Theorem 2, once the cannibalization of the current generation is taken into account, the next generation may lose money at the margin. That feature makes it increasingly difficult for next-generation development projects to survive an internal "business case" evaluation. For example, questions are being raised about the viability of microchip projects slated for production around the year 2000 because the escalating fixed costs of entry (R & D and wafer fab facility costs) will preclude a return given today's short life of product generations (*Business Week* 1994).

Third, a protection-through-preemption strategy may be sidelined by the management structure of the incumbent. For example, if the projects leading to two separate generations of advantages are managed by different people, the current-generation manager may demand that the next-generation launch be delayed so profits can accrue to the current generation advantage. That delay, which may occur at the business case stage rather than the launch stage, can result in the incumbent losing the race to launch. To counter such individually optimal but firm-suboptimal behavior, some companies such as Northern Telecom and Motorola Communications have taken steps to ensure that they are ready with the next generation on time.

Finally, Kim and Kogut (1996) show that firms having proprietary experience with a promising technology platform possess a strength that can be turned into a next-generation advantage. In a study of start-ups in the semiconductor industry, they found that firms founded on strong technology platforms were more likely to survive than those founded on weak platforms. A key to the success of surviving firms was the ability to grow by diversification into related subfields, developing next-generation technologies that replaced old ones. That process of survival and growth by going on to new advantages may explain the emergence and persistence of market-dominating firms—especially in technology-intensive industries. Indeed, several exemplars we use to illustrate our protection-through-preemption strategy (e.g., Intel and Motorola) have their origins in promising technology platforms.

The results of our model provide the foundation for future research in several areas. One area is the longer-run implications of a protection-through-preemption strategy for the entrant and the incumbent. First, if an incumbent following such a strategy leads in each generation, then the optimal strategy for the entrant is an open question. Second, although we illustrate that it may be optimal for the incumbent to launch a next generation that loses money at the margin, if that strategy is used repeatedly, then the rewards for achieving market-leading competitive advantage may diminish over time. The firm may be better off alternating as leader and follower in successive generations. Such a strategy would allow the firm to achieve a higher return on each generation it pursues by reducing cannibalization and lowering launch costs.

Another area is relaxation of the requirements imbedded in our Assumption 4 which, in essence, precludes a second launch of the next generation advantage. We have done some preliminary work showing that the results reported here continue to hold under less restrictive conditions where second launches of the next generation to occur—consistent with our argument that Assumption 4 is representative of many forms of price and quantity competition. Completely eliminating the restrictions associated with Assumption 4 is likely to change our results drastically—and may also be a fruitful avenue to pursue.

Yet another important area for future research is empirical validation of our model's results. Though many firms *seem* to be following a protection-through-preemption strategy (i.e., Intel in microprocessors and Hewlett Packard in its printer division), whether they are making their decisions as a result of that strategy or on some other basis is unclear. In-depth case analyses of a set of firms would be useful to clarify the relationship between their decision-making processes and our suggested strategy.

An alternative empirical approach would be to determine whether next-generation advantages have diminishing returns (when cannibalization is factored in) or are losing money at the margin. That issue has important implications for investment decisions in diversified firms because it may be in the best interest of the overall firm *not* to protect its advantage in some markets in favor of alternative investment opportunities. An investigation of the issue would require information about individual companies and their specific markets.

ACKNOWLEDGMENTS

The authors thank the reviewer and participants of the Conference on Innovation in new Product Development: Best Practice in Research and Modeling Applications at the Wharton School, University of Pennsylvania, the participants of the Marketing Science Conference in Sydney, Australia, and the guest editors of this special issue. Parts of the work were completed while the first author was visiting the University of British Columbia. support for the research was provided by the Natural Science and Engineering Research Council of Canada and the Social Science and Humanities Research Council of Canada.

Appendix

The proof of Theorem 1 makes use of the strategy spaces and payoff functions formalized in Section 4.B of Fudenberg and Tirole (1985: 392-393). Our notation is slightly modified as we employ superscripts to denote firms, and use T as a subscript in place of t as a superscript to the function G.

Strategy Spaces and Payoff Functions

DEFINITION 1. A simple strategy for firm i in the game starting at T is a pair of real-valued functions $(G^i, \alpha^i): [T, \infty) \times [T, \infty) \to [0, 1] \times [0, 1]$ satisfying

(a) G^i is nondecreasing and right-continuous.

(b) $\alpha^i > 0 \Rightarrow G^i(T) = 1$.

(c) α^i is right-differentiable.

(d) If $\alpha^i(T) = 0$ and $T = \inf(s \geq T \backslash \alpha^i(\cdot) > 0)$, then $\alpha^i(\cdot)$ has a positive right derivative at T.

Let the "first interval of atoms" be represented by

$$\tau^i(T) = \begin{cases} \infty & \text{if } \alpha^i(s) = 0 \; \forall s \geq T, \\ \inf(s \geq T \mid \alpha^i(\cdot) > 0) & \text{otherwise.} \end{cases}$$

$\tau(T) = \min(\tau^1(T), \tau^E(T))$. $\alpha^i(s) = \lim_{\epsilon \to 0}[G^i(s) - G^i(s - |\epsilon|)]$. Let $G^{i-}(T)$ be the left limit of $G^i(\cdot)$. at T. The game begins at $T \geq 0$ so set $G^{i-}(T) = 0$. Payoffs are

$$V^i(T, (G^I, \alpha^I), (G^E, \alpha^E)) = \left[\int_T^{\tau(T)^-} (L(s)(1 - G^j(s)) \, dG^i(s) \right.$$

$$+ F(s)(1 - G^i(s)) \, dG^j(s)) + \sum_{s < \tau(T)} a^i(s)a^j(s)M(s) \Bigg]$$

$$+ \left[\left(1 - G_T^{i-}(\tau(T))\right)\left(1 - G_T^{j-}(\tau(T))\right) \right.$$

$$\left. W^i\left(\tau(T), (G^I, \alpha^I), (G^E, \alpha^E) \right) \right],$$

where $W^i(\cdot)$ is defined as follows: If $\tau^j(T) > \tau^i(T)$, then

$$W^i(\tau(T), (G^I, \alpha^I), (G^E, \alpha^E))$$

$$= \left[\frac{G^i(\tau) - G^{i-}(\tau)}{1 - G^{i-}(\tau)} \right] [(1 - \alpha^i(\tau))F(\tau) + \alpha^i(\tau)M(\tau)]$$

$$+ \left[\frac{1 - G^i(\tau))}{1 - G^{i-}(\tau)} \right] L(\tau).$$

If $\tau^i(T) > \tau^j(T)$, then

$$W^i(\tau(T), (G^I, \alpha^I), (G^E, \alpha^E))$$

$$= \left[\frac{G^i(\tau) - G^{i-}(\tau)}{1 - G^{i-}(\tau)} \right] [(1 - \alpha^j)\tau))L(\tau) + \alpha^j(\tau)M(\tau)]$$

$$+ \left[\frac{1 - G^i(\tau)}{1 - G^{i-}(\tau)} \right] F(\tau).$$

Finally, if $\tau^I(T) = \tau^E(T)$, then

$$W^i(\tau(T), (G^I, \alpha^I), (G^E, \alpha^E)) = M(\tau) \text{ if } \alpha^i(\tau) = \alpha^j(\tau) = 1,$$

$$\frac{\alpha^i(\tau)(1 - \alpha^j(\tau))L(\tau) + \alpha^j(\tau)(1 - \alpha^i(\tau))F(\tau) + \alpha^i(\tau)\alpha^j(\tau)M(\tau)}{\alpha^i(\tau) + \alpha^j(\tau) - \alpha^i(\tau)\alpha^j(\tau)}$$

$$\text{if } 2 > \alpha^I(\tau) + \alpha^j(\tau) > 0,$$

$$\frac{\alpha^{i\prime}(\tau)L(\tau) + \alpha^{j\prime}(\tau)F(\tau)}{\alpha^{i\prime}(\tau) + \alpha^{j\prime}} \text{ if } \alpha^i(\tau) = \alpha^j(\tau) = 0.$$

DEFINITION 2. A pair of simple strategies (G^I, α^I) and (G^E, α^E) is a Nash equilibrium of the game starting at T (with neither firm having yet launched) if each firm's strategy maximizes its payoff, $V^i(T, \cdot, \cdot)$, with the other firm's strategy held fixed.

DEFINITION 3. A closed-loop strategy for firms is a collection of simple strategies $(G_T^i(\cdot),\ \alpha_T^i(\cdot))_{T \geq 0}$ for games starting at T satisfying the intertemporal consistency conditions:

(e) $G_T^i(T + v) = G_T^i(T + u) + (1 - G_T^i(T + u))G_{T+u}^i(T + v)$ for $T \leq u \leq v$.

(f) $\alpha_T^i(T + v) = \alpha_{T+u}^i + (T + v) = \alpha^i(T + v)$ for $T \leq u \leq v$.

DEFINITION 4. A pair of closed-loop strategies $\{(G_T^I(\cdot),\ \alpha_T^I(\cdot))\}_{T \geq 0}$ and $\{(G_T^E(\cdot),\ \alpha_T^E(\cdot))\}_{T \geq 0}$ is a perfect equilibrium if for every T the simple strategies $(G_T^I(\cdot),\ \alpha_T^I(\cdot))$ and $(G_T^E(\cdot),\ \alpha_T^E(\cdot))$ are a Nash equilibrium.

Let $\eta^i(T) = \inf\{s \geq T \mid G_s^i(s) > 0\}$. Note that if $\eta^i(0) < \tau^i(0)$, then $\eta^i(0)$ is the first time of an isolated jump. And let $\eta(0) = \min\{\eta^I(0), \eta^E(0)\}$.

PROOF OF THEOREM 1. $G_T^i(s)$ is the cumulative probability that firm i has launched by time s, in the game starting at T, given the other firm has not already launched. $\alpha^i(T)$ measures the intensity of G in the interval $[T, T + dT]$. Consider the following simple strategies for the two firms.

$$G_T^I(s) = \begin{cases} 0 & \text{if } s < T_1^E \\ 1 & \text{if } s \geq T_1^E \end{cases}$$

$$\alpha^I(s) = \begin{cases} 0 & \text{if } s < T_1^E \\ \dfrac{L^E(T) - F^E(T)}{L^E(T) - M^E(T)} & \text{if } s \geq T_1^E \end{cases}$$

$$G_T^E(s) = \begin{cases} 0 & \text{if } s \leq T_1^E \\ 1 & \text{if } s > T_1^E \end{cases}$$

$$\alpha^E(s) = \begin{cases} 0 & \text{if } s \leq T_1^E \\ \dfrac{L^1(T) - F^1(T)}{L^I(T) - M^I(T)} & \text{if } s > T_1^E \end{cases}$$

All games starting at T must be considered, $G_T^{i-}(T) = 0$. We examine strategies starting at T_1^E, that is, $T \in [T_1^E, \infty)$. Prior to T_1^E, waiting is a dominant strategy for both firms.

We begin by examining the incumbent's strategy and payoffs. Assume first that $T \in [T_1^E, \infty)$. From the entrant's equilibrium strategy $\alpha^E(T)$, $\tau = \tau^E(T) = T$. If $G_T^I(T) = 0$, then the resulting payoff is $F^I(T)$. If $G_T^I(T) = \lambda$, $0 < \lambda < 1$, then it must be that $\alpha^I(T) = 0$ and $\tau^I(T) > \tau^E(T)$. The resulting payoff is

$$\lambda[\alpha^E(T)M^I(T) + (1 - \alpha^E(T))L^I(T)] + (1 - \lambda)F^I(T) \tag{11}$$

$$= \lambda \left[\frac{(L^I(T) - M^I(T))(-L^I(T) + F^I(T))}{L^I(T) - M^I(T)} + L^I(T) \right] \tag{12}$$

$$+ (1 - \lambda) F^I(T) = F^I(T).$$

If $G_T^I(T) = 1$, then $\alpha^I(T) > 0$ and $\tau^I(T) = \tau^E(T)$. With $2 > \alpha^I(T) + \alpha^E(T) > 0$, the resulting payoff is

$$\frac{\alpha^I(T)(1 - \alpha^E(T))L^I(T) + \alpha^E(T)(1 - \alpha^I(T))F^I(T) + \alpha^I(T)\alpha^E(T)M^I(T)}{\alpha^I(T) + \alpha^E(T) - \alpha^I(T)\alpha^E(T)} \tag{13}$$

which, using (11) and (12), yields

$$\frac{\alpha^I(T)F^I(T) + \alpha^E(T)(1 - \alpha^I(T))F^I(T)}{\alpha^I(T) + \alpha^E(T) - \alpha^I(T)\alpha^E(T)} = F^I(T) . \tag{14}$$

Thus, the incumbent is indifferent between those strategies over $T \in (T_1^E, \infty)$.

Next, consider $T = T_1^E$. Again from the entrant's equilibrium strategy, $\alpha^E(T) = 0$ and $G_T^E(T) = 0$. If $G_T^I(T) = 0$, then $\alpha^I(T) = 0$. Thus, $\tau^I(T) \geq \tau^E(T) = \tau > T_1^E$, and $2 > \alpha^I(\tau) + \alpha^E(\tau) > 0$. The resulting payoff is calculated as in (13) and (14), and is therefore $F^I(\tau)$. If $G_T^I(T) = \lambda$, $0 < \lambda \leq 1$, then the situation is the same as when $G_T^I(T) = 0$, and the resulting payoff is equivalent, $F^I(\tau)$. If $G_T^I(T) = 1$, then $\alpha^I(T) > 0$, and therefore $\tau = T_1^E = \tau^I(T) < \tau^E(T)$. Because the remaining terms cancel, the resulting payoff is $L^I(\tau)$. Because $L^I(\tau) > F^I(\tau)$ when $\tau = T_1^E$, the incumbent prefers $G_T^I(T) = 1$.

Now we check the entrant's strategy and payoffs. Examine first $T \in (T_1^E, \infty)$. From the incumbent's equilibrium strategy, $\alpha^I(T) > 0$, thus, $\tau^I(T) = \tau(T) = T$. If $G_T^E(T) = 0$

then $\alpha^E(T) = 0$, and $\tau^E(T) > \tau^I(T)$. With the remaining terms dropping out, the resulting payoff is $F^E(T)$. If $G_T^E(T) = \lambda$, $0 < \lambda \leq 1$, then again $\alpha^E(T) = 0$, and $\tau^E(T) > \tau^I(T)$. The payoff is therefore

$$\lambda \left[\alpha^I(T)M^E(T) + (1 - \alpha^I(T))L^E(T) \right] + (1 - \lambda)F^E(T).$$

Analogous to (11) and (12), the result is $F^E(T)$. If $G_T^E(T) = 1$, then $\alpha^E(T) > 0$, $\tau^E(T) = \tau^I(T)$, and $2 > \alpha^I(T) + \alpha^E(T) > 0$. Similar to (13) and (14), the payoff is

$$\frac{\alpha^E(T)(1 - \alpha^I(T))L^E(T) + \alpha^I(T)(1 - \alpha^E(T))F^E(T) + \alpha^I(T)\alpha^E(T)M^E(T)}{\alpha^E(T) + \alpha^I(T) - \alpha^I(T)\alpha^E(T)} = F^E(T).$$

Consequently, the entrant is indifferent over those strategies for $T \in (T_1^E, \infty)$.

Consider $T = T_1^E$. From the incumbent's equilibrium strategy, $\alpha^I(T) > 0$, $G_T^I(T) = 1$, and $\tau = T_1^E$. If $G_T^E(T) = 0$, then $\alpha^E(T) = 0$, $\tau^E(T) > \tau^I(T)$. If $G_T^E(T) = \lambda$, $0 < \lambda \leq 1$, then again $\alpha^E(T) = 0$, and $\tau^E(T) > \tau^I(T)$. If $G_T^E(T) = 1$, then $\alpha^E(T) > 0$, $\tau^E(T) = \tau^I(T) = \tau$, and $2 > \alpha^I(\tau) + \alpha^E(\tau) > 0$. Each payoff is the same as when $T \in (T_1^E, \infty)$, $F_1^E(T)$. Hence, the entrant is also indifferent over those strategies.

Therefore, those simple strategies are a Nash equilibrium for every T, and are intertemporally consistent over T. As a result they are a perfect equilibrium.

We now show that there are no other perfect equilibria. Assume first $\tau(0) \leq \eta(0)$. Prior to T_1^I neither firm wants to launch because $F^i(T) > L^i(T)$, $M^i(T)$. Prior to T_1^E the entrant does not want to launch because $F^E(T) > L^E(T)$, $M^E(T)$. In fact, $F^i(T), L^i(T) > M^i(T)$ $\forall T$. For $T \in [T_1^I, T_1^E)$ the incumbent prefers to wait because $L^I(T + \in) > L^I(T)$ for small but positive $\in$. At any $T \in (T_1^E, \infty)$ each firm's best response is to launch at $\tau(T) + \in$ because $L^i(\tau(T) - \in) > F^{i}(T)$. Now consider $T = T_1^E$. The incumbent's dominant strategy is to launch because $L^I(T) > F^I(T)$. By definition of T_1^E, the entrant is indifferent between following and leading at that time. For both firms those payoffs exceed the payoff from simultaneous launch; therefore, the entrant is better off not launching at T_1^E.

Assume next that $\eta(0) < \tau(0)$. Prior to T_1^I waiting is optimal for both firms. For $T \in [T_1^I, T_1^E)$, $\eta(T) = \eta^I(T)$ because the entrant is still better off waiting. But $L^I(T)$ is increasing in this interval so launching at T is not optimal for the incumbent either. At $T = T_1^E$, if $\eta(T) = \eta^I(T)$, then the entrant can avoid a possible mistake (simultaneous launch) by waiting. For $T \in (T_1^E, \infty)$, if $\eta(T) = \eta^i(T)$, then firm j is better off launching with probability one at $T - \in$. Finally, at T_1^E the incumbent can avoid a positive probability of a mistake by launching with probability one.

REFERENCES

Aoki, R. (1991), "R & D Competition for Product Innovation: An Endless Race," *American Economic Review,* 81, 2, 252-256.

Balcer, Y. and S. A. Lippman (1984), "Technological Expectations and Adoption of Improved Technology," *Journal of Economic Theory,* 34, 292-318.

Business Week (1994), "Will We Keep Getting More Bits for the Buck?" July 4, 90-91.

―――― (1995a), "Intel: Far Beyond the Pentium," February 20, 88-90.

―――― (1995b), "The Man Who's Rebooting IBM's PC Business," July 24, 68-72.

Craig, T. (1996), "The Japanese Beer Wars: Initiating and Responding to Hypercompetition in New Product Development," *Organization Science,* 7, 3, 302-322.

D'Aveni, R. A. (1994), *Hypercompetition,* New York: Free Press.

Deutschman, A. (1994), "The Managing Wisdom of High-Tech Superstars," *Fortune,* October 17, 197-206.

Dixit, A. (1979), "A Model of Duopoly Suggesting a Theory of Entry Barriers," *Bell Journal of Economics,* 10, 1, 20-32.

―――― (1980), "The Role of Investment in Entry-Deterrence," *Economic Journal,* 90, March, 95-108.

Dolan, R. J. (1982), "Sealed Air Corporation," Cambridge, MA: Harvard Business School Case Services, No. 582-103.

Eaton, B. C. and R. G. Lipsey (1980), "Exit Barriers Are Entry Barriers: The Durability of Capital as a Barrier to Entry," *Bell Journal of Economics,* 11, 2, 721-729.

Fudenberg, D. and J. Tirole (1983), "Capital as a Commitment: Strategic Investment to Deter Mobility," *Journal of Economic Theory,* 31, 227-250.

―――― and ―――― (1985), "Preemption and Rent Equalization in the Adoption of New Technology," *Review of Economic Studies,* 52, June, 383-401.

―――― and ―――― (1986), *Dynamic Models of Oligopoly,* New York: Harwood Academic.

Gaimon, C. (1989), "Dynamic Game Results of the Acquisition of New Technology," *Operations Research,* 37, 3, 410-425.

Ghemawat, P. (1991), "Market Incumbency and Technological Inertia," *Marketing Science,* 10, 2, 161-171.

Golder, P. N. and G. J. Tellis (1993), "Pioneer Advantage: Marketing Logic or Marketing Legend?" *Journal of Marketing Research* 30, 158-170.

Henkoff, R. (1994), "Delivering the Goods," *Fortune,* November 28, 64-77.

House, C. H. and R. L. Price (1991), "The Return Map: Tracking Product Teams," *Harvard Business Review,* 69, January-February, 92-100.

Judd, K. (1985), "Credible Spatial Preemption," *Rand Journal of Economics,* 16, 1, 153-166.

Kalish, S. and G. L. Lilien (1986), "A Market Entry Timing Model for New Technologies," *Management Science,* 32, 2, 194-205.

Kamien, M. I. and N. L. Schwartz (1982), *Market Structure and Innovation,* Cambridge, MA: Cambridge University Press.

Katz, M. L. and C. Shapiro (1987), "R & D Rivalry and with Licensing or Imitation," *American Economic Review,* 75, 429-436.

Kerin, R. A., P. R. Varadarajan, and R. A. Peterson (1992), "First-Mover Advantage: A Synthesis, Conceptual Framework, and Research Propositions," *Journal of Marketing,* 56, October, 33-52.

Kim, D. J. and B. Kogut (1996), "Technological Platforms and Diversification," *Organization Science,* 7, 3, 283-301.

Lieberman, M. B. and D. B. Montgomery (1988), "First-Mover Advantages," *Strategic Management Journal,* 9 (Special Issue), 41-58.

Lilien, G. L. and E. Yoon (1990), "Timing of Competitive Market Entry," *Management Science,* 36, 5, 568-585.

Mamer, J. W. and K. F. McCardle (1987), "Uncertainty, Competition, and the Adoption of New Technology," *Management Science,* 33, 2, 161-177.

McCardle, K. F. (1985), "Information Acquisition and the Adoption of New Technology," *Management Science,* 31, 11, 1372-1389.

Mitchell, W. (1991), "Dual Clocks: Entry Order Influences on Incumbent and Newcomer Market Share and Survival when Specialized Assets Retain Their Value," *Strategic Management Journal,* 12, 85-100.

Norton, J. and F. M. Bass (1987), "A Diffusion Theory Model of Adoption and Substitution for Successive Generations of High-Technology Products," *Management Science,* 32, 9, 1069-1086.

Purohit, D. (1994), "What Should You Do When Your Competitors Send in the Clones?" *Marketing Science,* 13, 4, 329-411.

Reinganum, J. F. (1981), "On the Diffusion of New Technology: A Game Theoretic Approach," *Review of Economic Studies,* 153, 395-406.

——— (1983), "Uncertain Innovation and the Persistence of Monopoly," *American Economic Review,* 73, 4, 741-748.

——— (1985), "Innovation and Industry Evolution," *Quarterly Journal of Economics,* 100, February, 81-99.

——— (1989), "The Timing of Innovation: Research, Development and Diffusion," Chapter 14 in R. Schmalensee and R. D. Willig (Eds.), *Handbook of Industrial Organization,* 1, New York: Elsevier Science, 849-908.

Slutsker, G. (1994), "The Company that Likes to Obsolete Itself," *Forbes,* September 13, 139-144.

Spence, A. M. (1977), "Entry, Capacity, Investment and Oligopolistic Pricing," *Bell Journal of Economics,* 8, 2, 534-544.

——— (1979), "Investment Strategy and Growth in a New Market," *Bell Journal of Economics,* 10, 1, 1-19.

Telesis (1993), "Understanding New and Emerging Customer Values," 97, December, 15-21.

Tirole, J. (1988), *The Theory of Industrial Organization,* Cambridge: MIT Press.

Wilson, L. O. and J. A. Norton (1989), "Optimal Entry Timing for a Product Line Extension," *Marketing Science,* 8, 1, 1-17.

9

Vertical Integration and Rapid Response in the Fashion Apparel Industry

JAMES RICHARDSON

Fashion apparel is a highly competitive business where product life is short and differentiation advantages are built on brand image and product styling that can be quickly imitated. Over the past two decades, competition on price and quality has intensified as low cost global manufacturing became available to even small competitors. Recently, competition has shifted to the arena of timing and know-how where vertically integrated firms gained the lead in implementing a set of process innovations known as "quick response," designed to shorten the production cycle. Less integrated firms have begun to erode that advantage, but the integrated firms that have linked quick response into retailing continue to have superior capabilities. These firms demonstrate the elements of organization needed to link flexible and fast cycle manufacturing with rapid learning about demand and customer satisfaction.

(VERTICAL INTEGRATION;
QUICK RESPONSE;
HYPERCOMPETITION; FASHION APPAREL)

INTRODUCTION

In many industries the pace of competition has quickened and firms find it increasingly difficult to create and sustain competitive advantage. New foreign competitors, rapid technological change, and more aggressive competition are compelling firms to innovate more rapidly and denying them the opportunity to reap the rewards of sustained advantages. While such industries as personal computers and consumer electronics are prominent examples, the fashion apparel industry provides an interesting case of hypercompetitive behavior (D'Aveni 1994).

In hypercompetition, firms continually disrupt the status quo to create a series of temporary advantages (D'Aveni 1994). Fashion apparel makers are continually jockeying for position with new products and marketing efforts in an attempt to capture the imagination of the customer with styling and image. They create short-lived differentiation advantages that are easily and rapidly eroded through imitation and innovative new styles. The fashion apparel business is characterized by very short product life, fickle consumer preferences, numerous competitors, relatively easy entry and exit, and a myriad of manufacturing, marketing, and retailing alternatives. In such an environment, competitive advantage is difficult to create and nearly impossible to sustain.

Competition in the arena of price and quality has intensified over the last few decades. Low cost manufacturing in less developed countries initially gave an advantage to the larger fashion apparel firms that moved earlier and more aggressively. Today, the large number of sophisticated subcontractors in many developing countries has made low cost global manufacturing available to even small competitors.

Recently, a set of process innovations known as "quick response" (Hunter 1990, Hammond 1990, Blackburn 1991), has shifted the arena of competition to timing and know-how. Utilizing information technology, leading quick response competitors have developed new capabilities in rapid learning, communication, and coordination that have supplanted traditional core competencies in design and fashion sense. Rather than bet on a few new designs from the most savvy designers, they try out many, quickly imitate others, and continue to produce only what sells.

Vertically integrated fashion apparel firms have led the implementation of quick response, giving them an advantage. This study looks at how and why vertical integration has been used to advantage in this highly competitive and volatile environment. It also looks at the moves by less integrated competitors to implement quick response or otherwise erode their advantage.

Fashion apparel has also seen strong competition in the strongholds arena. In particular, vertical integration has been used to maneuver around distribution channel strongholds and penetrate brand strongholds. In a good example of the latter, The Gap used backward integration to transform itself from one of Levi's largest customers to one of its strongest competitors. In so doing, it dealt Levi's a serious blow (*Business Week*).

Here the focus is on competition in the arena of timing and know-how. Because fashion apparel makers have been operating in an intensely competitive environment for decades, they provide an excellent case for study. This study looks at how these firms have organized their activities to provide the flexibility and responsiveness needed for survival. In particular, it examines the organization of quick response. These process innovations overlay a production system involving a global chain of activities linked through a variety of contractual and ownership relations. The result is a rich environment for the study of organization (Uzzi 1995).

The chapter begins with a discussion of quick response and of the literature on organization and vertical integration in volatile environments. A strategic theory of organization based on agency theory provides deeper insight into the potential advantages and disadvantages of vertical integration. After a short description of the methodology, the empirical findings are presented. The conclusion relates the findings to the general question of organizing in volatile or hypercompetitive environments.

QUICK RESPONSE AND
VERTICAL INTEGRATION

Fashion Sense Versus Quick Response

Normal competitive behavior in fashion apparel involves introducing new product lines multiple times per year, typically in a seasonal cycle. But, creating new styles that will "catch on" is fraught with uncertainty. The risk is increased by the lengthy traditional product development and manufacturing process that requires committing most of the investment in inventory for a new product line well in advance of sales (Hunter 1990, Hammond 1990).

The traditional cycle of fashion apparel manufacturing revolves around the sales season for a line of clothing. The products are designed from several months to over a year ahead. Then most, if not all, of the expected season's production is done in advance. The retailer prefers to start the season with a shorter supply of a greater variety of products, then reorder based on sales. But because of the long lead times, manufacturers are committed to their production and prefer advance orders from retailers. The manufacturers' policies on initial orders, reorders, and returns vary, depending upon their capabilities and their relationship with the retailers.

The traditional approach to dealing with uncertainty has been to concentrate on designing and producing only products that sell, in other words, to accurately predict demand. Fashion sense and innovative designs are traditional core competencies. The set of process innovations known as quick response is aimed at shortening the manufacturing cycle and thereby reducing the initial production commitment, inventory levels, and the retailers initial purchasing commitment (Hunter 1990, Hammond 1990, Blackburn

1991). With these process changes, responsiveness can be used to effectively substitute for fashion sense and forecasting ability.

Simply stated, quick response is a strategy for linking retailing and manufacturing operations in order to provide the flexibility needed to quickly respond to shifting markets (Hammond 1990). The ideal quick response system would enable the manufacturer to adjust production in response to retail sales in order to deliver the styles and quantities needed to meet the demand revealed during the season. The benefits of quick response come from reduced inventory costs, fewer markdowns of overproduced items, and increased sales of popular items because of reduced stock outs. The objective is a more efficient, less risky, and more effective operation.

The quick response methods incorporate a number of technologies to increase processing speeds (Blackburn 1991, Hammond 1990, Hunter 1990, McPherson 1987). CAD/CAM (computer-aided design and manufacturing) equipment facilitate the design process as well as the transfer of designs to the manufacturer where programmable cutting and, to some extent, sewing machines are used. EDI (electronic data interchange) links enable electronic transfer of information between separate facilities and companies involved in the production process. Orders and POS (point of sale) data can be transmitted electronically from the retailer to the manufacturer.

In addition to the use of new information technologies, quick response depends on greater information sharing and closer working relationships throughout the supply chain (Hunter 1990, Hammond 1990). The apparel maker may participate in merchandising and assortment planning with the retailer. And the apparel maker may bring the fabric supplier and the retailer into the design process. The maximum benefits of quick response require close coordination between the marketing, sales, and purchasing activities of the retailer and the design, production, and distribution activities of the manufacturer.

Besides greater coordination, the logic of quick response calls for greater risk sharing along the supply chain. While the overall inventory risk in the entire chain is being reduced, the risk is also being distributed back up the chain (Hammond 1990). Each stage of the supply chain is looking to its suppliers to be more responsive to the shifting demands of the end market. Even with the shortest feasible production cycles, there will be some inventory risk. In order to be both efficient and responsive, each stage is looking to the previous one to help absorb the risk.

The concept of quick response is not unique to fashion apparel. Firms in a wide range of consumer products, from autos to health and beauty aids, are attempting to shorten production cycles and provide more rapid response to changing markets (Blackburn 1991, Davidow and Malone 1992). The ability to produce variety and make rapid product changes efficiently has become a competitive challenge in many industries. This has been facilitated by such able and aggressive quick response retailers as Wal-Mart (Stalk et al. 1992). Certain characteristics of a quick response organization in fashion apparel, such as investments in information technology, shortened production cycles, increased coordination, and reduced inventory, are common to all quick response systems. Other characteristics, in particular control over retailing, seem to be especially suited to fashion apparel.

Vertical Integration and Responsiveness

Vertical integration is not generally considered to be a superior form of organizing in volatile environments. But certain industry conditions, such as those found in fashion apparel, may make vertical integration advantageous for implementing rapid response to changing market demands.

As pointed out by D'Aveni (1994), there have been numerous ideas put forward recently on the subject of organizing in volatile competitive environments. Among these are outsourcing, strategic alliances, network organizations, and virtual corporations (Davidow and Malone 1992). Common to all of these concepts of organization is limited commitment and flexibility to adapt to changing circumstances. The consensus seems to be that firms in volatile competitive environments should focus on their core competence (Prahalad and Hamel 1990) and look for ways to apply it in more or less temporary arrangements with other firms (Quinn 1992). Extensive vertical integration would seem to be contrary to such advice. Vertical integration is thought to create and inflexible commitment to assets and capabilities at risk of losing their value as circumstances change (Teece 1992).

The subject of vertical integration has been extensively studied by economists and management scholars. But with regard to the question of vertical integration within volatile environments, Harrigan's (1983) study is probably unmatched. Harrigan concludes that extensive vertical integration is probably a liability in industries with volatile structure. Vertical integration can limit flexibility and reduce information about both input markets and product markets as the firm becomes more insulated. When inputs are readily available from competing suppliers and knowledgeable, capable, firms exist downstream to sell one's products, companies in volatile environments are advised not to vertically integrate, especially if they have some bargaining power. D'Aveni and Ilinitch (1992), found some empirical support for the notion that extensive vertical integration in a volatile environment increases risk.

On the other hand, there are some potential benefits from vertical integration, even in volatile environments. Harrigan (1983) and Porter (1980) note that forward integration can provide product differentiation advantages that are difficult to imitate as well as superior marketing intelligence. An indicator of the potential benefits from integration is the degree of value added at that stage. For fashion apparel, the retail environment appears to be a significant factor in product differentiation. Store appearance and atmosphere, merchandise mix, service, and local marketing efforts are all significant elements of the fashion apparel business.

Volberda (1996) points out the need to match organizational flexibility to the demands of the environment. He develops a classification of types of organizational flexibility—operational, structural, and strategic—and suggests conditions under which each type is needed. Vertical integration may provide fashion apparel firms with superior operational flexibility to achieve quick response. At the same time, it may constrain structural or strategic flexibility.

Finally, D'Aveni (1994) stresses the importance of providing superior customer satisfaction by creating new customer needs and predicting changes in needs before they happen. Whether creating new needs or predicting changes, it is essential that the organization be able to learn and respond quickly. In order to learn, the organization must identify mistakes, determine what explains the mistakes, and take corrective action (Ackoff 1993). Vertical integration may speed up the learning process with regard to customer satisfaction, enabling the firm to identify mistakes more quickly. Perhaps most important, integration may provide the necessary control to take corrective action rapidly.

The above findings and conclusions are suggestive, but a deeper understanding is possible using a strategic theory of organization that is grounded in agency theory. Agency theory provides a framework that aids in understanding the costs and benefits of vertical integration. Here, somewhat heretically, agency models (Jensen and Meckling 1976), transaction cost theory (Williamson 1988), and Principal-Agent models (Grossman and Hart 1986) are all included under agency theory. The central hypothesis of agency theory is that, in a competitive environment, firms will organize the value chain of activities in their industry in the most efficient manner. That is, they will either organize successive activities within one firm or use exchanges between separate firms depending on which approach minimizes agency and other transaction costs.

A firm is vertically integrated when it owns assets (Grossman and Hart 1986), organizes activities (Riordan 1990), or controls activities (Reve 1990) in successive stages of the value chain. Agency theory predicts that when exchanges are characterized by uncertainty over inputs, infrequent exchange, and the need for transaction specific investments, it may be more efficient to vertically integrate, that is, bring two successive activities within the firm (Williamson 1988, Grossman and Hart 1986, Riordan 1990). The basic tradeoff is between the improved information but reduced performance incentives that result from integration (Riordan 1990).

Reve (1990) has extended the agency theory of organization beyond efficiency into the realm of strategic management, making it more useful for understanding the use of vertical integration in volatile environments. In Reve's model, as in agency theory, the hierarchy of the firm is seen as a coordinating mechanism for managing exchanges with suppliers and buyers. Alternative coordinating mechanisms include various forms of alliances or bilateral vertical agreements as well as market exchanges. Reve posits that a firm should focus on a strategic core—a set of assets and capabilities that are highly specific and necessary to attain the firm's strategic goals. Management of these core assets and capabilities requires the full range of coordinating mechanisms that are available within the firm. Complementary assets and skills of medium specificity can be managed with bilateral vertical agreements. Bringing an activity within the firm, i.e., full vertical integration, is necessary only when the assets and capabilities are very highly specific.

Reve (1990) treats vertical integration as matter of degree, a concept adopted here. There are a range of vertical forms of organization, with full vertical integration through ownership at one end, and arms-length market exchanges or no integration at the other. Various forms of bilateral vertical agreements or alliances constitute vertical integration to some degree. The concept of degree of vertical integration is consistent with Williamson's (1988) notion of a spectrum of quasi-integrated forms of organization. The degree of integration is reflected in the arrangements for both ownership and control of assets in the successive activities.

Reve (1990) argues that, from a strategic perspective, the central issue in the use of vertical integration is control rather than ownership. Not that ownership is not a strategic issue. Ownership certainly affects risk and incentives important to strategy. The point is that the firm needs sufficient control over the assets and capabilities in the value chain to efficiently coordinate its activities and achieve its goals. Ownership is one way to achieve sufficient control. But the benefits of vertical integration that are afforded by greater control can often be more efficiently obtained through vertical agreements than through ownership (Reve 1990). The downside of full vertical integration (ownership) cited by Reve echoes those given above: "Full vertical integration ties up capital resources and creates considerable management problems as the firms gets involved in successive stages of production or distribution where it has very little experience."

The challenge for the firm is to find a combination of activities and coordinating mechanisms that pay off, given the dynamics of the industry (Reve 1990). When faced with a volatile competitive environment, the case for focusing on the strategic core and using markets or bilateral vertical agreements rather than full vertical integration would seem to be even more compelling. Full vertical integration would create additional risks in a volatile environment. The firm would be committed to investments in assets and capabilities that could lose their value when technology and markets change. In contrast, vertical agreements allow the firm greater flexibility to adjust capacity, change product and process technologies, or switch distribution channels at lower cost by withdrawing from alliances and forming new ones. At the same time, separate firms have greater incentive to innovate and adapt to changing circumstances than the integrated firm, as suggested by agency theory.

Summarizing the above arguments, it is the higher cost and lower incentive to change in response to market or technology changes that give the vertically integrated firm its reputation for sluggishness. Generally speaking, full vertical integration is seen as an inferior form or organizing the value chain in a volatile competitive environment. A corollary would seem to be, the greater the volatility, the lower the degree of integration that is desirable.

The key to understanding the use of vertical integration to achieve superior responsiveness in fashion apparel lies in the nature of the volatility within fashion apparel and in the strategic core needed to achieve rapid response. The nature of the volatility in fashion apparel makes vertical integration a less risky prospect. And the need for control to introduce the new technologies and coordinating mechanisms necessary for rapid response makes vertical integration a more attractive form of organization.

The volatility in fashion apparel is almost entirely in the end market. Assets and capabilities along the value chain are at low risk of obsolescence. Even though innovative new product introductions and demand changes can be rapid and somewhat unpredictable, new product introduction is routine in fashion apparel. All firms introduce new products on a regular seasonal basis. Moreover, the product and manufacturing technologies are fairly stable. New products involve mainly styling or fabric changes that do not usually require new technology. Hence, investments in design and manufacturing assets are not subject to great risk of obsolescence and could usually be redeployed or divested. Nor are long term alliances at great risk of becoming burdensome because of technical obsolescence. Perhaps the greatest need for flexibility in manufacturing is in terms of capacity. At the downstream end, the retail stores are also assets at fairly low risk of obsolescence that could be redeployed or divested. The brand is probably the asset at greatest risk of obsolescence and most in need of careful management as products and markets change. But the brand investment is at similar risk for all fashion apparel makers, regardless of degree of integration.

Given the relatively low risk of obsolescence of assets and capabilities, the major drawbacks to vertical integration in fashion apparel are the potential for management difficulties and reduced performance incentives. As noted above, vertical integration brings activities of greater variety and geographic extent into the firm, necessitating more extensive expertise. And, as pointed out by agency theory, it can also dull incentives for performance and innovation at each stage relative to having separate firms involved. However, these management drawbacks may be outweighted by the need to define a more extensive strategic core in order to achieve rapid response capability.

In order to implement quick response capability, fashion apparel makers needed to introduce a much higher degree of coordination along the entire value chain as described above. This required investment in new information technology at each stage as well as more integrated planning and decision making. The information technology investments could be substantial (Hammond 1990) and were seen initially as relationship specific by many firms. Further, although quick response has the potential to lower the inventory in the entire value chain, new arrangements for risk sharing were needed. Given these management challenges, it is reasonable to conceive of the strategic core as an extensive portion of the value chain, especially in the early stages of development of quick response. As the technology of quick response matures, it is likely to be manageable by less integrated forms of organization (Reve 1990). A key point stressed by Harrigan (1983) is that the advantages from vertical integration depend on the firm and the industry conditions, and thus can change over time.

ORGANIZATION AND RESPONSIVENESS IN FASHION APPAREL

Methodology and Data

In order to find how fashion apparel makers organize for quick response, three types of firms in two different market segments were studied. The three organizational types—independent, interdependent, and integrated—are defined in the next section. In the moderately priced casual fashion segment are firms like The Limited and Benetton, who are integrated from manufacturing into retailing, as well as design firms, like Liz Claiborne and Carol Little, that subcontract manufacturing and sell primarily through department stores and independent specialty retailers. Some of these latter firms have interdependent organizations while others are independents. Several of the

TABLE 9.1 Sample

	Independent	Interdependent	Integrated
Casual Fashion	2	2	3
Surfwear	5	2	

top competitors of all three types were looked at. The other segment studied is surfwear. These are smaller design firms that also typically subcontract manufacturing. The largest ones sell to department stores and a few have developed certain interdependent characteristics, but most are independents who sell to a very fragmented group of small independent specialty retailers. Most of the top firms in the surfwear segment, Quiksilver, Gotcha, Ocean Pacific, and so on were looked at. Table 9.1 summarizes the sample.

Most of the information was collected through a questionnaire and follow-up telephone interview with a manager in each firm responsible for manufacturing/purchasing. After initial telephone contact, a questionnaire was faxed and followed up with the telephone interview. Published information such as articles in the business trade press, business cases, and annual reports were quite useful for the top firms in the casual fashion segment, but the smaller firms and the surfwear firms are mostly privately held and not much published information is available.

The sample is designed to characterize how each type of apparel maker typically organizes and manages the supply chain. Operational and some financial performance data were collected for comparisons, but the sample sizes are not sufficient for statistical confidence. That was not the intent. The integrated firms are the clear and acknowledged leaders in quick response. The others were sampled to find out how leading but less integrated firms are responding to the challenge. Confidence that these are relatively effective organizations rests on the fact that these companies have been successful competitors for many years. And although quick response is a relatively recent innovation for some of the smaller firms, the larger ones have been refining their organizations for some time.

Organizational Types

For the purposes of this study, a fashion apparel maker is a firm that arranges for the design and production of clothing that it then sells, wholesale or retail. Pure subcontractors are excluded. The apparel manufacturing process consists of three basic steps: design, cutting, and sewing. Many

TABLE 9.2 Organization and Performance Characteristics

	Independent	Interdependent	Integrated
Organization			
Design	All in-house	Most to all in-house	Some to most in-house
Manufacturing			
Ownership	None	None	20 to 100%
Percentage offshore	50% (5 to 60)	80% (75 to 85)	75%[1]
Coordination	Domestically, some early season adjustments	Some late ordering and early season adjustments,	Open ordering adjustments, and cancellation
Initial production	85% (25 to 100)	100%	30%[2]
Lead time			
Domestic	5 weeks (3 to 8)	7 weeks (6 to 8)	5 weeks (4 to 8)
Offshore	3 mos. (2 to 4)	3 mos. (2 to 3)	4 weeks (3 to 6)
Retailing			
Ownership	None	None to < 1%	< 1% to 100%
Coordination	Typically very little	POS or other sales info. from key accounts, guidance and training on merchandising consult on designs	POS info, control or strong influence over merchandising and store operation
Initial purchase	75% (35 to 100)	80% (80 to 85)	30%[2]
Performance			
Product intros/year	4 lines	4 to 6 lines	2 lines plus continuous
Inventory turns	6 (4 to 8)	6 (4 to 7)	8 (6 to 9)
Markdowns	10% (4 to 25)	7% (5 to 10)	Not available

1. Numbers for The Limited. Benetton does nearly all production domestically in Italy.
2. Numbers for The Limited. Benetton initially produces around 80% and its retail stores initially purchase 80 to 100%.

apparel makers specialize. A firm may do only design, subcontracting the cutting and sewing, possibly to different sources in different locations. Because sewing remains by far the most labor intensive operation, that step may be done in a low-labor-cost country. Once the clothing is manufactured, the apparel maker usually manages distribution. But here again, firms specialize. Some do their own retailing, some distribute to other retailers, and some sell to distributors.

The findings are organized around the classification of firms by organizational type, i.e., independent, interdependent, and integrated. For each classification, the typical organizational characteristics and operational performance (as summarized in Table 9.2) are described in more detail. In concept, quick response should enable the apparel maker to make one or more of four possible production changes in mid-season—reduce volume, increase volume, drop a product, or add a product. In practice, only the integrated firms can do all four.

The three organizational types should be considered as categories along the spectrum from pure arms-length exchange to full vertical integration through ownership (Reve 1990, Williamson 1988). Each fashion apparel maker may have a variety of relationships with upstream and downstream firms, some arms-length, some quasi-integrated, and some fully integrated (i.e., involving ownership). The classification of an apparel maker as independent, interdependent, or integrated is based on the preponderance of its relations with manufacturing and retailing activities as described below.

1. *Independents.* An independent apparel maker deals with manufacturing subcontractors and retailers mainly in arms-length relationships. Contractural terms are usually according to industry standards and there is little or no coordination of activities.

Five of the surfwear makers and two of the casual fashion makers are classified as independents. These are smaller firms, with annual revenues from $10M to $100M. They do all or nearly all of their own designs and they subcontract all manufacturing. Lower-cost offshore manufacturing is utilized, but most of their production is done domestically. With offshore subcontractors, the independents must usually commit to an entire season's production in advance. Production lead times of 90 days make reorders during a season infeasible. Terms are typically based on letters of credit and there is little flexibility.

In order to shorten production cycles and gain some flexibility, independents have utilized domestic manufacturing, usually located near the company office. Even so, the four- to six-week response time enables only one or possibly two reorders in a three month season. Manufacturing close by does enable the independent apparel makers to monitor production and to some extent adjust it upward or downward just prior to and at the beginning of the sales season.

The independents make a tradeoff between the lower cost of offshore production and the quicker response and flexibility of domestic production. Stable items in their line can be made offshore at lower cost, but more fashionable, unpredictable, items may have higher overall profitability when done domestically.

Independents sell to department stores and specialty retailers who carry a variety of brand names. The independents create their designs and show samples to retailers who commit to purchases prior to the season. Independents with strong brands can get retailers to commit earlier, before the production period, and for a larger amount of the expected season's sales. Even so, independents absorb much of the risk. Several have commitments for less than half of their expected sales. One strategy used to deal with the risk is to produce only on firm retailer commitments, accepting the stockouts and forgoing the opportunity of reorders. But most produce and carry inventory to meet about 25% of expected orders during the season. A few retailers can provide sales information and sales representatives may provide reports about sales activity. Some independents use this information to adjust production early in the season. But most commit to the product line and volume before the season. A product can be dropped very early in the season, but products are not added.

2. *Interdependents.* Interdependent apparel makers have closer relationships with subcontractors and retailers. Ordering and production schedules with their network of subcontractors are more flexible (Uzzi 1995). Retailers provide sales information to the apparel maker and may coordinate their merchandising and marketing activities as well.

Like the independents, these firms are typically design focused. All or nearly all design is done in-house while manufacturing is subcontracted. These firms are mostly larger than the independents, with revenues ranging from $50M up to $2.2B for Liz Claiborne in 1992. They do a larger share of their production offshore than the independents. Because they are larger firms and have had longer relationships with subcontractors, they usually get better terms than the independents, but they have similar long production lead times offshore. Because they do more production offshore, they do not have the capability to adjust production much once the season begins. Like the independents, they commit to most of their production up front. They may carry inventory to meet expected reorders from retailers during the season. But, as with the independents, one strategy used is to produce only what is initially ordered by the retailers, forgoing the opportunity to take reorders. As mentioned above, a strong brand can get the retailers to commit earlier and for an entire season's order.

The interdependents differ from the independents in their relationship with retailers as well. They receive comprehensive sales information from key retailers, possibly to adjust production at the early part of the season, but also to feed into the design process for the next year. They consult with key customers during the design process, taking suggestions and ideas. The interdependent apparel makers also actively participate in the retailers' merchandising and marketing activities. This may take the form of visits from representatives and published materials on store layout, pricing, and so on. Or it may go as far as the apparel maker managing a department within the retailer's store.

The balance of the risk sharing between the apparel maker and the retailer is quite similar for the independent and interdependent firms. The degree of risk borne by the retailer depends more on the strength of the brand than the extent of coordination of activities with the apparel maker.

3. *Integrated Apparel Makers.* Integrated apparel makers also have close relationships with, if not ownership of, manufacturers, but they are distinguished by their ownership and control over retailing. For this group of well-known firms, published information is available. Benetton, The Limited, and Giordano, a relatively new Hong Kong firm were studied. Questionnaire and interview data were obtained from two of the three.

Perhaps the most difficult distinction to draw is between the interdependent and the integrated firms. None of these firms is fully integrated through 100% ownership of all manufacturing and retailing operations. The difference between the integrated and the interdependent firms is one of degree. Evidence for classification as integrated includes some ownership of both manufacturing and retailing operations (partial or tapered integration), ownership share or joint ventures in these activities, and a high degree of exclusivity in relationships with both subcontractors and retailers. All of these characteristics point to a greater degree of control over manufacturing and retailing than can be exercised by the interdependent firms.

A brief description of the organization and operation of an integrated apparel maker, The Limited, Inc. (Adams and Griffin 1989, Austin 1991), serves to illustrate the notion of integration and the operation of a quick response system. The Limited began as a retailer in the 1960s and has integrated backward into manufacturing. A quote from the founder and chairman, Leslie Wexner, summarizes the strategy behind The Limited's structure: "The future will belong to those retailers who can respond to the changing needs of their customers . . . and do it fast!" The Limited's marketing, distribution, and production are centrally managed as follows:

Retailing. The Limited's 780 retail stores throughout the U.S. are company owned and tightly controlled. Every other week, store layout is redone and all the stores follow; no deviations are allowed. Each week, store managers receive a plan that dictates pricing, presentation, and merchandise mix. POS data from all the stores enable the company to track sales, order replacements, and drop items from the product line rapidly.

Manufacturing and Distribution. The Limited subcontracts manufacturing to low labor cost regions worldwide. It has ownership interests in some manufacturing facilities and long standing relationships with many more. Through its subsidiaries, it owns steamships that transport fabric to the manufacturers, airplanes that transport apparel to New York, and trucks that bring it to the central distribution point in Ohio. Company owned trucks make two shipments per week to the stores.

Design. The Limited uses both in-house designers and supplier's designs. New designs (sometimes copies of others' fashions) are computerized and electronically transmitted to manufacturers. The target is a 1,000 hour turnaround time between design conception and delivery of the product to the stores. They have been able to make copies and have them on store shelves before the original design is produced for sale.

Overall Performance. In 1990, The Limited boasted that it had the highest sales per square foot in its segment and inventory turns of 10 per year compared to an industry average of 3.

The integrated fashion apparel makers also subcontract manufacturing, but the degree of integration into manufacturing varies across the three firms. Giordano largely owns its manufacturing in Hong Kong and the PRC, The Limited combines its own manufacturing with a large share of subcontracting, and Benetton is highly integrated, at least in certain stages. Despite moves to deintegrate manufacturing during the 1980s, Benetton remains relatively highly integrated according to the definition used here. Benetton has shifted most of its labor-intensive operations to subcontractors. But these subcontractors were spun off from Benetton or created by it and work exclusively for Benetton. The Benetton company or members of the Benetton family own interests in many of the key suppliers. Benetton has retained the most capital intensive and technically sophisticated part of manufacturing, the dyeing, in-house. Benetton purchases all the raw materials and exercises complete control over manufacturing as it plans production and coordinates the movement of materials and products between various subcontractors and Benetton's facilities during the manufacturing process.

As to location, The Limited does nearly all of its manufacturing offshore, Giordano is mixed between domestic (Hong Kong) and other Asian locations, while Benetton is mainly domestic (Italy). The integrated firms have developed quite flexible and responsive relationships with their suppliers, whether offshore or domestic. The Limited reports that it gets faster production offshore than it can get domestically (in the U.S.), though it may take air freight to achieve the desired turnaround time. There remains a tradeoff between cost and response time, but achieving better response from lower cost offshore manufacturers than competitors can get domestically (in the U.S.) gives The Limited a certain advantage.

The major distinction of the integrated apparel makers is the degree of control they exercise over retailing. Whether through ownership, or in the case of Benetton, a strong franchise-like license agreement, the integrated firms effectively control their retailing. The three firms studied all have their own branded specialty retail stores that carry their products exclusively. The Limited and Giordano own the stores (though Giordano has begun to franchise in the PRC), Benetton owns only a small percentage of their stores, but deals with the rest through a licensing arrangement that gives them substantial control. At all of the integrated firms, the look of the stores, merchandising, and pricing are centrally managed. Surprisingly little discretion is left to the store manager/owner. All of the integrated firms centrally monitor retail sales closely, e.g., daily, using POS data, in order to make production and distribution decisions. Benetton's retailers are involved in ordering products for their stores, but they are guided by regional reps and have limited discretion. The Limited and Giordano simply deliver what they determine is needed.

It is interesting to note that Benetton was considered a pioneer in organizing for quick response in fashion apparel (Signorelli and Heskett 1984). Today, firms such as The Limited, The Gap, and Giordano have surpassed Benetton in a number of ways. While Benetton receives POS data from a few select retailers, the others have all of their stores on line. Benetton, like The Limited, has two seasonal collections each year. But unlike The Limited or Giordano, Benetton offers their stores only minimal opportunity to adjust orders during the season. And unlike The Limited, The Gap, or Giordano, Benetton does not regularly introduce new products in mid-season. Although Benetton boasts by far the most global retailing, The Limited and The Gap are more capable of executing quick response across a global supply chain. Benetton's largely Italian production still relies on retailers who commit up front to most or all of their purchases for a season.

In terms of sheer speed, Giordano may be the current leader. Originally a Hong Kong retailer that has now entered Korea, Taiwan, and the PRC, Giordano can execute quick response with links to manufacturers in Hong Kong and nearby Guangdong Province in the PRC. Conceived in 1987,

Giordano's quick response process and other innovations brought it extraordinary success through 1992. By 1993, imitators and other similarly capable firms had begun to give them some competition.

As to relevant industry conditions, it should be noted that the use of small specialty stores by The Limited and other integrated apparel makers has benefited from the emergence of the shopping mall. With many small retailers in one location (often alongside major department stores) the department store no longer has a variety advantage.

Globalization of fashion has also facilitated the approach of the integrated apparel makers. Their centrally managed, highly standardized, approach to retailing works well in a market with broadly homogeneous tastes. If adaptation to local demand conditions were more important, the potential drawback of forward integration would be greater.

The most forward integrated firms, The Limited and Giordano, seem to have most effectively minimized the risk in the supply chain. Interdependent and even independent firms who receive frequent and comprehensive sales information from their retailers and who have gained some flexibility from shorter production cycles have reduced their inventory risks. But there remains a large element of uncertainty over the retailers' purchasing among competing brands. The firms with stronger brands can and do shift the risk to the retailer. Even Benetton largely shifts the inventory risk to its retailers. Only the most forward integrated firms have used quick response to lower the risk all the way through to the retailer.

Perhaps more significant, the integrated firms have begun to move away from the seasonal product line concept. A season may begin with a new line, but products are dropped and new ones are added as needed. The Limited has only two seasons for which a new line is introduced, Fall/Winter and Spring/Summer. There is greater use of new products during the season, making it more of a continuous process.

Vertical Integration, Flexibility, and Competition

Most apparel makers have benefited from quicker response in manufacturing and distribution, but only the integrated firms have been able to make full use of this capability for competitive maneuvering. Most independent and interdependent firms are now more efficient. They have lower inventory and fewer markdowns, which has reduced their risk. But within fashion apparel, it seems that only the most forward integrated firms have been able to manage the close coordination needed to bring quick response into the retail environment. Extending quick response into the retail environment is the most difficult challenge but probably the most beneficial (Hunter 1990).

Through greater control of the retail operation, the integrated apparel makers can better manage the creation of short term advantages. The most forward integrated firms can quickly change their product offerings, both to respond to changing fashion trends and to create new ones. In mid-season, they can introduce new products, change the merchandise mix, and adjust pricing. Moreover, they can take these actions with knowledge of sales activity at many stores as well as knowledge of production. For example, say a new product experiences sales several times greater than predicted within the first week. It may take three to six weeks to increase production and deliveries by that amount. In the meantime, the integrated firm can increase the price to reduce the likelihood of stocking out and get maximum benefit. These actions are significantly more difficult to coordinate for an interdependent and nearly impossible for the independent firm.

In terms of Volberda's (1996) types of organizational flexibility, the integrated fashion apparel makers have achieved a higher degree of operational flexibility than their less integrated competitors. Though product innovations and demand changes are rapid and somewhat unpredictable, introducing new products and responding to changing demands are routine maneuvering in fashion apparel. New styles and designs do not usually require new types of inputs or process technologies. The integrated firms simply have the operational flexibility afforded by greater operational control to adjust production and outmaneuver their competitors in the retail market.

Despite the superior maneuvering capability of the most forward integrated firms, it is arguable whether it affords them much advantage. Independents and interdependents introduce four or more product lines each year. Even though they cannot adjust production much or introduce new products in mid-season, the more able ones can and do use sales information to adjust offerings in the next season. Since it takes even the integrated firms 3 to 6 weeks to make significant changes, the lag suffered by the others is only a matter of weeks. But that may be enough to make a rewarding difference. To illustrate the possible benefits, consider a (hypothetical) gold mining analogy. Suppose gold mining is done under very short term (say 90 day) leases to mine and there are two types of gold mining firms. One type uses the best scientific methods, folk wisdom, and intuition to deploy its workforce, locate gold and mine it, and it is very successful—it almost always finds gold. The other type is also scientific in its approach, but a little less careful about where it looks. Instead, it focuses on rapid redeployment of its resources to the mines it discovers with the largest veins. Which firm will be more successful? It depends upon the predictability of the size of the veins. In fashion apparel, the size of the veins may be somewhat predictable, but the less responsive firms may also be leaving a lot of gold in the ground.

Advantageous or not, it is clear that quick response has quickened the pace of competition in fashion apparel.

DISCUSSION

The question initially asked was how and why certain fashion apparel makers have used vertical integration to their advantage in this volatile and highly competitive environment. The simple answer is that it gives them superior capability to respond quickly to competitors and to disrupt the status quo. More specifically, these firms have used vertical integration to escalate competition within the arena of timing and know-how. And in so doing, they have been able to achieve superior customer satisfaction. By linking design and production closely to retailing through integration, they are better able to manage flexible production to meet demand volatility. The operational flexibility of the integrated firms matches the flexibility required by their competitive environment (Volberda 1996). Integration of manufacturing and retailing provides the controllability that is needed to achieve the overall operational flexibility of quick response.

These integrated fashion apparel makers have managed to avoid one of the cited drawbacks to forward integration—that the firm cuts itself off from the efficiencies and innovations of a competitive buyer market. The notion is that knowledgeable and capable independent retailers will be able to adjust quickly to market conditions and provide the apparel maker with superior market information. Harrigan's (1983) example of the integrated men's suit maker that foists off unappealing products to its retail stores is instructive. But, as the integrated firms have demonstrated, these drawbacks are more a result of management than ownership. These firms have used forward integration to obtain superior market knowledge, respond better to customers, and reduce the risk of new product introductions.

The quick response advantages of the integrated firms are under attack. New, similarly structured firms, have and will continue to emerge. The large discount merchandisers, like Wal-Mart and K-Mart, and their suppliers are now the real pros at quick response (at least in terms of rapid stock replenishment), and they have been moving up the fashion scale. They may never become direct competitors with the fashion apparel makers who compete on image and style, but the discount merchandisers and their suppliers are quick imitators with low costs. The threat they pose helps to drive the pace of competition. Finally, the interdependent firms may form more integrated relationships with their retailers and implement quick response. For example, Vanity Fair, a capable quick-response supplier to Wal-Mart, is now successfully implementing it with department stores.

What lesson can be drawn from the successful use of vertical integration in fashion apparel? Is full integration between manufacturing and retailing through ownership a superior form of organization in markets where demand is volatile and shifts with quickly changing fashion and product features? Probably not, in general. Rather, the lesson seems to be that close coordination, rapid information exchange, and risk sharing between manufacturing and retailing are essential for responsiveness and timely innovation in fast changing markets. The extent and degree of integration needed to achieve these capabilities will depend on the industry and the firm.

On the manufacturing side, two of the three integrated firms have found it advantageous not to fully backward integrate. They have defined their strategic core more narrowly around the production planning and distribution functions. Vertical alliances, along with some partial and some tapered integration, appear to provide sufficient control over manufacturing.

In a related study, Uzzi (1995) has found that network embeddedness affects the survival of apparel subcontractors in New York City. The concept of embeddedness is related to the notion of integration. Indeed the measure used for embeddedness is based on the concentration or degree of exclusiveness in exchanges. Uzzi found that subcontractors are more likely to survive when they are highly embedded in a network that has mixed modes of relations, some embedded, some arms-length. Either too little or too much embeddedness in the overall network increased the subcontractor's probability of failure. While these results are not directly about responsiveness, flexibility and adaptability are cited by Uzzi as desirable network characteristics that should enhance survival. Uzzi's results suggest the notion of an appropriate degree of integration on the manufacturing side, at least from the subcontractor's perspective. Mixed mode would characterize the manufacturing side of The Limited, while Benetton's manufacturing network seems to be highly embedded.

On the retail side, a high degree of vertical integration gave these fashion apparel firms a clear advantage in implementing quick response. As in many industries, cooperative relationships along the value chain were not the norm in fashion apparel, and this has proven to be a barrier to implementing quick response (Hunter 1990, Hammond 1990). But the degree of vertical integration between manufacturing and retailing that is needed to achieve these organizational capabilities remains a question.

Bilateral vertical agreements appear to provide adequate coordination mechanisms for the quick stock replenishment capability that Wal-Mart and K-Mart have achieved. These firms and their (large) suppliers have managed to invest in the necessary information technology and achieve the close coordination and rapid information exchange required to lower inventory and rapidly restock products.

However, the required flexibility and the risks in fashion apparel are different from those in discount retailing. The fashion apparel retailer must join with the manufacturer in continually experimenting with new designs and styles. The required information exchange is richer than simple POS data. Moreover, the retailer must make substantial commitments to marketing and merchandising the manufacturer's products. Altogether, the degree of coordination, information exchange, and risk sharing needed to achieve quick response in fashion apparel is greater than needed for the commodity-like products handled by discount retailers.

It is certainly conceivable that a closely integrated vertical alliance could provide fashion apparel makers with sufficient control over retailing to implement quick response. For example, Benetton might develop a more flexible, responsive operation with greater risk sharing in its relationship with its retailers. Indeed, interdependent fashion apparel firms are moving in this direction with their relationships with retailers. The possible advantages of such alliances over ownership include lower capital commitments, simpler decentralized management, and improved incentives for performance, similar to franchising. These considerations no doubt influenced Benetton's method of organizing their retailing. On the other hand, The Limited has a simpler task controlling the retail environment and has developed a more effective quick response organization. The balance of the tradeoffs is not obvious and will no doubt change as the technology of quick response matures.

Despite the distinctive characteristics of this industry, the success of vertical integration in fashion apparel may provide some general insight into organizing for competitive maneuvering based on operational flexibility. New flexible and fast cycle manufacturing technologies in many industries are enabling firms to produce variety and customized products on a large scale. Effective use of these manufacturing capabilities requires another set of capabilities—rapid learning about demand and customer satisfaction. Some degree of vertical integration seems advantageous to achieve the required coordination, information exchange, and risk sharing between manufacturing and retailing. Few industries are as fashion sensitive or have such short product lives as fashion apparel. Hence few will require the same extent or degree of vertical integration to achieve the necessary control. But the integrated fashion apparel makers have demonstrated the elements of organization needed to link the two sets of capabilities into a rapid response system.

REFERENCES

Ackoff, R. L. (1993), "Foreword" in *Internal Markets,* W. E. Halal et al. (Eds.), New York: John Wiley.

Adams, S. and A. Griffin (1989), "Liz Claiborne, Inc.," Univ. of North Texas & Texas Woman's Univ.

—— and —— (1989), "The Limited, Inc.," Denton: Univ. of North Texas & Texas Woman's Univ.

Arpan, J. S., J. de la Torre, and B. Toyne (1982), *The US Apparel Industry: International Challenge, Domestic Response,* Business Publishing Division, Atlanta: Georgia State Univ.

Austin, M. J. (1991), "The Limited, Inc.—1991," Murfreesboro: Middle Tennessee State University.

Blackburn, J. D. (1991), "The Quick Response Movement in the Apparel Industry: A Case Study in Time-Compressing Supply Chains," in *Time-Based Competition,* J. D. Blackburn (Ed.), Homewood, IL: Business One/Irwin.

D'Aveni, R. A. (1994), *Hypercompetition: Managing the Dynamics of Strategic Maneuvering,* New York: Free Press.

—— and A. Y. Ilinitch (1992), "Complex Patterns of Vertical Integration in the Forest Products Industry: Systematic and Bankruptcy Risks," *The Academy of Management Journal,* 35, 3, 596-625.

Davidow, W. H. and M. S. Malone (1992), *The Virtual Corporation,* New York: HarperCollins.

Grossman, S. J. and O. D. Hart (1986), "The Costs and Benefits of Ownership: A Theory of Vertical and Lateral Integration," *Journal of Political Economy,* 94, 691-719.

Hammond, J. H. (1990), "Quick Response in the Apparel Industry," Cambridge, MA: Harvard Business School Case 9-690-038.

Harrigan, K. R. (1983), *Strategies for Vertical Integration,* Lexington, MA: Lexington Books.

Hunter, N. A. (1990), *Quick Response in Apparel Manufacturing,* Manchester, NH: Textile Institute.

Jarillo, J. C. and J. I. Martinez (1988), "Benetton S.p.A.," Cambridge, MA: Harvard Business School Case 9-389-074.

Jensen, M. C. and W. H. Meckling (1976), "The Theory of the Firm: Managerial Behavior, Agency Costs, and Ownership Structure," *Journal of Financial Economics,* 3, 305-360.

Ketelhoehn, W. (1990a), "Building the Benetton System," European Case Clearing House 390-042-1, Babson College, Wellesley, MA.

—— (1990b), "The Fashion Success Story of the 1980s: Benetton SpA," European Case Clearing House 390-043-1.

McPherson, E. M. (1987), *Apparel Manufacturing Management Systems: A Computer-Oriented Approach,* Park Ridge, NJ: Noyes.

Mitchell, R. (1992), "Inside the Gap," *Business Week,* March 9.

Porter, M. E. (1980), *Competitive Strategy,* New York: Free Press.

Prahalad, C. K. and G. Hamel (1990), "The Core Competence of the Corporation," *Harvard Business Review,* 68, 3, p. 79.

Quinn, J. B. (1992), *Intelligent Enterprise,* New York: Free Press.

Reve, T. (1990), "The Firm as a Nexus of Internal and External Contracts," in M. Aoki, B. Gustafson, and O. E. Williamson (Eds.), *The Firm as a Nexus of Treaties,* Thousand Oaks, CA: Sage.

Riordan, M. H. (1990), "What is Vertical Integration?" in M. Aoki, B. Gustafson, and O. E. Williamson (Eds.), *The Firm as a Nexus of Treaties,* Thousand Oaks, CA: Sage.

Signorelli, S. and J. L. Heskett (1984), "Benetton (A)," Cambridge, MA: Harvard Business School Case 9-685-014.

———— and ———— (1985), "Benetton (B)," Cambridge, MA: Harvard Business School Case 9-685-020.

Stalk, G., P. Evans, and L. Shulman (1992), "Competing on Capabilities: The New Rules of Corporate Strategy," *Harvard Business Review,* 70, 2, p. 57.

Teece, D. J. (1992), "Competition, Cooperation, and Innovation: Organizational Arrangements for Regimes of Rapid Technological Progress," *Journal of Economic Behavior and Organization,* 18, 1, 1-25.

Uzzi, B. (1995), "Through the Looking Glass: The Functional and Malfunctional Effects of Embeddedness on Economic Action in New York's Apparel Industry," unpublished manuscript, Evanston, IL: J. L. Kellogg Graduate School of Management, Northwestern University.

Volberda, H. W. (1996), "Toward the Flexible Form: How to Remain Vital in Hypercompetitive Environments," *Organization Science,* 7, 4, 359-374.

Williamson, O. E. (1988), "The Logic of Economic Organization," *Journal of Law, Economics, and Organization,* 4, Spring.

10

Hypercompetition in a
Multimarket Environment:
The Role of Strategic Similarity
and Multimarket Contact
in Competitive De-Escalation

JAVIER GIMENO
CAROLYN Y. WOO

The effect of intra-industry heterogeneity on hypercompetitive escalation and de-escalation in a multimarket environment is examined. The authors study two critical dimensions of intra-industry heterogeneity: strategic similarity, which captures similarity in competitive orientation, and multimarket contact, which captures the degree of overlap between rivals in the multiple markets of the industry. Theory predicts that both variables influence the intensity of rivalry and competitive disruption.

The predictions in the literature about the effect of strategic similarity on the intensity of rivalry are mixed. While strategic group theory proposes that strategic similarity may lead to lower rivalry, other theories (focusing on product differentiation, the resource-based view of the firm, and hypercompetitive escalation) predict that strategic similarity may actually increase rivalry. Those diametrically opposed propositions are captured as alternative hypotheses of the effect of strategic similarity. With respect to the effect of multimarket contact on the intensity of rivalry, the existing literature on multiple point competition predicts that multimarket contact should decrease rivalry, since it provides credible threats which discourage competitive escalation.

The chapter performs an empirical analysis of these hypotheses with data on over 3,000 city-pair markets of the U.S. airline industry. The chapter focuses on the effects of changes in strategic similarity and multimarket contact in a city-pair market on the prices charged by airlines in that market. Other important factors which influence prices, such as service attributes, market characteristics, cost positions, market structure and firm-specific advantages, are rigorously controlled. The methodology used for the empirical analysis, a panel data regression with fixed-effect intercepts, also serves to control for other sources of stable differences across airlines and city-markets.

The results show that strategic similarity moderately increases the intensity of rivalry, whereas multimarket contact strongly decreases it. Interestingly, the findings suggest that the effect of strategic similarity on intensity of rivalry may be biased if the effect of multimarket contact is not explicitly accounted for. This is due to the fact that strategic similarity may capture some of the strong de-escalation effect of multimarket contact when this variable is not controlled. This finding explains and challenges prior literature which found that strategic similarity reduces rivalry.

The findings have important theoretical implications. For strategic group theory, they suggest two distinct dimensions of strategic heterogeneity (strategic similarity, multimarket contact), which *should not* be aggregated because they have opposite effects on the intensity of rivalry. These two dimensions should be separately considered to produce more rigorous analysis of rivalry within and between strategic groups. For hypercompetition theory, the findings indicate that hypercompetition in the cost-quality arena and stronghold invasion arena may lead in the future to greater competitive restraint. If hypercompetition in the cost-quality arena leads to greater differentiation in the market positions of firms, this could de-escalate competition. In addition, if hypercompetition in the stronghold invasion arena leads firms to obtain a broader multimarket overlap with their rivals, this condition could also provide the basis for deterrence and hypercompetitive de-escalation.

(HYPERCOMPETITION; STRATEGIC SIMILARITY;
MULTIMARKET CONTACT; STRATEGIC GROUPS;
MULTIPLE POINT COMPETITION; RIVALRY)

The problem of competitive adaptation and response to new and heterogeneous rivals is at the heart of hypercompetition (D'Aveni 1994). When heterogeneous firms engage in competitive interaction, their heterogeneity affects the intensity of their rivalry in several ways. Firms tend to imitate and leapfrog each other in their positioning within their markets (hypercompetition in the cost-quality arena), in building their resource base (timing and know-how arena), in the competitive creation and destruction of dominant positions in product or geographic markets (stronghold creation/invasion arena), and in the use of attacks and counterattacks based on size and financial advantages (deep pocket use/neutralization arena). We examine the competitive disruption effect of two critical dimensions of interfirm differences: differences in the markets served by the firms (captured by the multimarket contact construct), and differences in the competitive orientation within those markets (captured by the strategic similarity construct).

As D'Aveni (1994) argues, the degree of intra-industry heterogeneity among competing firms (and potential entrants) may be an important force for hypercompetitive disruption and an obstacle to the tacit de-escalation that potentially could end it. Rivals with different skill bases, competitive orientations, and home market strongholds are likely to use their idiosyncratic differences to their own advantage, possibly leading to hypercompetitive escalation in the four competitive arenas (D'Aveni 1994, p. 221). Moreover, intra-industry heterogeneity may prevent tacit de-escalation among competitors by reducing firms' ability to tacitly coordinate a de-escalation move (Newman 1978, D'Aveni 1994, p. 225). Therefore, it is important to analyze the effect of intra-industry heterogeneity (i.e., heterogeneity among competing firms in terms of strategies, resource bases, home markets, etc.) on the onset of hypercompetition (through competitive escalation) and, possibly, on its ending (through competitive de-escalation).

Our study expands the literature by examining the effects of multiple dimensions of intra-industry heterogeneity on the intensity of rivalry experienced by firms within the context of an industry composed of multiple markets. Although multiple markets or niches within an industry are the norm rather than the exception (Abell 1980, Carroll 1985), little empirical work has explicitly considered the implications of multimarket environments within the context of an industry (Barnett 1993, Baum and Singh 1994, Smith and Wilson 1995). The consideration of a multimarket environment adds complexity and realism to the analysis of intra-industry heterogeneity. We define a multimarket environment as a group of distinct markets (i.e., markets for products or services that are not strong demand substitutes) that are strongly related on the supply side by the use of similar technologies and capabilities. Examples of multimarket environments include the chemical, pharmaceutical, airline, and electronics industries, among others. The concept can also be applied to the study of competition in industries with geographically defined markets, such as regional competition in the U.S. brewing industry (Carroll and Swaminathan 1992) or triad competition in international markets (Ohmae 1985).

Hypercompetition in a multimarket environment has special characteristics due to the multiplicity of markets present. Multimarket environments allow great firm diversity and strategic heterogeneity. Firms can differ
in their product-market scope in terms of breadth (narrow vs. broad scope)
as well as the specific markets targeted. Hence, the heterogeneous firms in
a multimarket environment vary in the degree to which their scope overlaps
with that of specific competitors, a construct known as multimarket contact
(Edwards 1955) or market commonality (Chen 1996). Multimarket overlap
presents opportunities for multiple point competition, "a situation when
firms compete against each other simultaneously in several markets"
(Karnani and Wernerfelt 1985, p. 87). Multimarket contact has a direct
relationship with D'Aveni's fourth arena of hypercompetitive interaction,
stronghold invasion. Firms with substantial multimarket contact hold positions
in each other's markets, and therefore have the ability to retaliate not only
in the markets where a competitive action occurs, but also in markets that
are more salient to the competitor. In contrast, firms with little multimarket
contact maintain a substantial portion of their markets out of the reach of their
rivals. Multimarket competition theory (Edwards 1955, Porter 1981, Karnani
and Wernerfelt 1985, Bernheim and Whinston 1990, Witteloostuijn and
Wegberg 1992) predicts that the lack of stronghold overlap may induce firms
with little multimarket contact to be bolder in their competitive actions. We used
that theory to develop predictions about the effects of multimarket contact.

In addition to multimarket contact, firms may differ in their competitive
orientation to the markets they serve (Caves and Porter 1977, Porter 1980).
For instance, different firms may position themselves at different points of
the cost/quality space, using unique resources and capabilities to serve the
market. Such lack of strategic similarity also has bearing on the intensity of
rivalry, because it influences how directly firms compete in the markets they
serve. Although D'Aveni (1994) recognizes that hypercompetition in the
cost/quality arena can occur both between firms with similar positioning and
between firms with different positioning, a large body of theoretical work,
particularly in the strategic group literature (Caves and Porter 1977, Peteraf
1993b) and the resource-based literature (Rumelt 1984, Barney 1991, Peteraf
1993a) provides conflicting predictions about the intensity of rivalry of firms
with similar or different strategic positions. We build on those conflicting
theories to illuminate the effect of hypercompetition in intra-market
positioning.

We investigate the *simultaneous* effect of the two dimensions of strategic
heterogeneity (multimarket contact and strategic similarity) on the intensity
of rivalry between U.S. airlines in the city-pair markets they serve. Our
multidimensional model enables us to make distinctions between different
dimensions of competitor heterogeneity and their effects on rivalry. For

instance, our work suggests a distinction between the "breadth" and the "intensity" of rivalry between two firms. In fact, theory suggests that broad rivals (rivals with multimarket contact) are not necessarily the most intense rivals. Our work also suggests a distinction between broad and similar rivals. Firms that compete in many markets may have very different competitive orientations in serving those markets. Moreover, firms that use similar competitive orientations in serving their markets may not actually compete with one another in any market. Our results suggest that the two dimensions of heterogeneity have diametrically opposed effects on the intensity of rivalry between airlines in their markets.

In the following section we develop the theoretical arguments for the effects of strategic similarity and multimarket contact on competitive de-escalation in multimarket environments, and suggest hypotheses obtained from the literature. We then specify our model and test the hypotheses with data from a large sample describing the position of 48 airlines in more than 3000 city-pair markets of the U.S. airline industry. Finally, we report the results, discuss the implications for hypercompetition theory, and suggest directions for future research.

INTRA-INDUSTRY HETEROGENEITY AND COMPETITIVE INTENSITY

Since its inception, the field of strategic management has paid close attention to the causes and consequences of intra-industry heterogeneity (Hatten and Schendel 1977, Rumelt 1984, Barney 1991, Peteraf 1993a). A dominant stream of work examining the effect of intra-industry hetero-geneity on competitive intensity has been strategic group research, particu-larly the studies following the Harvard tradition of such research (Hunt 1972; Porter 1976, 1979; Caves and Porter 1977; Newman 1978; Cool and Dierickx 1993; Peteraf 1993b), which has addressed the effect of strategic similarity on the intensity of rivalry by comparing the intensity of rivalry *within* and *between* groups (Peteraf 1993b).

The operationalizations of strategic similarity have c₁   .luded some measure of product-market scope similarity, commonly in terms of scope breadth (Hatten and Schendel 1977, Cool and Schendel 1987, Feigenbaum and Thomas 1990). Although that definition of strategic similarity can closely overlap the construct of multimarket contact in some situations (e.g., large multimarket generalist firms are likely to have a high degree of multimarket contact), the multimarket contact construct captures a dimen-sion that is not totally captured by current operationalizations of strategic similarity in strategic group research: the fact that firms compete in the *same* markets.

Nowhere in the literature does that distinction appear more clearly than in the work of Hatten and Hatten (1987, p. 333), who have argued that strategic groups should be formed by firms pursuing similar strategies, irrespectively of whether or not they actively compete against each other. Two firms that are strategically similar in their narrow product-market scope (e.g., two regional brewers in the U.S. brewing industry or two feeder airlines in different hubs) may in fact have no multimarket contact at all. In other words, in a multimarket environment, strategic similarity between two firms (as defined by current strategic group theorists) does not imply that they are broad rivals, or even that they compete at all.

Following Hatten and Hatten's (1987) definition, we can distinguish conceptually between two dimensions of interfirm similarity: *strategic similarity*, defined as similarity in the general pattern of resource deployments and competitive orientations independent of the specific markets served by the firm, and *multimarket contact*, which captures the homogeneity in terms of the specific markets served by the firms. Those two dimensions may in some cases be correlated in some industry contexts, but it is possible to find industry contexts in which their correlation is low enough to allow the empirical estimation of their idiosyncratic effects on the intensity of rivalry. The expected effects of those variables on the intensity of rivalry are discussed next.

Strategic Similarity

A leading theoretical view of the relationship between strategic similarity and intensity of rivalry is derived from the Harvard approach to strategic groups (Hunt 1972, Porter 1976, Caves and Porter 1977, Newman 1978), strongly influenced by the industrial organization economics paradigm. In that stream of research, strategic distance (the inverse of strategic similarity) is seen as an impediment to interfirm tacit coordination. When interfirm tacit coordination fails because of lack of strategic similarity, strong rivalry ensues that eventually drives down firm performance. Porter (1979, p. 218) defines strategic distance as "the degree to which strategies in different groups differ in terms of the key strategic decisions variables, such as advertising, cost structure, R & D, organization of production, etc. The greater this distance, other things being equal, the more difficult tacit coordination becomes and the more vigorous is rivalry likely to be in the industry." The logic is developed more extensively by Newman (1973, 1978), who argues that when firms differ in their strategies, such differences may lead to lack of goal congruence, which would reduce their ability to tacitly collude. That argument has become known as the Caves-Porter hypothesis (Peteraf 1993b).

Despite the centrality of the relationship between strategic similarity and rivalry (Cool and Dierickx 1993) for strategic group theory, only one test of the relationship has been reported in the literature. In a study of the pricing patterns of airlines in monopoly markets, Peteraf (1993b) found significant differences between monopolists facing a similar potential entrant (higher prices) and those facing a dissimilar potential entrant (lower prices). Although this finding is in agreement with the proposition that similar firms compete less intensely, the test lacks generalizability in terms of the competitive market structures considered (only monopoly markets).

The hypothesis that strategic similarity leads to reduced rivalry has been subject to significant caveats and challenges. Porter (1976, p. 86) warned that strategic similarity per se does not have a determinate effect on rivalry, because increased strategic similarity is often associated with increased market interdependence (the product offerings of the firms are closer substitutes). Hence, although similar firms may be able to coordinate their actions better in avoiding intense rivalry, their lack of differentiation also means that, if coordination were absent, their rivalry could be substantially more intense than that between differentiated firms. Such reasoning agrees with the predictions of IO models of product differentiation (Hotelling 1929, Beath and Katsoulakos 1991), which suggest that a critical advantage of product differentiation is the relaxation of direct price competition (D'Aspremont et al. 1979). Thus, strategic similarity in intra-market positioning could actually be associated with more intense rivalry if the effect of lack of product differentiation outweighs the effect of increased coordination. That notion is defended by D'Aveni (1994) in his view of hypercompetition in the cost/quality arena. He suggests that similarity positioned rivals are most likely to engage in intense price wars with little restraint (p. 44), but also explicitly recognizes that differentiated rivals may in some cases be just as active and disruptive as similar rivals (p. 49).

The resource-based view of competitive advantage suggests that similarity of rival firms in terms of resource endowments may increase rivalry (Barney 1991, Peteraf 1993a). Peteraf (1993a) contends that (resource) heterogeneity is a necessary condition for competitive advantage, because without it rent erosion can occur. Firms that do not have unique resources and capabilities are thus likely to compete away any supranormal profits. That argument closely mirrors the argument by Porter (1976) that the close substitutability of the products of similar firms may increase the likelihood of their rivalry if tacit interfirm coordination is not effectively recognized and exercised.

The hypothesis that tacit interfirm coordination is more successful among similar firms has also been challenged. For instance, strategic distance (lack of similarity) may facilitate tacit coordination by making it easier to know whether a rival has overstepped its tacit boundary. Thus, from the combined literature of strategic groups, product differentiation, and the resource-based view of the firm, conflicting predictions emerge, each with its own logic, about the effect of strategic similarity on the intensity of interfirm rivalry. Following Zajac and Kraatz (1993), we present two alternative, diametrically opposed predictions, the results of which illuminate the theoretical tension on the issue.

H1. *The average strategic similarity of a firm to competitors in a market will decrease the intensity of rivalry experienced by that firm in that market if everything else is constant.*

H1 (Alternative). *The average strategic similarity of a firm to competitors in a market will increase the intensity of rivalry experienced by that firm in that market if everything else is constant.*

Multimarket Contact

Another way in which intra-industry heterogeneity can affect the intensity of rivalry in a multimarket environment is by influencing the degree of multimarket contact with rivals. For any pair of competing firms in a market within the industry, multimarket contact reflects the number of other markets in the industry in which the same pair of firms meet as competitors. Thus, multimarket contact between two competing firms in a given market reflects the degree of market overlap between those firms in the other markets of the industry.

The theory of multimarket competition suggests that multimarket contact between two firms will reduce the intensity of rivalry between them in each of the markets in which they compete (Edwards 1955, Feinberg 1984, Bernheim and Whinston 1990, Witteloostuijn and Wegberg 1992). Thus, although multimarket contact implies that firms are competitors across a large set of markets ("breadth" of competition), the theory predicts that the intensity of rivalry in each of the mutually contested markets will be low. The reason for such an effect, according to the theory, is that firms with high multimarket contact have an extended scope for retaliation to actions taken by the rival (Feinberg 1984), because the opportunity for cross-market retaliation is added to the set of retaliation possibilities.

The development of multimarket contacts may spark episodes of intense rivalry, as firms enter each other's markets (Karnani and Wernerfelt 1985), in a process of hypercompetitive interaction in the stronghold invasion arena (D'Aveni 1994). However, once the multimarket contacts are in place, and as firms mutually recognize that actions taken in one market may have implications in other markets, the theoretical prediction (Karnani and Wernerfelt 1985, Bernheim and Whinston 1990), supported by substantial empirical work (Scott 1982, Phillips and Mason 1992, Evans and Kessides 1994), is that firms will forbear from additional disruption (Edwards 1955).

Although most of multimarket competition theory has evolved independently of strategic group theory, a few authors have studied the differences and connections between the two theories (Greening 1980, Broadman 1981, Barnett 1993). Greening (1980) argued that the effect of multimarket contact discussed in the multipoint competition literature is in fact evidence of the tacit coordination effect of strategic similarity postulated by strategic group theory. Greening's argument raises the important issue of empirically distinguishing between strategic similarity and multimarket contact, but his conception of strategic similarity is substantially broader than ours. From our definition, based on more current strategic group theory developments (Hatten and Hatten 1987), it is clear that firms can pursue similar strategies without necessarily being in the same markets of a multimarket environment.

Some empirical attempts to integrate the concepts of multimarket contact and strategic groups have been reported (Broadman 1981, Barnett 1993). Broadman (1981) studied geographic multimarket contact among petroleum firms classified into strategic groups based on their patterns of vertical integration, finding a strong performance effect for some groups. Barnett (1993) studied geographic multimarket contact within and across groups of telephone service companies defined by their core business, finding a forbearance effect for some groups. However, both researchers used the strategic group construct not as a possible alternative hypothesis to multimarket contact, but as a context variable for the effects of multimarket contact. That approach hinders the direct comparison of strategic similarity and multimarket contact as predictors of rivalry.

In summary, the theoretical predictions are in agreement about the rivalry-decreasing effect of multimarket contact. They are captured in our second hypothesis.

H2. *A firm's average multimarket contact with competitors in a market will decrease the intensity of rivalry experienced by that firm in that market if everything else is constant.*

MODEL SPECIFICATION

In a multimarket environment, the intensity of rivalry as a firm-level construct has meaning only as an aggregate, because the rivalry experienced by a firm will differ among markets depending on the firm's choice of markets, its competitive advantage in those markets, the set of competitors the firm meets in those markets, and other variables. Thus, a multimarket firm could experience very intense rivalry to win customers in one market while experiencing little rivalry for the customers in another. The implication is that the natural unit of analysis is the *rivalry experienced by a firm within a particular market*. Although aggregation of within-market rivalries to the firm level is possible (Cool and Direickx 1993), it is likely to sacrifice information about the intra-firm variation of the variables.

Studying the intensity of rivalry experienced *by a firm within a given market* of a multimarket environment facilitates controlling for the sources of rivalry. Because a multimarket environment, as defined here, is characterized by little or no cross-elasticity between the markets (products or services offered to different markets are not close substitutes), the only source of competition for a firm within a market is the set of relevant competitors (other incumbents and potential entrants) in that specific market. Hence, defining the focus of study at that level simplifies the specification and identification of the expected rivalry effects.

The intensity of rivalry experienced by a firm in a market can be captured by two alternative methods well established in the literature. A method used increasingly in strategy research is to evaluate rivalry from direct observation of competitive moves and countermoves by rivals (Smith et al. 1992, Smith and Wilson 1995, Chen 1996). The intensity of rivalry is evaluated by the aggressiveness, speed, and pattern of competitive actions and responses in the market (Chen 1996). Another method, well established in empirical IO economics, focuses on the impact of such a pattern of actions and reactions in the price-cost margin of a firm in a market. The former method has the advantage of directly observing the dynamic ordering of competitive actions (who moves and who responds), but the latter is superior in evaluating the magnitude of the actual impact of those interactions on the firm's operations. Given the data available for our study and their direct measurement of the impact or outcome of rivalry, we used the latter method. However, replications of our study using dynamic interaction data would add a very valuable perspective on the competitive effects of intra-industry heterogeneity.

Combining the IO and resource-based views of performance, we can specify the price-cost margin of a firm in a market as composed of firm-specific rents from its unique capabilities and product-market profits from reduced rivalry in the market. Product-market profits can be decomposed into three sources: (1) market structure effects, which capture the effects of number and size distribution of incumbents and potential entrants, regardless of their degree of heterogeneity, (2) firm-specific dominance effects, which capture the firm-specific market power, and (3) intra-industry heterogeneity effects, which represent the aggregate effect of intra-industry heterogeneity of relevant competitors in the specific market. Thus, the price-cost margin of a firm i in a market m at a period of time t can be specified as:

$$P_{imt} - C_{imt} = f(\text{rents}_{imt}, \text{market structure}_{imt},$$

$$\text{firm-specific dominance}_{imt}, \text{intra-industry heterogeneity}_{imt}).$$

Even if cost per unit information is not available at the market level, such information can be estimated on the right side of the equation by estimating the firm's cost per unit as a function of a set of independent variables X_{imt}:

$$P_{imt} = C(X_{imt}) + f(\text{rents}_{imt}, \text{market structure}_{imt},$$

$$\text{firm-specific dominance}_{imt}, \text{intra-industry heterogeneity}_{imt}).$$

We used that equation for estimating the effects of intra-industry heterogeneity (strategic similarity, multimarket contact) on the intensity of rivalry.

EMPIRICAL TEST

Sample

We selected a sample of city-pair markets in the U.S. scheduled passenger airline industry for the period 1984 through 1988 to test the hypotheses with the described specification. A city-pair market is defined as the set of customers demanding air travel between any given pair of cities, irrespectively of how that demand is satisfied in terms of the trip structure (direct flight, one-stop flight). Only city-pair markets at least 100 miles apart and with at least 10 passengers a day were considered. That sample provided an ideal context for our study of hypercompetition among heterogeneous firms for four reasons. First, hypercompetition swept the airline industry after deregulation in 1978, including increased differentiation of strategic orientation and a wave of stronghold creation/invasion. As Figure 10.1 shows, the sampled period is particularly dynamic because it included not only the largest drop in real (deflated) prices (1984-1986), but also a period of relative de-escalation with increasing real prices (1986-1988). Thus, it enabled us to explore both hypercompetitive escalation and de-escalation. Second, the definition of a market as a city-pair market is very convenient for narrowing the set of relevant competitors for a firm in a market, because there is no cross-elasticity across city-pair markets and firms serving the same market compete head-to-head with little differentiation. Third, there was great intra-industry heterogeneity in the strategies used by airlines (Bailey and Williams 1988). Fourth, the fact that air transportation was the primary business of almost all of the airlines provided control for the effects of diversification outside the industry.

A panel data sample describing the activities of 48 airlines across 3,171 markets for five periods (fourth quarters of 1984 through 1988), totaling 48,644 observations, was obtained from the U.S. Department of Transportation (DOT). The DOT databases used were the Ticket Price Origin and Destination Survey (DB1A), the service segment data, and the Form 41 reports of financial and operational data. The unit of analysis was defined as the *airline-route:* the position as incumbent that a given airline i has in a given city-pair market m. The sample included 15,207 airline-routes. For each airline-route, an observation was obtained for each time period in which the firm was incumbent in that market. The subscripts i, m, and t refer to the airline, city-pair market, and time period of the observation, respectively. A firm was considered to be an incumbent if it had at least a 5% share of the market *or* carried at least 10 passengers a day. That definition eliminated cases in which passengers flew an airline-route through combinations unintended by the airline, but maintained in the sample small competitors that target niches of demand in high density markets. A potential entrant was defined as a firm with operations at both end cities of the city-pair but not serving the demand in the city-pair market. Berry (1989) provides support for that definition by finding that the odds of entry for a potential entrant already established at both end points are more than 18 times greater than those for a firm established in only one end city and 77 times greater than those for a firm not established in either end city.

Operationalization of Variables

The *dependent variable* in our study (yield$_{imt}$) is the average price charged by a firm to passengers in a city-pair market divided by the distance of the

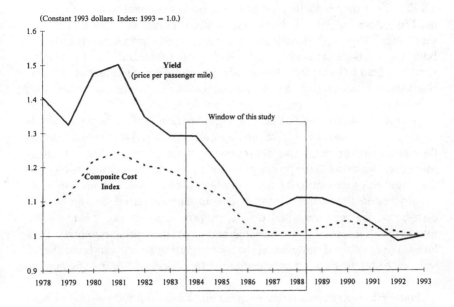

(Constant 1993 dollars. Index: 1993 = 1.0.)

Figure 10.1. Yield and Cost Changes in the U.S. Airline Industry Since Deregulation (constant 1993 dollars. Index: 1993 = 1.0.)
SOURCE: Air Transport Association.

market. The division of the price level by the market distance is a normal practice in the industry, which often reports such data as "yield" or "revenue per passenger-mile." Dividing by distance also scales all observations to be comparable for different markets, facilitating the use of linear methods (eliminating some heteroscedasticity). The use of actual prices rather than announced or advertised prices is important, because airlines can easily change prices by changing the availability of seats to different fare categories, without necessarily changing their advertised prices for those categories.

The critical *independent variables* describe the constructs of strategic similarity and multimarket contact. The operationalization of *strategic similarity,* the first dimension of interfirm heterogeneity, has received considerable attention and debate in the strategic groups literature (Hatten and Hatten 1987). Whereas early studies used simple dimensions specifically relevant for the industry under study, later studies have increasingly used multiple dimensions that are generalizable (product-market scope and resource deployments have been the dimensions most widely used to define strategic similarity). A data reduction method, usually cluster analysis, then has been used to reduce the pattern of strategic similarities among firms to a discrete set of strategic groups. Barney and Hoskisson (1990) have severely criticized both the variable selection methods (small differences in the selected variables lead to radically different results) and the data reduction methods (the assumption of having a few homogenous strategies in the market is not often met).

Instead of attempting to find the "right" measure of strategic similarity, we considered three alternative operationalizations and thus could evaluate the sensitivity of results to alternative measures of strategic similarity. Moreover, we avoided the problems raised by clustering techniques by using the actual pairwise similarity data without data reduction. For any pair of the 48 airlines in the sample, i and j, the measure of strategic similarity is distributed between zero and one, with zero representing the maximum interfirm difference in that dimension and one representing maximum similarity. We developed those measures by comparing some firm-level characteristics of the firms' strategies that are independent of the *specific* markets served.

The first operationalization of strategic similarity follows the discrete classification scheme used by the Department of Transportation, based on annual operating revenues of the airlines. DOT distinguishes between the following categories: majors (over \$1 billion), nationals (\$100 million to \$1 billion), large regionals (\$10 million to \$100 million), and medium regionals (up to \$10 million). The numbers of airlines in the sample in those categories are 12, 19, 13, and 4, respectively. Although the DOT classification is based strictly on revenues, it is strongly associated with the product-market strategies pursued by the firms (Bailey and Williams 1988). Firms with the same DOT classification are likely to be strategically similar in their intra-market positioning, which should influence the intensity of their rivalry. Hence,

$$d_{ij}^{\text{DOT}} = \begin{cases} 1 \text{ if firms } i \text{ and } j \text{ have different DOT classification,} \\ 0 \text{ if firms } i \text{ and } j \text{ have the same DOT classification.} \end{cases}$$

A second operationalization of strategic similarity can be obtained from Stinchcombe's (1965) hypothesis about structural stability and date of founding. Stinchcombe suggests that firms originating in a given period are "imprinted" by the environment prevalent at that time, and choose their structures and strategies accordingly. Those strategies and structures thus become ingrained in the firm and are difficult to change because of organizational inertia and path dependence. If Stinchcombe's hypothesis is correct, the date of founding can be used as a unidimensional proxy for strategy, and firms that are similar in year of founding (i.e., firms that experienced similar environments at their founding dates) are likely to follow similar strategies. A measure of strategic similarity is thus constructed by one minus the difference in years of founding (normalized to a zero-to-one range):

$$\text{similarity}_{ij}^{\text{date}} = \frac{|\,\text{Founding date}_i - \text{Founding date}_j\,|}{\max_{k,\,l} |\,\text{Founding date}_k - \text{Founding date}_l\,|}.$$

The measure takes the value of zero (minimum similarity) when the difference in founding dates between two firms equals the maximum difference in our sample (62 years) and it equals one (maximum similarity) when the founding dates are the same for two firms.

The third operationalization of strategic similarity is more attuned to the multivariate methods currently in use in strategic group research. We selected a set of seven variables (z_{i1} to z_{i7}) that describe the competitive strategy of the firm in terms of the type of markets in which it competes and its positioning within those markets. The strategic orientation variables are (1) the passenger-weighted average *density* of the markets in which the firm competes, (2) the passenger-weighted average *distance* of those markets, (3) the percentage of *tourist markets* among all markets served by the firm (tourist markets are defined as those for which one end-point is Aspen, Atlantic City, Las Vegas, Reno, and any destinations in Florida, Hawaii, Virgin Islands, Guam, American Samoa, Marianna Islands, and Puerto Rico), (4) the passenger-weighted percentage of *direct flights* over all flights, (5) the passenger-weighted average daily *frequency*, (6) the passenger-weighted *market share* of the firm in its markets, and (7) the passenger-weighted average *premium over standard industry fare level (SIFL)* per mile. The seven dimensions capture the most critical differences in the strategies of U.S. airlines, such as being short haul versus long haul, high frequency versus low frequency, and point-to-point versus hub-and-spoke systems. The variables were averaged across the multiple markets and time periods, so that only one seven-dimensional datapoint represents the strategy of each airline over the five-year period. Strategic similarity is then represented by one minus the Euclidean distances between the standardized points in the seven-dimensional space (normalized to the zero to one range):

$$\text{similarity}_{ij}^{\text{strat}} = 1 - \frac{\sqrt{\sum_{v=1}^{7} \left(z_{iv} - z_{jv}\right)^2}}{\max_{k,l} \sqrt{\sum_{v=1}^{7} \left(z_{kv} - z_{lv}\right)^2}}$$

The measure takes the value of zero (minimum similarity) when the Euclidean distance in the strategic space between two firms is the largest for all pairs in the sample, and it equals one (maximum similarity) when the Euclidean distance is zero (firms are equal in competitive orientation).

Because the intensity of rivalry experienced by a firm in a market is affected by the rivalry with all relevant competitors in the market (other incumbents and potential entrants), we aggregated the effect of strategic similarity to those competitors by calculating the average strategic similarity to all other (actual and potential) competitors j in market m. If total competitors$_{imt}$ represents the number of competitors, actual or potential, competing with firm i in market m at t, the aggregate measures are calculated as follows.

$$\text{average similarity}_{imt}^{\text{DOT}} = \frac{1}{\text{total competitors}_{imt}} \cdot \sum_{j \neq i} \text{similarity}_{ij}^{\text{DOT}}$$

$$\text{average similarity}_{imt}^{\text{age}} = \frac{1}{\text{total competitors}_{imt}} \cdot \sum_{j \neq i} \text{similarity}_{ij}^{\text{age}}$$

$$\text{average similarity}_{imt}^{\text{strat}} = \frac{1}{\text{total competitors}_{imt}} \cdot \sum_{j \neq i} \text{similarity}_{ij}^{\text{strat}}$$

For the second important construct, *multimarket contact,* several measures are available in the literature (Scott 1982, Feinberg 1985, Evans and Kessides 1994). For simplicity we used a count measure of multimarket contact, which sums the number of markets outside market m where firms i and j also compete. The average multimarket contact measure is the average of multimarket contacts with all of firm i's relevant competitors in market m. We go beyond the previous measurements of multimarket contact used in the literature by including potential contacts with competitors as well as actual contacts in the count of multimarket contact. Thus, an instance of multimarket contact occurs according to our definition when a firm i, an incumbent in a focal market m, and another (actual or potential) competitor j in market m meet in another market n, in which competitor j is an incumbent and firm i is an incumbent or potential entrant. That instance is coded as multimarket contact$_{ij,mn,t} = 1$. The multimarket contact of firm i with competitor j is the sum of multimarket contacts over all markets outside market m:

$$\text{multimarket contact}_{ij,m,t} = \sum_{n \neq m} \text{multimarket contact}_{ij,mn,t}.$$

The overall measure of multimarket contact is the average number of multimarket contacts with the competitors (actual and potential) in market m, calculated as:

$$\text{average multimarket contact} = \frac{1}{\text{total competitors}_{imt}} \cdot \sum_{j \neq i} \text{multimarket contact}_{ij,m,t}.$$

Several other *control variables* are used to control for the effects of relevant factors influencing prices and costs, including firm-specific factors designed to control for the heterogenous resource endowment and market positions of the firms. Those variables can be associated with four major constructs that have well-reported influence on airline yields: (1) controls for heterogenous *service attributes* (circularity of flight, being a direct flight, frequency of flights, percentage of first/business class passengers, and percentage of round trip tickets), (2) controls for *exogenous market characteristics* (cost of inputs captured by the SIFL, and density in the market), (3) controls for the *cost position* in the airline-route (load factor, scale of the firm, presence at end cities, and hub-and-spoke network effects), (4) controls for *market structure* (market's Herfindahl index of concentration, total number of potential entrants, and Herfindahl index of concentration at the end cities) and the *firm-specific dominance* in the market (firm's share of enplanements at the end cities and firm's market share in the city-pair market). In addition, sets of dummy variables are used to control for unobserved fixed effects of time periods (average industry trends in yields) and mergers. The exact definitions of the control variables are given in Table 10.1.

METHOD

The structure of the data, an unbalanced panel data sample of 15,207 airline-routes observed over five years, allowed use of panel data methodology (Hsiao 1986) with a fixed-effect intercept model, also known as the least squares dummy variable (LSDV) model. The LSDV model has the unique advantage (in comparison with other cross-sectional time-series methods) of being able to control for unobserved cross-sectional heterogeneity among the airline-routes by allowing the intercept of the testing equation to vary for each airline-route. We included a set of 15,207 dummy variables to control for any observed or unobserved effects that are constant for an airline-route for the five years of observation. This dummy variable intercept thus controls for a wide variety of factors that would otherwise be impossible to capture explicitly.

The practical implication of using LSDV must be well understood for correct interpretation of the results. An entirely equivalent method of estimation, known as *absorption* (Searle 1971), is to transform all dependent and independent variables to deviations with respect to the airline-route mean for those variables and run an OLS regression on the transformed variables. The implication is that the LSDV coefficients will not be influenced by cross-sectional differences among airline-routes that remain stable over the five-year period. That feature serves to control for any stable airline-route specific advantages (i.e., rents), such as slot constraints in airports or special landing rights for an airline. The LSDV coefficients are affected only by the covariations of variables from year to year within a given airline-route. Thus, an LSDV coefficient can be interpreted as describing longitudinal changes occurring *within* an airline-route, and closely approximates the marginal effect that a change in an independent variable would have on the yield of a heterogeneous firm in a given market, other things being constant.

We carried out a diagnosis of violations of the basic assumptions of the LSDV model, including heteroscedasticity, autocorrelation, and linearity of effects. Marketwise heteroscedasticity in the LSDV residuals was identified and corrected by using weighted least squares, with weights equal to the inverse of the market variance of residuals. No significant autocorrelation was found, which indicated lack of unaccounted-for lagged effects from one year to the next, a finding consistent with the fluid nature of airline prices. Through the use of spline linear regression, we found two variables to have a significant and meaningful nonlinear effect on yield: density and network economies. In response, we transformed the density variable to its squared root and defined a two-step function of network economies. The assumption that the airline-route specific intercepts are fixed effects rather than random

TABLE 10.1 Definition of Control Variables Used in the Study

Controls for heterogeneous service attributes:

$circularity_{imt}$ — Circularity of the firm's flights in the market (actual miles traveled by passengers/great circle distance between cities)

direct $flights_{imt}$ — Percentage of passengers flying direct (without connection) in the airline-route

$frequency_{imt}$ — Number of flights per day by the firm serving the city-pair market

round $tickets_{imt}$ — Percentage of round trip tickets of all the firm's tickets in the airline-route

$class_{imt}$ — Percentage of first and business class tickets in the airline-route

Controls for exogenous market attributes:

cost of $inputs_{imt}$ — Index of changes in the cost of labor and fuel inputs: the Standard Industry fare level (calculated by FAA and adjusted by changes in costs of inputs) divided by distance

$\sqrt{Density_{imt}}$ — Square root of total number of passengers traveling the market with any airline (1 = 100,000 passengers)

Controls for the cost position of the firm in the airline market:

load $factor_{imt}$ — Distance-weighted average of the load factors of the segments of the market

firm $scale_{imt}$ — Number of passengers carried in all other markets outside the market (m) under study (1 = 1,000,000 passengers)

hub $economies_{imt}$ — Average number of enplanements by the firm at both end-cities (1 = 100,000 passengers)

network $economies_{imt}$ — Percentage of the passengers traveling in the same flight segments as the passengers of the city-pair market who are not flying that city-pair market (a large number indicates high network economies)

high network $economies_{imt}$ — Max{network $economies_{imt}$ − 0.95,0}, which captures a change in slope of the network economies variable after the 95% level.

Controls for market structure and the firm's dominance within the market:

market $concentration_{mt}$ — Herfindahl-Hirshman index of concentration at city-pair

potential $entrants_{mt}$ — Number of potential entrants (firms with presence at both end-cities that do not serve the city-pair)

hub $concentration_{mt}$ — Average of the Herfindahl-Hirshman index of concentration of total enplanements at both end-cities

market $share_{imt}$ — Market share of the airline in the market

hub $share_{imt}$ — Average of the firm's share of total enplanements at both end-cities

Other controls:

airline-route controls — 15,207 dummies controlling for the observed and unobserved airline-route effects that are constant for the five year period.

merger controls — 11 dummy variables which compare pre-merger to post-merger main effect for 11 major mergers during the period: American Airlines-Air California, USAir-Pacific Southwest, Alaska Airlines-Jet American/Horizon, Braniff-Florida Express, Continental-People Express/New York Air, Delta-Western, Northwest-Republic, People Express-Frontier Airlines, Piedmont-Empire, TWA-Ozark, and Southwest-Muse.

time period controls — 4 dummy variables that control for unobserved year effects by comparing each year to the base year (1984) effects was tested by the Hausman (1978) test, which showed the fixed-effect specification to be appropriate for the data.

RESULTS

Table 10.2 gives the descriptive statistics of the dependent, independent, and principal control variables, including means and standard deviations of the original variables, as well as the within-airline-route correlation matrix. We report the within-airline-route correlation, rather than the zero-order correlation, because that is the correlation matrix underlying the LSDV model. A positive *within-airline-route* correlation coefficient between two variables indicates that, over the period of five years, values of the first variable above (below) its five-year mean for a given airline-route tended to be associated with values of the second variable above (below) its five-year mean for the same airline-route.

The descriptive statistics show that all three strategic similarity variables have positive and significant correlations with yield, indicating a negative bivariate association between strategic similarity and intensity of rivalry. The operationalizations of strategic similarity have a correlation between 0.60 and 0.81, indicating a high degree of reliability among the measures. All three measures of similarity are positively correlated with multimarket contact at levels between 0.23 and 0.38. Such moderate correlation between the two dimensions of heterogeneity is helpful, as it allows a better identification of the effects of each. Multimarket contact has a small but positive correlation with yield, indicating a negative bivariate association between multimarket contact and intensity of rivalry. Thus, univariate analysis provides some initial support for the de-escalation effects of both strategic similarity and multimarket contact.

The multivariate analysis was carried out in several steps. Only the strategic similarity variables were included in Models 1a, 1b, and 1c and only multimarket contact was included in Model 2 (see Table 10.3). Both strategic similarity and multimarket contact were included in Models 3a, 3b, and 3c (see Table 10.4). In addition to those independent variables, all the multivariate models included a large number of control variables, as is the norm in this literature (Borenstein 1989, Peteraf 1993b, Evans and Kessides 1994).

Table 10.3 reports the results for the multivariate test of H1 and H2 when we include one dimension of heterogeneity at a time. The results of the test of H1 (Models 1a, 1b, and 1c), which states that strategic similarity decreases/increases the intensity of rivalry, seem to partially support the coordination-enhancing view of strategic similarity. Changes in the set of relevant rivals that increase (decrease) the average strategic similarity to

TABLE 10.2 Descriptive Statistics

Variable	Units	Mean	SD	Within-Airline-Route Correlation																		
				[1]	[2]	[3]	[4]	[5]	[6]	[7]	[8]	[9]	[10]	[11]	[12]	[13]	[14]	[15]	[16]	[17]	[18]	[19]	[20]	[21]
[1] Yield	dollars/mile	0.17	0.10	.00																				
[2] Circularity	ratio of distances	1.09	0.16	-.01	-.49																			
[3] Direct flights	percentage	0.18	0.38	.04	.16	-.25																		
[4] Frequency	flights/day	3.27	1.99	.21	.03	-.02	-.04																	
[5] Class	percentage	0.01	0.03	-.16	.00	.05	.13	-.10																
[6] Round tickets	percentage	0.82	0.20	.24	-.02	.01	-.11	.11	-.08															
[7] Cost of inputs	dollars/mile	0.16	0.04	-.30	-.06	.11	.13	-.09	.15	-.14														
[8] √Density	100,000 pass.	0.42	0.41	-.14	.13	-.10	.04	-.03	.06	-.12	.21													
[9] Load factor	percentage	0.56	0.09	.03	-.01	.02	.26	-.09	.26	-.10	.21	.15												
[10] Firm scale	1,000,000 pass.	5.57	2.53																				
[11] Hub economies	100,000 pass.	1.99	2.95	.07	-.04	.11	.30	-.07	.16	-.12	.18	.17	.53											
[12] Network economies	percentage	0.87	0.24	.11	.39	-.80	.26	.03	-.08	-.03	-.15	.12	.04	.01										
[13] High network economies	percentage	0.02	0.02	.10	.30	-.26	.13	.04	-.14	-.03	-.12	.08	.04	-.03	.32									
[14] Hub share	percentage	0.16	0.11	.13	-.09	.13	.22	.03	.06	.01	.03	.14	.37	.60	-.04	-.08								
[15] Hub concentration	Herfindahl [0, 1]	0.25	0.10	.07	-.02	.00	.15	-.05	.14	-.10	.12	.10	.35	.34	.05	.02	.27							

(continued)

TABLE 10.2 Continued

Variable	Units	Mean	SD	[1]	[2]	[3]	[4]	[5]	[6]	[7]	[8]	[9]	[10]	[11]	[12]	[13]	[14]	[15]	[16]	[17]	[18]	[19]	[20]	[21]
																Within-Airline-Route Correlation								
[16] Market share	percentage	0.29	0.24	.06	−.21	.26	.13	−.01	.16	.06	−.11	.04	.06	.19	−.31	−.51	.36	.04						
[17] Market concentration	Herfindahl [0.1]	0.37	0.16	.12	−.02	.05	.04	.01	.01	.10	−.01	.01	.03	.10	−.05	−.03	.18	.19	.37					
[18] Potential entrants	number of p.e.	3.12	2.29	−.08	−.04	.06	−.08	.01	−.04	.02	−.07	.00	−.08	−.09	−.09	−.05	−.05	−.14	.08	.14				
[19] Average similarity (DOT)	range [0.1]	0.83	0.27	.03	.00	.00	.06	−.03	.08	−.09	−.02	.04	.11	.09	.02	.03	.05	.18	.02	.08	−.19			
[20] Average similarity (age)	range [0.1]	0.84	0.16	.04	.00	.00	.05	−.03	.07	−.01	−.02	.04	.12	.08	.02	.03	.05	.16	.03	.09	−.21	.81		
[21] Average similarity (strat)	range [0.1]	0.82	0.01	.04	.01	.00	.00	.00	.00	−.04	−.04	.01	.02	.01	.00	.00	.03	.08	.03	.05	−.21	.60	.60	
[22] Average multimarket contact	100 contacts	5.66	2.62	.03	.01	.00	.24	−.10	.26	−.20	.17	.12	.68	.41	.06	.05	.23	.36	.03	.03	−.22	−.38	−.37	−.23

NOTE: $N = 48,644$ observations; correlations above 0.018 are significant at the $\alpha < 0.001$ level.

252

those rivals appear to be associated with an increase (decrease) in yields, other things being constant. The coefficients for strategic similarity in terms of DOT classification and year of founding are both positive and significant at the $\alpha < 0.01$ level. The coefficient for strategic similarity in the seven-dimensional strategy space is also positive but not significantly different from zero ($\alpha = 0.19$). Thus, although the support is not entirely robust to alternative specifications of strategic similarity, all three alternative specifications point in the same direction, albeit with different degrees of significance. Those results apparently replicate Peteraf's (1993b) findings that similar firms compete less intensely, even after control for a much larger set of possible competing explanations.

Table 10.3 also reports the results when only multimarket contact is included (Model 2). The coefficient of multimarket contact on yield is positive and strongly significant ($\alpha < 0.001$), a finding strongly supporting the prediction of H2 that multimarket contact significantly reduces the intensity of rivalry experienced by a firm in a market. The standardized (beta) coefficient also shows that average multimarket contact$_{imt}$ has an effect on yield greater than that of any of the market structure and firm dominance variables commonly specified in strategy and IO economics as strong predictors of rivalry. Thus, the result strongly suggests that, at least in the airline industry, the ultimate outcome of hypercompetition in the stronghold creation/invasion arena may eventually facilitate competitive de-escalation, because as the mutually invading firms gain greater overlap of each other's strongholds, the likelihood of additional disruption is reduced by fear of cross-market retaliation.

Table 10.4 reports the results for the hypothesis when both strategic similarity and multimarket contact are *simultaneously* included in the model. The simultaneous inclusion of the two dimensions of similarity is important because, although the two dimensions are theoretically distinct, they are likely to be correlated empirically to some extent. That is in fact the case in our data, with correlations between multimarket contact and strategic similarity operationalizations ranging from 0.23 to 0.38. The correlation makes it important to evaluate the distinct effect of each measure of heterogeneity after controlling for the other. The findings for Models 3a, 3b, and 3c show that whereas the effect of multimarket contact remains stable with control for strategic similarity, the effect of strategic similarity is substantially different with control for multimarket contact. In fact, when multimarket contact is included in the model, all three measures of strategic similarity become negative and significant, indicating that when multimarket contact is kept constant, additional strategic similarity actually increases rivalry in a significant way.

TABLE 10.3 Sequential Tests of Hypotheses 1 and 2

Dependent Variable: Yield	Model 1a coeff.	Model 1a beta	Model 1b coeff.	Model 1b beta	Model 1c coeff.	Model 1c beta	Model 2 coeff.	Model 2 beta
15,207 airline route intercepts[a]	NOT SHOWN		NOT SHOWN		NOT SHOWN		NOT SHOWN	
4-year fixed-effects	NOT SHOWN		NOT SHOWN		NOT SHOWN		NOT SHOWN	
11 merger fixed-effects	NOT SHOWN		NOT SHOWN		NOT SHOWN		NOT SHOWN	
Circularity	-0.0056	-0.008	-0.0057 +	-0.008	-0.0058 +	-0.008	-0.0062 +	-0.009
Direct flights	0.0374***	0.143	0.0373***	0.143	0.0374***	0.143	0.0384***	0.147
Frequency	0.0016***	0.053	0.0016***	0.053	0.0016***	0.054	0.0017***	0.055
Class	0.1721***	0.207	0.1721***	0.207	0.1720***	0.207	0.1703***	0.205
Round tickets	-0.0418***	-0.162	-0.0417***	-0.162	-0.0417***	-0.162	-0.0416***	-0.161
Cost of inputs	0.6746***	0.242	0.6681***	0.239	0.6668***	0.239	0.5704***	0.204
$\sqrt{\text{Density}}$	-0.0913***	-0.216	-0.0914***	-0.216	-0.0917***	-0.217	-0.0878***	-0.207
Firm scale	0.0019***	0.111	0.0019***	0.112	0.0019***	0.110	0.0009***	0.055
Hub economies	0.0013***	0.042	0.0013***	0.042	0.0012***	0.041	0.0013***	0.045
Network economies	0.0498***	0.151	0.0497***	0.150	0.0496***	0.150	0.0515***	0.156
High network economies	0.1258***	0.049	0.1259***	0.049	0.1256***	0.049	0.1324***	0.052
Load factor	-0.0511***	-0.139	-0.0512***	-0.139	-0.0511***	-0.139	-0.0497***	-0.135

254

	(1)		(2)		(3)		(4)	
Hub share	0.0311***	0.053	0.0310***	0.053	0.0314***	0.054	0.0266***	0.045
Hub Concentration	0.0316***	0.057	0.0318***	0.058	0.0318***	0.058	0.0317***	0.057
Market share	0.0016	0.008	0.0016	0.008	0.0015	0.007	0.0024 +	0.011
Market concentration	0.0215***	0.087	0.0215***	0.087	0.0218***	0.088	0.0204***	0.083
Potential entrants	−0.0020***	−0.102	−0.0020***	−0.102	−0.0020***	−0.103	−0.0017***	−0.088
Average similarity (DOT)	0.0027**	0.012						
Average similarity (age)			0.0046**	0.012				
Average similarity (strat)					0.0063	0.006		
Average multimarket contact							0.0016***	0.124
$N = 48,644$ observations								
Overall R^2 (including airline-route intercepts)	95.40%		95.40%		95.40%		95.43%	
F-value of model (including airline-route intercepts)	45.49		45.49		45.48		45.85	
R^2 of absorbed model (deviations from airline-route means)	38.43%		38.43%		38.42%		38.89%	
F-value of absorbed model (deviations from airline-route means)	631.88		631.88		631.62		644.19	

a. The airline-route dummies are absorbed first. Based on Type I sum of squares, their F-value is 43.41, which is significant at the 0.0001 level. Hausman test supports fixed-effects specification.

Significance: + at $\alpha < 0.1$, * at $\alpha < 0.05$, ** at $\alpha < 0.01$, and *** at $\alpha < 0.001$.

TABLE 10.4 Simultaneous Test of Hypotheses 1 and 2

Dependent Variable: Yield	Model 3a		Model 3b		Model 3c	
	coeff.	beta	coeff.	beta	coeff.	beta
15,207 airline route intercepts[a]	NOT SHOWN		NOT SHOWN		NOT SHOWN	
4-year fixed-effects	NOT SHOWN		NOT SHOWN		NOT SHOWN	
11 merger fixed-effects	NOT SHOWN		NOT SHOWN		NOT SHOWN	
Circularity	−0.0063 +	−0.009	−0.0062 +	−0.009	−0.0062 +	−0.009
Direct flights	0.0385***	0.147	0.0385***	0.147	0.0384***	0.147
Frequency	0.0017***	0.056	0.0017***	0.055	0.0017***	0.055
Class	0.1701***	0.205	0.1701***	0.205	0.1701***	0.205
Round tickets	−0.0416***	−0.161	−0.0417***	−0.161	−0.0417***	−0.162
Cost of inputs	0.5605***	0.201	0.5677***	0.203	0.5739***	0.205
√Density	−0.0882***	−0.208	−0.0881***	−0.208	−0.0881***	−0.208
Firm scale	0.0009***	0.051	0.0009***	0.051	0.009***	0.052
Hub economies	0.0013***	0.044	0.0013***	0.044	0.0013***	0.044
Network economies	0.0514***	0.156	0.0515***	0.156	0.0514***	0.156
High network economies	0.1321***	0.052	0.1320***	0.052	0.1319***	0.052
Load factor	−0.0497***	−0.135	−0.0496***	−0.135	−0.0496***	−0.135
Hub share	0.0269***	0.046	0.0269***	0.046	0.0271***	0.046
Hub concentration	0.0319***	0.058	0.0317***	0.057	0.0318***	0.058
Market share	0.0023 +	0.011	0.0023 +	0.011	0.0023 +	0.011
Market concentration	0.0207***	0.084	0.0207***	0.084	0.0205***	0.083
Potential entrants	−0.0018***	−0.090	−0.0018***	−0.090	−0.0018***	−0.091
Average similarity (DOT)	−0.0028**	−0.013				
Average similarity (age)			−0.0045*	−0.012		
Average similarity (strat)					−0.0144**	−0.013
Average multimarket contact	0.0017***	0.131	0.0017***	0.130	0.0017***	0.130
N = 48,644 observations						
Overall R^2 (including airline-route intercepts)	95.44%		95.44%		95.44%	
F-value of model (including airline-route intercepts)	45.85		45.85		45.86	
R^2 of absorbed model (deviations from airline-route means)	38.90%		38.90%		38.91%	
F-value of absorbed model (deviations from airline-route means)	625.55		625.51		625.62	

a. The airline-route dummies are absorbed first. Based on Type I sum of squares, their F-value is 43.41, which is significant at the 0.0001 level. Hausman test supports fixed-effects specification.
Significance: + at $\alpha < 0.01$, * at $\alpha < 0.05$, ** at $\alpha < 0.01$, and *** at $\alpha < 0.001$.

Several potential conditions could account for the unexpected change of signs of the strategic similarity variables, and we investigate them in detail because the conclusion of that diagnosis would influence the credibility of our findings. A necessary condition for such sign reversal is a correlation between the two dimensions of heterogeneity after the effect of the remaining control variables is partialed out. If the correlation is very high, a multicollinearity problem is present that could lead to flawed results. It is well known (Judge et al. 1985, Greene 1990) that high levels of multicollinearity can lead to unstable and unreliable coefficients because of the near singularity of the cross-product matrix. We investigated that possibility by using two popular multicollinearity diagnostics: variance inflation factors and ridge regression (Neter et al. 1985).

Variance inflation factors (VIFs) reflect the impact of multicollinearity on each independent variable in the model. No multicollinearity appears as a VIF value of 1, but VIFs above 10 are commonly considered to reflect excessive multicollinearity (Neter et al. 1985). In Models 3a, 3b, and 3c, VIFs for the strategic similarity variables are 1.26, 1.24, and 1.19, respectively, whereas the VIF of the multimarket contact variable in those models ranges from 3.47 to 3.62. Thus, VIFs do not indicate the presence of multicollinearity in a way that could render the coefficients unreliable. In addition, we used ridge regression to evaluate the stability of the coefficients to the degree of multicollinearity. Ridge regression introduces a small bias in the cross-product matrix that reduces the impact of multicollinearity, although at the cost of slightly biasing the coefficients. If the sign reversal were due to multicollinearity, we would expect the coefficient estimates to be very sensitive to small ridges, even to the extent of reversing signs. Using ridges from 0 to 0.1, we found the coefficients to be relatively stable to increases in the ridge parameter. Those findings suggest that the sign reversal cannot be attributed to high levels of multicollinearity.

Another possible explanation of the sign reversal is the phenomenon known in the econometric literature as *bias from the omission of relevant variables* (Greene 1990, 259). It occurs when a variable that has a strong effect on the dependent variable is excluded from the model. Other variables that may be moderately correlated with the omitted variable then pick up part of the effect of the omitted variable, thus becoming biased. In that case, the sign reversal may hinge not on the high correlation between the independent variables (although some correlation is necessary for the effect to occur), but on the relative strength of the effect of the omitted variable. Because the direct effect of multimarket contact in our study is positive and very strong, and the correlation of multimarket contact with strategic similarity is positive though moderate, that combination has an effect of biasing the estimated effect of strategic similarity upward if we do not control for multimarket contact. The researcher would be led toward accepting the Caves-Porter hypothesis (rivalry-reducing effect of strategic similarity) when in fact, at least for the U.S. airline industry, the de-escalation effect originates in multimarket contact rather than in strategic similarity.

DISCUSSION AND CONCLUSIONS

Recent work on strategic group theory (Cool and Dierickx 1993, Peteraf 1993b) has stressed the importance of re-examining the relationship between intra-industry heterogeneity and intensity of rivalry as a way to strengthen the theoretical content of that literature. Our study contributes to the theoretical development by identifying two distinct dimensions of intra-industry heterogeneity that have different effects on the intensity of rivalry. In agreement with Chen (1996), we highlight the relevance of distinguishing between market overlap (captured in our research by the multimarket contact construct) and strategic similarity. Although those two dimensions may sometimes be correlated, unfolding them provides important insights. First, it forces the researcher to recognize cases in which the two dimensions are not collinear (strategically similar firms with little market overlap, and strategically different firms with substantial market overlap). Consideration of the two dimensions increases the quality of competitor analysis and provides new theoretical understanding of interfirm rivalry (Chen 1996). Moreover, our research shows that the dimensions actually have different effects on rivalry, an additional reason for considering them separately. Our findings, summarized graphically in Figure 10.2, suggest that the off-diagonal cases have a greater effect on rivalry. We find that the most intense rivalry is between similar firms with little multimarket contact, whereas the least intense rivalry is between strategically different firms with high multimarket contact. Further, our results suggest that not separating these dimensions empirically could lead to biased results about the effect of strategic similarity, as one might conclude that strategic similarity reduces rivalry when in fact it is the multimarket contact dimension that produces competitive restraint. We urge researchers interested in the heterogeneity-rivalry relationship to differentiate the two dimensions empirically.

For the competitive effects of strategic similarity, our robust results falsify the Caves-Porter hypothesis that similarity leads to lower rivalry. Multimarket contact being constant, similar competitors actually compete more intensely. The finding that firms with similar strategies compete more intensely is not foreign to strategy research. Research in product differentiation (D'Aspremont et al. 1979) and the proponents of the resource-based view

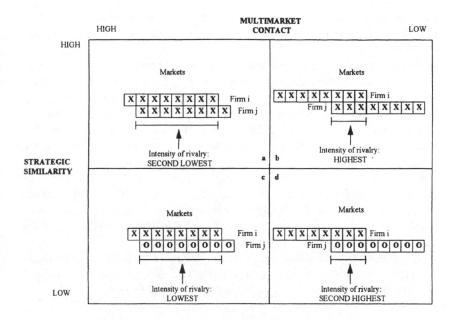

Figure 10.2. Graphic Representation of Results for the Effects of Strategic Similarity and Multimarket Contact

(Rumelt 1984, Barney 1991, Peteraf 1993a) and of organizational ecology (Carroll and Swaminathan 1992) have suggested that firms with similar strategies compete more intensely because of the high cross-elasticity of the products, the lack of unique resources, or the dynamics of competition in the same organizational niche. Our finding does not negate the possibility of tacit coordination among strategically similar rivals but tends to indicate that such coordination is not successful at eliminating all the potential for disruption when rivals seek similar market positions, use similar resources, or develop similar organizational capabilities. The finding is in agreement with D'Aveni's (1994, p. 45) suggestion that competitive restraint is difficult to exercise among rivals with similar market positions. Another possible explanation of the result is that strategically similar rivals develop similar competitive profiles, a set of organizational routines for how to engage and respond in competitive interaction. Such routines may be effective in coping with different rivals, but they may be incompatible with rivals using similar routines. For instance, firms such as Southwest that use low-price predatory competitive routines geared toward market dominance may be incompatible with rivals using similar competitive routines. More research is needed to study in detail the dynamics of hypercompetition in the positioning arena, as well as the compatibility of profiles among similar and differentiated sets of competitors.

For multimarket contact, our findings show that competitive de-escalation is strongly and significantly facilitated by increasing multimarket contact among competing firms, that is, by increasing overlap among competing firms in other markets in the industry. The strength of the de-escalation effect of multimarket contact is highly noticeable. Beta coefficients suggest that multimarket contact in other city-pair markets in the airline industry has a stronger effect on de-escalation among competing airlines than high seller concentration or low number of potential entrants in the focal city-pair market. Hence, at least in industries characterized by a multimarket environment, multimarket contact should be considered a leading factor in competitive de-escalation, similar in importance to the structural conditions of the local markets.

According to multipoint competition theory (Karnani and Wernerfelt 1985), the de-escalation effect of multimarket contact is due to managers' concern that an aggressive move in one market may provoke a response to in other mutually contested markets, thus leading to a multimarket escalation of rivalry. Managers therefore behave more conservatively toward multimarket rivals. Such a de-escalation effect does not come cheaply, however. To benefit from the mutual forbearance effect, competing firms need to increase their multimarket overlap, thus increasing the percentage of their activities that are at risk of attack by their competitors. Although multimarket contact decreases the mean level of intensity of rivalry in the overlapping markets, it may also have the effect of making any incidents of rivalry particularly virulent, as they would spread quickly throughout the range of overlapping markets. That is probably why, in the airline industry, price changes are matched quickly not only in the originating markets, but also in other markets where the same competitors overlap.

Our findings for multimarket contact contrast interestingly with D'Aveni's discussion of hypercompetition in the stronghold creation/ invasion arena, and other articles in this issue. D'Aveni presents a model in which market invasion spurs intense rivalry, leading to counterattack in the attacker's home markets. Craig (1996) observes a pattern of stronghold invasion in the Japanese brewing industry. Those episodes clearly represent escalating hypercompetitive interactions, but our research suggests that such mutual invasions carry the seeds of future de-escalation. As the markets of rivals become increasingly overlapping, the aggressiveness of the actions diminishes because of the risk of retaliatory reaction in some or all of the overlapping markets, thus decreasing the intensity of rivalry, at least in the price dimension we studied. Perhaps the apparently sustainable standoff actually means that hypercompetition has shifted to another arena, such as new product introductions (Craig 1996). An example of that type of shift, occurred in the case of the pet food industry (Collis 1991), in which a period of intense reciprocal entry that increased multimarket contact among the major firms in the industry was followed by a shift toward the introduction of new premium products. High multimarket contact may have also been a factor in the Japanese beer wars by preventing direct price competition and perhaps encouraging rivalry in new product development.

The temporal stability of our results is a potential concern. We calculated the strategic similarity variables by averaging strategic dimensions for a five-year period, thus ignoring possible shifts in competitive orientation by firms during the sample window. Future research with a longer time period should investigate firms' changes in strategic orientation (repositioning) and its effect on rivalry through shifts in strategic similarity among rivals. Another concern is the temporal stability of the coefficients of strategic similarity and multimarket contact. Cool and Dierickx (1993) found that rivalry within and between strategic groups changed over a 20-year period in the pharmaceutical industry. We minimized the impact on the results by selecting a sampling window that included periods of escalation and de-escalation. The temporal stability of the mutual forbearance effect also should be examined in future work.

Our findings have major implications for the theory of hypercompetition. First, they suggest that hypercompetition may occur in cycles, rather than being continuously escalating, and that hypercompetitive escalation may establish a basis for competitive de-escalation in the future. At the initial stages of hypercompetition, firms will try to outmaneuver each other in the different arenas, including entering each other's markets. As reciprocal entry occurs, firms become increasingly interdependent in multiple markets. The cost of an additional aggressive move increases as the opportunities of retaliation in multiple markets also increase. Eventually, aggressive behavior in localized markets becomes too risky, and firms relax their competitive activities to avoid extended confrontation. Thus, hypercompetition may occur in cyclical waves, originating from radical changes in the environment (such as deregulation) and the entry of new rivals, and eventually receding into more traditional forms of oligopolistic rivalry.

Second, the combined findings about strategic similarity and multimarket contact have value for predicting the evolution of industries entering hyper-competitive periods and those for which industry boundaries are becoming blurred. An interesting case in which our framework could be applied relates to the effects of deregulation in cable and local telephone communications. Deregulation will have the effect of bringing into competition firms with different positioning and capabilities (cable companies and the Baby Bells) that have not experienced multimarket contact in their service operations because of previous local market regulations. Our findings can be used to predict which particular competitive interactions will be more intense, helping managers develop strategies that enable them to motivate some restraint by rivals.

Third, our findings have implications for successful de-escalation strategies to cope with hypercompetition. They show that relying on strategic similarity as a method of competitive de-escalation is not effective, but multimarket contact is. Although strategic similarity may facilitate understanding of the competitors' strategies and intentions and promote tacit coordination, it does not by itself provide an economically credible rationale for reducing the aggressiveness of competition. In contrast, multimarket contact provides hostages that can be used effectively and credibly as a deterrence mechanism. The deterrence effect of multimarket contact will depend on the profits currently achieved by the rival in the market. Thus, hypercompetitive strategies, such as entering the home market of a foreign competitor, afford enforcement power over that competitor which could ultimately be used to reduce its disruptive power (Watson 1982, Karnani and Wernerfelt 1985). Paradoxically, aggressive escalation moves in the stronghold-invasion arena may carry the seeds of future competitive de-escalation.

In summary, our findings provide a more detailed understanding of how intra-industry heterogeneity may have a disruptive effect by influencing rivalry among heterogeneous rivals. That understanding has substantial implications for the development of a microdynamic view of how rivalry evolves in an industry, and how it affects and is affected by changes in heterogeneity in an industry. In turn, an understanding of those micro-dynamics would substantially contribute to our understanding of hypercompetition, strategic group formation and dissolution, and the sustainability or erosion of competitive advantage.

ACKNOWLEDGMENTS

The first author thanks the Ministry of Science and Education of Spain and the Purdue Research Foundation for financial support. The authors benefited from the comments of three anonymous reviewers, discussions with Tim Craig, Rich D'Aveni, Paul Hirsh, Anne Ilinitch, Ken Smith, and Greg Young, and very particularly the comments and suggestions of Ming-Jer Chen. A previous version of the articles, entitled "Do Similar Firms Really Compete Less? Strategic Distance and Multimarket Contact as Predictors of Rivalry Among Heterogeneous Firms," was presented at the

Whittemore Conference on Hypercompetition at Dartmouth College, Hanover, New Hampshire.

REFERENCES

Abell, D. F. (1980), *Defining the Business: The Starting Point of Strategic Planning,* Englewood Cliffs, NJ: Prentice Hall.

Bailey, E. E. and J. R. Williams (1988), "Sources of Economic Rent in the Deregulated Airline Industry," *Journal of Law and Economics,* 31, 173-202.

Barnett, W. P. (1993), "Strategic Deterrence Among Multipoint Competitors," *Industrial and Corporate Change,* 2, 249-278.

Barney, J. B. (1991), "Firm Resources and Sustained Competitive Advantage," *Journal of Management,* 17, 1, 99-120.

—— and R. B. Hoskisson (1990), "Strategic Groups: Untested Assertions and Research Proposals," *Managerial and Decision Economics,* 11, 187-198.

Baum, J. A. C. and J. V. Singh (1994), "Organizational Niches and the Dynamics of Organizational Founding," *Organization Science,* 5, 483-501.

Beath, J. and Y. Katsoulakos (1991), *The Economic Theory of Product Differentiation,* Cambridge, UK: Cambridge University Press.

Bernheim, D. and M. D. Whinston (1990), "Multimarket Contact and Collusive Behavior," *RAND Journal of Economics,* 21, 1-26.

Berry, S. T. (1989), "Entry in the Airline Industry," Ph.D. dissertation, Economics, University of Wisconsin-Madison.

Borenstein, S. (1989), "Hubs and High Fares: Dominance and Market Power in the U.S. Airline Industry," *Rand Journal of Economics,* 20, 344-365.

Broadman, H. G. (1981), "Intraindustry Structure, Integration Strategies, and Petroleum Firm Performance," Ph.D. dissertation, Economics, University of Michigan.

Carroll, G. R. (1985), "Concentration and Specialization: Dynamics of Niche Width in Populations of Organizations," *American Journal of Sociology,* 90, 1262-1283.

—— and A. Swaminathan (1992), "The Organizational Ecology of Strategic Groups in the American Brewing Industry from 1975-1988," *Industrial and Corporate Change,* 1, 65-97.

Caves, R. E. and M. E. Porter (1977), "From Entry Barriers to Mobility Barriers," *Quarterly Journal of Economics,* 91, 241-261.

Chen, M.-J. (1996), "Competitor Analysis and Interfirm Rivalry: Toward a Theoretical Integration," *Academy of Management Review,* 21, 100-134.

Collis, D. (1991), "Cat Fight in the Petfood Industry," cases (A), (B), (C) and (D), Boston, MA: Harvard Business School.

Cool, K. and I. Dierickx (1993), "Rivalry, Strategic Groups and Firm Profitability," *Strategic Management Journal,* 14, 47-59.

—— and D. Schendel (1987), "Strategic Group Formation and Performance: The Case of the U.S. Pharmaceutical Industry 1963-1982," *Management Science,* 33, 1102-1124.

Craig, T. (1996), "The Japanese Beer Wars: Initiating and Responding to Hypercompetition in New Product Development," *Organization Science,* 7, 3, 302-321.

D'Aspremont, C., J. J. Gabszewicz, and J.-F. Thisse (1979), "On Hotelling's 'Stability in Competition,'" *Econometrica,* 47, 1045-1050.

D'Aveni, R. (1994), *Hypercompetition,* New York: Free Press.

Edwards, C. D. (1955), "Conglomerate Bigness as a Source of Power," in *Business Concentration and Price Policy,* A Conference of the Universities-NBER, Princeton, NJ: Princeton University Press, 331-352.

Evans, W. N. and I. N. Kessides (1994), "Living by the 'Golden Rule': Multimarket Contact in the U.S. Airline Industry," *Quarterly Journal of Economics,* 109, 341-366.

Feinberg, R. M. (1984), "Mutual Forbearance as an Extension of Oligopoly Theory," *Journal of Economics and Business,* 36, 243-249.

———— (1985), " 'Sales-at-Risk': A Test of the Mutual Forbearance Theory of Conglomerate Behavior," *Journal of Business,* 58, 225-241.

Fiegenbaum, A. and H. Thomas (1990), "Strategic Groups and Performance: The U.S. Insurance Industry, 1970-84," *Strategic Management Journal,* 11, 197-215.

Greene, W. H. (1990), *Economic Analysis,* New York: Macmillan.

Greening, T. (1980), "Diversification, Strategic Groups and the Structure-Conduct-Performance Relationship: A Synthesis," *The Review of Economics and Statistics,* 62, 475-477.

Hatten, K. J. and M. L. Hatten (1987), "Strategic Groups, Asymmetrical Mobility Barriers and Contestability," *Strategic Management Journal,* 8, 329-342.

———— and D. E. Schendel (1977), "Heterogeneity Within an Industry," *Journal of Industrial Economics,* 26, 2, 592-610.

Hausman, J. A. (1978), "Specification Tests in Econometrics," *Econometrica,* 46, 1251-1271.

Hotelling, H. (1929), "Stability in Competition," *Economic Journal,* 39, 41-57.

Hsiao, C. (1986), *Analysis of Panel Data,* New York: Cambridge University Press.

Hunt, M. S. (1972), "Competition in the Major Home Appliance Industry," 1960-1970, unpublished Ph.D. dissertation, Harvard University.

Judge, G. G., W. E. Griffiths, R. Carter Hill, H. Lutkepohl, and T-C. Lee (1985), *The Theory and Practice of Econometrics,* New York: John Wiley.

Karnani, A. and B. Wernefelt (1985), "Multiple Point Competition," *Strategic Management Journal,* 6, 87-96.

Neter, J., W. Wasserman, and M. H. Kutner (1985), *Applied Linear Statistical Models,* Homewood, IL: Richard D. Irwin.

Newman, H. H. (1973), "Strategic Groups and the Structure-Performance Relationship: A Study with Respect to the Chemical Process Industries," unpublished Ph.D. dissertation, Harvard University.

———— (1978), "Strategic Groups and the Structure-Performance Relationship," *Review of Economics and Statistics,* 60, 417-427.

Ohmae, K. (1985), *Triad Power,* New York: Free Press.

Peteraf, M. A. (1993a), "The Cornerstones of Competitive Advantage: A Resource-Based View," *Strategic Management Journal,* 14, 179-191.

———— (1993b), "Intra-industry Structure and the Response Towards Rivals," *Managerial and Decision Economics,* 14, 519-528.

Phillips, O. R. and C. F. Mason (1992), "Mutual Forbearance in Experimental Conglomerate Markets," *Rand Journal of Economics,* 23, 395-414.

Porter, M. E. (1976), *Interbrand Choice, Strategy, and Bilateral Market Power,* Cambridge, MA: Harvard University Press.

———— (1979), "The Structure Within Industries and Companies Performance," *Review of Economics and Statistics,* 61, 214-227.

———— (1980), *Competitive Strategy,* New York: Free Press.

———— (1981), "Strategic Interaction: Some Lessons from Industry Histories for Theory and Antitrust Policy," in S. Salop (Ed.), *Strategy, Predation, and Antitrust Analysis,* Washington, DC: Federal Trade Commission, 469-521. Rumelt, R. P. (1984), "Towards a

Strategic Theory of the Firm," in R. B. Lamb (Ed.), *Competitive Strategic Management,* Englewood Cliffs, NJ: Prentice Hall, 556-570.

Scott, J. T. (1982), "Multimarket Contact and Economic Performance," *Review of Economics and Statistics,* 64, 368-375.

Searle, S. R. (1971), *Linear Models,* New York: John Wiley.

Smith, F. L. and R. L. Wilson (1995), "The Predicted Validity of the Karnani and Wernerfelt Model of Multipoint Competition," *Strategic Management Journal,* 16, 143-160.

Smith, K. G., C. M. Grimm, and M. J. Gannon (1992), *Dynamics of Competitive Strategy,* Newbury Park, CA: Sage.

Stinchcombe, A. L. (1965), "Social Structure and Organizations," in J. G. March (Ed.), *Handbook of Organizations,* Chicago: Rand McNally.

van Witteloostuijn, A. and M. van Wegberg (1992), "Multimarket Competition: Theory and Evidence," *Journal of Economic Behavior and Organization,* 18, 273-282.

Watson, C. M. (1982), "Counter-Competition Abroad to Protect Home Markets," *Harvard Business Review,* 60, 1, 40-42.

Zajac, E. J. and M. S. Kraatz (1993), "A Diametric Forces Model of Strategic Change: Assessing the Antecedents and Consequences of Restructuring in the Higher Education Industry," *Strategic Management Journal,* 14 (Summer Special Issue), 83-102.

11

Toward the Flexible Form

How to Remain Vital in Hypercompetitive Environments

HENK W. VOLBERDA

Hypercompetition has received much attention, but an important question has not been answered: What organizational forms lead to success in hypercompetitive environments? Hypercompetition forces firms to move more quickly and boldly and to experiment in ways that do not conform to traditional administrative theory. Bureaucratic vertical forms severely hamper the ability to respond to accelerating competition. Flexible forms, in contrast, can respond to a wide variety of changes in the competitive environment in an appropriate and timely way. The author examines several alternative flexible forms for coping with hypercompetitive environments.

Flexibility derives from the repertoire of managerial capabilities (management challenge) and the responsiveness of the organization (organization design challenge). On the basis of theories of control, the author argues that organizational flexibility is inherently paradoxical and requires a constructive friction between change and preservation. The paradox of flexibility is portprayed in a conceptual model that relates competitive environments, certain types of flexibility, and organizational conditions.

The author develops a rich typology of organizational forms for coping with hypercompetition, each of which reflects a particular way of addressing change and preservation. Furthermore, he explores different trajectories of organizational development over time, especially those relating to revitalization. The implications of

267

the typology for strategy and organization design research in hypercompetitive environments are profound.

(FLEXIBILITY; ORGANIZATIONAL FORM;
HYPERCOMPETITIVE ENVIRONMENTS;
REVITALIZATION)

INTRODUCTION

Although traditional organizational forms have worked well in relatively
stable environments of past decades, the globalization of markets, rapid
technological change, shortening of product life cycles, and increasing
aggressiveness of competitors have radically altered the ground rules for
competing in the 1990s and beyond. Instead of long, stable periods in which
firms can achieve sustainable competitive advantage, competition is increasingly characterized by short periods of advantage punctuated by frequent
disruptions (D'Aveni 1994). The behavior of firms in such hypercompetitive
environments has received much attention recently, but the characteristics of
firms that lead to success in hypercompetitive environments have not been
identified. This chapter addresses the question of how firms should be
organized to cope best with hypercompetitive environments.

In the traditional mode of low-intensity and moderate-intensity competition, firms must develop certain unique and difficult-to-transfer routines as
a part of their core competence. Their repositories of routines specify
behavior that is appropriate and a search process for new ideas that are
reasonable and consistent with prior learning (Nelson and Winter 1982).
Competition for rents depends on innovations in routines that are organizationally embedded. Such innovations tend to be incremental and sufficiently
infrequent that specialization is both feasible and desirable.

Teece (1984, p. 106), however, has argued that a limited repertoire of
available routines severely constrains a firm's strategic choice. Although this
suppression of choice is probably a condition for the exploitation of a core
competence, Leonard-Barton (1992) rightly remarks that in highly competitive environments a core competence can become a core rigidity; firms
develop core rigidities together with highly specialized resources to enhance
profits at the price of reduced flexibility. Similarly, Utterback and
Abernathy's (1975) model posits that a firm which does pursue the evolution
of its processes and products to the extreme may find that it has achieved the
benefits of high productivity only at the cost of decreased flexibility and
innovative capacity. It must face competition from innovative products that

are produced by more flexible firms. In the new mode of *hypercompetition,* therefore, rents do not derive from specialized routines but from *adaptive capability.* The reason is that, with hypercompetition, competitive change cannot be predicted but only responded to more or less efficiently ex post. Hence, superior organizational modes in hypercompetitive environments must generate superior adaptive capability.

A well-established stream of research in contingency theory has examined organic forms adapted to highly complex and dynamic environments (Burns and Stalker 1961, Duncan 1972, Lawrence and Lorsch 1967, Thompson 1967). Nonetheless, the defining characteristic of hypercompetition is that firms, in their struggle for control, continuously identify and develop new advantages, thereby creating a temporary disequilibrium. This dynamic process requires new organizational forms that are able to explore new opportunities effectively as well as exploit those opportunities efficiently, to change their strategic focus easily as well as develop some strategic direction, and to change their dominating norms and values as well as correct deviations from essential norms and values. These paradoxical requirements imply that balances must be struck if organizational forms are to remain vital. But how can firms reconcile the conflicting forces for change and stability?

Recently, several approaches have been suggested for coping with this paradox, such as the virtual corporation (Davidow and Malone 1992), the network form (Miles and Snow 1986), and the shamrock organization (Handy 1990). Most researchers are concerned with the logic of justification and rationalization of a particular organizational form, rather than the logic of discovery of new forms in general. In this chapter, a typology of alternative flexible forms is developed for coping with hypercompetitive environments. The empirical chapters of Hanssen-Bauer and Snow (Chapter 14, this volume), Liebeskind et al. (1996), Richardson (Chapter 9, this volume), and Smith and Zeithaml (Chapter 16, this volume) show that some of these forms are viable whereas others have not yet been found.

First, the inherently paradoxical nature of flexibility is examined. On the basis of some insights drawn from theories of control, organizational flexibility is argued to derive from the control capacity of the management and the controllability of the organization. This two-dimensional conception of flexibility as a managerial and organization design challenge is portrayed in a conceptual model. Specific propositions then are derived that connect types of competitive environments with effective types of flexibility and organizational conditions. The typology of possibilities consists of the rigid, planned, flexible, and chaotic forms; each form reflects a particular way of coping with the flexibility paradox of change versus preservation. Finally, trajectories of organizational failure and success are derived from the typology.

THE PARADOX OF FLEXIBILITY

Nearly all definitions of organizational flexibility emphasize the adaptive capacity of management in terms of an ability (Aaker and Mascarenhas 1984, Frazelle 1986, Kieser 1969, Scott 1965, Zelenovic 1982), a repertoire (Weick 1982), a degree of freedom (Sanchez 1993, Thompson 1967), or free options (Quinn 1985) to initiate or adapt to competitive change. In most definitions flexibility opposes stability, and only a few emphasize that if flexibility is to have value it must be combined with stability. That idea is not wholly new, for Scott (1965) observed that creating too great a capacity to respond by deliberate postponement of decisions resulted in a lack of decisiveness, progressively increasing costs, and a continual revision of plans. Too great a reaction capacity or too short a reaction time may lead to overreaction, excessive information search, and wasted resources, Weick (1982) concluded that total flexibility makes it impossible for the organization to retain a sense of identify and continuity; in other words, flexibility without stability results in chaos. More recently, Van Ham, Pauwe, and Williams (1987) stressed the stability component of flexibility as necessary to preserve the identify and maintain the controllability of the organization. Similarly, Adler (1988) claimed that flexibility is advantageous or a meaningful concept only against a backdrop of stability. Instability is a result of a lack or excess of flexibility, so flexibility is the middle course between rigidity and overreaction.

Control theory provides another way of looking at the paradox of flexibility (De Leeuw and Volberda 1992). A firm is "under control" when for each competitive change there is a corresponding managerial capability and firm response (see Figure 11.1). In hypercompetitive environments, in which competitive change is frequent and radical, organizations may easily become adrift because flexibility requires high responsiveness (controllability) of the organization and sufficient managerial capabilities (control capability of management). The flexibility of an organization is the outcome of an interaction between (a) the controllability or responsiveness of the organization and (b) the dynamic control capacity of management. This interaction is such that the elements must be in balance. If one outweighs the other, there is no gain. More controllability does not compensate for less capacity. The system is only as effective as the weakest dimension.

Hence, flexibility is a function of the interaction of two sets of variables. We can see this duality in two separate tasks (see Figure 11.2). First, flexibility is perceived to be a managerial task. Can managers respond at the right time in the right way? In this connection, the concern is with the managerial capabilities that endow the firm with flexibility; for example, manufacturing flexibility to expand the number of products the firm can profitably offer to the market or innovation flexibility to reduce the response

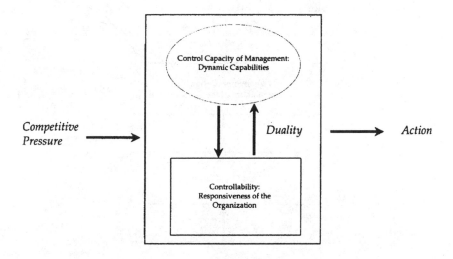

Figure 11.1. Paradox or Duality of Control Capacity and Controllability

time for bringing new products to the market. Second, flexibility is perceived to be an organization design task. Can the organization react at the right time in the directed way? The concern here is with the controllability or changeability of the organization, which depends on the creation of the right conditions to foster flexibility. For instance, manufacturing flexibility requires a technology with multipurpose machinery, universal equipment, and an extensive operational production repertoire (cf. Adler 1988). Similarly, innovation flexibility requires a structure of multifunctional teams, few hierarchical levels, and few process regulations (cf. Quinn 1985; Schroeder et al. 1986). These two tasks result in the following definition (Volberda 1998, Volberda and Cheah 1993).

> DEFINITION. *Flexibility is the degree to which an organization has a variety of managerial capabilities and the speed at which they can be activated, to increase the control capacity of management and improve the controllability of the organization.*

The Managerial Task: Developing Dynamic Capabilities

As a managerial task, flexibility involves the creation or promotion of capabilities for situations of unexpected disturbance. Developing such capabilities is not exclusively the role of the manager. Grant (Chapter 12, this

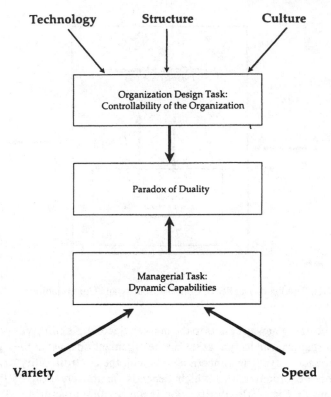

Figure 11.2. Organizational Flexibility and the Associated Managerial and Organization Design Tasks

volume) makes clear that in principle every organizational member participates in the process of capability development. Whereas authoritarian managers may restrict capability development to a limited number of people, more democratic and more participative forms of decision making in organizations can result in a much wider involvement. Figure 11.2 shows two core components of this managerial task, variety and speed.

Variety of Managerial Capabilities. Not only the currently used arsenal of capabilities is important, but also the collection of potential flexibility-increasing capabilities that are not yet activated. Currently used capabilities have already been deployed for a real flexibility need (Reichwald and Behrbohm 1983). The possible emergence of opportunities or threats requires management to have some potential capabilities as insurance against risk (see Scott 1965). Ashby (1964) demonstrated that to be able to respond

TABLE 11.1 Types of Flexibility

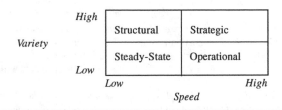

to all circumstances, a firm must have a variety of capabilities at least as great as the variety of disturbances in the environment. In a turbulent environment, management needs an extensive, multidimensional collection of capabilities. Variety can be in terms of either the quantity (the number) of capabilities or the quality of capabilities (such as temporary versus durable flexibility-increasing capabilities). For instance, the training of multiskilled personnel results in a durable improvement in flexibility, whereas the contracting out of certain peripheral activities or "hire-and-fire" employment practices result in a temporary improvement in flexibility. Temporary flexibility-increasing capabilities lead to a reduction of the potential for use once allocated, but durable flexible capabilities are not restricted in use.

Speed. Management may have the necessary capabilities, but may not be able to activate them in time. Flexibility is not a static condition, but a dynamic process. Speed is therefore an essential factor of organizational flexibility.

The dynamic capabilities that endow the firm with flexibility are manifested in the "*flexibility mix.*" Considering this flexibility mix as a hierarchy of capabilities (cf. Grant, Chapter 12, this volume), we can distinguish four types of flexibility (see Table 11.1): steady-state, operational, structural, and strategic (Ansoff and Brandenburg 1971, Volberda 1998). Each type represents a simple combination of more/less variety of capabilities and fast/slow response.

Steady-state flexibility (low variety, low speed) consists of static procedures to optimize the firm's performance when the levels of throughput and the nature of throughput remain relatively stable over time. It hardly seems to be a real type of flexibility, because under steady-state conditions there is only minor change and a relatively low premium on speed of response to external conditions.

For the other three types of flexibility a distinction can be made between internal and external flexibility (Ansoff 1965). Internal flexibility is defined

TABLE 11.2 Examples of Internal and External Types of Flexibility

	Internal	External
Routine maneuvering capacity	*Internal operational flexibility* • Variation of production volume • Building up of inventories • Use of crash teams	*External operational flexibility* • Use of temporary labor • Multisourcing • Reserving of capacity with suppliers
Adaptive maneuvering capacity	*Internal structural flexibility* • Creating multifunctional teams • Changing managerial roles • Alterations in control systems	*External structural flexibility* • Purchasing of components from suppliers with a short delivery time (JIT) • Purchasing of subassemblies from suppliers (co-makership) • Developing of subcomponents together with suppliers (co-design)
Strategic maneuvering capacity	*Internal strategic flexibility* • Dismantling of current strategy • Applying new technologies • Fundamentally renewing products	*External strategic flexibility* • Creating new product market combinations • Using market power to deter entry and control competitors • Engaging in political activities to counteract trade regulations

as management's capability to adapt to the demands of the environment. External flexibility is defined as management's capability to influence the environment so that the firm becomes less vulnerable to environmental changes. Examples of these types of flexibility are provided in Table 11.2. The table shows that the variety and speed of managerial capabilities may result in various levels of managerial maneuvering capacity and can be both internal and external.

Operational flexibility (low variety, high speed) consists of routine capabilities that are based on present structures or goals of the organization. It is the most common type of flexibility and relates to the volume and mix of activities rather than the kinds of activities undertaken within the firm. The routines used are directed primarily at the operational activities and are reactive. Operational flexibility provides rapid response to changes that are familiar. Such changes typically lead to temporary, short-term fluctuation in the firm's level of activity. Although the variety in the environment may be high, the combinations of conditions are sufficiently predictable for management to develop specialized routines to reduce uncertainty. Operational flexibility can be internal or external. Examples of internal operational flexibility are the variation of production volume, the building up of inventories, and the maintenance of excess capacity in terms of financial resources. Richardson (Chapter 9, this volume) shows that vertically integrated fashion apparel firms have developed "quick-response" routines aimed at shortening the manufacturing cycle, reducing inventory levels, and enabling manufacture in response to sales during the season. The object of internal operational flexibility is a more efficient, less risky operation in a volatile end market. External operational flexibility can be achieved by contracting out certain peripheral activities, using temporary labor to adjust the size of the workforce to shifts in product demand, or obtaining resources from more than one supplier.

Structural flexibility (high variety, low speed) consists of managerial capabilities to adapt the organization structure, and its decision and communication processes, to suit changing conditions in an evolutionary way (Krijnen 1979). When faced with revolutionary changes, management needs great internal structural flexibility or intraorganizational leeway to facilitate the renewal or transformation of current structures and processes. Examples of internal structural flexibility are horizontal or vertical job enlargement, the creation of small production units or work cells within a production line, changes in organizational responsibilities, alterations in control systems, the use of project teams, and even the transformation from a functional grouping to a market-oriented grouping with interchangeable personnel and equipment.

Structural flexibility can also be external in terms of interorganizational leeway in supporting and sheltering new technologies or developing new products or markets. Examples are various forms of JIT purchasing, comakership, codesign, or even joint ventures and other coalignments. By increasing such structural relations with outsiders, the organization can engage more easily in new developments. This point is perfectly illustrated by Hanssen-Bauer and Snow (Chapter 14, this volume), who note that for regional firms to cope with hypercompetitive environments, they need network relationships to expedite the learning process. From the regional firm's standpoint, external structural flexibility raises interesting questions about the relative efficacy of internal versus external avenues toward new products, technologies, and knowledge (cf. Pennings and Harianto 1992).

Strategic flexibility (high variety, high speed) consists of managerial capabilities related to the goals of the organization or the environment (Aaker and Mascarenhas 1984). This most radical type of flexibility is much more qualitative and involves changes in the nature of organizational activities. Strategic flexibility is necessary when the organization faces unfamiliar changes that have far-reaching consequences and needs to respond quickly. The issues and difficulties relating to strategic flexibility are by definition unstructured and nonroutine. The signals and feedback received from the environment tend to be indirect and open to multiple interpretations, "soft" and "fuzzy." Because the organization usually has no specific experience and no routine answer to cope with the changes, management may have to change its game plans, dismantle its current strategies (Harrigan 1985), apply new technologies, or fundamentally renew its products. The response may also be external, for example influencing consumers through advertising and promotions (Mascarenhas 1982), creating new product market combinations (Krijnen 1979), using market power to deter entry and control competitors (Porter 1980), or engaging in political activities to counteract trade regulations. New values and norms are necessary and past experience may not provide any advantage (Newman et al. 1972). The creation of new activities in new situations may be very important. Smith and Zeithaml (Chapter 16, this volume) show how regional Bell operating companies (RBOCs) developed strategic flexibility from international expansion activities because the international managers in the unregulated side of the business questioned past practices, raised new assumptions about the organization, and promoted significant changes in strategy.

The Organization Design Task: Creating Adequate Organizational Conditions

The ability to initiate the repertoire of managerial capabilities depends on the design adequacy of organizational conditions, such as the organization's technology, structure, and culture (Zelenovic 1982). Those conditions determine the organization's controllability or responsiveness. As Grant (Chapter 12, this volume) argues, capabilities can be utilized efficiently only if the hierarchy of capabilities corresponds to the architecture of the firm. If management tries to increase the flexibility mix beyond the limits of organizational conditions, the controllability of the organization will diminish.

Designing the appropriate organizational conditions requires identifying the type of technological, structural, or cultural changes necessary to ensure effective utilization of managerial capabilities. For many service and manufacturing organizations, recent developments in *technology* have created a range of programmable automation systems and general information systems that seem to afford much greater flexibility potential (Adler 1988). In this connection, "technology" refers to the hardware (such as machinery and equipment) and the software (knowledge) used in the transformation of inputs into outputs, as well as the configuration of the hardware and software. The design of technology can range from routine to nonroutine, corresponding to the opportunities for routine capabilities. Routine technology is often characterized by mass or process modes of production, a typical line layout, specialized equipment dedicated to specific products, and a limited production repertoire. Such technology is focused on volume to create learning by doing or economies of scale. Consequently, its potential for flexibility is minimal. Nonroutine technology is characterized by small batch or unit modes of production combined with a group layout. In addition, the means of transformation are often multipurpose and the operational production repertoire is large. Such a completely redeployable technology gives leeway for search processes. The potential for flexibility is not restricted by technological constraints. Various intermediate technological designs also are possible. Richardson's study (Chapter 9, this volume) of fashion apparel firms shows that redesigning their technology by implementing new information technologies such as CAD/CAM equipment and EDI resulted in a large potential for operational flexibility.

Increases in controllability might also involve changes in *organizational structure*. Organizational structure comprises not only the actual distribution of responsibilities and authority among the organization's personnel (basic form), but also the planning and control systems and the process regulations of decision-making, coordination, and execution. The structural design of the organization can range from mechanistic to organic (Burns and Stalker 1961), corresponding to the opportunities for adaptive capabilities. A functional type of organizing with many hierarchical levels is characteristic of a mechanistic structure. Processes may be highly regulated through elaborate planning and control systems, specialization of tasks, and high degrees of formalization and centralization. Only minor incremental changes are possible in such a highly formalized and centralized structure (Cohn and Turyn 1984).

In contrast, an organic structure can range from the divisionalized form to the project or matrix form consisting of few hierarchical levels. Essential for both the divisional and matrix forms are planning and control systems that are predominantly performance oriented instead of means oriented and allow for ambiguous information and necessary experimentation and intuition. Moreover, direct process regulation in the form of specialization and formalization is extremely low, whereas indirect process regulation by training and education is well developed. The preceding principles of organic structure are basic guidelines. Because of the "equifinality" of the various structural design parameters, different configurations of those parameters can constitute the organic structure. Such organic structures provide great leeway for structural flexibility.

Many large corporations are undertaking organizational restructuring to increase their responsiveness. For instance, Xerox was able to exploit its superior technological and market capabilities after fundamentally changing the organizational architecture of the firm by creating business divisions with self-organizing teams and developing new reward and recognition systems (Howard 1992). Similarly, Smith and Zeithaml (Chapter 9, this volume) illustrates that the newly developed capabilities of two RBOCs could be successfully deployed after drastic restructuring and organizational redesign.

Not only structural changes, but also cultural changes may be necessary to increase the controllability of the firm. *Organizational culture* can be defined as the set of beliefs and assumptions held relatively commonly throughout the organization and taken for granted by its members (Bate 1984). Essential features of such beliefs are that they are implicit in the minds of organization members and to some extent shared (Hofstede 1980). The beliefs may constrain managerial capabilities by specifying broad, tacitly understood rules for appropriate action in unspecified contingencies (Camerer and Vepsalainen 1988). The organizational culture can range from conservative to innovative, depending on the slack within the current norms and value systems for strategic capabilities. A conservative culture consists of a strong and homogeneous identity with a narrow scope. Leaders apply a directive leadership style. There are large repositories of unwritten rules as a result of a strong discipline dominance, socialization processes, and a low tolerance of ambiguity. Moreover, a conservative culture has a closed external orientation, which is mainly short-term and reactive. In contrast, an innovative culture has a weak and heterogeneous identity with a broad scope. Leaders apply a delegative leadership style and are biased toward improvisation. There are only a few unwritten rules as a consequence of a low discipline dominance (free exchange of knowledge and information between the various disciplines), weak socialization processes, and a high tolerance of ambiguity. Exceptions involving violations of the formal rules are possible. The external orientation is very open and long-term oriented.

The beliefs and assumptions of the organizational culture play a central role in the interpretation of environmental stimuli and the configuration of organizationally relevant strategic responses (Johnson 1987). Does the organization see new strategic options? Can it deviate from present patterns? The more innovative the culture, the greater the leeway for strategic flexibility within the organization. Hence, many large corporations have not only restructured the organization, but also tried to change the corporate culture (e.g., GE's workout program, Philip's Centurion program, and ABB's corporate bible). Craig's (Chapter 7, this volume) study of two players in the Japanese beer industry reveals that Asahi initiated and Kirin responded to hypercompetition by not only working on their functional structure, but also reconsidering their intolerant culture. Both firms fundamentally changed their corporate culture by corporate identity and empowerment programs.

THE CONCEPTUAL MODEL:
BASIC ASSUMPTIONS AND PROPOSITIONS

Combining the managerial and organization design tasks involves a process of matching, typically called duality or resolving paradoxes. Management must develop dynamic capabilities that enhance flexibility and the firm must have an adequate organizational design to utilize those capabilities. Consequently, management must cope with a constructive tension (Kanter 1983) between developing capabilities and preserving organizational conditions. If there is no balance, flexibility efforts will fail. For instance, if management develops dynamic capabilities but the organization remains inert, the firm will experience chaos. Management will overreact to competitive change and the organization will be unable to respond. Conversely, if the responsiveness of the organization is increased but the managerial capabilities are limited, the flexibility potential will be largely unrealized.

The process of matching represents *metaflexibility*. Management must reconfigure the flexibility mix and redesign the organizational conditions in line with future competitive changes. Because change is frequent and disruptive in hypercompetitive environments, effective flexibility requires the development of a supporting monitoring or learning system, particularly the intelligence-gathering and information-processing functions of management (Galbraith 1973). Such a system may contribute to the firm's vision of where the next advantage will be discovered, where the company should focus its disruption, and which capabilities it needs and which it does not. D'Aveni (1994, p. 246) calls this "strategic soothsaying," which is concerned with understanding the future evolution of markets and technology that will proactively create new opportunities to serve current or new customers. Ansoff (1980) calls the latter "surprise management."

The factors that determine the sufficiency of the flexibility mix and the design adequacy of the organizational conditions have not been examined explicitly. When can management combine operational flexibility with tight organizational conditions and when must it combine structural or even strategic flexibility with looser organizational conditions? The sufficiency of the flexibility mix and the adequacy of the organizational conditions are assumed to depend on the turbulence in the environment. That is, the more dynamic (frequency and intensity of environmental changes), complex (number and relatedness of environmental changes), and unpredictable the environment (extent to which cause-effect relationships are incomplete), the more difficult it is to handle the managerial and organization design tasks (Volberda 1998). However, the causal connection between the environment

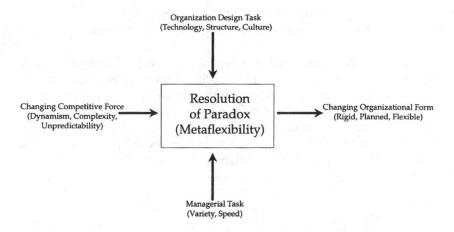

Figure 11.3. A Conceptual Model of Organizational Flexibility

and the firm is not assumed to be one way. Firms may drive their environment and vice versa. This two-dimensional conception of flexibility together with the turbulence characteristics of the organizational environment are portrayed in the conceptual model in Figure 11.3. The model relates the composition of the flexibility mix and the design of organizational conditions to the degree of environmental turbulence. The basic assumptions of the conceptual model follow.

ASSUMPTION 1. *Management's flexibility mix must match the degree of environmental turbulence (**sufficiency of the flexibility mix**).*

ASSUMPTION 2. *To activate a sufficient flexibility mix, the design of the organizational conditions must provide adequate potential for flexibility (**design adequacy of the organizational conditions**).*

ASSUMPTION 3. *The sufficiency of the flexibility mix and the design adequacy of the organizational conditions must be continuously matched with the degree of environmental turbulence.*

The first assumption reflects the managerial task of flexibility, the second reflects the design task of flexibility, and the third indicates the difficulty of matching the two tasks in a dynamic context.

Three propositions can be stated about optimal organizational forms for coping with various competitive environments.

PROPOSITION 1: RIGID FORM UNDER LOW COMPETITION. *In a static, simple, and predictable (**noncompetitive**) environment, the optimal organizational form employs a limited flexibility mix and has a routine technology, a mechanistic structure, and a conservative culture. In addition, the intelligence-gathering and information-processing aspects of metaflexibility are very elementary.*

The first proposition is very straightforward. In noncompetitive environments, firms have established positions that enable them to develop absolute sustainable competitive advantages and generate excessive profit potential. In such environments, there is little need for managers to expend effort on a flexibility mix or for the organizational conditions to generate potential for flexibility. Too much flexibility is a nuisance. Consequently, intelligence gathering and information processing can be restricted to the primary functions of the organization.

PROPOSITION 2: PLANNED FORM UNDER MODERATE COMPETITION. *In a dynamic and/or complex but largely predictable (**moderately competitive**) environment, the optimal form employs a more comprehensive flexibility mix dominated by operational flexibility and has a more nonroutine technology, a relatively mechanistic structure, and a conservative culture. In addition, intelligence-gathering and information-processing capacity is very extensive and directed toward proliferation of routines.*

For survival in a dynamic and complex but largely predictable environment, managers must activate many sophisticated routines to cope with complex changes. They need a potential for operational flexibility originating from a nonroutine technology. In moderately competitive environments, firms seek to establish stable "oligopolies" by implicit collusion or developing sustainable competitive advantages (D'Aveni 1994, p. 224). Creation of strong entry and mobility barriers can reduce intraindustry rivalry. Competition may be characterized by relatively long periods of incremental, competence-enhancing changes (Tushman and Anderson 1986). In Clark's (1985) terminology, the result is a narrowing of approach instead of the emergence of new management approaches. Although competitive changes can be very dynamic and complex, they may be predictable to a large extent and various routines (ranging from simple to sophisticated) can be developed. Management therefore needs an extensive information-processing capacity to anticipate complex changes and to facilitate development of routines.

PROPOSITION 3: FLEXIBLE FORM UNDER HYPERCOMPETITION. *In a funda-mentally unpredictable environment, which may also be dynamic and complex (**hypercompetitive**)* the optimal form employs a broad flexibility mix dominated by structural and strategic flexibility and has a nonroutine technology, an organic structure, and an innovative culture. The intelligence-gathering and information-processing aspects of metaflexibility are directed toward enhancing the receptiveness to new environments.

The third proposition suggests that in hypercompetitive environments, management must activate both strategic flexibility and structural flexibility originating from innovative culture and organic structure. The escalating degree of competition results in short periods of advantage punctuated by frequent disruptions. The disruptions are associated with departures from current approaches that reduce the value of established commitments and competence and require fundamentally new capabilities. The liability of newness plagues new firms confronting moderate competition within well-established markets, whereas the liability of age and tradition constrains established successful firms confronting hypercompetition (Stinchcombe 1965, Tushman and Anderson 1986). Hypercompetition is facilitated by the disequilibrium-creating activities of firms that are capable of breaking new ground, pioneering new fields, promoting radical innovation, and, in the process, partially or completely transforming the organization. Instead of building on current routines as a part of their operational flexibility, such firms develop high levels of structural and strategic flexibility.

A TYPOLOGY OF FORMS FOR
COPING WITH HYPERCOMPETITION

The conceptual model clarifies variations among organizations in the composition of the flexibility mix. Nonetheless, this instrumental model ignores the *process* of variation in the composition of the flexibility mix *over time*. In other words, how does management cope with change? The propositions raise serious doubts as to whether there is a permanently flexible organization. Shifts may occur in the level of competition, and the composition of the flexibility mix and the design variables of the organizational conditions must vary correspondingly. An ongoing process of variation in the flexibility mix and related organizational conditions is needed to overcome routinization and chaos. On the basis of the two central dimensions of organizational flexibility—the extensiveness of the flexibility mix and the controllability of the organizational conditions—many organizational forms are possible for coping with hypercompetition. Aside from the three ideal

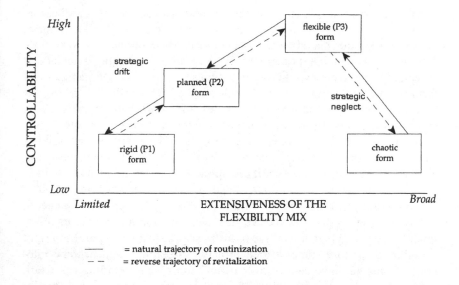

Figure 11.4. A Typology of Alternative Flexible Forms for Coping with Hypercompetition

types, *rigid, planned,* and *flexible,* there is at least one other, the *chaotic* form (see Figure 11.4). Each type represents a particular way of addressing the flexibility paradox of change versus preservation, and some are more effective than others.

The *rigid form* reflects Proposition 1. It has a very small flexibility mix and the controllability or changeability of the organization is low. The flexibility mix is dominated by simple procedures (steady-state flexibility). In addition, the choice and variation possibilities are limited; improvisation is forbidden in the organization. The mature technology (routine), the functionalized and centralized structure with many hierarchical layers (mechanistic), and the monotonous and narrow-minded culture (conservative) do not allow potential for flexibility and result in a fragile and vulnerable organization.

The *planned form* (Proposition 2) also has a narrow flexibility mix, but the variety of routines and the controllability are less limited than in the rigid organization. The flexibility mix mainly consists of specific rules and detailed procedures, which are sophisticated and complex and require an extensive information-processing capacity. Moreover, for every possible change, the management has developed a certain routine. The rigidity of this organizational form is not a result of the technology or the basic organiza-

HYPERCOMPETITIVE RESPONSES

tional structure, but of strong process regulations such as standardization, formalization, and specialization, and very detailed planning and control systems. Also, the shared cultural beliefs and assumptions give very little leeway for deviant interpretations of the environment, and dissonance is potentially threatening to the organization's integrity. This organizational form resembles the "ideal-type" bureaucracy of Weber (Perrow 1986). As long as there are no unexpected changes, the controllability of such an organization is high. However, if changes occur that are not anticipated in the planning repertoire and are threatening to the shared idea system, the result is a situation known as *"strategic drift"* in which consciously managed incremental changes do not necessarily keep pace with environmental changes (Johnson 1988, p. 88). Inertia sets in and the organization becomes rigid.

An illustration of the planned form is provided by Richardson (Chapter 9, this volume) in his discussion of vertical integration as a valuable organizational mode in a hypercompetitive industry such as fashion apparel. By tight coupling, firms lose some of their structural flexibility and become integrated firms that have control over manufacturing and retailing (cf. Clark 1985, Utterback and Abernathy 1975). Such integrated firms are very similar to the planned form in the typology. They have mainly operational flexibility in terms of managerial routines to respond quickly based on a nonroutine technology (CAD/CAM equipment, EDI). Such integrated firms are superior organizational forms for exploiting current opportunities through technological innovations known as "quick response." Nonetheless, their structural and strategic flexibility for developing new opportunities is low. Richardson's study shows that the exploitation of time and response opportunities requires further integration and may lead to new rigidities. The planned firms run the risk of being outperformed by flexible deintegrated firms that have more structural and strategic flexibility.

The *flexible form* (Proposition 3) has a large and rich flexibility mix dominated by strategic and structural flexibility. In addition, the controllability of the organizational conditions is reasonably high. Disturbances are met effectively with alert adaptations without the organization losing its distinctiveness. Resistance to signals of threat to the idea system is low, and the system adapts. Change can be implemented easily through adaptations within the current (nonroutine) technology and (organic) structure (Ansoff and Brandenburg 1971). The organization is able to resist being overwhelmed by its immediate environment and the consequently losing its distinctiveness. It develops some dominance over its environment to preserve its identity. The balance between change and preservation is well managed.

Of the organizational forms discussed in this volume, the social network form (Liebeskind et al., Chapter 15, this volume) and the cluster form (Hanssen-Bauer and Snow, Chapter 14, this volume) are closest to the flexible form. Liebeskind and her coauthors argue that the social network form is an appropriate organizational mode for sourcing scientific knowledge in the hypercompetitive new biotechnology industry. The social network form differs from the hierarchy and market exchange forms in the sense that it has a high degree of structural and strategic flexibility. This organizational form is characterized by a redeployable technology and an organic structure, but with strong ties between actors as a result of a strong professional culture. New biotechnology firms in a social network have much room to maneuver, but also preserve some commonly shared social norms. That is, the network requires a willingness to change and to renew and at the same time an unconditional commitment, concern, and loyalty to the social norms. It supports Kanter's (1988, p. 195) suggestion to encourage strong social ties within flexible forms and strong beliefs in fundamental values. Also, the regional cluster form of Norvest Forum Inc. in Norway described by Hanssen-Bauer and Snow might be considered a flexible form. Such a cluster form provides much strategic leeway for participating regional firms, but also preservation and self-control in terms of structural relationships.

Finally, the *chaotic form* in the typology has a very extensive flexibility mix dominated by strategic flexibility, but is totally uncontrollable. In such organizations, the possibilities for variation are unlimited, because there is no anchorage within the organizational conditions. The innumerable initiatives for change are impossible to implement. A distinct technology, administrative structures, and basic shared values stemming from the organizational culture are lacking. Consequently, the environment can force the organization in a certain direction; that is, the organization is controlled by the environment. The lack of administrative stability is caused by *strategic neglect*. According to Burgelman (1983, pp. 234-237), strategic neglect is the more or less deliberate tendency not to pay attention to the administrative structure of the organization. As a result, emerging administrative problems deteriorate from petty and trivial to severe and disruptive. In his study of new internal corporate ventures, Burgelman concluded that such administrative instability is exacerbated by lack of strong strategic orientation to counter opportunistic behavior on the part of some participants in the venture. The range of possible procedures is so large that making a choice is very difficult and managers' decision-making capacity is greatly reduced (Eppink 1978, Scott 1965). Decisions are delayed although the situation requires an immediate decision.

The chaotic form generally has a negative association, but Smith and Zeithaml (Chapter 16, this volume) show that it has a role for exploration of new opportunities when firms are facing advancing hypercompetitive conditions. By exploring how two regional Bell operating companies created new capabilities in their telecommunication service industry, she argues that resource-rich firms begin to develop new capabilities through chaotic forms in their unregulated business. The chaotic forms were characterized by no clear agreement on outcomes, uncrystallized or problematic relations between means and ends, and a lack of focused strategy (cf. Hrebiniak and Joyce 1985).

The four-cell typology of organizational forms is important for understanding the process of variation in the composition of the flexibility mix and the design of the organizational conditions over time. No such system of categorization related to flexibility has been proposed in the study of organizations. Forms are currently identified through such typologies as mechanistic-organic or bureaucratic-professional or through empirically developed typologies. Although these fragmentary typologies contribute rich insights to flexible technologies, structures, and cultures, they are often not complex enough or sufficiently developed to permit a very comprehensive analysis of organizational flexibility. Consequently, the difference between the planned form (in which operational flexibility dominates) and the flexible form (in which structural and strategic flexibility dominate) is frequently unclear or confusing. For instance, the vertically integrated form described by Richardson (Chapter 9, this volume) is perfectly able to exploit quick-response routines. The superior operational flexibility enables the firms to identify mistakes and take corrective actions quickly. Nonetheless, their structural and strategic flexibility diminishes as a consequence of an increased commitment to irreversible resources. The social network form, in contrast, has high levels of structural and strategic flexibility that enable it to engage more easily in radical new developments. Both the integrated form and the social network form are flexible, but in totally different ways.

TRAJECTORIES OF TRANSFORMATION

The typology illustrates that none of the forms is a permanent solution of the flexibility paradox of change versus preservation. However, we can obtain from the typology trajectories for coping with competitive change. Some likely trajectories are considered next, with examples based on the empirical studies in this volume and flexibility studies in Philips Semiconductors, the Dutch Postbank, and the Dutch National Gas Corporation (see Table 11.3).

TABLE 11.3 Trajectories for Coping with Hypercompetition over Time

	Rigid-Planned	Planned-Flexible	Flexible-Chaotic
Routinization (←)	*Strategic Drift*	*Maturation* • Exploitation of time and response opportunites in the fashion apparel industry resulting in further integration of firms (Richardson, Ch. 9)	*Strategic Focus* • Identification of capabilities created within unregulated business of two RBOCs forced by top management intervention (Smith & Zeithaml, Ch. 16)
Revitalization (→)	*Professional Revitalization* • RBOCs becoming more market-driven in their core activities after divestiture (Smith & Zeithaml, Ch. 16) • The Dutch National Postbank's movement from standardized to customized services (Volberda 1998)	*Entrepreneurial Revitalization* • Ability of two firms (Asahi and Kirin) in the Japanese beer industry to create new capabilities and to carry out radical internal change (Craig, Ch. 7) • Transition of Philips Semiconductors from a bureaucratic and conservative to an innovative and responsive company (Volberda 1998)	*Strategic Neglect* • Lack of administrative structures and a shared culture within the R & D Dept of Dutch National Gas Corporation (Volberda 1998)

The Natural Trajectory of Routinization: Decreasing Levels of Competition

The process of transition from a chaotic state to flexible, planned, and rigid forms can be described as a natural trajectory of routinization (see Figure 11.4). During this process of decreasing levels of competition, the accumulation of routines results in a natural trajectory. The trajectory corresponds with Nelson and Winter's (1982) evolutionary theory of economic change, which holds that radical change becomes less possible as the organization ages (Rumelt 1987, p. 151).

Smith and Zeithaml's (Chapter 16, this volume) study on international expansion of two RBOCs is illuminative. These RBOCs were ill-prepared for competition after divestiture, but their top managers allowed chaotic forms in the unregulated side of their business. Smith's study shows how strategic flexibility was created from the firms' chaotic international expansion activities but, because of organizational conditions, the new capabilities could not be utilized. A distinct technology, administrative structures, and shared values stemming from the organizational culture were lacking. The new strategic capabilities of the RBOCs could be deployed only through top management support to *focus* their international efforts on certain types of telecom services, project types, and countries and through drastic changes in organizational design. The chaotic forms are moving toward more flexible forms in which prior experiences with the chaotic forms can be maximally exploited.

As the level of competence-destroying competition (hypercompetition) decreases, the flexible organization faces a crisis. It must become more efficient in its operations to extract greater benefit from the hypercompetitive changes that it introduced previously. The transition from a flexible form toward a planned form can be portrayed as a process of *maturation*. According to Miller and Friesen (1980, p. 285), maturation creates a greater need to professionalize and institutionalize the intelligence-gathering and information-processing functions, and to integrate the efforts of decision makers by formal means (process regulations). This trajectory of maturation can be seen in Richardson's (Chapter 9, this volume) study, where the vertically integrated firm gained more competitive advantage from current technological opportunities (CAD/CAM, EDI) than the more flexible deintegrated firms. However, in the process of adapting and refining the organizational conditions to efficiently exploit time and response opportunities, the planned organization runs the risk of losing its strategic and structural flexibility as it concentrates increasingly on the accumulation of a large number of operational procedures and routines (operational flexibility). In such circumstances, it may become progressively more rigid.

The Reverse Trajectory of Revitalization: Escalating Levels of Competition

For many organizations, the transition from a chaotic state toward a rigid organization can be regarded as a natural trajectory. A transition in the reverse direction in the typology also can be perceived as a trajectory, though it may not be as easy to achieve or seem as "natural" as the former process. Such trajectories of revitalization, initiated for creating temporary disequilibria, are most likely to be effective under situations of hypercompetition.

Smith and Zeithaml's (Chapter 16, this volume) description of the transformation within the core activities (local telephone service activities) of the RBOCs after divestiture seems to expand this trajectory. During their 100-year history in AT&T, the rigid forms had functioned in the context of a monopoly. In 1982, however, the seven RBOCs were jolted from their rigid existence in AT&T. After divestiture, their core activities seemed to be moving toward the planned form. The same trajectory was evident within the Administrative Department of the Dutch National Postbank, the fifth largest bank of The Netherlands (Volberda 1998). The bank was recently privatized. In the past, its main line of business had been retail banking because of restrictions imposed by the Dutch government. It largely provided standardized services to more than six million account holders. After the deregulation, it intended to provide more customized services as a part of corporate banking. The bank was confronted with increasing national and international competition, new information technologies in banking, increased pressure on interest margins, and the introduction of new banking-related services. The Administrative Department Corporate Accounts, which was bureaucratically organized for a noncompetitive environment, had to adopt a more comprehensive flexibility mix dominated by operational flexibility, which in turn originated from a more adaptive technology (broadly applicable information systems) and a larger operational production repertoire of employees.

When such professional revitalization proves inadequate, the planned organization must transform itself further into a more flexible form. In terms of organizational conditions, this change in the composition of the flexibility mix can be realized only if the organization moves toward an even more flexible or multipurpose technology, develops a more organic structure, and adopts a more heterogeneous, open, and externally oriented culture. Such efforts help to promote asymmetry within and "unbalance" the previous organizational form while propelling the organization toward the creation of new temporary advantages better suited to hypercompetitive environments. This process of *entrepreneurial revitalization* is promoted by such changes as new leadership composed of visionary entrepreneurs, reduction of process regulations (specialization, formalization), loose basic organizational forms (grouping by target market, flat structure, and broad management tasks), a more open external orientation, and a high tolerance for ambiguity.

This kind of transition is perfectly described in Craig's (Chapter 7, this volume) study on hypercompetition in the Japanese beer industry. For a long period of time the Japanese beer industry was a stable oligopoly in which competition was limited to well-understood nonprice dimensions (moderate competition). Nonetheless, the hypercompetitive behavior of one firm with declining market share (Asahi) caused escalation of competition on the industry level. The only firms that could respond were ones that were able to revitalize their culture (e.g., corporate identity campaigns, empowerment) and structure (redrawing organizational boundaries between marketing and production, shifting from functional to product division structure, new evaluation and reward systems). A similar transition occurred within Philips Semiconductors (Volberda 1998). The rapidly escalating competition in cost and quality (price erosion and unforeseen volume developments) and in timing and know-how (introduction of plastic diodes, release of higher voltages versions, new crystal types, and the advance of integrated circuits in the application markets) forced the firm to increase its structural and strategic flexibility to more easily exploit unknown opportunities in those hypercompetitive areas. The transition of entrepreneurial revitalization was accomplished by radically transforming the firm from a bureaucratic, conservative company to one that is innovative and responsive. The development of autonomous task groups, interdisciplinary marketing-production-development teams, and less formal planning and control, combined with the development of a unique logo for the plant, the organization of social events, special training, and a news bulletin for employees, made the transformation possible.

If the organization is successful in achieving a major transformation, it faces the opposite danger of overshooting its target and becoming chaotic. For example, the R & D Department of the Dutch National Gas Corporation had unlimited potential for flexibility, but it was impossible for managers to activate (Volberda 1998). In other words, the department was too flexible. There were many initiatives for new research, but they could not be implemented because the department had no clear administrative structures or shared values stemming from its culture. Nor did the department have adequate information about man-hours, costs, or technical progress per project. The schizophrenia of the department resulted in distorted information with which managers could not make appropriate decisions. Consequently, the environment (board, internal clients) could force the department in a certain direction; that is, the department was controlled by its environment. This *strategic neglect* resulted in a lack of decisiveness about research priorities, a fragmented structure, and a loose constellation of subcultures. Kanter (1988, p. 195) points out that, ironically, creating change requires stability. Organizational structures and cultures must allow continuity and preserve the organization in the midst of change. In particular, Kanter proposes encouragement of strong social ties and strong beliefs in fundamental values. Liebeskind et al. (Chapter 15, this volume) discuss the social network form as a viable flexible form under conditions of hypercompetition.

DISCUSSION

Various alternative flexible forms enable firms to initiate or respond successfully to different kinds of competition including hypercompetition. On the basis of an elaboration of the flexibility paradox, a conceptual model is developed for describing flexible organizations. The model is used to construct a rich typology of organizational forms for coping with hypercompetitive environments. From the typology, trajectories of organizational success and failure in meeting various levels of competition are obtained. In the old mode of competition in which firms' attention is directed toward reducing the level of competition, a natural trajectory of routinization is most likely. Contrary to this evolutionary approach, in the new mode of hypercompetition in which firms are confronted with rapidly escalating competition, a trajectory of revitalization is more likely to be successful. In hypercompetitive situations, firms must continuously increase the variety and speed of managerial capabilities as well as the controllability of the organization.

The chapters I have mentioned here provide examples of superior organizational forms for use with particular kinds of hypercompetition. The studies show that the regional cluster form, the social network form, the vertically integrated form, and the garbage can form are viable organizational modes analogous to the forms identified in the typology. Still, in reconciling the "logic of discovery" presented here with the "logic of justification" applied in the empirical articles, a few remarks are necessary.

First, the logic of discovery in my chapter is to some extent speculative, based on a limited number of observations. The model and typology developed might be a fallacious attempt to reduce complex phenomena to simple dimensions. For instance, some dimensions might not be included in the model. Furthermore, the typology does not address the question of causality, the firm affecting the market and vice versa. Nonetheless, exploratory interviews with management consultants and flexibility audits within Philips Semiconductors, the Dutch Postbank, and the Dutch National Gas Corporation suggest that the ideal types are to some extent distinguished by practitioners and clearly have some empirical value (Volberda 1992).

Second, besides being speculative, the logic of discovery can never be as comprehensive as reality. Perhaps there are forms that span the boxes because the typology is restricted to only one level of analysis. Some evidence suggests that if multiple levels or multiple parts are considered, different trajectories of transformation for coping with hypercompetition can be found in a single firm. For instance, Smith and Zeithaml (Chapter 16, this volume) found two different trajectories within the same RBOC. After divestiture, the RBOCs shifted their core activities into more planned modes, but in their unregulated business they created more chaotic modes. The fact that RBOCs now complain about their split-brain personality is not surprising given the two trajectories, one through chaos and another through a more planned mode. One successful RBOC solved this paradox by knitting the regulated and unregulated sides into an integrated whole (synthesis), whereas another successful RBOC accepted the paradox by splitting the company in two to increase both parts' chances for survival. In the study by Galunic and Eisenhardt (Chapter 17, this volume), the paradox is solved by spatial separation (cf. Poole and Van de Ven 1989). That is, mature divisions confronted with moderate competition operate in a planned mode, whereas new ventures developed to create hypercompetitive disruption may operate in a chaotic mode. Nonetheless, to the extent that the relevant environment for the organization as a whole has been transformed from moderate competition to hypercompetition, the crisis confronts the entire organization and requires a comprehensive response, not a partial one. Craig's (Chapter 7, this volume) study shows that a dramatic redesign often is necessary to deploy new capabilities.

Another limitation of the typology is that only four forms are considered. Other combinations of levels of managerial flexibility and controllability of the firm are possible. One might think of the hollow corporation in the left upper corner in the typology; that form is highly controllable but the managerial flexibility repertoire of participating firms is restricted.

The most important contribution of this chapter is that it describes successful and unsuccessful ways to achieve superior flexibility. However, as is clear from the other chapters mentioned here, there will never be one best way to achieve the flexible state in hypercompetitive environments. The trajectories indicate that firms can arrive at the flexible form through strategic focusing of the chaotic mode or through entrepreneurial revitalization of the planned mode. In addition, the flexible form itself can be achieved in different ways, which suggests the likelihood of equifinality. There are several equally good ways to match high variety and speed of managerial capabilities with an adequate design of organizational conditions, solving the constructive tension between development of capabilities and preservation of stability within the organizational conditions. Both the social network form and the regional cluster form are considered as examples of the flexible form. Both forms have high levels of structural and strategic flexibility, but the preservation in the social network form is based on strong beliefs in fundamental values, whereas in the regional network form it is based on self-control of the network in terms of structural relationships.

Finally, the train of thought in this chapter on alternative flexible forms has been initiated in other areas, for instance, the work on strategy types (Miles and Snow 1978, Mintzberg and Waters 1985), archetypes of organizational transitions (Miller and Friesen 1980, Nelson and Winter 1982), and types of corporate entrepreneurship (Schumpeter 1934, Stopford and Baden-Fuller 1994). Although the logic of discovery was enriched by those works, the intention of this chapter is to develop theory and stimulate debate that goes beyond theory on traditional forms in stable competition. The conceptual underpinning of flexible forms as viable in situations of hypercompetition has not been discussed properly. The conceptual model and typology of alternative flexible forms may provide a useful guide for the study of effective organizational forms in the new world of hypercompetition. The logic of discovery has something to offer.

ACKNOWLEDGMENTS

The research was supported by a grant from GITP International. The author thanks Julia Liebeskind, Anna Grandori, Hans Pennings, Ard Pieter de Man, Frans van den Bosch, and especially Charles Baden-Fuller for helpful comments on drafts of the manuscript. In addition, the author thanks the managers of Philips Semiconductors, the Dutch National Gas Corporation, and the Dutch Postbank who participated in the study. Finally, the author owes a great debt of thanks to the editor, Arie Lewin, the participants of the Whittemore Conference on Hypercompetition, and three anonymous reviewers for their insightful and thought-provoking comments. All errors are the author's responsibility.

REFERENCES

Aaker, D. A. and B. Mascarenhas (1984), "The Need for Strategic Flexibility," *Journal of Business Strategy*, 5, 2, 74-82.

Adler, P. S. (1988), "Managing Flexible Automation," *California Management Review*, 30, 3, 34-56.

Ansoff, H. I. (1965), *Corporate Strategy*, New York: McGraw-Hill.

——— (1980), "Strategic Issue Management," *Strategic Management Journal*, 1, 131-148.

——— and R. Brandenburg (1971), "A Language for Organizational Design: Parts I and II," *Management Science*, 17, 12, 350-393.

Ashby, W. R. (1964), *An Introduction to Cybernetics*, London, UK: Methuen.

Bate, P. (1984), "The Impact of Organizational Culture on Approaches to Organizational Problem-Solving," *Organization Studies*, 5, 1, 43-66.

Burgelman, R. A. (1983), "A Process Model of Internal Corporate Venturing in the Diversified Major Firm," *Administrative Science Quarterly,* 28, 2, 223-244.

Burns, T. and G. M. Stalker (1961), *The Management of Innovation,* London, UK: Tavistock.

Camerer, C. and A. Vepsalainen (1988), "The Economic Efficiency of Corporate Culture," *Strategic Management Journal,* 9, 115-126.

Clark, K. B. (1985), "The Interaction of Design Hierarchies and Market Concepts in Technological Evolution," *Research Policy,* 14, 235-251.

Cohn, S. F. and R. M. Turyn (1984), "Organizational Structure, Decision Making Procedures, and the Adaptation of Innovations," *IEEE Transactions on Engineering Management,* EM31, November, 154-161.

D'Aveni, R. (1994), *Hypercompetition: Managing the Dynamics of Strategic Maneuvering,* New York: Free Press.

Davidow, W. H. and M. S. Malone (1992), *The Virtual Corporation,* New York: Harper Collins.

De Leeuw, T. and H. W. Volberda (1992), "On the Concept of Flexibility," in Robert Trappl (Ed.), *Cybernetics and Systems Research '92,* Vol. 2, Singapore: World Scientific, 1079-1086.

Duncan, R. B. (1972), "Characteristics of Organizational Environments and Perceived Environmental Uncertainty," *Administrative Science Quarterly,* 17, 3, 313-327.

Eppink, D. J. (1978), "Planning for Strategic Flexibility," *Long Range Planning,* 11, 4, 9-15.

Frazelle, E. H. (1986), "Flexibility: A Strategic Response in Changing Times," *Industrial Engineering,* 18, 3, 17-20.

Galbraith, J. R. (1973), *Designing Complex Organizations,* Reading, MA: Addison Wesley.

Handy, C. (1990), *The Age of Unreason,* Boston, MA: Harvard Business School Press.

Harrigan, K. R. (1985), *Strategic Flexibility,* Lexington, MA: Lexington Books.

Hofstede, G. (1980), "Motivation, Leadership and Organization: Do American Theories Apply Abroad?" *Organizational Dynamics,* 9, 1, 42-63.

Howard, R. (1992), "The CEO as Organizational Architect: An Interview with Xerox's Paul Allaire," *Harvard Business Review,* 70, 5, 106-121.

Hrebiniak, L. G. and W. F. Joyce (1985), "Organizational Adaptation: Strategic Choice and Environmental Determinism," *Administrative Science Quarterly,* 30, 336-349.

Johnson, G. (1987), *Strategic Change and the Management Process,* Oxford, UK: Basil Blackwell.

―――― (1988), "Rethinking Incrementalism," *Strategic Management Journal,* 9, 75-91.

Kanter, R. M. (1983), *The Change Masters,* New York: Simon & Schuster.

―――― (1988), "When a Thousand Flowers Bloom: Structural, Collective, and Social Conditions for Innovation in Organization," in B. M. Staw and L. L. Cummings (Eds.), *Research in Organizational Behavior,* Vol. 10, Greenwich, CT: JAI, 169-211.

Kieser, A. (1969), "Zur Flexibilität verschiedener Organisationsstrukturen," *Zeitschrift für Organisation,* 38, 273-282.

Krijnen, H. G. (1979), "The Flexible Firm," *Long Range Planning,* 12, 2, 63-75.

Lawrence, P. and J. Lorsch (1967), *Organization and Environment,* Boston, MA: Harvard School of Business Administration Press.

Leonard-Barton, D. (1992), "Core Capabilities and Core Rigidities: A Paradox in Managing New Product Development," *Strategic Management Journal,* Special Issue, 13, 8, 111-125.

Mascarenhas, B. (1982), "Coping with Uncertainty in International Business," *Journal of International Business Studies,* 13, 2, 87-98.

Miles, R. E. and C. C. Snow (1978), *Organizational Strategy, Structure, and Process,* New York: McGraw-Hill.

―――― and ――――, (1986), "Network Organizations: New Concepts for New Forms," *California Management Review,* 28, 3, 62-73.

Miller, D. and P. Friesen (1980), "Archetypes of Organizational Transition," *Administrative Science Quarterly*, 25, 2, 268-300.

Mintzberg, H. and J. A. Waters (1985), "Of Strategies, Deliberate and Emergent," *Strategic Management Journal*, 6, 257-272.

Nelson, R. R. and S. G. Winter (1982), *An Evolutionary Theory of Economic Change*, Cambridge, MA: Harvard University Press.

Newman, W. H., W. H. Summer and E. K. Warren (1972), *The Process of Management: Concepts, Behavior and Practice*, Englewood Cliffs, NJ: Prentice Hall.

Pennings, J. M. and F. Harianto (1992), "Technological Networking and Innovation Implementation," *Organization Science*, 3, 3, 356-382.

Perrow, C. (1986), *Complex Organizations—A Critical Essay*, 3rd ed., New York: Random House.

Poole, M. S. and A. H. van de Ven (1989), "Using Paradox to Build Management and Organization Theories," *Academy of Management Review*, 14, 4, 562-578.

Porter, M. E. (1980), *Competitive Strategy: Techniques for Analyzing Industries and Competitors*, New York: Free Press.

Quinn, J. B. (1985), "Managing Innovation: Controlled Chaos," *Harvard Business Review*, 63, 3, 78-84.

Reichwald, R. and P. Behrbohm (1983), "Flexibilität als Eigenschaft productions-wirtschaftlicher Systeme," *Zeitschrift für Betriebskunde*, 53, 831-853.

Rumelt, R. P. (1987), "Theory, Strategy, and Entrepreneurship," in D. J. Teece (Ed.), *The Competitive Challenge—Strategies for Industrial Innovation and Renewal*, Cambridge, MA: Ballinger, 137-158.

Sanchez, R. (1993), "Strategic Flexibility, Firm Organization, and Managerial Work in Dynamic Markets," *Advances in Strategic Management*, Vol. 9, Greenwich, CT: JAI, 251-291.

Schroeder, R., A. van de Ven, G. Scudder and D. Polley (1986), "Managing Innovation and Change Processes: Findings from the Minnesota Innovation Research Program," *Agribusiness*, 2, 4, 501-523.

Schumpeter, J. A. (1934), *The Theory of Economic Development*, Cambridge, MA: Harvard University Press.

Scott, B. W. (1965), *Long-Range Planning in American Industry*, New York: American Management Association.

Stinchcombe, A. L. (1965), "Social Structure and Organizations," in J. G. March (Ed.), *Handbook of Organizations*, Chicago, IL: Rand McNally, 142-193.

Stopford, J. M. and C. W. F. Baden-Fuller (1994), "Creating Corporate Entrepreneurship," *Strategic Management Journal*, 15, 3, 521-536.

Teece, D. J. (1984), "Economic Analysis and Strategic Management," *California Management Review*, 26, 3, 87-110.

Thompson, J. D. (1967), *Organizations in Action*, New York: McGraw-Hill.

Tushman, M. L. and P. Anderson (1986), "Technological Discontinuities and Organizational Environments," *Administrative Science Quarterly*, 31, 3, 439-465.

Utterback, J. M. and W. J. Abernathy (1975), "A Dynamic Model of Process and Product Innovation," *Omega*, 3, 6, 639-656.

Van Ham, J. C., J. Pauwe, and A. R. T. Williams (1987), "Flexibiliteit en stabiliteit vanuit individu en organisatie," in A. Buitendam (Ed.), *Arbeidsmarkt, Arbeidsorganisatie, Arbeidsverhoudingen, Sociaal Beleid*, Ch. 6, Deventer, The Netherlands: Kluwer, 74-90.

Volberda, H. W. (1998), *Building the Flexible Firm: How to Remain Competitive*, Oxford: Oxford University Press.

Volberda, H. W. and H. Cheah (1993), "A New Perspective on Entrepreneurship: A Dialectic Process of Transformation within the Entrepreneurial Mode, Type of Flexibility and

Organizational Form," in H. Klandt (Ed.), *Research in Entrepreneurship*, Aldershot, UK: Avebury, 261-286.

Weick, K. E. (1982), "Management of Organizational Change Among Loosely Coupled Elements," in P. S. Goodman and Associates (Eds.), *Change in Organizations: New Perspectives in Theory, Research, and Practice*, San Francisco, CA: Jossey-Bass, 375-408.

Zelenovic, D. M. (1982), "Flexibility—A Condition for Effective Production Systems," *International Journal of Production Research*, 20, 3, 319-337.

12

Prospering in Dynamically-Competitive Environments

Organizational Capability as Knowledge Integration

ROBERT M. GRANT

Unstable market conditions caused by innovation and increasing intensity and diversity of competition have resulted in *organizational capabilities* rather than *served markets* becoming the primary basis upon which firms establish their long-term strategies. If the strategically most important resource of the firm is *knowledge,* and if knowledge resides in specialized form among individual organizational members, then the essence of organizational capability is the integration of individuals' specialized knowledge.

This chapter develops a knowledge-based theory of organizational capability, and draws upon research into competitive dynamics, the resource-based view of the firm, organizational capabilities, and organizational learning. Central to the theory is analysis of the mechanism through which knowledge is integrated within firms in order to create capability. The theory is used to explore firms' potential for establishing integrated within firms in order to create capability. The theory is used to explore firms' potential for establishing competitive advantage in dynamic market settings, including the role of firm networks under conditions of unstable linkages between knowledge inputs and product outputs. The analysis points to the difficulties in creating the "dynamic" and "flexible-response capabilities" which have been deemed critical to success in hyper-competitive markets.

(KNOWLEDGE;
ORGANIZATIONAL CAPABILITY;
COMPETITIVE ADVANTAGE)

INTRODUCTION

The growing intensity and dynamism of competition across product markets has had profound implications for the evolution of strategic management thought during the 1980s and 1990s. Increasing turbulence of the external business environment has focused attention upon *resources* and *organizational capabilities* as the principal source of sustainable competitive advantage and the foundation for strategy formulation. As the markets for resources have become subject to the same dynamically-competitive conditions that have afflicted product markets, so *knowledge* has emerged as the most strategically-significant resource of the firm. This chapter seeks to extend our understanding of the determinants of competitive advantage in dynamically-competitive market environments by analyzing the role of knowledge in organizational capability. Building upon four major theoretical streams: competition as a dynamic process, the resource-based view of the firm, organizational capabilities and competences, and organizational knowledge and learning, this paper establishes the rudiments of a knowledge-based theory of the firm. At the heart of this theory is the idea that the primary role of the firm, and the essence of organizational capability, is the *integration of knowledge.* The chapter explores how knowledge is integrated to form organizational capability, and goes on to identify characteristics of capabilities which are associated with creating and sustaining competitive advantage in dynamically-competitive markets, including the achievement of *flexible integration* across multiple knowledge bases. Finally, I consider the relative merits of internal versus external knowledge integration and the benefits of firms networks in coping with hypercompetitive market conditions.

BACKGROUND

The displacement of static theories of competition associated with neoclassical microeconomics and the "structure-conduct-performance" school of industrial economics by the more dynamic approaches associated with the Austrian school of economics, especially with Schumpeter's concept of competition as a process of "creative destruction" (Schumpeter 1934), has had profound implications for strategic management thought (Jacobsen 1992). During the early part of the 1980s, strategy analysis was focused upon the quest for monopoly rent through industry and segment selection and the manipulation of market structure to create market power (Porter 1991). However, if market structure is in a state of flux, and if monopoly rents quickly succumb to new sources of competition, approaches to strategy based upon choices of product markets and positioning within them are unlikely to yield profit advantages that are more than temporary. The impact of the resource-based view of the firm on strategic management thinking can be attributed to two factors. First, given the lack of evidence that monopoly power is an important source of profit (Rumelt 1991), Ricardian rents (returns to resources over and above their opportunity costs) appear to be the primary source of interfirm profitability differences. Second, if external markets are in a state of flux, then the internal resources and capabilities of a firm would appear to be a more stable basis for strategy formulation than the external customer focus that has traditionally associated with the marketing-orientation to strategy (Levitt 1960).

This emphasis on the "supply-side" rather than the "demand side" of strategy has been closely associated with recent work on organizational capabilities. Prahalad and Hamel (1990) argue that sustainable competitive advantage is dependent upon building and exploiting "core competences"—those capabilities which are fundamental to a firm's competitive advantage and which can be deployed across multiple product markets. Porter's recent work emphasizes the need for firms and countries to broaden and upgrade their internal advantages in order to sustain and extend competitive advantages (Porter 1991, 1992).

While extreme forms of dynamic competition (termed "hypercompetition" by D'Aveni 1994) are characteristic of product markets, dynamically competitive conditions also are present in the markets for resources. Indeed, competitive conditions in product markets are driven, in part, by the conditions of competition in the markets for resources (Barney 1986). Thus, the speed with which positions of competitive advantage in product markets are undetermined depends upon the ability of challengers to acquire the resources needed to initiate a competitive offensive. Sustainability of competitive advantage therefore requires resources which are *idiosyncratic* (and therefore scarce), and not easily *transferable* or *replicable* (Grant 1991). These criteria point to knowledge (tacit knowledge in particular) as the most strategically-important resource which firms possess (Quinn 1992). Thus, this paper's focus upon knowledge and its integration is justified by two assumptions about the success in dynamically-competitive market environments:

> *First, under dynamic competition, superior profitability is likely to be associated with resource and capability-based advantages than with positioning advantages resulting from market and segment selection and competitive positions based upon some form of "generic strategy";*
>
> *Second, such resource and capability-based advantages are likely to derive from superior access to and integration of specialized knowledge.*

The literature on organizational knowledge and learning has explored the role of organizations in the acquisition, processing, storage, and application of knowledge (Argyris and Schon 1978, Levitt and March 1988, *Organization Science* 1991, Starbuck 1992). The primary emphasis of this literature is on the acquisition of information by organizations. Nonaka (1994) proposes a theory of knowledge creation built around dynamic interaction between two dimensions of knowledge transfer: transformations from tacit to explicit knowledge and vice-versa; and transfers between individual, group, organizational, and interorganizational levels. However, as Spender (1992) recognizes, firms are engaged not only in knowledge creation but also in knowledge application. The distinction between these two processes is crystallized in Demsetz's (1991) observation that efficiency in the acquisition of knowledge requires that individuals specialize in specific areas of knowledge, while the application of knowledge to produce goods and services requires the bringing together of many areas of specialized knowledge.

Much of the research into the management issues concerning the integration of different types of specialized knowledge has been within the context of new product development (Nonaka 1990, Clark and Fujimoto 1991, Wheelwright and Clark 1992). While some innovations are the result of the application of new knowledge, others result from reconfiguring existing knowledge to create "architectural innovations" (Henderson and Clark 1990, Henderson and Cockburn 1995). This ability of the firm to "generate new combinations of existing knowledge" and "to exploit its knowledge of the unexplored potential of the technology" is what Kogut and Zander (1992, p. 391) describe as "combinative capabilities."

The theory of organizational capability which follows represents an extension and synthesis of these contributions, based upon the idea that the essence of organizational capability is the integration of individuals' specialized knowledge.

THE MODEL: ORGANIZATIONAL
CAPABILITY AS KNOWLEDGE INTEGRATION

My model of organizational capability rests upon basic assumptions regarding the characteristics of knowledge and its deployment. From these assumptions I develop propositions concerning the nature of organizational capability, the linkage of capability to organizational structure, and the determinants of competitive advantage.

Assumptions

The focus of this chapter is upon a single resource: knowledge. This emphasis is justified by the assumptions that, first, knowledge accounts for the greater part of value added,[1] second, barriers to the transfer and replication of knowledge endow it with strategic importance. I define knowledge broadly to include both "explicit" knowledge which can be written down, and "tacit" knowledge which cannot. The emphasis is on tacit knowledge since, in the form of "know-how," skills, and "practical knowledge" of organizational members, tacit knowledge is closely associated with production tasks, and raises the more interesting and complex issues regarding its transfer both within and between organizations.

The key managerial issues arising from the characteristics of knowledge stem from the observation that tacit knowledge is acquired by and stored within individuals. Due to the cognitive limits of the human brain, knowledge is acquired in a highly specialized form: An increase in depth of knowledge implies reduction in breadth. Advances in knowledge tend to be associated with increased specialization. However, production—the creation of value through transforming input into output—requires a wide array of knowledge, usually through combining the specialized knowledge of a number of individuals.

Integrating Knowledge to
Form Organizational Capability

These assumptions provide the basis for a knowledge-based view of the firm. If knowledge is a critical input into all production processes, if efficiency requires that it is created and stored by individuals in specialized form, and if production requires the application of many types of specialized knowledge, then the primary role of the firm is the integration of knowledge. But why are institutions called "firms" needed for the integration of knowledge? It is because the alternatives are too inefficient. An individual's ability to integrate knowledge is constrained by cognitive limits: It is not feasible for each individual to try to learn the knowledge possessed by other specialists. Integration across markets is difficult: In the case of explicit knowledge it is difficult to appropriate the value of the knowledge through market contracts; in the case of tacit knowledge, transfer is both difficult and necessitates transaction-specific investment. This view of the firm as an institution for knowledge integration establishes a view of the firm based upon close integration between organizational members implying stability, propinquity and social relationships, but it does not readily yield precision definition of the firm and its boundaries. For this reason, Demsetz (1991) refers to "firm-like organizations."

Integration of specialist knowledge to perform a discrete productive task is the essence of *organizational capability,* defined as a firm's ability to perform repeatedly a productive task which relates either directly or indirectly to a firm's capacity for creating value through effecting the transformation of inputs into outputs. Most organizational capabilities require integrating the specialist knowledge bases of a number of individuals. A hospital's capability in cardiovascular surgery is dependent upon integrating the specialist knowledge of surgeons, anaesthetist, radiologist, operating-room nurses, and several types of technicians. L. L. Bean's order processing capability, Rubbermaid's new product development capability, and McDonald's Restaurants' capability in preparing and serving hamburgers are all examples of organizational capabilities requiring the integration of specialized knowledge across quite large numbers of employees.

The Architecture of Capabilities

The integration of knowledge into organizational capabilities may be viewed as a hierarchy. This hierarchy is not one of authority and control, as in the traditional concept of an administrative hierarchy, but is a hierarchy of integration. At the base of the hierarchy is the specialized knowledge held by individual organizational members. At the first level of integration are capabilities which deal with specialized tasks. Moving up the hierarchy of capabilities, the span of specialized knowledge being integrated broadens: Task-specific capabilities are integrated into broader functional capabilities—marketing, manufacturing, R & D, and financial. At higher levels of integration are capabilities which require wide-ranging cross-functional integration—new product development involves especially wide-ranging integration (Clark and Fujimoto 1991). Figure 12.1 illustrates this concept of hierarchy of capabilities by providing a vertical segment of the hierarchically-arranged organizational capabilities of a manufacturer of private-branch telephone exchanges (PBXs).

The wider the span of knowledge being integrated, the more complex are the problems of creating and managing organizational capability. The "quick response capability" which Richardson (1996) identifies among apparel suppliers Benetton, The Gap, and Giordano is an important competitive advantage primarily because it is difficult to achieve—it involves integrating across multiple vertical stages. The difficulties experienced by the Bell operating companies in transferring the new capabilities developed in their

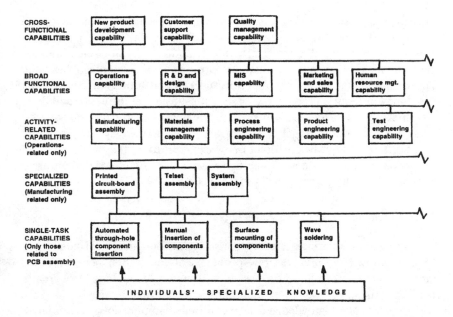

Figure 12.1. Organizational Capabilities of a PBX Producer: A Partial Vertical Segment

overseas businesses back to their domestic operations can be attributed to the fact that many of these new capabilities (e.g. wireless communication, fiber-optics, marketing within competitive markets, and managing joint ventures) require integration across broad-spans of knowledge and expertise (Smith 1996).

Although higher-level capabilities involve the integration of lower-level capabilities, such integration can only be achieved through integrating individual knowledge. This is precisely why higher level capabilities are so difficult to perform. New product development requires the integration of an extremely broad basis of knowledge, but communication constraints imply that the number of individuals who can be directly involved in the process is small.[2] Cross-functional product development teams are not so difficult to set up, the challenge (as confirmed by Imai et al. 1985 and Clark and Fujimoto 1991) is for the team to access the breadth and depth of functional knowledge pertinent to the product, and integrate that knowledge.

In most companies, hierarchies of capabilities do not correspond closely with their authority-based hierarchies as depicted by organization charts. In particular, some top management capabilities such as capital budgeting, strategic planning, and government lobbying may involve a limited scope of knowledge integration, and hence are closer to the base than to the apex of the capability structure. At the same time, if knowledge is to be integrated effectively by the firm, the architecture of capabilities must have some correspondence with the firm's structure of authority, communication, and decision making, whether formal or informal. For example, Clark and Fujimoto find that, within automobiles, superior capabilities in new product development require product managers with substantial influence and decision making authority—what they term "heavyweight product managers." The need for organizational capabilities to be supported by firm structure poses difficulties for the creation of new capabilities. In the case of the Bell telephone companies, new capabilities were created outside the formal structure through "garbage can" processes (Smith 1996).

Mechanisms for Integrating Knowledge

How is knowledge integrated by firms to create organizational capability? Explicit knowledge involves few problems of integration because of its inherent communicability. Advances in information technology have greatly facilitated the integration of explicit knowledge through increasing the ease with which explicit knowledge can be codified, communicated, assimilated, stored, and retrieved (Rockart and Short 1989). However, the most interesting and complex issues concern the integration of tacit knowledge. The literature points to two primary integration mechanisms:

(*i*) *Direction.* Demsetz (1991, p. 172) identifies direction as the principal means by which knowledge can be communicated at low cost between "specialists and the large number of other persons who either are nonspecialists or who are specialists in other fields." To optimize the operation of a McDonald's restaurant, it is more efficient for McDonald's to create an operating manual which covers almost every aspect of the restaurant's management than to educate every McDonald's manager in cooking, nutrition, hygiene, engineering, marketing, production management, human resource management, psychology, accounting and finance, and the other specialist areas of knowledge embodied in standard operating rules.

The more complex an activity, the greater the number of locations in which that activity must be replicated, and the more stringent the performance specifications for the outcome of that activity, the greater is the reliance on knowledge integration through direction. British Airways operates aircraft maintenance facilities in 67 locations distributed across the globe. Service and repair at these facilities is guided by a host of highly formalized procedures and directives based upon the standards established by the major regulatory authorities (the Federal Aviation Authority, the British Civil Aeronautics Board, and others), guidance and technical information provided by aircraft manufacturers, and the company's own policies and procedures. These directives, policies, and procedures embody the technical knowledge of a large number of specialists.

(*ii*) *Organizational Routines*. Direction involves codifying tacit knowledge into explicit rules and instructions. But since a characteristic of tacit knowledge is that "we can know more than we can tell" (Polanyi 1966), converting tacit knowledge into explicit knowledge in the form of rules, directives, formulae, expert systems, and the like inevitably involves substantial knowledge loss.

An organizational routine provides a mechanism for coordination which is not dependent upon the need for communication of knowledge in explicit form. March and Simon (1958, p. 142) "regard a set of activities as routinized to the extent that choice has been simplified by the development of a fixed response to a defined stimuli." Such patterns of stimulus and response may lead to highly complex and variable patterns of seemingly-automatic behavior. Within our knowledge-based view, the essence of an organizational routine is that individuals develop sequential patterns of interaction which permit the integration of their specialized knowledge without the need for communicating that knowledge.

Observation of any work team, whether it is a surgical team in a hospital operating room or a team of mechanics at a grand prix motor race, reveals closely-coordinated working arrangements where each team member applies his or her specialist knowledge, but where the patterns of interaction appear automatic. This coordination relies heavily upon informal procedures in the form of commonly-understood roles and interactions established through training and constant repetition, supported by a series of explicit and implicit signals (see Pentland and Rueter 1994, for a careful analysis). The advantage of routine over direction is in economizing on communication and a greater capacity to vary responses to a broad range of circumstances.

COMPETITIVE ADVANTAGE IN DYNAMICALLY-COMPETITIVE ENVIRONMENTS

Creating and Sustaining Advantage

Under conditions of dynamic competition, the potential of organizational capabilities to earn rents for the firm through establishing sustainable competitive advantage depends upon their capacity for both creating and sustaining advantage. Competitive advantage is determined by a combination of supply-side and demand-side factors. On the demand side, a firm's productive activities must correspond to a market need. On the supply side, the firm must have the capabilities not only to serve that market need, but to serve it more effectively or efficiently than other firms. For simplicity's sake, let us abstract from demand-side considerations and focus exclusively upon the supply side: the ability to create unique advantages and to protect these advantages against imitation.

The first observation is that the critical source of competitive advantage is knowledge integration rather than knowledge itself. Specialized knowledge cannot, on its own, provide a basis for sustainable advantage, first, because specialized knowledge resides in individuals, and individuals are transferable between firms; second, because the rents generated by specialized knowledge are more likely to be appropriated by individuals than by the firm. Of course, some knowledge (patents, copyrights, trade secrets) is proprietary to the firm, and is appropriate. However, empirical evidence suggests that the value of proprietary knowledge depreciates quickly through obsolescence and imitation (Levin et al. 1987). Hence, even in technology-intensive industries, the key to sustainable advantage is not proprietary knowledge itself, but the technological capabilities which permit the generation of new knowledge.

If knowledge integration is the basis for competitive advantage under dynamic market conditions, what are the characteristics of knowledge integration associated with the creation and sustenance of such an advantage? I identify three characteristics of knowledge integration pertinent to the competitive advantage and the rents associated with such advantage:

(i) The *efficiency of integration*—the extent to which the capability accesses and utilizes the specialist knowledge held by individual organizational members;

(ii) by the *scope of integration*—the breadth of specialized knowledge the organizational capability draws upon;

(iii) the *flexibility of integration*—the extent to which a capability can access additional knowledge and reconfigure existing knowledge.

My goal is to explore the performance requirements of systems of knowledge integration conducive to attaining competitive advantage. Given the uniqueness of each firm's stock of specialized knowledge and the idiosyncracy of each firm's institutional heritage, it is impossible to specify the organizational arrangements conducive to the formation of organizational capability through knowledge integration. Critical to the analysis of this paper is an equifinality view (Van de Ven and Drazin 1985) that, recognizing uniqueness of knowledge bases and institutional conditions, firms can achieve equally effective, yet highly differentiated approaches to knowledge integration. The key contribution of our analysis is in recognizing the common requirements of these different approaches.

The Efficiency of Integration

Competitive advantage depends upon how productive firms are in utilizing the knowledge stored within individual organizational members, which is dependent upon the ability of the firm to access and harness the specialized knowledge of its members. Three factors are important in determining the efficiency with which a firm integrates the specialized knowledge available within it:

(a) The Level of Common Knowledge. Both direction and routine require communication between individuals. Demsetz (1991) identifies the prerequisite for communication between different specialists as the presence of *common knowledge* between them. If specialized knowledge must be reduced to common knowledge in order to communicate it, there is inevitably substantial information loss. The size of this loss depends upon the level and sophistication of common knowledge. A basic prerequisite is a common language. Direction is almost entirely ability upon detailed articulation of instructions. Routines typically rely upon a much more limited set of cues and responses which serve not so much as to communicate knowledge, but to permit a sequencing of individual's application of knowledge inputs. For both integration mechanisms, efficiency of communication depends upon commonality of vocabulary, conceptual knowledge, and experience between individual specialists. Shared behavioral norms form a central part of the common knowledge which facilitates communication and understanding (Garfinkel 1967, Zucker 1987). Generally speaking, the wider the scope of knowledge being integrated (and, hence, the greater the diversity of the individuals involved), the lower is the level of common knowledge, and the more inefficient the communication and integration of knowledge. Thus, the effectiveness of social networks among biotechnologists as mechanisms for communicating and integrating knowledge reflected their high level of common knowledge arising from their comparatively narrow spread of knowledge and commonality of behavioral norms (Liebeskind et al. 1996). Organizational culture may be regarded as a form of common knowledge, one of the functions of which is to facilitate knowledge integration within the company.

(b) Frequency and Variability of Task Performance. The efficiency with which organizational routines integrate the specialized knowledge of team members depends upon the sophistication of the system of signalling and responsiveness which develops between team members as a result of repetition and improvement. The efficiency of an organizational routine derives from the fact that:

> While each organization member must know his job, there is no need for anyone to know anyone else's job. Neither is there a need for anyone to be able to articulate or conceptualize the procedures employed by the organization as a whole. (Nelson and Winter 1982, p. 105)

The critical requirement is the "ability to receive and interpret a stream of incoming messages from other members and from the environment" (ibid, p. 100). Integrative efficiency depends upon the effectiveness of this communication in eliciting appropriate responses from each organization member. This is a function of the frequency with which the particular pattern of coordinated activity is performed. The greater the variation in the routine which is required in response to variation in environmental circumstances, the lower is integrating efficiency likely to be. The ineffectiveness of the response by the National Guard to the Los Angeles riots of 1992 and the Russian Army to the Chechnya rebellion of 1994/95 reflects, in part, the infrequence with which these organizations were required to suppress insurrection.

(c) Structure. Efficiency of knowledge integration requires economizing upon the amount of communication needed to effect integration. Organization structures need to be designed with a view to organizing activities such as to reduce the extent and intensity of communication needed to achieve knowledge integration. Bureaucracy is a structure which (under certain circumstances) maximizes the efficiency of knowledge integration in an organization where direction is the predominant integrating mechanism. A key feature of organizational innovations such as Henry Ford's moving assembly line, the kanban system for just-in-time scheduling, multidivisional structure (or "M-form") is their promotion of efficiency through achieving higher levels of coordination with lower levels of communication.

The principle of *modularity* is fundamental to the structuring of organizations to achieve communication efficiencies. Simon's observation that "division of labor means factoring the total system of decisions that need to be made into relatively independent subsystems, each one of which can be designed with only minimal concern for its interactions with the others" (Simon 1973, p. 270) and Williamson's "principle of hierarchical decomposition" (Williamson 1981, p. 1550), may be viewed as organizational conditions for optimizing the efficiency of knowledge integration.

Modularity is especially important in organizing highly complex capabilities which involve broad-scope knowledge integration. Clark and Fujimoto (1991) show how the hugely complex task of developing a new model of automobile is facilitated by means of organizing the task

- into sequential phases (concept development, vehicle design and layout, component design, prototype building, process engineering);
- by function (marketing, product engineering, test engineering, process engineering);
- by product segment (body, chassis, engine, transmission, electrics and electronics).

The problem of many conventional approaches to modularity is that they rest heavily upon time-sequencing. Under conditions of hypercompetition such sequencing is simply too time consuming. The organizational challenge is creating modularity which permits either overlapping phases or full simultaneity.

The Scope of Integration

Increases in the span of knowledge which are integrated within an organizational capability increases the potential for both establishing and sustaining competitive advantages through two sources:

(i) Different types of specialized knowledge are *complements* rather than *substitutes* in production. Up to the point of diminishing relevance, the marginal revenue product of a unit of specialist knowledge increases with the addition of different types of knowledge.

(ii) The greater the scope of knowledge being integrated within a capability, the greater the difficulty faced by competitors in replicating that capability due to increases in "causal ambiguity" (Lippman and Rumelt 1982) and time-based diseconomies of replication (Dierickx and Cool 1989). The complexities associated with broad-scope integration are further increased when different types of knowledge require different patterns of integration. Toyota's lean production system combines cost efficiency, quality, flexibility, and innovation. These different performance dimensions involve different types of integration. While cost efficiency may be best served through organization around "sequential interdependence," flexibility is likely to require more complex patterns of "reciprocal interdependence" (Thompson 1967, p. 40). Similar complexities of integration are likely among suppliers of fashion apparel which combine low costs with fashion-based differentiation and quick response capability (Richardson 1996).

The Flexibility of Integration

While integration across a wide scope of specialist knowledge is important in sustaining competitive advantage, hypercompetitive conditions ultimately result in all positions of competitive advantage being eroded by imitative or innovative competition. Hence, maintaining superior performance ultimately requires the continual renewal of competitive advantages through innovation and the development of new capabilities. Within the context of our model, there are two dimensions to such renewal: extending existing capabilities to encompass additional types of knowledge, and reconfiguring existing knowledge into new types of capability.

The ease with which existing capabilities can be extended to encompass new knowledge depends heavily upon the characteristics of knowledge with regard to communicability. If new knowledge is explicit, or if tacit knowledge can be articulated in explicit form, then integrating new knowledge does not pose major difficulties. In designing its 777 passenger plane, Boeing was able to greatly extend its knowledge of electronics and new materials through an advanced CAD system which provided a common language for specialists across widely different knowledge areas and different companies to communicate and integrate. By contrast, General Motors' upgrading of its manufacturing capability to encompass the knowledge embodied in Toyota's system of lean production was a slow and painful process because much of that knowledge was tacit and the routines for its integration were deeply embedded with Toyota's history and culture.

The reconfiguration of existing knowledge through new patterns of integration is more complex, but may be even more important in creating competitive advantage. Such knowledge reconfiguration is central to Abernathy and Clark's (1985) concept of "architectural innovation." Subsequent research by Henderson and Clark (1990) and Henderson and Cockburn (1995) identifies the critical role of *"architectural knowledge"*—the "integration of knowledge across disciplinary and organizational boundaries within the firm" (Henderson 1995, p. 3)—in driving such innovation. Her studies of pharmaceuticals and the semiconductor photolithographic alignment equipment industry provide strong support for the role of broad-scope knowledge integration in supporting superior performance.

Such architectural innovations are concerned not only with product and process innovations, but also with *strategic innovations* which reconfigure knowledge into new approaches to competing. Such "new-game strategies" (Buaron 1981) are not specific to technology-based industries. Baden-Fuller and Stopford (1994, Chapter 3) show that strategic innovation is fundamental to creating competitive advantage in mature business environments. In fashion clothing for example, Benetton and The Limited have created "quick-response capability" through innovative approaches to value-chain reconfiguration (Richardson 1996).

Most examples of firms' reconfiguring knowledge into architectural innovations (EMI's CT scanner, the Polaroid instant camera, the Apple Macintosh, Pilkington's float glass process, Lanier's "virtual reality") and strategic innovations (Nucor in steel, Benetton in apparel, Starbuck's in coffee houses) point to these innovations as isolated successes rather than evidence of flexible capabilities which have the capacity to continuously and repeatedly reconfigure knowledge in new patterns of interaction. Given the difficulties inherent in integrating tacit knowledge and dependence of such integration upon routines and communication patterns developed over time, establishing organizational arrangements needed to achieve the "flexible integration" proposed by Henderson (1995) and "meta-flexibility" proposed by Volberda (1996) represents a formidable challenge to management. Continuous innovation in dynamically-competitive environments (e.g., Rubbermaid in plastic housewares, 3M in adhesive and thin-film products, Sony in consumer electronics, Motorola in communication products) tends to be the result of the deployment and extension of a continuing core of capabilities rather than the constant creation of new capabilities. Achieving flexible integration, either through continually integrating new tacit knowledge or through constantly reconfiguring existing knowledge, is likely to impose substantial costs in terms of reducing the efficiency of knowledge integration. The implication is that radical, discontinuous change in industry environments (such as the micro revolution in computing and the possible displacement of internal combustion engines by electric motors in autos) is likely to be accompanied by the decline of established market leaders. The noteworthy feature of IBM's performance during the 1980s and 1990s is not so much its decline during the 1990s, but its remarkable success in microcomputers during the 1980s.

INTERNAL VERSUS EXTERNAL INTEGRATION: THE CASE FOR NETWORKS

The need for flexibility in organizational capabilities poses complex issues with regard to firm boundaries and choices between internal and external knowledge integration. In common with other types of transactions, there are three basic alternatives for knowledge transfer and integration: internalization within the firm, market contracts, and relational contacts (which in multiple form create firm networks). Given uncertainties over appropriability and valuation, market contracts are typically inefficient means for transferring knowledge. In Demsetz's (1991) analysis, market transactions are only efficient in transferring knowledge when that knowledge is embodies within a product. Such transfer of product-embodies knowledge across markets is efficient when the effective utilization of the product by buyers is not dependent upon the buyers needing access to the knowledge embodies within the product. Thus, within the context of fashion apparel (Richardson 1996), Benetton does not need to integrate knowledge of the application of computer science to computer-aided design into its design capability, if it can purchase CAD software adequate to its needs. On the other hand, expertise in fashion design is tacit, and it cannot be embodied into expert-system software. Thus, Benetton cannot purchase fashion design knowledge packaged into software, neither can Benetton rely upon purchasing individual fashion designs from independent designers because of the need for garment design to integrate multiple knowledge bases: fashion design flair, Benetton's own market knowledge, and manufacturing expertise. The implication is that Benetton is likely to require internalization of at least some of fashion design capability. Similarly, in the case of the regional Bell companies' expansion into wireless communication. If knowledge concerning wireless switching and siting of cellular bases is not capable of embodiment within marketable products and services. then these companies will, ultimately, be required to extend their capabilities to embody such knowledge (Smith 1996).

Relational contracts, either in individual strategic alliances or broader interfirm networks, are an intermediate solution justified by a number of intermediate situations. For example, explicit knowledge which is not embodies in specific products cannot be efficiently transferred through market contracts, but diffusion of its sources or uncertainty over its applicability to the firm's products may not justify the internalization of its producers within the firm. Networks, either of firms or of individuals, may be well-suited to the transfer and integration of such knowledge. Thus, in biotechnology, social networks of scientists provide a powerful vehicle for the transfer of scientific knowledge since such networks provide the reputational assets and the repeated-game characteristics necessary to avoid the inefficiencies associated with market exchanges (Liebeskind et al. 1996).

Interfirm collaboration through relational contracts is also likely to provide efficient mechanisms for knowledge integration where there is a lack of perfect correspondence between the knowledge base of the firm and its set of products. The scope of a firm may be defined in terms of its range of knowledge or its range of products. Where the boundaries of both knowledge and products correspond perfectly, not only are firm boundaries unambiguous, but knowledge resources are fully utilized. Where a perfect correspondence does not exist, or where uncertainty exists over the linkages between knowledge and products, then two consequences follow:

(a) ambiguity is created over the optimal boundaries of the firm;

(b) internal provision of the full range of specialized knowledge needed for a particular set of products must result in the inefficient exploitation of at least some of that specialist knowledge.

In such circumstances, interfirm collaboration can increase the efficiency with which specialized knowledge is utilized. A consequence of hypercompetition is uncertainty over links between knowledge inputs and product outputs. In biotechnology, new knowledge may have applications in "human health, crop production and protection, chemical feedstock production and processing, food processing, and waste management" (Liebeskind et al. 1996). As a result, "these sources of technological and competitive uncertainty make it extremely difficult to determine which scientific knowledge is potentially valuable and which is not" (ibid). While my analysis points to the superiority of intrafirm relationships in integrating knowledge, the importance of networks in sourcing biotechnological knowledge suggests that the inefficiencies of interorganizational relationships are outweighed by the flexibility advantages associated with a wider set of knowledge-product linkages.

A final consideration concerns the speed with which new capabilities can be built and extended. Even if relational contracts are imperfect vehicles for integrating knowledge, a critical concern is that they can permit knowledge to be transferred and integrated with a comparatively short time. If competitive advantage in dynamic market settings is critical dependent upon establishing first-mover advantage then the critical merit of firm networks is in providing speed of access to new knowledge. Such considerations proved to be critically important both in biotechnology (Liebeskind et al. 1996, and in telecommunications Smith 1996). In fashion apparel where the need to access new knowledge was less apparent, firm networks did not provide any clear advantage over vertical integration (Richardson 1996).

Similar considerations explain the establishment of the Nordvest Forum regional learning network (Hanssen-Bauer and Snow 1996). Although such interorganizational contacts have limited potential for integrating knowledge across companies, such a network permits fuller utilization of knowledge by permitting firms to share knowledge that has application outside of each firm's product set. Second, it encourages investments in knowledge acquisition in the face of uncertainty over knowledge-product linkages.

SUMMARY AND CONCLUSION

I have established that knowledge is the preeminent resource of the firm, and that organizational capability involves the integration of multiple knowledge bases. The resulting theory of organizational capability provides a more cogent description of firm competence and analyzes more precisely than hitherto the relationship of organizational capability to competitive advantage in markets where market leadership and power is continually undermined by competition and external change. I show that the processes through which firms integrate specialized knowledge are fundamental to their ability to create and sustain competitive advantage. Figure 12.2 summarizes this theory of organizational capability and its implications for competitive advantage in hypercompetitive environments.

While making some progress in integrating prior research on organizational learning and organizational resources and capabilities, much remains to be done at both the empirical and the theoretical level, especially in relation to understanding the organizational processes through which knowledge is integrated. For example, while organizational routines are generally recognized as important mechanisms for coordination within firms, with a few notable exceptions (e.g., Pentland 1992, Pentland and Rueter 1994), detailed study of the operation of organizational routines is limited. Further progress is critically dependent upon closer observation of the processes through which tacit knowledge is transferred and integrated.

Despite its limited achievements so far, this analysis offers considerable potential—especially in building bridges between strategic management and organization theory and design. Conventional notions of organizational structure rest heavily upon concepts such as division of labor, unity of command, and grouping of similar tasks. The view of the firm as an integrator of knowledge provides a rather different perspective on the functions of organization structure. The analysis can also offer insight into many current developments in management practice. Cross-functional product development teams, TQM, and organizational change programs such as GE's "workout" can be viewed as attempts to change organizational structure and processes to achieve better integration across broad spectra of specialized knowledge. The trend toward "empowerment" takes account of the nature of knowledge acquisition and storage in firms: if each employee possesses unique specialized knowledge and if each employee has access to only part of every other employee's knowledge base, then top-down decision making must be a highly inefficient means of knowledge integration. The task is to devise decision processes that permit integration of the specialized knowledge held throughout the organization—not just in the boardroom, but on the shop floor as well.

ASSUMPTIONS

* Knowledge is the principal productive resource of the firm.
* Of the two main types of knowledge, explicit and tacit, the latter is especially important due to its limited transferability.
* Tacit knowledge is acquired by and stored within individuals in highly specialized form.
* Production requires a wide array of knowledge.

PROPOSITIONS

1. *The nature of the firm.* The fundamental role of the firm is the integration of individuals' specialist knowledge. Organizational capabilities are the manifestation of this knowledge integration.

2. *Capability and structure.* The capabilities of the firm are hierarchically structured according to the scope of knowledge which they integrate. Effectiveness in creating and managing broad-scope capabilities requires correspondence between the scope of knowledge and the structures needed for managing such integration.

3. *Integration mechanisms.* Two primary mechanisms exist to integrate knowledge: direction and routine. Reliance upon direction increases with complexity of the activity, the number of locations in which the activity is performed, and the stringency of performance specifications. The advantage of routine in integrating tacit knowledge is in economizing upon communication and permitting flexible responses to changing circumstances.

4. *Capability and competitive advantage.*

    (A) The competitive advantage conferred by an organizational capability depends, in part, upon the *efficiency of knowledge integration* which is a function of: (a) the level of common knowledge among organizational members; (b) frequency and variability of the activity; (c) a structure which economizes on communication (e.g., through some form of modularity).

    (B) An organizational capability's potential for establishing and sustaining competitive advantage increases with the span of knowledge integrated.

    (C) Sustaining competitive advantage under conditions of dynamic competition requires continuous innovation which requires flexible integration through either (a) extending existing capabilities to encompass new knowledge, or (b) reconfiguring existing knowledge within new patterns of integration. Since efficient integration of tacit knowledge requires experience through repitition, achieving flexible integration represents a formidable management challenge.

IMPLICATION: FIRM NETWORKS UNDER HYPERCOMPETITION

Firm networks based upon relational contracts are an efficient and effective basis for accessing knowledge:

- where knowledge can be expressed in explicit form;
- where there is a lack of perfect correspondence between the knowledge domain and product domain of individual firms, or uncertainty over the product-knowledge linkages;
- where speed in extending the knowledge base of the firm is critical in creating competitive advantage.

Figure 12.2. Summary: The Knowledge-based Theory of Organizational Capability

This chapter offers little solace to managers grappling with the uncertainties and demands of hypercompetitive environments. While establishing that, under conditions of intense and dynamic competition, internal capabilities provide a more stable basis for strategy than market positioning, my analysis points to the difficulties inherent in achieving the dynamic capabilities which for many are the "solution" to the problem of sustaining competitive advantage under conditions of hypercompetition. Volberda (1996) identifies these dynamic capabilities with "the repertoire of flexibility-increasing capabilities that management possesses." But, if such capabilities depend upon integration across a broad span of largely-tacit knowledge, then a firm's strategic flexibility is limited by two factors: First, its repertoire of capabilities is unlikely to extend far beyond those currently deployed within existing business activities; second, the time horizon and uncertainty associated with creating new capabilities. The "flexible integration" and network relationships I propose as responses to this problem identify what is required, but offer little guidance as to the management actions needed to achieve flexibility in knowledge integration.

ACKNOWLEDGMENTS

I am grateful to Jon Hanssen-Bauer, Duane Helleloid, Arie Lewin, Julia Liebeskind, Steve Postrel, James Richardson, Ann Smith, and Henk Volberda for helpful comments and suggestions.

NOTES

1. The part of national income attributable to knowledge may be calculated as wages and salaries over and above that which would be earned by unskilled manual labor, plus royalties and license fees. To this a major part of profit can be added, since profit is a return to the resources owned by the firm, a major part of which comprise or embody the knowledge of people. International differences in living standards and productivity are mainly due to differences in human capital. Denison's research into international differences in growth rates found that, in the case of Britain, advances in knowledge accounted for 46 percent increases in real national income per person employed between 1950 and 1960 (Denison 1968).

2. A key distinction between an administrative hierarchy and the hierarchy of capabilities is that, in the administrative hierarchy, the span of control can remain constant throughout the hierarchy. In the hierarchy of capabilities, the fact that each layer of capabilities cannot directly integrate the preceding layer of capabilities and must return to the base in terms of integrating individual's knowledge, means that the span of integration increases as one ascends the hierarchy.

REFERENCES

Abernathy, W. J. and K. B. Clark (1985), "Innovation: Mapping the Winds of Creative Destruction," *Research Policy,* 14, 3-22.

Argyris, C. and D. A. Schon (1978), *Organizational Learning,* Reading, MA: Addison-Wesley.

Baden-Fuller, C. and J. M. Stopford (1994), *Rejuvenating the Mature Enterprise,* Boston: Harvard Business School Press.

Barney, J. (1986), "Strategic Factor Markets: Expectations, Luck and Business Strategy," *Management Science,* 32, 1231-1241.

Buaron, R. (1981), "New-game Strategies," *McKinsey Quarterly,* Fall, 24-40.

Clark, K. B. and T. Fujimoto (1991), *Product Development Performance,* Boston: Harvard Business School Press.

Demsetz, H. (1991), "The Theory of the Firm Revisited," in O. E. Williamson and S. Winter (Eds.), *The Nature of the Firm,* New York: Oxford University Press, 159-178.

Denison, E. F. (1968), "Economic Growth," in R. E. Caves (Ed.), *Britain's Economic Prospects,* Washington: Brookings.

Dierickx, I. and K. Cool (1989), "Asset Stock Accumulation and Sustainability of Competitive Advantage," *Management Science,* 35, 1504-1513.

Garfinkel, H. (1967), *Studies in Ethnomethodology,* Englewood Cliffs, NJ: Prentice Hall.

Grant, R. M. (1991), "The Resource-based Theory of Competitive Advantage: Implications for Strategy Formulation," *California Management Review,* 33, 3, 114-135.

Hanssen-Bauer, J. and C. C. Snow (1996), "Responding to Hypercompetition: The Structure and Processes of a Regional Learning Network Organization," *Organization Science,* 7, 4, 413-427.

Henderson, R. and K. Clark (1990), "Architectural Innovation: The Reconfiguration of Existing Product Technologies and the Failure of Established Firms," *Administrative Science Quarterly,* 35, 9-31.

Henderson, R. and I. Cockburn (1995), "Measuring Competence? Exploring Firm Effects in Pharmaceutical Research," *Strategic Management Journal,* 15, Winter, 63-84.

Imai, K., I. Nonaka, and H. Takeuchi (1985), "Managing the New Product Development Process: How Japanese Companies Learn and Unlearn," in K. Clark, R. Hayes, and C. Lorenz (Eds.), *The Uneasy Alliance,* Boston: Harvard Business School Press.

Jacobsen, R. (1992), "The 'Austrian' School of Strategy," *Academy of Management Review,* 17, 782-805.

Kogut, B. and U. Zander (1992), "Knowledge of the Firm, Combinative Capabilities, and the Replication of Technology," *Organization Studies,* 3, 383-397.

Levin, R. C., A. K. Klevorick, R. R. Nelson, and S. G. Winter (1987), "Appropriating the Returns from Industrial Research and Development," *Brookings Papers on Economic Activity,* 3, 783-820.

Levitt, B. and J. G. March (1988), "Organizational Learning," *Annual Review of Sociology,* 14, 319-340.

Levitt, T. (1960), "Marketing Myopia," *Harvard Business Review,* July-August, 24-47.

Liebeskind, J. P., A. Oliver, L. Zucker, and M. Brewer (1996), "Social Networks, Learning, and Flexibility: Sourcing Scientific Knowledge in New Biotechnology Firms," *Organization Science,* 7, 4, 428-443.

Lippman, S. and R. Rumelt (1982), "Uncertain Imitability; An Analysis of Interfirm Differences in Efficiency Under Uncertainty," *Bell Journal of Economics,* 13, 418-438.

March, J. and H. Simon (1958), *Organizations,* New York: John Wiley.

Nelson, R. and S. Winter (1982), *An Evolutionary Theory of Economic Change,* Cambridge: Belknap.

Nonaka, I. (1990), "Redundant, Overlapping Organization: A Japanese Approach to Managing the Innovation Process," *California Management Review,* 32, Spring, 27-38.

——— (1994), "A Dynamic Theory of Organizational Knowledge Creation," *Organization Science,* 5, 1, 14-37.

Organization Science (1991), Special Issue, "Organizational Learning: Papers in Honor of (and by) James G. March," 2, 1, 1-163.

Pentland, B. T. (1992), "Organizing Moves in Software Support," *Administrative Science Quarterly,* 37, 527-548.

——— and H. H. Rueter (1994), "Organizational Routines as Grammars of Action," *Administrative Science Quarterly,* 39, 484-510.

Polanyi, M. (1966), *The Tacit Dimension,* New York: Anchor Day.

Porter, M. E. (1991), *The Competitive Advantage of Nations,* New York: Free Press.

—— (1992), "Towards a Dynamic Theory of Strategy," *Strategic Management Journal,* 12, Winter Special Issue, 95-118.

Prahalad, C. K. and G. Hamel (1990), "The Core Competences of the Corporation," *Harvard Business Review,* May-June, 79-91.

Quinn, J. B. (1992), *Intelligent Enterprise,* New York: Free Press.

Richardson, J. (1996), "Vertical Integration and Rapid Response in Fashion Apparel," *Organization Science,* 7, 4, 400-412.

Rockart, J. F. and J. E. Short (1989), "IT in the 1990s: Managing Organizational Interdependence," *Sloan Management Review,* 30, 2, 17-33.

Rumelt, R. P. (1991), "How Much Does Industry Matter?," *Strategic Management Journal,* 12, 167-185.

Schumpeter, J. A. (1934), *The Theory of Economic Development,* Cambridge, MA: Harvard University Press.

Simon, H. A. (1973), "Applying Information Technology to Organization Design," *Public Administration Review,* 106, 467-482.

—— (1991), "Bounded Rationality and Organizational Learning," *Organization Science,* 2, 125-134.

Smith, A. and C. Zeithaml (1996), "Baby Bells, Garbage Cans, and Hypercompetition," *Organization Science,* 7, 4, 388-399.

Spender, J-C. (1992), "Limits to Learning from the West: How Western Management Advice May Prove Limited in Eastern Europe," *International Executive,* 34, 5, September/October, 389-410.

Starbuck, W. H. (1992), "Learning by Knowledge-intensive Firms," *Journal of Management Studies,* 29, 713-739.

Thompson, J. D. (1967), *Organizations in Action,* New York: McGraw-Hill.

Van de Ven, A. H. and R. Drazin (1985), "The Concept of Fit in Contingency Theory," in L. L. Cummins and B. Staw (Eds.). *Research in Organizational Behavior,* 7, Greenwich, CT: JAI, 333-365.

Volberda, H. W. (1996), "Toward the Flexible Form: How to Remain Vital in Hypercompetitive Environments," *Organization Science,* 7, 4, 359-374.

Wheelwright, S. C. and K. B. Clark (1992), *Revolutionizing Product Development,* New York: Free Press.

Williamson, O. E. (1975), *Markets and Hierarchies,* Englewood Cliffs, NJ: Prentice Hall.

—— (1981), "The Modern Corporation: Origins, Evolution, Attributes," *Journal of Economic Literature,* 19, 1537-1568.

Winter, S. G. (1987), "Knowledge and Competence as Strategic Assets," in D. Teece (Ed.), *The Competitive Challenge,* Cambridge, MA: Ballinger.

Zucker, L. (1987), "Institutional Theories of Organizations," *Annual Review of Sociology,* 13, 443-464.

13

Social Capital, Structural Holes,
and the Formation of an Industry Network

GORDON WALKER
BRUCE KOGUT
WEIJIAN SHAN

The formation of a network is determined by the opposition of two forces. The first is the reproduction of network structure as a general social resource for network members. The second is the alteration of network structure by entrepreneurs for their own benefit. The idea of reproduction is a conventional one in organizational sociology but has taken on increased importance due to the work of Bourdieu and Coleman. In contrast, Burt stresses the entrepreneurship of individual agents in exploiting structural holes that lie between constrained positions. Though complementary, the theories of social capital and structural holes have fundamentally different implications for network formation.

This chapter investigates these theories by examining empirically the formation of the interorganizational network among biotechnology firms. We propose that network structure determines the frequency with which a new biotechnology firm (or startup) establishes new relationships. Network structure indicates both were social capital is distributed in the industry and where opportunities for

EDITOR'S NOTE: This chapter is of interest because of its comparison of social capital theory and structural hole theory in explaining network formation. The chapter demonstrates, in the case of biotechnology start-ups, that network formation and industry growth are significantly influenced by the development and nurturing of social capital. The chapter raises several important implications: structural hole theory may apply more to networks of market transactions than to networks of cooperative relationships, and that the study of the structure of interfirm collaborations over time requires an analysis of the network as a whole.—Arie Y. Lewin entrepreneurial action are located. The reproduction of network structure depends on how startups value social capital compared to these opportunities. The critical test is, consequently, whether new relationships reproduce or alter the inherited network structure. We find strong support for the power of social capital in reproducing the network over time.

(SOCIAL NETWORK; SOCIAL CAPITAL;
STRUCTURAL HOLES;
NETWORK FORMATION;
BIOTECHNOLOGY)

INTRODUCTION

There is a fundamental conflict in the formation of a network. On the one hand, there are powerful forces toward the reproduction of dense regions of relationships. Reproduction is powerful because it is based upon the accumulation of social capital that requires the maintenance of and reinvestment in the structure of prevailing relationships. Yet, it is exactly this principle of conservation that generates the opportunities for entrepreneurial actors to bridge these regions and alter the structure of the network.

The formation of interfirm networks is a critical point of contention between otherwise complementary views of network structure. For Pierre Bourdieu (1980) and James Coleman (1990a), a network tends toward the reproduction of an inherited pattern of relationships due to the value *to the individual* in preserving social capital. The notion of social capital implies a strategy of maintaining the structure of existing relationships. To Bourdieu, "social capital is the sum of the resources, actual or virtual, that accrue to an individual or a group by virtue of possessing a durable network of more or less institutionalized relationships of mutual acquaintance and recognition" (Bourdieu and Wacquant 1992, p. 119). Similarly, Coleman notes that an advantage of modern society is that organizations provide stability, even if people are mobile. "The social invention of organizations," he notes, "having positions rather than persons as elements of the structure has provided one form of social capital that can maintain stability in the face of instability of individuals" (Coleman 1990b, p. 320). Similarly, firms may tend toward the reproduction of existing interfirm relationships to maintain the value of their inherited social capital.

Ronald Burt (1992) has a different view of the conservative tendency of networks toward reproduction. To him, the emphasis should be placed on the opportunities for entrepreneurs to exploit the "structural holes" between dense pockets of relationships in the network. It is exactly the structural constraints on what people know and can control, created by the inheritance of past relationships, that presents the opportunities for brokers. These brokers seek out partners with whom they can form unique, or "nonredundant," relationships that bring new information and the possibility of negotiating between competing groups. Through forming these new and unique relationships, entrepreneurs transform network structure.

The theories of social capital and structural holes have important implications for understanding the formation of relational networks in high growth, technology-intensive industries. In these industries, the extensive innovative activities of small firms (Bound et al. 1984, Acs and Audretsch 1989) push out industry boundaries into new subfields and increase the level of competition in traditional markets. However, opportunities for cooperation are created by unintended spillovers and intended agreements. Organizations are also related through their members' professional connections, joint suppliers and customers, and industry associations. These commonalities may be sources of information about competitor behavior, new technological developments, and other industry trends. However, formal agreements are the most salient and reliable indicator of resource and information sharing between firms and the origin of information regarding a firm's cooperative strategy. This information is critical for future decisions regarding cooperation for product development and commercialization.

The emergence of the network of formal cooperative agreements influences the course of industry growth and innovation. A swelling network of cooperative agreements may provided a positive externality to which potential investors respond (Hagedoorn and Schakenraad 1992). Also, since poorly positioned firms may have access to less than adequate resources to achieve their economic goals, the network may act as a selection mechanism, culling out some firms on the basis of their partners' weakness.

Early in the history of an industry, social capital among firms is low, and yet it is critical for the identification and acquisition of new relationships. Rapid industry growth aggravates this problem of acquiring valid information on other firms. In this early period, firms enter relationships according to their differences in need and capability, and these relationships initialize the network (Kogut et al. 1994). In biotechnology, for example, small startups have extensive expertise in technological innovation but lack resources in marketing and distribution possessed by large incumbents. Cooperation between a startup and incumbent gives each access to a resource necessary for product commercialization. Variation in firm-level attributes, especially the effective management of interfirm cooperation, contributes to network growth. But this contribution is partial. As an unintended outcome of their cooperative strategies, firms build the network that serves as a map for future association.

Network formation occurs as new relationships by incumbent firms or startups exploit the opportunities inherent in the network, reinforcing the existing network structure or reshaping it (Galaskiewicz and Wasserman 1981, Marsden 1983, Kogut et al. 1994). Two types of opportunity drive the process of network formation. First, network structure is a vehicle for inducing cooperation through the development of social capital. Firms draw upon network structure as a system-level resource to facilitate the governance of their relationships. Second, however, gaps in the pattern of information flows reflect potentially profitable opportunities for establishing connections between unlinked firms (Burt 1992). These opportunities stimulate entrepreneurial action to broker different segments of the industry.

The relative advantages and risks of inducing cooperation and exploiting brokering opportunities have an important implication for network formation. The structural conditions inducing cooperation free resources for the establishment of new relationships that in turn strengthen the structure as a useful system for controlling noncooperative behavior. If the structure is reinforced by new relationships, early patterns of cooperation should persist, resulting in a path dependence analogous to the imprinting effect on an industry of the era in which it was formed (Stinchcombe 1965). However, if some firms have specific capabilities for information arbitrage, they may choose to broker relationships between organizations in different regions of the network. In this case, the existing structure is not strengthened but repeatedly reshaped. The early pattern of relationships is blurred as more organizations are linked together.

To address these issues, we examine network formation in terms of its structural development, positing network structure as a social fact interacting with firm-level behavior over time. Our theory below follows most closely recent developments in structural sociology, especially the ideas of Coleman (1990) and Burt (1992). The tests of our propositions on data from the biotechnology industry show strong support for this approach to analyzing the process of network formation.

THEORY

Social Capital

Social capital is a means of enforcing norms of behavior among individual or corporate actors and thus acts as a constraint, as well as a resource. Successful cooperation cannot be achieved in interorganizational relationships without constraints on the partners to perform according to each other's expectations. These constraints allow firms to risk greater investment with a partner in a relationship that would otherwise be hindered by the threat of opportunism. Lower levels of constraint are associated with difficulties in finding information about current or potential partners and therefore impede effective cooperation. Because cooperation is less frequent, network and consequently industry growth are hindered.

The network serves an important function in the development of social constraint directing information flows in the building and maintaining of social capital. Consider two extreme examples of network structure. If all firms in an industry had relationships with each other, interfirm information flows would lead quickly to established norms of cooperation. In such a dense network, information on deviant behavior is sanctioned. Firms in this industry would benefit equally from the network as a reputation building mechanism. Coleman (1990; see also Loury 1977, Bourdieu 1980) characterizes the extreme case of a fully connected network as "closed." Members of closed networks are connected to each other. In a closed network, firms as institutional actors have access to *social capital,* a resource that helps the development of norms for acceptable behavior and the diffusion of information about behavior. As the predictability of behavior is increased in a system that is already connected, self-seeking opportunism is constrained and cooperation enabled.

At the other extreme is an "open" network. Firms in open networks have no social capital on which to rely. If firms are not connected to each other extensively, norms regarding cooperation are more difficult to achieve, and information on behavior in relationships diffuses more slowly. Without relationships that determine behavior and carry information, firms are less able to identify or control opportunism. In support of this conjecture, Raub and Weesie (1990) use a Prisoner's Dilemma framework to show that a firm embedded in a closed network is constrained to be more cooperative that a comparable firm embedded in an open network. Similarly, Granovetter (1985) argues, through extensive examples, that embeddedness in dense networks leads to effective interfirm cooperation.

However, a common result of research on interfirm network structure is that it is neither uniformly dense nor sparse (Knoke and Rogers 1978, Van de Ven et al. 1979, Nohria and Garcia-Pont 1991). The structure is uneven, composed of regions that are more or less filled with relationships. The positions firms occupy in the network are embedded in these regions. Some firms occupy positions that are embedded in regions filled with relationships, indicating a high level of available social capital, but other positions are located in regions with few relationships, suggesting a low social capital. In such a complex network, the degree of social capital available to a firm is thus determined by its position in the network structure.

A central premise of the present chapter is that social capital influences how the network forms. Network formation proceeds through the establishment of new relationships, building on the base of existing interfirm ties. Managing these ties requires ongoing attention and resources, of which organizations have only limited amounts. Social capital is thus a valuable additional asset for managing interorganizational relationships since it constrains a firm's partners to be more cooperative. Firms with less social capital are more vulnerable to opportunistic behavior and less able to build an enduring history of effective cooperative behavior with their partners over time. They, therefore, are required to expend greater time and effort monitoring the relationship. In contrast, the more social capital available to a firm, the fewer resources it needs to manage existing relationships and the more resources it can use to establish new ones. Coleman explains:

> Social capital is defined by its function. It is not a single entity but a variety of different entities, with two elements in common: they all consist of some aspect of social structures, and they facilitate certain actions of actors—whether persons or corporate actors—within the structure. (Coleman 1988, p. S98)

In the present study, the social structure is the interorganizational network. The amount of social capital depends on the firm's position in the network structure. The action facilitated by this structure is the formation of new relationships. These arguments lead to the central proposition that firms in network positions with higher social capital are likely to have more relationships with new partners in the following time period.

An important question follows: how do a firm's new cooperative relationships affect the social capital available to it? If social capital improves cooperation, then it seems likely that firms would seek partners that are more rather than less constrained by network structure. That is, firms should try to increase the social capital available to them through the new relationships they establish. Thus, the value of social capital motivates firms to reproduce the existing network structure, building the social capital available to them.

The amount of social capital that can be increased by new relationships should be related to the base amount. Mayhew and Levinger (1976) show that network density tends to attenuate as the network grows larger. Thus, firms that begin a year with high social capital cannot improve their network positions as much as those firms that are structurally less advantaged. Therefore, the more social capital available to a firm, the less the firm can increase it through forming new relationships.

Structural Holes

Burt (1992) presents an alternative to the social capital argument. Emphasizing the importance of open rather than closed networks, he argues that the network positions associated with the highest economic return lie *between* not *within* dense regions of relationships. He calls these sparse regions *structural holes*. Structural holes present opportunities for brokering information flows among firms. These opportunities have greater economic payoffs because the broker's information advantage creates the potential for arbitrage in markets for goods and services.

Burt assumes that partner selection, more than social capital, determines effective cooperation between firms (Burt 1992, p. 16). Burt's argument subtly weaves between normative implications and positive theory. He places more emphasis than Bourdieu or Coleman on the strategic action of entrepreneurs. In Burt's view, the benefits of increasing social constraint from establishing relationships in closed regions of the network are offset by a reduction in independence. Firms with relationships in open networks have greater latitude in their cooperative strategies. These firms have higher economic gains because they are most able to parlay their superior, i.e., less redundant, information into increasing their control. Burt (1992, p. 37) argues:

> The higher the proportion of relationships enhanced by structural holes, the more likely and able the entrepreneurial player, and so the more likely it is that the player's investments are in high-yield relationships. The result is a higher aggregate rate of return on investments.

Structural hole theory therefore raises the problem of free-riding on the public good of social capital. Over time, firms will seek to exploit the holes between the islands of social capital in which relationships are embedded. As a result, the social capital available to an entrepreneur should decrease as the firm forms new relationships.

In each year, new relationships change network structure. Firms are much more likely to experience these changes as they happen, rather than all at once at the end of each year. If structural constraint represents social capital, the change in structure should determine the resources available to a firm to form new relationships. From Coleman and Bourdieu's perspective, increasing social capital in a period should enable more relationships. Alternatively, if, as Burt asserts, trust is determined only by careful partner selection, increases in social capital should have no effect on the number of new relationships. The arguments regarding network formation from both the

Social Capital Perspective	Tests of Propositions
1. Firms with higher social capital are likely to have more relationships with new partners in the following time period.	Regression of new relationships on social capital (for incumbent and entering partners), see Table 2.
2. The more relationships a firm forms, the more likely its social capital will increase.	Regression of change in social capital on new relationships (for incumbents and entering partners), see Table 3.
3. The more social capital at the beginning of a time period, the lower the increase in social capital in the next time period.	Regression of change in social capital on level of social capital in the previous time period, see Table 3.
4. The more a firm's social capital increases over a time period, the more relationships it should have during this time period.	Regression of new relationships (for incumbent and entering partners) on change in social capital, see Table 2.

Structural Hole Perspective

5. The more relationships a firm forms in a year, the more its social capital should decrease.	Regression of change in social capital on new relationships (for incumbents and entering partners), see Table 3.
6. Lack of empirical support for Proposition 4 above would be consistent with the Structural Hole Perspective.	Regression of new relationships (for incumbent and entering partners) on change in social capital, see Table 2.

Figure 13.1. List of Propositions Developed in the Theory Section and Their Tests

social capital and structural hole perspectives are set out as propositions in Figure 13.1.

Control Variables

We test these propositions against the view that only organizational attributes determine interfirm cooperation. Since firms with similar attributes may occupy the same network position (Burt 1992, chapter 5), controlling for these attributes makes the analysis of network formation more robust. We identify five control variables: firm size, firm experience in cooperating with other firms, public offering of the firm's equity, the concentration of the firm's partners across global regions, and the average number of relationships of the firm's partners. The last two of these variables might be viewed more properly as partner characteristics. However, since they are aggregated by firm, they are included as firm-level controls.

Firm size is a measure of a firm's capacity to cooperate and a measure of its capacity to do without cooperation. Whereas Shan (1990) found a negative relationship between size and cooperation, Boyles (1968) and Powell and Brantley (1991) found that the frequency of cooperative relationships more than proportionally rises with size. Whether this difference rises from a nonlinearity in the association between size and the frequency of cooperation is partly addressed below.

Firm experience with cooperation, represented as the number of relationships it has established, presents a similar set of issues. The more relationships a firm has, the more it should know about how to manage them and so the less costly it should be to form new relationships. On the other hand, the lower incremental learning from new relationships may attenuate their formation. Again, we address this potential nonlinearity in our analysis.

The effect of issuing public equity on interfirm cooperation also has an ambiguous interpretation. First, a public offering is one form of getting resources. As a publicly held corporation, an entrepreneurial startup can probably go to the capital markets to finance projects, thereby decreasing the need to cooperate for this purpose. However, going public may also be an indicator of the legitimacy of the firm and signal a strong position in the network. Firms with higher legitimacy are likely to attract more partners for cooperative ventures.

Regional concentration represents how a firm's partners are distributed across three major global regions: United States, Europe, and Japan. As Hofstede et al. (1990) have shown, national cultures have a significant impact on work behavior. Managing partners across different regions should therefore be a more complex and difficult task than managing partners from the same region. The higher the concentration, the more partners from a single region are represented in the firm's organization set and the less difficult its task of managing them.

The experience of an organization's partners in interfirm agreements may influence its tendency to cooperate. The more agreements a firm's partners currently have, the more likely they are to be embedded in closed regions of the network and therefore to be constrained from acting opportunistically (see Baker 1990). However, partners with more relationships may also be less dependent on the firm for its information, goods and services, releasing normative pressures for equitable behavior. Partner experience may therefore either heighten or dampen the firm's tendency to cooperate.

Finally, in studying the reproduction of network structure, it is important to differentiate between relationships with partners entering the network and relationships with partners already in the network. The first are called entering partners and the second incumbent partners. Splitting partners in this way provides a robust test of the social capital argument. In the broadest sense, social capital releases resources to firms for further cooperation whether the firm engages partners that are new to the network or already network members. A narrower view of social capital suggests that social capital theory applies to network formation only for relationships with network incumbents. If this is the case, future research must consider network incumbency as a moderator of social capital's effect.

DATA

We test these hypotheses by examining network formation in the biotech-nology industry.[1] As most earlier studies have shown, the frequency of interfirm relationships in this industry is quite high, primarily between large established firms in a variety of businesses (pharmaceuticals, chemicals, agricultural products, food products) and small, entrepreneurial startup firms (Barley et al. 1992, Powell and Brantley 1992, Kogut et al. 1995). These relationships have been shown to increase the capabilities of startup firms, indicating a motivation for continuing cooperation (Shan et al. 1994). The incidence of these relationships has been explained both by network (Kogut et al. 1992) and firm-level variables (Shan 1990, Pisano 1990).

Biotechnology is typical of industries with high rates of innovation and a significant entrepreneurial sector. The motivation for interfirm cooperation in these industries is quite strong, based on the complementarity of large and small firm capabilities. Because of the tremendous potential market for new biotechnology products, established companies have sought access to this new technology both by starting up biotechnology operations in-house and by forming cooperative agreements with startup firms, typically begun by scientists. Startup firms, in turn, have been willing to enter into cooperative agreements to provide established firms with new technologies and products in order to receive funding and to breach the barriers to entry in marketing, distribution, and government certification (Shan 1987). As firms become connected through these agreements, a broad network, typically global in scope, is formed.

To analyze network formation in biotechnology, we examine new relationships by startups rather than those by established firms, for several reasons.[2] Kogut et al. (1994) showed that startups have a much greater propensity to cooperate than established firms over time and correspondingly have more relationships. Network growth is therefore determined more by the expansion of startup organization sets than by the organization sets of their established firm partners. Startups also have much higher variability than established firms in number of relationships over time and are more central in the network (Barley et al. 1992).

Although startups have relationships with each other, their relationships with established firms are far more prevalent. Only six percent of relationships existing in 1988 were between startups. A description of the timing of foundings of startups and the pattern of their relationships with established firms is given in Figures 13.2 to 13.5. (See Appendix A for a description of data sources and the characteristics of our sample.) The distribution of cooperative relationships is shown in Figures 13.2 and 13.3. Startup foundings (shown in Figure 13.2) lead the formation of these relationships by three to five years (shown in Figure 13.3). Startup foundings peak in 1981, while the number of relationships with partners peaks in 1984 with a second mode in 1986. This second (1986) mode can be partly attributed to the entry into the network of established firms (see Figure 13.4). The modal year for all relationships, by both new and incumbent startups, is also 1986 (see Figure 13.5).

Since the process of developing, testing, and commercializing biotechnology products takes many years, cooperative relationships endure for a long time. Only 18 percent of the relationships in the industry from its beginning until 1988 had a fixed duration (that is, their termination date was formally specified when they were initiated); and only 31 percent of fixed duration relationships ended before 1988. Furthermore, only 11 percent of the relationships with unfixed durations were terminated before 1988. Thus, in 1988 some 85 percent of all the agreements that had ever been formed were still in effect.

METHOD

Measuring Social Capital

Our measure of social capital is based on the idea of structural equivalence, which has been frequently used in the analysis of interorganizational networks (Knoke and Rogers 1978, Van de Ven et al. 1979, DiMaggio 1986, Schrum and Withnow 1988, Nohria and Garcia-Pont 1990, Oliver 1988). Determining the structural equivalence of firms is also central to network

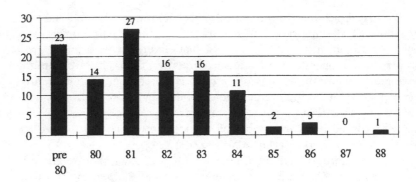

Figure 13.2. Number of Sample Startups Founded in Each Year

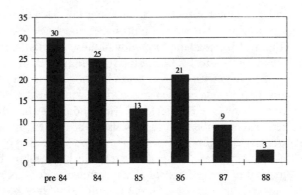

Figure 13.3. Number of Sample Startups Entering Network in Each Year

analysis in structural hole theory (Burt 1992, chapter 2). Firms that are structurally equivalent have relationships with the same other firms in the network. In principle, structurally equivalent startups have the same established firms as partners and structurally equivalent established firms have the same startups as partners. The emergence of this type of structure therefore depends on the pattern of partner sharing.[3]

An idealized example of this type of network structure is shown in Figure 13.6. Rows represent startups and columns their established firm partners. An "X" indicates a relationship and a "0" the absence of a relationship. Note that the intersections of row and column groups are either dense with relationships or sparse.

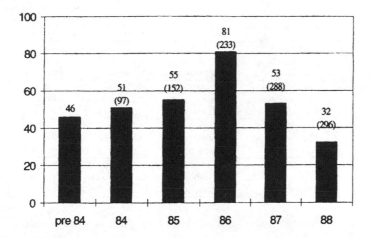

Figure 13.4. Number of Established Firms Entering Network in Each Year

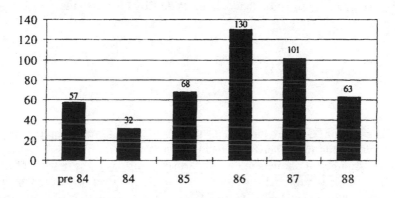

Figure 13.5. Number of Cooperative Relationships Formed in Each Year

A network where all groups of firms are densely related to each other is rare, since it would be almost fully connected. Therefore, measuring structural equivalence in practice almost always depends on an assessment of relative partner overlap. While some groups may have firms that share almost all their partners, firms in other groups may share hardly any of their partners.

One way of measuring how much firms in a group share partners is to examine the dispersion of intergroup densities around the network average. A group of firms that share partners extensively should have dense relationships with some partner groups and sparse or no relationships with other

Partners

		Group 1	Group 2	Group 3	Group 4
Startups	Group 1	XXXOOXXX XXXXOOXX OXXXXOXX	000000000000 0000000000 000000000000	000000000000 000000000000 000000000	000000000000 000000000000 000000
	Group 2	000000000000 000000000000 000000000	XXXXXXOOOX XXXOXXXXOX XXOXXXOXXX	000000000000 000000000000 000000000	XXXXXXXOOX XOXXOXXXOX XXXXOXXOX
	Group 3	000000000000 000000000000 000000000	000000000000 000000000000 000000000	OOXXXXXXXX XXXXOXXXXO XOXOXXOXXXX	000000000000 000000000000 000000
	Group 4	000000000000 000000000000 000000000	000000000000 000000000000 000000000	000000000000 000000000000 000000000	XXXXXOXOOX XXOXXOXXXO OXXXXOXXOX

Figure 13.6. An Idealized Network Structure Based on Structural Equivalence

partner groups. This pattern is found for all the groups, both row and column, in Figure 13.6. An equation that calculates density dispersion is:

$$G_i = n_i \sum_j m_j (d_{ij} - d*)^2.$$ (1)

In this equation, G_i is the measure of the dispersion of intergroup densities for the ith group in the network, n_i is the number of firms in the ith group, m_j is the number of partners in the jth partner group, d_{ij} is the density of the intersection of the ith and jth groups, and $d*$ is the overall density of the network.[4] A higher value of G_i indicates greater dispersion of a group's densities and therefore more partner sharing by the firms in group i. Note that this measure penalizes small groups of firms with small partner groups.

To show how the structure of the biotechnology network differs from the idealized network of Figure 13.6, we use a method that builds on G_i to analyze the biotechnology network of relationships formed before 1984. Since G_i reflects the deviation of intergroup relationships from the average network density, summing G_i over all groups produces a measure of network structure:[5]

$$G = \sum_i \sum_j n_i m_j (d_{ij} - d*)^2.$$ (2)

The details of the methodology are presented in Appendix B, which shows how the pre-1984 network was analyzed.

Figure 13.7a shows the partitioned raw data. There are four startup groups and six partner groups. Group I has the largest number of firms, which have relationships predominantly with partner groups A, B, and C. Because the number of relationships Group I has with each of the partner groups is much smaller than the number of possible relationships, the densities of these intergroup relationships are quite low (see Figure 13.7b). Unlike Group I; Groups II, III, and IV are densely related to their partner groups. Group II contains only one firm, the only startup to have agreements with Group E. Furthermore, this firm has only one other relationship in the network, with a partner in Group F. Finally, both Groups III and IV are composed of several startups that have established relationships with Groups D and F, respectively.

Only a few firms contribute significantly to the structure of biotechnology network. To demonstrate this, we divide Equation (1) by Equation (2) to get a measure of each group's percentage contribution to network structure. This variable, bounded by zero and one, represents the dispersion of startup group densities normalized by a measure of how structured the network is in a time period.

Startup groups in the network occupy distinct positions which vary in their social capital. A group's contribution to network structure in a time period indicates how tightly packed are its relationships with partners. Higher density means greater partner sharing within a startup group, creating a stronger focal point for conversation.[6] Startups in groups with higher contributions have greater social capital available to them.[7] If a group's contribution to network structure increases with new relationships, we assume that startups have chosen partners so that social capital is increased. However, increased social capital also means increased social constraint. Following Burt's argument (Burt 1982, p. 57), if startups are searching for lower social constraint, the startup group's contribution to network structure should decline over time.

Testing the Propositions

Although structurally equivalent startups that occupy the same position will have the same amount of social capital, they will differ in the number of relationships they establish in each year and in the control variables. We therefore designed the empirical tests at the firm level, consistent with the way they are stated, over each pair of years from 1984 to 1988. The data are

Partner Groups

```
                         A              B    C       D        E           F
             OOOOOOOOOOOOOOOOOOOO •OO •OOXOO •OOOOO •OOOOOO•OOOOOOOOO
             OXOOOOOOOOOOOOOOOOOO •OO •OOOOO •OOOOO •OOOOOO•OOOOOOOOO
             OOOOOXOOOOOOOOOOOOOO •OO •XOOOO •OOOOO •OOOOOO•OOOOOOOOO
             OOOOOOOOO•OOOOOOOOXO •OO •OOOOO •OOOOO •OOOOOO•OOOOOOOOO
             OOOOOOOOOOOOOOOOOOOX •OO •OOOOO •OOOOO •OOOOOO•OOOOOOOOO
             OOOXOOOOOOOOOOOOOOOO •OO •OOOXX •OOOOO •OOOOOO•OOOOOOOOO
             OOOOOOXXOOOOOOOOOOOO •OX •OOOOO •OOOOO •OOOOOO•OOOOOOOOO
             OOOOOOOOXOOOOOOOOOOO •OO •OOOOO •OOOOO •OOOOOO•OOOOOOOOO
        I    OOOXOOOOOOOOOOOOOOOO •OO •OOOOO •OOOOO •OOOOOO•OOOOOOOOO
             OOOOOOOOOOOOOOOOOOOO •OO •OOOOO •OOOOO •OOOOOO•OOOOOXOOO
             OOOOOOOOOOOOOOOOOOOO •XO •OOOOO •OOOOO •OOOOOO•OOOOOOOOO
Startup      OOOOOOOOOOXOOOOOOOOO •OO •OOOOO •OOOOO •OOOOOO•OOOOOOOOO
Groups       XOOOOOOOOOOOOOOOOOOO •OO •OOOOO •OOOOO •OOOOOO•OOOOOOOOO
             OOOOOOOOOOOOOOOOOOOO •OX •OOOOO •OOOOO •OOOOOO•OOOOOOOOO
             OOXOOOOOOOOOOOOOOOOO •OO •OOOOO •OOOOO •OOOOOO•OOOOOXOOO
             OOOOOOOOOOOOXOOXOOO  •OO •OXOOO •OOOOO •OOOOOO•OOOOOOOOO
             OOOOOOOOOOXOOOOOOOOO •OO •OOOOO •OOOOO •OOOOOO•OOOOOOOOO
             OOOOOOOOOOOOOXOOOOO  •OO •OOOOO •OOOOO •OOOOOO•OOOOOOOOO
             OOOOOOOOOOOOOOOOOOOO •XO •OOOOO •OOOOO •OOOOOO•OOOOOOOOO
             OOOOOOOOOOOOOOOXOO   •OO •OOOOO •OOOOO •OOOOOO•OOOOOOOOO
             OOOOOOOOOOOXOOOOOOO  •OO •OOOOO •OOOOO •OOOOOO•OOOOOOOOO
             OOOOOOOOOOOOOXOOOO   •OO •OOOOO •OOOOO •OOOOOO•OOOOOOOOO
       II    OOOOOOOOOOOOOOOOOOOO •OO •OOOOO •OOOOO •XXXXXX•XOOOOOOOO
             OOOOOOOOOOOOOOOOOOOO •OO •OOOOO •OXXXO •OOOOOO•OOOOOOOOO
       III   OOOOOOOOOOOOOOOOOOOO •OO •OOOOO •XXOOX •OOOOOO•OOOOOOOOO
             OOOOOOOOOOOOOOOOOOOO •OO •OOOOO •OOOOO •OOOOOO•XOXOXOOOO
       IV    OOOOOOOOOOOOOOOOOOOO •OO •OOOOO •OOOOO •OOOOOO•XXOOOXXOO
             OOOOOOOOOOOOOOOOOOOO •OO •OOOOO •OOOOO •OOOOOO•XOOOXOOOO
             OOOOOOOOOOOOOOOOOOOO •OO •OOOOO •OOOOO •OOOOOO•OOOXOXOOX
             OOOOOOOOOOOOOOOOOOOO •OO •OOOOO •OOOOO •OOOOOO•OOOXOXOXO
```

Figure 13.7a. Partitioned Raw Data for 1983 Network

	A	B	C	D	E	F
I	.05	.09	.05	0	0	.01
II	0	0	0	0	1	.11
III	0	0	0	.6	0	0
IV	0	0	0	0	0	.33

Figure 13.7b. Density Matrix of 1983 Network

pooled cross-sections of year pairs from 1984 to 1988; e.g., 1984-1985. Dummy variables for each year pair are included to correct for time period effects.

We use several regression techniques: negative binomial, two-stage least squares and generalized least squares regression. Like Poisson regression, the negative binomial model treats the dependent variable as a count variable but allows for a direct measure of heterogeneity (see Cameron and Trivedi 1986). Estimating heterogeneity not only relaxes the stringent Poisson assumption of equal mean and variance in the error term but also accounts for omitted variable bias.

However, the negative binomial model does not correct for the potential bias due to the simultaneity of new relationships and change in social capital over time. To make this correction, we assume that the dependent variable is not a count but continuous and use two-stage least squares. Generalized least squares permits corrections for serial correlation in the error term and unobserved firm-level effects. Figure 13.1 shows how these regressions test the propositions based on the theories of social capital and structural holes.

RESULTS

Table 13.1 shows the means, standard deviations, and correlations among the variables, and Table 13.2 presents the findings for regressions. Five of the explanatory variables have consistent results: the social capital and change in social capital, startup experience, partner experience, and public offering (IPO). Both network variables explain the frequency of new relationships strongly, as social capital theory predicts. Interestingly, neither startup nor partner experience has an effect on new relationships, controlling for the network variables.[8] This finding shows that new relationships are not explained by how many relationships a startup or its partner has, but how the relationships are distributed across partner groups. Public offering has a positive, significant effect on establishing relationships with entering partners but no influence on relationships with incumbents.

The results for startup size and regional concentration are not as clear. Neither has an effect for incumbent partners. However, for entering partners, the results for the two techniques differ in significance but not in sign.

Table 13.3 reports the results of testing whether social capital and the number of new startup relationships influence change in social capital. Included in the model are dummy variables for each year and a variable indicating the number of firms in a startup's group. Controlling for this variable is necessary since G (in Equation 1) is linearly related to it. The two-stage least squares regression shows that more new relationships increase social capital. Also, the increase in social capital is lower when a startup has more social capital in the beginning period.

Startup propensities to cooperate may vary to some extent. There may be unobserved firm-level factors that influence how frequently cooperation occurs. The α term in the negative binomial regression captures these unobserved variables to a degree.

TABLE 13.1 Means, Standard Deviations, and Correlations

Variables	MN	SD	Correlations									
			1	2	3	4	5	6	7	8	9	10
1. Social capital	0.039	0.036	1.00									
2. Change in social capital	-0.001	0.027	-0.52	1.00								
3. Number of relationships with entering partners in each period	0.73	1.16	0.25	0.17	1.00							
4. Number of relationships with incumbent partners in each period	0.52	0.95	0.17	0.14	0.27	1.00						
5. Size	170.08	245.99	0.38	0.01	0.27	0.07	1.00					
6. IPO	0.74	0.44	0.12	0.01	0.19	0.12	0.16	1.00				
7. Regional concentration	1.79	0.61	0.03	-0.001	0.04	0.03	0.41	0.10	1.00			
8. Startup experience	3.94	4.64	0.55	-0.08	0.14	0.18	0.41	0.26	0.05	1.00		
9. Partner experience	2.45	1.52	-0.09	0.04	-0.14	-0.11	-0.12	0.12	0.06	0.03	1.00	
10. Number of startups in group	40.16	28.09	-0.65	0.37	-0.19	-0.13	-0.20	-0.06	-0.07	-0.32	0.14	1.00

TABLE 13.2a Results for Regression Explaining New Startup Relationships

Explanatory Variables	Entering Partners		Incumbent Partners	
	Negative Binomial	2SLS[a]	Negative Binomial	2SLS
Constant	−1.35***	−0.15	−1.97***	−0.13
	(0.42)[b]	(0.28)	(0.67)	(0.23)
Social capital	8.08*	17.94***	13.08**	11.82***
	(4.27)	(5.39)	(5.32)	(4.26)
Change in social capital	13.06***	27.52***	18.84***	16.95***
	(3.12)	(8.26)	(5.74)	(6.28)
Startup experience	0.002	−0.03	0.023	0.0042
	(0.031)	(0.024)	(0.038)	(0.02)
Partner experience	−0.057	−0.035	0.089	−0.59
	(0.057)	(0.043)	(0.27)	(0.38)
Size	0.0004	0.0004	−0.001	−0.0004*
	(0.0003)	(0.0003)	(0.0006)	(0.0003)
IPO	0.79***	0.39***	0.39	0.12
	(0.23)	(0.15)	(0.27)	(0.13)
Regional concentration	0.09	0.0004	0.089	0.0001
	(0.15)	(0.0001)	(0.27)	(0.0009)
D86	0.52**	0.73**	1.04***	0.64***
	(0.26)	(0.25)	(0.39)	(0.21)
D87	−0.30	−0.056	0.77*	0.39**
	(0.29)	(0.24)	(0.44)	(0.20)
D88	−0.99***	−0.34	0.26	0.16
	(0.35)	(0.26)	(0.48)	(0.22)
α	0.081		0.59*	
	(0.13)		(0.32)	
F-value		12.49		5.27
df		10,262		10,261
R^2		0.32		0.16
Adjusted R^2		0.29		0.13

NOTE: R^2 Terms pertain to unadjusted estimates.
a. 2SLS coefficients are adjusted for serial correlation in the error term.
b. Standard errors are reported in parentheses.
*$p < 0.10$; **$p < 0.05$; ***$p < 0.01$.

To explore this problem further, we regressed the frequency of new startup relationships on the explanatory variables including firm-specific dummy variables to account for unobservable effects. Since our sample draws from a larger population of startup firms, a random effects specification is appropriate. The hypotheses are therefore tested, without simultaneity, using Generalized Least Squares. The results of this GLS regression are stronger than those of the negative binomial and two-stage least squares regressions.[9] Consequently, we can be reasonably confident that unobserved firm-level variation in the propensity to cooperate does not confound our findings.

TABLE 13.2b

Explanatory Variables	Entering Partners		Incumbent Partners	
	Negative Binomial	OLS[a]	Negative Binomial	OLS
Constant	−1.08***	0.51***	−1.50**	−0.32*
	(0.40)[b]	(0.19)	(0.69)	(0.17)
Social Capital				
Change in social capital				
Startup experience	0.029	0.026*	0.056	0.042***
	(0.020)	(0.016)	(0.037)	(0.014)
Partner experience	−0.057	−0.037	−0.12	−0.057
	(0.066)	(0.044)	(0.084)	(0.039)
Size	0.0008***	0.0009***	−0.0002	−0.0001
	(0.0003)	(0.0003)	(0.0006)	(0.0003)
IPO	0.87***	0.47***	0.47*	0.16
	(0.24)	(0.15)	(0.27)	(0.13)
Regional concentration	0.17	0.0004	0.18	0.0003
	(0.16)	(0.001)	(0.28)	(0.0009)
D86	0.15	0.26	0.63	0.35*
	(0.23)	(0.19)	(0.42)	(0.18)
D87	−0.67***	−0.45**	0.31	0.13
	(0.26)	(0.19)	(0.42)	(0.17)
D88	−1.43***	0.79***	−0.26	−0.14
	(0.29)	(0.19)	(0.48)	(0.18)
α	−0.27		0.99**	
F-value		9.94		3.15
df		8,263		8,263
R^2		0.22		0.087
Adjusted R^2		0.19		0.059

a. The OLS regression results reported are adjusted for autocorrelated error. The F-statistic reported is not adjusted for this error.
b. Standard errors are reported in parentheses.

DISCUSSION

We have posed two theories to explain the incidence of new relationships. One theory emphasizes the positive effect of social capital, as structural constraint, on new cooperation. The other argues that highly constrained cooperation has lower rewards and is therefore avoided. Our analysis of biotechnology startups shows that social capital theory is the better predictor of cooperation over time. More constrained firms cooperate with partners that can be firmly embedded in the historical network structure. The network is thus increasingly structured over time. Network formation, and industry

TABLE 13.2c

Explanatory Variables:	Entering Partners		Incumbent Partners	
	Negative Binomial	2SLS[a]	Negative Binomial	2SLS
Constant	-0.94***	0.15	-1.87***	-0.13
	(0.26)	(0.18)	(0.39)	(0.16)
Social capital	11.91***	14.75***	12.17***	9.62***
	(2.34)	(1.97)	(3.73)	(1.77)
Change in social capital	17.22***	21.14***	18.16***	13.09***
	(3.41)	(2.66)	(5.003)	(.38)
D86	0.72***	0.69***	1.12***	0.60***
	(0.25)	(0.19)	(0.38)	(0.17)
D87	-0.1	-0.095	0.75*	0.36**
	(0.28)	(0.19)	(0.38)	(0.17)
D88	-0.80**	-0.42**	0.27	0.10
	(0.32)	(0.19)	(0.41)	(0.17)
α	-0.24		0.75**	
	(0.16)		(0.34)	
F-value		22.93		9.82
df		5,266		5,266
R^2		0.30		0.16
Adjusted R^2		0.29		0.14

a. The 2SLS regression results reported are adjusted for autocorrelated error. The F-statistic reported is not adjusted for this error.

growth, are therefore significantly influenced by the development and maintenance of social capital.

Why have biotechnology startups chosen to increase social capital rather than exploit structural holes? First, relationships in the biotechnology network last a long time. Long durations entail extensive, ongoing interaction over a broad range of technical and commercial problems. Were partners to behave in a self-interested way during the course of such a long relationship, a substantial investment in time and effort would be jeopardized. Structural stability is therefore desirable. In a network where relationships are of shorter duration, the structure would undoubtedly be less stable and less available as a resource for action. Enduring interfirm ties sustain the structure that facilitates new cooperation. Second, structural hole theory may apply more to networks of market transactions than to networks of cooperative relationships. Lacking the requirement to cooperate over time, firms may not experience structural constraint in their relationships. Third, interfirm relationships in biotechnology are based on a kind of mutual dependence that may prevent either startups or established firms from gaining control over

TABLE 13.3 Results of Two-stage Least Squares Regression on Change in Social
Capital

Explanatory Variables:	Dependent Variable: Change in Social Capital	
Constant	0.0043	0.0049
	(0.0054)	(0.0077)
Number of startup relationships with entering partners	0.018***	
	(0.0038)	
Number of startup relationships with incumbent partners		0.036***
		(0.017)
Existing social capital	−0.44***	−0.41***
	(0.056)	(0.86)
Number of startups in group	0.0001*0.0003**	
	(0.00007)	(0.0001)
D86	−0.025***	−0.037
	(0.0054)	(0.010)
D87	−0.0047	−0.023***
	(0.0051)	(0.009)
D88	0.0018	−0.014*
	(0.0054)	(0.0075)

$*p < 0.10; **p < 0.05; ***p < 0.01.$

the other. Biotechnology startups and their established firm partners have complementary resources that are jointly necessary for product development and commercialization.

Such mutuality may not be present to such an extent in other technology-intensive industries. For example, Kogut et al. (1992) argue that cooperative agreements between startups and established firms in the semiconductor industry are based on the technical standards which large firms own. Large firms dominate the network structure of the semiconductor industry as they compete for technological dominance through their alliances with startups. In such a structure, embeddedness clearly has a different meaning than in the biotechnology network (compare, e.g., Marsden 1983).

Our results lead to the conclusion that some firms continuously improve their already strong social endowments, although at a decreasing rate, while other firms have less social capital to draw upon in forming new relationships. This conclusion holds for relationships with both incumbent and newly-entering partners, indicating that the effect of network structure on forming new relationships is not moderated by partner incumbency. Although the results for network formation are similar for both incumbent and entering partners, these partner types differ in two important ways. First, entering partners tend to establish relationships with startups whose equity is publicly traded while the choice of incumbents does not depend on the characteristics of individual startups. *IPO* (Initial Public Offering) appears to signal organizational legitimacy to entering firms rather than represent a source of potential startup capital substituting for a partner's financial resources. A second difference between incumbent and entering partners is in the time trends. For relationships with entering firms, the signs on the year dummy variables turn from negative to positive to negative over the four years. Relationships with entering partners decline in the later years simply because there are fewer firms coming into the network. But, as shown in Figure 13.5, the trend for incumbent partners remains positive, though declining in the later years. When there are fewer entrants, incumbent partners attract more attention.

PATH DEPENDENCE IN
NETWORK FORMATION

The firms in the industry recreate a stable network structure whose foundation was laid at an early point in the industry's history. Firms' early partner choices thus have a significant impact on the course of future cooperation. To examine this conjecture, we analyze and compare the network structures from 1984 to 1988. Examining structural equivalence over time indicates how much network structure is altered by network growth through entry and new relationships among incumbents.

Table 13.4 presents cross-tabulations showing whether pairs of firms remained structurally equivalent or nonequivalent from one year to the next. Entries on the main diagonal in each table indicate persistence. To assess whether these entries are larger than the off-diagonal entries, we calculated the cross-product ratio for each table. The cross-product ratio is a commonly used statistic for estimating the degree of association between two variables (see Agresti 1984, p. 15). A cross-product ratio of zero indicates no association between the variables, and values of the ratio greater than one imply a positive relationship. Because the logarithm of the cross-product ratio is less skewed than the ratio itself, we use the log of the ratio to test for structural persistence (Wickens 1989, pp. 218-222). These log ratios are all positive and strongly significantly different from zero for both startups and partners. Except for the 1983-1984 period, the tables show that once a pair of startups are structurally equivalent, the odds are significant that they will continue to be so. Furthermore, the reverse is also generally true: if a pair of startups are not structurally equivalent, they are likely to remain this way.

TABLE 13.4 Structural Equivalence of Organizations over Time

1. Startups

	1984				1985				1986	
	Str. eq.	Not Str. eq.			Str. eq.	Not. Str. eq.			Str. eq.	Not. Str. eq.
1983	52*	190	1984		189	99	1985		917	528
Not. Str. eq.	4	189	Not. Str. eq.		605	592	Not. Str. eq.		270	631

Log cross product ratio = 2.56	Log cross product ratio = 0.62	Log cross product ratio = 1.40
Std. error = 0.53	Std. error = 0.14	Std. error = 0.09

	1987				1988	
	Str. eq.	Not. Str. eq.			Str. eq.	Not. Str. eq.
1986	1162	1067	1987		1609	519
Not. Str. eq.	426	1261	Not. Str. eq.		903	1722

Log cross product ratio = 1.17	Log cross product ratio = 1.78
Std. error = 0.07	Std. error = 0.07

2. Established Firms

	1984				1985				1986	
	Str. eq.	Not. Str. eq.			Str. eq.	Not. Str. eq.			Str. eq.	Not. Str. eq.
1983	56	187	1984		141	270	1985		257	651
Not. Str. eq.	15	777	Not. Str. eq.		187	4058	Not. Str. eq.		377	10190

Log cross product ratio = 2.74	Log cross product ratio = 2.43	Log cross product ratio = 2.47
Std. error = 0.03	Std. error = 0.13	Std. error = 0.09

	1987				1988	
	Str. eq.	Not. Str. eq.			Str. eq.	Not. Str. eq.
1986	339	1097	1987		368	1561
Not. Str. eq.	784	24808	Not. Str. eq.		971	37855

Log cross product ratio = 2.28	Log cross product ratio = 2.22
Std. error = 0.03	Std. error = 0.07

Predicting partner groups over time depends mostly on the persistence of structural dissimilarity, however. Between 1987 and 1988, for example, the odds that a pair of partners will continue to be structurally equivalent are roughly one to five (368/1561), while the odds that they will remain structurally nonequivalent are roughly forty to one (37855/971). The reason for this pattern is the large number of entering partners relative to partners already in the network.

The structural development of the industry, based on the building and reinforcement of social capital, offers a simple insight into the rigidity of organizational forms. Since an organization depends on the resources available in its network, organizational inertia may be less an inherent property of organizations than a product of the organization's position in a rigid network. The persistence of these positions, as shown in Table 13.4, suggests that a startup's characteristics may endure because of structural conditions (see Shan et al. 1994).

CONCLUSION

Social capital, as outlined by Coleman and Bourdieu, is a powerful concept for understanding how interfirm networks in emerging industries are formed. It is important to note that network formation need not lead towards an optional structure for innovation or product commercialization.[10] Although there is evidence that interfirm cooperation and startup patent activity are related (Shan et al. 1994), the local benefits of partner sharing may not be distributed so that the most productive and useful technological advances are commercialized successfully.

The importance of network formation for interfirm cooperation has important consequences for organization theory. Taking the transaction as the unit of analysis is inadequate to capture the structural effects we have identified. The study of interfirm cooperative agreements over time requires an analysis of the network as a whole.

The persistence of network structure has subtle implications for entrepreneurial behavior. Structural persistence does not imply that firms are equally situated to exploit profitable opportunities for cooperation. Because the structure is relatively inert, brokering positions are established early in the history of the network. In fact, if structure did not persist, all firms would be potential brokers but with few enduring opportunities. Given the relative fixity of brokering positions, the kind of enterpreneurship Burt proposes, as the exploitation of structural holes, should be especially profitable. An intriguing hypothesis is that the pursuit of these rewards explains the current wave of mergers and acquisitions among biotechnology firms.

The persistence of the past is welcomed if alternative futures look less promising, especially scenarios with free-rider or prisoner-dilemma problems. But social capital can also be associated with encumbering commitments that impede competition and change. If biotechnology firms could rewrite their histories of cooperation, few would be surprised that an alternative path of network formation would emerge. It is this gap between the desired and the actual that expresses most clearly the idea that structure both enables and constrains entrepreneurial ambitions.

ACKNOWLEDGMENT

This research was supported through a grant from AT&T administered under the auspices of the Reginald H. Jones Center. We would like to acknowledge the helpful comments of Arthur Stinchcombe.

Appendix A

Data Sources

The primary source of data is BIOSCAN (1988, 1989), a commercial directory of biotechnology firms, published and updated quarterly by ORYNX Press, Inc. Because it has generally been considered the most comprehensive compendium of information on relationships in the industry, any relationship listed in BIOSCAN is included in our sample. However, because BIOSCAN may have omitted some relationships terminated before 1988, we collected data from the three other sources: (1) a proprietary database obtained from a leading biotechnology firm (called the "black volumes") in 1986; (2) a database developed by the North Carolina Biotechnology Center, based on published announcements of cooperative agreements; and (3) a direct mail survey of and telephone interviews with startups.

Because these latter three sources had neither BIOSCAN's history of direct contact with startups and their partners nor its depth of information about agreements, we relied less on their data. We added an agreement if it appeared in at least two of these sources. We found 46 relationships in this category. As they do not appear in the 1988 BIOSCAN directory we assumed that these relationships had been terminated before 1988; the network analysis for 1988 therefore excluded them.

All startups in the final sample were independent businesses specializing in the commercialization of biotechnology products. Their portfolio of products must include diagnostic or therapeutic pharmaceuticals. The agreements consisted of joint ventures, licensing, and long term contracts between startups and their partners. Powell and Brantley (1992) found that different types of relationships—e.g., licensing, joint venture, research and development limited partnership—were not statistically related to how much firms engaged in cooperative agreements. Consequently, the network we analyze contains these types of relationship together. Since only firms that have engaged in at least one agreement can contribute to network structure, startups without relationships are excluded from the sample.

Application of these criteria produced a sample of 114 startups that had cooperative agreements before 1989. These startups differed in their time of entry into the network, as Figure 13.3 shows. Thirteen have agreements only with universities, government agencies and research institutes. (Many of these relationships represent licenses of the original patents stemming from university research.) We dropped these startups from the sample in order to retain a group of partners whose interest were clearly commercial. Whereas university ties are important for the initial licensing and subsequent consulting services, our focus is on the structuring of relationships among commercial partners.[11]

Appendix B

Operationalization of Measures of Network Structure

We analyzed the asymmetric matrix of cooperative relationships with CONCOR, a network analysis algorithm (Breiger et al. 1975) that has been used frequently in interorganizational research (Knoke and Rogers 1978, Van de Ven et al. 1979, DiMaggio 1986, Schrum and Withnow 1988). The usual practice of applying CONCOR (see Arabie et al. 1978) is to dichotomize the full set of network members; then to split these two groups separately; then to split these results; and so on until either (1) a desired number of groups are obtained or (2) groups are obtained with a specific number of members. We used the following rules for applying CONCOR to both startups and their partners: (1) groups with fewer than 10 members were not split; and (2) when splitting a group produced a singleton subgroup, the group was kept whole. We followed this practice separately for both the startups (rows) and their partners (columns) of the matrix of relationships. The purpose of these rules is to avoid groups with small sizes that are inappropriate relative to the size of the network (see Walker 1985).

Although CONCOR's results at the two group level have been benchmarked against an optimality criterion (Noma and Smith 1985), the results of subsequent splitting have not been evaluated. Because of potential variation in decision rules for subsequent splits of the data, different results may be achieved for the same data set. To address this problem, we applied a second algorithm to the partition of network members produced by CONCOR. This algorithm, called CALCOPT, reallocates network members from group to group in the partition if the shift in group membership improves a target function consistent with Lorrain and White's (1971) original definition of structural equivalence. This target function is Equation (2). Thus CALCOPT reallocates network members from one group to another if the move increases the dispersion of densities in the density matrix. CALCOPT evaluates the CONCOR row partition and then the column partition iteratively until no reassignment improves the target function.

CONCOR and CALCOPT were applied to each year of data from 1984 to 1988. The data for each year are all cooperative relationships that were established between the startups and their partners up to that year minus any relationships that were terminated during the year. For example, the 1985 network includes the 1984 network plus all agreements begun between 1984 and 1985 minus terminated relationships. Thus five separate networks, one for each year, were analyzed to identify (1) groups of structurally equivalent startups and groups of structurally equivalent partners and (2) the pattern of intergroup densities used to measure social capital.

NOTES

1. Biotechnology includes all techniques for manipulating micro-organisms. In 1973 Cohen and Boyer perfected genetic engineering methods, an advance that enabled the reproduction of a gene in bacteria. In 1975, Cesar Millstein and Georges Kohler produced monoclonal antibodies using hybridoma technology; and in 1976 DNA sequencing was discovered and the first working synthetic gene developed. These discoveries laid the technological base for the "new biotechnology."

2. Our definition of interfirm cooperative relationships is inclusive. For our purposes a cooperative relationship may be organized as equity or nonequity joint ventures, licensing, marketing or distribution agreements, or research and development limited partnerships (see Appendix A). Further, we define a relationship between firms rather than between projects so that new relationships entail new partners rather than old partners attached to new projects. This definition coincides with our focus on network formation, rather than the evolution of a single interfirm relationship.

3. We do not observe the actual communication of information regarding partner behavior among startups. However, conversations with board members of startup firms confirm that such communication is quite common (Hamilton 1992).

4. Density is defined as: k/mn, where k is the number of actual relationships a group of n structurally equivalent startups and a group of m structurally equivalent partners. The densities of each intersection can be calculated to form a density matrix. This matrix is the basis for the construction of a blockmodel, a binary matrix representing relations among groups of structurally equivalent firms in the network (White et al. 1976, Arabie et al. 1978). Blockmodels typically are constructed only for symmetric networks—i.e., network that are formed by relationships between only one type of firm, say, startups. Consequently, we do not develop a conventional blockmodel for our data.

5. This function has been used to analyze sparse networks, in a number of studies (Boorman and Levitt 1983; Walker 1985, 1988) which found it to have strong construct and predictive validity.

6. See Note 3.

7. This measure of social capital is structural, consistent with Coleman's (1990) usage and arguments. Alternative measures based on attributes of specific interfirm relationships may be useful when global network data are not available (see Baker 1990).

8. To test whether the effect of startup experience on new startup relationships might be quadratic, we included experience^2 in the equation, without significant results. We made the same test for startup size, also without significant results.

9. The GLS results are not shown and are available from the authors on request.

10. For different perspectives on this topic see Baker (1987) and Delany (1988).

11. See Barley et al. (1992) on the sparseness of the university/NBF density matrix, as well as a breakdown of agreements by type (e.g., licensing, joint venture).

REFERENCES

Acs, Z. and D. B. Audretsch (1989), "Entrepreneurial Strategy and the Presence of Small Firms," *Small Business Economics,* 1, 3, 193-213.

Agresti, A. (1984), *Analysis of Categorical Data,* New York: John Wiley.

Arabie, P., S. A. Boorman, and P. R. Levitt (1978), "Constructing Blockmodels: How and Why," *Journal of Mathematical Psychology,* 17, 21-63.

BIOSCAN (1988, 1989), Phoenix, AZ: Oryx.

Baker, W. (1984), "The Social Structure of a National Securities Market," *American Journal of Sociology,* 89, 775-811.

—— (1990), "Market Networks and Corporate Behavior," *American Journal of Sociology,* 96, 589-625.

Barley, S. R., J. Freeman, and R. C. Hybels (1992), "Strategic Alliances in Commercial Biotechnology," in N. Nohria and R. G. Eccles (Eds.), *Networks and Organization,* Cambridge, MA: Harvard Business School Press.

Boorman, S. A. and P. R. Levitt (1983), "Blockmodelling Complex Statutes: Mapping Techniques Based on Combinatorial Optimization for Analyzing Economic Legislation and Its Stress Points over Time," *Economic Letters,* 13-19.

Bound, J., C. Cummins, Z. Griliches, B. H. Hall, and A. Jaffe (1984), "Who Does R & D and Who Patents?" in Z. Griliches (Ed.), *R & D, Patents, and Productivity,* 21-54, Chicago: University of Chicago Press.

Bourdieu, P. (1980), "Le Capital Sociale: Notes Provisaires," *Actes de la Recherche en Sciences Sociales,* 3, 2-3.

—— and L. Wacquant (1992), *An Invitation to Reflexive Sociology,* Chicago: University of Chicago Press.

Boyles, S. E. (1968), "Estimate of the Number and Size Distribution of Domestic Joint Subsidiaries," *Antitrust Law and Economics Review,* 1, 81-92.

Breiger, R. L., S.A. Boorman, and P. Arabie (1975), "An Algorithm for Clustering Relational Data, with Applications to Social Network Analysis and Comparison with Multidimensional Scaling." *Journal of Mathematical Psychology,* 326-383.

Burt, R. L. (1980), "Models of Network Structure," *Annual Review of Sociology,* 6, 79-141.

—— (1987), "Social Contagion and Innovation, Cohesion versus Structural Equivalence," *American Journal of Sociology,* 92, 1287-1335.

—— (1992), *Structural Holes,* Cambridge MA: Harvard University Press.

Calhoun, C. (1993), *Bourdieu: Critical Perspective,* C. Calhoun, E. Lipuma, and M. M. Postone (Eds.), Cambridge, UK: Polity.

Cameron, A. and P. Trivedi (1986), "Econometric Models Based on Count Data: Comparisons and Applications of Some Estimators." *Journal of Applied Econometrics,* 1.

Clark, K., W. B. Chew, and T. Fujimoto (1987), "Product Development in the World Auto Industry," *Brookings Papers on Economic Activity,* 3, 729-782.

Coleman, J. (1990a), "Social Capital in the Creation of Human Capital," *American Journal of Sociology,* 94, S95-S120.

—— (1990b), *Foundations of Social Theory,* Cambridge, MA: Harvard University Press

Delany, J. (1988), "Social Networks and Efficient Resource Allocation: Computer Models of Job Vacancy Allocation through Contacts," in B. Wellman and S. Berkowitz (Eds.), *Social Structure: A Network Approach,* Cambridge, UK: Cambridge University Press.

DiMaggio, P. and W. W. Powell (1983), "The Iron Cage Revisited: Institutional Isomorphism and Collective Rationality in Organization Fields," *American Sociological Review,* 43, 147-160.

DiMaggio, Paul (1986), "Structural Analysis of Organizational Fields: A Blockmodel Approach," *Research in Organizational Behavior,* 8, 335-370

Doz, Y. (1988), "Technology Partnerships Between Larger and Smaller Firms: Some Critical Issues," in F. Contractor and P. Lorange (Eds.), *Cooperative Strategies in International Business,* 317-338, Lexington, MA: Lexington Books.

Evan, W. M. (1972), "An Organization-set Model of Interorganizational Relations," in M. Tuite, R. Chisolm and M. Radnor (Eds.), *Interorganizational Decision-Making,* 181-200, Chicago, IL: Aldine.

Fruen, M. (1989), "Cooperative Structure and Competitive Strategies: The Japanese Enterprise System," Unpublished Manuscript, INSEAD.

Galaskiewicz, J. and S. Wasserman (1981), "A Dynamic Study of Change in a Regional Corporate Network," *American Sociological Review,* 46, 475-484.

Grabber, G. (1988), *De-Industrialisierung odor Neo-Industrialisierung?* Berlin, Germany: Wissenchaftszentrum Berlin fur Sozialforschung.

Granovetter, M. (1985), "Economic Action and Social Structure: The Problem of Embeddedness," *American Journal of Sociology,* 78, 1360-1380.

Hagedoorn, J. and J. Schakenraad (1992), "Leading Companies and Networks of Strategic Alliance in Information Technologies," *Research Policy,* 21, 163-190.

Herrigel, G. (1991), "Politics of Large Firm Relations with Industrial Districts: A Collision of Organizational Fields in Baden Wurtemberg," in *Country Competitiveness,* B. Kogut (Ed.). London, UK: Macmillan.

Hofstede, G., B. Neujien, D. Daval Ohayv, and G. Sanders (1990). "Measuring Organizational Culture: A Qualitative and Quantitative Study Across Twenty Cases," *Administrative Science Quarterly,* 3, 286-316.

Judge, G., W. E. Griffiths, R. C. Carter, H. Lutkepohl, and T.-C. Lee (1985), *The Theory and Practice of Econometrics,* New York: John Wiley.

Knoke, D. and D. L. Rogers (1978), "A Blockmodel Analysis of Interorganizational Networks," *Social Science Research,* 64, 28-52.

Kogut, B. (1991), "Joint Ventures and the Option to Expand and Acquire," *Management Science,* 37, 19-33.

———, W. Shan, and G. Walker (1994). "Knowledge in the Network and the Network as Knowledge," in G. Grabher (Ed). *The Embedded Firm,* London, UK: Routledge.

———, G. Walker and D.-J. Kim (1995), "Cooperation and Entry Induction as a Function of Technological Rivalry," *Research Policy.*

———, ———, W. Shan, and D.-J. Kim (1995), "Platform Technologies and National Industrial Networks," in J. Hagedoorn (Ed.), *The Internationalization of Corporate Technology Strategies.*

Lorrain, F. and H. C. White (1971), "Structural Equivalence of Individuals in Social Networks," *Journal of Mathematical Sociology,* 1, 49-80.

Loury, G. (1977), "A Dynamic Theory of Racial Income Differences," in P. A. Wallace and A. Le Mund (Eds.), *Women, Minorities, and Employment Discrimination,* Lexington, MA: Lexington Books.

Mansfield, E. (1988), "The Speed and Cost of Industrial Innovation in Japan and the U.S.: External vs. Internal Technology," *Management Science,* 34, 10, 1157-1168.

Marsden, P.V. (1983), "Restricted Access in Networks and Models of Power," *American Journal of Sociology,* 88, 4, 686-717.

Mayhew, B. H. and R. L. Levinger (1976), "Size and the Density of Interaction in Human Aggregates," *American Journal of Sociology,* 82, 86-110.

Meyer, J. W. and B. Rowan (1977), "Institutionalized Organizations: Formal Structure as Myth and Ceremony," *American Journal of Sociology,* 83, 340-363.

Nohria, N. and C. Garcia-Pont (1991), "Global Strategic Linkages and Industry Structure," *Strategic Management Journal,* 12, 105-124.

Noma, E. and D. R. Smith (1985), "Benchmarks for the Blocking of Sociometric Data," *Psychological Bulletin,* 97, 583-691.

Office of Technology Assessment (1984), *Commercial Biotechnology, An International Analysis,* U.S. Congress.

Oliver, C. (1988), "The Collective Strategy Framework: An Application to Competing Predictions of Isomorphism," *Administrative Science Quarterly,* 24, 405-424.

Pisano, G. (1990), "The R & D Boundaries of the Firm: An Empirical Analysis," *Administrative Science Quarterly,* 35, 153-176.

—— (1991), "The Governance of Innovation: Vertical Integration and Collaborative Arrangements in the Biotechnology Industry," *Research Policy,* 20, 237-250.

Powell, W. W. and P. Brantley (1992), "Competitive Cooperation in Biotechnology: Learning through Networks?," in N. Nohria and R. G. Eccles (Eds.), *Networks and Organization,* Cambridge, MA: Harvard Business School Press.

Raub, W. and J. Weesie (1990), "Reputation and Efficiency in Social Institutions: An Example of Network Effects," *American Journal of Sociology,* 96, 626-654.

Scherer, F. M. (1986), *Innovation and Growth: Schumpeterian Perspectives,* Cambridge: MIT Press.

Schrum, W. and R. Withnow (1988), "Reputational Status of Organizations in Technical Systems," *American Journal of Sociology,* 93, 882-912.

Schumpeter, J. A. (1934), *The Theory of Economic Development,* Cambridge: MA: Harvard University Press.

Shan, W. (1987), "Technological Change and Strategic Cooperation: Evidence from Commercialization of Biotechnology," Ph.D. Dissertation, University of California, Berkeley.

—— (1990), "An Empirical Analysis of Organizational Strategies by Entrepreneurial High-Technology Firms," *Strategic Management Journal,* 11, 129-139.

——, G. Walker, and B. Kogut (1994), "Interfirm Cooperation and Startup Innovation in the Biotechnology Industry," *Strategic Management Journal,* 15, 5, 387-394.

Stinchcombe, A. L. (1965), "Social Structure and Organizations," in J. G. March (Ed.), *Handbook of Organizations,* 142-193, Chicago, IL: Rand McNally.

Teece, D. (1988), "Capturing Value from Technological Innovation: Integration, Strategic Partnering and Licensing Decisions," *Interfaces,* 18, 46-61.

Van de Ven, A., G. Walker, and J. Liston (1979), "Coordination Patterns within an Interorganizational Network," *Human Relations,* 32, 19-36.

Walker, G. (1985), "Network Position and Cognition in a Computer Software Firm," *Administrative Science Quarterly,* 30, 103-130.

—— (1988), "Network Analysis for Interorganizational Cooperative Relationships," in F. Contractor and P. Lorange (Eds.), *Cooperative Strategies in International Business,* Lexington, MA: Lexington Books.

White, H., S. A. Boorman, and R. Breiger (1976), "Social Structure from Multiple Networks, I, Blockmodels of Roles and Positions," *American Journal of Sociology,* 81, 730-780.

Wickens, T. D. (1989), *Multiway Contingency Tables Analysis for the Social Sciences,* Hillsdale, NJ: Lawrence Erlbaum.

14

Responding to Hypercompetition

The Structure and Processes of a
Regional Learning Network Organization

JON HANSSEN-BAUER
CHARLES C. SNOW

The authors present a model of the learning process in a regional network organization. The model is based on a six-year study of Nordvest Forum, perhaps the only multifirm network in the world to have been purposefully formed to help its member companies learn how to develop and apply knowledge about management and organizational change. The network, composed of 46 companies located in and around Ålesund, Norway, has been an effective mechanism for helping many of the region's firms respond to today's hypercompetitive global marketplace. Implications for research on hypercompetition, learning networks, and regional development policy are discussed.

(HYPERCOMPETITION;
NETWORK ORGANIZATIONS;
ORGANIZATIONAL LEARNING PROCESS)

Increasingly, firms are facing environments that are hypercompetitive (D'Aveni 1994). Such environments are highly changeable and even discontinuous, requiring organizations to respond flexibly and rapidly. In the most hypercompetitive industries, competitors act boldly and aggressively to disrupt the status quo, forcing countermoves that are equally powerful.

Perhaps most troublesome for many firms is the fact that hypercompetitive environments are unforgiving. Firms whose responses are inappropriate, incomplete, or too slow are severely penalized, and their ability to experiment, learn, and adapt is reduced.

Today hypercompetition is a reality throughout most of the industrialized world. The declining cost of technology and the ability to transfer it quickly from one industry and country to another have intensified competition in many businesses. Moreover, many competitors have achieved world-class status by adopting continuous improvement, benchmarking, and other modern management practices.

Global hypercompetition's demands for simultaneous efficiency, responsiveness, and speed mean, quite simply, that firms must become better learners. Now competitive fitness is measured by a firm's ability to develop and apply knowledge, often in collaboration with other firms (Alter and Hage 1993; Hamel, Doz, and Prahalad 1988). In addition, firms need to learn how to influence their environments—to help shape in a proactive way an infrastructure that will support their efforts to become more competitive. Without the ability to learn and to restructure internal and external relationships, companies in hypercompetitive environments inevitably will lose the ability to compete successfully.

We describe the structure, processes, and outputs of a regional learning network organization. Our report is based on an in-depth study of Nordvest Forum (Northwest Forum), a group of 46 small- and medium-size firms in and around the city of Ålesund on the northwestern coast of Norway. Nordvest Forum was created specifically to help its member firms upgrade their management and adaptive capacity so that they could compete more effectively in both the national and international marketplaces. Hence, lessons learned from the Nordvest Forum experience should be helpful to other organizations that are trying to respond successfully to hypercompetitive environments.

We begin by discussing the basic elements of hypercompetition as well as the role of organizational learning in companies' responses to it. Next, we identify four distinct types of competitors found in the Ålesund region, describing how they are differentially affected by hypercompetitive forces and therefore face different learning challenges. We then describe Nordvest Forum, a regional learning network organization, emphasizing its structure, major activities, and objectives. We identify the key features of Nordvest Forum's learning process and present a model of how they interact. Finally, we offer several recommendations for future research on hypercompetition, learning networks, and regional development policy.

HYPERCOMPETITION AND
ORGANIZATIONAL LEARNING

As described by D'Aveni (1994, Chapter 6), hypercompetition has affected virtually every industry, from financial services and telecommunications to cat foods and children's toys. Moreover, hypercompetition is not restricted to the industrialized world; it has also appeared, or is expected soon, in Third World countries. Most assuredly, hypercompetition is here to stay and companies must learn to live with it.

A New Construct. Hypercompetition is both a new competitive reality and a new theoretical construct. It is not merely a speeded-up version of traditional competition. For example, perfect competition and hypercompetition each can be characterized by such factors as erodable entry barriers, low prices, and limited profitability, but hypercompetition differs from perfect competition primarily in the fact that a hypercompetitive industry does not have an equilibrium state in which competitors have no advantage over each other. Instead, "hypercompetitive behavior is the process of continuously generating new competitive advantages and destroying, obsoleting, or neutralizing the opponent's competitive advantage, thereby creating disequilibrium, destroying perfect competition, and disrupting the status quo of the marketplace" (D'Aveni 1994, p. 218). Hence, a perfectly competitive environment is not an endpoint but a transitional stage between periods of disruption.

Hypercompetition is also a theoretical concept of firms' competitive behavior. In contrast to the traditional view of firms as vying against each other in the marketplace by developing profitable and sustainable advantages over the long run, hypercompetition reflects a Schumpeterian view of firms as continuously disruptive—escalating or restarting competition in a particular arena or switching the locus of competition to a new, previously dormant arena.

In a hypercompetitive environment, the only enduring competitive advantage is the ability to generate new advantages (D'Aveni 1994). Having the lowest cost, the highest quality, the most know-how, or the deepest pockets is not enough—a firm's skill in generating such advantages must be sustainable. Such skill comes from the ability to envision the next series of disruptions in the market, some general capabilities needed to cause disruption, and the ability to use specific tactics that create disruptions with great effectiveness. In other words, companies that want to be successful in hypercompetitive businesses must be able to learn continuously and to apply their knowledge rapidly to the ever-changing marketplace.

The Learning Organization

Developing the ability to learn continuously is enormously difficult for the typical organization. Practical learning approaches, such as that of Senge (1990, 1994), appear to be founded on the following logic.

1. The ability to create and apply knowledge can be a competitive advantage. Knowledge is potentially the most productive resource of a company and can be a key source of competitive advantage (Barney 1991, Grant 1991, Quinn 1992). Knowledge is both tacit and explicit (Nonaka 1991), and it consists of individual know-how, skills, and beliefs that enable organization members to make distinctions and ascribe meaning to observations (von Krogh, Roos, and Slocum 1994). For individually held knowledge to be useful in a competitive situation, it must be mobilized into focused collective action (Kim 1993, Grant 1996). Such focusing is especially challenging in hypercompetitive environments that regularly require the creation and application of new knowledge. Moreover, in such environments the conversion of knowledge into improved organizational practice must be quick and achieved at minimal psychological and economic cost. Therefore, firms that have the ability to institutionalize various types of specialized new knowledge quickly and effectively into their operational routines may achieve superior returns.

2. Knowledge is created by learning to act. A company's stock of knowledge is created and expanded through a learning process (Daft and Huber 1987, Daft and Weick 1984, Huber 1991). According to the information-processing view, learning occurs when information is obtained, processed, and stored for future use. However, that essentially passive view of the learning process has limited value in describing how knowledge is created in an organization, particularly one in a hypercompetitive environment. "Information processing is viewed as a problem-solving activity which centers on what is given to the organization—without due consideration of what is created by it" (Nonaka 1994). In contrast, a proactive view of knowledge creation characterizes learning as an innovative process in which the organization creates and defines problems and then actively develops new knowledge to solve them (Nonaka 1994). Thus, learning occurs in stages within a context of purposeful interaction by individuals seeking to understand, and trying to adjust to, fluctuations in their environment, or attempting to recover from misguided previous perceptions. Individual knowledge is enlarged and shared among members of the organization in order to be justified and internalized into new norms and behavior. Learning breakdowns can occur if the various process elements are poorly designed or if the mechanisms linking them are not functioning properly.

3. Organizational learning is enhanced by commonality and diversity. Paradoxically, organizational learning must build on commonality and be nurtured by diversity, and it requires an environment that is conducive to interaction. To learn, individuals must explore and share their tacit knowledge with each other, as well as combine their explicit knowledge into new conceptualizations (Nonaka 1994). The essential characteristics of a favorable learning environment include committed interest, trust, and shared language and cognitive maps for interpreting information (Stata 1989). Organizational learning also is facilitated if knowledge that is taken for granted is challenged by diverse and novel information in an open dialogue linked to practice. Learning occurs, for example, when organization members reach agreement on the framing of issues while they debate their content (Fiol 1994). Company knowledge structures evolve as organization members adjust their diverse views and reach consensus on the value and legitimacy of new meanings and approaches through debate. The process of constructing collective meaning is enhanced when organization members have the opportunity to engage in self-managed problem solving with adequate access to others' experiences and backgrounds. Often, learning requires the establishment of flexible organization structures that enable members to cut across previous communications channels and the implementation of nurturing managerial styles (Nonaka 1994). Last, the firm needs efficient ways of diffusing and routinizing new knowledge throughout the organization.

4. Key outcomes of learning and knowledge creation are flexibility and adaptability. As industrial environments become too unstable or complex to comprehend and too imposing to defy, firms must become flexible enough to adapt (Volberda 1996). Operationally, increased flexibility means being able to anticipate changes in the environment, becoming more proficient at learning from competitors and collaborators, integrating knowledge within and across organizations more efficiently, making greater use of the ideas of all managers and employees, and so on (Marquardt and Reynolds 1994). Searching for an optimal fit with environmental characteristics, firms adjust their organizations to include a particular flexibility mix (Volberda 1996). Increased levels and types of flexibility lead to greater adaptability, enabling organizations to both reshape and adapt to their environments.

DYNAMICS OF HYPERCOMPETITION
IN A GEOGRAPHIC REGION

A successful response to hypercompetition requires great organizational flexibility and adaptability, which are generated by the ability to develop and apply new knowledge quickly and consistently. However, beyond those general relationships, the dynamics of hypercompetition are not well understood. For example, D'Aveni (1994) argues that hypercompetition in a particular industry is manifested in four areas: cost and quality, timing and know-how, strongholds, and deep pockets. Therefore, one might trace the impact of hypercompetition among firms in an industry by analyzing it along the value chain and in each of the four areas. Such an analysis, however, may not uncover hypercompetition's impact on the various firms in a particular geographic region where numerous industries are represented and where most of the firms do not compete against each other.

The region in which our study was conducted is centered around the city of Ålesund on the northwestern coast of Norway. Protected by deep fjords but facing the North Sea and the Atlantic Ocean, the region has for centuries been an externally oriented part of Norway. The area's links to the sea have made access to international markets traditionally easy, and long ago the region became a major fish-processing center. A marine equipment industry developed to serve the fishing fleet and began to flourish when the change from sails to diesel engines made long-distance ocean fishing possible. Today, the fish processors, ship builders, and furniture manufacturers in the region are highly export oriented and compete successfully in the global marketplace. The region is recognized throughout Norway for its industrious, entrepreneurial, business-minded people. Companies are typically small by international standards, even when they are part of large Norwegian corporations, and the family-owned firm is a prominent feature of the Ålesund region.

Our study uncovered four distinct types of firms in the region, all of which experienced hypercompetition in different ways and therefore faced different challenges in how to respond. One type of firm is the preferred supplier, which manufactures products or components for large international companies. It experiences the demands of global hypercompetition through its large customer(s), including the requirement to keep pace with technological developments, quality improvements, and other market needs. The preferred supplier's primary stronghold is its relationships with its large customers. To protect its position as a preferred vendor, the supplier may have to not only meet its major customers' specifications, but also anticipate and even exceed them faster than its competitors. Thus, the key suppliers of large international companies often are pressured to become active learners in areas such as technology development, total quality management, and fast cycle times.

Preferred-supplier firms face a dilemma in deciding whether to join a learning network. They may be better off acting alone, focusing only on learning that improves relationships with their major customers. Alternatively, to avoid becoming too dependent on their major customers, preferred suppliers may choose to develop strategic flexibility by cooperating with other firms to learn more about what these firms are thinking and doing.

A second type of firm is the large company that has been competing for a long time in an international business. It experiences global hypercompetitive forces directly. In Norway, this type includes companies in industries such as fishing, furniture, shipbuilding, and marine equipment. The largest firms in those industries have a lengthy history of international competition, and they fully realize that to be successful they must keep abreast of technological and market developments in their respective business. In shipbuilding, and increasingly in furniture production, being second best may not be good enough. Companies in those businesses must win contracts, and doing so requires a record of demonstrated ability to produce and deliver high-quality products on schedule. Also, because of their size and leading positions, such firms typically perform their own scanning of the competitive landscape, so they know first-hand what it takes to be successful in their respective industries.

In the international companies, learning tends to focus internally on the management of change and the ability to do things quickly and efficiently. Such response mechanisms have been called structural and operational flexibility (Volberda 1996). The firms may become leading participants in regional learning networks. Banding together to learn has the potential to reduce their individual learning costs and to increase the supply of available information and experience. As long as the exposure to mutual competition is not too high, cooperation does not entail major risks.

A third type of firm in the Ålesund region is the secondary supplier to the international market. It is partially buffered from the effects of hypercompetition. Most of its business is within the region, and it may have only limited relationships with firms that compete internationally. Such a firm may supply parts and components to other companies in the area, or it may provide a service to the region (e.g., electricity). The secondary supplier clearly faces a dilemma as it seeks to respond to hypercompetition. It can choose, for example, to capitalize on its relationships with its most demanding, internationally oriented customers and learn how to compete aggressively in a hypercompetitive environment. That is what one of the municipal electricity agencies did, as it sought to become more market-driven and to restructure its production and selling operations along private-sector lines.

A firm choosing that competitive approach is interested in cooperating with other firms whose first-hand experience with global competition can aid its efforts to increase strategic flexibility. Further, it is likely to review its management capability and its basic operating practices, thus possibly achieving increased operational flexibility. Alternatively, the secondary supplier may decide to continue to compete only on a regional basis. A firm choosing that approach is unlikely to be selected as a preferred supplier by large international companies, and its growth potential may diminish.

A fourth type of regional firm simply does not know how it is being affected by global hypercompetition. Such an organization might be a local retailer, a transportation company, a hotel chain, or other business. It does not compete in the international market, either directly or indirectly, and therefore experiences little or no external pressure to learn new approaches. In a few cases, however, managers sense that the organization may have to compete differently in the future. For example, a bus company in the region anticipated deregulation of the transportation market. It wanted to differentiate itself from its future competitors early. Instead of fighting deregulation, it chose to develop strategic flexibility and managerial competence in competing head-to-head with major firms with which it previously had collaborated, such as the Norwegian Railroad and national and international bus companies. However, this type of organization does not know how to learn on its own, nor can it afford the cost of learning how to become a strong competitor. Its only recourse is to join the ranks of firms already engaged in the learning process. One such regional learning network, Nordvest Forum, is described in the next section.

NORDVEST FORUM

Nordvest Forum (NVF), a multifirm regional network, was founded in 1989. At the same time, Nordvest Forum Inc. (NVF Inc.) was established as a service company to manage the network's activities. The owners of NVF Inc. are 46 shareholding companies located in and around Ålesund. Nordvest Forum is a network not a cooperative, and companies may join or leave the network as they choose. Nordvest Forum's stated purpose is to improve regional competitiveness by upgrading the management capacity of the shareholding companies and other firms in the region (see Figure 14.1).

Our description of Nordvest Forum is based on a variety of data sources. For example, the first author has followed the development of NVF through participant observation since its inception. He has participated as a consultant to the leaders of the network and has helped to obtain funding for the network from various sources. He also participated in most of NVF's initial decision-making meetings and has met in some capacity with most of the network's key members. He is currently acting as the co-supervisor of two doctoral students who are working in NVF companies.

Another major data source is an evaluation of NVF's effectiveness performed by both authors in the latter half of 1992. The evaluation study was funded by the Norwegian Research Foundation and the Norwegian Work Life

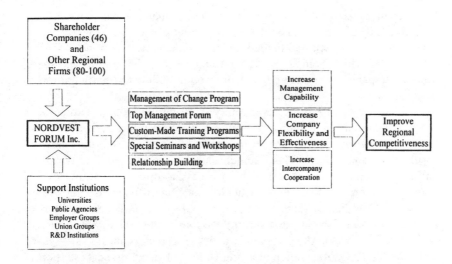

Figure 14.1. Nordvest Forum: Components, Activities, Objectives, and Purpose

Center. Two main research methods were used. First, interviews were conducted with key stakeholders such as the founders of the network, members of NVF Inc.'s board of directors, and other appropriate executives. The interviews afforded substantial insights about the goals and activities of the network as perceived by its core members, as well as an overall evaluation of the network's perceived achievements. Second, a survey based on a specific evaluation model was conducted by means of questionnaires distributed to all past participants in an NVF management development program and to the mentors of those participants. At the time, the management development program was one of NVF's main activities. The survey results were presented to the board of directors as well as to several groups of participants for validation and interpretation before publication of the final report.

Brief History

Many of the region's most influential companies are members of Nordvest Forum. They recognized the need to cooperate and improve if they were to be successful in attracting managerial talent to the area and in competing in the increasingly hypercompetitive international marketplace. In addition, the Ålesund region has many small, entrepreneurial enterprises that could not afford to undertake significant developmental efforts on their own. In 1989, several leading executives met in a conference to discuss their firms' common needs and to identify the areas in which their companies could cooperate.

The group agreed on two initial activities: a management development program (subsequently named the Management of Change Program) and a forum for senior executives (called the Top Management Forum). NVF Inc. was charged with organizing and managing those activities, and the share-holder companies were ensured control through their active participation on NVF Inc.'s board of directors.

NVF Inc. recognized that its primary contribution would be to act as a facilitator of learning and change within the member companies. Also, the owners decided at the outset that every aspect of the Nordvest Forum network would be based on "world-class" standards. NVF Inc. was to be self-financed and self-sustaining, and it was to gain access to up-to-date knowledge of management practices and develop mechanisms for diffusing that knowledge among the member companies. The regional representative of the Confed-eration of Norwegian Business and Industry supported the establishment of NVF Inc., serving on the company's board of directors in the early years. The Norwegian Confederation of Trade Unions also expressed its support of Nordvest Forum's basic network concept and activities.

The formation of the network moved ahead steadily, and the establishment of NVF Inc. as its management company went smoothly. Nevertheless, certain tensions and conflicts arose. For example, recruiting companies to NVF's programs was difficult in the beginning. Some companies were reluctant to take part until NVF had proven its ability to deliver practical information on global management practices. Further, the managers who actually launched the network also participated in the first class of the Management of Change Program. Although they were highly supportive of the concept of Nordvest Forum as a learning network, they were rather impatient and critical of the management development program and demanded that all sessions be made directly relevant to their own work situations. Several instructors were criticized for being too theoretical, and the designers of the program were asked to find other speakers on certain topics.

Because the network concept was new and unproven, obtaining outside financial support was initially difficult. In each of its first four years, NVF Inc. overspent its operating budget and the shareholding companies had to provide additional funds beyond those budgeted. Also, tensions developed between the internationally oriented companies and the regionally oriented firms over NVF's emphasis on management knowledge and practice. Some of the smaller, regionally oriented firms thought NVF Inc. put too much emphasis on "world-class" standards and the "best practices" of large inter-national corporations. They wanted programs geared more to their needs. The larger internationally oriented firms complained that the regional companies were too slow to learn and not active enough in supporting the network.

Today, even though Nordvest Forum is well established and very successful, some tension persists among the network's member firms. As NVF's visibility and achievements have grown, companies outside the Ålesund region have asked to join the network. Their requests have created an ongoing discussion about how large Nordvest Forum can become and how diverse its membership should be.

Initial Structure and Activities

Nordvest Forum's main activities were established in the fall of 1989 and throughout 1990. Two senior professionals in the field of management training and development were invited by NVF Inc. to help design and launch the first learning vehicles, the Management of Change Program and the Top Management Forum. The first class of the Management of Change Program was held in 1990-1991, and approximately 200 managers from nearly 100 companies have participated in the program to date. A key part of the program is a management development project that is required of every participant. The best projects are ones that involve interdepartmental change in the participant's company and contribute to the company's ability to compete internationally. Each project has a mentor, an experienced manager from the same company or another company in the region. Several of the management development projects have resulted in successful major organizational changes. The methods and results of the change projects have been communicated to the other NVF companies in various ways, particularly in subsequent sessions of the Management of Change Program. That approach has helped to build a stock of knowledge and experience that is widely shared by firms in the region.

The Top Management Forum was developed at the same time as the Management of Change Program. The Forum is a periodic two-day gathering for senior executives in the region. Fifteen Forum meetings have been held. The primary objective of the Forum is to provide a meeting place where executives can hear presentations on international management subjects and discuss issues of importance to companies in the region. The meetings also provide a convenient setting for personal and professional networking.

The corporate owners of NVF Inc. decided in the beginning that the service company should remain small. They wanted it to draw on resources from all appropriate institutions, and they wanted it to be a model of a network approach that companies in the region could use to locate needed resources rapidly. During the early years, most of NVF Inc.'s work was performed by its managing director on a full-time basis and the two senior professionals on a part-time basis. In addition to those three individuals, a substantially larger set of professional and institutional resources was called upon at times to provide needed inputs.

Linking with Resource Institutions

NVF Inc. worked aggressively to find individuals and institutions to serve as resources in developing the management capacity of the region's companies. As a result, influential people from Norway and other European countries have visited the region and have made presentations in either the Management of Change Program or the Top Management Forum. Today, Nordvest Forum is widely acknowledged as having developed one of the best networks in the country for quickly accessing management-oriented professionals and institutions in Norway, Europe, and the United States.

Throughout the six-year history of NVF Inc., its stakeholders have insisted that the company establish links to various "research and development" institutions in Norway and abroad. For example, one important linkage is with the highly regarded Institute for Management Development (IMD) in Switzerland, where NVF Inc. is a Business Associate. That relationship gives Nordvest Forum companies access to the "best practices" of notable global corporations. In addition, NVF Inc., in collaboration with key Norwegian research, employer, and union organizations, decided in 1992 to employ two University of Trondheim doctoral students in business administration. Several of NVF's member companies use the doctoral students to help them understand new management approaches and to implement business development projects.

Network Effectiveness

According to several indicators, Nordvest Forum has been an effective network organization. When in 1992 NVF's board of directors commissioned the authors to conduct an evaluation of the network's effectiveness, both perceptual and unobtrusive measures indicated that NVF had made substantial progress in achieving its overall objective of increasing regional competitiveness. For example, managers in NVF's member companies reported in a questionnaire survey that Nordvest Forum's activities had affected them positively as individual managers (e.g., by helping them form professional networks). They also reported that NVF had helped to improve their companies (e.g., through organizational change projects) and the region in general (e.g., by upgrading its image in the business press). Those generally positive perceptions were confirmed by the managers' mentors in a separate questionnaire.

Several unobtrusive measures supported the finding of overall network effectiveness, particularly with respect to company outcomes. For example, prior to NVF's founding (1989), none of the firms in the region had applied for financial resources allocated by the central employer federations or the national government for business development projects. In 1994, central institutions cited four projects in the Ålesund region, all conducted within NVF's learning framework, as showcase examples of successful business development. Further, at least a dozen NVF companies have engaged in major strategic change programs using the network for guidance and support. Subclusters among the more active companies now meet regularly with each other to share experiences and develop solutions to common problems. Five companies are currently engaged with NVF Inc. to use the two doctoral students to help them with organizational change projects. The Norwegian Research Foundation has decided to support an extension of that successful way of combining business development with academic training and research, and it has funded three more doctoral students to be employed by NVF Inc. The Foundation has also funded research to guide and document the further development of the regional learning network model. A national commission studying how public support can best be invested to increase the competitiveness of Norwegian business, headed by the office of the Norwegian Prime Minister, has invited NVF Inc. to participate in the study to provide its experience with the learning-network approach.

Although NVF's effectiveness can be demonstrated, the efficiency of the network is much less clear. That is, the learning process clearly works, but whether successful knowledge creation and organizational change could have occurred more quickly or with fewer resources is not known.

A MODEL OF REGIONAL
LEARNING NETWORK STRUCTURE,
PROCESSES, AND EFFECTIVENESS

Nordvest Forum was designed according to an explicit learning philosophy linking theory and practice. The architects of NVF believed that theoretical ideas and information should be converted into understanding and skills within a trust-inducing environment and through the implementation of organizational development projects under sound mentorship. In addition, the learning environment should encourage the building of personal and professional networks among managers.

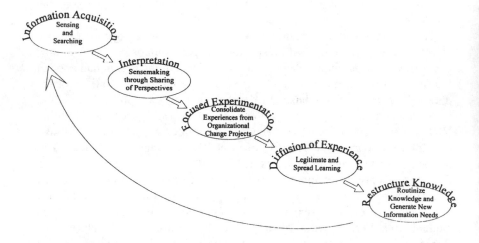

Figure 14.2. Nordvest Forum's Learning Cycle

Figure 14.2 is our representation of Nordvest Forum's "learning cycle." Effective learning occurs within and across the network's member firms because NVF Inc. has worked hard to improve each stage of the learning cycle. Over the network's six-year history, several factors have emerged that we believe are important facilitators of the organizational learning process. Specifically, two main categories of variables must be taken into account in designing the structure and processes of a multifirm learning network: (1) the stage of development of the region's companies and infrastructure and (2) the various levels at which learning can and should take place.

Launch Stage

The design of a multifirm learning network must fit the regional environment from which the network draws its members and in which it seeks to exert influence. The Ålesund region contains a mix of small and medium-size companies in various stages of internationalization. Therefore, Nordvest Forum believed that eventually it had to reflect that diversity in its operations. Four factors (or variables in the model) were particularly important to NVF's effectiveness during the launch stage: (1) individual and company leadership, (2) network ownership and structure, (3) broker behavior, and (4) shared vision and focus (see Table 14.1).

TABLE 14.1 Design Characteristics of a Regional Learning Network Organization, by Stage of Development

Launch Stage	Development Stage	Maturity Stage
Individual and company leadership	Structural stability	Thematic renewal
Network ownership	Membership variety	Professional input support and structure
Broker behavior	Modern management paradigm	Flexible subnetwork building
Shared vision and focus	Professional network development	Core and peripheral membership
	R & D institutional links	Environmental impact
	Local demonstration projects	
	External financial support for network development	

The concept of Nordvest Forum was hatched by a small group of business leaders in the region. The group had a strong desire to improve the competitiveness of the entire region as well as that of their own companies. Their notion of a regional learning process was articulated by working with a wider group of well-known and respected senior managers in the area. Together, all of those leaders called on other companies in the region to cooperate to meet their common management and international business challenges. For the most part, the core leaders came from the larger firms already facing international hypercompetition and from the preferred-supplier companies that were vendors to global competitors. Both types of companies serve as a channel to hypercompetitive markets and environments. By focusing on those companies' problems, NVF Inc. was able to demonstrate to the less internationally oriented firms the kinds of problems they would have to solve to become strong competitors in the future. As a result, many smaller firms chose to participate in NVF programs.

The leaders believed that Nordvest Forum should be widely owned by its members. Economic ownership came from a one-time membership fee that entitled each firm to a single share in NVF Inc. Limiting shareholding companies to a single share ensured that no firm could dominate NVF Inc. However, psychological ownership was also considered important, and NVF's leaders were sensitive to the need for NVF to be perceived as belonging to all companies in the region regardless of whether they were shareholders.

The managing director of NVF Inc. and the two senior professionals in organizational development played the role of network broker. All three individuals knew the region's business life very well, and all had a good grasp of the international business situation. Together they provided the member companies with the expertise required to launch the network.

Nordvest Forum was formally launched through a "search conference" (Emery and Emery 1978) that provided an initial vision and a focused set of activities. The network's purpose and objectives were accepted by the shareholding companies, its proposed learning approach was thoroughly discussed, and its ambitions were set so that shareholder members felt the organization could meet their expectations.

Development Stage

In the three-year developmental period that followed NVF Inc.'s formation, various activities were begun and refined while others were considered and discarded. From a learning perspective, seven specific factors were crucial to NVF Inc.'s success in progressing through the development stage: (1) program stability, (2) membership variety, (3) modern management paradigm, (4) professional network development, (5) R & D institutional linkages, (6) local demonstration projects, and (7) external financial support (see Table 14.1).

It was important during the development stage for NVF Inc. to stabilize its two main service offerings, the Management of Change Program and the Top Management Forum. Program stability enabled companies in the region to participate in the activities according to their own needs and timing. Nordvest Forum became a visible and open arena for participation and learning. Over time, many companies increased their involvement and eventually became NVF Inc. shareholders.

The brokers attempted to have a mix of companies in the network that mirrored the region's business community and included all of the main industries. They also urged the companies to send multiple managers to participate in NVF programs. Company diversity would substantially increase the number of learning locations and experiences. Having multiple participants would make learning in each company more comprehensive and more easily diffused. Both factors would foster the creation of intercompany relationships. Ultimately, Nordvest Forum grew to have a rich mix of company sizes and businesses.

Learning was facilitated across the different types of member companies by use of the common management terminology and communication approaches taught in the Management of Change Program. Participants in the program were offered a modern management paradigm that included the globalization process, strategic thinking, total quality management, participation and collaboration, interpersonal skills, and other key concepts needed to understand how companies transform themselves to compete in the international marketplace.

Program participants were further urged to develop their own professional networks and to initiate intercompany contacts as appropriate. NVF Inc. was especially adept at matching younger managers with more experienced individuals who served as mentors, thus transferring managerial know-how across both generations and companies. Many mentors, in turn, increased their own knowledge of the latest global management concepts and practices.

Throughout the development stage, NVF Inc. increased its linkages to R & D institutions and professionals. Those individuals and institutions were the main information providers to the network's member companies. As new ideas and approaches were imported into the network, they were turned into practical demonstration projects within interested member companies. Successful projects were then described and analyzed in subsequent sessions of the Management of Change Program or in separate project workshops. That follow-through provided both a means of diffusing learning and a form of organizational memory (Walsh and Ungson 1991).

Finally, NVF Inc. had sufficient financial backing to sustain it through the development stage. The original funding came from the member companies. Later, funds were obtained from other sources such as participation fees from NVF Inc.'s own operations and grants obtained from national development programs and research foundations.

Maturity Stage

After six years of operation, Nordvest Forum arguably is a mature network organization. Many firms in the region regard themselves as active members of the network, recognize their interdependence with other companies, and value the benefits obtained from cooperating on learning issues. Further, NVF Inc. now has a stable set of activities and an appropriate funding base. Five final factors help to explain NVF's effectiveness as it continues to pursue its mission as a learning organization: (1) thematic renewal, (2) professional input support, (3) flexible subnetwork building, (4) expansion of core and peripheral members, and (5) environmental impact (see Table 14.1).

As hypercompetition in international markets changes the parameters for doing business, and as knowledge deepens and spreads within NVF companies, the needs for information and knowledge change. In some areas companies need more advanced information, whereas in others they need to explore entirely new learning themes. Changing needs created pressure for renewal on NVF Inc. The network brokers responded in three main ways. One was to create new services for network members. Another was to enlarge

TABLE 14.2 Learning Features of a Regional Learning Network Organization, by
Level

Individual	Company	Regional and National
Combination of theoretical and practical knowledge	Multiple company participants in network	Use of communications media (TV, newspapers, etc.)
Learning through experience	Professional networking by top managers	Center of discussion and debate
Effective learning environment	Awareness of potential company partners	Influencing regional and national institutions
Top management support	Critiques of and advice on change projects	
Excellent teaching and mentoring	External financial support for company change projects	

the set of professionals and institutions from which the network members
could draw resources. A third response was to facilitate the creation and
administration of subnetworks of companies wanting to explore their common management challenges together.

As Nordvest Forum matured as a network, its shareholding companies
began to measure its effectiveness according to how quickly and profession-
ally NVF Inc. met their renewal needs. They also measured effectiveness by
NVF Inc.'s ability to attract additional companies into the network. In six
years, NVF's core members doubled in number, and its peripheral members
tripled. Finally, the core members increasingly have expected NVF Inc. to
influence regional and national policy organizations.

Levels of Learning

The intent of Nordvest Forum was to have an impact at three distinct
levels: individual, company, and regional/national. The main learning factors
associated with each level are listed in Table 14.2. Learning at the individual
and company levels has resulted in substantial improvement in the region's
management capacity. The region now has a critical mass of managers who
share a common management paradigm, as well as a comprehensive stock of
knowledge and experience based on the change projects conducted in the
companies over the past six years.

Some limited but important changes have occurred at the regional and
national levels because of NVF's efforts, and most observers believe the
region's overall competitiveness has improved. First, Nordvest Forum has

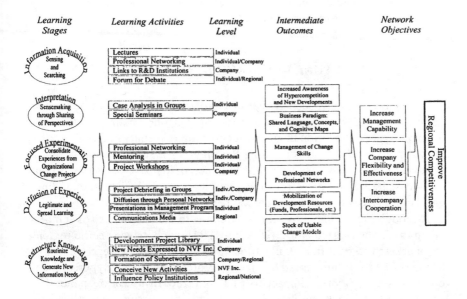

Figure 14.3. A Model of Regional Learning Network Effectiveness

had a high profile in the communications media. Information about its activities has raised regional awareness of the importance of responding effectively to hypercompetitive forces. Second, NVF increasingly has served as a center for discussion and debate of international business issues and challenges. Third, NVF Inc. has implicitly challenged regional institutions to improve themselves by taking the position that only the best is good enough for its member companies. The result has been increased cooperation from the region's R & D institutions, public agencies, and other stakeholders. Fourth, NVF Inc. has been able to influence national policy institutions to give funds to some of the network's member companies for specific development projects.

By combining the learning factors listed in Tables 14.1 and 14.2 with Nordvest Forum's learning cycle illustrated in Figure 14.2, a comprehensive model of regional learning network effectiveness can be specified. As shown in Figure 14.3, each stage of the learning cycle (column 1) has been implemented by developing a particular set of learning activities listed in column 2. Each activity targets a specific learning level(s) as noted in column 3. The six intermediate outcomes listed in column 4 are, in our judgment, the main features of the regional learning process that have helped Nordvest Forum pursue its objectives (columns 5 and 6).

FUTURE RESEARCH DIRECTIONS

A single case study, such as that of Nordvest Forum, cannot be used to test hypotheses about hypercompetition. It can only help to refine and improve hypercompetition theory by identifying relevant variables, describing their interaction, and suggesting the range of their applicability. Also, Nordvest Forum arose as a response to hypercompetitive pressures, so our study essentially addressed organizational learning and adaptation and not the driving forces behind the hypercompetition process.

Although hypercompetitive forces continue to raise the stakes of competing in the industrialized world (D'Aveni 1994), we believe specific regions and markets will be differentially affected by those forces. Therefore, it will be important for future research to try to predict areas where hypercompetition will strike, what its impact will be, and how firms can respond. The various experiences of Nordvest Forum's member firms suggest that successful organizational responses to hypercompetition in many industrial regions will require the collective efforts of companies to learn new approaches, as well as the support of regional and national institutions. That is particularly true when the companies are too small to foster the diversity needed to enhance internal learning processes or too lean in professional staff to form effective links with traditional sources of knowledge such as courses, consultants, or research institutions. Hence, we believe three specific topics warrant further theorizing and empirical research: (1) the concept and dynamics of hypercompetition, (2) the evaluation of network learning processes, and (3) the shaping of competitive business environments.

Hypercompetition: Impact and Response

Hypercompetition is a corollary of the globalization process. That is, the factors associated with globalization—increasing ease of technology transfer, faster communications, homogenization of consumer tastes, internationalization of factor markets, and so on—are spurring hypercompetition in many industries and regions. As globalization proceeds, so too will hypercompetition. Further, a significant contribution of the hypercompetition concept, both theoretically and practically, is the reorientation toward the view of competition as continuously disruptive. If equilibrium disappears as a feature of competitive arenas, strategic theory and practice will require substantial rethinking.

A necessary first step in the reorientation process is to predict where hypercompetition will appear and what its impact will be. For example, hypercompetition certainly has surfaced in the Ålesund region of Norway, but its impact has been considerably less pronounced there than that in, say, Silicon Valley, California, where hypercompetitive pressures on companies to be responsive and act fast are intense (Saxenian 1990, 1994). Research on hypercompetition would be well served by the development of a comprehensive typology of industrial regions so that areas in Norway, California, and elsewhere can be examined according to theoretically important similarities and differences. A valid typology would reflect the key drivers of hypercompetition, which appear to include the area's stage of economic development, the ease of technology transfer in the region, and the quality of the area's support infrastructure.

Moreover, within the Ålesund region, the impact of hypercompetition has varied among firms. For example, the large international companies in shipbuilding and furniture were the first in the region to feel the effects of hypercompetitive forces, followed by the preferred suppliers to large global corporations. Hypercompetition may be manifested even at the level of a specific business function such as marketing or manufacturing. One recent study of the globalization process in a single international company suggests that globalization affects a firm at the functional rather than the enterprise level (Malnight 1995). Hence, hypercompetition seems likely to vary in its impact across the functional, firm, industry, and regional levels.

Future research also should address patterns of response to hypercompetition. The position of the firm on the industry value chain appears to be an important factor. For example, direct competitors in a given industry, especially large integrated companies, appear to respond to hypercompetition by climbing one or more of the key "escalation ladders" such as cost, quality, or deep pockets (D'Aveni 1994). Other firms may respond by forming network organizations in which each firm performs only a few functions along the value chain and then outsources remaining functions to specialist partners (Miles and Snow 1986, 1994; Thorelli 1986). Such cooperation can be temporary, as in the case of a past alliance among IBM, Intel, and Microsoft in the computer industry, or it can endure as in the long-standing relationships between Nike and its production partners in the athletic footwear and apparel business. Firms that are not direct competitors may respond to hypercompetition by forming regional learning networks that can help them to understand such competition and how to cope with it. Nordvest Forum is a case in point.

Hypercompetition and Organizational Learning

The need to link the theory of organizational learning to the theory of hypercompetition is clear. Nordvest Forum's learning cycle was specifically designed to capitalize on what was known about organizational learning at the time. For example, the designers were careful to create a process whereby individual learning could be converted into collective action, knowledge creation was directly related to competitive needs, diffusion would occur across firm boundaries, and so on. That behaviorally sound learning model was tailored to fit the regional multifirm network it served. Other industrial regions, however, might develop different, perhaps less cooperative, means of learning about how to respond to hypercompetition.

As learning networks begin to appear in other regions, their efficiency and effectiveness must be evaluated. According to most measures, Nordvest Forum Inc. has set up effective mechanisms for developing knowledge and diffusing it throughout the network's member firms. However, a question remains about the efficiency of that learning process in terms of speed and cost. Also, because of its pioneering nature, NVF's learning process has not been compared directly with other learning and change modes. As different types of regional learning networks appear elsewhere in the world, such evaluation studies will be necessary.

The evaluation studies should involve cross-disciplinary approaches to grasp and assess learning mechanisms on all levels, from the individual and company levels to the intercompany or network level. Particularly useful would be studies to determine the critical mass of a given company's linkages to the network that enables the company to benefit most efficiently from the overall learning process. In addition, it would be useful to examine the proper mix of a firm's managers and employees who are directly involved in the acquisition and interpretation phases of the learning cycle. For example, NVF Inc. has recently considered extending its training program to trade union leaders, lower-level managers, and certain functional areas such as purchasing. NVF Inc. currently believes that such extensions would increase the breadth of learning within each company and facilitate change processes that involve multiple departments.

Shaping the Competitive Business Environment

As companies attempt to respond to hypercompetitive conditions, they are inevitably drawn into efforts to shape their own environment. For example, to implement its learning cycle, NVF Inc. had to influence various resource and policy-making institutions. Over time, the behavior of those institutions has been altered by the presence of Nordvest Forum in the region, and in general they have become more responsive to the region's business needs. An important university changed its doctoral curriculum on the basis of the experiences of networking and organizational change in Nordvest Forum companies. Numerous research projects have been launched to examine particular international competitiveness issues emerging in the region. Further, several national policy agencies have incorporated the concept of a regional learning network into their funding processes and are now willing to grant development funds to such organizations as NVF Inc.

Every regional network example in the literature (e.g., Italian industrial districts and Japanese regional industrial policy) has demonstrated the value of a supportive public policy environment. Therefore, future research should describe and assess systematically the roles, processes, and mechanisms involved in effectively shaping such an environment. NVF Inc. developed a nontraditional approach to organizing business firms and influencing regional policy institutions in Norway. It went directly to national policymakers with its message and funding requests. It also used the communications media to influence regional planning and decision making. The usual approach has been to try to influence regional planning and policy formulation by participating in political parties or lobbying groups. It is essential to examine the most efficient and effective ways of linking the policy process of national and regional agencies with the learning process of firms participating in regional business networks.

CONCLUSION

As more industries become hypercompetitive—that is, require their member companies to be simultaneously efficient, responsive, and fast—the ability to develop, apply, and diffuse knowledge for continuous change will become a major competitive advantage. The best competitors in hypercompetitive industries—companies that continually meet their customers' needs in a timely way—will also be the best learners. In some cases, such as in cooperative regional networks, they may also be the best teachers, helping their fellow network participants learn and practice new approaches for coping with hypercompetitive conditions.

ACKNOWLEDGMENTS

This chapter is based on an ongoing research project started within the framework of a national program for business development in Norway (The Norwegian Work Life Center, SBA). The SBA program, which ran from 1988 through 1993, was funded by the major work life organizations and the Norwegian government. The authors are grateful to SBA's director, Dr. Thoralf U. Qvale, for his generous support throughout the project. The chapter builds on an evaluation of NVF Inc. performed by the authors in 1992-1993 that was funded by SBA and the Norwegian Research Foundation. The authors are indebted to the three main brokers of NVF Inc. for their helpful explanations and judgments: Knut Åsebø, Managing Director of NVF Inc., Professor Svein Kile, and Director Ragnar Østrem. The chapter benefited from the constructive comments of the participants at the Whittemore Conference held at the Amos Tuck School, Dartmouth College, in September 1994 and from the authors' colleagues Oğuz Babüroğlu and James Thomas.

REFERENCES

Alter, C. and J. Hage (1993), *Organizations Working Together,* Newbury Park, CA: Sage.

Barney, J. (1991), "Firm Resources and Sustained Competitive Advantage," *Journal of Management,* 17, 99-120.

Daft, R. L. and G. P. Huber (1987), "How Organizations Learn: A Communication Framework," *Research in the Sociology of Organizations,* 5, 1-36.

———— and K. E. Weick (1984), "Toward a Model of Organizations as Interpretation Systems," *Academy of Management Review,* 9, 284-295.

D'Aveni, R. A. (1994), *Hypercompetition: Managing the Dynamics of Strategic Maneuvering,* New York: Free Press.

Emery, M. and F. E. Emery (1978), "Searching: For New Directions, In New Ways, For New Times," in J. Sutherland (Ed.), *Management Handbook for Public Administrators,* New York: Van Nostrand Reinhold.

Fiol, C. M. (1994), "Consensus, Diversity, and Learning in Organizations," *Organization Science,* 5, 403-420.

Grant, R. M. (1991), "The Resource-Based Theory of Competitive Advantage: Implications for Strategy Formulation," *California Management Review,* 33, 114-135.

———— (1996), "Prospering in Dynamically Competitive Environments: Organizational Capability as Knowledge Integration," *Organization Science,* 7, 4, 375-387.

Hamel, G., Y. L. Doz, and C. K. Prahalad (1988), "Collaborate with Your Competitors—and Win," *Harvard Business Review,* 66, 133-139.

Huber, G. P. (1991), "Organizational Learning: The Contributing Processes and the Literatures," *Organization Science,* 2, 88-115.

Kim, D. H. (1993), "The Link Between Individual and Organizational Learning," *Sloan Management Review,* 35, 37-50.

Malnight, T. W. (1995), "Globalization of an Ethnocentric Firm: An Evolutionary Perspective," *Strategic Management Journal,* 16, 119-141.

Marquardt, M. and A. Reynolds (1994), *The Global Learning Organization,* Burr Ridge, IL: Richard D. Irwin.

Miles, R. E. and C. C. Snow (1986), "Network Organizations: New Concepts for New Forms," *California Management Review,* 28, 62-73.

——— (1994), *Fit, Failure, and the Hall of Fame: How Companies Succeed or Fail,* New York: Free Press.

Nonaka, I. (1994), "The Knowledge-Creating Company," *Harvard Business Review,* 69, 96-104.

——— (1994), "A Dynamic Theory of Organizational Knowledge Creation," *Organization Science,* 5, 14-37.

Quinn, J. B. (1992), *Intelligent Enterprise,* New York: Free Press.

Saxenian, A. (1990), "Regional Networks and the Resurgence of Silicon Valley," *California Management Review,* 33, 89-112.

——— (1994), *Regional Advantage,* Cambridge, MA: Harvard University Press.

Senge, P. (1990), *The Fifth Discipline,* New York: Doubleday.

——— (1994), *Field Guide to the Fifth Discipline,* New York: Doubleday.

Stata, R. (1989), "Organizational Learning—The Key to Management Innovation," *Sloan Management Review,* 30, 63-74.

Thorelli, H. B. (1986), "Networks: Between Markets and Hierarchies," *Strategic Management Journal,* 7, 37-52.

Volberda, H. W. (1996), "Toward the Flexible Form: How to Remain Vital in Hypercompetitive Environments," *Organization Science,* 7, 4, 359-374.

von Krogh, G., J. Roos, and K. Slocum (1994), "An Essay on Corporate Epistemology," *Strategic Management Journal,* 15, 53-72.

Walsh, J. P. and G. R. Ungson (1991), "Organizational Memory," *Academy of Management Review,* 16, 57-91.

15

Social Networks, Learning, and Flexibility

Sourcing Scientific Knowledge in New Biotechnology Firms

JULIA PORTER LIEBESKIND
AMALYA LUMERMAN OLIVER
LYNNE ZUCKER
MARILYNN BREWER

We examine how two highly successful new biotechnology firms (NBFs) source their most critical input—scientific knowledge. We find that scientists at the two NBFs enter into large numbers of collaborative research efforts with scientists at other organizations, especially universities. Formal market contracts are rarely used to govern these exchanges of scientific knowledge. Our findings suggest that the use of boundary-spanning social networks by the two NBFs increases both their learning and their flexibility in ways that would not be possible within a self-contained hierarchical organization.

(SOCIAL NETWORKS;
ORGANIZATIONAL LEARNING;
ORGANIZATIONAL FLEXIBILITY;
BIOTECHNOLOGY)

INTRODUCTION

In a recent editorial, Daft and Lewin (1993) called for more midrange and grounded studies of the new flexible learning organizations that are currently displacing older bureaucratic and hierarchical structures in what they

377

describe as an "organizational revolution." Commenting that "managers, not organization scholars, practice organization design and redesign," Daft and Lewin express concern that without grounded studies, organization theory will become "isolated and irrelevant." In response to Daft and Lewin's call, we examine how two highly successful new biotechnology firms (NBFs) use boundary-spanning social networks to source their most critical input— scientific knowledge. Our findings suggest that the use of boundary-spanning social networks by these NBFs increases both their learning and their flexibility in ways that would not be possible within a self-contained hierarchical organization. However, in defense of hierarchy, we argue that the NBFs' own rules and procedures play a critical role in supporting their use of social networks.

ORGANIZATION AND COMPETITION IN THE BIOTECHNOLOGY INDUSTRY

Background

Biotechnology comprises three different technologies: recombinant DNA or "rDNA" technology, first discovered by Boyer and Cohen in 1973; monoclonal antibody, or "Mabs" technology, first discovered by Kohler and Milstein in 1975; and protein engineering technology, developed during the 1980s. Together, these three technologies offer the prospect of producing an array of highly valuable processes and products in areas such as human health, crop production and protection, chemical feedstock production and processing, food processing, and waste management. The *biotechnology industry* consists of firms involved in the research, development, and commercialization of such processes and products.

Organization of the Biotechnology Industry

The development of the U.S. biotechnology industry has been characterized by the founding of large numbers of new biotechnology firms (NBFs) dedicated to researching and developing new products. Powell and Brantley (1992) attribute the development of NBFs to the fact that biotechnology was a competence-destroying innovation for established firms in client industries such as pharmaceuticals and chemicals. Lacking an understanding of biotechnology, established firms channeled their investments in biotechnology research to NBFs through long-term contracts or by forming joint ventures (Arora and Gambardella 1990, Pisano 1990). NBFs, in turn, entered into long-term contracts with established firms to obtain such complementary assets as product testing, production, marketing and distribution capabilities that NBFs lacked at the outset of their development (Barley et al. 1992, Pisano 1990, Powell and Brantley 1992, Shan 1990, Teece 1989). Consequently, the biotechnology industry is characterized by a network structure of interorganizational alliances that govern the exchange of complementary assets among NBFs, scientists, and established firms. NBFs are central to these interorganizational networks of alliances because of their role as intermediaries between scientists, who make basic discoveries, and large firms that have established capabilities in product testing, production, and distribution, but which lack critical biotechnology knowhow (Barley et al. 1992, Powell and Brantley 1992). The survival and success of NBFs within the industry network structure therefore depends on their ability to capture rights to scientific knowledge in the form of commercially valuable discoveries made by scientists.

Competitive Conditions in the Biotechnology Industry

The two NBFs we studied are both involved in the production of human health care products, including human diagnostic and therapeutic products, and associated treatment delivery systems. This industry segment is characterized by hypercompetition, compounded by appropriation problems, high levels of uncertainty, and critical resource immobility.

Hypercompetition. According to D'Aveni's (1994) criteria, the health care segment of the biotechnology industry can be classified as a "hypercompetitive" environment. Biotechnology itself is a revolutionary technology, and rapid technological innovation within biotechnology threatens to render even current biotechnological products obsolete within a relatively short time. Therefore, NBFs can sustain a competitive advantage only by continuous innovation that results in valuable and patentable products. The capacity of an NBF to achieve that goal depends critically on its supply of scientific knowledge. Meanwhile, the rapid pace of innovation in biotechnology demands that NBFs maintain strategic flexibility by minimizing their sunk cost investments in any particular line of research.

Uncertainty. Because biotechnology is a leading edge technology, NBFs cannot determine in advance if any particular research program in which they invest will lead to a valuable discovery. In some cases, biotechnology research has produced unique and highly valuable new health products.[1] In other cases, products that were expected to succeed have failed dramatically.[2] NBFs also face uncertainty about competitive conditions. New products developed by rival firms may render an NBF's research programs, or even its products, immediately obsolete. Meanwhile, the locus of innovation in biotechnology is constantly changing. University-based expertise is diffusing rapidly as new generations of biotechnology scientists are trained and move away from the early centers of innovation such as Stanford and UCSF (Kenney 1986). New NBFs continue to be founded, often to capitalize on key discoveries from these new centers of university research (Zucker et al. 1994). The high levels of technological and competitive uncertainty make it extremely difficult for NBFs to determine which scientific knowledge is potentially commercially valuable and which is not.

Appropriability. The rapid pace of innovation in the health care sector of biotechnology is fuelled and accelerated by strict property rights regimes. According to United States patent laws, only firms that are first to discover a product or process can reap any financial rewards from it. Firms therefore have incentives to "race" for patents by intensifying their research efforts (Grossman and Shapiro 1985, Lippman and McCardle 1987). Each NBF faces numerous committed competitors in these patent races, including established firms, other NBFs, and potential new NBF entrants. Established firms fuel competition by using their deep pockets to fund their own research or to fund NBFs' research efforts (Arora and Gambardella 1990, D'Aveni 1994). Moreover, all NBFs can be expected to be intensely competitive because they are strategically dedicated to the biotechnology industry (Ghemawat 1991, Porter 1980). This intense competition for patentable know how in biotechnology creates incentives for rival firms to appropriate scientific knowledge that is not already protected by patent laws. NBFs must therefore guard against appropriation in sourcing scientific knowledge.

Intellectual Resource Immobility. Although the number of biotechnology scientists has increased rapidly in the last decade, only a few "star" researchers have made numerous commercially valuable discoveries, and many of these stars work in universities. For example, Zucker et al. (1994) identify only 337 star researchers in biotechnology. Of the 213 stars in their sample who were trained in the United States, fully 163 (77%) worked in universities and another 44 (21%) worked in other nonprofit research institutes; only six stars (3%) worked in firms. Therefore, NBFs need to develop organizational arrangements that give them access to these valuable external intellectual resources.

In all, the biotechnology industry is an extremely challenging, hypercompetitive environment for NBFs. To survive and succeed, NBFs must devise organizational arrangements that enable them to source their critical input—patentable scientific knowledge—at minimum sunk cost while overcoming problems of uncertainty, appropriability, and intellectual resource immobility.

SOCIAL NETWORKS IN THE
BIOTECHNOLOGY INDUSTRY

Hierarchies, Markets, and Social Networks

We consider three organizational options available to NBFs for sourcing scientific knowledge: internal sourcing through the use of hierarchy, external sourcing through market exchanges, and external sourcing through social networks.[3] Transaction costs economics traditionally has distinguished between only two types of organizational arrangements for conducting exchanges: markets and hierarchies (Coase 1937, Williamson 1975). Markets organize the firm's external exchanges through price mechanisms and/or legal contracting; hierarchy organizes the firm's internal exchanges through direct employment and asset ownership (Camagni 1989, Masten 1988, Reve 1990, Teece 1989).

A common critique of this traditional analytical framework is that it ignores the importance of social values in the exchange process (Granovetter 1985). Both "markets" and "hierarchies" are social constructions whose existence and efficacy depend on broad social consensus about norms of behavior. (See, for example, Belshaw 1965 and Geertz 1978.) Hence, exchanges in both markets and hierarchies can be understood to be both supported, and shaped by, the norms of the social groups involved (Dore 1983, Granovetter 1985). In some situations, social norms supplement the operation of markets and hierarchies. In other situations, social norms may actually substitute for markets or hierarchies in the organization of exchange. For example, Ouchi (1980) identifies three distinct types of organization for conducting exchanges: markets, bureaucracies, and "clans." In clans, shared norms and values ensure fairness in exchange without resort to market pricing, contracts, or managerial authority. In a similar vein, Bradach and Eccles (1989) define price, authority, and "trust" as alternative methods of supporting exchange, where trust is engendered by shared norms. Powell (1990) argues that exchanges through social networks constitute a separate and distinct form of organization in which exchange is predicated on trust. According to these definitions, and following the theoretical frameworks of Coase (1937), Masten (1988), and Williamson (1991), we can distinguish social networks from markets or hierarchies as a means of governing exchanges by two criteria:

1. Unlike hierarchies, but like markets, social networks involve *exchanges between legally distinct entities.* Network exchanges, like market exchanges, are external to the firm (Reve 1990). Therefore, such exchanges are not for-

mally excluded from the rule of law, as are exchanges that take place within hierarchies.

2. Unlike markets, but like hierarchies, *social networks support exchanges without using competitive pricing or legal contracting.* Specifically, exchanges between individuals or organizations that are conducted through social networks have no need for price competition or legal contracts because the shared norms of the exchange partners alone will ensure that outcomes are fair.

Shared norms of trustworthy behavior may be instilled through socialization and tradition among members of a specific social group such as a tribe, social class, region, profession, religion, industry, or organization (Brusco 1982, Dore 1983, Elster 1989, Ross 1906, Zucker 1986). Norms of trustworthy behavior may also evolve over time as exchanges are repeated between friends or members of the same social group (Axelrod 1984, Kreps 1990). In addition, trustworthy behavior may be elicited by such mechanisms as posting a bond, testing, or performance monitoring, all of which are commonly used conditions of membership of professional or social groups (Evans-Pritchard 1940, Klein and Leffler 1982, Williamson 1979). Therefore, a social network can be defined as *a collectivity of individuals among whom exchanges take place that are supported only by shared norms of trustworthy behavior.* Social networks may or may not be contiguous with the boundaries of legally defined organizations. We describe a social network that includes members of more than one legally-defined organization as a "boundary-spanning" social network.

Social Networks, Learning, and Flexibility

According to Powell (1990) and Zucker (1991), social networks may make an important contribution to organizational learning. Powell (1990) argues that social networks are the most efficient organizational arrangement for sourcing *information* because information is difficult to price (in a market) and to communicate through a hierarchical structure. He states (p. 304):

Networks are particularly apt for circumstances in which there is a need for efficient, reliable information. The most useful [valuable] information is rarely that which flows down the formal chain of command in an organization, or that which can be inferred from price signals. Rather, it is that which is obtained from someone you have dealt with in the past and found to be reliable. You trust information that comes from someone you know well.

Powell's argument is that social networks serve as sources of reliable information, which is essential to efficient organizational learning. Hence, organizations whose employees are members of a social network would learn more efficiently than organizations whose employees are not members of a social network, because the quality of the former's information would be higher. That may be particularly true when social networks span the boundaries of the firm. According to Zucker (1991, p. 164) bureaucracies (i.e., firms) often lack "expert" information and must therefore seek it externally:

> While bureaucratic authority is by definition located within the firm's boundaries, expert authority depends on the information resources available to an individual, and not on the authority of office. Thus, authority may be located within the organization . . . but when an external [expert] authority market can provide information that leads to greater effectiveness, then [expert] authority tends to migrate into the market.

In addition, if expert authority is external to a firm, sourcing knowledge through social networks may enable the firm to integrate that knowledge more effectively than information acquired through market arrangements such as licensing, which do not allow for learning-by-doing or open-ended learning (Grant 1996).

Social networks may also enhance flexibility—a firm's capacity for responding to unpredictable changes in its competitive environment (D'Aveni 1994, Volberda 1996). Each time a firm internalizes and routinizes an activity, it makes a sunk cost investment in organization that is specific to that activity. When technology is changing rapidly, the value to a firm of undertaking certain activities and/or certain combinations of activities will also change rapidly; internalization therefore may result in excess sunk costs that are avoided in external exchanges (Camagni 1989, Teece 1989). In addition, rapid technological change undermines firms' abilities to assess the value of information accurately because they cannot learn and institutionalize appropriate assessment routines in short periods of time (Camagni 1989). An external "informational network" of experts can provide the firm with multiple evaluations of the value of its own information and know-how, thereby increasing its efficiency in searching for valuable information, screening information, codifying information for managerial use, selecting appropriate investments, and applying managerial control (Camagni 1989, Zucker 1991). Therefore, sourcing information from external experts not only increases learning, but also increases the flexibility of a firm's boundaries because each external expert represents a "strategic sourcing option" that the firm can exercise only when necessary (Volberda 1996).

Social Networks in Biotechnology

All NBFs have the option of sourcing scientific knowledge through the social network of academic scientists, because typically they are founded and staffed by university-trained scientists. For example, Herbert Boyer, a founder of Genentech, is one of the discoverers (and patenters) of gene-splicing technology and is a renowned academic scientist (Kenney 1986).

Consistent with Powell's (1990) arguments, the social network of academic scientists is characterized by norms of trustworthy behavior in exchanges of information. Indeed, the network exists to ensure the reliability of scientific information (David 1991, Merton 1973). Among academic scientists, these norms are well defined and socially enforced, and include reciprocity, respect for individuals' intellectual property rights, and honesty in research (Blau 1973, Crane 1972, Merton 1973, Nelkin 1984). Individual scientists' intellectual property rights are protected through presentations and authorship of published research reports. Norms of honesty in research are instilled through long and rigorous training and are enforced through research that seeks to replicate and validate the findings of other scientists (David 1991, Merton 1973). Reputations for trustworthy behavior can be established in the social network because academic scientists conduct repeated exchanges of information through shared research programs, attendance at meetings, presentations, and reviewing and refereeing written work (Merton 1973). The system of repeated exchange allows detection and punishment of plagiarism and falsification (Klein and Leffler 1982). Finally, scientists who do not conform to accepted norms can be excluded from exchanges of information (such as participation in research teams and access to the latest research findings), which will severely damage their future careers (Crane 1972, Merton 1973). In extreme cases, plagiarism or falsification of research findings will lead directly to job loss. In sum, trustworthy behavior among academic scientists is instilled, motivated, and maintained through a variety of mechanisms. Such behavior facilitates the production and sharing of reliable, valuable information, allowing the frontier of knowledge to advance rapidly and at minimal cost.

Given the competitive conditions in the biotechnology industry, and given that social networks can increase organizational learning and flexibility, NBFs might be expected to depend heavily on the social network of academic scientists in sourcing scientific knowledge. First, by sourcing scientific knowledge from a wide variety of external scientists and organizations, an NBF can increase the likelihood that it will be the first to gain access to, or knowledge about, new discoveries. Sourcing knowledge externally through a social network rather than a market may also increase the reliability of externally acquired scientific knowledge (Powell 1990). Not only will that knowledge be subject to the norms of scientific enquiry, it will also be sourced by the NBF's own experts—its scientist-employees. In addition, when an NBF's scientists conduct collaborative research with external scientists, the latters' knowledge is integrated directly into the ongoing R & D program of the NBF, something that could not be achieved with pure market exchanges (Cohen and Levinthal 1990, Grant 1996).

Second, social network exchanges enable NBFs to reduce their costs. Such exchanges give NBFs access to cutting-edge research in universities that is funded by taxpayers, reducing the firm's sunk R & D costs (DeBresson and Amesse 1991, Teece 1989). By seeking evaluations from external experts, NBFs can better evaluate their own research programs and further avoid excess sunk costs of R & D (Camagni 1989). In addition, using social networks eliminates the costs of using markets. Contracts are costly to negotiate, may involve substantial commitments of specialized resources, and may impose high costs of exit or renegotiation (Ghemawat 1991, Williamson 1991). Such costs can be avoided when exchanges are conducted through social networks, which allow an NBF to be flexible in terms of switching from one external supplier of scientific knowledge to another as competitive and technological conditions change.

Third, social networks may provide more protection against appropriation than markets, where even legal contracting may not prevent misappropriation (Arrow 1962, Levin et al. 1987). For example, some knowledge that is contributory to the discovery process may not be patentable. In addition, patent coverage may be too slow and/or too narrow to prevent appropriation of knowledge that can lead to follow-on products (Levin et al. 1987). Under such circumstances, the norms of scientists may protect an NBF against appropriation of unprotected knowledge. However, appropriability concerns may impel NBFs to govern certain knowledge exchanges exclusively through their own hierarchies if the returns to appropriation are so high as to render any external exchange risky. In particular, as research programs progress, their value becomes more certain, reducing the marginal value of external inputs of scientific knowledge, whereas the incentive for appropriation increases. By internalizing exchanges of more certainly valuable knowledge, an NBF can use managerial authority to restrict the flow of that knowledge beyond its boundaries. An NBF also increases the likelihood that it can establish undisputed property rights if it is the undisputed locus of discovery (Von Hippel 1982).

Finally, social network exchanges may enable an NBF to gain access to unique resources. Expert knowledge that is critical to an NBFs' survival and success may be produced by scientists who are not willing to work for any firm and who cannot sell their research services through market contracting. In particular, many universities restrict the amount of time their employees can work for other institutions and/or the amount of income they can receive from outside sources (Giamatti 1982, Kennedy 1982). However, university scientists may be willing and able to supply scientific knowledge to an NBF through scientific collaboration, if they can receive resources in return to satisfy norms of reciprocity (Mauss 1950, Ouchi 1980, Zucker 1991). An NBF may also be able to attract and retain more talented scientists itself if it permits its employees to participate in external exchanges of scientific knowledge. Such external exchanges enable an NBF's scientist-employees to continue to gain prestige and friendships from their professional social network, reducing divergence between scientists' goals and those of the organization (Deutschman 1994). In turn, increasing the status of an NBF's scientist-employees in the social network of scientists through research exchanges has the potential to increase the number and importance of external exchanges an NBF can enter into.

In sum, an NBF can benefit substantially from supporting and promoting external exchanges of scientific knowledge, especially those conducted through social networks, so long as the benefits of those exchanges are greater than any costs of misappropriation that might result.

METHOD

Sample

This study describes the organizational arrangements used to source scientific knowledge in two highly successful NBFs—firms that have succeeded in sourcing and commercializing valuable scientific knowledge. As both firms requested anonymity, we refer to them as Firm X and Firm Y. Both firms are involved in the most profitable segments of the biotechnology industry: human therapeutic and diagnostic products. In some product markets the two firms are head-to-head competitors. In addition, the two firms are diversified into similar numbers of different product areas. The firms operate under identical regulatory and property rights regimes. The products of both firms are biomedical products that are governed by FDA regulations, and most of their products are patentable under U.S. intellectual property laws. Both firms are located in California.

We used a sample of only two firms because collecting data on social network exchanges is difficult and time-consuming. Our approach therefore represents a choice of depth over breadth. We chose to study two firms with similar transactions, operating under similar regulatory regimes, to provide some comparison of our findings and theoretical interpretations. The data we report detail each firm's organizational arrangements for its supply of scientific knowledge after its founding; we have 10 years of data for Firm X and nine years of data for Firm Y. To preserve the two firms' anonymity, the year of founding of each firm is designated as Year 1. The two firms were founded relatively closely in time, so their development is unlikely to have been differentially influenced by changes in their competitive environments over time.

Data and Measures

We considered three alternative organizational arrangements for governing the exchange of scientific knowledge: hierarchies, markets, and social networks. We measured both organization-level and individual-level exchange arrangements.

Although ultimately all exchanges of knowledge take place between individuals (Grant 1996), individual-level exchanges can be supported by organization-level arrangements. We classified exchanges that take place between individuals who are scientist-employees of the same NBF as being governed by the firm's hierarchy, because a firm's managers are legally empowered to establish and enforce terms and conditions of employment (Masten 1988). We classify "market" exchanges as (1) exchanges between the scientist-employees of an NBF and employees of other organizations with which the NBF has some type of formal contractual agreement for the supply of scientific knowledge, or (2) exchanges between the scientist-employees of an NBF and individuals (a) who are not employees of the firm, and (b) are not employees of any other organization with which the NBF has some type of formal contractual agreement for the supply of scientific knowledge, but (c) are parties to a formal, legally enforceable, individual contract with the NBF for the supply of scientific knowledge. Finally, consistent with our preceding definition, we classify "social network" exchanges as exchanges of scientific knowledge between scientist-employees of an NBF and individuals who are not employees of the firm or of any other organization with which the NBF has some type of formal contractual agreement for the supply of scientific knowledge, and who are not parties to any formal, legally enforceable, individual contract with the NBF.

We measured exchanges of scientific knowledge in terms of scholarly publications on which scientists at the two NBFs studied were named as authors. Scholarly publications measure the production of scientific knowledge because research findings are published only if they are considered to contain valid, reliable information that is of value to other scientists (Irvine and Martin 1985). Publication data also provide impartial records of patterns of scientific collaboration at the individual level, and of knowledge production at the individual and institutional level (Irvine and Martin 1985, Zucker et al. forthcoming).

Possibly, not all research collaborations conducted by scientists at a firm lead to knowledge that is directly useful *to that firm*. For example, scientists who have discretion to design their own research programs may choose to conduct research that interests them rather than research that meets the goals of the firm. We have no direct data on the "usefulness" of the research collaborations we measured. Indeed, "usefulness" may be impossible to measure: Discoveries (and their associated patents) typically emerge from long programs of research, and the contribution of publications to the development of scientific knowledge necessarily varies (Irvine and Martin 1985). Interviews conducted at Firm X and Firm Y suggested that collaborative research between employee-scientists and external scientists served several purposes. Some collaborative research represented a continuation of ongoing research programs between scientists who had joined the two firms and their colleagues who had remained at universities. Much of this research was evidently valuable to the two firms because it was the reason for their employing these scientists in the first place. In addition, some external collaborative research was strategic, in the sense that key external scientists were sought out to work on specific problems that the firms themselves lacked the resources or knowledge to pursue, consistent with Zucker's (1991) arguments. Finally, some external research collaborations were "prospecting," allowing the firms to "peek" at others' knowledge at low cost, consistent with the arguments of Camagni (1989) and Teece (1989). Although much of the last type of research may not prove useful, both firms encouraged prospecting research collaborations in the expectation that some would pay off in the future.

We recognize that using publication data provides an incomplete measure of exchanges of scientific knowledge at Firms X and Y. First, publication data exclude information on research collaborations that did not yield publishable results, even though that outcome may have provided valuable information to the two firms (e.g. a line of research is not worth continuing). Conversely, a collaboration may have provided knowledge so valuable that the NBF withheld it permanently from publication. Second, scientific knowledge can be exchanged in ways other than through research collaborations. For example, scientists at both firms attend scientific meetings and colloquia both at their own firm and at outside institutions (Martens and Saretzki 1993). However, much of the knowledge exchanged in that way may be of limited value to any individual firm because it is publicly available and so cannot be patented.

Firms X and Y both keep detailed records of scholarly publications in which their scientists are listed as authors. Using these records, we looked up the original articles in libraries and recorded each institution of origin of each external author as listed on each article. We were then able to compile data on the number, identity, and type of institutions at which external collaborating scientists worked. We also recorded the number of scholarly publications in which scientists at Firms X and Y did not collaborate with outside scientists. Altogether, these publication data enable us to examine each firm's research exchanges in terms of the extent and frequency of research collaborations between scientists at Firms X and Y and external scientists, the number of external institutions involved in the collaborations, the types of institutions involved, the frequency of collaborative research endeavors with specific institutions, the degree to which the two firms' external exchange networks overlap, and the evolution of external research collaborations over time.

We gathered patent data from the *U.S. Patent Database* and from individual patent listings for the purpose of identifying the assignees of each patent. Additional patent data were obtained from corporate records. Data on patents were used only if the public and corporate records matched; sometimes patents that had been applied for but were not yet granted were listed in the corporate records.

The data were collected during the period 1989 to 1992. In addition to collecting proprietary data from the corporate records of the two firms, we obtained data from interviews with scientists and managers in the two firms, from public data sources such as the *North Carolina Biotechnology Database, BioScan,* the *Wall Street Journal Index,* and from various reports on the biotechnology industry published by consulting or investment firms such as Ernst & Young, Kidder Peabody, and Shearson Lehman.

EVIDENCE

Interorganizational Arrangements

The extent of inter- and intraorganizational governance of exchanges supplying scientific knowledge to Firms X and Y is shown in Tables 15.1, 15.2, and 15.3. Table 15.1 gives the number of scientists directly employed by Firms X and Y. Firm X employed 197 scientists by Year 10 and Firm Y employed 146 scientists by Year 9. These numbers indicate that each firm was making substantial direct investments in intellectual resources that could be governed by its own hierarchy. Table 15.1 also shows that, despite the newness of the two firms, 47% of scientists at Firm X and 35% of scientists at Firm Y had been employed for five or more years. This finding indicates that the hierarchies of the firms supported long-term employment which is critical to building organizational learning and knowledge integration routines (Grant 1996).

TABLE 15.1 Hierarchical Governance of Exchanges at Firms X and Y: Numbers of Employee-Scientists[a] and Year of Hiring

	Firm X	Firm Y
A. Number of scientists employed by NBF		
Year 10	196	Not available
Year 9	—	146
B. Longevity of employment: Percentage of scientists who have been with the firm:		
10 years	13.3	Not available
9 years	7.7	8.9
8 years	4.6	8.2
7 years	8.7	8.9
6 years	2.6	11.6
5 years	10.7	4.1
4 years	14.3	6.8
3 years	16.3	28.8
2 years	17.4	17.1
1 years	4.6	12.3
5 years or more	47.4	35.0

SOURCE: Corporate records.
a. Employee-scientists are classified as all individuals whom the two firms identified as being "scientists" in their corporate records. Most of these individuals had Ph.D.s or other education qualifications in relevant disciplines such as microbiology and biochemistry.

Table 15.2 provides evidence on the market arrangements of Firm X and Y for sourcing scientific knowledge. Panel A shows that both Firm X and Firm Y had numerous market arrangements. However, panel B shows that very few of those arrangements provided for knowledge sourcing: Firm X had only two knowledge-sourcing arrangements by Year 10 and Firm Y had only six by Year 9. Of the eight arrangements, five were long-term R & D contracts; there was only one R & D joint venture, one equity investment in another research-based firm, and one licensing agreement. This evidence is somewhat surprising. Previous studies show that NBFs are imbedded in a dense network of interorganizational market agreements for sourcing complementary assets (Barley et al. 1992, Powell and Brantley 1992). Moreover, Barley et al. (1992) found that 30.5% of the 2,206 alliances they studied were R & D alliances, but did not distinguish between R & D alliances in which NBFs *source* scientific knowledge from other organizations and those in which NBFs *supply* scientific knowledge to other organizations. Our data suggest that NBFs make very few market arrangements for sourcing scientific knowledge. At the organizational level of analysis, therefore, our data

TABLE 15.2 Inter-organizational Market and Quasi-Market Arrangements for Sourcing Scientific Knowledge at Firms X and Y

| | Type of Institution Involved | | | | |
| | Universities | | Firms | | |
	U.S.	Int'l.	U.S.	Int'l.	Total
A. All market arrangements[a]					
Firm X	0	0	15	5	20
Firm Y	2	2	21	16	41
Total	2	2	36	21	61
B. Market arrangements for sourcing scientific knowledge[b]					
Firm X					
Number	0	0	2	0	2
Percentage of total					10
Firm Y					
Number	1	1	4	0	6
Percentage of total					15
Both firms					
Number	1	1	6	0	8
Percentage of total					13

SOURCES: Corporate records, *North Carolina Biotechnology Database, BioScan, Wall Street Journal Index.*
a. Defined as all market and quasi-market organizational arrangements (Williamson 1991).
b. Defined as all market and quasi-market arrangements in which the NBF is primarily sourcing scientific knowledge from other organizations. These include five long-term R & D contracts, one R & D-sourcing joint venture, one equity investment in another R & D firm, and one licensing agreement.

appear to suggest that Firms X and Y are almost entirely self-sufficient in terms of sourcing scientific knowledge. However, the evidence on individual-level exchanges leads to a different conclusion.

Individual-level Exchanges of Scientific Knowledge

Table 15.3 reports the extent of individual exchanges of scientific knowledge at Firms X and Y, measured in terms of counts of published research findings. The table shows that scientists at both firms were highly involved in research that resulted in published research findings. At Firm X, scientists had produced 503 research publications by Year 10; at Firm Y, scientists had produced 345 research publications through Year 9. In both firms, a large number of publications involved scientists from other institution; 257 collaborations at Firm X and 256 at Firm Y involved external scientists. In addition, Table 15.4 shows that these external collaborations represented a large number of external institutions. Scientists at Firm X were involved in research collaborations with scientists at 144 different external institutions;

TABLE 15.3 Number of Scientific Collaborations Resulting in Published Research
Classified by Exchange Governance Mechanism

Number of Research Publications

	Firm X	Firm Y	Total
1. Total number of publications	503	345	848
2. Number of publications based on research			
collaboration with external scientists	257	256	513
Percentage of total	51	74	60
Of which are governed by market arrangements			
that are			
(a) Interorganizational	0	2	2
(b) Individual-level	0	0	0
3. Number of publications produced only by			
scientists-employees	246	89	335
Percentage of total	49	26	40

scientists at Firm Y took part in research collaborations with scientists at 147
different external institutions. These large numbers of collaborations and
external institutions illustrate the very high degree to which both firms relied
on scientists to increase the scope of their organizational learning and to
increase their strategic and organizational flexibility. They are also supportive of the argument that NBFs "prospect" for valuable scientific knowledge
at many different institutions to reduce uncertainty about the loci of innovation, and to discover valuable scientific knowledge that they can subsequently absorb.

Remarkably, almost none of the external exchanges of scientific knowledge entered into by Firms X and Y were governed by contracts or other
market mechanisms. Table 15.3 shows that only two publications involved
institutions with which Firms X or Y had an interorganizational contract, and
no exchanges were governed by individual-level contracts. The reason for
this result may have been that most of the external exchanges involved
scientists at universities and other nonprofit research institutions where
contracting restrictions apply: Table 15.4 shows that 86% of all institutions
involved in published collaborative research with Firms X and Y were
universities and other nonprofit research institutions. Moreover, panel B
shows that the rates of collaboration per institution were far higher for
external universities than for external firms. This finding suggests that the
two NBFs were willing to conduct a large number of external collaborations
at a large number of different institutions, governed only by the norms of the
scientific social network. In addition, Table 15.4 shows that many scientific
collaborations at Firms X and Y involved scientists outside the boundaries

TABLE 15.4 Frequency of Collaboration in Published Research Between Scientists at Firms X and Y and External Scientists by Type of Institution of Affiliation of External Scientists

| | Type of Institution | | | | |
| | Universities and Other Nonprofit Research Institutions | | Firms | | |
	U.S.	Int'l.	U.S.	Int'l.	Total
A. Number of institutions:					
Both firms					
Number	157	93	28	13	291
Percentage of total	54	32	10	4	100
Firm X					
Number	85	36	17	6	144
Percentage of total	59	25	12	4	100
Firm Y					
Number	72	57	11	7	147
Percentage of total	49	39	8	4	100
B. Mean number of collaborations per institution by type:					
Both firms	3.28	2.05	1.53	1.08	
Firm X	3.31	2.08	1.88	1.16	
Firm Y	3.25	2.03	1.18	1.00	

SOURCES: Corporate records of Firms X and Y, journal references.

of U.S. jurisdiction on intellectual property rights: 29% of all institutions participating in collaborative research with Firm X and 43% of all institutions participating in collaborative research with Firm Y were located outside the U.S.

Table 15.5 provides further evidence of the "prospecting" nature of external collaborations at Firms X and Y. Very few of the external research collaborations conducted by the two firms produced numerous publications, which are an indication of a long-lived research program. At Firm X, 130 of a total of 144 (90%) collaborative research relationships yielded five or fewer research publications; in Firm Y, 134 out of 147 (91%) collaborative relationships yielded five or fewer publications.

Other studies have shown that NBFs decrease their number of market agreements involving complementary assets over time (Kogut et al. 1992, Shan 1990). Therefore, we investigated whether Firm X and Firm Y became more autonomous in terms of research capabilities over time. The evidence in Table 15.6 shows that annual rates of external research collaborations at Firms X and Y did not decline with time during the period studied. At Firm X,

TABLE 15.5 Number of External Research Collaborations at Firms X and Y by Institution (all years combined)

Number of Publications per Institutional Collaboration	Number of Collaborations by Institution and by Frequency Category		
	Firm X	Firm Y	Total
1-5	130	134	264
6-10	9	7	16
11-15	2	3	5
16-20	1	0	1
21-25	1	1	2
26-30	1	0	1
31 +	0	1	1
Total	144	147	291

scientists steadily increased their number of external collaborations over time to a high of 62 collaborations in Year 10; at Firm Y, scientists maintained a rate of about 40 external collaborations from Year 5 onwards, although the rate fluctuated from year to year. This evidence suggests that Firms X and Y continued to gain benefits from research collaborations during the period studied in terms of prospecting for innovations, reducing their direct R & D costs, accessing the knowledge of immobile external scientists, and attracting and retaining scientist-employees. Table 15.6 also shows that scientists at Firms X and Y continued to publish their own research findings, even when research did not involve collaboration with external scientists. However, the two NBFs differed in the degree to which they encouraged (or permitted) their employee-scientists to enter into network exchanges of scientific knowledge that did not involve external collaborations. The number of publications at Firm Y involving only its own scientists ($n = 89$) was far lower than the number at Firm X ($n = 246$), even though the numbers of external collaborations in published research were essentially identical for the two firms.

One question raised by this evidence is whether conducting numerous external research collaborations without the protection of legally enforceable contracts covering intellectual property rights led to appropriability problems for Firms X and Y. Table 15.7 shows that both Firm X and Firm Y obtained clear property rights to scientific discoveries during the period studied. Of the 28 patents owned by Firm X, only three were shared, none of them with scientists or institutions in their collaborative network. Of the 21 patents owned by Firm Y, two were shared with institutions with which

TABLE 15.6 Number and Rate of External Collaboration at Firms X and Y by Year

	Firm X			Firm Y		
	Total Number of Publications per Year	Proportion of Publications per Year Involving		Total Number of Publications per Year	Proportion of Publications per Year Involving	
		External Scientists	No External Scientists		External Scientists	No External Scientists
1	0			0		
2	0			0		
3	18	0.22	0.78	13	0.77	0.23
4	39	0.23	0.77	21	0.81	0.19
5	56	0.45	0.55	50	0.86	0.14
6	56	0.32	0.68	56	0.77	0.23
7	82	0.60	0.40	47	0.66	0.34
8	73	0.58	0.42	56	0.68	0.32
9	82	0.59	0.41	60	0.75	0.25
10	107	0.58	0.42	42[a]	0.80[a]	0.20[a]
Total:	503	0.50	0.50	345	0.74	0.26

a. Data for Year 10 for Firm Y is not complete.

TABLE 15.7 Exclusive Versus Shared Patent Rights of Firms X and Y

	Firm X	Firm Y
Total number of patents[a]	28	21
Number of exclusive patents	25	19
Number of shared patents	3	2
Number of patents shared by NBF with institutions, or scientists at institutions, with which NBF has a formal contractual agreement	3	2
Number of patents shared by NBF with institutions, or scientists at institutions, with whose scientists NBF scientists have collaborated in published research	0	2

SOURCES: Corporate records, patent records.
a. Defined as major patents in force at the time of writing; numbers do not include patents applied for and not received and do not include separate claims made under each patent.

the firm conducted collaborative research. However, Firm Y also had market agreements with those two institutions that may have specified that intellectual property be shared. Perhaps the reason for the lack of shared patents at Firms X and Y was that only "basic" (i.e., not directly commercializable) research was conducted with external scientists through social networks. In the case of biotechnology, however, basic scientific discoveries and commercially valuable products are typically indistinguishable. We therefore believe the evidence at least partially supports the interpretation that the norms of the social network of professional scientists protect against the risk of knowledge appropriation.

DISCUSSION

The evidence presented in the preceding section shows that social networks play an important role in promoting organizational learning and in fostering organizational flexibility in the two NBFs studied. Using a very wide network of external scientist-collaborators, Firms X and Y were able to access scientific knowledge at numerous institutions in the United States and abroad, increasing both their organizational learning and their operational and strategic flexibility.

Our findings suggest that social network exchanges make two important contributions to organizational learning. First, they contribute by extending the *scope* of organizational learning. The two NBFs sourced knowledge from a large number of other institutions. The reliability of this externally sourced knowledge was ensured by that fact that it was exchanged among members of the same social network (Powell 1990) and by the fact that it was sourced by the firms' own experts —scientist-employees (Zucker 1991). Second, social networks contributed to the *integration of knowledge* at the two firms. Because collaborative research took place at the operating (research) level of the two NBFs, the knowledge held by external experts could be integrated directly into the routines of the firm. Indeed, the evidence is consistent with Grant's (1996) argument that, because all learning involves collaboration between individuals, markets are not good mechanisms for transferring knowledge. We find that almost none of the individual-level exchanges of knowledge through research collaboration involved organizations with which either NBF had a market agreement. In his study, Grant (1996) considers only firms and markets as alternatives for integrating knowledge. Our study suggests that social networks also warrant serious consideration as mechanisms for organizing the transfer and integration of knowledge between both individuals and organizations.

Our findings also illustrate how social networks can contribute to organizational flexibility. Volberda (Chapter 11, this volume) characterizes flexible firms as being able to adapt rapidly to changing circumstances at the operating, organizational, and strategic levels. Social networks can be considered to have increased the *operating flexibility* of the two firms. Because social networks in the two NBFs supported collaborative research, they facilitated the integration of new scientific knowledge into the two firms' operations through learning-by-doing. Also, social networks can be considered to have increased the *organizational flexibility* of the two NBFs by enabling them to switch from one source of knowledge to another without incurring the costs or commitments inherent in either hierarchical or market exchanges. Finally, using external sourcing of scientific knowledge permitted the firms to reduce the costs of their own hierarchies, which is essential to maintaining *strategic flexibility* in a rapidly changing industry characterized by high sunk costs (Camagni 1989, Teece 1989).

The evidence we report in this chapter highlights the importance of social networks in sourcing scientific knowledge, but the importance of the two firms' own hierarchies in supporting those exchanges must not be overlooked. During the early stages of their development, Firms X and Y were both staffed and managed by academic scientists who imported the norms and values of academic science into the two firms. From the outset, therefore, norms of external collaboration were implanted in each firm as a core practice. In addition, each NBF's staff of highly skilled research scientists could initiate and support social network relationships with key external scientists (Cohen and Levinthal 1990). To attract and retain such scientists, however, each NBF needed to maintain a "university-like" organizational context as it developed. That is, the NBF's organizational policies had to support both the formation and maintenance of boundary-spanning social network relationships as well as numerous other complementary activities such as rapid publication of research results and freedom of scientific inquiry (Deutschman 1994). Therefore, the hierarchies of Firms X and Y clearly played a critical role in supporting and governing their internal exchanges in ways that supported their external exchanges, and vice-versa (Reve 1990). This model is illustrated in Figure 15.1.

Daft and Lewin (1993) observed that new flexible learning organizations are replacing "structures that provide central control over activities." However, that change does not imply that the hierarchy of the firm is no longer important. Rather, our results suggest that the role of hierarchy in new learning, flexible organizations such as NBFs has shifted from *coordinating the on-going internal activities of the firm through a command and control structure to providing appropriate organizational support for both the internal and external exchanges* that are essential to the firm's survival and success. Indeed, providing such support may be *the* critical capability for

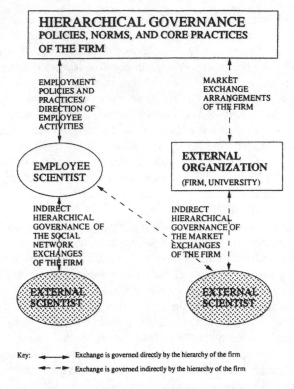

Figure 15.1. Hierarchies as Support for Both Markets and Social Networks in the External Exchanges of an NBF

knowledge-based firms (Adler 1989, Henderson and Cockburn 1994). In all such firms, self-coordination among experts is more efficient than coordination by managers (Thompson 1967). However, self-coordination across organizational boundaries cannot take place without (at the very least) organizational permission or (at the very best) active organizational support.

One question that must be addressed is whether our findings are generalizable to other NBFs. We know of no other study that has examined the role of boundary-spanning social networks in biotechnology firms in detail. However, Kenney (1986) and Zucker et al. (1994) argue that ties between NBFs and major research universities are an essential condition for NBF founding and survival. In addition, several studies suggest that market-type alliances are critical to the survival and success of NBFs. For example, Shan (1990), Kogut et al. (1992) and Oliver (1993) find that NBFs tend to form more interorganizational market-type alliances when they are newer and otherwise more likely to fail (Singh et al. 1986). Our findings suggest that social networks should also be considered in the calculus of NBF survival. In addition, our findings point towards an explanation for the failure of established pharmaceutical firms to enter biotechnology directly (Arora and Gambradella 1990): Those firms lacked access to the social networks that are critical to sourcing scientific knowledge. Deutschman (1994) argues that historically, large pharmaceutical firms discouraged their scientists from publishing research findings and therefore had difficulty attracting and retaining top scientists from academia. Yet without such scientists, access to social networks in biotechnology would be blocked and the absorptive capacity of the firm would be undermined (Cohen and Levinthal 1990). Consequently, it is possible that large pharmaceutical firms could enter biotechnology only via strategic alliances with NBFs which were able to support social network exchanges of scientific knowledge.

An additional question that must be addressed is whether our findings are generalizable outside California, where both Firm X and Firm Y are located. California has provided a fertile breeding ground for new firms in several industries including biotechnology and electronics. Saxenian (1994) argues that the Silicon Valley area in particular has provided an exceptionally munificent environment for knowledge-based firms because the area's culture supports free exchanges of ideas. Possibly, NBFs located elsewhere in the United States may have different patters of social network exchanges. However, Firms X and Y conducted social network exchanges with many institutions outside California, and even outside the United States, reducing the strength of the argument that biotechnology collaborations are regionally embedded. We believe it more likely that scientific collaborations in biotechnology are culturally embedded within the social network of professional scientists, wherever those scientists are located.

Our findings may also be generalizable to other emerging industries that depend on university research. Evidence shows social networks to be critical in certain industries such as publishing (Coser et al. 1982) and investment banking (Eccles and Crane 1988), but few industries at present are as embedded in the social network of academic science as biotechnology. Universities are now on the cutting edge of research in several other areas that hold great commercial promise, such as materials engineering. Our findings suggest that social networks will play a critical role in giving firms access to this new university-based knowledge.

Two emerging trends may change patterns of social network exchanges in biotechnology in the future. One is change in the locus of innovation. Many of the pathbreaking discoveries in biotechnology are now being made within firms. For example, Genentech is now ranked fourth in number of citations among all research institutions in genetics and molecular biology, ahead of prestigious research universities such as Harvard, Princeton, and MIT (Deutschman 1994). If this trend continues, the reliance of many NBFs on universities for scientific knowledge may decline, reducing the importance of access to, and participation in, social networks. The second trend that may change current patterns of exchange is increasing awareness of the value of scientific knowledge. When biotechnology was in its infancy, the potential value of biotechnology products was highly uncertain. As more products are brought to market, much of this uncertainty is being resolved— many products are proving to be very valuable. In an interview, the research director at one of the two firms we studied remarked that the firm was intending to introduce contracts to govern certain external research collaborations involving knowledge, materials or technologies that were highly valuable to the firm. At the same time, universities are becoming more vigilant in protecting their intellectual property rights, placing additional restrictions on, and increasing the costs of, flows of valuable scientific knowledge from universities to firms.[4]

We see several promising avenues for further research. First, our study did not examine the processes whereby scientists in NBFs form relationships with external scientists, or how such boundary-spanning relationships evolve over time.[5] It would be particularly interesting to investigate what organizational policies NBFs have in place to promote the creation and development of boundary-spanning social networks. Second, our study provides evidence that the social networks of Firms X and Y are global in scope, which raises questions of how long-distance collaborative relationships are formed, maintained, and governed. We hope that future research on social networks in biotechnology will address these issues.

ACKNOWLEDGMENTS

The authors thank Paul Adler, Michele Bolton, participants at the Academy of Management Meeting in Dallas and the Whittemore Conference on Hypercompetition held at the Tuck School, Dartmouth College, two anonymous referees, and the Editor-in-Chief for useful comments and suggestions. This research was partly funded by a National Science Foundation dissertation improvement grant to Dr. Oliver, and by research grants from the National Science Foundation and from the University of California System Biotechnology Research Program to Dr. Zucker and Dr. Brewer (principal investigators).

NOTES

1. For example, the drug Neupogen (produced by Amgen Inc.), which is uniquely able to reduce anemia in chemotherapy patients, had sales of $544 million in 1992 (*Businessweek,* April 26, 1993, p. 86).

2. For example, the failure of Cetus Inc. is commonly attributed to its strategy of concentrating its R & D efforts on interleukins: In 1990, the FDA failed to approve the firm's product interleukin-2 as a treatment for cancer. (The firm was subsequently rescued by being taken over by Chiron Corporation.) Genentech's "wonder drug" TPA, designed to treat thromboses, proved to afford little more benefit than established treatments, although it was far more costly. In 1993 and 1994, the FDA failed to approve several toxic shock treatments developed by Centocor and other NBFs, causing their market value to drop dramatically.

3. A distinction can and should be made between social networks as an *exchange governance mechanism* and *network structures* of exchanges that describe exchange patterns at the individual, organizational, industry or societal level. We use the phrases "social network" and "network" interchangeably to describe an *exchange governance mechanism*: A definition is given at the end of this subsection. Also note that we use the term "hierarchy" to describe governance of exchanges within a firm, following Coase (1937) and Williamson (1975), we do not use the term to describe the structure of the reporting system of the firm.

4. It is now common practice for universities to require faculty to sign contracts that award rights to all intellectual capital they generate in the course of their university duties to the university. Universities are also enforcing their property rights through the courts.

5. One paper on this topic is Kreiner and Schultz (1993) who discuss collaborative networks in biotechnology research in Denmark.

REFERENCES

Adler, P. (1989), "When Knowledge Is the Critical Resource, Knowledge Management Is the Critical Task," *IEEE Transactions on Engineering Management,* 36, 87-94.

Arora, A. and A. Gambardella (1990), "Complementary and External Linkages: The Strategies of Large Firms in Biotechnology," *Journal of Industrial Economics,* 38, 361-379.

Arrow, K. (1962), "Economic Welfare and the Allocation of Resources for Invention," in *The Rate and Direction of Inventive Activity,* National Bureau of Economic Research, Princeton University Press, Princeton, NJ.

Axelrod, R. (1984), *The Evolution of Cooperation,* Basic Books, New York.

Barley, S., J. Freeman, and R. Hybels (1992), "Strategic Alliances in Commercial Biotechnology," in *Networks and Organizations,* N. Nohria and R. Eccles (Eds.), Harvard University Press, Boston, MA.

Belshaw, C. S. (1965), *Traditional Exchange and Modern Markets,* Prentice-Hall, Englewood Cliffs, NJ.

Blau, P. (1973), *The Organization of Academic Work,* John Wiley, New York.

Bradach, J. and R. Eccles (1989), "Markets Versus Hierarchies: From Ideal Types to Plural Forms," in *Annual Review of Sociology,* W. R. Scott (Ed.), 15, 97-118.

Brusco, S. (1982), "The Emilian Model: Productive Decentralization and Social Integration," *Cambridge Journal of Economics,* 6, 167-184.

Camagni, R. (1989), "Cambiamento Technologico, 'Milieu' Locale e Rete di Imprese: Verso Una Teoria Dinamica dello Spazio Economico," *Economia e Politica Industriale*, 64, 209-236.

Coase, R. (1937), "The Nature of the Firm," *Economica*, 4, 386-405.

Cohen, W. and D. Levinthal (1990), "Absorptive Capacity: A New Perspective on Learning and Innovation," *Administrative Science Quarterly*, 35, 128-152.

Coser, L., C. Kadushin, and W. Powell (1982), *Books: The Culture and Commerce of Publishing*, Basic Books, New York.

Crane, D. (1972), *Invisible College: Diffusion of Knowledge in Scientific Communities*, University of Chicago Press, Chicago, IL.

Daft, R. and A. Lewin (1993), "Where Are the Theories for the 'New' Organizational Forms? An Editorial Essay," *Organization Science*, 4, i-vi.

D'Aveni, R. (1994), *Hypercompetition: The Dynamics of Strategic Maneuvering*, Basic Books, New York.

David, P. (1991), "Reputation and Agency in the Historical Emergence of the Institutions of Open Science," Paper presented to the Conference on the Economics of Conventions, Centre de Research en Epistemologie Applique, Ecole Polytechnique, Paris (this paper is available from the first author on request).

DeBresson, C. and F. Amesse (1991), "Networks of Innovators," *Research Policy*, 20, 363-379.

Deutschman, A. (1994), "The Managing Wisdom of High Tech Superstars," *Fortune*, October 17, 197-206.

Dore, R. (1983), "Goodwill and the Spirit of Market Capitalism," *British Journal of Sociology*, 34, 459-482.

Eccles, R. and D. Crane (1988), *Doing Deals: Investment Banks at Work*, Harvard Business School Press, Boston, MA.

Elster, J. (1989), "Social Norms and Economic Theory," *Journal of Economic Perspectives*, 3, 4, 99-117.

Evans-Pritchard, E. (1940), *The Nuer: A Description of the Modes of Livelihood and Political Institutions of the Nilotic People*, Clarendon Press, Oxford, England.

Geertz, C. (1978), "The Bazaar Economy: Information and Search in Peasant Marketing," *American Economic Review*, 68, 2, 28-32.

Ghemawat, P. (1991), *Commitment: The Dynamics of Strategy*, Free Press, New York.

Giamatti, B. (1982), "The University, Industry, and Cooperative Research," *Science*, 218 (December 24), 1278-1289.

Granovetter, M. (1985), "Economic Action and Social Structure: A Theory of Embeddedness," *American Journal of Sociology*, 91, 481-510.

Grant, R. M. (1996), "Prospering in Dynamically-competitive Environments: Organizational Capability as Knowledge Integration," *Organization Science*, 7, 4, 375-387.

Grossman, G. and C. Shapiro (1985), "Dynamics of R & D Competition," *Economic Journal*, 97, 372-387.

Henderson, R. and I. Cockburn (1994), "Measuring Core Competence? Evidence from the Pharmaceutical Industry," *Strategic Management Journal*, 15, 63-84.

Irvine, J. and B. Martin (1985), "Basic Research in the East and West: A Comparison of the Scientific Performance of High Energy Physics Accelerators," *Social Studies of Science*, 15, 293-341.

Kennedy, D. (1982), "The Social Sponsorship of Innovation," *Technology in Society*, 4, 4, 253-266.

Kenney, M. (1986), *Biotechnology: The University-Industrial Complex*, Yale University Press, New Haven, CT.

Klein, B. and K. Leffler (1982), "The Role of Market Forces in Assuring Contractual Perfor-mance," *Journal of Political Economy,* 89, 615-641.

Kogut, B., W. Shan, and G. Walker (1992), "The Make or Cooperate Decision in the Context of an Industry Network," in *Networks and Organizations,* N. Nohria and R. Eccles (Eds.), Harvard University Press, Boston, MA.

Kreiner, K. and M. Schultz (1993), "Informal Collaboration in R & D. The Formation of Net-works Across Organizations," *Organization Studies,* 14, 2, 189-209.

Kreps, D. (1990), "Corporate Culture and Economic Theory," in *Perspectives on Positive Political Economy,* J. Alt and K. Shepsle (Eds.), Cambridge University Press, Cambridge, England.

Levin, R., R. Klevorick, R. Nelson, and S. Winter (1987), "Appropriating the Returns from Individual Research and Development." *Brookings Papers on Economic Activity,* 3.

Lippman, S. and K. McCardle (1987), "Dropout Behavior in R & D Races with Learning," *Rand Journal of Economics,* 18, 287-295.

Martens, B. and T. Saretzki (1993), "Conferences and Courses on Biotechnology: Describing Scientific Communication by Exploratory Methods," *Scientometrics,* 27, 237-260.

Masten, S. (1988), "A Legal Basis for the Firm," *Journal of Law, Economics and Organization,* 4, 3-47.

Mauss, M. (1950), *The Gift,* W. W. Norton, New York.

Merton, R. (1973), *The Sociology of Science,* University of Chicago Press, Chicago, IL.

Nelkin, D. (1984), *Science as Intellectual Property: Who Controls Scientific Research?* Macmil-lan, New York.

Oliver, A. (1993), "New Biotechnology Firms: A Multilevel Analysis of Inter-Organizational Relations in an Emerging Industry," Unpublished Ph.D. dissertation, University of Cali-fornia, Los Angeles, CA.

Ouchi, W. G. (1980), "Markets, Bureaucracies and Clans," *Administrative Science Quarterly,* 28, 129-141.

Pisano, G. (1990), "The R & D Boundaries of the Firm: An Empirical Analysis," *Administrative Science Quarterly,* 35, 153-176.

Porter, M. (1980), *Competitive Strategy,* Free Press, New York.

Powell, W. (1990), "Neither Market nor Hierarchy: Network Forms of Organization," *Research in Organizational Behavior,* 12, 295-336.

―――― and P. Brantley (1992), "Competitive Cooperation in Biotechnology: Learning Through Networks?" in *Networks and Organizations,* N. Nohria and R. Eccles (Eds.), Harvard University Press, Boston, MA.

Reve, T. (1990), "The Firm as a Nexus of Internal and External Treaties," in *The Firm as a Nexus of Treaties,* M. Aoki, B. Gustafsson and O. Williamson (Eds.), Sage, Newbury Park, CA.

Ross, E. (1906), *Social Control,* Macmillan, New York.

Saxenian, A. (1994), *Regional Advantage,* Harvard University Press, Cambridge, MA.

Shan, W. (1990), "An Empirical Analysis of Organizational Strategies by Entrepreneurial High-Technology Firms," *Strategic Management Journal,* 11, 2, 129-140.

Singh, J., D. Tucker, and R. House (1986), "Organizational Legitimacy and the Liability of Newness," *Administrative Science Quarterly,* 31, 171-193.

Teece, D. (1989), "Concorrenza e Cooperazione Nelle Strategie di Sviluppo Technologico," *Economia e Politica Industriale,* 64, 17-46.

Thompson, J. (1967), *Organizations in Action,* McGraw-Hill, New York.

Volberda, H. W. (1996), "Toward the Flexible Form: How to Remain Vital in Hypercompetitive Environments," *Organization Science,* 7, 4, 359-374.

Von Hippel, E. (1982), "Appropriability of Innovation Benefit as a Predictor of the Source of Innovation," *Research Policy,* 11, 95-115.

Williamson, O. (1975), *Markets and Hierarchies,* Free Press, New York.

——— (1979), "Transaction Cost Economics: The Governance of Contractual Relations," *Journal of Law and Economics,* 22 (October), 3-61.

——— (1991), "Comparative Economic Organization: The Analysis of Discrete Structural Alternatives," *Administrative Science Quarterly,* 36, 269-296.

Zucker, L. (1986), "Production of Trust: Institutional Sources of Economic Structure 1840 to 1920," *Research in Organizational Behavior,* 8, 53-111.

——— (1991), "Markets for Bureaucratic Authority and Control: Information Quality in Professions and Services," *Research in the Sociology of Organizations,* 8, 157-190.

———, M. Brewer, M. Darby, and Y. Peng (forthcoming), "Collaboration Structure and Information Dilemmas in Biotechnology: Organizational Boundaries as Trust Production" in *Trust in Organizations,* R. Kramer and T. Tyler (Eds.), Sage, Thousand Oaks, CA.

———, M. Darby, and M. Brewer (1994), "Intellectual Capital and the Birth of U.S. Biotechnology Enterprises," Working Paper # 4653, National Bureau of Economic Research, Cambridge, MA.

16

Garbage Cans and Advancing Hypercompetition

The Creation and Exploitation of New Capabilities and Strategic Flexibility in Two Regional Bell Operating Companies

ANNE D. SMITH
CARL ZEITHAML

How does an organization functioning in a regulated, monopoly environment transform itself to prepare for hypercompetitive conditions? Two of the regional Bell operating companies (RBOCs) found one answer to that question: create self-contained areas of chaotic activities with the potential to spawn new managerial capabilities and flexibility.

After diverstiture from AT&T, the RBOCs maintained their local telephone service monopolies, but they all became involved in numerous unregulated activities, such as international expansion. For two of the seven RBOCs, the international activities led to new skills; learning and capabilities developed inside their stodgy bureaucracies. By the early 1990s, the RBOCs' local telephone service was facing dramatic change. Powerful potential entrants such as long-distance, wireless, and cable companies were surrounding and converging on the local telephone service industry through their new wireless licenses, collaborations crossing traditional industry borders, and new network development. The RBOCs saw clear signs of impending hypercompetitive conditions.

How the two RBOCs changed over an eight-year period and prepared for hypercompetition illustrates several aspects of Volberda's model of organizational transformation. The two RBOCs proceeded through two parallel trajectories of change, which after several years converged and necessitated reorganization. Only through a major organizational change were the two RBOCs able to redeploy the capabilities acquired from international activities into their regulated core business, thereby creating the flexibility they needed to prepare for advancing hypercompetition. With the imminent removal of regulatory barriers and legal roadblocks to competition in local telephone service in the United States, the RBOCs' flexibility and ability to manage hypercompetition may soon be tested.

(CAPABILITY DEVELOPMENT;
TELECOMMUNICATIONS SERVICE INDUSTRY;
INTERNATIONAL EXPANSION;
HYPERCOMPETITION)

The U.S. local telecommunications service industry has proceeded through two distinct periods: pre-divestiture and post-divestiture. In the pre-divestiture period, local telephone service was controlled by AT&T through its 22 Bell operating companies. For more than 100 years, AT&T's vertically integrated hierarchy provided end-to-end service through a rigid bureaucracy. This first period of local telecommunications service ended in 1982, when AT&T agreed to an out-of-court settlement, known as the modified final judgment (MFJ), with the Department of Justice. Pursuant to that agreement, AT&T divested its local telephone service (as well as yellow pages, directory assistance, and cellular rights), but gained the freedom to move into competitive markets such as computers.

The second era of local telecommunications service began on January 1, 1984, when seven new corporations were spun off from AT&T. They were known as Baby Bells, regional holding companies (RHCs), or, as the managers in those firms refer to them, regional bell operating companies (RBOCs). Each of the seven firms had its own assets, debt, and shareholders. In its exclusive territory, each RBOC would provide telephone service to business and residential customers, but because of the MFJ was not allowed to manufacture equipment, offer long distance service, or provide information services over its network. With their monopoly on local service, the RBOCs were subject to close scrutiny by the Department of Justice (specifically by Judge Harold Greene, who was overseeing the MFJ), the Federal Communications Commission (for cellular regulation and long-distance interconnection), and state regulatory bodies (for local rates). Severe restrictions defined their local service activity, but the RBOCs were allowed to pursue businesses unrelated to their core telephone service. All new lines of business, including international pursuits, had to be approved by Judge Greene. Because the new lines of business were in nonmonopolistic industries, the RBOCs struggled to develop new skills with which to compete.

We chronicle how two RBOCs created strategic flexibility in one unregulated area, international expansion, during the second era of local telecommunications service. Although the RBOCs were ill equipped for competition after divestiture, their top managers allowed areas of chaos or "garbage can" activities to develop in the unregulated side of their business. One of those areas was international expansion. All seven RBOCs became involved in international activities, but by early 1992 only two RBOCs had created new capabilities and strategic flexibility in that area. Those two firms maintained a pocket of capabilities in international activities that was separate from their overall local exchange service activities. However, by 1992, the growing threat of hypercompetitive conditions in the RBOCs' traditional local telephone service had become a catalyst for the organizationwide integration of capabilities acquired through international pursuits.

Hypercompetition is characterized by a series of short-term advantages, whereby competitors constantly and rapidly redefine the nature of competition (D'Aveni 1994). By the mid-1990s, industry experts agreed that such competition was inevitable and rapidly approaching (Kupfer 1994, Mason 1992a, Roetter 1993, 1994, Wilson 1994). "The local telephone business is going to be wide open to competition in the very near future" (Cauley et al. 1994, p. A3).

As seen in Figure 16.1, long-distance competitors, global satellite consortia, public utilities, bypass operators, wireless consortia, and cable companies are poised with new technology, ample resources, alliances, and/or segmentation strategies to enter the $90 billion local telephone service monopoly. The RBOCs will need to develop new capabilities and strategic flexibility to be responsive to approaching hypercompetitive conditions (Volberda 1996). Developing such strategic flexibility in an organization poses a paradox (Van de Ven and Poole 1988, Volberda 1996). On one side, an organization must create and easily deploy actual and potential managerial capabilities that enhance present and potential flexibility (Volberda 1996). On the other side, a firm must develop an appropriate, stable structure to utilize the new capabilities. Organizations need both stability and rapid-response capabilities (Itawi 1987), and reconciling that paradox is critical for firms such as the RBOCs that are preparing for fierce, unpredictable, and continuous assaults on their core business activity.

To compete in the third era of local telecommunications, an era of hypercompetition, the RBOCs' overall organization must become highly flexible. We examine two RBOCs and how the flexibility they created

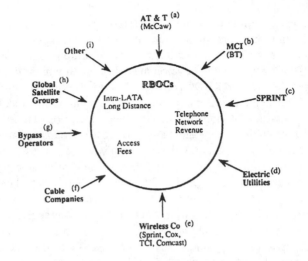

Figure 16.1. Entities Poised to Enter the Local Telephone Service Industry

NOTE: (a) AT&T is poised to reenter local telephone service through its acquisition of McCaw coupled with its winning bids for 21 personal communication licenses to fill out a national wireless network. AT&T, with deep pockets, has been fierce in lobbying to keep the RBOCs out of long distance. AT&T also has the know-how to service local subscribers and compete in hypercompetitive markets because of its decade-long battle in the U.S. long-distance industry. AT&T is allied with other large foreign telephone companies targeted on corporations in the RBOC's territories.

(b) MCI, the second largest U.S. long-distance company, is pushing the regulatory window to enter local telephone service through its MCI Metro service in many major U.S. cities. That service, fully implemented, would eliminate the access fees paid by MCI's long-distance operations to the RBOCs and would eliminate the RBOC's monthly telephone revenues from subscribers. MCI is offering telecommunications outsourcing services for businesses in the RBOCs' territories.

(c) Sprint, the third largest U.S. long distance company, purchased a major independent telephone company that has an extensive cellular network. The acquisition puts Sprint into local telephone service around the U.S. that could be applied in new territories, such as the RBOCs'. Sprint has extended its wireless network through its bidding with Wireless Co. for the new PCS wireless licenses (see item e). In 1995, Sprint obtained a significant equity infusion from France Telecom and Deutsche Telecom.

(d) Electric utilities have already laid and stubbed-in fiber optic cable in their rights-of-way under many major and medium-sized U.S. cities. They await regulatory change to become a new competitor for business customers in the RBOC territories.

(e) Wireless Co. is an alliance of Sprint and three large cable operators (Cox, Comcast, TCI). In 1995, this consortium was the largest winner of PCS licenses; it won 29 licenses across the U.S. at a cost of $2.1 billion. The PCSs operate in micro-cells and require small, lightweight handsets. The technology is lower cost than traditional cellular and wireline service and is targeted for mass utilization to potentially replace the local wired telephone, serviced by the RBOCs. These PCS systems, coupled with existing cellular licenses, could erode the RBOCs' customer base and its monthly subscriber revenues.

(f) Cable companies (e.g., Cox, Prime, Comcast, TCI, and Jones) have wired the majority of U.S. households. They have the content and bandwidth to offer television, cable, and multimedia to households. For example, Time-Warner's cable operations are offering telephone service in New York City. Many U.S. cable companies are gaining experience in offering both telephone and cable service in the United Kingdom. Most cable companies are involved in alliances or partnerships outside the cable industry.

(g) Bypass operations, such as MFS and Teleport, have already gained 1.5% of total local telephone service revenues by taking away business subscribers. These companies are developing alliances with long-distance carriers and cable companies to penetrate further into the RBOC's business customers with their highly efficient fiber optic network.

(h) Many global satellite consortia, such as Iridium, Inmarsat, Globalstar, Odyssey, ECCO, and Aces, are building satellite networks that are focused on global businesses that could be RBOC customers.

(i) Other possible entrants into the RBOCs' local telephone service include other long distance companies, other cellular players, independent telephone companies (GTE), and other companies that are PCS license winners.

through international pursuits began to be integrated throughout their organizations. A radical change in their overall organizational structure took place to incorporate new capabilities and strategic flexibility in the face of advancing hypercompetitive conditions. The purpose of our chapter is twofold: (1) to examine how capability in one unregulated activity was created during the second era of U.S. telecommunications and (2) to report how that capability was exploited to prepare the overall RBOC organization for an era of hypercompetitive telecommunications competition.

Methodologically, the two RBOCs present a unique, natural field experiment in that they were created at the same time from the same culture and are similar in size. We used a case study method to examine their international activities (see Appendix). Both companies initially had no international experience and both developed an articulated strategy. We conducted openended, structured interviews with international managers to explore the companies' international expansion from 1984 through the beginning of 1992. Complete details of every international activity were compiled before RBOC visits, and a detailed timeline of international transactions was used during each interview. The RBOC executives requested and were granted anonymity. We chose a pseudonym reflecting a key concept related to each RBOC's international activities to avoid linking specific comments with any one RBOC. The two pseudonyms are Rings and Layers.

CREATING CAPABILITIES FROM INTERNATIONAL GARBAGE CANS

After divestiture, all seven RBOCs became involved in many unregulated activities. Some were successful and others, such as real estate ventures and computer service/leasing, were not. Still others, such as international expansion, were neither outright failures nor successes. Judge Greene's laissez faire approach allowed the RBOCs wide discretion in their international activities (Gilroy 1990). International expansion was initially chaotic and without direction but, with guidance by their top managers, Rings and Layers eventually developed important new managerial capabilities and areas of flexibility.

International Garbage Cans

Initially, international expansion was chaotic, nonlinear, and fragmented. Rings and Layers were opportunistic and experimental in their international activities, as seen in the diverse products/services and markets they pursued. International involvement often resulted from an acquisition, an international partner, or simply the efforts of an aggressive RBOC marketing representative. Top RBOC executives allocated few financial and managerial resources to the exploration of international markets. Only short-term, small projects were pursued that would pose no risk to the RBOC's financial health. Top managers tolerated such dabbling around the world because, as one RBOC international manager explained, "Our top managers were concentrating on getting us through divestiture . . . learning how to run a ten billion dollar public corporation from a standing start." The wide variety of small international projects did not suggest any clear purpose or consistent strategy. According to a Rings manager, "We acted like a body without a brain, actions without a plan, motions without strategic thinking." This phase was marked by trial-and-error learning through the entry mode, product/service, and geographic decisions made by international managers at Rings and Layers.

As indicated in the first two columns in Table 16.1, most entry modes were short-term and represented relatively small commitments to international projects. After divestiture, Layers set up numerous offices and subsidiaries around the world to enhance its exposure to opportunities developing in overseas markets. Those subsidiaries and international management efforts led to numerous short-term contracts, many of which were projects for the World Bank and lasted less than a year. The projects did not provide large consulting fees; as one Layers manager claimed, "These contracts hardly paid the light bills for our subsidiary." The minority ownership activities were small joint ventures related to such diverse activities as voice mail, intelligent buildings, and paging. Strategic agreements were formal documents signed by the RBOC and a telephone provider in another country; such agreements did not give Rings and Layers much involvement with the non-U.S. telephone companies. Rings was involved in several acquisitions of U.S. firms that had international subsidiaries. The acquisitions were not pursued for their international activities, and they were managed independently of the international development area.

Rings and Layers pursued a wide variety of products and services internationally with the scant resources made available by top managers. One Rings executive, characterizing its early international expansion, stated, "We could have been doing Pizza Huts in Pakistan." As indicated in the first two columns in Table 16.2, the two RBOCs were involved in many projects related to their core business, such as telephone consulting and systems upgrades. Activities that the RBOCs were given from AT&T at divestiture, such as directories and paging, were explored internationally during this period. The two firms also became involved in even more diverse activities, such as computer leasing and finance, computer applications software, credit card verification systems, and construction of an R & D center for a European

TABLE 16.1 Entry Modes

	Phase 1: Garbage Cans		Phase 2: Strategic Focusing	
	Rings	Layers	Rings	Layers
Strategic agreements	1	2	0	0
Short-term contracts, less than a year	9	4	1	0
Minority ownership of international license/ venture (< $50MM)	3	7	0	10 (mostly catv)
Majority ownership of international license/ venture (< $50MM)	0	0	1	0
Acquisition of nondomestic firm or U.S. firm with significant international holdings	4	1	2	1
One of many partners in major consortium project (> $50MM)	1	0	5	4
Total	18	14	9	15

NOTE: The counts indicate the number of actual activities by the two RBOCs during the two phases.

TABLE 16.2 Product/Service Diversity

	Phase 1: Garbage Cans		Phase 2: Strategic Focusing	
	Rings	Layers	Rings	Layers
Telephone systems upgrades and installations	5	1	1	0
Telephone consulting	4	6	0	0
Privatizations	0	0	1	0
Large telephone system upgrades	0	0	0	1
Directory publishing and advertising	0	1	0	0
Equipment distribution	2	0	0	0
Cellular	2	0	6	5
Other wireless ventures	1	1	1	1
Value-added services (e.g., voice mail)	1	5	0	0
Cable television	1	0	0	8
Leasing and finance	2	0	0	0
Total	18	14	9	15

NOTE: The counts indicate the number of actual activities by the two RBOCs during the two phases.

telephone company. One Layers executive explained the lack of focus in international products and services by saying. "The benefit of this phase was that we were experimenting and learning what we were good at and what we were bad at offering internationally . . . as well as domestically during this time."

TABLE 16.3 Geographic Diversity (all numbers in %)

| | Phase 1: Garbage Can | |
	Rings	Layers
U.K. and Western Europe	50	30
Eastern Europe and Russia	0	0
South America	6	0
Mexico, Central America	7	0
New Zealand and Australia	6	0
Canada	0	0
Japan	0	15
China	12	15
Other Asia	7	26
Middle East, India, Other NEC	12	14
	100%	100%

NOTE: Counts of Phase 1 international transactions are indicated as percentages for each geographic category.

During the early international exploration, the activities of Rings and Layers were geographically dispersed. According to a Rings international manager, "We were scatterpoints on a map . . . just popcorned around the world to whatever area was hot and trendy . . . we would go anywhere." As indicated in Table 16.3, 50% or more of their activity was outside Western Europe and the United Kingdom, which are markets considered traditionally to be similar culturally and economically to the United States. Rings and Layers pursued projects in such diverse countries as China, India, Japan, Thailand, South Korea, Kuwait, Guatemala, and Mexico.

Both companies continued their opportunistic, unfocused, and chaotic international expansion for several years. Those early international activities typify several aspects of a garbage can decision-making process (Cohen, March, and Olsen 1972). One aspect of garbage can processes seen in the RBOCs' early expansion is a lack of clear goals and preferences for international activities. One reason for the lack of goals and the resulting opportunistic dabbling was that RBOC top executives had almost no international experience. Those executives had spent their careers in insular, domestic AT&T, and many of them did not even have a passport at the time of divestiture. They were therefore unable to provide guidelines for international pursuits. However, they did not allow a small amount of resources to be allocated, either because the other RBOCs were expanding internationally or because of a vague feeling that international activities eventually may be important.

A second aspect of garbage can processes seen in the early international expansion of Rings and Layers is a lack of understanding about how to achieve successful international outcomes. After divestiture, a group of ambitious managers in Rings and Layers (referred to as "marketing mavericks" or "corporate renegades") were attracted to the international business development area. Like the RBOC top executives, these international managers had no international market knowledge, but they were enthusiastic and willing to learn about international activities. Because of their lack of knowledge, the RBOC managers affiliated themselves internationally with well-connected individuals (called "gypsies" or "bandits") who were knowledgeable about local markets. Few, if any, managers in the international area had combined product and market knowledge.

A third aspect of garbage can processes was the fluid participation of a variety of entities in the RBOCs' international expansion. While the international managers were searching for opportunities in a country or region, many "gypsies" and "bandits" would contact them. For a fee, those country experts would describe the market conditions and introduce the RBOC managers to local corporate executives. The international managers moved in and out of relationships with the local contacts. Once the international managers worked out an international project, they had to bring in managers and technicians from other areas of the RBOC to execute the project. Thus, the inside and outside people associated with the RBOCs' international decisions and activities were constantly changing.

Over time, the chaotic garbage can activities caused tension in Rings and Layers. As international managers began to develop confidence and to learn about larger international opportunities, they pushed their top managers for more resources. However, because of their domestic focus and persistent lack of international knowledge, the top managers at Rings and Layers still were leery of large international investments and did not allocate larger amounts of resources for international pursuits.

The tension was resolved by a change in the CEO or the CEO's mindset. In Layers, a new CEO was promoted who was not convinced that international activities should be continued. The new CEO shut down international subsidiaries and suspended development of new international activities for a year. After he developed an understanding of international opportunities, the new CEO became convinced of his RBOC's long-term international growth potential. Rings did not have a change in CEO, but commitment to international pursuits was facilitated by a change in the CEO's mindset. The CEO became convinced that international opportunities could bridge the impending gap between its local exchange growth of about 3% and its shareholder growth expectations of 6%. The CEO brought in consultants who advised his top management team of the importance of aggressively pursuing markets outside the United States for long-term growth opportunities.

Bounded, Focused International Activities

Despite their visible commitments to international efforts, the CEOs of Rings and Layers did not give international managers carte blanche in their pursuits. Rather, the CEOs and several top executives were closely involved in subsequent international decision making. While those top executives were still learning about international markets and opportunities, they were instrumental in making large, long-term international commitments to certain product/service offerings and geographic locations.

Rings and Layers bid on projects that were much larger and longer term than their previous garbage can activities. As seen in the last two columns of Table 16.1, the size of the international projects increased, the majority being over $50 million; most projects reflected commitments of more than 10 years. Eight of the 10 minority ownerships of international ventures, seen in Layers' second phase, were U.K. cable television licenses that it won. Those licenses, collectively, were similar to two large projects because they were won with similar sets of partners and constituted much more than $50 million.

Partner selection was mentioned by international managers as a critical factor in winning licenses. A Rings executive stated, "Many times, you strive to pick the 'right local partner' that is looked upon favorably by the government." International managers in both companies mentioned the need to get over the "control thing" in international relationships. A Layers executive asserted, "We need partners who are experienced, who add value, and who know what they are doing . . . selection of local partners was critical." Clearly, the large, long-term projects hinged on strong partnering relationships.

The product/service and geographic diversity was more focused than it had been in the earlier international activities of Rings and Layers. The top managers' preferences were reflected in international product/service choices. Layers was comfortable investing in U.K. cable, whereas Rings did not bid on U.K. cable television licenses. Rings managers also indicated that they were not interested in privatizations because they were, in the words of one Rings executive, "one-trick ponies. . . . We would have to fight the same battle in Mexico or Argentina or Venezuela that we are going to have to fight on our own territory in the coming years." As indicated in the two right columns in Table 16.2, Rings and Layers concentrated on wireless ventures. The total counts in Table 16.2 reflect only international projects that were won; many bids, which required substantial managerial resources and a year of bid preparation, were lost. Each RBOC developed a distinct geographic orientation, again reflecting top executives' preferences. Rings concentrated primarily on Europe and Latin America whereas Layers concentrated on Asia and Europe.

This phase of international expansion involved a more focused, intendedly rational approach to making large bids, especially in comparison with the first phase of garbage can activities. The international expansion of Rings and Layers reflected many aspects of a boundedly rational process (Cyert and March 1963). First, neither Rings nor Layers had an articulated strategy after the CEO's commitment to large, long-term international investments. Top managers' general preferences or guidelines for certain services or geographic areas narrowed the range of international activities, but many of the large projects were awarded through an auction process and executing a specific strategy was difficult with intense competition for a license. Second, each bid was assessed independently from other international projects. Working on several large bids simultaneously, international managers learned to satisfice. International projects were not scrutinized in relation to a specific strategy, but a decision to bid and the price offered were determined independently and on the project's own merit. Third, bidding on large international projects was not a straightforward process. A limited, localized search for information characterized many of the bids, and the process was described by one RBOC manager as "a circuitous route to a final bid." A project could change many times from the point of initial announcement, through the technical bid stage, to the final bid, and to the final selection. One government, for example, initially offered a digital cellular license, but six months later added an international satellite and a nationwide domestic bypass operation as part of the final project offering. "We had to be flexible," said one Rings manager.

After a large bid was won that put Rings and Layers, individually, over $1 billion in long-term commitments to international markets, tension grew in the firms; top executives wanted to know if their "critical mass" of international commitments had strategic value and would be a future growth engine for the firms. By the end of 1991, the top managers had stopped all bidding in order to rationalize their international commitments. The two RBOCs did not plan and articulate a strategy at the outset of their inter-national deal making; rather, international strategy and managerial capabilities at Rings and Layers emerged from their winning bids and resulting international positions.

New Managerial Capabilities

New managerial capabilities in Rings and Layers evolved from initial chaos, subsequent focusing, and eventual strategic identification. The capabilities acquired through the development of new markets created a pocket of strategic flexibility within the overall RBOC organization.

First, in the words of one Rings manager, "We became good at winning bids." Rings and Layers had both become skilled at forming winning consortia to bid on new projects. They had learned how to price a large deal and to select partners that would increase their chances of winning it. Rings and Layers had developed a cadre of managers, referred to as "adult children of AT&T" by one manager, who had strong domestic product knowledge, excellent international market knowledge, and strong deal-making skills.

Second, the international managers had learned how to manage partnerships in large, long-term projects and to execute ventures around the world, working shoulder-to-shoulder with both large non-U.S. telephone companies and local partners.

Third, some of the international projects enabled Rings and Layers to acquire experience in telecommunication activities from which they were barred in the United States. One of these RBOCs, for instance, had created a competing national long-distance service in a foreign country, while domestically, under the MFJ, it was not allowed to compete in long-distance activity.

Fourth, operational managers and personnel in Rings and Layers had learned to build and start up advanced wireless systems quickly throughout the world. Those systems required "on the fly" modifications to procedures used in the United States. Some of the systems had more advanced technology or different standards than those in the United States, but the team learned how to implement them. In one Rings project, international managers, in consultation with domestic managers, purposely chose a digital switch that they did not have in their network at home to experience the switch "off line" from their domestic network.

Several other important managerial capabilities developed from the two RBOCs' international activities. The Rings and Layers international managers learned to share learning across similar international ventures, "to create synergy," in the words of one Rings manager. They learned how to add content to their existing international networks and thus generate more revenue with current investments. The Rings and Layers pseudonyms reflect managers' comments about how they were now trying to "ring" and "layer" current investments with new products and services.

Many Rings and Layers international managers gained significant experience building and running an operation with a skeleton support staff because for most international projects "it was very expensive to send a full staff of ex-pats," according to one Rings manager. Hence, international managers and operational personnel developed the ability to work without the large, bureaucratic support staff that is typical in their U.S. operations.

By the end of 1992, many of Rings' and Layers' international operations were not only described as "cash positive," but were also perceived as a long-term growth engine for the two firms. Despite their success, international operations were still a very small portion (less than 5%) of these firms' total revenues in 1992. Most revenues were derived from domestic local telephone service, which in the mid-1990s was facing the onset of hypercompetitive conditions.

New capabilities developed from international activities were redeployed or, in the words of one Layers manager, "backward integrated" into the domestic operations. International managers held the potential for RBOC flexibility because they had learned to adjust to varying competitive conditions, country conditions, partners, equipment, technologies, and time frames. Because knowledge and learning are imbedded in individuals (Grant 1996, Itawi 1987), new international capabilities were transferred by moving international managers back into domestic operations. As early as 1992, managers and their capabilities were being redeployed to help create overall flexibility in Rings' and Layers' domestic local telephone activities.

EXPLOITING CAPABILITIES TO PREPARE FOR LOCAL SERVICE HYPERCOMPETITION

In 1992, Rings and Layers undertook drastic restructuring and organizational redesign, after which their international capabilities began to be utilized in a larger context throughout their organizations. Those actions seem to have been motivated by top managers' recognition of the growing "split brain personality . . . based on the range of conflicting needs and responsibilities" in their organizations (Mason 1992b, p. 12). An organizational redesign reconciled the growing tension between the RBOCs' regulated and unregulated activities. In the new structure, managerial capabilities acquired through international activities were redeployed to prepare for domestic hypercompetition. The redesign was dramatic in both RBOCs, but Rings' and Layers' new organizations were not the same and they redeployed their international capabilities very differently. Therefore, Rings and Layers are not specifically named in the next two sections because it would be very easy to identify them.

Integrating the Regulated
and Unregulated Activities

One RBOC committed itself to erasing the line between regulated and unregulated activities, which represented a fundamental change in the way the RBOC had been run. The CEO tried to change the conservative culture under which the regulated side of the RBOC had operated for many years, and to do so tried to integrate the learning, experiences, and capabilities of managers of unregulated activities into the regulated operations. Training programs, for instance, were in place for many levels of employees in the domestic telephone business to make them aware of the impending changes in the industry. The transfer of new capabilities from international to domestic operations took place primarily through the transfer of international project and operational managers. The utilization of new capabilities from international operations was achieved through a coordinated effort among top marketing and operations managers on the regulated side, corporate human resource managers, and international managers. The cross-fertilization took place at both the operational and strategic levels. Operational managers involved in international turn-key operations and business startups and project managers responsible for the overall implementation of an international project and who managed the operational managers were strategically placed in important positions on the regulated side upon their return to the United States.

Returning operational managers were valued and desired by managers on the regulated side. For instance, this RBOC sent back over 50 operational managers to start an alternate network against an entrenched national telephone company. Several months before their return, their resumes were circulated around critical regulated wireline functions, and top executives reinforced the need to bring the managers back into significant positions in the wireline operations. When the operational managers started to return from this assignment, they were "literally fought over," according to one RBOC international manager, because their understanding of how bypass operators thought and acted would help managers on the regulated side compete better in the domestic territory. According to another international manager, "International, enterpreneurial experience was valued, and it began to change the culture as employees who had taken individual career risks [going abroad] were rewarded."

Another example of the transfer of knowledge and capabilities from international operations to domestic network operations was the placement of international project managers. One international manager, who had been involved in bidding on the bypass project and improving the operations of international properties, was promoted to head one RBOC domestic market segment. In that new position, the manager was responsible for developing strategy and marketing plans to prepare for competition in a particular market segment.

According to a former international project director, the cross-fertilization was helpful in "awakening our wireline operations to the realities of coming competition and need for employees to be flexible, strategic thinkers." In reference to the personal communication system (PCS) auctions, one manager mentioned the potential for using managers involved in international deal making for selecting potential partners, determining the price, and bidding in the auctions. This RBOC utilized its new managerial capabilities by transferring operational and strategic managers from its international activities into the traditional wireline side of the business, thus increasing the adaptability of its domestic wireline operations in the face of advancing hypercompetitive conditions.

Splitting the Company Apart

In 1992, the other RBOC undertook a study to assess the consequences of splitting into two distinct, publicly held companies. It was thought that one company could be the regulated domestic wireline telephone company, and the other a new company that would focus on wireless activities both in the United States and worldwide. At the end of 1993, this RBOC did split into two companies to reconcile the "split brain" personality between the regulated and unregulated sides (Mason 1992b). The RBOC's CEO stated, "To be successful, we must fundamentally rethink the way we do things," and he believed that a regulated and an unregulated company would have better chances of developing flexibility by refocusing their separate activities rather than by meshing them together.

In the new company, all international activities unrelated to wireless activities (e.g., a U.K. cable operation) were shed. Capabilities developed through the international activities were rationally, specifically, and directly applied to the wireless activities. Experience in building and operating a digital system based on the GSM standard outside the United States was

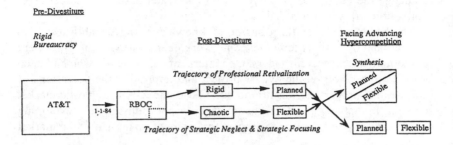

Figure 16.2. Overall Transformation of Rings and Layers

transferred from the international to the domestic operations. International deal-making skills were applied in bidding for new international licenses and, with the hope of being unshackled from MFJ restrictions, the new company began to penetrate the RBOC's base of traditional domestic local exchange customers with wireless or long-distance services, using the deep knowledge and proven managerial capabilities it had acquired by working with wireless technology around the world.

The existing regulated wireline company was free to bid on PCS licenses anywhere in the United States, whereas the new wireless company was more constrained in its bidding. Splitting the RBOC enabled the two companies to become direct competitors, in essence cannibalizing each other's service. In this RBOC, international capabilities were transferred to the new wireless company to increase flexibility in response to threats from new domestic wireless competitors. A fundamental organizational change enabled the RBOC to backward integrate its international capabilities rationally into the domestic wireless area and to free the wireline company to bid on new wireless systems in the face of advancing hypercompetitive conditions.

DISCUSSION AND
THEORETICAL IMPLICATIONS

The approaches taken by the two RBOCs illustrate how the flexibility paradox can be reconciled over time in an organization (Van de Ven and Poole 1988; Volberda, Chapter 11, this volume). Figure 16.2 is a model of the dual trajectories of organizational transformation that builds on Volberda's framework. It represents how new knowledge and capabilities were created from an isolated garbage can, thus illustrating some of Grant's propositions.

Pre-Divestiture: Rigid Form

Before 1984, local telephone service activities were protected within the bureaucracy and natural monopoly status of AT&T. AT&T has been characterized as inflexible, centralized, and conservative, elements of Volberda's rigid organizational form (Volberda, Chapter 11, this volume). For instance, AT&T required, "a centralized staff . . . to insure physical and managerial connections" (Feldman 1986, p. 43). Before 1984, the local telephone companies (the 22 Bell operating companies that later became grouped together and known as the RBOCs) were focused on "internal processes of the organization as opposed to market processes" (Feldman 1986, p. 57).

After divestiture, the RBOCs' activities were clearly divided between delivery of domestic local telephone service and unregulated ventures in competitive industries. Those two distinct areas in Rings and Layers changed along different paths, following two different trajectories from Volberda's framework: (1) *professional revitalization* of core telephone activities and (2) *strategic neglect and subsequent focusing* of early garbage can international activities.

Post-Divestiture: Professional Revitalization Trajectory

The traditional wireline activities could be characterized initially as rigid because they still operated in highly regulated environments, had received a windfall local rate increase in 1984, and held a monopoly on local service.

Over time, the rigidity in their core business activities gave way to a more planned organizational form (Volberda 1996). Several years after divestiture, top managers in the two RBOCs worked to reduce the strict regulations on their local service, especially because of competition for business subscribers from bypass companies. Rings and Layers were extremely active in lobbying and judicial efforts to rescind MFJ restrictions on domestic lines of business and to reduce domestic regulation. They also worked with state regulators to change the traditional rate-of-return regulation, helping to develop incentive-based local rate regulation that resulted in greater flexibility in pricing services in the wireline area of their business. With more than 88% of their state utility commissions adopting some form of incentive rate-making in 1991, Rings and Layers were far ahead of the other RBOCs in establishing incentive-based rate-making. Such initiatives reflect movement in the early 1990s from extreme rigidity toward a more planned organizational form in the regulated side of these RBOCs' business.

Post-Divestiture: Garbage Cans
and Strategic Focusing Trajectory

While RBOC managers were trying to understand their new regulatory environment, they essentially neglected many of their more speculative unregulated activities, such as international expansion. This neglect reflected their top managers' (and Judge Greene's) laissez faire approach to their international expansion. Lack of supervision allowed chaotic "global trotting." After a point, however, top managers in the two RBOCs had to make hard decisions about whether to maintain, terminate, or grow their diverse unregulated activities. Some RBOC unregulated activities, such as real estate, applications software, and computer maintenance, were severely curtailed or terminated. However, Rings and Layers judged international activities to be valuable for long-term RBOC growth and, with some focusing, top managers allocated more managerial and financial resources to that area. The top management intervention and focusing enabled international managers to create new specialized knowledge, such as how to bid in a competitive auction process, how to partner with nondomestic firms, how to build new businesses with minimal staff, and how to deliver new services outside the United States. Strategic flexibility subsequently developed through integration of that knowledge.

Preparing for Hypercompetition:
Reconciling the "Split Brain" Paradox

Within Rings and Layers, the flexibility in international activities contrasted with the more planned nature of the rest of the RBOC activities. The two trajectories had to be reconciled through an organizational redesign to redeploy the international strategic flexibility. Such reorganization reinforces Grant's second proposition that the architecture of capabilities and the overall organizational structure must correspond if a company is to use international knowledge and prepare for hypercompetition (Grant 1996). Despite the different organizational changes in Rings and Layers, international activities became legitimized within the companies which facilitated knowledge integration in other parts of the organization. International managers were promoted to new positions in the domestic side of the business to bring in their new perspectives and knowledge. The capability integration relied on what Grant (1996) calls the "routine mechanism." International managers' tacit knowledge was communicated by transferring key managers into new areas facing changing circumstances. Such a beneficial consequence of garbage can processes in an organization's transformation is ironic, especially when the relevancy and usefulness of garbage can approaches have been questioned recently (Eisenhardt and Zbaracki 1992).

LIMITATIONS AND
MANAGERIAL IMPLICATIONS

Given the limited cases and the uniqueness of the RBOCs' divestiture and industry, under what conditions should executives intentionally create areas of chaos as part of an overall organizational transformation process? Organizations that have gone through a discontinuous organizational change should consider the development of dual trajectories. For instance, a firm that breaks into two pieces (as ICI did in 1992 and Marriott considered doing in 1993) or a part of a firm that is divested (like several food units of Borden in 1994) may find the creation of a few garbage can activities to be a long-term growth hedge; those activities could be reviewed once the core business is under control and functioning. Many organizations are preparing for privatization, such as many of the European national telephone companies, and the dual-trajectory model may have value for executives faced with operating and growing firms that have new, demanding shareholders.

Companies facing dramatic external changes, such as the introduction of competition in a nearly monopolistic industry, may find value in creating garbage cans. The creation of chaos could lead to new capabilities that could be deployed to cope with increasing competition. The dual-trajectory model of organizational transformation may be of value to companies such as electric utilities that are facing dramatically changing industry conditions. A firm that is emerging from affiliation with a larger corporate entity, government ownership, or monopoly status could find a dual trajectory, replete with garbage cans, to be valuable for the development of new capabilities to fuel long-term growth.

If a dual transformation path is pursued, top managers should allocate enough time, managers, and money to see the changes through. Such transformation requires the presence of inside "corporate renegades" and entrepreneurial managers who are attracted to an unstructured, noncore area. Those managers should be given enough time and money to learn about a new area, but the activities should not distract top executives or jeopardize the overall financial health of the firm. Top managers must be able to tolerate the presence of a garbage can of chaos so that learning takes place. They should recognize that tension between themselves and the operational managers, who are demanding more sources for their chaotic pursuits, is an inevitable and expected part of the development of new capabilities. Discernment by top managers will be needed to determine when to stop and "tip" the garbage cans to see which activities should continue, stop, or be given additional resources. The need to integrate the learning and capabilities gained through the initially chaotic activities will be intensified by deteriorating industry conditions that require new capabilities and growth.

Overall, pockets of new capabilities and strategic flexibility can be created from initially chaotic conditions and with subsequent top management focusing. Those new capabilities highlight the paradox of transformation, as seen through the RBOCs' dual trajectories and reconciliation of their "split brain" personality. An isolated area of flexibility can be exploited to increase the overall flexibility of the organization in the face of discontinuous change and impending hypercompetitive conditions. Much more empirical research is needed on how capabilities are created and how organizations should be transformed to cope with hypercompetition.

ACKNOWLEDGMENTS

The authors thank Henk Volberda, Robert Grant, Julia Porter Liebeskind, James Richardson, and Jon Hanssen-Bauer for their helpful comments on previous versions of this chapter.

Appendix

Research Method

A case study methodology (Yin 1989) was selected to examine the international activities of the RBOCs. Case study research is empirical inquiry investigating a contemporary phenomenon within its real-life context. The focus is on the dynamics present within a small number of cases. A case study method was appropriate for the research because it addresses recent calls for more holistic or longitudinal approaches to research on international expansion (Melin 1992). It was consistent with the guidelines developed by Yin (1989) and with the methods used in previous organizational research (Eisenhardt and Bourgeois 1988).

Data Collection

Data were collected from both qualitative and quantitative sources, including trade journals, the general business press, market research reports, Federal Communications Commission documents, company records, and field interviews with investment bankers and industry experts. The most important data sources, however, were extensive field interviews conducted with senior RBOC executives, as well as detailed survey instruments they completed. The data collection process consisted of three phases.

The first phase was designed to develop a significant understanding of the RBOC context. Over several months, a variety of industry experts and consultants were interviewed. All domestic and international issues facing the RBOCs were identified. That process eventually yielded a field interview protocol.

In the second phase, the field interivew protocol guided semistructured interviews with senior RBOC international executives. The executives were very candid, cooperative, and remarkably critical of their firm's international experiences. In addition to a wide variety of open- and closed-ended items relevant to the research questions, a timeline that charted the history of the firm's international activities was provided. The timelines were an overwhelming success, as they demonstrated researcher expertise on key international issues and events and allowed the interview to proceed with a very substantive and collegial tone.

The third phase consisted of gathering detailed information about each RBOC's international history and important influences on their international expansion. A survey was sent to a key informant, and archival data were collected. The survey was designed to confirm every international transaction in which the RBOC was involved, identify every international deal on which the RBOC bid without winning, determine the structure and personnel of international divisions, and update any current and future international issues confronting the RBOC. Secondary data were collected from a vast array of government and company documents.

Data Analysis

The data collection and data analysis components of the case study method are not discrete, separate, sequential activities. Rather, the researcher iterates toward clarity over time (Eisenhardt 1989, Yin 1989). Preliminary relationships identified during each RBOC field visit were compared with an emerging model of international expansion. The formal data analysis consisted of three phases.

The first phase involved a full review of each RBOC and its international expansion experience. Qualitative information on each RBOC was organized by using Miles and Huberman's (1984) table shells. The grids were organized to reflect the dimensions of international expansion. Diagrams of each firm's international growth pattern and capability development were generated. The second phase of the data analysis compared the RBOCs' international expansion experiences. Several cross-case comparison techniques were used (Eisenhardt and Bourgeois 1988). Finally, the quantitative data were reviewed in relation to the emerging model derived from qualitative information. They were used to supplement and provide objective measures of relationships found in the qualitative analyses.

REFERENCES

Cauley, L., J. J. Keller, and D. Kneale (1994), "Battle Lines Harden as Baby Bells Fight to Kill Restrictions," *Wall Street Journal* (July 15), A1, A3.

Cohen, M. D., J. G. March, and J. P. Olsen (1972), "A Garbage Can Model of Organizational Choice," *Administrative Science Quarterly,* 17, 1-25.

Cyert, R. M. and J. G. March (1963), *A Behavioral Theory of the Firm,* Englewood Cliffs, NJ: Prentice Hall.

D'Aveni, R. (1994), *Hypercompetition: Managing the Dynamics of Strategic Manoeuvering,* New York: Free Press.

Eisenhardt, K. M. (1989), "Building Theories from Case Study Research," *Academy of Management Review,* 14, 4, 532-550.

——— and L. J. Bourgeois (1988), "Politics of Strategic Decision Making in High-Velocity Environments: Toward a Midrange Theory," *Academy of Management Journal,* 31, 4, 737-770.

——— and M. J. Zbaracki (1992), "Strategic Decision Making," *Strategic Management Journal,* 13, 17-38.

Feldman, S. P. (1986), *The Culture of Monopoly Management: An Interpretive Study in an American Utility,* New York: Garland.

Gilroy, A. A. (1990), "Information Services: What Role for Bell Operating Companies?" *Congressional Research Service Report for Congress* (July 13), Report No. 90-348E.

Grant, R. (1996), "Prospering in Dynamically Competitive Environments: Organizational Capability as Knowledge Integration," *Organization Science,* 7, 4, 376-387.

Itawi, H. (1987), *Mobilizing Invisible Assets,* Cambridge, MA: Harvard University Press.

Kupfer, A. (1994), "The Future of the Phone Companies," *Fortune,* (October 3), 95-106.

Mason, C. F. (1992a), "RHCs Face Long, Tough Transition to World of Competition," *Telephony* (July 7), 7, 16.

——— (1992b), "Study Calls for Divestiture II," *Telephony* (August 3), 12.

Melin, L. (1992), "Internationalization as Strategy Process," *Strategic Management Journal,* 13, 99-118.

Miles, M. B. and A. M. Huberman (1984), *Qualitative Data Analysis: A Sourcebook of New Methods,* Beverly Hills, CA: Sage.

Roetter, M. R. (1993), "Will Past LEC Giants Become Information Age Dinosaurs?" *Telephony* (July 19), 21-25.

——— (1994), "The Genie in the Bottleneck: Competition in Local Telephone Service," *Telephony* (October 3), 32-36.

Van de Ven, A. and M. S. Poole (1988), "Paradoxical Requirements for a Theory and Organizational Change," in *Paradox and Transformation: Toward a Theory of Organization and Management,* R. Quinn and K. Cameron, eds., Cambridge, MA: Ballinger, 19-63.

Volberda, H. W. (1996), "Toward the Flexible Form: How to Remain Vital in Hypercompetitive Environments," *Organization Science,* 7, 4, 359-374.

Wilson, C. (1994), "Telephony's Competitive Landscape," *Telephony,* May 3, 74-114.

Yin, R. K. (1989), *Case Study Research: Design and Methods,* Newbury Park, CA: Sage.

17

The Evolution of Intracorporate Domains

Divisional Charter Losses in High-Technology, Multidivisional Corporations

D. CHARLES GALUNIC
KATHLEEN M. EISENHARDT

Modern corporations have become synonymous with the multidivisional form of organization. Variously interdependent divisions are "chartered" to look after one or more business areas, in effect defining the "turf" of the division and its purpose within the corporation, and collectively defining the corporate domain. However, once created, these divisional charters should not be regarded as rigid; they are susceptible to change. Particularly in fast-paced environments, such as in high-technology industries, divisional charters are liable to change as divisions add or subtract businesses to their charter responsibilities. These charter changes are seen as an adaptive device for large, multidivisional corporations in fast-paced environments.

This chapter presents a process model of how divisions change their domains in hypercompetitive contexts, focusing on the specific question of how divisions lose all or portions of their business charters. The chapter is based on a larger inductive study of charter changes in ten divisions, both domestic and foreign, of a large, multinational, high-technology corporation. Data were collected over an 18-month period and included formal interviews, questionnaires, company documents, group interviews, media publications and direct observations of strategy formation sessions. Over 80 informants were interviewed across several managerial levels.

Our data revealed three distinct patterns and logics of charter loss depending upon what phase of core business development a division found itself: (1) Divisions starting-up new core businesses lost these charters because of a combination of their failure in the new area and competition with other divisions in the company—the process revealed a competitive market for new charters; (2) Divisions rapidly growing new core businesses lost peripheral business areas in order to focus on the core business—the process emphasized a focus logic for charter change; finally (3) Divisions with mature charter areas were found to shed their core business areas because of an emerging misfit between their skills and culture and the nature of competition in the industry—the process emphasized the emerging nature of corporate misalignment and the abrupt charter changes that can follow. This chapter contributes to organizational theory by exploring the evolution of large, diversified corporations, focusing on the organizational responses to fast-moving, competitive environments. It also contributes to strategy by revealing a "re-combinant" multidivisional organizational form, by which timely charter changes can be used by large corporations to keep pace in these turbulent contexts.

(EVOLUTION; STRATEGIC PROCESS;

MULTIDIVISIONAL FIRM;

ORGANIZATIONAL STRUCTURE AND CHANGE)

The multidivisional organizational form has become the dominant paradigm for organizing diversified corporations (Chandler 1962; Rumelt, Schendel, and Teece 1994). Globally, "M-form" organizations account for trillions of dollars in worldwide assets and employ tens of millions of people (Fortune 1992). Traditionally, the M-form has been justified on the basis of transaction and information processing efficiency (Chandler 1962, Williamson 1975). In recent years, however, rapid change and unrelenting erosion of competitive advantage have made speed, flexibility, and adaptation central to the organization of large corporations (Eisenhardt 1989b, D'Aveni 1994). This chapter attempts to offer new insights into the nature of M-form organization, particularly its adaptive capabilities in these turbulent business environments.

Fundamental to the multidivisional form is the concept of domain (Levine and White 1961, Scott 1981, Thompson 1967). An organizational domain consists of the goods or services an organization provides and the markets or populations it serves (Thompson 1967). In the case of the entire corporation, corporate domain entails very broad, often abstract, claims, defining the turf that the corporation occupies. For example, corporate domains are often synonymous with industries, such as agriculture, chemicals, or electronics.

Domains, however, are often more sharply articulated at the divisional level as divisional "charters." For example, within a corporate domain of transportation, a more concise and definitive division charter for producing luxury cars may exist. Moreover, several closely related businesses can make up a divisional domain or charter. For example, a division charter could include both personal computers and related peripheral devices such as monitors, keyboards, and perhaps modems. Thus, divisions are "chartered" to look after one or more business areas and these constitute the "turf" of the division. Specifically, we define a "charter" as the businesses (i.e., product and market arenas) in which a division actively participates and for which it is responsible within the corporation. In turn, divisional charters represent the building blocks of the corporate domain.

Substantial research exists on the multidivisional form (see Ramanujam and Varadarajan 1989 and Galunic and Eisenhardt 1994 for related reviews). Figure 17.1 summaries the major perspectives on the M-form, which we briefly outline below. Two early streams highlight the fit between strategy and structure, with one focusing at the corporate level and the other at the strategic business unit level. *"Corporate Strategy and Structure Fit"* represents the founding literature, focusing on diversification and the question of which form of organizational structure "fits" this corporate strategy ("fit" meaning what structure is theoretically most suitable and/or positively impacts performance). *"SBU Strategy and Structure Fit,"* on the other hand, focuses on the fit between SBU strategy and structure. Corporate level issues are largely ignored, although useful archetypes for SBU strategies and structures are developed and used in subsequent perspectives. More recently, additional streams have emerged. In the *"Intracorporate Fit"* stream, emphasis is no longer on purely Corporate or SBU level issues, but the perspective on the M-form broadens to examine the interrelationship between these two levels in the corporation. In particular, fit is examined between SBU strategies and the nature of corporate governance and control. A second perspective *"Intracorporate Networks,"* centers on the horizontal relationships among SBUs, emphasizing potential interdependence amongst SBUs and the need for synergistic integration. This stream, with a particularly normative slant, includes the popular Asea-Brown-Boveri exemplar (Taylor 1991) and the "Transnational Solution" for structuring multinational firms (Bartlett and Ghoshal 1991). Finally, the stream we label *"Corporate Entrepreneurship and Renewal"* contains two major foci. One emphasizes the process by which new businesses (and, often, new divisions) are created within large corporations (e.g., Burgelman 1983), and the other emphasizes

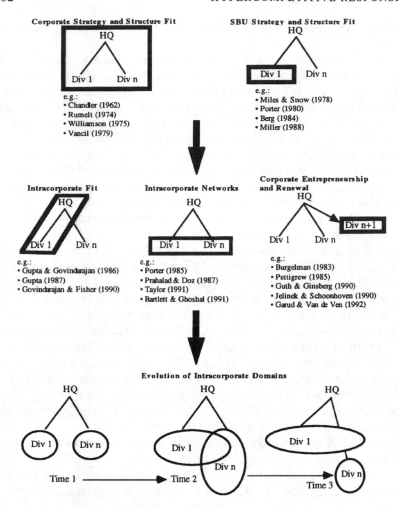

Figure 17.1. Brief Review of Research Perspectives on the M-Form

how pre-existing businesses are transformed and renewed (such as major changes in marketing, product development, and/or operations) (e.g., Pettigrew 1985, Guth and Ginsberg 1990, Chakravarthy and Lorange 1991). Yet, while this latter literature stream considers changes to existing divisional structures (typically moments of cataclysmic organizational restructuring), regular, reoccurring patterns of charter change have not been studied. Indeed, despite variations among these research streams, the underlying vision is that M-form corporations are divided into subunits focused on *fixed* business domains.

In contrast, real divisional charters are not always timeless creations. Businesses may be added to divisions, taken away, or switched from one division to another. Therefore, division charters are not once-and-for-all creations. Indeed, our data suggest charter changes can be made on a continual basis in the course of a corporation's development. One of the informants in this study said it best:

> A charter is really a time dependent concept, since it is not something that remains forever with the division. Generally, it is a statement of purpose. It includes the task, market, and the customer the division is concerned with. It also tells you something about how the division is linked to the rest of the company, but these things can change.

Charter change can be viewed as a critical adaptive device for M-form corporations. In essence, charter changes are an organizing strategy by which M-form corporations continually align evolving business areas with pockets of corporate resources. This stems from our conception of divisions as, fundamentally, consisting of underlying resources (i.e., skills, routines, competencies, etc.) and product-market areas where these are utilized (i.e., divisional charters). Although these two components certainly require one another, we point out that these two components are also separable—product-market areas can be matched with different divisions and the resource pools they represent. Moreover, we can conceive of some division-charter match-ups being potentially superior or inferior to others. Charter changes, therefore, via a process of dynamic realignment, have a potential to offer greater adaptability to the corporation.

The motor behind charter changes is often evolving technologies and markets. For example, new technologies (e.g., RISC computing, gene-splicing) and new products (e.g., cellular phones, mini-vans) open new charter opportunities. Such new businesses might become the charters of new divisions or be added to the charters of established ones, perhaps through a competitive intracorporate market for charters. Sometimes business opportunities converge (e.g., fax products combine print and telecommunications know-how) such that the charters of once separate divisions collide and compete. In this case, businesses may be moved between divisions to redraw the charter boundaries, and therefore, reassert distinctions between divisions. At other times, the market of a particular division can explode, spawning many new business opportunities (e.g., microprocessors expanded to personal computer, workstation, and lap top products). In this case, redistribution of business responsibilities may be necessary to focus the burgeoning division and find appropriate homes for spillover charter areas. Existing divisional charters might again be readjusted to better fit the expanding marketplace.

Finally, sometimes markets simply fade and charter-division match-ups must be appropriately reconsidered. Overall, because markets and technologies are dynamic, so to division-charter match-ups may need to coevolve.

Charter change is particularly relevant as an adaptive strategy in high-velocity settings. When technologies and markets are evolving rapidly, the match between existing charters, divisional skills, and business opportunities is most likely to fall out of alignment. Moreover, if the business areas are highly competitive and advantages erode quickly, such as in hypercompetitive contexts, there may be even greater pressure to shift charters in order to maintain competitiveness. Thus, rapidly evolving markets and technologies create opportunities to change charters and competition makes it imperative to do so. Indeed, we argue that *the continual assessment, movement, and recombination of divisional charters may be an important adaptive device used by corporations to remain competitive in high-velocity settings.* Yet, given the static conception of charters in previous research, there is little conception of how these processes operate, an important next step for research on diversified corporations to take.

So, the question arises, how do charters change? Is charter change fundamentally a selection or an adaptation process (e.g., Mintzberg 1990, Burgelman 1991)? Does charter change involve long periods of relative stability followed by short bursts of tremendous change (e.g., Tushman and Romanelli 1985)? Or is it more a case of frequent, incremental, and quasi-planned changes (e.g., Quinn 1980)?

The purpose of this chapter is to explore the evolution of divisional charters. Given the complexity of this topic, we focus our attention in this chapter on one research question: *How do divisions lose all or portions of their business charters*? Specifically, we ask: What initiates such losses? What roles do various entities in the corporation play in these losses? How can we characterize these changes?

As noted above, since past research usually takes a static view of charter domains, there is little theory to guide our thinking. So, in taking this next step in multidivisional research, we conducted an inductive study of 9 charter losses in a major, U.S. multinational firm. This firm competes in a number of hypercompetitive industries (e.g., telecommunications, computers, electronics, semiconductors) where opportunities for divisional domain changes are frequent.

We begin by discussing the inductive methodology that this chapter employed. We then turn to our findings, which reveal three distinct patterns of charter loss contingent upon a division's phase of business development. One ("start-up losses") revolves around divisional failures to launch new businesses. The second ("growth losses") involves the shedding of charters by booming divisions in search of focus. The third ("maturity losses") is associated with divisions in mature markets falling into misalignment with the market. Within each pattern, we note the interplay between the focal division, other divisions, and corporate executives.

We conclude with the observation that Omni, our focal firm, effectively relies on the strategic use of charter changes as a means of adaptation with rapidly coevolving markets and technologies. This "recombinant" view of organizations, where charters, like genes in DNA, are respliced to fit changing conditions, is the conceptual contribution of the paper. It is intended to be a more dynamic vision of large, diversified firms than the static conceptions of the past. We see this as an important next step in research on the diversified corporation.

METHODS

We pursued our research inductively using nine cases of charter loss in a major, U.S. multinational firm. The use of multiple cases allowed a replication logic whereby each case was used to test emerging theoretical insights. This method also allowed for a close correspondence between theory and data, a process whereby the emergent theory is "grounded" in the data (Glaser and Strauss 1967, Eisenhardt 1989a). No hypotheses or theories were constructed prior to the research effort. This research strategy is appropriate given the inductive nature of the study and its focus on strategic process modeling.

The study captured multiple sources of influence on the charter change process, including industry forces and various levels of authority in the corporation. It also involved understanding the history of the company and the division being studied, linking the past to the events and actions surrounding specific charter changes (Pettigrew 1990). Finally, the design included both retrospective and real-time data on charter change, the former increasing the economy of multiple case studies while the latter allowing greater depth of understanding of this longitudinal process (Leonard-Barton 1990).

Research Setting

This research is the result of a broader, 18-month study of charter changes in 10 divisions, both domestic and foreign, of a large, multinational, high-technology corporation based in the United States. "Omni" corporation is a Fortune 500 high-technology firm whose interests lie across a wide, but related, spectrum. Customers include large private businesses, scientific and academic institutions, the government sector, and individual consumers. The corporation is divided into multiple groups and divisions. Each group consists of related divisions, and each division is treated as a profit center and holds strategic and operational control over its business(es). The corporate structure is of a global product-division type (Beamish et al. 1994), that is divisions have global responsibilities and are not distinguished on geographical dimensions. Rather, divisions are distinguished according to product, market (i.e., nature of enduser), and technological dimensions. Divisions were sampled according to the following criteria: (1) Divisions had experienced one or more recent charter changes (typically within two years) or else were currently undergoing a charter change; (2) Divisions were selected from different business groups, thus increasing the likelihood of differences in divisional business contexts and thereby increasing the generalizability of findings (five of Omni's 15 groups were represented); (3) Two divisions were typically sampled per group to allow us to observe the interdivisional dynamics that constitute these charter changes. Table 17.1 outlines the cases that comprise this study.

The unit of analysis was the charter change experienced by a division. A division's charter typically included the responsibility over one or more related businesses. Charter changes were found to be of two basic types: *gains* and *losses*. A charter gain occurs when a division is made responsible for a new product to produce, market to serve, and/or new area to develop. A charter loss, in turn, occurs when a product or market area of responsibility is removed from a division.[1] Of the 10 divisions sampled, nine cases of charter loss were found. This paper analyzes these nine cases of charter loss.

Data Collection

Data were collected primarily through semi-structured individual interviews and questionnaires. Informants in the interview process included corporate vice presidents responsible for the group to which the division belonged, division general managers (one per division), division functional managers (multiple), and occasionally lower level project managers, although informants mostly comprised of the division's top management team (general manager and functional staff). Also, numerous discussions regarding charter change processes were held with corporate-level staff responsible for organizational design support (and who were familiar with the charter change events). Two feedback sessions were also used to gather further insights from informants on charter change processes. A total of 82 informants were interviewed.

Interviews were usually conducted during a site visit to the division. Informants were briefed beforehand as to the nature of the research and most of the interviews were tape recorded and transcribed. In all cases, the occurrence of charter change had been confirmed through telephone conver-

TABLE 17.1 Description of Cases

Charter Loss Case	Phase of Business Development	Total Interviews	Division Location[a]	Data
1. Venture	New charter	5-pilot, div. level 7-division level 1-corporate level	Group B	Retrospective
2. Pioneer[b]	New charter	5-division level 1-corporate level	Group D	Retrospective
3. Scout	New charter	7-division level 2-corporate level	Group D	Retrospective
4. Dynamo	Growing charter	7-division level 2-corporate level	Group C	Retrospective
5. Zeus	Growing charter	8-division level 1-corporate level 2-group sessions	Group B	Retrospective and real time
6. Marvel	Growing charter	8-division level 1-corporate level	Group E	Retrospective
7. Patriarch	Maturing charter	10-division level 2-corporate level	Group A	Real time
8. Omega	Maturing charter	4-division level 1-corporate level	Group E	Retrospective
9. Faust[b]	Maturing charter	5-division level 1-corporate level	Group D	Retrospective

a. Charter losses were only from U.S.-based divisions. However, data connected from 2 foreign divisions (which gained charters lost by Faust and Omega) were used extensively in the data analysis.
b. Each case of charter loss consisted of a separate division, except in the cases of Pioneer and Faust, which occurred in the same division although at two different points in its recent history and under a different management team. We identify the cases under separate names in order to fully distinguish the processes of loss experienced.

sations with the general manager or functional staff member before a site visit was scheduled. Informants were selected on the basis of their presence during, and involvement in, charter changes. Early contacts with managers also helped to establish a list of "must" interviews during the site visit, although other actors were pursued if their involvement in the charter changes became obvious after the initial interviews. Interviews typically lasted 90 minutes, although some interviews went on for several hours. Notes taken during the interview were entered into a database created on a notebook computer, typically during that same 24-hour period. The focus here was on quickly getting the story of the change recorded in as much detail as possible in order to help understand the interview transcripts. In addition, an ordinary paper notebook was used to collect impressions and new ideas regarding the charter change process for every site completed.

An interview guide was used to conduct the investigations. There were three sections to the interview guide. First, questions were asked regarding the informants' history with the company and division, along with their understanding of the division charter, both past and present. Questions regarding the division's performance were also asked. Second, the informants were asked to provide a detailed account of the charter change(s). Informants were given freedom to develop the story as they observed it, although probing questions were used to flesh-out details (e.g., "When did you first hear about the change?" "Who were the key players involved?" "What were the arguments in favor of the change?" "Was the change resisted? how? by whom?" etc.). The final section focused on specific constructs and their change over the course of the charter change, including: division goals, strategy, internal structure, technology, extent of decentralization, conflict, and communication patterns. We regarded these as key issues in the study of large corporations and therefore wanted more focused comment on how these may have been affected by the change process.

Retrospective data collection occurred during 2-3 day site visits to divisions. Real-time data collection, where the charter change was in progress, involved at least two entries. In the case of Patriarch division, data were collected via a site visit shortly following an initial decision to transform the domain and then 7-8 months later, via telephone interviews, as the charter changes were being implemented. In the case of Zeus division, data were collected over a 2-3 month period with five points of entry. Information was gathered both retrospectively, regarding a recent charter change, and in real-time, concerning current decision making that sought to transform division boundaries.

Questionnaires, including a financial data sheet, were also used to gather quantitative data on some of the constructs discussed in the third section of the interview. In particular, the questionnaire attempted to gather information on changes in divisional goals, strategy, and decision making influence. Secondary sources of data included company documents, group interviews, media publications, and direct observations of several strategy formation sessions.

Data Analysis

Data analysis used familiar approaches for qualitative, inductive data analysis (Glaser and Strauss 1967, Miles and Huberman 1984, Eisenhardt 1989a, Yin 1989). Analysis began with detailed written accounts and schematic representations of charter changes at each division. Initial versions of the charter change story were written immediately after each site visit was completed. These were followed by much more extensive accounts of the charter change process, making full use of quotes from transcripts and combining accounts of multiple informants. We usually found high agreement between respondents over critical issues, such as who were the main players involved and what were the key actions. Secondary data were useful in confirming or verifying events. We met frequently to discuss the events of the cases and to exchange information.

After construction of the case histories, within case analysis was conducted by answering the focal research question for each case. These answers were the basis for developing early constructs surrounding patterns of charter change for each division, involving at least two investigators in the construct development and confirmation of findings. We analyzed the cases separately, and then came together to discuss each case and our interpretations of the events in the loss process, referring frequently to the data and our personal notes. Significant dimensions emerged in describing each loss through an iterative process of going into the data for insights, suggesting constructs, dipping back into the data to check for inconsistencies, emerging with refreshed constructs, and so on. These constructs were kept "close to the case." That is, we described the loss process in very case-specific terms. When common dimensions of the charter loss process began to emerge, as we moved from case to case, we noted these but refrained from further refinement of the emerging dimensions until we finished our analysis of each case and began our cross-case analysis.

Cross-case analysis produced the working framework of the charter loss process. Charter change cases were compared and contrasted using methods suggested by Miles and Huberman (1984) and Eisenhardt (1989a). These typically involved the use of tables and matrices to examine the emergent dimensions across the cases. Typically, a series of two or three cases were compared at a time before attempting to generalize the constructs across the whole sample. This allowed us to still focus deeply on the data before trying to elevate the level of abstraction. Constructs were lifted to higher levels of abstraction as we compared across the whole sample.

In particular, we found that three entities were reappearing as significant factors in each case of change and that they could be used effectively to categorize other constructs. The three entities were: the focal division, other divisions, and corporate executives. Interactions among these players, both horizontal (between divisions) and vertical (between hierarchical levels) interactions, also appeared important. Overall, this triad provided an effective lens through which to view each case and examine other constructs, such as performance, charter overlaps, and conflict. We also noticed that three patterns, contingent upon the phase of business development at the division, were emerging across the cases. What resulted was a rough framework of the overall process, revealing three patterns of loss that involved distinct pro-

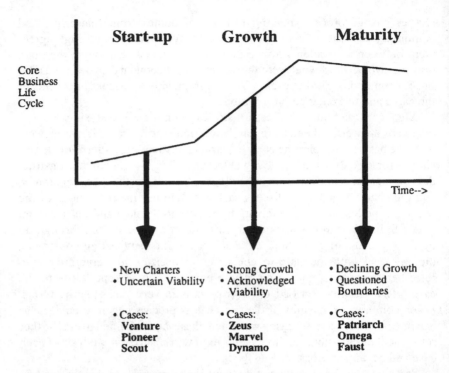

Figure 17.2. Business Life Cycle Phases Within Which Divisions Losing Charters Were Found

cesses of interaction. Taking this framework, we then went back into the data to re-examine our emergent model. This began another iterative process of going back-and-forth between the emergent model and the data. This further grounded our findings and shaped the development of a process model of charter losses, to which we now turn.

PATTERNS OF CHARTER LOSS

How do divisions experience charter losses? Figures 17.2 and 17.3 summarize the process model that emerged from our analysis of nine charter losses at Omni. As Figure 17.2 displays, we found three patterns of charter loss that correspond to three phases of core business development. These phases are consistent with the well-known concept of a product life-cycle (e.g., Porter 1980). Divisions were either attempting to launch new busi-

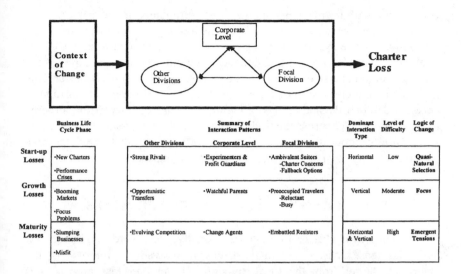

Figure 17.3. Charter Loss in a Large, Multinational, High-Technology Corporation

nesses ("start-up phase"), growing their businesses ("growth phase"), or managing maturing businesses ("maturity phase") when they suffered charter losses.

Second, we found that each business phase had a distinct pattern of charter loss (see Figure 17.3). The patterns varied in terms of the logic of change (i.e., the underlying theoretical motor), the importance and nature of interactions between particular corporate actors, and the difficulty of the change. For example, in the start-up phase, the divisions competed with one another in a kind of Darwinian competition to create viable new businesses. Although there were "losers," the loss process itself was relatively free of conflict. In the growth phase, the group executive played a decisive role in a more difficult change process that was motivated by the need to keep booming divisions focused on their burgeoning markets. In the maturity phase, once-dominant divisions had lost touch with their markets and the result was a wrenching, charter battle between competing divisions.

Third, although the pattern in each phase was unique, the actors, consisting of *group executives,* the *focal division,* and *other divisions,* were always the same. That is, the interplay among these three actors consistently shaped charter losses, although in no single fashion. Of particular importance was divisional interdependence ("horizontal" interplay), vacillating between competition with one another in the corporate marketplace for charters and cooperation with fellow divisions who were ultimately on the same "team." Similarly, tensions arose between divisions looking out for their own interests and corporate executives trying to take the corporate perspective ("vertical" interplay). So, charter loss depended not only on characteristics of the focal division, but also on the needs and successes of other divisions and the interests of the corporation as a whole. Moreover, there existed a duality between competitive and collaborative mechanisms of interaction, a theme that will be evident across the three patterns of charter loss and one that we will return to in our discussion. We now turn to an explication of the three patterns and logics of charter loss that comprise our model.

START-UP LOSSES: SURVIVAL OF THE FITTEST

One pattern of charter loss occurred as divisions were launching new business areas. Charter loss in these cases involved the removal of the emerging charter from the focal division. The charter loss process was characterized by four key elements: (a) performance crises in the focal divisions as they attempted to build new businesses; (b) availability of competing and typically more successful divisions as alternative sites for the charter; (c) "fluid" commitments to any specific charter-division match-ups by corporate level managers; and (d) ambivalence within focal divisions surrounding the new charters. Overall, these losses were characterized by a logic of quasi-natural selection and a consensus among all concerned about the wisdom of the loss. Venture, Scout, and Pioneer divisions experienced this pattern of charter loss as we explain below.

The Setting: Novelty, Excitement, and Crisis (Table 17.2, column 1)

In large corporations, there is often intense pressure to grow. Growing a division carries with it significant rewards, including higher salaries, promotions, and prestige within the company. And, growth ensures the future of the corporation. Thus, at Omni, seeking growth had become a powerful norm, driving managers to seek new charters as sources of expansion. As one manager put it, "Everybody's going nuts trying to find ways to grow at phenomenal growth rates . . . and if you're not growing at that rate, you might want to be considering getting out." Not surprisingly then, three of our divisions (Venture, Scout, Pioneer) went after new opportunities.

There was excitement surrounding these promising markets. For example, in the case of Pioneer, an emerging business area provided an opportunity to take part in an intriguing new market that was projected to grow wildly. As

TABLE 17.2 Cross-Case Illustrations of "Start-Up" Charter Loss Pattern

Case	Setting	Other Divisions (Horizontal Interactions)	Corporate Level (Vertical Interactions)	Focal Division
VENTURE	New charter: —2 years old at loss "We really wanted to grow . . . this can do it for us!" Performance crisis: No demand —Growth = Insignificant —Net margins = 0% "We didn't even live up to [our] most pessimistic forecast . . . it just never took off."	Strong rivals: —Up-and-coming site in search of charter —Critical competencies —Successful "the [group executive] was being pressured to create an entity [overseas]. And he was looking for a charter for this entity . . . they had come up to speed and had done a very good job with [their small charter] . . . it seemed to make sense to [the group executive] to have them focus on our charter area, since we were kind of floundering."	Experimenter and profit guardian: "[the executive's] thinking was . . . start trawling." "Venture had not found a way that we could achieve [the executive's] growth goals and [the executive's] profit goals."	Concern: Rapid schedule "It had an extremely aggressive schedule." Fallback option: "I requested that we get out of this business and get back on the business that's paying the bills." (GM) Consensus over loss: "So both [the GM and corporate executive] felt the same thing. And so it was a pretty easy thing to do at the meeting."
SCOUT	New charter: —1 year old at loss "Our manager pushed hard [to get this charter]" Performance Crisis: No direction —Growth = Poor forecasts —Net margins = 28% drop "We were never really clear that we could produce the miracle breakthroughs."	Strong rivals: —Needing charter —Relevant competencies —Successful in highly related areas —Ease of people transers "Closing the division was discussed . . . [but a senior VP] has told me a couple of times that we [Scout's rival] . . have all this	Experimenter and profit guardian: "[The executive] came in and really provided a lot of enthusiasm and excitement [around this new charter]." "[Highest corporate levels] put some reasonable pressure, I would guess, on [our executive] to dig in and face off with this cost	Concern: Extent of change "It fundamentally didn't make sinse to [employees] that you could [make that change]." Fallback Option: "We were trying to make a transition but we had these nice things [from our pre-existing charter]." Consensus over loss:

(continued)

443

TABLE 17.2 Continued

Case	Setting	Other Divisions (Horizontal Interactions)	Corporate Level (Vertical Interactions)	Focal Division
		[relevant expertise] here, we've been in the business a long time." "From a corporate management of people standpoint, it worked really well [to make this move]."	[crisis] . . . and make a decision and do it quickly."	"I think that for the most part, most of the writing was already on the wall."
PIONEER	New charter: —1 year old at loss "This was just the hottest thing . . . there was excitement about this new product charter." Performance crisis: No viable product —Growth = 0% —Net margins = Large losses "It became clear that this wasn't going to work and at the same time in the external environment it became clear that people [weren't ready yet for this concept]."	Strong rivals: —Competing in same area —Further along in related business —More promising venture "At the time there were not good clear boundaries." "What [this other division] is doing is [our new area], so why are we building this stuff?"	Experimenter and profit guardian: "The other reputation [the executive] has is great visionary." "Profit was a remote concept to most of these people! (executive)	Concern: Pace and complexity "I think [the mood] was mixed . . . people liked the charter, I mean it's fun . . . I think the mixed reaction was more that people's bandwidth [was stretched]. [Our] ability to juggle all the different balls in our court." Fallback option: "We had a good business understanding of [an older area] . . . and we lost it because we got diddled and daddled in other things. But, the core capability and skill set was here." Consensus over loss: "[The executive] was looking at it. I was looking at it and we said this thing ain't going to cut it."

444

one manager emphasized, "This was just the hottest thing . . . there was excitement about this new product charter." At Venture, the new charter created excitement as well. As one manager put it:

> We really wanted to grow. And when all of a sudden, we kind of said "we really can't do it with [our existing business]," and the new business came in and we said "this can do it for us! Now let's go do it."

As time went on, this early optimism waned as within a few years of starting the new core charter, performance problems became apparent. We defined performance problems in terms of difficulties in generating sales, profit, and strategic direction for the new business. At Scout, falling margins and lack of a viable strategy signalled performance problems. Scrutiny intensified over Scout's charter performance when profit margins fell 6% in the first year, a surprising amount given the fact that early (and costly) product development was conducted in another division. More importantly, Scout failed to devise a future direction for the business. Despite their time with the charter, Scout managers remained uncertain about where to go. As a manager stated, "Our problem was figuring out where the hell to go once we needed to be tuned to this new charter, and figure out where was the market headed, what were the customer needs, and we thrashed a long time on that."

Pioneer faced similar problems. The division had mounting financial losses as they spent tremendous resources in developing the new charter. First, Pioneer faced major problems defining their new charter, as one manager noted:

> The new business was a very difficult concept to explain to people. On the surface it seemed simple. When you get into trying to explain it to somebody it's difficult to grasp.

Pioneer also faced the realization that its product, in its existing form, would not sell well. One manager summarized:

> We couldn't get it cheap enough. So we said, "Let's scale it down." It still wasn't cheap enough. . . . It became clear that this wasn't going to work and at the same time in the external environment it became clear that . . . the move wasn't going to happen as fast as people thought.

Finally, Venture division experienced abysmal market response to its new charter product. Profit margins plunged. Since this charter was expected to be a new core product for Omni, it had aroused excitement and inflated hopes.

The dismal early returns, therefore, were particularly shocking, quickly triggering attention and raising serious concerns. One manager summarized the final months:

> I don't think that reality set in until the end of the first month of sales. Our first day was actually a very exciting day, because we sold enough units that would put us on track with expectations. But then we didn't sell any more! . . . We didn't even live up to our most pessimistic forecast.

In sum, poor performance in terms of weak revenues, falling profit margins, failure to develop viable products, and inability to provide future direction signalled crises in these divisions. Although in all cases divisions had placed great hopes in the new charter areas, expectations were not met, early performance measures were poor, and the businesses were lost. On the surface, simple financial considerations explain these charter losses. Yet, our data reveal that these are not complete explanations. After all, executives could have waited longer, invested more money, changed management, or reshaped strategy and processes.[2] Rather the loss process was heavily influenced and shaped by other factors.

Other Divisions: Strong
Rivals (Table 17.2, column 2)

Omni competes in many highly competitive and fast changing markets. Theirs is an aggressive "have lunch or be lunch" world. Not surprisingly then, as we mentioned before, senior executives at Omni encourage divisional managers to go after new markets. Thus, not surprisingly, divisional managers went out looking for new businesses. However, they ended up with charters that bumped and overlapped with other divisions from time to time, particularly as "hot" new business areas emerged that attracted divisions from several vantage points. The fuzziness of new markets made it even more likely to run into other divisions even when not trying to do so. Indeed, in each of the three cases, while the focal division was going after a new domain, so too were others either pursuing the same domain or posturing to do so. Sometimes the divisions knew about each other, but sometimes not. These overlaps eventually created competition and were a critical element in the charter loss process.

Sometimes there was direct competition within the same emerging business area. For example, both Pioneer and another division were actively developing products in Pioneer's new domain, each approaching the domain from a unique technical vantage point. This created confusion over where the charter for this business area belonged. As one manager stated, "At the time there were not good clear boundaries." Moreover, since they were part of the same group, these divisions were striving for the same set of resources. As a corporate level executive reflected on this emerging situation in the group:

> One of our biggest problems was that we still had too many entities, and too much overhead . . . for our size in the industry we were in, we had too many organizations.

In the case of Venture, another division was also developing a very similar business, creating confusion and friction over who was the actual owner of the charter. As one manager claimed:

> It was a war! And who owns this entire new area? Do we own it? Do they own it?

Competition was also emergent, coming in the form of other divisions posturing or lobbying to attempt the same business opportunities. Venture also faced competition of this sort, most notably from a site with similar (if not advantageous) competencies that created a strong alternative to Venture as a home for the charter. Venture was developing a new product that relied on several technical competencies. Venture could deliver in one critical area, but the competitive division could deliver on another. Also, the other site was considered "up-and-coming," was concurrently searching for a brand new business charter, and was generally keen about this new area. Moreover, having successfully managed its existing business duties, the other site was in a good position to seek greater responsibilities. The combination of having developed a critical expertise, being successful in this undertaking, and needing a new business charter created a powerful rival for Venture's charter.

Unfortunately, Scout, Pioneer, and Venture did not measure up against their internal competition. For example, Pioneer failed to develop a product in its emerging business area. The other division's development, on the other hand, looked promising, particularly since they had recently developed a successful, related product which they were using as a source of leverage into the new domain. As one Pioneer manager stated, "They were experiencing [the necessary] expertise." In the end, problems with their approach, mounting losses, and the recognition of ever increasing overlaps with a more successful division led Pioneer managers to reconsider their new charter, a business area they eventually chose to terminate.

Similarly at Venture, the presence of another division served as an important facilitating factor in the charter loss process. As one manager summarized:

What happened concurrently was that the group manager was being pressured to create a charter at this other site. He was looking for a charter for this new entity . . . they had done well and the company was looking for a charter for them . . . it seemed to make sense to him to have them focus on our charter area, since we were kind of floundering with it and not doing well. He agreed, and took advantage of the opportunity to move it out of our division and over to the new site as their official charter.

Finally, Scout faced a rival that was considered very competent in Scout's new business area. As one manager of the rival division said, "[a senior VP] has told me a couple of times that we . . . have all this [relevant expertise] here." Scout's rival also faced possible closure and massive relocation of employees if they could not gain a new charter, because the division recently lost its current charter to a third division. Thus, their acknowledged competence within Scout's domain and Scout's mounting performance problems led Scout managers to agree to transfer their new business to their rival, particularly since Scout employees could readily relocate to nearby sites.

Corporate Executives: Fluid Commitments (Table 17.2, column 3)

Corporate executives played an intriguing dual role. They were often among the instigators of forays into new markets. They wanted divisions to try new markets and new ideas since they, just like divisional managers, were concerned about future growth possibilities. But, while the divisions became emotionally invested in their new charters, these senior executives were more detached regarding the division-charter match per se. They were more generally concerned with the well being of the new opportunity wherever it may reside. To them, most attempts at starting-up new businesses were experiments. If one bet did not work, another might. These executives were consummate experimenters, as reflected in this description of Venture's corporate executive by a Venture manager:

Strategically, [the executive's] thinking was sound in the sense that he felt like we don't know a lot about this market, so don't spend a lot of time designing a product. Get something out there, we'll learn more from having even a poor product on the market than we would to take two years to get what we think is the perfect product.

Moreover, although Venture's executive showed tremendous interest in the new venture per se, the concern was more from the perspective of the entire business group. As another manager reflected, "He was fascinated with the concept, liked it, though it was a great concept, and wanted to go forward with it from his business group standpoint."

Simultaneously, corporate executives were also guardians of corporate profit and they passed that pressure onto the divisions. For example, one manager at Pioneer worried, "You've got like a one-year transition time where the [old] business is going to keep you alive, but if you want to maintain the size of this organization you've got to find several hundred million dollars worth of revenue from the [new] business." So, much like Gersick's (1994) venture capitalist, these executives experimented, but usually with limits on time and funds available. The result was that corporate executives were only weakly committed to any *particular* attempt to start-up a new charter. They wanted new charters to succeed, but were willing to attempt different charter-division match-ups for the new charter area. Indeed, executives apparently preferred to have multiple experiments in the early going, allowing charter overlaps and boundary issues to be played out between divisions instead of dictated from above. As one Scout manager recounted:

> [The executive] delegated a great deal to [our GM] with respect to shoring up the charter. [The executive] would swoop in everyone once in a while, kind of give us a tune-up on what the group was doing, the vision of his organization, and then he'd go away. And [our GM] was left to develop the relationships between his compatriots [in the group]—we were then trying to share charters . . . it was my sense that [our GM] was out on his own, trying to duke it out with the other GM's, to define what Scout's charter was.

Focal Division: Ambivalent Suitor (Table 17.2, column 4)

As mentioned earlier, great enthusiasm accompanied attempts to start-up new business areas. But division members also had substantial concerns. For example, some division members were concerned about the changes that the new charters involved. At Scout, managers worried that the change was taking them too far from their pre-existing domain. As a manager reflected:

> It was a lot of work to get the organization to accept and believe that we could jump in this vicious battle that was going on in the marketplace . . . a lot of the aspects of it were outside of the troops comfort zone . . . the pace and the pressure of the new business was much different than what people were coming from. The people who were highly suspect of the change were . . . especially the engineers.

Another example is Venture. Here there was skepticism about the realism of schedules. The division was expected to develop a complex charter under tight time pressure. As two managers stated:

> It had an extremely aggressive schedule. We knew nothing about the new area, and we were asked to produce a product in 15 months . . . and the proposal there was 24 months. We felt that was aggressive.

> As we started looking at it, you know, we've been talking about this [downsized] version, and we began to say, "I'm afraid we're going to get into trouble with this."

Likewise, Pioneer managers were skeptical about whether they could generate revenues quickly enough as they transitioned from the old business to the new one. Pioneer managers also worried that the new charter contained too many complex pieces. The possible strain on employee "bandwidth" (i.e., extent of job responsibilities and duties) created mixed feelings. As one manager stated:

> I think [the mood] was mixed . . . the mixed reaction was more that people's bandwidth [was stretched], [our] ability to juggle all the different balls in our court.

In general, the dynamics of "start-up losses" reflected an uneasy emotional duality. Moods swung between excitement and apprehension, as a manager from Venture vividly claimed:

> We went through cycles. There'd be periods of time when people'd get pretty excited about the potential for the program, what it could do for us, that it could give us growth, and them we'd go through periods of nonexcitement when we'd hit the problems.

A second source of ambivalence was fallback options. In all cases, these divisions concurrently managed older charter areas along with starting-up their new domains. The ties to their previous core charters, therefore, were often strong. For example, Venture was still considered a market leader in the old charter area and they maintained active investment in this charter. The move back was, therefore, natural. As one manager said, "I requested that we get out of this business and get back on the business that's paying the bills." Similarly, in the case of Scout, their pre-existing business provided a viable alternative, as a manager stated, "We were trying to make a transition, but we had these 'nice things' [from our pre-existing charter]."

At Pioneer, the maintenance of relevant core competencies and the success of their final product in their former core charter area (which they were in the midst of dissolving) provided a path for their return to this domain. As one manager stated:

> We had a good business understanding of [the old charter] . . . and we lost it because we got diddled and daddled in other things. But, the core capability and skill set was here.

Losses: Consensus (Table 17.2, column 4)

The combination of competing divisions, weakly committed corporate executives, and ambivalent losing divisions made for a relatively painless charter loss. For example, as the situation within Pioneer worsened, and as the competition with another division became more apparent and their success more obvious, both the divisional general manager and the corporate vice president came to the same conclusion to terminate Pioneer's new charter, as reflected by the general manager's comment, "The executive was looking at this charter, I was looking at this charter and we said 'this thing ain't going to cut it!' "

Similarly, Venture managers and the corporate executive decided simultaneously that the charter responsibilities for the new area should be moved from Venture. As a Venture manager recounted:

> [We] made a decision to go to the [corporate level executive] and recommend at the quarterly review that we get out of the [new] business. And it turns out they had come to the quarterly review with a similar idea!. . . . So both felt the same thing, and so it was a pretty easy thing to do at the meeting.

In fact, in all three cases the charter loss showed very little top-down forcing of any kind. Most of the writing, as one Scout manager put it, was "on the wall." Arguably, this reflects Omni's culture. We observed Omni to be a team-oriented institution. However, it is important to remember that this did not preclude these divisional competitions from being generated in the first place. Nor does this culture explain the greater harshness of the loss process that we observe in subsequent patterns. Rather, the circumstances and structural conditions (e.g., ambivalence and shallow organizational roots in the new charter) apparent during this phase were important in explaining the relatively consensual atmosphere surrounding the losses.

In summary, charter losses in this phase are triggered by performance problems. Losing divisions could not find a clear charter, could not develop a product, or could not sell. Perhaps these situations might have turned around with more time, money, or different management. But, other factors were key. The presence of *competing divisions* was critical in pulling the charter away from the focal division. These divisions gave these attractive charters somewhere else to go. *Senior executives* displayed fluid commitment. In their minds, attempts to start-up new businesses were experiments, tempered by demands for profits. Finally, within the *focal divisions,* rather than escalating commitments, there were doubts and fallback positions.

Overall, this charter loss pattern resembles a *quasi-natural selection* mechanism of adaptation. Variation (emergence of novel forms) was evident in the number of divisions attempting to develop the same charters from different vantage points. For example, Pioneer was engaged in creating the new charter using one expertise, while a rival division approached it from strength in a different technical arena. Selection (i.e., choice among forms) was based on internal comparisons (typically of performance and skills) of alternative homes for the emergent businesses. For example, Scout was selected out because of slumping financial performance when compared with another division with the requisite skill set in a closely related area. Finally, retention (i.e., perpetuation of selected form) occurred as the redrawn boundaries were implemented around new charters. In short, "start-up losses" display an example of a natural selection process within an organization (e.g., see also Burgelman 1991, Miner 1994).

Our data, however, also revealed a more complex process than simply natural selection. There were critical time and resource constraints on variation. Consistent with Gersick's (1994) venture capitalists, corporate executives here were instrumental in triggering variations. More importantly, they thought of variations in terms of limited experiments—experiments with only so much time or so much money. For example, Venture was given only 15 months to deliver a product, while Pioneer was given a rigid, two-year window in which to make money. Thus, rather than purely blind and random variation, attempts at launching new charters (i.e., variations) were always constrained.

Second, although performance was a key selection criterion, selection was a more social process than simply financial "winners" and "losers." The data revealed a self-selection component, whereby internal attitudes within focal divisions helped to explain the losses. For example, as noted above, there was substantial ambivalence in each division about the new charter. In addition, despite internal competition among divisions for the best charters, there was also a sense of equity and cooperation towards other divisions. For example, Pioneer managers were sensitive to the fact that in past disputes their rival division had been mistreated. Leaving the charter area graciously partially redressed these past injustices towards a fellow division. Thus, efficiency-based decision making was coupled with social dynamics that recognized that competing divisions were ultimately in the same corporation. Finally, factors beyond performance weighted heavily in the selection process. Scout lost to a rival division not only because of poor performance, but also because the other division needed to maintain the employment base in a sensitive geographic region. Similarly, Venture partially lost because the corporation wanted to expand its presence in a key overseas location. So, in addition to the relative performance of divisions, the social fabric of these divisions and the broader corporate context influenced the selection process.

The findings also illustrate the link between "shallow structures" and the natural selection mechanism. The mixed feelings over new business domains and the brief time with the new charters were symptomatic of the shallow roots of these charters within divisional homes. In contrast, Gersick (1991) observed the presence of "deep structures" as organizations become entrenched in some endeavor over time. Deep structures are interlocking configurations of organizational structures (formal and informal) and processes that develop and, more importantly, persist around some endeavor within organizations. History is particularly important in their development. They are difficult to change, often requiring "revolutionary periods" (Gersick 1991). Clearly, divisions facing start-up losses had not had time to form deep structures around these charters. Since structures were shallow, uprooting new charters proceeded relatively smoothly.

GROWTH LOSSES: TRACKING THE
MARKET AND FOCUSING THE DIVISION

A second pattern of charter losses was found among divisions that had survived the launch of new core charters and were successfully growing their new businesses. Charter losses occurred as peripheral charter areas (both older businesses and new ventures) were stripped from these divisions in order to ensure focus on the booming business areas. "Growth losses" were characterized by four essential elements: (a) focus problems created by very rapid growth in market size and divisional revenues; (b) needy alternative divisions; (c) watchful corporate leaders; and (d) burgeoning charter responsibilities limiting divisional resistance to change. Overall, the process was marked by a teleological logic of change, as corporate executives continuously focused the focal division on riding its booming core charter. Zeus, Dynamo, and Marvel divisions all experienced charter losses of this pattern, to which we now turn.

TABLE 17.3 Cross-Case Illustrations of "Growth" Charter Loss Pattern

Case	Setting	Other Divisions (Horizontal Interactions)	Corporate Level (Vertical Interactions)	Focal Division
ZEUS	Booming Business/Marketplace: —6 years old —Growth = 40%-50% —Net margins = 9%-12% "It was an unbelievable time for all of us here ... very fast paced. It was phenomenal!" Focus Problems: Old Business and New Opportunities "[We had shed the old charter] primarily because of the fact that we really needed heavy-duty focus to deal with the [core]." "The perception was that with the structure that existed at Zeus, you could not make [new ventures] happen here."	Needy Division "[A foreign division] was needing a product charter." New Division Created "[Other divisions] had their hands full."	Watchful Parent: "[Corporate executives] saw that there was this [new business] empire to build here."	Reluctance: "I need to feel more comfortable with the [loss], but I don't." Busy: "Our hands were full at Zeus!" Top-Down Push: "No, I wasn't behind it ... much of it was driven by [a corporate executive]." {GM}
DYNAMO	Growing Business/Booming Marketplace: —4 years old —Growth = Core 50% of Total —Net Margins = 18%	New Division Created "the decision was made to break the [pre-existing] business out from under Dynamo."	Watchful Parent: "[Corporate] wanted ... complete focus on [the new business]." "Well, [the new executive]	Reluctance: "[division managers] were getting a lot of pressure from their people to kind of keep things going as they are."

	"dollars are starting to flow." Focus Problems: Boom Business "Generally I thought we had pretty good technology but we were slow. Slow to react to changes. . . . People were not very well focused on productivity improvements, time to market, cost." {Corporate Executive}	comes on board and starts looking and realizing that it is good for Dynamo to have to live [with the new conditions]. "	Busy: "Dynamo was just a huge division that just was becoming unruly in terms of managing it." Top-Down Push: "There were a few of the top management people that recognized this and said these are changes that are going on in industry and we need to face up on them."
MARVEL	Booming Business/Marketplace: —8 years old —Growth = 100% —Net Margins = 11% "Marvel division [had grown] from nothing to a big success." Focus Problems: New Opportunities "this other business was there and not clearly a high focus of the team." {Corporate Executive}	Watchful Parent: "Marvel had to be successful. . . . Because heart of the program at that time was in Marvel." {GM in a "needy division" in Marvel's group} Needy Division "it was a business that wasn't doing well . . . so it was pretty low risk to say let's get [needy division focused on this [new and bring all the energy of a dedicated management team, a dedicated resource of people who deal as though their lives and their future depends on this." {Corporate Executive}	Reluctance: "there were a group of people who felt that they had started the business and they were losing something so [the boss] was difficult." {Corporate Executive} Busy: "I looked at what was going on in Marvel and they had [their core charter] business by the tail, a tiger by the tail, trying to make that a success." {Corporate Executive} Top-Down Push: "Marvel was to focus on the [core] . . . it's focus, focus, and focus!" {GM in Marvel's group}

The Setting: Booming Business
(Table 17.3, column 1)

Large corporations occasionally have "big winners," divisions that perform enormously well. But, ironically, these wins set the stage for a second pattern of charter losses that we found in three divisions (Zeus, Marvel, Dynamo). Charter losses occurred as peripheral charter areas (both old businesses and new opportunities) were shed while these divisions focused on growing their burgeoning core charter area.

Zeus, Marvel, and Dynamo were riding exploding markets. For example, six years after entry into this business area, Zeus was growing sales at 40%-50% and adding employees at the same rate. They were among a small number of companies that had entered this rapidly rising sector of their industry. And, they were winners. One manager colorfully described, "It's like drinking out of a fire hose. . . . And we haven't stopped to get air yet!"

Marvel was also an early participant in a growing market area. Six years after the charter began, Marvel was booming, doubling revenues and enjoying healthy profits. A manager within Marvel's group stated what was generally acknowledged when he said "Marvel division [had grown] from nothing to a big success."

Dynamo was also tracking a lucrative market area. As one manager testified, "It's growing and gaining customer acceptance, and dollars are starting to flow through." Although not as firmly entrenched on the growth curve of the life cycle as Marvel and Zeus, Dynamo was also successfully competing in an exploding business.

As time went on, however, it became more difficult for divisional managers to keep track of their enterprises. Managers became cognitively overburdened as divisions attempted simultaneously to manage their booming core charters, older business areas that preceded the boom, and new opportunities spawned by the exploding markets. As one Zeus manager said, "I could not deal with both business issues, I was stretched."

These difficulties were manifest in focus problems. Some involved neglect of new opportunities. Booming divisions were often teeming with new ventures, some of which these divisions could and should pursue. However, despite their lucrative nature, these opportunities could not always be accommodated in the overburdened divisional structures. For example, Zeus's labs had expanded to where it was difficult for the R & D manager to guide strategically more than incremental innovations. As one manager described, "we had too many technologies that we were mucking around with." Thus, although attempts to champion new businesses were encouraged, straining internal structures and systems usually slowed their progress. A Zeus manager said:

> The strategy was to pursue the neat opportunities that were emerging from Zeus. (But), the perception was that with the structure that existed at Zeus, you could not make them happen here. You could not get the results.

Marvel experienced similar problems with new opportunities. Marvel had enjoyed tremendous success since its inception, as one manager stated, "the heart of the [group] at that time was in Marvel." However, Marvel also spawned new charter opportunities that could not be given adequate attention within the division. As one corporate executive stated, "I looked at what was going on in Marvel and they had [their core charter] business by the tail, a tiger by the tail, trying to make that a success and this other business was there and not clearly a high focus of the team." Managing old businesses was a problem as well. Although they had passed their primes, these businesses were often still valuable generators of profit and brand image. At Zeus, these businesses were ignored. In contrast, at Dynamo managers paid too much attention to them. As one executive related, "Although net margins were strong for the entire charter at the time of the split (18%), the new core area had only managed to make up 50% of the overall revenues for the division in the four years of its existence. This was substantial, but still disappointing for divisional managers given the rapid growth of the new marketplace. For Dynamo, the old business was easy since it involved selling to captive internal customers. In contrast, the booming marketplace was more competitive. As a result, the distraction of the old business damaged Dynamo's competitiveness. One manager testified:

> Generally, I thought we had pretty good technology but we were slow to react to changes because we had this umbrella of [secured internal customers]. People were not very well focused on productivity improvements, time to market, cost . . . it was really a nice protective environment.

These problems led to periodic "shedding" of the old and new businesses that surrounded the primary charter area. For example, Dynamo split off the old charter. The division subsequently refocused on its booming business while the old business was spun-off to form a new division. Marvel grafted a new opportunity onto another existing division. Zeus spun-off both the old and the new. The rationales were the same. As a Zeus manager said regarding the older business, "[We lost the business] primarily because of the fact that we really needed heavy duty focus to deal with the [booming business]." The result—"more focus for us!"

On the surface, a simple focusing rationale explains these charter losses. Yet, there were other options, such as adding administrative staff and expanding divisional structures, that might have worked. Rather, the loss process was also influenced by other factors.

Other Divisions: Opportunistic Transfers
(Table 17.3, column 2)

Corporations such as Omni are portfolios of businesses. Thus, while divisions such as Zeus, Dynamo, and Marvel were booming, it occurred that others were not faring so well. Not surprisingly then, to some of these latter divisions, the cast-offs from the corporate titans looked attractive. Thus, losses occurred not only to focus the corporate "golden geese," but also to help other divisions.

For example, at Marvel, their charter loss was facilitated by a fellow division (Omega) that was desperately seeking new business domains. Omega, as we shall detail later, was facing a maturing business and needed new business opportunities to remain viable. Moreover, Marvel was not able to exploit this new part of their domain, straining, as we saw above, merely to keep up with managing an explosive core business. However, other than Omega's high technical competence and ability to devote total attention to the new venture, there were no particular advantages to Omega. Rather, Omega was in need and Marvel had excess. One corporate executive recounted, "[Marvel's new venture] was small at the time and so it was pretty low risk to say let's get a new organization focused on this and bring all the energy of a dedicated management team, a dedicated resource of people who deal as though their lives and their future depends on this, then you get different results."

Similarly, Zeus transferred an older charter area to another division that was seeking a new charter. Although this site did not necessarily contain competitive advantages for the older business, their need for charter was itself a facilitator of the charter loss. As one manager said, "it was real clear that [the other division] needed a product charter."

Overall, these divisions facilitated charter loss by providing somewhere for excess charters to go. However, unlike "start-up losses," interdivisional relationships were not competitive in the sense that the recipient divisions were rivals, with selection based on performance. The recipient divisions were in no position to challenge the corporate engines of growth. Rather, other divisions were convenient parking spaces for the excess businesses of corporate titans. In fact, there were no existing recipient divisions in several cases. For example, in Dynamo's charter loss, a new division was created by "spinning-off" a peripheral business area since a suitable alternative division was not readily available to absorb the business.

Corporate Executives: Watchful Parents
(Table 17.3, column 3)

Corporate executives were invariably instrumental to the "growth losses" process. Our data revealed that in all cases corporate executives closely monitored the performance, market conditions, and divisional structures of these emerging giants. Strategically, these were now the engines of growth in the corporation and were carefully tracked. As Burgelman (1991) found, these businesses often come to dominate corporate strategic thinking. A manager at Zeus described, "[Corporate executives] saw that there was this [new business] empire to build here."

As corporate executives followed these divisions, the divisional bandwidth problems described previously became increasingly acute, suggesting the need for shedding charters. However, bandwidth problems were not the whole story. Our interviews with corporate executives suggested there were political issues as well. Corporate executives worried that large divisions would build ever bigger domains, perhaps becoming too powerful in directing the future of the group for which the corporate executives were ultimately responsible. These executives favored spreading the wealth by slicing out business areas to reduce dependence on one division. Moreover, they worried that such powerful divisions would not show the financial returns that could be expected from more tightly managed charters. This is reflected in one corporate executive's lament about a division that historically had enormous reach and control over group businesses but did not, presumably as a result, perform well. He claimed, "They were basically the Vienna of [their "Hapsburg"] empire that retained all the structure, but didn't have the majority of the revenue" (i.e., this division was retaining more control over charter areas in the business group than they were effectively able to direct and manage). Thus, unlike executive actions in the previous phase, where executives stepped in to redraw boundaries in a consensual situation, executives in this phase preemptively redrew existing divisional domains. By so doing, executives not only ensured divisional focus, but also retained greater political control over charters in their domains.

Focal Division: Preoccupied Travelers
(Table 17.3, column 4)

Division managers were reluctant to lose pieces of their charters. Their reluctance partially stemmed from a fear of losing a source of steady revenues and profit. For example, Dynamo resisted losing their older business area because of the financial security this business brought. It provided extensive divisional profit margins and thus shielded the division from competitive forces mounting against the core charter. As one manager reflected, "the core charter was hiding under the cloak and profit of the past."

Divisions also feared losing strategic control over the general business area. This was a particular concern when a new business was closely coupled to the core business. For example, Zeus had an opportunity to develop a new business that was a technically advanced version of its booming product line, catering, however, to a different customer, Although Zeus managers acknowledged that their current divisional structure could not handle both businesses, they feared that the two businesses were so related that they would lose some control over the general business area. This attitude is reflected by a manager's comment:

> One of my fears . . . if we split this division, you lose this power [over the business].
> . . . Right now we have controlling power. . . . I need to feel more comfortable with
> [the loss], but I don't. So everybody is thinking, is there some way to keep this thing
> together?

These divisions also had remedies that differed from corporate cures for focus problems. For example, Dynamo and Zeus attempted intradivisional reorganizations by forming separate business teams around the charter areas and using matrix structures. Indeed, divisional managers, agreeing that divisions were becoming simply too large to manage effectively, joined corporate executives in recognizing the problems of focus. They were not, however, so convinced that a charter loss was the solution.

These divisions, however, were also very busy. Although the focal divisions typically opposed the charter losses, the exploding market conditions surrounding them provided enough distraction and, more importantly, security for divisional managers to prevent full blown resistance to change. They ended up simply being too busy to block charter losses. As one Zeus manager recalled:

> It was an unbelievable time for all of us here . . . very fast paced. . . . It was phe-
> nomenal! . . . I actually had to leave my phone off the hook to just go to the rest
> room.

Similarly, in Marvel, they were trying to wrestle with their "tiger" business, which needed full attention in order to ensure continued growth and profits. In the case of Dynamo, the enormous size to which the division had grown made change, perhaps of any sort, highly desirable, and thus strong divisional resistance less likely:

> Dynamo was just a huge division that just was becoming unruly in terms of managing it. And Dynamo had grown beyond traditional size even of a large division.

Losses: Top-Down Push (Table 17.3, column 4)

The combination of available and needy divisions, motivated corporate executives, and preoccupied focal divisions led to losses that were driven by corporate executives. For example, Dynamo's executive stepped in to streamline Dynamo's charter responsibilities and separate the division from an older, lucrative business that was distracting managers from the central, but more competitive, core charter. As one Dynamo manager recalled, "Well, [the new executive] comes on board and starts looking and realizing that it is good for Dynamo to have to live [with the new conditions]." Similarly, in the case of Zeus, the executive played a critical role in pushing through the charter loss. As the general manager recounted, "No I wasn't behind it . . . much of it was driven by [the corporate executive]." Finally, in the case of Marvel, as we noted previously, the corporate executive was key in noticing the focus problems at Marvel, the lack of attention to a new business area, and the opportunity to place the new area within Omega. This executive subsequently pushed through the charter loss despite reluctance at Marvel.

In summary, booming divisions shed old charter areas and new opportunities that defocused them from their burgeoning charter areas. Losing divisions could not keep track of old businesses and new opportunities while simultaneously managing their exploding businesses. They could, of course, have added more staff and expanded structures. But, other divisions often were searching for charters and so provided homes for excess businesses. Corporate executives were taking no financial or political chances with their engines of growth, preferring to keep them focused. Finally, division managers themselves were usually too busy to mount significant protests. Like Eisenhardt's strategic decision makers in high-velocity environments (1989b), these managers (particularly the more successful ones at Zeus and Marvel) became absorbed by their fast moving, increasingly complex core areas. They naturally gravitated towards these "real-time" businesses, neglecting past and future opportunities. Generally, therefore, the underlying logic was one of *focus*.

This process of charter change relates to the information processing perspective on organizational design. That is, information processing failures are seen as leading to reorganizations which either increase processing capacity or decrease the need to process information (e.g., Galbraith 1973), with charter losses representing this latter logic. However, unlike these reorganizations, consisting of major structural changes to the core activities of an organization, the reorganization process here is a shedding of peripheral activities around the core business. This trimming of excess businesses suggests an additional design strategy for the information processing perspective.

This process of charter change also relates to Van de Ven and Poole's (1995) description of teleological adaptation. Teleological processes are characterized by highly purposeful, adaptive actions. Entities evolve towards readily identifiable endstates or goals through explicit actions. Similarly, "growth losses" involved a central and clearly understood mission to focus on the cardinal task of growing the core businesses, and thus to shed new ventures or old business areas as needed. There was no doubt among all concerned regarding the primary of these engines of corporate growth. However, our data also reveal that the evolutionary processes of Marvel, Dynamo, and Zeus were not purely teleological. Rather, executives were focused on keeping pace with their changing businesses, rather than arriving at some endstate per se, as in a purely teleological process. So, they were directing their energies towards tracking and exploiting the present, rather than reaching some future goal.

Charter losses of this pattern also revealed the critical role played by group executives. Whereas the predominant interaction in the previous pattern was among rival divisions, this pattern reveals strong vertical interactions. Partially, the vertical interactions reflected power struggles. Division general managers were pitted against corporate executives attempting to maintain control over these business areas. By dividing up charters, corporate executives were able to exert, and assert, greater control over these business areas. However, there was also a strategic role evident in the group executives' conduct. These executives went to great lengths to ensure the continued viability of these engines of growth in the company. By matching up needy divisions with excess opportunities that "fell off the plate" of these burgeoning divisions, corporate executives also better aligned these market opportunities with corporate "homes" within which they could be nurtured. In this way, these executives influenced the strategic direction of the company. They protected corporate "empires" while enabling experimentation into potential future "empires" that we saw in the previous loss pattern. These charter losses were, therefore, a key executive tool for shaping corporate strategy within Omni.

MATURITY LOSSES:
EMERGENT TENSIONS AND UPHEAVAL

The third pattern of charter losses occurred among divisions with maturing businesses. Charter losses occurred as these divisions lost their mature
businesses in order to pursue new business areas that better matched their
organizational competencies and cultures. "Maturity losses" were characterized by four essential elements: (a) a fundamental misfit between the
competencies, structure, and culture of the focal division and the nature of
competition in the industry; (b) competition with closely related and ambitious corporate divisions/subsidiaries that better fit the need of the maturing
business areas; (c) heavy top-down forcing by corporate executives, marked
by upheaval in group and division management; and (d) extensive resistance
in the focal division. Overall, this pattern of charter loss was characterized
by an *emergent tensions* logic, marked by confrontations between the focal
division's normal mode of operation (e.g., heavy emphasis on R & D,
innovative culture, high overheads) and both the changing nature of competition in the industry (e.g., low-cost emphasis, modest extensions of existing
technological platforms, downsizing) and the availability of other divisions
to accommodate this approach. Faust, Omega, and Patriarch divisions all
experienced this pattern of charter loss.

The Setting: Maturing Businesses
(Table 17.4, column 1)

Success is not eternal and businesses tend to mature (Harrigan 1988). At
Omni, that was certainly the case for three of our divisions (Faust, Omega,
Patriarch). Each had been a corporate powerhouse. In the late 80s, Omega
had been known as "Mecca." Patriarch had been a market leader for almost
a decade. Faust had prospered as well in a rapidly expanding market. As one
manager recalled:

> If you look through the second half of the 80s they were just phenomenal! And we
> were just going like crazy. For a few years we just doubled the size of the division
> every year.

But, by the early 90s, these divisions were slumping. As one Faust
manager stated, "Performance was pretty crummy really. Nothing to be proud
of." Similarly, Omega's boom years gave way to struggles with new competitors and lost competitiveness. After years of high margins, Omega's costs
became too high and profits disappeared. As one manager reflected, "I think
that there was the perception that Omega . . . enjoyed tremendous leadership

TABLE 17.4 Cross-Case Illustrations of "Maturity" Charter Loss Pattern

Case	Setting	Other Divisions (Horizontal Interactions)	Corporate Level (Vertical Interactions)	Focal Division
FAUST	Maturing/Slumping Core Business: —9 years old —Growth = flat —Net Margins = mounting losses "[Performance] was pretty crummy really. Nothing to be proud of being in [this] business." Misfit: —Innovation-focused versus low-cost-focused marketplace "There was a lot of competence in taking new technologies and developing them to specific products in Faust, and the feeling was that the market was moving to where you didn't need that as much."	Emergent Competition: —Well-positioned subsidiary —Successful —Active lobbyist "It was logical [to put Faust's old charter here] because [we] had proven [we were] able to be successful in [this area] . . . therefore, [we] must have something that was right." "I'd been pushing people extremely strongly." (GM)	Change Agent: —New group executive "We had very long discussions about (misfit) and took inventory of what skill sets we hreally ad in each of the 1 ocations. What are the core competencies that we really command as opposed to the one's that we wish we did or other hoped for criteria . . . So, I guess we can shorten that by saying we took a good census of skills, knowledge, and where the time was going."	Resistance: "People in our organization would question us giving away everything but either you're going to give it away or you're not going to give it away." Upheaval Over Loss: —New general manager/New functional staff "I have a completely different functional staff. Everybody has changed."
OMEGA	Maturing/Slumping Core Business: —20 years old —Growth = flat —Net Margins = n/a	Emergent Competition: —Well-positioned subsidiary —Successful —Active lobbyist	Change Agent: —New group executive "[The new executive] wanted to make something positive	Resistance: —Politicking —Emotional attachment "Omega never wanted [rival

"[top managers were] convinced that Omega became too . . . noncompetitive.

Misfit:
—Innovation-focused versus low-cost-focused marketplace

"[we] enjoyed tremendous leadership in the marketplace, tremendous profit . . . but that allowed Omega to have a fat cost structure . . . that was okay until there were many [competitors] in the world."

PATRIARCH Maturing/Slumping Core Business:
—11 years old
—Growth = flat
—Net Margins = "Poor relative to others."

"we don't want to get trapped into the buggy whip scenario."

Misfit:
—Innovative focused versus low-cost focused marketplace

"I think we were very R&D creative driven. We weren't thinking cost of sales and leaverage . . . we didn't have to . . . But, that has changed in the last couple of years."

"You would see always a constant in every, every one of our steps [the division took in its progression] which is always exceeding expectation."

"[Our GM] said 'we want a charter' . . . it was [the GM's] speech for 2 years or 3 years."

Emergent Competition:
—Well-positioned division
—Successful
—Lobbyist for change

"I'm not very egotistical but it seems to me to be fairly obvious that we had almost a step function higher performance . . . We took more out of manufacturing costs and improved speed in manufacturing, more than some of them."

"I think [our GM] pushed for some of these concepts in the past."

happen, and languishing as it had for a couple years of not sure what to do, that he firmly believed [there was a change needed]."

Change Agent:
—Executive pushes change

"The actual initiation of [change] probably occurred when [the corporate executive] decided that it was time to make a structural change."

division]. They said it was a big waste . . . they saw it as a real drain."

"very difficult when you work so hard on a particular market to be successful."

Upheaval Over Loss:
—New general manager/
    New functional staff

"we basically changed 2/3s of the management team in Omega so it was very very tough, it was very difficult."

Resistance:
—Rivalry/Politicking
—Emotional attachment

"It was even described by a few people as a hostile take-over."

"I think there is a real emotional attachment. . . . We are the experts in the world on this stuff."

Upheaval Over Loss:
—High disagreement over decision

"I was actually amazed at how little consensus . . . had developed."

in the marketplace, tremendous profit . . . but that allowed [them] to have a fat cost structure . . . that was okay until there were many [competitors] in the world."

As time went on, misfit grew. Markets became more competitive and cost sensitive. These divisions increasingly lost their alignment between core competencies and the evolving demands of their chartered areas. For example, although Faust grew wildly when the market was unexplored and customers appreciated novel product features, the division gradually became misaligned with the marketplace when efficient production and "no-frills," low-cost products captured interest. Faust maintained a large R & D department, complex matrix structures, high costs (40% above other competitors by one manager's estimates), and an innovative culture. The competitive environment, on the other hand, became focused on low cost, low price, and small extensions of standard designs. One manager summarized:

> There was a lot of competence in taking new technologies and developing them to specific products in Faust, and the feeling was that the market was moving to where you didn't need that as much, there wasn't so much value in all that engineering and so we felt that [we did not fit] . . . if we want to stay in the [old] business, the gross margins that you can make in that business in order to fund R & D, marketing and things like that are so much smaller that if we stay in that business we're going to have to tear this place apart.

Omega experienced similar growing misalignment. Omega retained an R & D focus while competitive conditions evolved towards efficient manufacturing and low cost. Omega became less and less able to compete effectively. Omega's strong engineering culture played a particularly strong role in creating misfit. One manager explained:

> That goes back to culture . . . it came from the strong engineering environment, so Omega tended to be feature oriented, Omega was not a low cost site, Omega did not have manufacturing efficiencies.

At Patriarch, the charter marketplace moved away from military applications towards commercial ones. Patriarch found its operations uncompetitive, too focused on development of expensive novelties while the market placed greater emphasis on price. One manager summarized the misfit:

> We designed this stuff in the heydays of the boom. We did not design for manufacturability back in the 80s . . . we had no cost of sales pressure . . . we had the world's greatest idea every three years. . . . But, that has changed.

One response could have been to divest these businesses, as suggested by portfolio planning models (e.g., Berg 1984). However, none was. Rather, these were seen as still important businesses in the overall brand image of the company, and in some cases, they held promise of some future growth. A second response could have been to realign and downsize these divisions. But, there was a desire to preserve expertise and avoid layoffs. One manager described the typical situation:

> We had this core expertise here, we had this skill set. We didn't necessarily want to break that apart.

The result was that old charters were replaced by new ones which better matched the division. For example, Faust was stripped of its old charter, but given the charge of finding new businesses that fit their existing competencies. The guiding principle was to enter emerging niches. One manager noted that they were "really trying to go off and establish a new area." Only new niches were likely to have the growth potential to maintain the employment base and to exploit the innovative skills of the division. As another Faust manager stated, "[so we said] 'let's see if we can find another market where we can take these technologies and keep high gross margins.'" Similarly, Omega lost its core charter, but, as noted in the previous section, gained a new venture opportunity from Marvel. Omega had the technical expertise and desire to drive the new business. Patriarch also lost its core charter and refocused on an emerging marketplace that provided a better match with, as one manager said, Patriarch's "world-wide expertise" in new product development.

Thus, "maturity losses" involved an emerging misfit between divisional competencies and the nature of competition in core businesses. Rather than divest or realign, these divisions switched charters. However, these losses were also greatly influenced by other divisions and corporate executives. Indeed, whereas "start-up losses" were marked largely by intradivisional dynamics (horizontal interaction), and "growth losses" were marked largely by hierarchical dynamics (vertical interaction), "maturity losses" were significantly affected by both.

Other Divisions: Evolving Competition (Table 17.4, column 2)

Rival divisions played an important role in charter loss. In each case, rival divisions began to outcompete focal divisions. However, the dynamics of this competition differed from those in "start-up losses." Whereas competition in the earlier phase was marked by relatively autonomous forays into emergent business domains by divisions that were sometimes even unaware of each other's actions, competition in this later phase was often the result of the complex structures and relationships that had been developed over the long histories of these divisions. These typically came in the form of long-existing charter overlaps between these former engines-of-growth and other corporate divisions. These overlaps created the potential for charter competition, as market changes caused commensurate shifts in the appropriateness of existing charter-division alignments and suggested new match-ups. Indeed, as a result these rivals often targeted the charters of the focal divisions.

Consider, for example, the complex structures that evolved around Faust and Omega. As noted above, both divisions had enjoyed substantial success during their long existence. Their emergence as vibrant divisions had required elaboration of their structures and systems to cope with increasing size, including, most significantly, the establishment of divisional subsidiaries within lucrative global markets. Although the subsidiaries were initially set-up as assembly sites to serve foreign markets, they were eventually given a broaded range of responsibilities, including the design of second-generation products and the full compliment of manufacturing duties. Strategically, these subsidiaries operated as cost-centers and not surprisingly their strengths lay in efficient production. As a manager from Faust's subsidiary noted, "We were focusing more on second generation type of product where the main interest is focused on reducing costs, increasing manufacturing [attention]."

As marketplace demands evolved, the competencies developed by these subsidiaries became more closely matched with the needs of the marketplace. Moreover, both subsidiaries established excellent performance records, as, for example, a manager from Omega's subsidiary noted, ". . . our history is a succession of small successes." Their management actively lobbied for more responsibilities. For example, the management of Omega's rival admitted to lobbying regularly for two or three years for domain changes. Similarly, the management of Faust's rival also lobbied for the main part of Faust's charter and clandestinely attempted to develop competing products.

Similarly, Patriarch's rival evolved from structural complexities as well, driven by 11 years of co-existence and interweaving of its charter and those of other divisions. The divisions began with distinct domains. Gradually however, their technologies converged and their markets overlapped, particularly as a result of increasing similarities in their basic product platforms. Yet, these overlaps (or redundancies) in basic platform design and manufacturing were tolerated because of the lucrative nature of their business areas and the greater design and operational freedom available to each division in serving customers who were often willing to spare no expense in order to ensure the most reliable, custom-made product. One manager described the situation:

There was redundancy occurring between the organizations . . . we had at various times as many as three or four of the divisions developing [basic platforms]. We were able to get away with that in the early 80s because of the amount of defense money that was being spent.

These overlaps, however, did not preclude divisions taking different paths to develop their charters. As we have noted, Patriarch chose to maintain a highly innovative mentality. A fellow division, however, chose to focus more heavily on manufacturing and cost reduction. As one manager stated, "We took more out of manufacturing costs and improved speed in manufacturing, more than some of [the other divisions]." Not surprisingly, when the marketplace shifted and the redundancies became too costly, the other division was in a better position than Patriarch. Moreover, the management of the rival division explicitly lobbied corporate executives to take over a portion of Patriarch's business.

In sum, while focal divisions slipped into misalignment with their markets, other parts of the corporation came into alignment. Whereas previously described overlaps (i.e., divisions experiencing "start-up losses") were the result of experimental forays into emergent domains, these latter overlaps were often the result of previously created structures. In all cases, as market conditions changed, the better fit between the competitive demands of the marketplace and the competencies of the rival sites created a powerful pull on the focal division's core business. Moreover, rival managers also explicitly attempted to strengthen their positions and lobby for the change. Thus, once again we see interdivisional competition as a powerful factor in the charter loss process.

Corporate Executives: Change Agent
(Table 17.4, column 3)

Despite growing misalignment and pressures from rival divisions, charter loss was slow. Although problems were often apparent for several years, existing corporate executives often tolerated the evolving misalignment. Indeed, the impression was that corporate executives were too much a part of the divisional arrangements for them to comfortably make the changes that were required. Nevertheless, performance deteriorated to the point where some action at the highest levels in the company was unavoidable.

Key events broke the logjam. At Faust and Omega, key corporate level executives were replaced (one retired, one resigned), representing the first steps in relieving the tensions building in the system. These new executives saw themselves as change agents with a mission to "shake things up." As a Faust manager explained, "I think [the new corporate executive] wanted to make something positive happen, and languishing as it had for a couple years of not being sure what to do, that he firmly believed [there was a change needed]." In describing the new corporate executive overseeing Omega, one executive said, "I saw a change, a very important change." At Patriarch, pressure to change emanated from the CEO, although the group executive stayed the same.

These corporate executives instigated a detailed evaluation of the competencies and charter options of focal divisions and neighboring divisions—a fundamental rethinking of divisional domains and alignments. These evaluations were instrumental in the decisions to remove maturing businesses from focal divisions and transplant them to other sites. For example, at Faust, as a corporate executive explained:

> We had very long discussions about it and took inventory of what skill sets we really had in each of the locations. What are the core competencies that we really command as opposed to the one's that we wish we did or other hoped for criteria . . . we took a good census of skills, knowledge and where the time was going and what we were spending our time and effort on.

At Omega, the new corporate executive also brought together divisions and asked "nasty" questions regarding division directions, as one manager noted:

> [The corporate executive] did a great job in asking the right tough questions. . . . He will go and visit the division and say "okay, show me your numbers or can't you do any better" . . . he didn't make a lot of friends. What he did is make people aware of the business environment.

At Patriarch, the corporate executive spent several months privately interviewing divisional managers in order to gather ideas and, perhaps more importantly, create expectations of change within the divisions, having been shoved into action by top corporate officials.

These evaluations gave the corporate executives the insight and the basis to push through what were often unpopular changes. In all three cases, corporate executives drove the change. At Patriarch, the corporate executive was described as "the main mover and shaker." Likewise, the corporate executive at Omega was quoted as saying, "I moved here to do something and I'm going to and really not wait for the bottoms up reaction, but put on a lot of top-down pressure." Thus, although the stresses that emerged in the system may have forced some change, corporate executives, operating as change agents, pushed them through.

Focal Divisions: Embattled Resistors
(Table 17.4, column 4)

As mentioned earlier, these divisions had been very successful in the past. Thus, it was not easy to face the loss of a charter that had done so well. Part of the resistance was nostalgia and a sense of history in the business area. For example, the old charter would be missed within Patriarch. As one manager explained:

> I think there is just a real emotional attachment—it's been the heart of this division's charter for 40 years. We are the experts in the world on this stuff.

There was also fear and a sense of imminent devastation. Engineers at Omega were particularly hard hit. As one manager described:

> The engineers had a very hard time, it's very difficult when you work so hard on a particular market to be successful . . . and the division was being shaken out like hell, so their motivation . . . well, I hope I never see this again.

Divisions also worried about the new charters they would pursue. There were tremendous uncertainties associated with changes of this magnitude. On the one hand, divisions faced some downsizing as they lost large, older businesses. On the other hand, they were expected to create new growth in emerging markets. This generated worries in divisional managers, as two Patriarch managers explained:

> We reviewed our business plan and we said [to the corporate executive], "here is the problem we are facing, You're telling us to fund this growth opportunity—we need to do that. But, we need dollars and people to do that. How are you going to handle that?"

> I was afraid that [the charter change] would be a convenient way to shift all the down-sizing headaches to Patriarch.

Resentment was also a factor. At Patriarch, there was a belief that the rival division had become too close to the corporate executives and obtained a "good deal" at the expense of Patriarch. In fact, Patriarch managers resented the rival division and, as one executive related, "it [charter loss] was described by some people as a hostile takeover!" In the case of Omega, one manager described how Omega managers viewed their rival, "they never wanted (rival division). They said it was a big waste . . . they saw it as a real drain."

Not surprisingly then, the focal divisions engaged in intense politicking. Omega managers attempted to undermine their rival by lobbying corporate executives into having it closed. They argued that any downsizing should happen outside of Omega. Then, when it appeared that the rival would succeed, top managers from Omega went uninvited to meetings between corporate executives and the rival division to plead their case.

At Patriarch, the 10-month period after the announcement of the charter loss was filled with misunderstandings, politicking, and conflict. Patriarch managers lobbied a senior corporate executive to intervene on their behalf. As the Patriarch general manager recalled, "I started talking to him directly when I started thinking 'shit, I wonder if we are going to lose this battle.' " Patriarch managers attempted to stall the process. One tactic was described as "sacrifice the knight." It involved agreeing to give up a portion of the core charter—but one that they did not really want. Sometimes they just stonewalled. Overall, as one manager described, "In the ensuing months I was actually amazed at how little consensus [the corporate executive] had developed."

Losses: Upheaval (Table 17.4, column 4)

The combination of a frightened focal division, determined corporate executives, and ambitious rivals lead to a turbulent process. At Faust there was almost a complete turnover of the top management team preceding the charter loss, including the division manager and functional staff, as the new general manager noted:

I have a completely different functional staff. Everybody has changed.

Omega also experienced a similar change in the top management team. Although not all functional staff members were replaced, the process was nevertheless wrenching. As a corporate executive observed, "we basically changed two thirds of the management team in Omega so it was very very tough, it was very difficult." At Patriarch, however, although there were no management changes, the implementation of the charter switch, as we noted, dragged out and became increasingly politicized. It was well summarized by one manager, "I viewed the [charter loss decision period] as the [group executive] putting on his black and white striped shirt and refereeing how [the divisions] carved-up some of the activities."

Overall, this pattern relates to a punctuated equilibrium process of evolution (e.g., Miller and Friesen 1984, Tushman and Romanelli 1985), which is characterized by long equilibrium periods of mounting tensions and short periods of intense change. In these cases, we observed mismatches building between divisions and their environments, often over several years. The eventual recognition of these mismatches by corporate executives was particularly instrumental in catalyzing the change process. That the process was so wrenching and difficult is suggestive of the deep structures that had built up over many years in the focal divisions and that are so often related to punctuated change processes.

However, our data also reveal a more complex process than simply the building of tensions within the focal division in the face of growing environmental misalignment. Rather, competitive divisions were central to the process. Their managers were persistent advocates of change, often over several years. They lobbied and engaged in covert activities to force change. Just as importantly, these divisions were strong performers and moved into positions of better fit with the maturing charter. So, while the focal divisions were being pulled apart internally by misalignment, these other divisions exerted a strong, external pull to strip charters. Also striking was the level of politicking. The interdivisional competition created bitter, political battles among the divisions, especially when the divisional managers or executives remained unchanged.

Finally, and perhaps most noteworthy, in most exemplars of punctuated change in organizations (e.g., Tushman and Romanelli 1985), strategies, structures, processes, and culture are dramatically shifted. In contrast, the major change here was the domain in which the divisions operated. Strategies, competencies, and culture remained relatively intact (i.e., high innovation and development focus, attack emerging market). As a result, these fundamental organizational features, arguably more difficult to re-engineer and more valuable to maintain, were kept in tact while businesses were switched. Singh and colleagues (1986) have noted the important distinction between adaptation of peripheral versus core features. What we see here is that Omni executives treat charters as peripheral while structures, culture, and processes are more immutable core features.

DISCUSSION AND IMPLICATIONS

This chapter is intended as a first step towards building a more dynamic vision of large, diversified firms. Although the last three decades have seen significant research on diversified companies, the fundamental concept of divisional domains remains static. Chandler's (1962) articulation of multidivisional organization assumes that divisions are neatly boxed into static business charters. This assumption endures. Yet, it seems likely that the divisional domains of real firms, especially those in highly competitive and high velocity industries, will coevolve with changing markets and technologies.

Our model highlights three patterns of charter loss, each operating with a different logic and associated with a different phase of charter development. The loss pattern associated with early charter development, as divisions attempt to launch new business areas, reflects a *quasi-natural selection* logic. Initial excitement about new charters gives way to problems in defining the charter, developing strategy, and creating successful products. Eventually, lagging performance brings on charter loss. In addition, the loss process is importantly influenced by other experimenting divisions, fluidly committed corporate executives, and ambivalence within the focal division. A second pattern of loss is associated with divisions riding the crest of booming charter areas. Here the logic is *focus*. Initially, divisions are able to manage old businesses, current growth, and new opportunities. As time goes by, this becomes more difficult to do. Eventually, the pattern of loss depends on powerful corporate executives concerned with focusing the corporate engines of growth in the face of reluctant focal divisions. Finally, the loss pattern associated with maturing charters reflects an *emergent tensions* logic. Initial success yields to increasing mismatch as the demands of the marketplace diverge from the competencies and culture of the division. Loss occurs as the misfit becomes too extreme to ignore, particularly as rivals come to provide a better fit with changing market conditions. Since the three patterns of charter loss occur across the broad range of product life-cycle phases within which most divisions find themselves, our model of charter losses is perhaps a modest first step towards a more general model of how M-form organizations adapt in fast-paced environments. Table 17.5 compares these three patterns.

From an organization theory perspective, these patterns of charter loss have implications for central debates surrounding change. A fundamental debate centers around whether adaptation or selection better capture organization change processes. That is, are organizations able to adapt or do new forms arise primarily from selection processes? Our data allow us to examine this issue at the intracorporate level of analysis. First, natural selection mechanisms are found to operate within Omni. Specifically, the results of the "start-up losses" process suggest that a kind of natural selection was at work. Divisions were found to be competing, sometimes unknowingly, for charters, and certain division-charter match-ups were selected out while others were retained. This is consistent with recent papers that use evolutionary theories and intra-corporate ecology to understand how strategies unfold *within* a firm, a novel and emerging use of ecological perspectives (e.g., Burgelman 1991, Miner 1994). Our chapter extends this perspective by exploring divisional selection processes within a corporation, a complement to the more common corporate level of analysis.

TABLE 17.5 Comparison of Loss Patterns

	Start-Up Losses	Growth Losses	Maturity Losses
Overall logic	Quasi-natural selection	Focus	Emergent tension
Nature of horizontal interaction	Experimentation: Competitive behavior	Opportunistic transfers: Mutualistic behavior	Evolving overlaps: Competitive behavior
Nature of vertical interaction	Fleeting commitments and consensus	Strategizing and top-down push	Upheaval and heavy top-down forcing
Dominant interaction type	Horizontal	Vertical	Horizontal and vertical
Difficulty of loss	Low	Moderate	High

However, we also found support for other logics of change, including more adaptive responses. Charter change processes borrow from several logics of change, not just one. For example, adaptation through a teleological process is apparent in the "growth" loss pattern. Here group executives engaged in purposive action to focus divisions onto their evolving markets by altering their charter responsibilities. The change process of these divisions was adaptive-competitive selection mechanisms were relatively absent. The "maturity" loss pattern exhibits bits of both processes. Selection occurred among competing divisions, but losses involved purposive action by group executives and major adaptive shifts by divisions. Thus, charter loss in M-form firms is a complex mixture of selection and adaptation processes.

Our work also relates to questions surrounding the fundamental nature of social interactions in M-form corporations. First, as others have argued, M-form organizations behave a lot like markets (e.g., Henderson 1979, Vancil 1979, Eccles and White 1986). That is, corporate divisions, like independent firms, often have overlapping claims on (typically scarce) corporate resources. What results is a process of competition such that these resources can be efficiently allocated between divisions—a process, in essence, that tries to mimic the price mechanism in a marketplace. However, the traditional conception of competition within the M-form focuses on the favorable re-allocation of *financial* resources. Divisions compete, typically within fixed product-market areas, for the retained earnings of the firm, offering-up to corporate headquarters different investment opportunities that are measured with the aid of some form of net-present-value analysis. The more lucrative investments, in theory, are endowed with the necessary capital. The resulting conception of the M-form organization as a marketplace, therefore, is centered on the way corporate profits are internally redistributed among divisions. In contrast, at Omni, the competition among divisions is for more than financial resources. The dynamism of evolving markets and technologies creates a market for business opportunities, that is a market for *charters* among divisions. So, divisions are competing not only for financial resources, but more importantly, within an "economy of charters" for the opportunities to pursue choice business areas. For example, constant flux in markets and technologies made it more likely that divisions would collide with each other from time to time in emerging product-market areas, creating competition for charters, as was particularly evident in "start-up losses." The evidence suggested that the division better able to survive and compete in this marketplace would be awarded the charter. Moreover, the running-down of certain marketplaces, and the subsequent misfit of some divisions while others gained in fit, also introduced opportunities for charter competition, as was seen in "maturity losses." Overall, therefore, market-like competition is seen as a defining feature of the M-form organization, with a particular emphasis in this paper on a marketplace for charters.

On the other hand, although Omni behaves like a marketplace for charters, it also behaves much like a hierarchy. For example, "winning" firms were not always granted the plum charters. In the "growth losses" pattern, neighboring, needy divisions were often given charters because they were in trouble and faced possible demise (e.g., Omega). The spoils of successful divisions, in Robin Hood fashion, were passed on to wanting divisions. In other cases, charter assignments were affected by needs for maintaining employment in particular locations or developing a presence in important geographic areas. Several explanations of these charter decisions strike us as plausible. First, a sense of cooperation and equity among divisions coexisted with the market-style competition described above. Managers certainly felt part of a strong corporate heritage and culture, and seemingly altruistic, sacrificial behavior was not out of place, if it was seen as "best for the corporation." Of course, this behavior may have been a signaling attempt by up-and-coming divisional managers of their loyalty to the whole company, thus not truly altrustic—it is difficult for us to discern the exact motives. Yet, what is clear is that charter decisions were sometimes made without a hint of market analogies, but rather a strong sense of collaboration, mutualism and even a social welfare mentality. Finally, political activities played a role in charter change. That is, outside of market-like conduct and mutualistic behavior, charters were sometimes altered simply because of the power and authority accumulated by those who wanted the change. For example, "growth losses" reflected, to some extent, a struggle for power between corporate and division executives, with corporate authority winning-out in our sample. Of course, it is unclear whether these "hierarchical" aspects of Omni are efficient (i.e., in terms of providing "optimal" charter-division match-ups). Yet, at firms such as Omni, the fast pace of the business environment may make a quick adaptation process (teamwork, flexibility, etc.) more desirable than one that is slower and more methodical in matching charters to divisions. Speed and experimentation is particularly valuable where the product-market conditions change quickly, frequently, and are often difficult to interpret. In sum, the nature of interactions within Omni reflected both intense market-like activities and hierarchical features (i.e., a concern for mutualism and the use of top-down decision making). To us, therefore, it seems unbenificial to identify large corporations are purely markets or hierarchies, but rather we should observe more closely under what conditions and circumstances they can exhibit either trait (see also Hill et al. 1992).

Finally, an important contrast with the traditional M-form organization is the critical role played by group executives at Omni. These executives were experimenters, profit guardians, and change agents. But, their most critical role was as corporate matchmaker. Whether wielding an "iron fist" in "maturity losses" or an "invisible hand" in "start-up losses," these executives continually matched and re-matched charters with divisions, a response to the dynamism of markets and technologies. Theirs was a challenging job. Focal divisions could not give up their charters without having new ones. They could not gain new ones without finding homes for the old. Every division needed a charter, every charter needed a division. In this "recombinant" view of organizations where charters, like genes in strands of DNA, are continually spliced and moved throughout the corporation, group executives were critical. This role adds an important new dimension to the potential contribution of corporate headquarters. During the 80s we witnessed agnosticism towards the value of corporate headquarters, evident in increased LBO activity and commensurate break-ups of large divisified corporations: The message was that corporations were worth more in pieces than when managed as a whole. We would argue that "charter changes" afford corporate headquarters new opportunities to create value. In particular, these changes highlight the fundamental task of corporate leadership—to continuously align business charters with divisional skills in order to keep pace with coevolving markets and technologies. The task is no longer just to choose what business areas are to be entered or exited (i.e., without considering organizational issues), nor just to re-engineer troubled operating units (i.e., without considering charter issues). Rather, via charter changes, the task is to manage both aspects of corporate reality.

CONCLUSION

We conclude this chapter with a question: Are the results from Omni generalizable? Although generalizability is, of course, an empirical question, it does seem likely that some firms may rely more on acquisitions to enter new domains, may let booming businesses burgeon, and may divest mature businesses more often than did Omni. In particular, firms in slower-paced industries would probably show less frequent charter change. So, Omni is not "everyfirm."

On the other hand, Omni can be thought of as one way to organize complex, diversified firms. Seen in this way, Omni's organizing strategy is to 1) attack new markets through limited thrusts by several divisions, 2) restrict the scope of divisions in booming markets, and 3) preserve skills and culture by appropriate switching and matching of charters. Overall, the organizational hallmark of Omni is the *strategic use of charter changes* to align and realign, on an apparently continual basis, the competencies of various divisions with coevolving markets and opportunities. It is this dynamism which weeds out inferior match-ups, nurtures and protects productive ones, and, therefore, offers greater adaptability to the diversified corporation.

How has this affected Omni's performance? Although it is impossible to tie performance to one element of a corporation's strategy, it is worthwhile to note that Omni has been a very successful firm in the time period relevant to this study. During the 1988-1993 fiscal period, Omni experienced significant overall growth (over 50% growth in revenue), remarkable given the stagnant nature of most economies where Omni participated during that period. Omni is also considered by many to be a superbly managed firm and a leader in a number of markets that could be termed "hypercompetitive." This superior performance, therefore, suggests that Omni's organizing model may also be an exemplar for effectively managing large, diversified firms in hypercompetitive markets. That is, Omni's ability to shift businesses among divisions may be a key organizational competence. In an age when greater emphasis is being placed on organizational capabilities and processes as sources of high performance (as opposed to just industry position), the effective recombination of corporate charters may be a worthwhile consideration for other managers of large, diversified corporations. Given the limitations of an inductive study with a limited number of cases, we hope that this study will offer ideas and lessons towards future empirical tests of this phenomenon, thus helping to build a new, more accurate model of the operation of our largest and perhaps most influential organizations.

ACKNOWLEDGEMENTS

This chapter has benefited from the generous support of the Alfred P. Sloan Foundation. The first author also benefited from a fellowship from the Social Sciences Research Council of Canada. The second author was also generously supported as the Finmeccanica Faculty Scholar at Stanford during the preparation of this chapter. We particularly appreciate the invaluable assistance of Bob Sutton, Jeff Pfeffer, and the seminar participants at the Organization Science/Whittemore Conference on Hypercompetition at Dartmouth College, plus our anonymous reviewers.

NOTES

1. Distinguishing between gains and losses served as convenient way in which to analyze the data, creating a distinction in the charter change outcome that was both naturally occurring and useful for data analyses purposes. Most importantly, it introduced parsimony into the modeling process. This is not to say that the two are totally independent—certainly some losses lead to a search for new charters, and some lucrative new opportunities lead to losses of older charter portions. But we found losses and gains also to have a life of their own. More to the point, within the confines of one research study that seeks to develop new theory, it would be unnecessarily complex to introduce, contrast, and compare both processes. This we leave for a later date. We begin with an exploration of losses, although gains could have served equally well as a starting point.

2. Indeed, there were divisions within Omni that faced similar early crisis but that did not lose their charters. Although the study of how these divisions successfully survived their rough beginnings is an interesting issue, the focus of this chapter is in explaining the process of charter losses.

REFERENCES

Bartlett, C. A. and S. Ghoshal (1991), *Managing Across Borders: The Transnational Solution.* Boston, MA: Harvard Business School.

Beamish, P. W., J. P. Killing, D. J. Lecraw and A. J. Morrison (1994), *International Management: Text and Cases.* Burr Ridge, IL: Richard Irwin.

Berg, N. A. (1984), *General Management: An Analytical Approach.* Homewood, IL: Richard Irwin.

Burgelman, R. A. (1983), "A Process Model of Internal Corporate Venturing in the Diversified Firm," *Administrative Science Quarterly,* 28, 223-244.

——— (1991), "Intraorganizational Ecology of Strategy Making and Organizational Adaptation: Theory and Field Research," *Organization Science,* 2, 3, 239-262.

Chakravarthy, B. S. and P. Lorange (1991), *Managing the Strategy Process: A Framework for a Multibusiness Firm.* Englewood Cliffs, NY: Prentice Hall.

Chandler, Jr., A. D. (1962), *Strategy and Structure: Chapters in the History of the American Industrial Enterprise.* Cambridge: MIT Press.

D'Aveni, R. A. (1994), *Hypercompetition,* New York: Free Press.

Eccles, R. G. and H. C. White (1986), "Firm and Market Interfaces of Profit Center Control," in J. S. Lindenberg, J. S. Coleman, and S. Nowak, eds., *Approaches to Social Theory.* New York: Russell Sage, 103-220.

Eisenhardt, K. M. (1989a), "Building Theories from Case Study Research," *Academy of Management Review,* 14, 488-511.

———— (1989b), "Making Fast Strategic Decisions," *Academy of Management Journal,* 32, 543-576.

Fortune (1992), "The Global 500," July 27th issue: 176-232.

Galbraith, J. R. (1973), *Designing Complex Organizations.* Reading, MA: Addison-Wesley.

Galunic, D. C. and K. M. Eisenhardt (1994), "Renewing the Strategy-Structure-Performance Paradigm," *Research in Organizational Behavior.* B. M. Staw and L. L. Cummings (Eds.).

Garud, R. and A. H. Van de Ven (1992), "An Empirical Evaluation of the Internal Corporate Venturing Process," *Strategic Management Journal,* 13, 93-109.

Gersick, C. J. G. (1991), "Revolutionary Change Theories: A Multilevel Exploration of the Punctuated Equilibrium Paradigm," *Academy of Management Review,* 16, 1, 10-36.

———— (1994), "Pacing Strategic Change: The Case of a New Venture," *Academy of Management Journal* 37, 9-45.

Glaser, B. and A. Strauss (1967), *The Discovery of Grounded Theory: Strategies for Qualitative Research.* London, UK: Wiedenfeld and Nicholson.

Govindarajan, V. and J. Fisher (1990), "Strategy, Control Systems, and Resource Sharing: Effects on Business-Unit Performance," *Academy of Management Journal,* 33, 259-285.

Gupta, A. K. (1987), "SBU Relations, Corporate-SBU Relations, and SBU Effectiveness in Strategy Implementation," *Academy of Management Journal,* 30, 477-500.

———— and V. Govindarajan (1986), "Resource Sharing Among SBUs: Strategic Antecedents and Administrative Implications," *Academy of Management Journal,* 29, 695-714.

Guth, W. D. and A. Ginsberg (1990), "Corporate Enterpreneurship." *Strategic Management Journal* 11 (Special Issue), 5-15.

Harrigan, K. R. (1988), *Managing Maturing Businesses.* Lexington, MA: Lexington Books.

Henderson, B. D. (1979), *Henderson on Corporate Strategy.* Cambridge, MA: Abt.

Hill, C. W. L., M. A. Hitt and R. E. Hoskisson (1992), "Cooperative versus Competitive Structures in Related and Unrelated Diversified Firms," *Organization Science,* 3, 501-521.

Leonard-Barton, D. (1990), "A Dual Methodology for Case Studies: Synergistic Use of a Longitudinal Single Site with Replicated Multiple Sites," *Organization Science,* 1, 3, 248-266.

Levine, S. and P. E. White (1961), "Exchange as a Conceptual Framework for the Study of Interorganizational Relationships," *Administrative Science Quarterly,* 583-601.

Miles, M. and A. M. Huberman (1984), *Qualitative Data Analysis.* Beverly Hills, CA: Sage.

Miles, R. E. and C. C. Snow (1978), *Organizational Strategy, Structure, and Process.* New York: McGraw-Hill.

Miller, D. (1988), "Relating Porter's Business Strategies to Environment and Structure: Analysis and Performance Implications," *Academy of Management Journal,* 31, 280-308.

———— and P. H. Friesen (1984), *Organizations—A Quantum View,* Englewood Cliffs, NJ: Prentice Hall.

Miner, A. S. (1994), "Seeking Adaptive Advantage: Evolutionary Theory and Managerial Action," in Baum, J. A. C. and Singh, J. V. *Evolutionary Dynamics of Organizations.* Oxford, UK: Oxford University Press.

Mintzberg, H. (1990), "The Design School: Reconsidering the Basic Premises of Strategic Management," *Strategic Management Journal,* 11, 171-195.

Pettigrew, A. M. (1985), *The Awakening Giant: Continuity and Change in ICI.* Oxford, UK: Blackwell.

——— (1990), "Longitudinal Field Research on Change: Theory and Practice," *Organization Science,* 1, 3, 267-292.

Porter, M. E. (1980), *Competitive Strategy—Techniques for Analyzing Industries and Competitors.* New York: Free Press.

——— (1985), *Competitive Advantage.* New York: Free Press.

Prahalad, C. K. and Y. Doz (1987), *The Multinational Mission.* New York: Free Press.

Quinn, J. B. (1980), *Strategies for Change: Logical Incrementalism.* Homewood, IL: Irwin.

Ramanujam, V. and P. Varadarajan (1989), "Research on Corporate Diversification: A Synthesis," *Strategic Management Journal,* 10, 523-551.

Rumelt, R. P. (1974), *Strategy, Structure, and Economic Performance,* Boston, MA: Harvard Graduate School of Business.

———, D. E. Schendel and D. J. Teece (1994), *Fundamental Issues in Strategy,* Boston, MA: Harvard Business School Press.

Scott, W. R. (1981), *Organizations—Rational, Natural and Open Systems.* Englewood Cliffs, NJ: Prentice Hall.

Singh, J., House, R. and D. Tucker (1986), "Organization Change and Organization Mortality," *Administrative Science Quarterly,* 31, 587-611.

Taylor, W. (1991), "The Logic of Global Business: An Interview with ABB's Percy Barnevik," *Harvard Business Review,* March-April, 1991.

Thompson, J. D. (1967), *Organizations in Action,* New York: McGraw-Hill.

Tushman, M. and E. Romanelli (1985), "Organizational Evolution: A Metamorphosis Model of Convergence and Reorientation," *Research in Organizational Behavior,* B. Staw and L. Cummings, (Eds.), 7, 171-222.

Vancil, R. F. (1979), *Decentralization: Managerial Ambiguity by Design.* Homewood, IL: Dow Jones-Irwin.

Van de Ven, A. H. and S. M. Poole (1995), "Explaining Development and Change in Organizations," *Academy of Management Review,* Volume 20, no. 3, 510-540.

Williamson, O. E. (1975), *Markets and Hierarchies: Analysis and Antitrust Implications.* New York: Free Press.

Yin, R. K. (1989), *Case Study Research: Design and Methods.* Newbury Park, CA: Sage.

18

Spontaneous Organizational Reconfiguration

A Historical Example
Based on Xenophon's *Anabasis*

KENNETH E. AUPPERLE

This chapter examines an ancient historical event that has profound implications regarding the role of organizational culture in facilitating spontaneous organizational reconfiguration. Xenophon's *Anabasis* documents the successful retreat of a Greek army trapped in Persia in a setting that is comparable to the hypercompetition of today. Spontaneous reconfiguration is seen here to be a vital survival element in hypercompetitive environments, past and present. As a result, a historical case is used as a time-bridge to reveal the importance of rapid and substantive organizational redesign when confronting highly competitive and quickly shifting environments. The *Anabasis* is also used to animate several of Gareth Morgan's (1986) metaphors. In particular, metaphors pertaining to a biological organism, the brain, and culture are used to parallel the Greek emphasis on body, mind, and spirit. While Xenophon's army is depicted here in terms of being an organic, biological organism, as well as a brain with holographic properties, it is culture that emerges as the truly defining metaphor.

The Greek supraculture appears to have played a vital role in facilitating nearly instantaneous organizational restructuring. This was a culture that emphasized an integrative balance between the ethic of community and individuality. Such redesigning properties were essential for an isolated, leaderless army which faced a variety of hostile competitors, rapidly shifting environmental conditions, and starvation. The culture metaphor enables us to see how widely shared values and beliefs can facilitate an organic type of behavioral programming capable of enabling Xenophon's army to transcend the formal attributes of organizational structure. Ultimately, it was culture, not strategy, qualitative and informal properties, not well defined roles and structures, that produced the Greek success. Contemporary organizations that attempt to become more horizontally focused, team oriented, and process driven are adopting a paradigm that is now 2,400 years old. Toynbee would not be surprised:

> What light have we that we can project upon the darkness of the future? We have the precious light of experience, which has always been Mankind's guide to action in public, as in private affairs. No sensible person, of course, has ever imagined that a mechanical application of past experience to present problems will grind out automatic solutions of these. Experience gives us enigmatic hints, not blueprinted instructions. Yet these hints are invaluable, since they are the only light on the future that we can bring to bear, and where the future that is in question is a society's not an individual's the experience of other societies has the same significance for us as the experience of our contemporaries and our elders is the ordering of our personal lives. (Toynbee 1953, p. xii)

(ARMY; CHANGE; CULTURE;
ENVIRONMENT; HISTORICAL; HORIZONTAL;
HYPERCOMPETITION; LEADERSHIP; METAPHOR;
ORGANIZATIONAL; PARADIGM;
RECONFIGURATION; RENEWAL; SOCIETAL;
SPONTANEOUS; TRANSFORMATIONAL)

A major contribution of the eminent historian Arnold Toynbee (1953) lies in drawing interesting and useful parallels between differing societies, events, and time frames. As Toynbee has argued, the past can provide clues to the future. It is argued in this chapter that all types of organizations, for-profit and not-for-profit, can benefit from a study of historical parallels, particularly given the nature of the competitive global marketplace. The specific concern of this chapter is to relate Xenophon's *Anabasis* to organizational culture and contemporary organizational theory. The intent is to ground Morgan's (1986) metaphors through the *Anabasis* while linking them to organizational redesign and the reality of hypercompetition as described by D'Aveni (1994). The overall goal is to be integrative.

Although culture is a relatively recent field in management studies, as a phenomenon, its importance dates back to the earliest civilizations. Numerous examples can be readily found to demonstrate the role culture played in the success of a particular society. Perhaps one of the most intriguing involves the culture of classical Greece dramatized by the "March of the Ten Thousand." While societal culture may be quite different in many instances from corporate culture, the approach taken here is to downplay such differences. This is done because many of the ancient societies possessed a degree of homogeneity, scale, and scope not unlike that of a contemporary firm.

In classical Greece 400 B.C., a "unique" culture existed. While perhaps all cultures are unique, it is the renowned Greek translator, W. H. D. Rouse, who observes that "The distinctiveness of spirit, wherever it came from, was real; and it consisted chiefly of a love of freedom in both mind and body. . . . In this spirit they stood alone in the world, like a garden of flowers in a jungle" (1959, p. vi). The historian Leonard Cottrell (1957) also observed the classical Greeks to be driven by a passion for freedom and individualism that "gave full play to the growth of the spirit and intellect" (p. 184). In the ancient world they were often democratic, adventuresome, and innovative regardless of what part of the Mediterranean they settled. They were also "different in their art, their literature, moral outlook, political and social organizations, in their way of thinking and feeling about life" (p. 185). Cottrell goes on to observe that "What held them together was their language and culture. They seem always to have regarded themselves as different from other people" (p. 187). However, because no culture is perfect, it is not surprising to find Greek culture relying on slavery, women subordinated to menial roles, and a "machismo" orientation. Overall, Greek culture reflected many positive characteristics, some of which are relevant for contemporary organizations.

One of the objectives of this paper is to explore the use of Morgan's (1986) metaphors, particularly the culture metaphor, within the context of Xenophon's *Anabasis:* "The March Up Country." The *Anabasis* is a 2,400-year-old account of a diverse group of Greek mercenaries engaged in a struggle for survival in a hostile and foreign society, much as many firms face in today's hypercompetitive environment. While this account may not be entirely objective, it provides a vivid example of the importance of organizational culture from which contemporary business could greatly benefit. Considerable effort is made to examine the *Anabasis* within the metaphorical framing provided by Morgan. The metaphors of particular concern include: biological organisms and ecology, brains and organizations as holographic systems, and organizations as cultural entities. These metaphors, while not all inclusive regarding what Morgan provides, are selected in part because they best relate to the Greek emphasis on body, mind, and spirit, respectively.

The use of metaphors is important in that they provide a qualitative means by which to better understand the more quantitative meanings of literal language. Tsoukas (1991) argues that "metaphors are better 'sensors' than literal terms for capturing and expressing the continuous flow of experience. They allow the transfer of concrete bands of experience, whereas literal discourse segments experiences" (p. 581). It can be argued that metaphors are, metaphorically speaking, the "soul" to the mechanistic process of information processing. Metaphors play a valuable integrative role in facilitating understanding. In addition, metaphors can dramatically alter how we view a particular subject. In a recent *Newsweek* (1993) article addressing the issue of "genius," a Nobel chemist, Hoffman, is quoted on the subject of metaphors. He states that "the imaginative faculties are set in motion by mental metaphor. Metaphor shifts the discourse, not gradually, but with a vengeance" (p. 50). Perhaps they can also help organizational theory to shift dramatically given a context of highly competitive, dynamic environmental realities.

Tsoukas (1991) makes a strong case for the use of metaphors and observes that understanding is better achieved when both metaphors and literal terminology are used as complementary devices. He states:

> The question therefore is not whether either metaphors or literal terms ought to be used in theory development in organizational science, but rather how can metaphorical language be used in such a way as to contribute to the development of literal language. (p. 582)

Tsoukas' work implicitly suggests that there is a need for benchmarking examples that link metaphors to literal descriptors. As a result, this paper seeks to achieve this integration by using Xenophon's detailed historical account. While Morgan's metaphors are linked here to organizational science through the *Anabasis,* the particular focus is on the role culture can play in facilitating organizational adaptability in a hostile environment.

The various objectives of this paper are linked closely to one another. The first is to examine Xenophon's *Anabasis* in order to ascertain the strategic role organizational culture plays in facilitating organizational adaptability and reconfiguration. The second objective is to address three of Morgan's metaphors within the context of the *Anabasis* and provide the pragmatic base capable of animating them. The final objective is integrative in that both Xenophon's historical account and Morgan's metaphors are used in support of new organizational theories and concerns, such as those of D'Aveni (1991) pertaining to hypercompetition.

THE IMPORTANCE OF
ORGANIZATIONAL CULTURE

While organizational culture has been an important concept and popular topic for several years, it is becoming increasingly evident that it is a key element in global competition. An insightful and pragmatic means by which to comprehend culture is provided by Hofstede (1991), a leading scholar in the area. He notes that "culture is the collective programming of the mind which distinguishes one group or category of people from one another" (p. 89). Similarly, Morgan (1986) perceives culture to reflect a pattern of shared meanings, understanding, and sense making (p. 128). Another eminent scholar, Schein (1986), perceives culture on three levels. First, culture pertains to overt behaviors and physical artifacts. Next, culture is concerned with values. Finally, and most fundamentally, culture is linked to basic assumptions as to how to behave in our environment. Culture is viewed in this paper as a societal gestalt reflecting "some" basic values, norms, and beliefs about the what, why, and how things are done. Because culture is a qualitative and elusive phenomenon, any effort that attempts to provide a definitional "straightjacket" is likely, as Morgan notes, to be mechanistic and self-defeating.

No effort is made here to provide an exhaustive review of the culture literature. Still, a number of interesting issues have emerged. Is culture as an immutable variable or is it one that can be managed (Morgan 1986)? Are strong cultures always desirable (Safford 1988)? Is culture reflective of integration, differentiation, or ambiguity (Morgan 1993)? Because the intent of this paper is to focus in particular on a historical example that contains useful insights regarding the implied role of culture in spontaneous organizational design, an extensive literature review would detract from the "story to be told."

A number of research efforts in culture do link up well with Xenophon's *Anabasis.* For instance, the notion that culture can be a guidance mechanism or behavioral blueprint that provides purpose and structure amidst conditions of ambiguity and change as demonstrated by Xenophon's *Anabasis,* relates well to the work of Hofstede (1991), Frost et al. (1991), and Martin (1992). As such, culture can assist in the implementation process by removing, in part, the need for costly, limiting, and time-consuming bureaucratic control mechanisms. Also, as Van Cauwenbergh and Cool (1982) observe, culture may act in strategy formulation decisions as "a kind of 'conventional wisdom' about what range of activities are deemed favorable for maintaining organization equilibrium (survival)" (p. 254). This certainly appears to be the case of the Greek army in its "March Up Country."

The *Anabasis* also reveals that the primary means of organizational control was a reliance on culture. Here, the besieged Greek army relied on a cultural blueprint which, in Hofstede's (1991) words, provided the behavioral software essential to survival. When Martin's three cultural perspective are considered, a kind of "unity in diversity" can be concluded when observing that an ambiguous, turbulent environment forced the Greeks to employ a flexible and often fragmented system of organizational control.

The study of organizational culture offers insights as to why General Motors, IBM, and Sears are found by Loomis (1993) to be capitalistic dinosaurs. Perhaps culture can help in confronting the apocalyptic demise of the West that Kennedy (1987) describes in his, *Rise and Fall of the Great Powers*. It currently appears that the individualistic cultural ethic of the West, inherently rooted in the ancient Greeks, is often struggling poorly against the collectivistic cultural ethic of the East. This would be hardly surprising to Parkinson (1963), a cultural historian who has analyzed cultural conflict and the volatile shifts in ascendancy between the East and West.

Because *empirical* research has yet to provide strong, unambiguous, quantitative support for the managerial importance of organizational culture, an effort is made here to use case method in affirming the validity of culture's importance. This historical account of Xenophon's *Anabasis* dramatizes in a highly qualitative fashion what can be accomplished under severely adverse conditions when the "right" cultural properties exist. Acquiring such properties is, of course, another problematic issue. The next section summarizes the *Anabasis, The March Up Country.*

THE MARCH UP COUNTRY

Xenophon, the Greek historian and student of Socrates, has provided a poignant, firsthand account of the exodus from Persian territory of nearly 13,000 Greek mercenaries in 401 B.C. Mercenaries from various Greek city-states had been recruited by the young Persian prince, Cyrus, to dethrone his older brother, King Artaxerxes. In a famous battle, Cunaxa, Cyrus and his Greeks were victorious, but Cyrus himself was killed in combat by his brother. After the battle, Cyrus's Persian troops defected to Artaxerxes, resulting in the isolation of the Greeks. The Greek leaders were cleverly and falsely persuaded to meet collectively as a negotiating team with the Persians to discuss their army's peaceful departure. During the lavish proceedings, the Greek leaders were killed. However, Artaxerxes underestimated the resolve and resilience of the Greek army, which now appeared leaderless.

Xenophon's account, *Anabasis,* describes in detail how the Greek army persevered and successfully left the confines of the Persian Empire. What is particularly interesting are the cultural strengths described by Xenophon to have been essential in surviving a march of 1,500 miles. This march was undertaken despite the loss of the army's original leadership. In addition, large, well-supplied armies and treacherous terrain blocked a peaceful exit.

What stands out in Xenophon's *Anabasis* is the superiority of the Greek culture when contrasted with other rival societies. It was the content of their culture rather than charismatic leadership, strategic prowess, or luck that enabled the Greeks to survive in a foreign and hostile society. Xenophon describes what Bourgeois and Brodwin (1984) depict to be true regarding the cultural process: the ability of organizational members to respond in an impromptu, ad hoc manner. The *Anabasis* observes Xenophon's comrades to be spontaneously resourceful and quick to reorganize when they discover the execution of their senior officers. New leadership naturally emerges through a democratic process, and this leadership is revealed to be strongly participative and humanistic. A cultural blueprint or guidance mechanism for organizational response to a volatile, unexpected crisis is implicitly revealed. It was their common heritage, education, and values, as well as their sense of independence and enterpreneurship, that facilitated a unified response to a "barbarian" that twice in a 100-year period tried to destroy their civilization.

While it was the culture of the Greeks that made them unique, it was also the cohesive glue behind the spontaneous unity and mutual adjustment of individuals from very different, and often warring, city-states. Xenophon provides numerous examples where discipline, organization, and unity coupled with energy, enthusiasm, and entrepreneurial insight are able to sustain a most difficult but successful retreat. The "March Up Country" is an instance where culture appears to have made a dramatic difference.

The literal march up country begins at Cunaxa, a city adjacent to the Euphrates river, close to the juncture with the Tigris river and 50 miles from ancient Babylon. Cunaxa is near the site of the battle fought between Cyrus and Artaxerxes. Once the Greek army regroups and elects new leadership, it moves north along the Tigris river through Assyria and Media. The route closely approximates the border between modern Iraq and Iran. Further north, they pass through the land of the Kurds into Armenia, which represents the eastern provinces of modern Turkey. The Greeks finally reach the Black Sea at Trebizond, not far south of the former Soviet state of Georgia. At this point the worst of dangers, but certainly not the last, are over.

As can be imagined, the "March" was an extensive trek over rugged terrain of all sorts while engaging an active enemy force. Culture, training, military zeal, and organizational skill were the Greek weapons. Botsford and Robinson (1956) note that Xenophon's army was a unique phenomenon of mercenaries.

The homeward march of the Ten Thousand across rivers, over mountains, and through deep snows of Armenia, ever harassed by the enemy and in wont of food and clothing, was a heroic achievement. It proved the Greeks had not lost their virility, and it laid bare the weakness of Persia. (p. 271)

The authors go on to note that this army's success led indirectly to the independence of the Greek cities in Asia Minor. The remnants of the Ten Thousand later joined with Spartan forces in directly freeing Greek cities from the Persians. Also, a path was set for Alexander the Great.

A factor to consider when relying on Xenophon is his objectivity and accuracy. While there is some debate by Fox (1980), Hornblower (1986), Murray (1991), and Stone (1988), as to Xenophon's reliability as a valued source, he is generally viewed as a reasonably objective writer who, as an Athenian, could easily relate to both Sparta and Persia. A reading of the *Anabasis* reveals a focus that is more about how the Greeks escape than on the failures of Persia and its culture. However, what Xenophon does describe and the approach taken by this chapter might lead the reader to believe an ethnocentric portrait has been drawn.

THE ETHNOCENTRIC DILEMMA

In an atmosphere of political correctness it is perhaps prudent to ascertain whether a given research thrust is driven by an ethnocentric bias. Critics of Western historical traditions might question whether the Greeks of Xenophon were truly unique and superior relative to other Mediterranean and Near Eastern societies. Parkinson, in his discussion of Eastern and Western societies, warns against adopting discriminatory and biased views when examining the strengths and weaknesses of the contrasting parties (societies) (p. xviii).

The focus of Parkinson's text, *East and West* (1963), is on the "alternating phases of Oriental and Western ascendancy" (p. xiii). He examines the factors that result in the rise and fall of various civilizations. In his examination of the East and West, it is noted that successful military initiatives are usually preceded by a cultural invasion of sorts (p. 65). Much like Kennedy later (1987), Parkinson is concerned about arresting ensuing decadence and decline, about forestalling the inevitable. However, he clearly views the conflict between East and West as mutually beneficial in that societal and human progress is facilitated (p. xvii).

Parkinson provides a useful portrait of the fifth and fourth century Greeks that contrasts sharply with that of Eastern societies, and in particular, the Persian. The Greeks believed in intellectual inquiry and that such inquiry should be *debated* whether before the walls of Troy or in the "March Up Country" (p. 74). In many ways it was the Greek polis that differentiated Xenophon's men from the Persians. The cultural rites, rituals, and practices associated with the gymnasium, agora, stadium, theater, as well as the acropolis and council house facilitated the rise of an individualistic ethic within the confines of a relatively small, homogeneous community. This community might demand conformity but it also, paradoxically, encouraged individualism (p. 77). However, there is another interesting dimensions to Greek culture that is often overlooked.

Reinforcing Parkinson's arguments regarding the superiority of Greek culture are recent military texts by Hanson (1989) and Keegan (1993). Both are distinguished military historians. Keegan (1993) notes that the battle traditions of the Greeks were culturally different from that of peoples in the Near and Middle East and of the Steppe where soldiers preferred the indirect, evasive, stand-off style that facilitated quick departure or safe victory (p. 332). He argues that the Greeks' major contribution to warfare is that of the pitched battle where soldiers fought to the death and sought quick, decisive victory (p. 332). The cultural differences between East and West are observed by Keegan when he refers to a new form of warfare

> wielded by small farmers who were equal citizens, and used to wage battles of an intensity and ferocity perhaps never before seen. The battles of earlier and other peoples—even those of the Assyrians, though we lack exact details of their conduct on the battlefield—had continued to be marked by elements that had characterized warfare since its primitive beginnings—tentativeness, preference for fights at a distance, reliance on missiles and reluctance to close to arm's length until victory looked assured. The Greeks discarded these hesitations and created for themselves a new warfare that turned on the function of battle as a decisive act, fought within the dramatic unities of time, place and action and dedicated to securing victory, even at the risk of suffering bloody defeat, in a single test of skill and courage. (p. 244)

Hanson (1989) amplifies these differences by noting the maniacal, almost barbaric attitude of the Greeks regarding the killing of their enemy. He states:

> Like so much of their art and literature, the Greek manner of battle was a paradox of the highest order, a deliberate attempt to harness, to modulate, and hence to amplify if not sanctify the wild human desire for violence through the stark order and discipline of the phalanx. To the Persians, who reversed these concepts—their disordered, moblike frightening hordes had no fondness for methodical killing—the approach of a Greek column was especially unsettling. At Marathon they thought a "destructive madness" had infected the Greek ranks as they saw them approach on the run in their heavy armor. Surely, as those outnumbered Greek hoplites crashed

into their lines, the Persians must have at last understood that these men worshipped not only the god Apollo but the wild, irrational Dionysus as well. (p. 16)

It is revealing to find such an enigmatic reality with the Greeks given our usual view that they possessed only the most positive attributes of a refined civilization. Rooted deep in the soul of the typical Greek soldier was a pathos that was at once both cultured and barbaric, heroic and demonic, humane and corrupt, visionary and psychotic. The Greek soldiers appear to suffer en masse from that which afflicts Joseph Conrad's Major Kurtz in *The Heart of Darkness* (1899).

Still, to understand the intense, warlike behavior of the Greeks it is important to understand its cultural and historical context. Perhaps a military-type barbarism was viewed as the best means by which to bring armed conflict to a quick end as it was for the Allies in 1945 (e.g., Hiroshima and Nagasaki). Griffin (1991) also observes that the Greeks believed "poverty was their instructor in hardihood and self-reliance, unlike the soft and wealthy peoples of the East" (p. 4). While Griffin is careful to observe the role other cultures played in shaping that of the Greeks, he goes on to argue that the latter became quite competitive in nature. Griffin's portrait of Greek culture relates very closely to the Japanese notion of "continuous improvement" (pp. 5-7). Even though many in the U.S. espouse the virtues of "continuous improvement," it rarely appears to be employed in practice. For the Greeks, "continuous improvement" was a full-time ethic as it is for the Japanese today.

Another interesting aspect of Greek culture was the way their society was mutually integrated and differentiated. Murray (1991) observes that

> multiple ties limited the freedom of the individual, and there is certainly an important sense in which the conception of the autonomy of the individual apart from the community is absent from Greek thought: the freedom of the Greeks is public, externalized in speech and action. This freedom derives precisely from the fact that the same man belongs to a deme, a phratry, a family, a group of relatives, a religious association; and, living in this complex world of conflicting groups and social duties, he possesses the freedom to choose between their demands, and so to escape any particular dominant form of social patterning. It is this which explains the coexistence of the group mentality with the amazing creativity and freedom of thought of classical Athens. (p. 248)

Such a description readily relates to Japanese management practices and the notion of the *keiretsu*.

To comprehend these cultural factors it is important to go to the base-root of Greek culture: the polis and its direct link to the citizen-farmer. Except for Sparta, most of Greece centered on the polis (Keegan, p. 242). Both Keegan (1993) and Hanson (1989) reveal the importance the polis had with its citizen-farmers. This was an intimate relationship which facilitated a democratic ethic even in Greek societies that were nondemocratic. Keegan and, in particular, Hanson, observe that the citizen-farmer was rooted to the polis through land ownership. When war broke out between two or more city-states, these individuals became part of the militia. As a result, war became a regular way of life even if for but a few months each year.

Keegan (1993) and Hanson (1989) note that the Greek attitude for fighting is culturally linked to the citizen's close link to the polis. For the Persian, fighting was generally for conquest while for the Greek, fighting was out of loyalty to the city-state, as well as for personal freedom, thus reflecting both the integration and differentiation perspectives of Martin (1992). Because, according to Keegan, slavery was generally in the minority in city-states, most male inhabitants were linked to a community committed to annual warfare. Hanson even observes the Greek phalanx to be a community of fighting men who depend intimately on each other for survival and military success.

The final outcome of Greek culture on the battlefield was to produce a warlike ethic committed to a complete victory, even if at great personal loss. While this ethic was "machismo" in its orientation, it was grounded on loyalty to the polis as well as one's homestead and family. The Greeks went into battle fully prepared to kill or be killed. As Hanson (1989) observes, the goal was to literally get into the face of their enemy and engage them at very close quarters. The Greeks believed that a bloody, visceral confrontation was the most efficient way to bring a quick resolution to the most inhumane of behaviors: war. This was a practice Alexander personally used against his Persian nemesis Darius in their last two confrontations (Issus and Gaugamela).

It has been argued here that the Greeks were in many ways culturally superior to the East and the Persians in particular. However, there is a particularly dark side to this superiority in regard to warfare. The "Kurtzian" type demeanor of the Greeks appears to have given them a decisive advantage in battle. Were the Greeks ethnocentric? Keegan (1993) notes they were. He observes that the Greeks were conscious of their differences from non-Greeks and even to participate in the Olympic games, one had to be able to speak Greek (p. 252). In addition, the role for women in Greek society reveals another "dark" dimension that is consistent with the machismo aspect of Greek culture. However, the intent here is not to endorse ethnocentrism but to reveal how a unique culture provided for competitive advantages in warfare as demonstrated by the "March Up Country."

THE METAPHORS
OF GARETH MORGAN

One of the more thought-provoking organizational texts of recent years is Morgan's *Images of Organization* (1986). The significant contribution of Morgan is that he examines the dynamics of human organization through a wide assortment of metaphors. His intent is to force the reader to view management and organizational principles through uniquely defining metaphors. Each metaphor provides a new perspective and in the process requires the reader to reassess old assumptions. While the various metaphors are not intended to be entirely compatible with one another, collectively they facilitate a holistic framing. Each metaphor provides a new way to define organizational problems, assess viable solutions, encourage creative processes, and collectively function as a managerial "CAT scan."

While the *Anabasis* facilitates a pragmatic grounding for several of Morgan's metaphors, only those directly linked to the Greek notions pertaining to body, mind, and spirit are considered here in detail. The metaphors that relate to and are amplified by Xenophon's *Anabasis* include: biological organisms and organizational ecology, brains and organizations as holographic systems, and organizations as cultural phenomena. As a result, considerable reciprocity is found between the *Anabasis* and Morgan's work.

While Morgan is creative in his "literal" use of metaphors, he is deficient in providing sustainable examples to ground his elaborate qualitative arguments. To a certain extent, Morgan resolves this problem through his recent text, *Imaginazation* (1993). However, the intent of this effort is to link a new array of highly specific metaphors to correspondingly focused examples. Unfortunately, the broadly conceived metaphors of *Images* still lack pragmatic animation.

One possible explanation for the lack of grounding in Morgan's *Images* text is fear of imposing a mechanistic linking on a qualitative concept. However, he does recognize the limitations with metaphors:

The population ecology view of organization in effect develops an equivalent ideology for modern times, holding up a mirror to the organizational world and suggesting that the view we see reflects a law of nature. In effect, natural law is invoked to legitimize the organization of society. *Obviously there are real dangers in doing so because when we take the parallels between nature and society too seriously, we fail to see that human beings in principle have a large measure of influence and choice over what their world can be.* (p. 76, emphasis added)

The Biological Metaphor

In his chapter "Organizations as Organisms," Morgan examines the biological metaphor where molecules, cells, complex organisms, species, and ecology are observed to parallel individuals, groups, organizations, industries, and societies. Much of the analysis is done in the context of systems thinking whereby the elements within the organization impact and reinforce one another while mutually interacting with and being influenced by the external environment. Systems theory is viewed by Morgan to have parallel relevance for biological phenomena and human ecology. There is a reciprocal and synergistic relationship between lateral as well as nesting elements. The biological metaphor provides examples of evolution and adaptation that dramatically exceed in value the metaphor of the "machine" (another Morgan metaphor), particularly regarding the issue of *survival*. However, Morgan does see a limitation with the biological metaphor. He observes:

> The task of successful organizational change and development thus often hinges on bringing variables into closer alignment so that the organization can meet the challenges and opportunities posed by the environment. In nature we find that organisms are endowed with a harmonious pattern of internal and external relations as a result of evolution. In organizations, however, the degree of internal harmony and fit with the environment is a product of human decision, action, and inaction, so that incongruence and conflict are often the rule. (p. 65)

Later, Morgan goes on to state:

> If we look at most organizations, however, we find that the times at which their different elements operate with the degree of harmony discussed above are often more exceptional than normal. For most organizations are not as functionally unified as organisms. The different elements of an organization are usually capable of living separate lives, and often do so. While organizations may at times be highly unified, with people in different departments working in a selfless way for the organization as a whole, they may at other times be characterized by schism and major conflict. (p. 70)

One can take issue with Morgan here by arguing that most advanced living organisms, particularly mammals, possess numerous biological subsystems that are often in conflict with one another. Many parts of the human body benefit at the expense of other parts, as in the case of athletic over-training.

Despite Morgan's cautionary stance, the biological metaphor takes on particular relevance when Morgan notes that both species and organizations evolve through a pattern of relations whereby they embrace their environment in a manner of mutual adjustment and survive by fitting in (rather than merely representing a survival of the fittest). He notes that "organizations and their environments are engaged in a pattern of cocreation, where each produces the other" (p. 69). Clearly, what Morgan describes is very compatible with the *Anabasis*.

A reading of the *Anabasis* reveals the Greek army proceeding over the hostile environment as if it were a single, highly complex biological entity capable of spontaneously responding and evolving in a unified manner to external as well as internal threats. The best example of this is when the Greek leaders chose to reconfigure the army's organizational structure. In order to traverse narrow ravines and mountain paths or to cross streams and rivers, the army's marching structure was quickly redesigned to provide maximum flexibility. Xenophon notes how the marching formations had broken down early in the exodus and became vulnerable when moving through difficult, changing terrain.

> When the commanders perceived this they made six companies of a hundred men each, and appointed a lieutenant to command each, and officers for each half-company and quarter-company.[1] When the wings drew in on the march these companies fell to the rear so as not to confuse the wings, and they lined up outside the wings. When the wings expanded again they filled up the gap in the line between, in line of companies in column if narrow, half-companies if wider, quarter-companies very wide, and so the gap was always filled. Thus they were not disordered if they had to cross a ford or a bridge, but the companies crossed in turn; and when they needed the line these were ready. (p. 81)[1]

> "These were taken from the front or rear rank of the square, which had to be shortened." (Xenophon's footnote.)

Later in the *Anabasis* another example is provided where spontaneous adjustment like a biological entity is required. Xenophon notes that attacking an enemy positioned high on a mountain required new thinking. Instead of relying on an extended linear formation that was likely to break, self-contained company columns were proposed. However, the independent columns were also expected to provide support to other fellow columns that were under heavy assault. Xenophon reasons that

> we form in company columns, leaving the columns so far apart that the extreme columns overlap the enemy wings; thus we shall overlap the whole enemy line, and

by leading in column the strongest will go on first, and where the way is easy, each of the other columns may follow in turn. It will not be easy for the enemy to penetrate the spaces between the columns, and it will not be easy to cut up a company standing in column. If one of the columns is hard pressed the nearest shall help. And if one of the columns can get to the top, not a man of the enemy will stand. (p. 109)

These examples of how the Greeks adjusted their formation are consistent with Bennis' (1966) concept of "adhocracy" to which Morgan frequently refers. "Adhocracy" is the constant mutual adjustment an organization makes in response to complex, turbulent environments. Clearly, the environment faced by the Greek army required new approaches that facilitated maximum flexibility (see Figure 18.1).

Xenophon also describes how the Greek army leadership was highly adaptable and not tied to singular roles. In one revealing incident it was necessary for Xenophon to switch roles quickly with another captain (Cheirisophos, the Spartan). Xenophon, who was normally the officer responsible for the rear guard, found it necessary to borrow troops from the army's vanguard (front) in order to lead a charge against enemy troops posted on a nearby hill intending to block passage. Meanwhile, the vanguard was rapidly and efficiently reinforced with troops from the center of the formations (p. 84).

The Brain Metaphor

Morgan observes that the brain possesses remarkable properties—the capacity for flexibility, resilience, and inventiveness as well as communication, command, and control. His particular concern is with the degree that human organizations can operate like a brain. Morgan is reasonably optimistic that organizations can partly emulate a brain. However, he suggests they need to adopt three essential ingredients. First, encourage openness and accept uncertainty as a fact of organizational life. Second, encourage analyses that explore divergent and unorthodox viewpoints. Finally, avoid imposing bureaucratic structures on organizational processes.

Morgan goes even further by viewing both brains and organizations as being holographic systems.

To compare the brain with a hologram may seem to be stretching reason beyond the limits. However, the way a holographic plate enfolds all the information necessary to produce a complete image in each of its parts has much in common with the functioning of a brain. And it is possible to extend this image to create a vision of organization where capacities required in the whole are enfolded in the parts, allow-

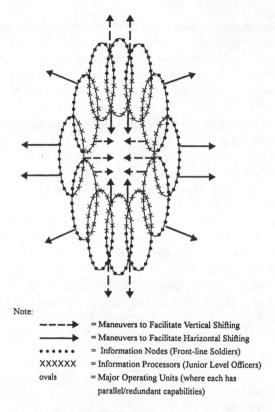

Note:

- - - ▶	= Maneuvers to Facilitate Vertical Shifting
───▶	= Maneuvers to Facilitate Harizontal Shifting
••••••	= Information Nodes (Front-line Soldiers)
XXXXXX	= Information Processors (Junior Level Officers)
ovals	= Major Operating Units (where each has parallel/redundant capabilities)

Figure 18.1. The Dynamic Organizational Form of Xenophon's Army: A Means by Which to Facilitate Spontaneous Realignment While Traversing Hostile Terrain in the "March Up Country"

    ing the system to learn and self-organize, and to maintain a complete system of functioning even when specific parts malfunction or are removed. (p. 95)

The principles of holographic design are viewed by Morgan to be: learning to learn, requisite variety, simultaneous specialization and generalization (and minimizing the ground rules), a capacity to self-organize, and redundancy (p. 97). The intent is to enable the organization to "be developed in a cellular manner around self-organizing, multidisciplined groups that have the requisite skills and abilities to deal with the environment in a holistic and integrated way" (p. 101). Xenophon's army clearly fits this description.

    Morgan also observes that if a self-organizing system encourages or permits too much random or independent behavior on the part of organizational members, chaos is possible, and too much time could be consumed in performing ordinary tasks. However, if an organization can learn how to establish functional patterns of connectivity, novel and creative solutions can be found to complex problems. "Such systems typically find and adopt a pattern graded in a hierarchical manner, in that sets of subsystems link to higher-order systems, but the pattern is emergent rather than imposed" (p. 103).

In the *Anabasis,* many holographic instances are detailed. The unique Greek culture enabled the leaderless troops to elect new officers to replace those deceived and executed by the Persians (pp. 68-72). Xenophon and other emergent leaders observe the importance of unity (pp. 71, 73, 76, 127) as well as the need for fresh ideas (pp. 76, 85, 94). However, it is also noted that in some situations the emphasis on unity must supersede independent thought in order to avoid anarchy (pp. 88, 133-136). In addition, the value of unity is demonstrated late in the *Anabasis* when part of the Greek army goes off on its own only to discover near annihilation until rescued by the main army (pp. 145-146).

Xenophon's account relates closely to Morgan's brain metaphor by observing the holographic elements of redundancy, requisite variety, self-organizing, and the ability to learn and adjust. Each Greek soldier was an entity inside a larger entity and was capable of spontaneous adjustments to unique situations. Incidents are detailed where individuals take informal, independent action to cope with a suddenly surfaced problem (Martin's differentiation, 1992). However, each soldier also knew how far their independent action should proceed so as not to jeopardize either the army's security or the need for unified behavior and commitment (Martin's integration, 1992). The delicate balance achieved in the "March Up Country" is remarkable and can be likened to an army of organized ants operating as if bound by a central nervous system but still independent enough to have individual members respond spontaneously to the unexpected, nonprogrammed problems. As such, it relates the brain metaphor both to the biology metaphor as well as to the culture metaphor.

The Culture Metaphor

Another metaphor that Morgan uses and that seems to be especially appropriate for the *Anabasis* is one pertaining to culture. This metaphor is strongly linked to the holographic metaphor. The connection is made evident when Morgan cites the research of Peters and Waterman (1982).

> The emphasis that Peters and Waterman place on the ability of these organizations to develop a shared sense of identity, mission, and "corporate culture" also

resonates with the holographic model. For it is by building this shared sense of the corporate whole into each and every employee that holographic organization achieves its coherence. Though not usually discussed in this way, the role of corporate culture is important in modern organizations because of its holographic potential. (pp. 104-105)

While the culture metaphor is portrayed by Morgan as vital to organizational success (p. 121), he also notes that it is usually misunderstood.

Our understanding of culture is usually much more fragmented and superficial than the reality. This is an important point, since many management theorists view culture as a distinct entity with clearly defined attributes. Like organizational structure, culture is often viewed as a set of distinct variables, such as beliefs, stories, norms, and rituals, that somehow form a cultural whole. Such a view is unduly mechanistic, giving rise to the idea that culture can be manipulated in an instrumental way. It is this kind of mechanistic attitude that underlies many perspectives advocating the management of culture. However, from the inside, culture seems more holographic than mechanistic. . . . Managers can by attempting to foster desired values, but they can never control culture in the sense that many management writers advocate. The holographic diffusion of culture means that it pervades activity in a way that is not amenable to direct control by any single group of individuals. (p. 139)

When turning to the *Anabasis,* it is reasonably evident that the distinguishing difference between Greek and Persian or Greek and "barbarian" is with culture. The Greek army was thoroughly rooted in a "humanistic" culture that had evolved over several centuries while the Persian army relied on a bureaucratic and autocratic control system. The leaders of the Greek army were a product of the Hellene culture rather than its creators. Consistent with Morgan's observations just noted, the Greek leadership was reasonably astute enough to know the value of relying on a less than evident weapon, their cultural heritage.

While Xenophon's mercenary army may appear on the surface to be a mere collection of soldiers recruited from very different as well as frequently warring city-states, there was certainly an ethos of being Hellene. In fact, in one passage, Xenophon condemns those soldiers who wish to discuss surrendering to the Persians. He states: "This man is a disgrace to his own country and to all Hellas, because he is a Hellene and yet behaves this way" (p. 70). A supracultural ethic appears to pervade the entire army despite the existence of strongly clashing Ionian and Dorian subcultures within Greece proper. The soldiers may have viewed themselves to be first an Athenian, a Corinthian or a Lacedaemonian, but in the final analysis, they all saw themselves as Hellenes.

More recently, historians have questioned the actual existence of a single Greek culture. Grant (1987) implies such a position when he observes:

> For the Greeks, by way of contrast, were highly, intensely and deliberately decentralized. Nearly 700 city-states are known to have existed; it would not be surprising if we discovered, eventually, that the real number was twice as large. It was asserted, according to Herodotus, that the Greeks were a single people, united by common blood, customs, language and religion. But they were also very sharply divided among themselves, since every one of these hundreds of city-states was politically independent of every other. (p. xiii)

It is interesting to note that Grant also implicitly observes a real Greek culture to have existed when he states:

> We have seen, throughout this study, a continuing contrast and counterpoint between the Panhellenic spirit, represented by common race, language and religion, and the centrifugal trends involved in the divisive relationships between one city-state and another. Now, faced with a Persian threat to all, unity just managed to prevail against disunity. (p. 281)

Murray (1986) also argues that Greece possessed a unique culture that centered around the polis—the city. He observes that "society is composed of interrelating phenomena, and there is fascination in seeing how the pieces fit together" (p. 232). Murray goes on to state that it was the existence of the Greek city-state that set in motion the complexities of public and private life that produced a conflict with traditional society. The city-state phenomenon nurtured complexities that "liberated the individual from the constraints of tradition without causing him to lose his social identity" (p. 232). It appears that the Hellene culture possessed the unique, performance-driven properties such as the loose-tight features identified by Peters and Waterman (1982) and the differentiation-integration qualities described by Lawrence and Lorsch (1967).

More significantly, the Hellene culture was paradoxical in that it reflected the three perspectives described by Frost et al. (1991) and Martin (1992): integration, differentiation, and fragmentation. Both Frost and Martin provide case examples depicting each of these cultural perspectives. Integration represents the view that a given culture possesses "clear and consistent values, interpretations and/or assumptions that are shared on an organization-wide basis" (Frost et al., p. 13). The differentiation perspective about culture observes that shared meanings can exist but do so more on a subcultural level. Finally, fragmentation and ambiguity are also seen as reflective of a given culture. Here, Frost et al. observe: "organizational ambiguities emerge from complex, apparently unsolvable problems, such as pollution, drug abuse, and poverty. Ambiguities also arise from the multiplicity of vantage points and belief systems represented in today's culturally diverse organizations" (p. 115).

A detailed analysis of the *Anabasis* suggests that the norms, values, and heritage of the Greeks truly facilitated a unifying process (integration) that also permitted individual differences (differentiation) and ambiguity characterized through unstructured, ad hoc self-serving behavior. The Spartan alliance with Persia against Athens at the end of the Peloponesian war, and the desire of some of Xenophon's men to surrender to the Persians once their leaders were executed, are self-serving examples of ambiguity which contrast sharply with integration and differentiation. In providing a definition to his concept of culture as mental software, Hofstede (1991) notes that "it is the collective programming of the mind which distinguishes the members of one group or category of people from another" (p. 5). This aptly fits the supra-Hellene culture which provided a unique, qualitative blueprint on how to respond spontaneously to a hostile enemy in a foreign land. As a result, the Greek leadership in their "March Up Country" had no need to impose a new set of competitive values to facilitate a successful escape. However, these paradoxical properties (perspectives) collectively enabled Xenophon's soldiers to know when and how to respond: as a whole, as a team, as individuals.

A relevant analogy is argued here that Hellas was to the individual Greek city-states as a contemporary corporation is to its separate departments and strategic business units. While the various departments and business units will often exhibit unique subcultures, in many corporations these will be subordinated to a strong, integrative organizational culture. Even though societal culture and corporate culture are reflective of different properties and realities, there are some useful similarities to be considered. In some ways, societal culture is merely a higher level of abstraction when compared to corporate culture. In regard to the ancient Greek societies the level of abstraction may not be nearly so great as would be a comparison today of American culture to that of its industrial corporations.

Xenophon's army provides us with a unique example of the importance of societal culture and its impact on organizational culture. Because this collection of mercenaries and adventurers was essentially a "temporary" organization, there was little time to forge a potent and distinctly unique organizational culture. Given the severe problems the besieged and leaderless army faced, the integrative Hellene culture *became* the organizational culture, and fragmentation was minimized when strong leadership emerged in response to the Persian treachery. As was noted above, strong subcultures (differentiation) did exist among the polis-centered Greeks, but these were subordinated more to the rational concerns of survival than to the vanity of political self-interest (ambiguity and fragmentation). Still, the sub-cultural differences may have served the Greeks well. Gordon (1991), in looking at the role industry determinants can have on organizational culture, provides considerable insight on the value of subcultural differences. He notes that "under certain conditions the degree to which subcultures from multidivisional and multi-industry firms exist may have a significant effect on the capacity of a company to change its culture" (p. 398). Hence, the distinct subcultures in the Greek army may have facilitated functional adaptation to a hostile environment in a manner consistent with Morgan's biological and holographic metaphors.

The ability of the Greek subcultures to reinforce and complement an overall Hellene culture can also be likened to a new conceptual area, cultural diversity. Taylor and Blake (1991) argue that cultural diversity within an organization facilitates creativity and the ability to adapt and change. Their observations fit well with Xenophon's account in the "March Up Country."

The *Anabasis* does provide a revealing portrait of the supra-culture of Hellas in operation when a number of junior Greek officers complain that many of the army's captains like Xenophon had not brought any troops of their own to Persia. What in essence was being asked of many of the captains was "how could an Athenian command troops he did not personally recruit?" More importantly, how could he command troops from a rival city-state like Sparta (p. 143)? However, none of Xenophon's accusers could demonstrate that he had failed in being a fair and wise leader or that he was partial to Athenians and his home state. Here, integration prospered over differentiation and fragmentation. Ironically, Xenophon was so impartial that he was later censured and ostracized by an Athens skeptical of his apparent fondness for Sparta.

While it is argued here that the Greeks possessed cultural advantages over their Middle East rivals (Persians), it is also true that such advantages were forged over several centuries. Even though culture can be shown in some cases to play a "positive" role and facilitate a competitive advantage, as Morgan observes, it also fails to be a managerial tool that is easily accessible and malleable (p. 139). In the short-term, culture may simply be a "static" managerial variable.

What is remarkable about the Greek army here is its ability to reconfigure itself spontaneously. The army behaved as if it were a living organism that possessed an ability to grown and evolve at a very rapid rate. This ability, however, is predicated on the organization's having strong, "humanistic" information processing skills well beyond the mechanistic state of contemporary artificial intelligence. Figure 18.1 reveals the existence of brain-like information nodes in the form of front line soldiers and information proces-

sors in the form of junior-level officers. This distributive information processing system is linked through the distinctive culture of the Greeks and is
not a common feature for most armies.

The culture of Xenophon's army was in many ways quite complex. On
one hand, it provided for a set of rational rules and procedures (Hanson 1989,
Murray 1991). The scientific rationality of the warlike Greeks facilitated the
mechanistic development of set military procedures and behaviors. This was
particularly true for the Spartans but, to a lesser degree, also relevant
regarding all Greeks, even non-Dorian. However, this army also reveals an
organic ability to learn how to learn and to know when to break with rules
and procedures. The Hellene culture imparted an intuitive ability to each
organizational member. In sharp contrast to the profound rigidity normally
observed in most soldiers throughout history, the Greek soldier depicted in
the *Anabasis* is able to assess the external environment and make a determination as to whether independent, personal action is required or whether the
information should be relayed upward and group (unit) action (depicted as
large ovals in Figure 18.1) or perhaps even system-wide organizational
action is desirable. Such an organizational entity as displayed in Figure 18.1
can quickly expand horizontally in a phalanx manner to offset an enemy
attack or contract vertically into narrow marching columns in order to cope
with difficult, constricting terrain. Few armies and even fewer firms can
reconfigure so easily.

Remaking the Modern Corporation

Much of what is reflected in Xenophon's army and depicted in Figure 18.1
is becoming recognized by both the popular business press and a number of
progressive firms. The theme of the popular business press is that the modern
business corporation needs to be reconfigured and not just by downsizing.
Both *Fortune* (1992, 1993, 1995) and *Business Week* (1992) have recently
argued the need for major change. They observe that companies are beginning to rely on both small, self-contained teams and large, cross-functional
super teams. These microenterprise units are facilitating lateral, diagonal,
and vertical communication and integration. In addition, these teams make
it possible to respond more quickly to environmental shifts because of the
new emphasis on organizing around *processes* rather managerial *functions*
and hierarchies.

Fortune's (1992) Stewart observes what management writers like Drucker
have argued for some time. There is a need for flat, decentralized structures
that possess few internal boundaries in order to respond quickly to fluid

environmental conditions. The ultimate intent is to let information flow wherever it's needed in order to produce a self-managed organization where traditional hierarchies disappear. As a result, "for the organization of the future, information technology will be the load bearing material—as hierarchy is now" (p. 97). Drucker (1992) also observes that the modern corporation must be prepared for constant change and will need to acquire new knowledge continuously. He dramatically argues that "every organization has to prepare for the abandonment of everything it does" (p. 97).

However, to create and sustain the new organizational paradigm, a key ingredient is required: culture. *Business Week*'s special issue, *Reinventing America* (1992), notes the important role culture must play in the transformational process. Ironically, much of what is being argued today regarding the "new organization" and the philosophy of "continuous improvement" is something that Gardner (1963) reflected on more than a generation ago. Gardner is particularly concerned about the issue of organizational and societal renewal. However, he believes renewal is impossible when we enslave ourselves with traditional organizational forms.

An important question Gardner raises in regard to the problem of organizational decay is "what would be the ingredients that provide immunity" (p. 1)? He notes that young organizations are "flexible, fluid, not yet paralyzed by rigid specialization and willing to try anything once" (p. 3). With maturity, these properties are lost when confronting unexpected challenges. As a result, the key to survival in the long run is in creating an ethic, a *cultural norm* of renewal.

Gardner also focuses on the notion of "continuous improvement," even though it has been primarily Japanese firms to pragmatically implement this philosophy. He observes that "In the ever-renewing society what matures is a system or framework within which continuous innovation, renewal and rebirth can occur" (p. 5). The ultimate challenge lies in developing a design that is able to "continuously reform itself." However, to do this requires the existence of youthful leadership that is able to recast an organization's cultural values that are presently trapped in a "drying reservoir." He argues that

Instead of giving young people the impression that their task is to stand a dreary watch over the ancient values, we should be telling them the grim but bracing truth that it is their task to re-create those values continuously in their own behavior, facing the dilemmas and catastrophes of their own time. Instead of implying that the ideals we cherish are safely embalmed in the memory of old battles and ancestral deeds we should be telling them that each generation refights the crucial battles and either brings new vitality to the ideals or allows them to decay. (p. 126)

Remaking the Organizational Paradigm

The shift in the organizational paradigm observed by the popular business press has also been addressed by a few academics. In an atmosphere of hypercompetition, as described by D'Aveni (1994), the old paradigm is observed to be dysfunctional given the quantum shift in competitive responsiveness and environmental change (pp. 217-218). Smircich, Calas, and Morgan (1992) also argue that there is a need to "broaden what can be called theory in the Academy of Management" (p. 608). In addition, Aktouf (1992) notes that there is a need for new management theories which distance themselves from managerial functionalism while grounding themselves in sincere humanism.

Aktouf is consistent with the popular business press and Gardner (1963) by arguing for a radical shift in how firms are managed and organized. He notes that

> The era of quality has been extended to the business firm; now all employees must be active and intelligent participants. Yet traditional management lacks the conceptual and theoretical means to grasp the magnitude of coming upheavals. Straight-jacketed in traditional theory, solidly anchored in functionalism and the ideology of consensus, many management theorists cannot see that dramatic shifts in the factors of success require an equally dramatic shift in management philosophy and in the conception of work and the worker. (p. 410)

The solution to today's organizational quagmire is seen by Aktouf to be a synergistic culture which encompasses the renewal properties observed earlier by Gardner (1963), and the "mental software" described by Hofstede (1991). These notions collectively support Kiernan's (1993) arguments regarding the "New Strategic Architecture." He notes that this architecture provides the normative "DNA" and "the enabling platform upon which specific strategies can then be built" (p. 7). Such an architecture is essential for spontaneous reconfiguration in an increasingly hypercompetitive environment.

Reflections of the New Paradigm

If there is a contemporary prototype of Xenophon's army, it might be AT&T. Despite its age and size, AT&T has recently developed the ability to reconfigure itself quickly. Kirkpatrick recently observed in *Fortune* (1993) that the company now possesses a team-driven structure that is flexible and nontraditional. In addition, AT&T places a high priority on individuality and respect for employees, something which Aktouf (1992) notes to be essential to any new paradigm. It appears that the major ingredient to AT&T's renewal is CEO Allen's emphasis on an open, organic culture. As a result, the firm's transformational culture has enabled it to move rapidly in the marketplace.

The new organizational theory that is gradually emerging suggests that there is a need for transformational cultures characterized by human and visionary values which openly encourage renewal and continuous improvement. This process of completely reengineering the firm cannot be left to a select few as is implied by Tichy and Ulrich (1985) when they articulate the properties of the transformational leader. Perhaps the greatest transformational leader we have ever known is former Soviet statesman, Mikhail Gorbachev. Because Soviet society lacks the entrepreneurial values associated with growing societies, as well as other cultural ingredients of renewal, Gorbachev's initiatives appear stillborn.

What "our" capitalistic society could benefit from in regard to the global economic wars is the existence of transformational organizations which embody the organic properties Morgan (1986) identifies through his metaphors and exemplified by the *Anabasis*. Such a transformational organization would possess a cultural ethic where all employees personalize the need to advocate and facilitate change. This kind of organization is more likely to respond to the critical turning points noted by Intel's CEO, Grove. He recently observed in *Fortune* (1993) that "there is at least one point in the history of any company where you have to change dramatically. Miss the moment, and you start to decline" (p. 39). The challenge is also in being able to act on the moment as did Xenophon's army, a forerunner of the new organizational paradigm.

CONCLUSION

The relevance of the "March Up Country" relative to contemporary organizations is given to us by Griffin (1991) when commenting on the Greeks:

> To see that such things can be true of people whom in some ways we find intelligible and recognizable can help to deliver us from the tyranny of the present, from the assumption that our own habits of action and thought are really inescapable, and from the idea that there are no alternatives. That is the liberating power of the past. (p. 8)

This chapter makes an effort to produce the linkage between metaphors and organizational science, a quest recently raised by Tsoukas (1991), by making use of a classic historical case. It is argued here that the *Anabasis* implicitly reveals Greek culture to be the essential factor that enabled Xenophon's besieged army to escape successfully. This military account not only animates in pragmatic fashion the metaphorical arguments of Morgan (1986), but reveals the importance culture can play in reconfiguring organizational structure. While culture is not a phenomenon easily defined or quantitatively assessed, both Keegan (1993) and Hanson (1989) argue strongly that culture is a major factor in producing military successes. It is also noted here that additional case studies and qualitative means need to be used to ascertain culture's importance given that empirical efforts to assess culture quantitatively are insufficient by themselves. This is consistent with Frost (1991) who, in regard to future research endeavors, states: "we advocate broad and flexible thinking in order to provide a rich array of ideas and information about a phenomenon that, in our view, can never be understood by one frame, through a single study, or by using one research technique" (p. 339).

The Greek military crisis dramatized by this chapter links up with the three perspectives described by Martin (1992) and advocated by Frost et al. (p. 338). It depicts a call for unity (integration) as well as independence (differentiation), self-creation, and "adhocracy" (ambiguity). New leaders were elected (redundancy and self-organization), dynamic flexibility was maintained (ability to learn), and differences were tolerated and encouraged (requisite variety). Most importantly, the Greek army succeeded *not* because it possessed a superior strategy, better soldiers, greater resources, or advanced technology. As Morgan observes, the culture metaphor "provides a new focus and avenue for the creation of organized action" (p. 135). The Greek culture *became the strategy*—the strategy of continuous, ad hoc adjustment to unique and adverse conditions. The *Anabasis* describes no game plan of escape. Nor is great leadership found to be indispensable. Instead, Xenophon details a biological and holographic entity that relied on a holistic culture supplying the right qualitative balance between dependence and independence. Interestingly enough, Ambrose (1994), a distinguished American historian, in his text, *D-Day June 6, 1944: The Climactic Battle of World War II,* sees much the same regarding the U.S. forces. He notes that the democratic values of independent thought and heroism of American GIs were the critical factors that facilitated success in Normandy rather than strategic planning and military superiority. It appears that the "right" culture can be an effective substitute for formal organizational design and strategic planning in an environment of hypercompetition.

Because the culture found in Xenophon's army is not easily reproduced or easily managed, many American corporations are likely to find it difficult to learn how to effectively evolve and restructure themselves. In particular, large firms like General Motors, IBM, and Sears as well as large, complex societies like the former Soviet Union have recently discovered the difficulty of reorganizing themselves in order to compete effectively in an ever increasingly turbulent, demanding environment. The value of a free-enterprise ethic is largely dependent on the notion of being able to organize for competitive action. American industry can clearly benefit from the organizational example of Xenophon's army. While the Greek emphasis on an ethic of individualism may have declined as a useful competitive attribute by the end of the 20th century, their emphasis on adaptability in an ambiguous environment remains quite relevant. The ability of a firm to reconfigure itself spontaneously like a futuristic creature out of science fiction is a competitive asset truly essential in a hypercompetitive, dynamic, and global environment.

ACKNOWLEDGMENTS

The author gratefully recognizes the valuable contributions of the reviewers and editors, as well as those of Dr. Robert Gaebel (University of Akron, Classics) and Dr. Paul Maier (Western Michigan University, History).

REFERENCES

Aktouf, O. (1992), "Management and Theories of Organizations in the 1990s: Toward a Critical Radical Humanism," *Academy of Management Review,* 17, 3, 407-431.

Ambrose, S. E. (1994), *D-Day June 6, 1944: The Climactic Battle of World War II,* New York: Simon Schuster.

Begley, S. (1993), "The Puzzle of Genius," *Newsweek,* June 28, 46-51.

Bennis, W. G. (1966), *Changing Organizations,* New York: McGraw Hill.

Boardman, J., J. Griffin, and O. Murray (1986), *The Oxford History of the Classical World,* Oxford, UK: Oxford University Press.

———, ———, and ——— (1991), *The Oxford History of Greece and the Hellenistic World,* Oxford, UK: Oxford University Press.

Botsford, G. W. and C. A. Robinson (1956), *Hellenic History,* New York: Macmillan.

Bourgeois, L. J. and D. R. Brodwin (1984), "Strategy Implementations: Five Approaches to an Elusive Phenomenon," *Strategic Management Journal,* 5, 241-284.

Byrne, J. A. (1992), "Paradigms for Postmodern Managers," in *Business Week Special Issue,* "Reinventing America," 62-63.

Conrad, J. (1899), *Heart of Darkness,* W. Blackwood's Edinboro Magazine.

Cottrell, L. (1957), *The Anvil of Civilization,* New York: Mentor.

Cox, T. H. and S. Blake (1991), "Managing Cultural Diversity Implications for Organizational Competitiveness," *Academy of Management Executive,* 5, 3, 45-56.

D'Aveni, R. A. (1994), *Hypercompetition: The Dynamics of Strategic Maneuvering,* New York: Free Press.

Drucker, P. F. (1992), "The New Society of Organizations," *Harvard Business Review,* 95-104.

Fox, R. L. (1980), *The Search for Alexander,* Boston: Little, Brown.

Frost, P. J., L. F. Moore, M. R. Louis, Craig C. Lundberg, and J. Martin (1991a), *Reframing Organizational Culture,* Newbury Park, CA: Sage.

———— (1991b), "Looking Back," 337-340 (found in previous cite).

Gardner, J. (1963), *Self-Renewal: The Individual and the Innovative Society,* New York: Harper/Colophon.

Gordon, G. (1991), "Industry Determinants of Organizational Culture," *Academy of Management Review,* 16, 2, 396-415.

Grant, M. (1987), *The Rise of the Greeks,* New York: Charles Scribner's Sons.

Griffin, J. (1991), "Introduction," in J. Boardman, J. Griffin and O. Murray (Eds.), *The Oxford History of Greece and the Hellenistic World,* 1-8, Oxford, UK: Oxford University Press.

Hanson, V. D. (1989), *The Western Way of War,* New York: Alfred A. Knopf.

Hofstede, G. (1991), *Cultures and Organizations,* London, UK: McGraw-Hill.

Hornblower, S. (1986), "Greece: The History of the Classical Period," in J. Boardman, J. Griffin, and O. Murray (Eds.), *The Oxford History of the Classical World,* 124-155, Oxford, UK: Oxford University Press.

Keegan, J. (1993), *The History of Warfare,* New York: Alfred A. Knopf.

Kennedy, P. (1987), *The Rise and Fall of the Great Powers,* New York: Random House.

Kiernan, M. J. (1993), "The New Strategic Architecture: Learning to Compete in the Twenty-first Century," *Academy of Management Executive,* 7, 1, 7-21.

Kirkpatrick, D. (1993), "Could AT&T Rule the World?" *Fortune,* May 17, 55-63.

Lawrence, P. and J. Lorsch (1967), *Organization and Environment,* Boston: Harvard Business School Press.

Loeb, M. (1995), "Empowerment That Pays Off," *Fortune,* March 20, 145-146.

Loomis, C. J. (1993), "Dinosaurs?" *Fortune,* May 3, 36-42.

Martin, J. (1992), *Cultures in Organizations: Three Perspectives,* New York: Oxford University Press.

Morgan, G. (1986), *Images of Organization,* Newbury Park, CA: Sage.

———— (1993), *Imaginization: The Art of Creative Management,* Newbury Park, CA: Sage.

Murray, O. (1991), "Life and Society in Classical Greece," in J. Boardman, J. Griffin, and O. Murray (Eds.), *The Oxford History of the Classical World,* 240-276, Oxford, UK: Oxford University Press.

Parkinson, C. N. (1963), *East and West,* Boston: Houghton Mifflin.

Peters, T. J. and R. H. Waterman (1982), *In Search of Excellence: Lessons From America's Best-Run Companies,* New York: Harper and Row.

Rouse, W. H. D. (1959), *The March Up Country, a Translation of Xenophon's* Anabasis, New York: Mentor.

Smircich, L., M. Calas and G. Morgan (1992), "Afterward/Afterwords: Open(ing?) Spaces," *Academy of Management Review,* 17, 3, 607-611.

Stewart, T. A. (1992), "The Search for the Organization of Tomorrow," *Fortune,* May 18, 92-98.

Stone, I. F. (1988), *The Trial of Socrates,* Boston: Little, Brown.

Tichy, N. M. and D. O. Ulrich (1985), "The Leadership Challenge—Call for the Transformational Leader," *Sloan Management Review,* 26, 1, 59-68.

Toynbee, A. J. (1953), *Greek Civilization and Character,* New York, Mentor.

Tsoukas, H. (1991), "The Missing Link: A Transformational View of Metaphors in Organizational Science," *Academy of Management Review,* 16, 3, 566-585.

Van Cauwenbergh, A. and K. Cool (1982), "Strategic Management in a New Framework," *Strategic Management Journal,* 3, 24-38.

Part III

OTHER PERSPECTIVES

19

The Dark Side of the
New Organizational Forms

An Editorial Essay

BART VICTOR
CARROLL U. STEPHENS

> I suppose one might have persuaded oneself that this was but the replacement of
> an ancient tranquility, or at least an ancient balance, by a new order. Only to my
> eyes, quickened by my father's imitations, it was manifestly no order at all. It was
> a multitude of uncoordinated fresh starts, each more sweeping and destructive
> than the last, and none of them ever worked out to a ripe and satisfactory
> completion. Each left a legacy of products—houses, humanity, or whatnot—in its
> wake. It was a sort of progress that had bolted; it was change out of hand, and
> going at an unprecedented pace nowhere in particular.
>
> —*H. G. Wells, from* New Machiavelli, 1910

(NEW ORGANIZATIONAL FORMS;
BUREAUCRACY; WEBER; JOB DESIGN)

The field of organization theory is rife with discussion of new organizational forms (Daft and Lewin 1993). So is the popular business press. It is no exaggeration to claim that the emergence of the organizational form variously termed post-industrial, post-bureaucratic, network, cluster, and perpet-

513

ual matrix has rejuvenated organization theory. Not only do scholars have a panoply of novel challenges facing turn-of-the-millennium organizations to address, but—as evidenced by coverage in magazines including *Fortune*, *Forbes*, and *Business Week*, and the best-seller status of books such as *Reengineering the Corporation* (Hammer and Champy 1993)—practitioners actually seem to care about organization design.

As we career into the brave new world of the 21st century organization— networked, information rich, delayered, lean, hypercompetitive and boundaryless—an unanticipated, undesirable and indirect consideration has been overlooked. Radical redesign of organizations throughout the society— indeed globally—necessarily entails losses as well as gains. We believe that the time is right to break the silence about the dark side of the new organizational forms. In this essay we wish to call attention to moral as well as pragmatic questions about the new forms.

These fundamental alterations in the nature of organizational forms are occasioned by changes of a magnitude that have not been seen since the industrial revolution and the consequent emergence of bureaucracy. New organizational forms tend to arise in response to social and technological advances (Weber 1978, orig. 1910; and Chandler 1962, 1977). Particular forms of organizations arise at particular times, within particular sets of conditions. Bureaucracy evolved in response to post-enlightenment rational thought, the weakening of primary institutions such as family and church, and the technological advances of the industrial revolution (Lewin and Stephens 1993, p. 400). The mechanization of the industrial revolution led many former artisans, craftspeople and farmers to leave the sphere of community and self-sufficiency (*Gemeinschaft*) in order to enter the labor markets of the large modern organization (*Gesellschaft*). This shift was propelled by the labor power demands of the industrial organization, which created net economic gains for society at large. Yet even a cursory review of the literature from the time that the bureaucratic organization was dawning reveals at least as much trepidation as heralding. Writers as disparate as Kafka, LePlay, Orwell, Durkheim, Huxley, Marx, Tonnies, and Michels powerfully depicted the social and human costs of modernization. Nowhere is this expressed more poignantly than by Weber himself—simultaneous chronicler and critic of bureaucracy:

> It is as if we were deliberately to become men who need order and nothing but order, who become nervous and cowardly if for one moment the order wavers, and helpless if they are torn away from their total incorporation in it. That the world should know no men but these: It is in such an evolution that we are already caught up, and the great question is therefore not how we can promote and hasten it, but what we can oppose to this machinery in order to keep a portion of humankind free from this

parcelling-out of the soul, from this supreme mastery of the bureaucratic way of life.
(in P. J. Mayer, *Max Weber and German Politics,* 1944)

Although chroniclers of and apologists for the new organizational forms
are multitudinous, critics are rare—at least in the organization theory literature. Yet a juxtaposition of the flossy "new org form" language—empowerment,
high commitment, downsizing, restructuring, reengineering—against the
hard economic data presents a jarring image. The lean, flexible organization
has far-reaching consequences for the downsized worker, and hence for
society: One third of all American workers now hold temporary, part-time,
or short-term contract jobs (U.S. Bureau of Labor Statistics). The number of
temporary workers tripled between 1982 and 1990. Although the U.S. economy is, by conventional measures, in recovery following the recession of the
late '80s and early '90s, a record number of companies announced layoffs in
1993 and, although the trend showed signs of slowing, it picked up again in
late 1997 and early 1998. More than 90% of new jobs being created are
part-time. After the four previous recessions, nearly half of all laid-off
workers returned to their original jobs; the current figure is 15%.

These figures, taken together, suggest that the U.S. economy and workplace are undergoing profound structural alterations, not merely cyclical ups
and downs. This is not necessarily a bad thing. According to theories of
modernization (Weber 1978, orig. 1910; Schumpeter 1934), economic progress generally brings about both a bigger pie for all to share, and a more-
equitable distribution of that pie, even when changes involve cataclysmic
dislocations such as the shift from an agrarian to an industrial economy. Furthermore, arguments can be made that trimming the workforce—
downsizing—is necessary to succeed in today's hypercompetitive environment. However, in contrast to earlier economic upheavals, the post-industrial
changes have led to heightened income disparities rather than shared benefits. Between 1980 and 1990 the richest 1% of the US population became
50% wealthier while the poorest 20% found themselves 8% more disadvan-
taged. Over the last decade, America's CEOs stretched their pay advantage
over production workers from 40/1 to 93/1; for *Fortune* 500 CEOs in 1996,
the differential was 200/1.

Of course, any far-reaching organizational change involves destruction as
well as creation. As Durkheim wrote, "What is in fact characteristic of our
development is that it has successively destroyed all the established social
contexts: One after another they have been banished either by the slow usury
of time or by violent revolution, in such a fashion that nothing has been
developed to replace them" (Durkheim 1893). The destructive aspects of the
industrial revolution were well reported. Those of the post-industrial revolution and the concomitant new organizational forms seem to be passing almost

unobserved. Over 20 years ago a few prescient scholars such as Herbert Marcuse (1968) and Daniel Bell (1973) posed the seemingly science-fiction question of how organizations, society, and economy would be restructured once technological advances rendered the full-time industrial employment of the majority of adults obsolescent. This is precisely the eventuality that we believe has come to pass at the turn of the millennium.

If quantum leaps in technology have enabled organizations to become leaner, thus leading to widespread job loss that our society has yet to address in a systematic manner, so too have technological changes had profound impact on those who remain members of the organization. Sophisticated computer-mediated telecommunications have permitted the development of the "virtual office"; where organizational boundaries begin and end is unclear. And, as Burns and Stalker warned in 1961 when they first described the flexible organic organization, post-bureaucratic organizational forms carry the hazard of blurring the boundaries of the demands that may be placed upon workers.

Looking ahead, the new organizational forms are supplanting jobs with what amount to virtual occupations. Total quality organizational cultures would have workers perform whenever tasks are required to satisfy the customer, or reach the quality wishdream of continuous improvement. Instead of a role anchored by the organization and codified in a job description, the new forms are offering a role defined by the task of the moment and location of the worker. Time, space, and shifting group membership are becoming the primary definers of responsibility and accountability for the virtual wage slave. Traditional indicators of status are becoming blurred as a result of obligations that are networked and diffused, and rights that are increasingly ephemeral in this new world of ours. At just the time that organizational commitment to the employee has been thoroughly violated, the employee is expected to exhibit feverishly enhanced commitment to the organization. And, fearing job loss, many are compliant despite the increasing one-sidedness of the deal.

There is much discussion about the empowering, challenging, and equalizing advantages of the new organizational form. But there is also a justified fear and loathing. Bureaucracy may have led to alienation and anomie; we tend to overlook the fact that bureaucracy also fostered procedural if not substantive justice for workers. Furthermore, not every person will be at ease with the free-floating demands of the hyperflexible workplace. As Erich Fromm (1941) pointed out, many if not most people thrive on predictability and routine.

The boundaryless, adaptive, learning organization will extract a price from everyone involved. One notable and distinctly unromantic consequence of the transformation from the craft form to the new bureaucracy was the impact on traditional know-how and skill. Confidence gained from inheritance and apprenticeship was stripped away by the machines and procedures of the new factory. As Elton Mayo described the fate of the Welsh workers in the newly mechanized coal mines of Pennsylvania,

> these men, many in late middle age, found themselves without an avocation and without means of continuing to support themselves and their families in the way of life to which they had become accustomed. This was for them a personal calamity of the first magnitude; as former pillars of society they did not lapse readily into revolutionary attitudes. They drifted downwards toward unemployment as their savings became exhausted and toward profound personal depression. (Mayo 1945)

In the new organizational form, the periodic deskilling that comes with technical progress in bureaucracy is replaced with an incessant demand for innovation and adaptation. To accommodate this, the new "learning organization" insists that everyone become a self-motivated, continuous learner. Absent this obsession with learning about work, workers are threatened with rapid obsolescence—and little hope of getting back on the treadmill of continuous progress.

This impact of new forms extends to our social selves as well. Flat organizations force interpersonal relations in more demanding and intrusive modes than ever before. Private self, benign eccentricities, and social warts become new terms of employment, even as we hope for a more diverse and unbiased workplace. Teams and networks call for new levels and kinds of cooperation. No one can expect to escape the demands to interact and be interactive. Even the values of the employee are offered up as fodder to be transformed by management for organizational ends (Stephens, D'Intino, and Victor 1995). Yet these high-velocity, high-commitment workplaces—flash-in-the-pan collectives—offer no ongoing relationships, no safe haven, no personal space.

Concepts such as loyalty, dedication, and belonging have at best a radically new place in the emerging workworld. We still wax nostalgic about the concept of family in a fashion that harkens to a lost (and mostly fictitious) past. How much more distant will the future take us? Concepts such as the expropriation of surplus value, rate busting, union busting, impression management, careerism, and dehumanization emerged from the bureaucratic form, along with the work ethic, affordable luxuries, corporate social responsibility, and meritocracy. In the discussion of the new organizational form we hear a great deal about valuing diversity, empowerment, and customized solutions. But what of the potential negative values and consequences? Perhaps it is our time to think critically enough of the future to warn our descendants of some of the potential dangers.

We cannot stop the emergence of the new form, just as the critics of bureaucracy could not stem the ineluctable reach of the iron cage. Less all its ills, the emergence of bureaucracy has probably been a net benefit for humankind. The same may be true of the new form. Organizational scholars are eagerly examining the implementation of the new forms. Perhaps we should expand our research agenda to address questions that have far-reaching moral as well as economic consequences: How can companies assist surviving workers in making the transition to the brave new workplace? How can stress be minimized, rather than accentuated, in the ambiguous new form? And, most importantly, what is to become of the superfluous downsized workers? It is worth repeating for our times the moral exhortation that Durkheim issued: "Science can help finding the direction in which our conduct ought to go, assisting us to determine the ideal that we gropingly seek. But we shall only be able to raise ourselves up to that ideal after having observed reality, for we shall distill the ideal from it" (Durkheim 1933).

REFERENCES

Bell, D. (1973), *The Coming of Post-industrial Society: A Venture in Social Forecasting,* New York: Basic Books.

Burns, T. and G. Stalker (1961), *The Management of Innovation,* London: Tavistock.

Chandler, A. (1962), *Strategy and Structure in the History of the Industrial Enterprise,* Cambridge: MIT Press.

——— (1977), *The Visible Hand: The Managerial Revolution in American Business,* Cambridge, MA: Belknap Press of Harvard University Press.

Daft, R. and A. Lewin (1993), "Where Are the Theories for the New Organizational Forms? An Editorial Essay," *Organization Science,* 4, 4(i-vi).

Durkheim, E. (1893), *Suicide,* New York: Free Press.

——— (1933), *The Division of Labor in Society,* New York: Free Press.

Fromm, Erich (1941), *Escape from Freedom,* New York: Avon.

Hammer, M. and J. Champy (1993), *Reengineering the Corporation: A Manifesto for Business Revolution,* New York: Harper Business.

Lewin, A. and C. Stephens (1993), "Designing Post-industrial Organizations: Combing Theory and Practice," in G. Huber and W. Glick (Eds.), *Organizational Change and Redesign,* New York: Oxford University Press, 393-409.

Marcuse, H. (1968), *Negations: Essays in Critical Theory,* London: Penguin.

Mayer, P. (1944), *Max Weber and German Politics,* London: Faber and Faber.

Mayo, E. (1945), *The Social Problems of an Industrial Civilization,* Boston: Havard Business School Press.

Schumpeter, J. (1934), *The Theory of Economic Development,* Campbridge, MA: Harvard University Press.

Stephens, C., R. D'Intino and B. Victor. (1995), "The Moral Quandary of Transformational Leadership: Change for Whom?" in R. Woodman and W. Pasmore (Eds.), *Research in Organizational Change and Development,* vol. 8, Greenwich, CT: JAI Press, 123-143.

Weber, M. (1978, orig. 1910), *Economy and Society* (G. Roth and C. Wittich, Trs.), Berkeley: University of California.

20

Refining Our Understanding of
Hypercompetition and Hyperturbulence

ASAF ZOHAR
GARETH MORGAN

INTRODUCTION

Kenneth Aupperle presents a strong case for the relevance of an ancient Greek story for the "new realities" faced by present-day organizations. Aupperle's *story of the story* of the "March Up Country" is intended to highlight the historical parallels of this remarkable event with current "hypercompetitive" conditions. He identifies some of the critical factors that contributed to the Greek army's successful organizational "reconfiguration" under the "hypercompetitive conditions" of war. Basically, his argument is that, by analogy, Hellenian culture, "was to individual city-states as a contemporary corporation is to its separate departments and strategic business units," and that the episode offers useful insights into some of the critical ingredients necessary for meeting the challenges of current organizational conditions and circumstances.

There are many notable strengths in Aupperle's cultural interpretation of "The March." At the same time, however, several critical aspects of his argument raise important, and highly evocative, issues. In this commentary, we will address one of these: Namely, the role and nature of metaphor in revealing the insights of this case in particular, and in the development of organizational science in general. Turning to the case itself, we will extend his reading of "The March" by adopting the metaphor of self-organization as a way of broadening our understanding of the theoretical and practical implications of the case. We will also use the insights gained from this discussion as a way of exploring the relevance and implications of the

519

self-organizing metaphor for the further development of hypercompetitive theories of organization.

THE SEARCH FOR "LITERAL"
VERSUS "METAPHORICAL KNOWLEDGE"

Our first point of critique of Aupperle's position is epistemological, and lies in his representation of the role of metaphor in administrative theory and research. Following others (e.g., Tsoukas 1991), Aupperle's position appears to avoid the extremes that have typified past debates on this issue. Instead of arguing that metaphors are either detrimental or essential to the development of organizational science (e.g., Pinder and Bourgeois 1982), he suggests that metaphorical and literal knowledge are "complementary." This complementarity, however, seems to flow in a single direction: "The use of metaphors is important in that they provide the qualitative means by which to better understand the more quantitative meanings of literal language." From his perspective, metaphors have an instrumental value in furthering literal knowledge. As he puts it, they are the "soul of the mechanistic process of information processing"; they may be valuable "sensors" for "capturing and expressing a continuous flow of experience"; and they can serve as a means of generating creative insights into aspects of concrete reality that otherwise could not be engaged through the inherent limitations of literal language.

In our view, this positioning of metaphor is limited and is caught in the trap of drawing misleading distinctions between metaphorical and literal knowledge. As has been argued elsewhere (Morgan 1993), while Aupperle and others (e.g., Tsoukas 1991) regard the empirical as the source or arbiter of "truth" or "literal knowledge," our view is that knowledge *always* emerges and develops as a domain of extended metaphor. An image becomes a root or generative source of knowledge by allowing the observer to engage reality in new ways. This sets the stage for studying reality in greater detail through metonymical or reductive processes that entail the detailed elaboration of the guiding image (White 1978, Morgan 1983). There is no clear separation between the "literal" and the metaphorical.

Organization science has always been constructed on this combination of metaphorical-metonymical understanding. Take, for example, the concept of organizational structure. The concept derives primarily from the metaphor that "the organization is a machine." The image allows a reductive focus on "structure" that then becomes treated as the defining essence of organization. As we know, this abstracted concept of structure became so powerful during the middle decades of this century that it eventually replaced the initial generative metaphor of "machine," being treated as a concrete, objective, "literal" feature of organizational life.

One can never disengage oneself from the interconnection between subject and object, and the role of metaphor as the constitutive force that creates the interpretive domain within which we talk about the literal. To seek literal truth independent of metaphorical construction is an illusion. The process of understanding and knowledge creation always occurs within the context of the limitations and strengths of a particular way of seeing, which is rooted in a particular metaphor or image of organization. As observers, we are forever locked into an autopoietic or self-referencing relationship with whatever we are studying.

METAPHOR AS A GENERATIVE
SOURCE OF KNOWLEDGE

One of the central implications of this approach is that since any particular way of seeing is problematic and incomplete, literal "truths" will always be partial truths. The challenge of knowing "the truth" of anything thus becomes connected with the art of understanding, reading, and interpreting organizational situations in multiple ways. By engaging situations from diverse standpoints or experiences generating admittedly partial "views," it becomes possible to avoid the search for universal, authoritative, "literal" explanations of social reality that end up elevating certain perspectives over others. The search for the "literal" is replaced by an iterative, dynamic process of framing and reframing multiple, and frequently paradoxical interpretations that can help us engage central aspects of the multifaceted phenomenon that we are studying.

One possible methodological approach was presented in *Images of Organization* (Morgan 1986). This is the approach Aupperle has used as a point of departure for his critical account of "The March." Aupperle's interpretation of this approach, however, represents a limited application and differs significantly from the one presented in *Images*, precisely because Aupperle's underlying assumptions about the nature and process of knowledge generation seem to differ from those that served as a basis for the book. *Images of Organization*, and the methodology it represents, is not just about choosing multiple reference points for viewing a phenomenon, but of coping with the relativity and fundamental epistemological implications that this entails. Any frame of reference or paradigm for studying a phenomenon is bound to be partial. In creating one kind of insight, it obscures others. This recognition of the subjective construction of "truth" demands that any attempt to understand a phenomenon be accompanied by a reflective stance that highlights and works with both the insights and distortions we are creating.[1]

This is of vital importance in interpreting the whole issue of hypercompetition as illustrated in Aupperle's analysis, and in the hypercompetition literature in general. Aupperle's analysis and interpretation of The March offers an excellent illustration of how the metaphors of "culture," "body," and "brain" can contribute to an integrated understanding of the Greek army's ability to engage in spontaneous responses to rapid, unpredictable change. He emphasizes the importance of what he terms "information processing skills" that enabled the army to act as a "distributive information processing system" which, at a local level, consisted of brain-like information nodes (front line soldiers) and information processors (junior level officers). This unique information processing capacity enabled individual units or, when necessary, the entire body of the Greek army to react in a timely, creative way to emergent challenges posed by the changing circumstances of the retreat. At the leadership level, this capacity was manifested in a highly adaptable approach that was not tied to singular, specialized roles. Xenophon's account of occasional switching of roles between captains illustrates that, like a biological entity, the army made spontaneous adjustments at all levels in order to assure its survival.

Aupperle emphasizes, however, that the most critical factor that accounted for this historic episode was the triumph of the Greek "humanistic" culture over a Persian army based on a bureaucratic and autocratic control system. The Greeks basically used their cultural heritage as their "subtle weapon." According to Aupperle, the Greek culture was paradoxical in that it simultaneously thrived on integration, differentiation, and fragmentation of multiple city-states. His analysis suggests that the norms, values, and heritage of the Greeks facilitated integrative or unifying processes that at the same time permitted individual differences. In this way, the distinct subcultures in the Greek army actually facilitated adaptation to a hostile and unfamiliar environment. These differences reinforced the dominant culture, while at the same time complementing it through the translation of diversity and difference into creativity and spontaneous organizational reconfiguration. Consequently, "the Greek leadership . . . had no need to impose a new set of competitive values to facilitate a successful escape. These paradoxical properties collectively enabled Xenophon's soldiers to know when and how to respond: as a whole, as a team, as individuals."

We agree with the details of Aupperle's analysis, but part company in seeing "culture" as the preeminent influence. In line with what we have said above, the culture metaphor provides an important lens for grasping aspects of the behavior of Xenophon's army, but it does not grasp the "literal truth" of this episode. Aupperle's search for this kind of "terra firma" tends to close off other options or "probes" into the case that can lead to additional insights. For example, using perspectives drawing on theories of chaos and self-organization, it is possible to reframe and understand much of what Aupperle describes as an example of how dynamic and complex social systems create novel patterns of order out of disorder (Gleick 1987, Goldstein 1994, Stacey 1992, Wheatley 1990), and how, perhaps as a corollary of certain cultural values, Xenophon's army had an inherent capacity for inner spontaneity and adaptiveness that allowed it to reorganize and renew itself in meaningful ways.

Following this perspective, a robust interpretive account would elevate the importance of understanding the nature of self-organizing processes, and the way in which cultural values can support or hinder the way these processes are allowed to surface. The interpretation of this episode is not, however, a question of adopting a position that stresses either "culture" *or* "self-organization" as the main explanation of this episode. The point is that both these perspectives can be integrated to provide powerful insights on organizational qualities and competencies in hyperturbulent conditions. The cultural values that lend a holographic, brain-like quality to Xenophon's army are intertwined with important features of self-organizing systems: the spontaneous emergence of novel patterns and configurations; the amplification and incorporation of random events; the self-guided discovery of creative alternatives for functioning by individual soldiers and leaders; and the emergence of new coherence and coordination at all levels of this military organization.

This self-organizing interpretation embellishes Aupperle's position by highlighting the holographic aspects of the culture of military organization evident in this episode. It allows us to reframe the significance of culture not merely as an artifact, but as a living process that can reproduce values, attitudes, capacities, and competencies that are necessary for sustaining a particular form of reality. Culture becomes part of the multidimensional context of enabling conditions that allow the army's inherent capacities for self-organization to emerge and shape organizational actions in meaningful ways.

This extended interpretation in no way detracts from Aupperle's insights into the cultural dimensions of the case. Our aim is to demonstrate the problem of premature interpretive closure and illustrate the benefits of remaining open to new insights. As noted above, the point of which metaphor (culture or self-organization) offers the "best" interpretation or reveals the "literal" truth of these events is not the most relevant one. The real question should be about how to gain the most insight and "leverage" into this episode. What can the various metaphors, in isolation or in combination, do to help us appreciate and understand the phenomenon being examined? How can they help us to come to grips with the phenomenon of hyperturbulence and hypercompetition?

HYPERTURBULENCE AND
HYPERCOMPETITION AS METAPHOR

The same kind of critique that we have advanced in relation to Aupperle's article can be extended to the topic of hyperturbulence and hypercompetition more generally. In advancing the metaphor of hypercompetition as a way of exploring new insights, D'Aveni (1994, 1995) takes conventional strategic wisdom to task by suggesting that organizations need to deliberately speed up the pace of change in order to manage it more successfully. He does not attempt to tinker with the controls of existing strategic navigational panels. By using hyperturbulence as a metaphor for dealing with the nature and pace of current realities, he calls for a fundamental reframing of our basic assumptions about organizational strategy. As with all metaphorical excursions, however, the argument is developed in a way that elevates the importance of certain aspects of our current reality and downplays others. For example, he paints a picture of a world characterized by "escalation ladders," "creative destruction," "warfare," "fencing," "hurricanes," and "earthquakes." He urges us to redefine the essential rules of organizational play under conditions of constant uncertainty, turbulence, and dis-equilibrium, suggesting that the most effective strategy is to proactively pursue market disruptions that enhance the increasingly prevalent forces of organizational chaos and upheaval. Downplayed or missing from the analysis are the moderating forces that play a role in countering such turbulence or provide alternative ways of coping.

There can be little doubt that we are entering an era of hypercompetitive environments, or what Emery and Trist (1965, 1973) described as "turbulent fields." But unlike Emery and Trist, D'Aveni's analysis and approach glosses over the fact that complex social environments are characterized by forces of both positive *and* negative feedback. While the former destabilize, the latter stabilize. Systems can be transformed through both routes. One can stimulate and escalate the destabilizing forces or one can stimulate counter patterns of connectivity that shift a system into new configurations. Emery and Trist's call for domain-based "referent organizations" and strategic alliances that can moderate competing lines of action in pursuit of shared values and objectives provides an example of strategy designed to deal with hyperturbulent conditions directly counter to the direction advocated by

D'Aveni. The cybernetic-systems inspiration of Emery and Trist takes them into a completely different direction.

Hyperturbulence is *not* an imperative system condition that *demands* hypercompetitive strategy as a response. Such strategies represent a *possible* response, but ones that will inevitably increase the positive feedback characteristics of the system as a whole. Some of the potential dangers have been well-captured in the comments of Jonathan Canger (1995), a senior executive at Motorola, who aptly presents the implications of a deliberate strategy of creative destruction by comparing an organization that adopts these strategies to driving a brakeless car. The idea of speeding up a runaway car as a way of negotiating the perils of high speeds seems dysfunctional and counterintuitive, especially, as Canger argues, if we are at the wheel of a '65 Volkswagen bus with bald tires instead of a Ferrari. As we slam down on the strategic accelerator, should we expect organizational members to sit placidly in the back seat as we negotiate hairpin turns? By imagining ten cars with the same problem, one begins to engage the sense of fear and despair that the metaphor is likely to inspire. "Creative destruction" may well prove a powerful competitive strategy for a single, well-prepared organization seeking to outmaneuver a rival. But practiced by many organizations, it can have disastrous systemic consequences, not least for the employees left riding in the back seat.

Space does not permit a full evaluation of D'Aveni's position. Suffice it to say that his approach represents a metaphor "gone wild." Just as the machine theorists extracted "structure" from their favored image, D'Aveni is abstracting creative destructiveness from his, to produce a new kind of "corporate anarchism." Just as the nineteenth century French anarchists declared that, "the most creative desire is the desire to destroy" to mobilize the overthrow of capitalism, a similar philosophy of systematic negation is now being advocated to help us cope with some of the contradictions of advanced capitalism. If pursued in a broad manner, it is likely that its effects will be much more dramatic than runaway vehicles screaming down a hill. Canger offers an excellent image. But it is one that probably underestimates the scale and complexity of the potential consequences.

The challenge presented by the hyperturbulence and hypercompetition metaphor is to grasp its lessons and overcome its weaknesses. As suggested above, there is much in existing theorizing in the disciplines of cybernetics and chaos theory that can help us here, to name but two useful sources of inspiration. As we have shown in relation to Aupperle's analysis of "The March," the challenge is to find ways of mobilizing a variety of powerful yet practical insights and ideas that can improve our ability to influence hyperturbulence in new and creative ways.

NOTE

1. In view of the above, it's clear that we want to extend Aupperle's view of *Images of Organization* as a kind of closed "CAT scan" with predetermined images into a much more open organic interpretive process. As shown in Morgan (1993), the same method can be used to embrace spontaneous "metaphors of the moment" that create penetrating reframings of a situation, as well as metaphors that have achieved the status of formal analytical models (e.g., the eight broad metaphors in *Images*).

REFERENCES

Aupperle, K. E. (1996), "Spontaneous Organizational Reconfiguration: A Historical Example Based on Xenophon's Anabasis," *Organization Science,* 7, 4, 444-460.

Canger, J. A. (1995), Executive Commentary on A. R. D'Aveni (1995), "Coping with Hyperturbulence: Utilizing the New 7S's Framework," *Academy of Management Executive,* 9, 3, 57-59.

D'Aveni, R. A. (1994), *Hypercompetition: Managing the Dynamics of Strategic Maneuvering,* New York: Free Press.

———— (1995), "Coping with Hyperturbulence: Utilizing the New 7S's Framework," *Academy of Management Executive,* 9, 3, 45-60.

Emery, F. E. and E. L. Trist (1965), "The Causal Texture of Organizational Environments," *Human Relations,* 18, 301-321.

———— and ———— (1973), *Toward a Social Ecology,* London: Tavistock.

Gleick, J. (1987), *Chaos,* New York: Viking.

Goldstein, J. (1994), *The Unshackled Organization,* Portland, OR: Productivity Press.

Morgan, G. (1983), "More on Metaphor: Why We Cannot Control Tropes in Administrative Science," *Administrative Science Quarterly,* 28, 610-607.

Morgan, G. (1986), *Images of Organization,* Newbury Park, CA: Sage.

———— (1993), *Imaginization: The Art of Creative Management,* Newbury Park, CA: Sage.

Pinder, C. C. and W. V. Bourgeois (1982), "Controlling Tropes in Administrative Science," *Administrative Science Quarterly,* 27, 641-653.

Stacey, R. D. (1992), *Managing the Unknowable: Strategic Boundaries Between Order and Chaos Between Organizations,* San Francisco: Jossey-Bass.

Tsoukas, H. (1991), "The Missing Link: a Transformational View of Metaphors in Organizational Science," *Academy of Management Review,* 16, 566-585.

Wheatley, M. (1990), *Leadership and the New Science: Learning About Organizations from an Orderly Universe,* San Francisco: Berret-Koehler.

White, H. (1978), *The Tropics of Discourse,* Baltimore, MD: Johns Hopkins University Press.

Index

Adaptive capability, 269
Agency theory, 212-213
Airbus, 8
Airline industry. *See* Intra-industry hetero-
geneity
Anabasis (Xenophon). *See* Metaphorical per-
spective
Appropriability conditions, 13
Architectural knowledge, 310-311
Asahi brewery (Japan). *See* New product de-
velopment, Japanese breweries
Austrian economics, 47-49, 50, 51-52, 55, 62-
64

Benchmarking, 81-82, 84, 86
Benetton, 215, 221-223, 226, 227
Biotechnology industry. *See* Network forma-
tion; Networks, scientific knowledge
Brewery industry (Japan). *See* New product
development, Japanese breweries

Capability development, flexibility and:
adaptive, 269
managerial, 267, 270-276
operational, 273, 274-275
speed of, 273-276
steady-state, 273
strategic, 273, 275-276, 282
structural, 273, 275, 282
variety of, 272-273
Capability development, knowledge integration and:
capability hierarchy, 302-304
organizational capability model, 300-305,
314-316
Capability development, new product:
general, 131, 147-148, 160-161
specialized, 131, 147-148, 159-160
Capability development, telecommunications
industry:
and hypercompetition, 405-406, 407-409

and hypercompetition response, 417-420
and revitalization, 421
focused activities, 414-415, 421-422
garbage can activities, 407, 409-414, 423-
424
industry history, 405-409
managerial capability development, 416-
417
managerial implications, 423-424
planned flexibility, 421
rigid flexibility, 420-421
strategic flexibility, 407, 409, 422, 424
theoretical implications of, 420-422
Chamberlinian competition, 132, 161-162
Chaotic flexibility, 283, 285-286
Chrysler, 8
Citibank Bankcard. *See* Deep pockets paralysis
Common knowledge, 307
Competitive activity, firm-level:
and Austrian economics, 47-49, 50, 51-
52, 55, 62-64
and structure-conduct-performance
model, 47-49, 50, 51-52, 54, 62-64
dynamic model of, 49-52
hypotheses of, 52-56
influence of cooperative mechanisms on,
47, 49-56, 58, 62-64
influence on firm performance, 47, 49-
52, 53-56, 59, 62-64
study methodology, 56-61, 65n1
study results, 61-64
Consumer demand, 13
Container wars (Japan), 135-136, 138
Control theory, 270
Corporate identity campaign (Japan), 149-
151, 154, 157
Culture, organizational:
and flexibility, 278
metaphorical perspective, 483-488, 499-
504, 505, 506-509

About the Editors

Richard D'Aveni is Professor at the Amos Tuck School of Business Administration, Dartmouth College in Hanover, New Hampshire, where he teaches business policy, industry and competitive analysis, and organization design from a general manager's perspective. He has also taught at the University of North Carolina at Chapel Hill, INTEGER; Centro de Exelencia Empresarial in Monterrey, Mexico; and the International University of Japan in Urasa, Japan. He earned his B.A. cum laude at Cornell University, his M.B.A. cum laude at Boston University, his J.D. cum laude at Suffolk University, and his Ph.D. in strategic management at Columbia University. He was an attorney and a member of the Bar, as well as a C.P.A., formerly associated with Coopers & Lybrand. He also served as a project manager on the governor's staff in Massachusetts. He has been and is a consultant to several major corporations (including several firms in the Fortune 500) and is frequently sought for executive education programs on strategy and top executive leadership, and organizational politics. He had consulted with or spoken to firms such as Aetna Insurance, AT&T, Bell Atlantic, Boston Technologies, Coopers & Lybrand, DEC, Fininvest Italia, General Electric, General Motors, Heafner & Co., IBM, Instinet, Mercuri International, PepsiCo, Philip Morris, Schering-Plough, US West, Wilson Learning, World Economic Forum, and numerous professional and industrial organizations in Switzerland, Italy, Vietnam, Holland, Belgium, Germany, Mexico, Israel, and elsewhere around the world. He has been extensively written about or quoted in the popular press, including *Business Month, Chicago Tribune, Christian Science Monitor, Financial Manager, Fortune, Los Angeles Times, Newsweek, Success Magazine, The New York Times, Time*, and over 200 other

535

newspapers and magazines worldwide. Much of his research on why and how large firms fail has been published in *Administrative Science Quarterly, Management Science, Organization Science,* and the *Academy of Management Journal.* He has or is currently serving on the editorial boards of *Administrative Science Quarterly, Strategic Management Journal, Academy of Management Journal,* and *Organization Science.* He is currently undertaking several studies looking at turnaround strategies, outsourcing versus vertical integration, top management team structure, and strategies for the reinvention of industries. In 1987, he was awarded the A. T. Kearney Award for his research on why large firms fail, He was named a Richard D. Irwin Fellow in 1985. He was also named a Sol C. Snider Fellow in 1992 by the Wharton School of the University of Pennsylvania. He was profiled in *Wirtschafts Woche,* the German equivalent of *Business Week,* as one of the next generation's promising new management thinkers most likely to have a major impact on management in the 1990s. He is currently speaking about his recent book, *Hypercompetition: Managing the Dynamics of Strategic Maneuvering,* which was published in 1994.

Anne Y. Ilinitch is Assistant Professor of Business Administration at the Kenan-Flagler Business School at the University of North Carolina at Chapel Hill, where she received her Ph.D. Her research involves strategies for managing change and improving the corporate performance of firms in mature, commodity-based industries, including the impact of vertical integration, diversification, the natural environment, and global exporting. Her publications have appeared in *Organization Science, Academy of Management Journal, Strategic Management Journal,* and *Long Range Planning.*

Arie Y. Lewin is Professor of Business Administration and Sociology at Duke University. He is Director of the Center for International Business Education and Research (CIBER) and of the recently established Center for Research on New Organization Forms. He was program director for decision, risk, and management science at the National Science Foundation (1986-1988); Chairman of the Academic Council of Duke University for two terms (1982-1986); 1986 recipient of Duke University Presidential Award for Meritorious Service; DKB Visiting Professor Keio University Graduate School of Business (Spring 1993); and Visiting Research Professor Institute for Business Research, Hitotsubashi University (1984-1995). His primary research interests involve the analysis of organization effectiveness and the design of organizations. Current research is focused on new forms of organizations distinguished by new adaptive capabilities. He is presently engaged in a major long-term cross-cultural—Germany, Japan, Korea, Sweden, Switzerland, the United Kingdom, and the United States—comparative study of strategic reorientations and organization restructurings. He is author of four books and his research articles have appeared or are forthcoming in many different journals, including *Academy of Management Journal, Decision Sciences, European Journal of Operation Research, Journal of Applied Psychology, Journal of Mathematical Sociology, Management Science, Organization Science, Organization Studies, Personnel Psychology, Policy Sciences, Science, Simulation* and *Accounting Review.* He has also published columns in *Business Week, Dun's Review,* and *Planning Review.* He has been a management consultant to government and several major corporations; was department editor of management science for the department of organization analysis, performance, and design (1984-1987), and is the founding Editor in Chief of *Organization Science,* a new journal, now in its eighth year, published by INFORMS. At the Fuqua School, he has chaired the Curriculum Committee, is organizer and academic leader of Annual Fuqua MBA Tour of Asia and is academic program director for the new six-weeks Global Executive Program (GEP). He is a member of the Academy of Management, Association of Japanese Business Studies, Institute for Operations Research and Management Science, Society of Judgement and Decision Making, and Strategic Management Society. He also serves on the editorial boards of the *European Journal of Operations Research, Information Systems Research,* and *Journal of Productivity Analysis,* and is a member of the editorial advisory board for the *Asia Pacific Journal of Management.*

About the Contributors

Kenneth E. Aupperle ("Spontaneous Organizational Reconfiguration: A Historical Example Based on Xenophon's *Anabasis*" is Professor of Management at the University of Akron. He received his Ph.D. in strategic management at the University of Georgia in 1982. His research interests are in the areas of corporate social responsibility, as well as organizational culture, structure, design, and performance. Historical and ethical considerations are also a particular concern.

James L. Bailey ("The Paralysis of Deep Pockets") is Executive Vice President in charge of quality control at Citicorp/Citibank. Prior to this position, he had been Executive Vice President for Global Transaction Services, which is part of Citicorp's Global Finance business. Before that, he was Executive Vice President for the North American Consumer Bank, covering all of Citicorp's consumer business in the United States. Prior to that, he had been Group Executive for the U.S. Card Products Group, which included all U.S. card businesses and the international Diners Club businesses, as well as the insurance and investment initiatives, for three years. He received his B.S. from Bowling Green State University in 1967 and a M.S. in mathematics from New York University in 1970. He began his career at Bell Telephone Labs in 1967 and moved to Booz, Allen & Hamilton in 1970. He joined Citicorp in 1972 and advanced through several assignments in the Bankcard Division. He was named Director of Credit Management in Bankcards in 1978. He moved to the New York Retail Banking Division as Regional Business Manager for lower Manhattan in 1984. He returned to the Bankcard Division in 1985 as General Manager. He was named Division

Executive for Bankcards in 1987, and Group Executive for Card Products in 1989.

Marilynn Brewer ("Social Networks, Learning, and Flexibility: Sourcing Scientific Knowledge in New Biotechnology Firms") is currently Ohio State Regent's Professor of Social Psychology at Ohio State University, and was previously Professor of Psychology and Director, Institute of Social Science Research at UCLA (1982-1993). Brewer is also recent President of the American Psychological Society (1993-1995). She is the author of numerous books, monographs, and research articles on intergroup relations, organizational diversity, and social dilemmas.

Tim Craig ("The Japanese Beer Wars: Initiating and Responding to Hypercompetition in New Product Development") is Associate Professor of International Business in the Faculty of Business of University of Victoria in Victoria, British Columbia, Canada. His research focuses on strategic and organizational issues in international business. He has lived in Japan for twelve years, where he has taught at the high school and university levels, worked for Matsushita Electric Industrial Co., Ltd. (Panasonic), and conducted doctoral research at Kobe University. He is also Japan Program Director for the University of Victoria's Centre for Asia-Pacific Initiatives.

Kathleen M. Eisenhardt ("The Evolution of Intracorporate Domains: Divisional Charter Losses in High-Technology, Multidivisional Corporations") is Professor of Strategy and Organization at Stanford University. Her current research interests center on complexity and game theories, and their application to strategy and organization in high-velocity, high-competition industries. She has published on a variety of topics including strategic decision making, alliance formation, product innovation, managing global firms, case study methods, and agency theory. She is a Fellow of the Academy of Management, Senior Editor at *Organization Science,* on the editorial boards of *Administrative Science Quarterly* and *Strategic Management Journal,* and is the President-elect of OMT. She has received several awards for her research including the Pacific Telesis Foundation Award for her work on fast decisions, the Stern Prize for alliance formation among entrepreneurial firms, and the Whittemore Prize for research on managing global firms in hypercompetition. For her teaching, she has also been named by students as one of Stanford's top 8 professors. She is currently working on a book (with S. L. Brown), *Competing on the Edge: Strategy as Structured Chaos.*

D. Charles Galunic ("The Evolution of Intracorporate Domains: Divisional Charter Losses in High-Technology, Multidivisional Corporations") is

Assistant Professor of Organizational Behavior at INSEAD Business School, Cedex, France, and earned his Ph.D. at Stanford University. He works within the field of organizational theory and strategy. His area of research is the management of strategic processes and resources in firms. He focuses particularly on large, multiunit corporations, examining how their methods for coordinating and supporting the internal exchange of company resources (i.e., information, know-how, political support) is a source of value and competitive advantage. He has worked with firms in the high-technology and pharmaceutical industries, in both the United States and Europe. His work on the structural evolution of multidivisional firms has been recognized in several places, including awards from *Organization Science* and most recently from the Academy of Management. At INSEAD, he lectures on organizational change (M.B.A.), strategic process management (Ph.D.), and organizational theory (M.B.A.).

Javier Gimeno ("Hypercompetition in a Multimarket Environment: The Role of Strategic Similarity and Multimarket Contact in Competitive De-Escalation") is Assistant Professor of Management at Texas A&M University. He holds a Ph.D. (1994) in strategic management from the Krannert School of Management at Purdue University. His research interests include the study of competitive interaction in multimarket competition, competitive strategy, and the interface between industrial organization economics and strategic management. His dissertation on multimarket competition in the airline industry received the 1995 Free Press Outstanding Dissertation Award from the Business Policy and Strategy Division of the Academy of Management. He has also researched the determinants of survival and performance of new entrepreneurial ventures. He has articles published or forthcoming in *Administrative Science Quarterly, Organization Science, Journal of Business Venturing*, and *Advances in Strategic Management,* among others. In addition to ongoing research in multimarket competition, he is currently studying the effects of organizational information processing constraints, executive compensation, and corporate governance structures on the intensity of rivalry in the airline industry.

Robert M. Grant ("Prospering in Dynamically-Competitive Environments: Organizational Capability as Knowledge Integration") is Professor of Management at Georgetown University. He has taught at St. Andrews University (Scotland), City University, London Business School, University of British Columbia (Canada), California Polytechnic, UCLA, and INSEAD Business School (France). He was formerly economic adviser to the British Monopolies Commission. He is known for his work on corporate diversification, the resource-based view of the firm, and organizational change among the oil majors. His book, *Contemporary Strategy Analysis: Concepts, Techniques, Applications* (2nd edition, 1995), is used widely in leading business schools in North America and Europe. His current research focuses on the determinants of competitive advantage with particular emphasis on exploitation of the firm's knowledge resources. Together with Paul Almeida he is investigating cross-border knowledge building among semiconductor companies. He is coeditor (with J.-C. Spender) of a recent issue of *Strategic Management Journal* on knowledge and the firm. He is a member of the editorial boards of *Strategic Management Journal* and *Strategy & Leadership,* and the executive board of the Business Policy and Strategy Division of the Academy of Management.

Curtis M. Grimm (" 'Austrian' and Industrial Organization Perspectives on Firm-Level Competitive Activity and Performance") is Professor in the College of Business and Management, University of Maryland at College Park, and Chair of the Transportation, Business, and Public Policy Department. He received his B.A. in economics from the University of Wisconsin–Madison and his Ph.D. in economics from the University of California–Berkeley. He has conducted extensive research on the interface of business and public policy with strategic management, with a particular emphasis on competition, competition policy, deregulation, and microeconomic reform both in the United States and overseas. This research has resulted in more than 50 publications. He has consulted for a number of government agencies and private firms, including the Interstate Commerce Commission, the General Accounting Office, the Postal Rate Commission, the Canadian Consumer and Corporate Affairs Department, and several railroads.

Jon Hanssen-Bauer ("Responding to Hypercompetition: The Structure and Processes of a Regional Learning Network Organization") is Research Director for the International Department at the FAFO Institute for Applied Social Science in Oslo, Norway. He also manages a business development research project in cooperation with enterprises in the Nordvest Forum and is a consultant to major Norwegian companies. As a research fellow at the Work Research Institute in Oslo from 1983 to 1989, he researched and published on such topics as organizational design, work environment, sociotechnical optimization, and management of project organizations for design of offshore oil and gas installations. From 1989 to 1993 he worked for the Norwegian Work Life Center, an enterprise development program supported by the Norwegian labor market partners and the government. He received his academic degree in social anthropology from the University of Oslo in 1982 with a thesis on peasant markets in the Highland Andes.

Hiroyuki Itami ("Hypercompetitive Strategies, Japanese Style") is Professor of Management, Department of Commerce, Hitotsubashi University, Japan. Prior to that, he was Visiting Assistant Professor, Graduate School of Business, Stanford University; and Assistant Professor, Department of Commerce, Hitotsubashi University. He received his B.S. in 1967 and M.S. in 1969 from Hitotsubashi University and a Ph.D. from Carnegie Mellon University in 1972. His teaching and research interests include corporate strategy, economic analysis of internal organization, economic theory of the firm, and management control. He received the Fulbright Exchange Fellowship (1969-1970), the Best Literature in Economics and Management Award and the Ohta Prize of Japanese Accounting Association for Adaptive Behavior (1978), the Best Literature in Economics and Management Award for the Diversification Strategy of Japanese Firms (co-authored) in 1981, and the Management Science Literature Award for the Logic of Corporate Strategy in 1981. He is a member of the board of trustees of the Matsushita International Foundation. He also serves as an editorial board member of *Sloan Management Review* and *Organization Science*. He is the author of many books and articles, including *Mobilizing Invisible Assets,* 1987; "Dynamic Interaction between Strategy and Technology," *Strategic Management Journal,* May 1992 (co-authored); and *Why Is Japan Stumbling: Japanese Computer Industry,* 1996 (co-authored).

Dong-Jae Kim ("Technological Platforms and Diversification") is Assistant Professor at the Graduate School of International Studies of Yonsei University, Korea. He received his Ph.D. in strategy and multinational management from the Wharton School of the University of Pennsylvania in 1992. Before joining the faculty of Yonsei, he was a consultant with McKinsey & Company and Assistant Professor at the University of Illinois at Urbana–Champaign. His research has evolved around the themes of interfirm heterogeneity and knowledge of the firm in the context of global competition.

Bruce Kogut ("Social Capital, Structural Holes, and the Formation of an Industry Network," "Technological Platforms and Diversification") is Professor of Management at the Wharton School of the University of Pennsylvania and has published on the knowledge of the firm, business history, economics of direct investment, regional spillovers, joint ventures as real options, and strategy. He has been a visiting professor or scholar at the Stockholm School of Economics, Wissenschaftszentrum, and the Centre de Recherche en Gestion.

Julia Porter Liebeskind ("Social Networks, Learning, and Flexibility: Sourcing Scientific Knowledge in New Biotechnology Firms") is Associate

Professor in the Department of Management and Organization at the Marshall School of Business, University of Southern California. Her research interests include theories of the scope of the firm, corporate restructuring, corporate governance, organization in diversified firms, interorganizational transactions, and the governance of exchanges of intellectual property. Her research has appeared in the *RAND Journal of Economics, Academy of Management Review, Strategic Management Journal, Journal of Industrial Economics, Organization Science,* and *Industrial and Corporate Change.* She serves on the editorial boards of the *Strategic Management Journal* and *Organization Science.*

Gareth Morgan ("Refining Our Understanding of Hypercompetition and Hyperturbulence") is author of seven books, including *Images of Organization, Imaginization: New Mindsets for Seeing, Organizing and Managing, Riding the Waves of Change, Beyond Method, Creative Organization Theory,* and *Sociological Paradigms and Organizational Analysis.* He acts as a consultant to and seminar leader at numerous organizations throughout Europe and North America and is Distinguished Research Professor at York University in Toronto. He holds degrees from the London School of Economics and Political Science, the University of Texas at Austin, and the University of Lancaster, and he has been elected a Life Fellow of the International Academy of Management.

Amalya Lumerman Oliver ("Social Networks, Learning, and Flexibility: Sourcing Scientific Knowledge in New Biotechnology Firms") is Assistant Professor of Sociology at the Hebrew University, Israel. Her research focuses on intellectual capital collaborations, interorganizational networks, trust and new organizational forms, and cognitive maps.

Barrie R. Nault ("Eating Your Own Lunch: Protection Through Preemption") is Associate Professor at the Graduate School of Management, University of California, Irvine. His current research is on ownership, incentives, membership and investment in new organizational forms such as alliances and network organizations. His most recent work applies these concepts to advanced logistics, electronic markets for transport services, and supply-chain management. He also does research on new technology diffusion, examining when new technologies should be released and what incentives can be put in place to make them successful. He has articles published or forthcoming in *Information Systems Research; Journal of Money, Credit and Banking; Management Science, Management Information Systems Quarterly; Marketing Science;* and *Organization Science,* among others. He is Associate Editor for *Information Systems Research,* and is a reviewer for various journals. He holds a Ph.D. from the University of British Columbia, Canada.

Peter Neupert ("Building a Leadership Position in a Hypercompetitive Technology Market") is Vice President of News and Commentary for Microsoft Corporation's Interactive Media Division. He is the driving force behind Microsoft's participation in the media business with NBC via the MSNBC cable and interactive joint ventures. Since joining Microsoft in 1987, he has held a variety of senior management positions. He was responsible for international product development strategy for Microsoft's worldwide products division, managed business operations and product development for Microsoft's Far East region (including Japan, Korea, Taiwan, Hong Kong, and Mainland China), and served as director of operating systems where he managed the development of OS/2 versions 1.0 and 1.1 while overseeing the IBM joint development relationship. Before joining Microsoft, he served as Vice President of Operations and Chief Operating Officer of Graphic Software Systems in Portland, Oregon. He holds a master's degree in business administration from the Amos Tuck School of Business at Dartmouth College and a Bachelor of Arts degree from Colorado College.

James Richardson ("Vertical Integration and Rapid Response in the Fashion Apparel Industry") is Associate Professor of Management at the University of Hawaii College of Business Administration, where he teaches business strategy and international business. His current research concerns strategy and structure for organizing the supply chain—supplier relationships, vertical integration, and alternative forms of vertical organization. He has published articles on these topics in *Strategic Management Journal, Managerial and Decision Economics,* and *Management International Review.*

Weijian Shan ("Social Capital, Structural Holes, and the Formation of an Industry Network") is Managing Director of J.P. Morgan. He was previously Assistant Professor of Management at the Wharton School of the University of Pennsylvania. He received his Ph.D. from the University of California at Berkeley in 1987.

Anne D. Smith ("Garbage Cans and Advancing Hypercompetition: The Creation and Exploitation of New Capabilities and Strategic Flexibility in Two Regional Bell Operating Companies") is Assistant Professor of Management and International Business at the School of Business at Florida Atlantic University, Broward Campus. Her primary research interests are international expansion processes and strategies for deregulating industry.

Ken G. Smith (" 'Austrian' and Industrial Organization Perspectives on Firm-Level Competitive Activity and Performance") is Professor of Management and Organization at the University of Maryland at College Park. He holds a Ph.D. from the University of Washington. His research centers on competitive dynamics or how firms achieve advantage by competing, cooperating, or both. His work has appeared in *Academy of Management Journal, Administrative Science Quarterly,* and the *Strategic Management Journal.* His most recent book, *Strategy as Action* (with Curtis M. Grimm) was published in 1997.

Charles C. Snow ("Responding to Hypercompetition: The Structure and Processes of a Regional Learning Network Organization") is Mellon Bank Professor of Business Administration in The Smeal College of Business Administration, The Pennsylvania State University. He has been a visiting scholar at Dartmouth College (The Amos Tuck School) and the Norwegian School of Management. He is currently working on a book tentatively titled *Managing the Global Enterprise.*

Carroll U. Stephens ("The Dark Side of the New Organizational Forms: An Editorial Essay") is Assistant Professor of Management at Virginia Tech, where she teaches organization theory, business ethics, and a seminar on critical theories of organization. She received an undergraduate degree in sociology and a Ph.D. in organization studies from Duke University. Her research interests include economic sociology, neo-institutionalism, post-bureaucratic organization forms, and the effects of organizations on macro-social structures. Her articles have appeared in journals such as *Organization Science, Administrative Science Quarterly, Academy of Management Review,* and *Business Ethics Quarterly.*

L. G. Thomas, III ("The Two Faces of Competition: Dynamic Resourcefulness and the Hypercompetitive Shift") is Associate Professor of Management at Goizueta Business School, Emory University. He received his Ph.D. in economics from Duke University. His research examines the interfaces between corporate strategy and government industrial policy, and between economics and strategic management.

Mark B. Vandenbosch ("Eating Your Own Lunch: Protection Through Preemption") is Assistant Professor of Marketing at the Richard Ivey School of Business at the University of Western Ontario, Canada. He holds a Ph.D. from the University of British Columbia, Canada. His research interests center around competitive strategy, product positioning and marketing research—primarily in technology-based markets. His most recent work is concerned with understanding the implications of competitive behavior in multigenerational product markets. His research has appeared in *Marketing Science, Organization Science, International Journal of Research in Marketing, Marketing Letters,* and the *Journal of Business Research.*

Bart Victor ("The Dark Side of the New Organizational Forms: An Editorial Essay") is Professor of Management at the International Institute of Management Development (IMD), Lausanne, Switzerland. Before joining IMD, he was Professor of Management at the Kenan-Flagler Business School, University of North Carolina at Chapel Hill. He received his B.A. in sociology from the University of California at Berkeley. After college, he founded and operated a number of businesses in California, Illinois, and New York. He then went on to earn his Ph.D. in management from the University of North Carolina at Chapel Hill. His research interests have focused on ethical climates in organizations and applications of social psychological theory to problems in organizational design. His work has been published in academic and professional journals including *Academy of Management Journal, Academy of Management Review, Harvard Business Review, Administrative Science Quarterly,* and *Organization Science.*

Henk W. Volberda ("Toward the Flexible Form: How to Remain Vital in Hypercompetitive Environments") is Professor of Strategic Management and Business Policy of the Rotterdam School of Management, Erasmus University, The Netherlands, where he teaches strategic management, strategy implementation, corporate entrepreneurship, and strategic flexibility. He has also been a visiting scholar of the Wharton School at the University of Pennsylvania and City University Business School, London. He obtained his doctorate cum laude in business administration at the University of Groningen, The Netherlands. His research on organizational flexibility and strategic change received the NCD Award, the ERASM Research Award, the Erasmus University Research Award, and the Igor Ansoff Strategy Award. He has worked as a researcher for many large European corporations and published in many refereed books and journals. His new book *Building the Flexible Firm* was published this year. He is director of the Erasmus Strategic Renewal Centre and secretary of the Dutch-Flemish Academy of Management. He is also a member of the editorial board of *Organization Science* and of *M&O.*

Gordon Walker ("Social Capital, Structural Holes, and the Formation of an Industry Network") is Professor of Business Policy at the Cox School of Business, Southern Methodist University. He received his Ph.D. from the Wharton School of the University of Pennsylvania. His research interests are organizational boundaries, organizational growth models, and the organizational implications of deregulation.

Carolyn Y. Woo ("Hypercompetition in a Multimarket Environment: The Role of Strategic Similarity and Multimarket Contact on Competitive De-Escalation") is Dean and Ray and Milann Siegfried Professor of Management, College of Business Administration, University of Notre Dame. Her specialties are strategic planning, entrepreneurship, management of innovation and technology, implementation structures and systems, and continuous improvement and total quality systems. Since 1995, she has served as Associate Executive Vice President of Academic Affairs at Purdue University and as Director of the Professional Master's Programs in the Krannert School of Management, Purdue University (1993-1995). In these roles, her administrative responsibilities encompass strategic planning, continuous improvement, department chair leadership development, oversight for conflict of interest, and academic reinvestment programs. She joined Purdue University as Assistant Professor in 1981 and was promoted to Full Professor in 1991. Her teaching and research interests include corporate and competitive strategy analyses, manufacturing strategy, entrepreneurship, management of innovation and change, enterprise integration, and organizational systems. She has received a number of research and teaching awards including the Distinguished Scholar Award sponsored by the International Council for Small Business (1987), Best Paper Award (Entrepreneurship Division, Academy of Management, 1991, 1992), second place in the A. T. Kearney Award for Outstanding Research in General Management (1980), second place in the Competition for Best Paper Award on Entrepreneurship and Innovation (1988), and second and third places in the same competition (1991). She was elected Chair of the Business and Policy Division of the Academy of Management (1988-1989). For excellence in teaching, she received the Salgo-Noren Award for Outstanding Teaching in the Professional Master's Programs (1987). She has consulted with both large and small corporations and has taught extensively in executive education programs. She has published in the *Harvard Business Review, Management Science, Strategic Management Journal, Journal of Management, Journal of Business Venturing, Advances in Strategic Management, Organization Science, Academy of Management Best Paper Proceedings,* and *Frontiers of Entrepreneurial Research.*

Greg Young (" 'Austrian' and Industrial Organization Perspectives on Firm-Level Competitive Activity and Performance") received his Ph.D. from the University of Maryland at College Park. He is currently Assistant Professor of Management at the College of Management, North Carolina State University, Raleigh. His research interests focus on the dynamics of competitive strategy, strategic alliances, entrepreneurship, and the management of technology and innovation. His work has been published in several prestigious journals, including the *Strategic Management Journal, Organization Science,* and the *Journal of Management Inquiry.* He is a member of the Academy of Management, the Strategic Management Society, and the Institute for Operations Research and the Management Sciences.

Carl Zeithaml ("Garbage Cans and Advancing Hypercompetition: The Creation and Exploitation of New Capabilities and Strategic Flexibility in Two Regional Bell Operating Companies") is Dean and F. S. Cornell Professor of Free Enterprise, McIntire School of Commerce, University of Virginia. His primary research interests focus on global strategy, strategic decision processes, knowledge-based competition, and corporate governance.

Asaf Zohar ("Refining Our Understanding of Hypercompetition and Hyperturbulence") is Assistant Professor in the Department of Organizational Behavior and Industrial Relations at the Schulich School of Business at York University in Toronto, Canada. He divides his energies among a variety of teaching, research, and consulting activities. He directs courses in organizational theory and analysis, organizational behavior, and creative problem solving in York's MBA program. His present research and consulting activities explore the implications of the self-organizing evolutionary paradigm and complexity theory for managing organizational change. He has authored several articles and made numerous executive and academic presentations on how we can create organizations that self-organize—continually creating new, emergent organizing processes and contexts that successfully respond to current challenges.

Lynne Zucker ("Social Networks, Learning, and Flexibility: Sourcing Scientific Knowledge in New Biotechnology Firms") is Professor of Sociology (1989 -) and Policy Studies (1996 -), Director of the Organizational Research Program at the Institute for Social Science Research (1986 -), and Director of the Center for International Science, Technology, and Cultural Policy (1996 -) in the School of Public Policy and Social Research at UCLA. Concurrently, she holds appointments as Research Associate with the National Bureau of Economic Research, as Consulting Sociologist with the American Institute of Physics, and is a member of the affiliated faculty of the UCLA School of Education.